Library of
Davidson College

Configurations

Configurations
A Topomorphical Approach to Renaissance Poetry

Maren-Sofie Røstvig

SCANDINAVIAN UNIVERSITY PRESS
Oslo - Copenhagen - Stockholm

Scandinavian University Press (Universitetsforlaget AS),
PO Box 2959 Tøyen, N-0608 Oslo, Norway
Distributed world-wide excluding Scandinavia by
Oxford University Press, Walton Street, Oxford OX2 6DP

Oxford New York Toronto
Dehli Bombay Calcutta Madras Karachi
Kuala Lumpur Singapore Hong Kong Tokyo
Nairobi Dar es Salaam Cape Town
Melbourne Auckland Madrid
and associated companies in Berlin Ibadan

Oxford is a trade mark of Oxford University Press

Published in the United States
by Oxford University Press Inc., New York

© Universitetsforlaget 1994

ISBN 82-00-21909-7

Published with a grant from the Norwegian Research Council

All rights reserved. No part of this publication may be reproduced, stored in a retrieval system, or transmitted, in any form or by any means, without the prior permission in writing of Scandinavian University Press. Enquiries concerning reproduction outside these terms and in other countries should be sent to the Rights Department, Scandinavian University Press, at the address above

This book is sold subject to the condition that it shall not, by way of trade or otherwise, be lent, re-sold, hired out or otherwise circulated without the publisher's prior consent in any form of binding or cover other than that in which it is published and without a similar condition including the condition being imposed on the subsequent purchaser

British Library Cataloguing in Publication Data
Data available

Library of Congress Cataloguing in Publication Data
Data available

Printed in Norway by Engers Boktrykkeri A/S, Otta 1994

*Oh that I knew how all thy lights combine,
  And the configurations of their glorie!
    Seeing not onely how each verse doth shine,
But all the constellations of the storie.*

George Herbert, "The H. Scriptures II"

Contents

Acknowledgements ix
Introduction xi

PART ONE: FROM AUGUSTINE TO TASSO

I Mirabilis Ordo: Augustine and the Vision of Unity 3
1. Augustine, Bonaventura, Cusanus, and Ficino 6
2. Pico and Giorgio 18
3. Pietro Bongo and Pierre de la Primaudaye 39
4. Philip of Mornay, Marin Mersenne, Peter Sterry, and Père André 54
5. From Theology to Poetics 62

II Fitly Framed Together: Augustine's *Confessions* 75
1. The Pre-planned Poem 79
2. The Autobiography (Books 1–9) 86
3. The Symmetrical Structure of Books 1–13 98
4. The Graded Arrangement of Books 1–13 116
5. Concluding Remarks 126

III Structural Exegesis 131

IV From Exegesis to Composition 169
1. Some Early Latin Poems and Plays 169
2. Torquato Tasso, *Sette Giornate del Mondo Creato* (1607) 188

V Patterns of Return: Tasso's *Jerusalem Delivered* 203
1. The Extended Centre 205
2. Triads and Tetrads 212
3. Recessed Symmetry 232
4. The Graded Arrangement 246
5. Canto Structure 249
6. Concluding Remarks 258

PART TWO: FROM SPENSER TO DRYDEN

VI Spenser's "Tunefull Diapase": *The Faerie Queene* I and II ... 267
1. Book I: Canto Structure ... 269
2. Book I: The Symmetrical Structure ... 292
3. Book I: The Graded Arrangement ... 305
4. Book II: The Ethical Crux ... 312
5. Concluding Remarks ... 365

VII The Religious Sequence: Francis Quarles, *Emblemes* (1635) ... 371

VIII The Religious Lyric ... 403
1. George Herbert ... 403
2. Henry Vaughan ... 425
3. Thomas Traherne ... 436

IX John Milton, *Paradise lost. A Poem Written in Ten Books* (1667) ... 461
1. Theologizing by Means of Numbers ... 470
2. Linking the Beginning, Middle, and End ... 487
3. Linking Books 3 and 8–9 ... 500
4. Linking Books 4–5 and 7 ... 512
5. The Structure of Book 7 ... 518
6. Concluding Remarks ... 522

X Dryden and the Art of Praise ... 535

Postscript ... 561

Appendix: John Keats, *The Eve of St. Agnes* (1820) ... 567

Index of Names ... 573

Subject Index ... 578

Acknowledgements

I wish to express my gratitude to the Norwegian Research Council for Science and the Humanities for its generous support of my research, and for the grant which made possible the publication of this study. I am particularly grateful for being nominated Senior Research Fellow for 1988, 1989, and the first quarter of 1990.

While he was a Research Fellow in the University of Oslo, Roy T. Eriksen gave valuable assistance beyond the call of duty, and, during the last phase of my work, H. Neville Davies of the University of Birmingham read my bulky manuscript, and provided the kind of response (in matters small and great) which is so useful and so hard to come by. My colleague in the University of Oslo, Michael Benskin, read my chapter on Milton with an eye to detail worthy of the best philological tradition; there are mysteries in punctuation, and logic in the choice of words. Among those who have given valuable moral support, I would like to mention Alastair Fowler, A. C. Hamilton, Jerry Leath Mills, and Thomas P. Roche.

Introduction

This is a study of the relevance, to Renaissance poetics, of the interrelated patterns of creation and redemption. Augustine derived the principle of unity in a work of art from these divinely created patterns in space and time; all artists ought to embody these spatial and temporal constructs in their own works so that their unity would similarly point to God as the source of all unity. To Augustine the universe was God's *carmen*, just as a poem would be a universe if arranged in number, weight, and measure (*Wisdom* 11:21) by the Wisdom which disposes everything sweetly (*Wisdom* 8:1). In the Renaissance this argument was echoed by Cristoforo Landino and Torquato Tasso, and in practice it entailed making use of symmetrical and graded structures, as Augustine explains in the *De musica* VI and the *De vera religione*.

The analytical technique called for in the study of works informed by this concept of unity may be referred to as topomorphical. The term has been coined from the Greek words *topos* and *morphē*, since we often perceive the unifying patterns by observing the placing of *topoi* within the body or *morphē* of the text.[1] A topos will be repeated (suitably varied) to create linkage between parts, and the focus in this study, therefore, will be on systems of linkage. The discovery of the similarity that links events is a source of delight as well as of a deeper understanding. Such a reading is mandatory, especially in romance epics; thus when we read about the torture suffered by Redcrosse Knight when his armour has become burning hot from the dragon's fiery breath (*The Faerie Queene* I.xi.26–28) we are meant to recall Fradubio's suffering within his "wooden wals" (*FQ* I.ii.33–43). The juxtaposition provides new insights: the fiery armour, like the "wooden wals", is that which encloses and torments fallen man until released by the grace of God.

Today Augustine's vision of unity seems curiously abstract and intellectual, but it was felt to appeal directly to the emotions and the imagination, as Marin Mersenne testifies in the early years of the seventeenth century.[2] Another point is that it appealed just as much to Protestants as to Roman Catholics; I have found no difference on this score. Augustine's basic idea is that, when we contemplate

God's work of creation or a work of human art, we shall ascend from the visible to the invisible as Paul commands us (see *Romans* 1 : 20) by observing how sweetly all has been ordered (*Wisdom* 8 : 1). Another proof passage often cited is *Hebrews* 8 : 5, where the pattern of the Tabernacle (interpreted as that of our threefold world)[3] is said to be "a shadow of heavenly things"; hence this is the pattern that artists must copy.

The presence of pre-planned textual structures in medieval and Renaissance poetry is well documented, but a theory capable of accounting for them has not been found, nor has the character or the scope of the compositional practice been fully understood. Reference to such compositions as numerical (or numerological) proves that the structural principles have been grasped only in part. The verbal texture is, in fact, more important than the patterns formed by symbolic numbers,[4] although there are exceptions. Tasso's *Il Mondo Creato* is a case in point, perhaps because of its subject.

The supposed absence of contemporary evidence has bothered many. One scholar states that "disappointingly little" was written in the Renaissance about numerical patterning, "perhaps because there was no clear classical precedent for such a discussion or perhaps such techniques were supposed to be kept semi-secret; yet Du Bartas used them."[5] But secrecy was not involved, and a great deal was actually written about numerical and related compositional techniques, though we have to turn to long neglected sources. It is above all in biblical exegesis that we find discussions of textual patterns and their meaning, but who today reads Cassiodorus on the Psalms? Chapter III presents a few examples of the kind of exegesis which functioned as literary criticism, so that logic invited a progress from exegesis to composition. There must have been ample classical precedent, but we have no evidence showing how classical poetry was read – with what awareness of what structures. All we have are modern attempts to discover textual structures in the poetry of, for example, Virgil and Apollonius of Rhodes.[6] I have therefore chosen to focus on a tradition that can be documented – an uninterrupted tradition of structural exegesis extending from late Antiquity into the Renaissance and beyond. The strength of this tradition is shown when a Renaissance author attributes biblical structures to the *Aeneid*.[7]

Patristic, medieval, and Renaissance theologians often write about the mystery of numbers; Augustine is one of them. But the "mystical" meaning of a text and of the numbers it may contain simply means the spiritual meaning in contrast to the literal one, and the spiritual meaning was open, not concealed. Augustine explains that on the subject of numbers he has consulted the authority of the Church, the tradition of his forefathers, the testimony of the Bible, and finally "the nature itself of numbers and of similitudes." This has convinced him of their significance, and so he concludes magisterially that "No sober person will decide against reason, no Christian against the Scriptures, no peaceable person against the church."[8] Numbers, then, are similitudes; their meaning enables them to function as such. Augustine's argument that artists should adopt the creative procedure of the Deity would not have had such an impact if it had not been supported by such a wealth of examples adduced from the structures attributed to Holy Writ. Symmetrical patterns were traced everywhere, and the ratio of the diapason (2 : 1) as well. Creation and redemption history reflect the harmony of the octave proportion, a proportion that contains within itself all the other ratios that create musical harmony (see Augustine's *De Trinitate* IV). In the course of time Plato's theory of creation was modified so that *idea* was replaced by *pattern*, as seen for example in Torquato Tasso's *Discorsi del Poema Eroico* (1957);[9] the transcendental reality capable of rational apprehension became, quite simply, the structure of things – the way in which they are disposed. By virtue of such an apprehension a poet may imitate more than the surface appearance of things, and it was because Moses was supposed to have had such a perception that he was referred to as the perfect pattern of a poet.[10]

"Mystical" is not the only term which calls for clarification; Renaissance Neoplatonism is another.[11] As I have argued in earlier publications, it is more in keeping with Renaissance thought to speak of Renaissance *syncretism*.[12] The fact that this term is so often avoided reflects an aversion to the phenomenon itself – an aversion based on non-comprehension or a reluctance to adopt a Renaissance perspective which we cannot share. We meet this attitude in Robert Ellrodt's study of *Neoplatonism in the Poetry of Edmund Spenser* (1960). Ellrodt admits that, whenever he uses the term Neoplatonic, reference is also intended to Pythagoras, Hermes Trismegistus, Zoroaster, Orpheus, the Cabala, and Arab philosophy, and this terminological inexactitude clearly stems from a dislike of the syncretistic tradition as "a seething mass of confused thinking" loosely related to Christianity.[13] Paul Oskar Kristeller affords a second example. It is with great reluctance that he concedes that Erasmus, in the *Enchiridion militis Christiani* (1503), displays what he calls a "persistent tendency to identify a simplified Platonic philosophy and a simplified Christian religion." This concession causes acute discomfort; Erasmus' position is neither historically accurate, philosophically defensible, nor theologically accurate; but "there is an aspect and an element of Platonic philosophy that Erasmus consciously endorses and that he believes to be compatible with the religious and theological position he is trying to present and defend."[14] Kristeller is on the verge of realizing that this bias should be connected with the patristic studies of the humanists,[15] but he fails to take the decisive step, and so merely concludes that "there is at least a Platonic element in Erasmus." S. K. Heninger's characterization of Erasmus as a "syncretic humanist" is surely more just,[16] but he too fails to honour syncretism as such, his purpose being to replace Neoplatonism by Pythagoreanism (see his *Touches of Sweet Harmony*, 1974). O. B. Hardison finds Heninger's approach lacking in focus: "Pythagoreanism" becomes just as meaningless as "Neoplatonism" when explained "by mosaic-like accumulations of heterogeneous sources." But Hardison, too, distances himself from the syncretistic tradition with something like contempt: Renaissance thinkers "often seem to have absorbed ideas in the uncritical manner of sponges absorbing water. The historian of ideas is not, however, obliged to imitate them."[17] Students of literature, though, are certainly obliged to study them on their own terms, and, the moment that this is done, their structural orientation emerges with almost startling clarity, and so does the relevance of this orientation to Renaissance poetics.

My point of departure, then, is the nature of the vision of unity as expressed in many exegetical treatises and in theological and philosophical works with a syncretistic slant. One authoritative source is Eusebius' *On the Preparation for the Gospel*, written early in the fourth century. E. K. refers to it in one of his glosses to Spenser's *The Shepheardes Calender* (1579), and so does Milton in the *Areopagitica* and in the Trinity College Manuscript.[18] Eusebius makes it plain that syncretism does not posit equality between Moses and Plato; the latter is subordinated to the former. The truth of revealed religion remains supreme; indeed, its supremacy is increased by viewing it as that toward which everything points with varying degrees of clarity. This kind of syncretism is a manifestation of faith and not of doubt, let alone of a confused mind requiring a selection of what is best in all traditions. The attitude was all-embracing in the sense that everything was subsumed under divine revelation, a revelation conveyed dimly at first, but in the end with complete clarity in the life of Christ. If this had not been so, it would scarcely have recommended itself to men like John Colet and Erasmus.

The syncretistic system of cross-references between Christ and Plato, which we trace for example in Pico della Mirandola,[19] finds an echo in the discovery of Christian truths in pagan myth. Don Cameron Allen's *Mysteriously Meant. The Rediscovery of Pagan Symbolism and Allegorical Interpretation in the Renaissance* (1970) provides a splendid survey. However, the absurdity of interpreting classical myth typologically bothers the modern scholar who knows only too well that Pan is not a type of Christ, nor is Apollo. Like Robert Ellrodt and Paul Oskar Kristeller, Don Cameron Allen deplores the phenomenon he investigates; such was the perverseness of the Renaissance that "the conviction that pagan theologies and histories were wastings of Adam's teachings" persisted despite "the solid efforts" of rationalists like Bayle and Fontenelle.[20] It is possible to write like this only when Renaissance mythographers are assessed from a modern perspective so that only those trends are honoured that live on into the next centuries.

The concept of unity itself, though, is the greatest stumbling-block of all. Today the idea that unity depends on a conscious arrangement of parts seems contrary to the workings of the poetic imagination as expressed for example by John Keats when he wrote that "if poetry comes not as naturally as the leaves to a tree, it had better not come at all." Compared with Keats's image, Augustine's concept of an *ars aeterna* must perforce seem "inorganic," to employ the term used by Robert M. Jordan in his description of Chaucer's poetics.[21] The connotations of the term "inorganic form" are pejorative, and this hostility has surfaced in the critical response to the so-called "numerological" studies published since the early 1960s. However, it must give us pause to consider that Keats himself adopted Spenser's compositional technique, and with excellent results, when he wrote one of his best poems, *The Eve of St. Agnes* (see the Appendix). This makes one wonder exactly how Keats looked at trees. When Augustine contemplated the 22 groups of 8 verses which constitute Psalm 119 (Vulg. 118), he saw a tree which is Christ – the Tree of Life in the garden and the Tree of the Cross.[22] Bonaventura compared the order of nature and the order of Scripture, and found them similar: "Scriptura ordinatissima est, et ordo eius est consimilis ordini naturae in germinatione terrae" (*Collationes in Hexaemeron* XIV.5). This order is traced in the growth of a plant from the root and the stem to the leaves and the flower, a ladder of 4 steps which parallels the growth of man: man is first *sensualis* or devoted to the life of sense, then *animalis* when he learns to speak and to use the images conveyed through the senses, and then *rationalis* and finally *intellectualis* as he proceeds from discursive to intuitive rational perception.[23] In the Scriptures these 4 levels are represented by the patriarchs, the law, the prophets, and Christ (*Collationes in Hexaemeron* XIV.10–11). These easy transitions from one level to another obliterate distinctions in favour of the *order* or *scale* which they have in common. When we perceive the order, we ascend *per visibilia ad invisibilia* (cf. *Romans* 1 : 20). This is why John Smith (*Select Discourses*, 1660) praised the Platonists for their "*Mathemata*, or Mathematical Contemplations" which enable us to shake off our dependency upon sense, "and so be a little inur'd, being once got up above the Body, to converse freely with Immaterial natures, without looking down again and falling back into Sense."[24] Regenerate man was by definition re-possessed of the inner vision required for this ascent, but all this changed in the mid-eighteenth century when a decisive line of division in the history of European civilization coincides with a similar line of division in biblical exegesis, both falling at the point where a belief in the overriding importance of sense perception finally ousted the traditional belief in an inner vision divorced from the world of sense. It was at this time that the habit of tracing spiritual meanings in the text of the Bible became discredited so that what had once seemed an exercise of highest reason began to be confused with the esoteric and the occult.

Swift pinpoints the issue and dramatizes the conflict in *A Tale of a Tub* (1704), where he attacks inner vision by setting up an unpleasant association with the discredited Puritan sects and with notorious occultists like Thomas Vaughan. Swift marks the beginning of a new era, but the reception accorded his satire in ecclesiastical circles proves that he was ahead of his generation in this as in so many other respects. John Locke's view of human understanding could not prevail overnight; it took a generation or two before it swept all before it so that an important Augustinian tradition no longer made sense even within the conservative confines of the established church. Once this had happened, a poem could no longer achieve transcendence by embodying the structures of time and space; these structures no longer carried conviction. It is difficult to tell when poets began to discredit the belief, yet continued to use pre-planned textual structures for the sake of their poetic effectiveness. For Tasso the patterns of redemption history clearly were a matter of personal belief, nor can we doubt Spenser's stand on this point. I would argue that Dryden, too, was a believer, while Pope and Fielding surely employed balanced and graded textual structures as a purely aesthetic phenomenon. Number symbolism reaches something of a grand climax in Dryden's poetry, where it helps to account for his fondness for triplets, but I find little or no evidence of it in Pope or Thomas Gray.

My analyses show that close attention must be paid to the verbal texture; it is never enough just to count lines or stanzas. The repetition of identical or similar words or phrases, whether in epics, poems of praise, or religious lyrics, serves to verify the presence of textual structures that may, or may not, be based on symbolically significant numbers. The poetry of Samuel Daniel proves that textual structures may be created by means of complex patterns of verbal repetition, yet without attention to the number of lines or stanzas.[25] The most common practice, though, is illustrated by Spenser, who consistently fuses numerical and verbal structures so that the latter verify the presence of the former. Tasso's *Il Mondo Creato* represents an extreme with regard to the use of symbolic numbers and ratios: Tasso counts verse paragraphs and their line totals as if his life depended on it; he must have felt that his faith (and hence his salvation) somehow was validated by this numerical technique of composing. Tasso therefore provides the best possible proof of the perfect orthodoxy of biblical number symbolism. There are three possibilities, then: textual structures may be based (1) on verbal repetitions, (2) on verbal repetitions combined with numerically significant unit totals, and (3) almost entirely on numeration or counting. The extremes are rare. The mean is the favoured position, but within this mean the balance may veer in favour of numbers or of verbal texturing.

This structural variety is complemented by structural complexity: it is the rule rather than the exception that symmetrical structures coexist with an arrangement in the ratio 2:1, as we see from Augustine's *Confessions*. The ratio finds expression in two ways. the 13 books are divided into the sequence 8 — 1 — 4, at the same time that books 1–2 are linked with book 13, 3–4 with 12, 5–6 with 11, and 7–8 with 10, thus leaving book 9 to function as a pivotal point of rest for both divisions (see Chapter II). Such structural complexities soften what might otherwise have been a too rigid outline, while at the same time posing a very real artistic challenge. Similarly challenged, the reader responds by developing an increased spatial sensitivity.

I have made extensive use of diagrams to encourage such spatial awareness. They present the "fore-conceit" so highly praised by Sir Philip Sidney and the system of linkage advocated by Père André some 160 years later. The structural conceit should not be separated from the contents: both encourage an ascent from the particular to the universal, from the visible to the invisible, like the ascent from types to antitypes.

The structural view of poetic unity was particularly useful to writers of romance epics; in a topomorphical reading, interpolated tales, extended descriptions, and other departures from the main narrative fall into place as logical parts of an overall design. To see the design, we must proceed from a particular passage to the *concept* it embodies, and this process in its turn takes us to the heart of the allegory. As I have suggested elsewhere, Fielding's *Tom Jones* shares the structural characteristics of the romance epic, at the same time as his hero has a great deal in common with Tasso's Rinaldo and Spenser's Guyon: all three dramatize the idea of the Choice of Hercules so dear to the heart of the Renaissance and the early eighteenth century.[26] The choice made by Augustine under the fig tree in his garden is of course the basic choice, and in the early years of the seventeenth century Francis Quarles exploited the popular emblem sequence to present his own version. Poems of praise, too, are concerned with moral and religious choices, especially since praise functions as exhortation to virtue, as no one knew better than John Dryden.

One virtue of the topomorphical approach is that it compels us to engage with the text in its entirety; it forbids us to pick and choose as our fancy takes us. The approach invites honesty: what the author places at a structurally significant point must for that reason be significant, and its significance emerges from a consideration of the structure of which it is a part. In other words, authorial intent may be revealed once a structure has been ascertained. A splendid example is afforded by Francis Quarles's *Emblemes* (1635); with the perception of its structures the sequence of 5 × 15 emblems can be seen to pursue a perfectly logical pattern with a clear beginning, middle, and end. From the very moment of the Fall as presented in the first emblem, the pattern of ascent (promised in the division into groups of 15) is undoubtedly present, as it must be if Christ is indeed King. No seventeenth-century Protestant (or Roman Catholic for that matter) would take the life of man to be a meaningless labyrinth of steps that lead forward only to double back again at the next moment. Quarles's position echoes that of Augustine, as one would expect: "for the steps of a man are directed by the Lord, and he shall dispose his way" (*Confessions* 5 : 7). This belief in a Providence that orders everything sweetly lent substantial support to the structural tradition outlined in this study; its continued popularity even in the eighteenth century must owe a considerable debt to this religious persuasion. As God orders the life of man, so does the poet order his words. In this way the poet, too, points the way to God, and his words reflect the power of the Word.

Notes to Introduction

1. I am indebted to Professor Roy T. Eriksen for this useful term.
2. See below, p. 56.
3. See the sections on Pico della Mirandola and Francesco Giorgio in Chapter I.
4. On number symbolism see my article in *The Spenser Encyclopedia*; see also Christopher Butler, *Number Symbolism* (London, 1970) and S. K. Heninger, Jr, *The Cosmographical Glass. Renaissance Diagrams of the Universe* (San Marino, The Huntington Library 1977), chs 1 and 4.
5. Anne Lake Prescott, *French Poets and the English Renaissance* (New Haven, 1978), p. xii. The belief in the supposed secrecy of number lore is hard to get rid of. Thus Christopher Butler speaks of the "secrecy and esotericism of the numerological tradition" (*Number Symbolism*, p. 103), and in his review of Butler's book S. K. Heninger rightly blames him for this view (see *Renaissance Quarterly* 25, 1972, 352–56). Heninger nevertheless places his own discussion of numerical analyses of Renaissance poetry (in *Touches of Sweet Harmony*, San Marino, 1974) in his chapter on the occult sciences. Heninger labels anything that cannot be classified as "Pythagorean" or "cosmic" as esoteric or even occult. Neither Heninger nor Prescott has studied the syncretistic tradition as it affected orthodox theology, and so Prescott believes that it is unorthodox (*French Poets*, pp. 225f.). Frances Yates's books, too, excellent though they are in many respects, have strengthened the tendency to characterize as occult ideas that are presented by perfectly orthodox theologians.
6. For Virgil, see Alastair Fowler, *Triumphal Forms* (London, 1970), pp. 91–95 and the sources cited there. The *Argonautica* is analyzed by André Hurst, *Apollonius de Rhodes. Manière et Cohérence*, Bibliotheka Helvetica Romana Vol. VIII (Institut Suisse de Rome, 1967). W. F. Jackson Knight discusses "Vergil's Secret Art" in Appendix 2 of his book on *Roman Vergil* (Harmondsworth, 1966), pp. 419–439. For a negative assessment of such analyses, see William S. Anderson, "The Theory and Practice of Poetic Arrangement from Vergil to Ovid," in *Poems in Their Place*, ed. Neil Fraistat (Chapel Hill and London, 1986), pp. 44–65. Anderson's review of various attempts to discover numerically conditioned structures in Virgil's *Eclogues* reveals that such analyses are lacking in stringency and consistency. In the absence of a clearly expressed classical theory to the effect that poems should be written so as to create such patterns, all modern analyses are bound to be conjectural. One may, of course, argue that the circumstance that Augustine does, in fact, express such a theory necessarily speaks in favour of its prior existence. Its connection with rhetorical schemes certainly warrants consideration.

7. R. M. Cummings, "Two Sixteenth-Century Notices of Numerical Composition in Virgil's 'Aeneid'", *Notes & Queries*, January 1969, pp. 26–27.
8. Augustine, *De Trinitate* IV.vi.10. All quotations from this work are from *On the Trinity*, tr. Arthur West Hadden (Edinburgh, 1873). I have preferred not to use the modern translation by Stephen McKenna (*The Fathers of the Church*, vol. 45, the Catholic University of America Press, 1963 and 1970).
9. For a useful study of these discourses, see Annabel M. Patterson, "Tasso and Neoplatonism: the Growth of His Epic Theory," *Studies in the Renaissance* 18 (1971), 105–133.
10. See below, pp. 21, 29, 46, and 132.
11. A. H. Armstrong calls for "more precise studies to determine exactly what we mean when we speak of a particular thinker as being Platonically or Neoplatonically influenced," "We must bear in mind that "neither emphasis on number and mathematical structure nor emphasis on the excellence and beauty of light is in any way exclusively Neoplatonic." A. H. Armstrong, "Later Platonism and Its Influence," in *Classical Influences on European Culture A.D. 500–1500*, ed. R. R. Bolgar (London, 1971), p. 200. A similar warning is in order with regard to "Pythagoreanism."
12. See, for example, my essay on "Structure as Prophecy: the Influence of Biblical Exegesis upon Theories of Literary Structure," in *Silent Poetry. Essays in Numerological Analysis*, ed. Alastair Fowler (London, 1970). pp. 32–72.
13. Robert Ellrodt, *Neoplatonism in the Poetry of Edmund Spenser* (Geneva, 1960), p. 9.
14. Paul Oskar Kristeller, "Erasmus from an Italian Perspective", *Renaissance Quarterly* 23 (1970), 1–14.
15. In his footnote 40 Kristeller draws attention to the fact that "Similar statements about the Platonists are repeatedly found in Augustine".
16. S. K. Heninger Jr, "Pythagorean Symbols in Erasmus' *Adagia*," *Renaissance Quarterly* 21 (1968), 162–165.
17. O. B. Hardison Jr, "Pythagoras and the Renaissance." (*Shakespeare Quarterly* 28 (1977), 123.
18. See p. 34 of John Milton, *Poems Reproduced in Facsimile from the Manuscript in Trinity College, Cambridge* (Scolar Press, 1970).
    Abraham Cowley refers to "Euseb. 1. 9 Præparat. Evang." in a footnote to his Pindaric ode on "The Plagues of Egypt".
19. See Pico, *On the Dignity of Man, On Being and the One, Heptaplus* (Indianapolis, The Bobbs Merrill Company Ltd., 1965), pp. 5 f., where Pico submits a Christian interpretation of the classical idea of metamorphosis.
20. Don Cameron Allen, *Mysteriously Meant* (Baltimore and London, 1970), p. 79.
21. Robert M. Jordan, *Chaucer and the Shape of Creation* (Cambridge, Mass., 1967).
22. Augustine saw the psalm as a tree with 22 branches, each of which has 8 twigs. The Jesuit Lorinus, *Commentarium in librum Psalmorum* (1611–1616), III, 479, explains that *sub similtudine arboris, quae in medio paradisi erat, Augustino hunc psalmum revelatum fuisse*. I have been unable to locate the passage in Augustine's works. Since this psalm supposedly contains all that is needed for salvation, its association with Christ is sufficiently logical.
23. The parallel with *Paradise Lost* 5.479–88 is striking.
24. Quoted from *The Cambridge Platonists*, ed. C. A. Patrides (London, 1969), p. 136.
25. See my study of "A Frame of Words: On the Craftsmanship of Samuel Daniel," *English Studies* 60 (1979), 122–137.
26. Some of these balanced structures are discussed in my essay on "*Tom Jones* and the Choice of Hercules," in *Fair Forms*, ed. M.-S. Røstvig (Cambridge 1975), pp. 147–177 and 222–226.

Part One
From Augustine to Tasso

Chapter I

Mirabilis Ordo
Augustine and the Vision of Unity

> Scriptura ordinatissima est et ordo eius est consimilis ordini naturae in germinatione terrae.
>
> Bonaventura, *Collationes in Hexaemeron*, XIV.5.

To the Renaissance, cosmic and poetic unity were of the same kind, each being the consequence of the imposition of a pre-planned design where parts are balanced against parts and made to cohere through various forms of linkage. Behind this cosmic and poetic unity was felt to be the unity manifested in divine revelation: God's works in space (creation) and time (as recorded in the Scriptures) bear the imprint of God who is highest unity. There are no firm lines of division between aesthetic, cosmic, and biblical concepts of unity, nor does Augustine separate them, although his emphasis may differ from work to work. Works like the *De ordine* and the *De musica* focus primarily on aesthetic principles, the *De libero arbitrio* on intellectual issues, while the providential pattern for our redemption is the subject of *De Trinitate* IV. As Augustine puts it in the *De vera religione*: to be made in the image of God means to be made for unity, so that we instinctively love the Wisdom which orders everything so sweetly (*Wisdom* 8:1). Nothing can be more beautiful than its ordering and adorning of the visible physical universe, and it is this order we admire in a work of art. By contemplating this order, therefore, the mind is led back to God.[1] The aesthetic argument is both simple and profoundly moving, highly intellectual though it is. The test of our understanding is to perceive how Augustine's constructivist principles function in practice, and perhaps to respond with the emotional fervour that Augustine himself experienced.

Augustine's thinking about the unity of creation (whether human or divine) is syncretistic, and the widespread popularity of syncretistic views in the Renaissance helps to explain the appeal of his aesthetics. Even reformers like Zwingly and Martin Luther reveal a syncretistic bias – Zwingly probably as a result of his strong indebtedness to Pico della Mirandola – nor was Calvin entirely untouched. When Roy Battenhouse, therefore, cites Philip of Mornay in France and Edmund Spenser in England as examples showing that Calvinism could combine with Neoplatonism,[2] it would be more correct to state that even Calvinism found room for the belief that much of what we read in Plato and the other "ancient theologians" had its origin in Moses. As is well known, the reformers turned to the earliest period in the history of the Church to get rid of what they considered human additions and falsifications, and so were clearly influenced (to a greater or lesser extent) by the syncretistic policy of early theologians like Eusebius.

Since syncretistic arguments so often depend on allegorical interpretations, it may perhaps seem surprising that Protestants should have joined the syncretistic fold. But the Protestant insistence on the one plain, literal meaning of the text of the Bible was not as unanimous or unambiguous as has been thought. In the first place, it had to be strongly modified by typological exegesis, since the typological meaning is part of the literal sense; if an event were not truly historical, it could not be a type. Then, secondly, we must remember how important it was not to be what Henry Bullinger calls a "carnal gospeller", but to proceed from the letter to the spirit. As the radical theologian, John Everard, was so fond of saying in his sermons: "The letter kills, but the spirit gives life" (2 *Cor.* 3 : 6). The ability so to proceed was proof of regeneration. A strong interest in types marks Renaissance sacred art as well as its theology, and types were found outside the Old Testament, too, for example in classical myth or in the realm of Nature. It is reasonable to posit a connection between syncretism and typology. If Moses and the prophets had not spoken about Christ in "veils and shadows," classical myth and philosophy could not similarly have been subjected to an interpretation in terms of *vela & umbra*.

Another important assumption was that divine revelation concerning the scheme of redemption extends back in time to Adam, which accounts for the many veiled allusions to it in Moses and the prophets. Milton relied on this well-established tradition when he concluded *Paradise Lost* with the revelation, to Adam, of the whole course of history to the end of time. The reputable Protestant Swiss theologian Henry Bullinger (1504–1575), to whom I have just referred, repeatedly asserts in his influential sermons that the gospel is one and eternal: "For the very same gospel which is at this day preached to us was at the beginning of the world preached to our first parents."[3] The first sermon in his five *Decades* (1577 and later editions) traces the generations from Adam to Moses and Christ to show how the gospel was passed on orally until we reach Moses, the seventh witness from Adam. In this way Moses learnt all about creation, the Fall, and the scheme of redemption "by a certain middle mean, that is, by the Word incarnate." The reference to Christ as a "middle mean" incidentally shows that Bullinger thought about Christ in the same mathematical way that we find in Augustine's *De Trinitate* IV.[4] Moses, then, was simply the first to commit all this to writing, but everything relating to Christ was presented through the veil of types. In so doing he was guided by the Holy Ghost: "The Holy Ghost, which was wholly in the mind of Moses, directed his hand as he writ. There was no ability wanting in Moses, that was necessary for a most absolute writer."[5] Descriptions could furnish types as well as events, for example the structure of the Ark of Noah or of the chariot seen by Ezekiel. Or should one perhaps rather speak of a spiritual interpretation of these structures? Whatever the term, the result is the same: a web of unifying links connects all of the Bible from beginning to end. Augustine, Pico della Mirandola, and Henry Bullinger may seem a strange triad, but they are at one in their praise of the skill with which Moses compressed so much meaning into his apparently simple narrative.

But why bother to unravel hidden meanings when the gospels contain all we need in a form capable of being understood by all? Augustine calls the obscurity of the Bible "part of a kind of eloquence through which our understandings should be benefited not only by the discovery of what lies hidden but also by exercise".[6] God constantly challenges us to use our gifts to the full to grasp as much of the divine plenitude as possible. He is not content with what we today would call a "sympathetic response"; he wants every detail in the text to be scrutinized so that we can grasp the truly amazing extent to which divine Providence "orders everything sweetly" (*Wisdom* 8:1). Our modern suspicion of intellectual subtlety cuts us off from the beauty which inheres in a highly rational plan or structure. Profoundly un-Platonic as our age is, beauty and intellect seem at odds, and so do emotion and thought. That the Renaissance could fuse the two and as a consequence create an art of unparalleled fullness, should be attributed more to Augustine and those who followed his lead than to Renaissance

"Neoplatonism". Augustine not only provided the main concepts, he gave to these concepts the all-important function of elevating the mind to God.

To present the vision of unity that inspired so many, I have chosen a handful of theologians or philosophers from Augustine to Père André in the eighteenth century. I have devoted more pages to Francesco Giorgio than the rest, because his presentation is so full and so poetical; also his influence was considerable. I have included the popular encyclopedia written by Pierre de la Primaudaye, *The French Academie*, to illustrate that here, too, we find the same basic ideas as in Augustine, Pico, and Giorgio. Peter Sterry represents the Cambridge Platonists, while Père André proves the great attraction of Augustine's aesthetics as late as in the mid-eighteenth century.

1. Augustine, Bonaventura, Cusanus, and Ficino

The fusion, in Augustine's thought, between the classical concept of harmony and the Christian concept of the perfection of God's works, is truly basic. Throughout his career Augustine used the language of the former as a gloss on the latter, which is logical enough. If God is the creator of harmony and Christ its restorer, then a knowledge of the principles of harmony is required for a proper understanding of the Christian message, and the artist who conveys it must see to it that his own work embodies these principles.

Augustine reveals the importance attached to ordered arrangements when he writes that he has considered "what spiritual truths" God "intended to be expressed by the order in which the world was created and the order in which the creation is described".[7] In other words, it is not enough that the work of creation be given a spiritual interpretation, this must apply to the *structure* of the Mosaic narrative as well. In the thirteenth century Bonaventura put this idea even more succinctly when he wrote that the Scriptures display an organic or ordered form like the created universe and all things in it. An ordered form, then, *is organic*. The Scriptures were not written by adding sentence to sentence; Holy Writ is most highly ordered (*ordinatissima est*), and its order is like that of Nature (*consimilis ordini naturae in germinatione terrae*).[8] In other words, the structures attributed to the Bible are identical with natural organic forms. All of the Bible, then, rests on a structure as firm as that of the universe, and as beautiful. Augustine's *De doctrina*

Christiana explains how numbers and patterns of numbers are placed in the sacred books "by way of similitudes," and a figurative action (i.e. a type) can be properly understood only when such similitudes, too, have been elucidated. Thus "Moses, Elias, and the Lord himself all fasted for forty days," and these three occurrences of the same event, limited by the same number, form a pattern which must be considered. I omit the rest of the argument since my purpose here is to draw attention to the parallels constantly drawn between biblical structures and those that we see in the world around us. Thus the 40 days should be seen as the product of 4 and 10, and 4 relates to all temporal cycles (of the day and the year), and these should remind us of the greatest circle of all, to wit Eternity, and so induce us to "condemn temporal things and desire the eternal" (II.xvi.25). But exegetical arguments of this kind will be considered in another chapter; here my concern is with the general principle of unity, which entails symmetrical and graded arrangements.

My discussion of Augustine's aesthetic principles must begin with a summary of the *De ordine*.[9] Since beauty is order, highest beauty is highest order. The beauty of all the arts and sciences depends on order, since beauty entails proper arrangement in terms of number or proportion. When surveying earth and heaven, reason estimates that beauty alone pleases it, in beauty the figures, in the figures the dimensions, and in the dimensions the numbers. The regular course of the seasons, the circles of the stars and the intervals that separate them, all is nothing but the reign of numbers. Reason sees that all sciences are subject to numbers, and that these numbers manifest themselves in proportions that represent absolute truth, while the world of sense contains only the shadows or vestiges of these numbers (*De ordine* II.iv.42–43).

There are three ways of so arranging things that they become beautiful: (1) by division into equal parts, (2) by placing an equal number of units to each side of a mid-point or centre, and (3) by arranging the units so that they form one of the ratios that create harmony. Such arrangements are beautiful because they reflect the divine Unity and hence absolute truth. This truth is grasped by rational thought alone. Rational thought is not subject to mortality, and the highest reason (*ratio*) may be found in the ratios created by the ordered sequences listed above. The ratio of the diapason (1:2), for example, conveys absolute truth. Its truth was not greater yesterday than today, nor will it be more true tomorrow or after a year. Even when the whole world perishes, this ratio cannot cease to exist. It remains always the same. Soul and reason may not be identical, but the soul employs rational thought and is improved by it so that it can proceed from lower to higher things, from mortality to immortality. If the soul comprehends the value and power of numbers – *numerorum vim atque potentiam* – she will deem it a useless pursuit to employ her reason to fashion splendid poetry and recite it to music as long as her own existence and she herself as soul can be seen to pursue a path of error (*devium iter*), so that, dominated by the passions, she produces the discordant noise of vice. (*De ordine* II.iv.1–li; see also *De musica* VI.xi.33).[10]

If Augustine had lived in the Renaissance, the phrase about the *power* of numbers could easily have led a modern scholar to accuse him of an occult bias. But the "power" of numbers is of course in their rational truth, which persuades the soul to establish in herself the same harmony that she so much admires in the work of poets. Augustine explains the relationship between the Creator and the numbers used in the act of creation in his *De Genesi ad litteram* (VI.xiii.23): the laws of numbers have been invested in the created universe through the power of God, but this power has not been tied to these laws.[11] Francesco Giorgio echoes this statement in his collection of Biblical cruxes, the *Problemata* (1536 and later editions). There is no virtue in the numbers themselves; they are characters or symbols only, showing how things are done (*Problemata* VI.viii.321). The world was made not by means of numbers and letters, but by what these signify (*Problemata* VI.vii.246). When Robert Greville wrote *On The Nature of Truth* (1640), this leading Puritan praised the Platonic philosophers for their use of numerical concepts, adding his regret that Satan, who can turn everything to his use, has taught his followers to abuse "even this sweet point of learning" to "charmes and spells".[12]

But the tenor of Augustine's argument is such that it cannot possibly lend itself to abuse. He applied it to the art of poetry in the sixth book of the *De musica*, written immediately after his conversion. Here, too, he explains the three ways in which unity may be achieved, and he does so in greater detail. He says for example that when the number of units is odd, so that unity must be achieved by distributing an equal number of parts around a centre, then this centrally placed unit becomes a unifying nexus. Augustine takes his examples from the quantitative measures of Latin poetry, so that he speaks in terms of quantitative movements (long and short syllables), but he expands his frame of reference from metrical rhythms to those of the universe: we may trace single and double intervals, as in iambic rhythms, also in the progression of hours, days, months, and years. Although after the Fall we can no longer perceive the harmony inherent in the structure of the universe, we may nevertheless infer what it is like from smaller units, because these are placed in a harmonious relationship to the whole. Man is of course part of this universal pattern, and God, the author of all harmony and concord, prevents us from indulging in irregular movements (*imparibus motibus*) and imposes regularity. The highest things are where an eternal and changeless equality prevails; here there is no time because there is no change, but Time proceeds from this sphere in imitation of Eternity – the imitation being the circular pattern seen in the revolution of the heavenly spheres, which return to the point whence they issued in obedience to the law of equality, unity, and order. This is how things on Earth are subservient to those in Heaven, so that by the harmonious succession of their time intervals they become part of the poem of the universe (*Ita coelestibus terrena subjecta, orbes temporum suorum numerosa successione quasi carmini universitatis associant. De musica* VI.xi.29). We return to God through a love of rational harmony, abandoning what is irrational or lascivious, so that we are restored to the enjoyment of rational numbers in which our whole being is turned towards God. In this manner our bodies are ordered by the numbers of health (*numeros sanitatis*) so that the corrupt, external man is changed into a spiritual being.[13]

The argument presented in the *De ordine* and *De musica* VI retained its validity for Augustine. As he puts it in the *De vera religione*, when the Bible states that God created man in his image, this means that the *res creatae* represent multiplicity harmonized through the imposition of an order reflecting the unity which is God. Man was formed for unity: "We worship one God by whom we were made and his likeness by whom we are formed for unity, and his peace whereby we cleave to unity".[14] This numerical terminology pervades the entire treatise on true religion: regeneration, for example, is referred to as a return to the One or Unity, which in its turn is the head or beginning of all concord (*omnis concordiae caput*). Unity alone is eternal and immutable; if we love what is mutable and temporal, we embrace death, but by loving God we achieve a return from the mutable Many to the One that is immutable. As we read on in this treatise, which manages to present abstract intellectual arguments with profound religious fervour, we see how consciously and persistently he argues that poetry and the arts in general lead man back to God. This is because man's ability to effect a return to Unity depends on his ability to perceive the nature of beauty. The beauty of verse is corporeal insofar as it depends on words spoken in time, but the abstract art of metrical movement is constant and changeless. For this reason it is perverse to love that which is perceived by the ear better than what is in the mind – the art of poetry itself. An art or discipline can be discovered only by rational inquiry, never by sense perception, and, since the standard of all the arts is absolutely unchangeable while our minds suffer the mutability of error, the standard called truth must be above our minds. This standard is the divine mind, and it is by this standard that we perceive that beauty is harmony (*convenientia*):

> In all the arts that which pleases is harmony, which alone invests the whole with unity and beauty. This harmony requires equality and unity, either through the resemblance of symmetrical parts, or through the graded arrangement of unequal parts. (*De vera religione* xxx.55).

The reason we delight in harmony is that we delight in absolute equality, which is the similitude of Him who created it. By perceiving this *aequalitas* in the created universe *or in a work of art*, the mind is led back to God. Size is irrelevant to beauty; the universe is beautiful, not because of its size but through its organization (*figurarum ratione*). An ordered fitness imposes beauty on spatial and temporal rhythms, irrespective of extension or duration. The norm or law governing this order is above time or space as it is above all movement, because it is in the unity which is the image of God.

Augustine's concluding paragraphs constitute a powerful rhetorical climax. If we cannot as yet establish union with the One, we must at least drive away from the theatre of our minds all futile and deceptive phantasms. To prevent us from being lost in idle speculations, God plays with us like the babies we are, teaching us by means of parables and comparisons until our inner vision becomes sufficiently clear to perceive the truth itself. If we are pleased with the spectacles of the stage, we ought to consider the art of Him who has imposed order on the theatre of the world as stated in *Wisdom* 8:1 (*disponit omnia suaviter*). The objects that we judge should invite us to consider the rules by which we judge, thus turning our attention away from the work of art to the art itself, so that we may contemplate the beauty without which nothing can be said to be beautiful. This is the message conveyed by Paul when he writes that the invisible things are understood by the things that are made

(*Romans* 1 : 20), and this is how one may achieve a return from the temporal to the eternal and the transformation of the old man into the new.

If the "poem of the world" is fully structured so as to display highest unity, the problem of free will obtrudes itself, since free will would seem incompatible with the idea of a pre-ordained pattern. (In the same manner, the freedom of poetic inspiration has seemed incompatible with the idea of preconceived structures). For this reason Augustine's treatise on the freedom of the will, the *De libero arbitrio*, devotes a great deal of attention to exactly this problem. God knows everything because he views all of time at once – past, present, and future. He sees the whole pattern of history from the first day to the last, and he has fashioned it so as to produce the highest order of beauty. God made all things, including men who would sin: "He did not make them so that they might sin, but so that they might adorn the universe whether they will to sin or whether they do not so will" (III.xi). If no creature existed who could choose whether to sin or refrain from sin, the order of the universe would not be diminished, but it would lack an important element. The order would be diminished if there were no beings capable of attaining "the very peak of the order in the whole creation – such that, if they chose to sin, the universe would be weakened and would totter". This is true of the heavenly powers, but even if all of them fell, this could not debase the order that rightly excludes them.[15]

As he considers the immutable form which is divine Providence, Augustine touches on the relationship between divine and artistic creation, Nature and Art. As he orders his creation, the artist performs the same function as divine Providence. Since divine Providence is immutable form, and since it is through this form that everything exists, this means that things exist because they embody the numbers appropriate to them (II.xvii). And if things exist only because they have number, then the artist, too, organizes his work by numbers; he produces works whose external form corresponds to his "inward light" or idea, and, when this has been fully achieved, the work "delights the inner judge who gazes upward upon numbers". A beautiful body is numbers held in space, while dancing is numbers involved in time, but there is neither space nor time in the art itself from which these numbers come. If we go beyond both the work and the workman, we shall see eternal number or the eternal form through which every created thing is permitted to complete its temporal course by measured movements (II.xvi).

Augustine's aesthetic principles are unusually clear and explicit, and to this clarity he adds the powerful appeal of a fervent religious faith; it is this faith which transforms the classical substratum so that the system may be felt as genuinely Christian. The *Confessions*, too, may be quoted to illustrate Augustine's constant concern with the principle of order. Thus, as he ponders *Genesis* 1 : 31 ("And as you saw all that you had made, O God, and found it very good"), Augustine concludes that, although each day's work is good, the vision of the whole completed work of creation is superior: "For a thing which consists of several parts, each beautiful in itself, is far more beautiful than the individual parts which, *properly combined and arranged*, compose the whole, even though each part, taken separately, is itself a thing of beauty" (*Confessions* 13 : 28; emphasis added).

Once it is understood how Augustine related his aesthetics to his theology, one sees how often he alludes to the former. His aesthetic principles are an integral part of his religious thought so that they must by no means be related only to his youthful addiction to classical learning. If this had been the case, they would scarcely have inspired Bonaventura, that medieval *doctor ecstaticus*, to some of his highest flights. No wonder, therefore, that they inspired the poets as well; the artist who took Augustine's advocacy of an *ars aeterna* seriously would have to incorporate into his work such rhythmical movement as would lead the mind to contemplate *summam aequalitatem*. Like the universe, his work would provide evidence of what is invisible. Imitating the hand of Providence, he would create harmonious successions of temporal or spatial units in structures ranging from a few lines to segments and cantos and the poem as a whole, or from a few hours or days of the epic action to the whole epic chronology.

The validity of Augustine's adaptation of the classical doctrine of harmony for Protestant theology also is seen when Calvin quotes Paul in support of his statement that "the exact symmetry of the universe is a mirror in which we may contemplate the otherwise invisible God" (*Institutes*, I.v.1).[16] Behind Calvin's phrase – "the exact symmetry of the universe" – lies a tradition valid for all the arts and not just for architecture and painting. The nature of the building unit may vary, and the size of the work created, but behind the work and the workman should always be seen the *ars aeterna* that is in the mind of God.

Anyone reading the *Itinerarium mentis in Deum* by Bonaventura (1221–1274) after having studied these works by Augustine, will at once recognize not only the quotations but also the general drift of the argument about the beauty of the created universe. Chapters II and III contain sustained quotations from, or summaries of, the passages on structure in Augustine's *De musica* VI, *De vera religione*, and *De libero arbitrio*. Chapter II quotes Augustine's definition of beauty as *aequalitas numerosa* (*De musica* VI.xiii.38); the *ratio pulchri* is *proportio aequalitatis* – a proportion that establishes equality – which is why beauty is independent of size or temporal duration, and exists wherever we find proportions that establish equality. In contemplating the laws of beauty, therefore, we rise above the world of sense towards a perception of the Deity. The laws by which we judge are from God, indelibly impressed upon our minds, and Augustine is again quoted: no one judges these laws, they are that by means of which we judge (*nullus de eis iudicat, sed per illas. De libero arbitrio* II.xiv.38). As Bonaventura explains, they are not made but increate, existing eternally in the eternal art: *non factas, sed increatas, aeternitaliter existentes in arte aeterna*.

This is followed by an explanation of the six categories of numbers posited by Augustine, beginning with the numbers found in physical bodies and those perceived by the senses, and concluding with those by means of which we judge (*iudiciales*). To these Bonaventura adds the *artificiales* (included in the *iudiciales* by Augustine): these are numbers impressed upon our minds. A consideration of these seven categories is in fact an ascent or *itinerarium* from the world of matter to the divine mind. As Boethius stated in the first chapter of his *De arithmetica*, numbers form the supreme *exemplar* in the mind of God, and for this reason the numbers found in all created things provide the clearest traces of the Deity. This quotation from Boethius enables Bonaventura to conclude that we are led to God when we consider the numerical proportions of all bodily things, delighting in these proportions and judging by them alone. And, since beauty and delight cannot exist without proportion, and since proportion is a matter of numbers, everything must necessarily consist of numbers: *omnia esse numerosa*.[17]

Bonaventura illustrates the complete fusion between the theory of proportion and number symbolism in his comments on the Mosaic account of creation, the *Collationes in Hexaemeron*, thus following Augustine's lead also in this respect. He traces balanced patterns through the Bible and the created universe, and he opposes for example an infernal triad to the Trinity, and an infernal group of twelve to the twelve connected with the scheme of redemption.

The view that all human arts are reflections of the infinite and divine art was advocated by Nicholas Cusanus (1401–1464), for example in the second chapter of his *Liber de mente*. It is in the works of Cusanus, and especially in the *De coniecturis*, that we find the intellectually most challenging use of numerical concepts. Cusanus draws a sharp distinction between the numbers in the human mind and those in God, the former being a mere reflection of the latter; this means that we are using symbols when we philosophize by means of numbers, like the Pythagoreans (*Liber de mente*, ch. 6). Numbers are types representing the first product of the eternal mind, which cannot be grasped except by means of symbols (*enigmate vel figura*). The eternal unity of the exemplar cannot manifest itself except through apt proportions, and proportions are created by numbers. The eternal mind works like a musician who desires to make what is in his mind capable of being perceived by the senses: he takes a multiplicity of tones (*pluralitatem vocum*) and joins them so that they create harmony – or, to put it more precisely, so that harmony finds its own reflection in these proportions. Since the beauty of all things consists of proportion, and proportion resides in numbers, number is the road to wisdom (*numerus ... ducens in sapienciam*). Intellectual perception is possible only through number, as the numbers in the divine mind create the numbers in the mind of man, and these in their turn the various concepts we use in thinking.[18] Cusanus is much too important a thinker to be dismissed in a single paragraph, but the frequent references to Cusanus in the works of Francesco Giorgio and Pietro Bongo ensure an indirect consideration while at the same time avoiding tedious repetition. Then, too, these later writers move on a less exalted intellectual level so that they are widely read. Suffice it, therefore, to stress the important role of "le docte Cusanus" in the dissemination of what Andrew Marvell calls "holy mathematics" ("Upon Appleton House").

On turning to Marsilio Ficino (1433–1499) one remarks at once that, although he draws directly on Plato and the Neoplatonists, he nevertheless reveals a surprising interest in Augustine. Not only are his references to Augustine frequent, he even incorporates extended passages from Augustine in his *Theologia Platonica*, the passages being exactly those that had attracted the attention of Bonaventura. The *Theologia Platonica* XII.5 contains almost all of Augustine's *De vera religione* xxix.53–xxxix.73, and the chapter which follows contains excerpts from Augustine's *De musica* VI. Ficino's *Theologia Platonica* therefore contains the most extensive and authoritative Renaissance version of Augustine's argument that beauty is harmony and that harmony is a reflection of the divine unity. Hence the act of creation – whether divine or artistic – consists in the imposition of unity on multitude through harmonious proportions. Every created thing, so Ficino writes, which consists of many things, achieves its greatest perfection when its parts are so closely linked that it seems one and indivisible because equally solid and harmonious throughout (III.2). Thus the four elements form one by means of the just proportions which prevail between them, and this is true of the universe as a whole, since the work of the one God must itself possess unity. The artist is no slave of Nature, but rather her competitor or emulator: he imitates the divine nature and corrects and improves *naturae inferioris opera* (XIII.3).[19]

Ficino develops Augustine's argument in an important direction when he adds his interpretation of Plato's account of creation in the *Timæus* to Augustine's theory of harmony as symmetrical or proportioned arrangement. True, Augustine uses the ratio of the diapason (1 : 2) in his exposition of the harmony of creation and the scheme for our redemption in the *De Trinitate* IV, but Ficino's account of the ratios which create harmony is much more elaborate and comprehensive. He presents this account in the *Commentarium in Timæum*,[20] but even here he never permits his reader to forget the religious perspective: these ratios depend on, and reflect, the unity that is God. Ficino's *Philebus* commentary uses Platonic terminology far more consistently, but even here there are Scriptural allusions, as when the intelligence is said to arrange "all things according to number, weight, and measure" (*Omnia enim mens in numero, pondere, et mensura ... transigit*).[21] Since all things are from God, as he puts it in the *Commentarium in Timæum*, the divine unity prevails everywhere. Through this unity all things continue to exist and are drawn towards God as in a circle; if this were not so, they would instantly hurtle out into nothingness. All things issue from the divine unity and carry its imprint by means of which they are called back to it, thereby finding their fulfilment. This very image impels souls to prayer through which we make earnest intercession for unity with God. This is a fairly close rendering of a passage in ch. 6, and it must be explained that the "imprint" is the harmonious arrangement set out in the *lambda* numbers. As ch. 32 explains, the ratios which create harmony reflect unity since through them what is dissimilar is made similar, and what lacks equality is provided with it. Thus the difference between the last two numbers – 8 and 27 – disappears when each is considered as a cube, or when they are related through the mean numbers 12 and 18. Thus 8 relates to 12 as 12 to 18 and as 18 to 27, the progression being created by always adding one half of the preceding number. The ratio, therefore, remains constant. The formula 8 : 12 :: 12 : 18 :: 18 : 27 gives arithmetical expression to the harmony imposed on the four elements, earth and fire being connected through the interposition of water and air.

Ficino identifies Plato's account of creation with that of Moses, both having used the same number of steps in the creative process. The "week" of creation gives us six phases, and Plato, too, posits six phases in his formula where six numbers issue out of Unity to create an ordered universe. Chapter 19 states that Plato compressed the mysteries of nature into mathematical images (*per Mathematicas imagines*), and that Moses used similar numerical concepts in his account. Plato therefore agrees with Moses, both arguing that God created everything in number, weight, and measure.

Ficino's radical syncretism can be studied in the pages of the *De Christiana religione*, a work translated into French by the poet Guy le Fèvre de La Boderie in 1578. Like Eusebius, Ficino explains how the whole course of history points towards the revelation given through the incarnation of Christ; before this moment the revelation was conveyed through types and symbols, and Ficino finds such types also in Greek myth, in the Sibylline prophecies, and in Plato and Hermes Trismegistus. But this is not all: Chapter XXII cites Augustine to the effect that Plato was divinely inspired, a much more extreme position than the one which posited a process of borrowing from Hebrew sources. (Ficino conveniently ignores Augustine's recantation in his *Retractationes*). Ficino's syncretism, however, rather increases the importance of Christ than the opposite. When Christ finally makes his appearance on the stage of the world, all imperfect prophecies cease at once: these relate to the truth as shadow to substance.

If the establishing of harmony is the process which leads man back to God, then the image of the circle will express the same idea of a return. The harmony of the diapason in fact constitutes a circle, since the last note returns to the first, but in a higher register. Ficino therefore conducts his discussion of unity as much in terms of the circle as of mathematical ratios. *The Theologia Platonica* I.3 proclaims that the circular form comes closest to *aequalitas*, but when assessing Ficino's use of this geometrical symbol we must not forget that it occurred so often in biblical exegesis that its connotations would have been felt as Christian. The biblical narrative was believed to have a circular form, the end being linked to the beginning in several ways. As I explain in Chapter III, the tree in the garden of Eden (*Gen.* 2:9) and that in the heavenly Jerusalem (*Rev.* 22:2) were types of Christ, so that the biblical narrative begins and concludes with the same image of Christ as a tree placed *in medio*.[22]

Many Renaissance theologians agreed with Ficino that the Mosaic seven-day week of creation should be interpreted as a metaphor for the ordered process which Plato explains by means of the heptachord of numbers constituting his *lambda* formula. Of the mathematical ratios, that of the diapason or the octave deserves special attention; its importance was partly a matter of the ratio, partly of its association with the number 8. Since in the octave the last tone returns to the first, it illustrates the circular return to God, and this return is of course to an eighth age of Eternity succeeding the seven ages of all of Time. The number 8 should also be related to Christ, who rose on the eighth day after Palm Sunday, thus securing the harmony that ensures a return to God or Unity. Augustine persistently associates Christ with the number 8 and with the harmony of the octave, as we may see from his sermons on the Psalms. In the diapason or the octave, therefore, three symbols coincide: that of the ratio, that of the circle, and that of the number 8. This illustrates the conceptual richness engendered by the syncretistic approach so admirably illustrated by Ficino's *Commentarium in Timæum*. No wonder, therefore, that it proved attractive to artists, as Ficino himself remarks in ch. 40. He opens this chapter with the statement that it would require considerable time and effort to list those among his contemporaries who had found that their purpose was best served by mathematics. Thus Leone Battista Alberti produced a magnificent book on architecture by exploiting this science, just as Francesco Berlinghieri composed a versified treatise on cosmography on a mathematical basis. André Chastel quotes this sentence in French translation in his *Marsile Ficin et l'art* (Geneva, 1954),[23] a work which rightly stresses the point that Ficino aligned the creative artist with the Deity on the basis of their *modus operandi*. However, Chastel is completely silent with regard to the Augustinian tradition outlined here; even in his discussion of Ficino's architectural metaphor – that all acts of creation presuppose a preconceived pattern – there is no acknowledgement of a tradition extending back through Bonaventura to Augustine and Philo Judæus. It is fortunate that Raymond Marcel's Latin–French edition of the *Theologia Platonica* not only makes the text available in a modern edition with a reliable translation, but also provides editorial annotations identifying Ficino's indebtedness to Augustine, pseudo-Dionysius, and other sources. It is regrettable that Ficino's *Commentarium in Timæum* is accessible only in Latin,[24] thus preventing his syncretistic interpretation of Plato's account of creation from being better known.

The relevance of such accounts of creation to Renaissance poetics is, perhaps, self-evident; Augustine had stated that the world is God's "poem" so that a poem in its turn should constitute a "world" arranged, like the universe, in "number, weight, and measure", and this argument became one of the great commonplaces of the Renaissance. It is echoed by Christoforo Landino (1424–1498)[25] who wrote that the literary artifact comes very close to being a creation, so that we may say, conversely, that "God is the supreme poet, and the world his poem. Just as God when he arranges his creation, that is the visible and the invisible world which is his work, in number, measure, and weight ... in a manner similar to this the poets establish their poems with the numbers of their feet, with the measure of long and short syllables, and with the weight of the sentences and the affections".[26] More than a hundred years later Tasso was to repeat the metaphor in his discourses on the art of poetry and on epic poetry,[27] and the fact that Tasso connects the harmony of poetry so firmly and unequivocally with an ordered arrangement of parts is evidence of the influence exerted by the Florentine humanists. We know that Tasso possessed a copy of Pico's *Heptaplus*,[28] and both Donne and Milton are among the English poets who refer to Pico.[29] In the work of Ficino, and even more so in that of Pico della Mirandola and Francesco Giorgio, the harmony of the universe is directly related to the art of poetry. To the Augustinian system of aesthetics they added a syncretistic interpretation of the work of creation, thus extending its range and providing further directions for artists to follow.

2. Pico and Giorgio

Pico della Mirandola (1463–94) must be considered together with the disciple whose fame was to eclipse his own – Francesco Giorgio (1453–1540). Giorgio in a way took over where Pico left off, and it may have been his surprising longevity which enabled him to produce what must surely be the most comprehensive Renaissance account of the harmony of creation, the *De harmonia mundi* (1525). Giorgio writes in a way which shows that his purpose was to move his readers to embrace the truths he presented, and these truths are his elaboration of the ideas conveyed by Augustine in the *De vera religione*. The chief difference between the two works is Giorgio's elaborate exposition of the order imposed by God on his works in space and time. Giorgio was not content merely to advocate an *ars aeterna*; this art must condition the structure of his own argument. The preconceived structure guides his thought. This is equally true of Pico's *Heptaplus* (1489), and both authors explain the meaning invested in the textual structures selected as appropriate. Pico favoured the number of creation (7), Giorgio that of harmony restored through Christ (8). Both combine symbolic numbers with circular structures and with balanced symmetries.

That the age itself recognized the kinship between the two is shown by the fact that a one-volume French translation of the *Heptaplus* and the *De harmonia mundi* appeared at Paris in 1578 and 1579. The translators were the brothers Guy and Nicholas le Fèvre de La Boderie. Guy le Fèvre was a poet of some distinction who explains in his preface that he was attracted to Giorgio's treatise because of its strong relevance to his own poetry. Giorgio's presentation is itself highly poetical but, although Pico's shorter treatise is somewhat schematic, it, too, is sufficiently imaginative to appeal to poets as well as to philosophers. Both may be said to have poetisized the syncretistic vision of world harmony.

The two proems to *Heptaplus*[30] contain ideas of great literary relevance. Like Augustine (cf. *Confessions* 12:18–32), Pico discovers a wealth of meaning in the simple words of Moses. Moses was "deeply learned in all the lore of the Egyptians", and he passed his insights on to Pythagoras; if Moses seems to write like "an unpolished popularizer" rather than a master of wisdom, we must remember that he could not write "openly and without figures". He screened the light "lest it hurt the bleary-eyed. He neither ought nor could nor wished to help the learned less than the unlearned" (p. 73). Although it is possible that Pico here may be speaking like a Christian Magus, the veiled character of the Mosaic narrative is a typological commonplace. That the creation of the sun on the fourth day is a type or prophecy of the advent of Christ is one of the most familiar of biblical types, and Raymond B. Waddington has shown how Pico, like Moses, created a structure for his work which "hides at its midpoint the prophecy of Christ's advent".[31] Pico's treatise, then, is clearly Christocentric. As Pico explains in his second proem to the whole book, he has divided his discourse into seven books of seven chapters each in order to establish correspondence with the seven days of creation. And, because the seventh day was a day of rest, "we have taken care that every exposition of ours shall always in the seventh chapter be turned to Christ, who is ... our Sabbath, our rest, and our felicity" (p. 84). However, through the typological significance of the creation of the sun on the fourth day, the fourth chapter of Book IV – the mathematical centre – shows what Waddington calls a hidden Son. This links the centre to the end of the book (IV.7), since each seventh chapter considers Christ directly and openly. An even stronger link is between IV.4 and VII.4, since VII.4 announces the arrival of the incarnate Son in the fullness of time "in the very middle of the fourth millennium" (p. 159). "For if the number four is the fullness of numbers [cf. the Pythagorean tetractys], will not the fourth day be the fullness of days?" (p. 157).

The overall structure, as Waddington explains, is that of a pyramid. We begin with the elements in Book I, Book II elevates us to the celestial spheres, and Book III to the angelic and invisible world. Book IV summarizes all these spheres since its subject is the microcosmos of man (with the hidden Son at the centre), and in Book V we are gradually led through an inverted sequence from the angelic world (V.1), the heavenly (V.2), and the elemental (V.3) via the heavenly bodies and the animals (V.4) to man (V.6). In the last two books this vertical movement is exchanged for one which is strictly linear or horizontal.

The best commentary on this structural technique is Pico's assessment of Moses. His ability as a writer (or poet) was such that his account of creation is "the exact image of the world":

> since a writer copies nature... it is believable that his teaching about the worlds is arranged just as God, the almighty artificer, arranged them in themselves, so that truly the scripture of Moses is the exact image of the world; just as we also read that on the mountain where he learned these things, he was commanded to make everything according to the pattern he had seen on the mountain (p. 79).

A piece of writing, then, becomes the "exact image of the world" when arranged, or put together, in the same way. The pattern Moses saw on the mountain was that of the created universe, and he gave it physical form in the building of the Tabernacle and literary form in his account of creation.

When Pico praises Moses as "the pattern for perfection in a writer", excelling "all other progeny of the human mind in doctrine, eloquence, and genius" (p. 95), a major reason is his alignment of his narrative with the structure of God's creation. By performing the same compositional *tour de force*, Pico emulates Moses and challenges his readers to study his own book with the same kind of attention. Pico's praise must have helped to strengthen the view that prophets are true poets so that, conversely, true poets are prophetic. It is interesting that such a very minor poet as John Collop should have echoed this view in his *Poesis Rediviva: or, Poesie Revived* (1656). The first poem in this collection, on "The Poet", proclaims that the prophets were poets and that the world is God's poem, made in number and measure, so that "Poets are Prophets, and the Priests of Heav'n." God himself "descends to us by Poesie."

Pico may not have been the first to explain the nature of allegory by referring to the correspondences between the three worlds, but his exposition must have carried a lot of weight; thus Pierre de la Primaudaye copies this passage verbatim, but without acknowledgement.[32] As Pico explains, the prophets could refer to an object in one world or sphere by means of its corresponding object in another. "In our world there is the elemental quality of heat, in the heavens there is a heating power, and in angelic minds there is the idea of heat ... But see how they differ. The elemental fire burns, the celestial gives life, and the supercelestial loves". As in the case of biblical types, then, the similarity is combined with a significant difference between lower and higher levels. These three worlds are one, in part because "regulated by appropriate numbers", and in part because "there is no one of them in which is not to be found whatever is in each of the others" (p. 77). The microcosmos of man is a fourth world, and all these worlds are governed by a Deity defined as primal Unity through whose agency they are "bound by the chains of concord". "From this principle ... flows the science of all allegorical interpretation" (p. 78). Moses was a great writer because he selected terms and so arranged his discourse "that the same words, the same context, and the same order in the whole passage are completely suitable for symbolizing the secrets of all the worlds and of the whole nature" (pp. 94 f.).

We feel the influence of Dionysius the Areopagite when each of the three worlds is organized in groups of nine (seen as three times three), and the definition of God as Unity probably owes more to the Areopagite than to Augustine. As the Areopagite was believed to have been the disciple of Paul, his writings possessed great authority, and one reason why the *lambda* numbers are so often found in Renaissance discussions of the cosmic scheme is surely that the triadic scheme of the Dionysian hierarchies overlaps with the Platonic formula, thus providing an authoritative warrant for their validity. The *lambda* sequence concludes with the two cubes, 8 and 27, and 8 could be used as a mathematical image of the eighth day of the resurrection (and the eighth age of eternal bliss),[33] while 27 reflects the threefold structure of the world as set out by Dionysius or again by Nicholas Cusanus (*De coniecturis* I.16) or by Nicholas le Fèvre de La Boderie in the preface to his translation of Pico's *Heptaplus*.[34]

Evidence of Pico's influence is easily discovered. John Colet's interpretation of the Mosaic account of creation agrees with Pico's on so many points that his direct reference to the Italian merely confirms what is already plain. A major Renaissance work strongly indebted to Pico is the *Cosmopoeia Vel, De Mundano Opificio, Expositio trium capitum Genesis* (Lyon, 1535) by Augustinus Steuchus Eugubinus (1496–1549), director of the Vatican Library. This is a thoroughly syncretistic treatise abounding with references to Plato, Hermes, Pythagoras, and other *prisci theologi*.[35] In England, references to Pico can be located in John Donne's *Essays in Divinity* (bracketed with Giorgio), in Abraham Cowley's footnotes to his own poems, in the prose of Thomas Traherne, and in Henry Reynolds' *Mythomystes* (1633). It is worth noting that Reynolds was interested in Pico because of his concern with poetic allegory, and this is true also of the brothers Guy and Nicholas le Fèvre de La Boderie. With these two Frenchmen we have reached an interesting group of poets and philosophers associated with the French Academies, whose influence reached across the Channel to England just at the time when Sidney and Spenser began their careers.[36] It is both possible and likely that *The Shepheardes Calender* (1579) was inspired by the many publications with a syncretistic bias published in France during the 1570s. Guy le Fèvre was extremely active as a transmitter of such ideas, both in his own poetry and as a translator, and his brother Antoine connects directly with England in his capacity as ambassador to the English court. A link between French and English literary circles has been discovered as early as in the 1560s, when the Daniel Rogers referred to by Gabriel Harvey in one of his letters frequented the group of poets who found inspiration in de Baïf's French Academy. Rogers met and conversed with Pierre Ronsard and listened to him recite his lyrics or perhaps chant them to musical accompaniment. On his return to London in 1570 he came to enjoy the friendship of the group known as the Areopagus, a fact which suggests that its members were already interested in the ideas expounded by Jean Antoine de Baïf and his circle.[37] The story of this circle has been told by Frances Yates (*The French Academies of the Sixteenth Century*, 1947), and in another of her books (*Giordano Bruno and the Hermetic Philosophy*, 1964) Frances Yates has shown that Bruno, too, helped to connect French and English literary milieus.[38] Considerable importance must also be attached to the one-volume French translation of Pico and Giorgio, as well as to the many Paris editions of Giorgio's *De harmonia mundi* and the *Problemata* in the original Latin. Thus the *De harmonia mundi* appeared at Paris in 1545, 1546, and 1564, but this time with a new title, *Promptuarium*, while *Problemata* appeared in 1574, 1575, and 1622.

Editions of the Hermetic dialogues, with editorial commentaries, strengthened the syncretistic trend considerably.[39] Thus the extensive commentary by the French nobleman and prelate François de Foix de Candale (Bourdeaux, 1579) professes to find all the Christian doctrines in the dialogues, and so does Robert Fludd in his detailed commentary on the Hermetic account of creation (*Mosaicall Philosophy*). Frances Yates mentions that John Dee owned a copy of the Latin edition of Giorgio's *De harmonia mundi* and copies of works by Ficino, Pico, and Pontus de Tyard. "The whole Renaissance", she writes, "is in this library", but it is a Renaissance seen as tinged by the occult. However, there is no magic and no occult lore in Giorgio and, although references to Hermetic and Cabalistic ideas are relatively frequent, it is quite misleading to call the book a "Hermetic–Cabalist work" largely responsible for Robert Fludd's leanings towards the occult.[40] As J.-F. Maillard has pointed out, Giorgio's *magnum opus* is on the contrary orthodox to a surprising extent.[41] I would also characterize as orthodox a letter written by Dee to the Archbishop of Canterbury, which Frances Yates takes as evidence that Dee "believed that the divine creation was held together by magical forces". The passage she quotes cannot possibly serve as a basis for such a conclusion. In it Dee merely states that one may ascend "(as it were) *gradatim*, from things visible to consider of things inuisible: from things bodily to conceiue of things spirituall"; in short, to be led by a consideration of "the most meruailous frame of the *whole world*" to love, honour, and glorify the Creator. Nothing could be more orthodox than this pious wish framed in terms taken from *Romans* 1 : 20.

If in the following I discuss Giorgio's ideas in some detail, this is in part because Giorgio is so close to Dee and Fludd, and these are important figures in the intellectual milieu of their time. Sir Philip Sidney studied under Dee, who enjoyed the support of Sidney's uncle, the Earl of Leicester, and it is a measure of Dee's international reputation that he is one of the sources that Pietro Bongo used when he compiled the material for his *Numerorum mysteria*.[42] In the early seventeenth century Marin Mersenne defended the doctrines of Giorgio after these had been modified so as to agree with "the full rigour of Christian orthodoxy" to quote Désirée Hirst,[43] and Fludd agreed with Giorgio to an extent which goes far beyond a possible common indebtedness to Augustine and Cusanus. To all this may be added that a man like Alexander Gill, Milton's teacher at St Paul's grammar school, could refer to Giorgio's *Problemata* in his discussion of the Christocentric nature of Time.[44] Via Dee, then, Giorgio's sphere of influence may be seen to extend to the Sidney–Spenser circle, and, via Alexander Gill, to the young Milton.

The transmission of these ideas across the English Channel may be traced in the English translations of Pierre de la Primaudaye's *The French Academie* (1586 and later editions) and of Philip of Mornay's *A Woorke concerning the trewnesse of the Christian Religion* (1587). It is a boon that Pico's *Heptaplus* has been translated into English, and that Giorgio's *De harmonia mundi* can be read in the French translation of 1578; Giorgio's *Problemata*, however, must be read in its original Latin and so must that useful late sixteenth-century encyclopedia of number symbolism, Pietro Bongo's *Numerorum mysteria*.[45] To these sources must be added a selection of representative theological treatises and biblical commentaries in order to assess the extent of overlapping, otherwise the orthodoxy of Pico's and Giorgio's structural arguments cannot be assessed. It has been assumed that they are unorthodox, but this is not so.

Christopher Butler's *Number Symbolism* (1970) illustrates the risks incurred if one's reading is too limited. Because he has failed to see how Giorgio's key arguments connect with the Augustinian tradition, Butler exaggerates Giorgio's singularity. When Giorgio for example uses a whole chapter to show how all things issue out of the Deity by means of the number 6 (*De harmonia mundi* I.viii.8) this argument should of course be referred back to Augustine's *De Trinitate* IV. This is true of Bongo, too, whose comments on this number contain frequent references to Augustine's exposition. A third writer who refers to it is Simon Goulart in his account of Du Bartas's passage on number symbolism.[46] Giorgio himself brackets Augustine with the "mathematicians" when he cites "les Mathematiciens et sainct Augustin" as authorities for his chapter on the reasons why God is said to have worked for six days and to have rested on the seventh (I.ii.11). Giorgio's references to Augustine are frequent and by basing his argument so extensively on the science of numbers he is in fact insisting on its impeccable rationality.

Giorgio's syncretism is his outstanding characteristic, but his syncretism fully deserves to be labelled as moderate, and his views were largely orthodox. True, in 1554, 14 years after his death, Giorgio's two books were placed on the *Index librorum expurgandorum*, but they were not burnt as heretical and they were often referred to by theologians.[47] The objections raised by the church concerned not so much Giorgio's ideas as his method – the fact that he drew on sources other than divine revelation entailed a very real risk of contamination.[48] Giorgio constantly juxtaposes Plato and Moses, or Plato and St John, but the Bible is always his point of departure and philosophy is adduced only to the extent that it agrees – or can be made to seem to agree – with divine revelation. Because this supposed agreement is taken seriously and is seen as extensive, the many references to Plato, Plotinus, Orpheus, or Pythagoras may seem to prevail at the expense of Holy Writ, but, if read with some care, the text proves clearly enough that Giorgio's sole concern is with the Christian message of salvation. Like Eusebius, Giorgio uses pagan sources in order to show that the truths they contain are from God. Giorgio actually has little to say about the harmony of the world which cannot be found in Augustine, Bonaventura, Cusanus, Ficino, and Pico; he is merely more elaborate and systematic.

True, he will occasionally resort to Cabalistic lore, but we must in all fairness remember that Cabalistic *gematria* were popular among orthodox theologians, too, for example when considering the four letters in the name of Jehovah (the *Tetragrammaton*). Since Hebrew letters are numbers as well, the four letters (two of which are identical) yield the numbers 5, 6, and 10, and in the mathematical quality of these numbers we are supposed to find a reflection of the nature of the Deity. Ten is circular since in it all numbers return to unity (in the sense that we begin all over again once we reach 10), and 5 and 6, too, are circular since they return to themselves in the last digit when multiplied with themselves. This "proves" that the nature of the Deity resembles that of the circle in being without beginning or end, and in encompassing everything. This was also "proved" by construing *Revelation* 1 : 8, 1 : 11, 21 : 6, and 22 : 13 ("I am Alpha and Omega, the beginning and the end, the first and the last") as meaning that the nature of God is like that of the circle. This argument is found in traditional exegesis as well, for example in the pages of Cornelius à Lapide.[49] Giorgio believes the nature of the Deity to be indicated not only by the *Tetragrammaton* but also by the dimensions of the heavenly Jerusalem: the four letters, like the squareness of the city (*Rev.* 21 : 16), symbolize firmness and stability, but the city must perforce also be circular. In God, then, the circle is squared. When Milton lets the heavenly Jerusalem seem "undetermined square or round" (*Paradise Lost* 2.1048) he was surely glancing in this direction rather than revealing uncertainty.

This may serve as an example of the kind of exposition that a modern reader will dismiss as unorthodox unless he consults traditional exegesis. Although the argument about the *Tetragrammaton* is fairly unimportant in itself, its assumption is truly basic, and that assumption is of course that the meaning inherent in the form helps to explain what is thus expressed. This is why so many could state that the mental ascent to God may be achieved by means of a contemplation of number, and this, in short, is what Giorgio's book is about.

As Giorgio explains in his prefatory epistle to the Pope, those who dedicate themselves to such an ascent achieve it because there is perfect alignment between the visible and the invisible world. The technique entails a contemplation of the harmony which joins Heaven and Earth, until one becomes part of it. Since this harmony (so he writes) is created by means of numbers, the most effective approach is by means of a knowledge of numbers. What Orpheus chanted, Pythagoras taught after him; Plato proposed the same doctrine, Porphyrius affirmed it and so did Chalcidius, Proclus, and Syrian his master, and all who have followed Pythagoras. No knowledge is more ancient or more precious than this which tells us how everything which has been created or will be is governed by the laws of harmony. The divine prophets have pondered many truths which must be revealed only as far as is permitted to avoid giving offense. Thus Isaiah in a vision saw the Lord on a throne elevated above all things, which constitute as it were his palace, full of the glory of the Workman. This "palace" is joined together (organized) by means of the Ideas in the mind of the Workman, which is why there is complete concord and mutual love between the Workman and his "Fabrique". The two seraphim proclaiming that the earth is full of the glory of God can do so because this glory is communicated through the ratios or proportions by means of which all things are disposed. The prophets left the mere "earthly" numbers behind in the porch, philosophizing instead by means of the divine and better numbers, thus proceeding to the species and forms and the ideas themselves. Ezekiel achieved this ascent when he contemplated the divine throne that the Hebrews call the Merkaba or chariot with four wheels made from divine ministers and saintly animals "pour tirer la consonance de toutes choses". They appear like wheels within wheels because this world is spherical and placed in the middle of the intellectual supreme sphere, that is the Word (the Logos) "qui tient le milleu [sic] en la Roue surmondaine" according to St John. (This juxtaposition of *Ezekiel* 1 with *Rev.* 1 : 13–16 is commonly found in biblical exegesis, since both visions are supposed to show Christ as the creative Logos in the middle of the created universe.) In what follows, Giorgio identifies the vision of the universe shown to Moses on the mountain with that of St John; to Giorgio, as to Bonaventura, Moses is the *inchoator sapientiae Dei, et Ioannes, terminator* (*Collationes in Hexaemeron* I.10). In the words of Giorgio, as translated from the French,

> that which St John, true prophet, saw on the mountain of Parnassus with its two hills, that is, on the breast of Jesus Christ or the double summit of Nature divine and human, this was seen also by Moses on the mount of Sinai with its two hills, who as the first revealed these mysteries .... But he hid and enveloped these secrets under obscure enigmas in his most rich and full description of the fabric of the world.

Moses employed historical narrative, then, for the purpose of concealment, but, by the wisdom of the few who are capable of proceeding from the unstable visible world to what is stable and invisible by means of the affinity of numbers and harmonious proportions, this narrative was seen to possess a moral, allegorical, and anagogical level of meaning.

Nothing could be more typical of Giorgio and the syncretistic approach in general than this bracketing of Moses and Ezekiel with the Apocalypse in order to prove that the divine *ordo* is based on the principle of harmonious proportions. Equally typical is the introduction of the mountain of Parnassus as one of three hills, each of which has two peaks representing the divine and the human sphere, respectively. The vision experienced on these mountains – one real (Sinai), one mythical (Parnassus), and one purely symbolical (the breast of Christ with its two "hills") – is of the harmonious concord between the two spheres. Spenser reflects this tradition when he describes how Redcrosse Knight has his vision of the heavenly Jerusalem on a hill compared first to Sinai, then to Mount Olivet, and finally to Parnassus (I.x.53–54). James E. Phillips has related Spenser's description to the syncretistic tradition,[50] and so suffice it here to draw attention to the fact that we find the same nexus of images in Giorgio's prefatory letter to the Pope. The similarity is sufficiently pronounced to suggest direct influence.[51]

Giorgio next touches on one of the great commonplaces of the Renaissance – that music represents a higher harmony of which the world is only a reflection, which explains why music can exert the power testified to by Timotheus and David. It was awareness of this power which caused harmonious chants to be introduced into the sacred rites by the royal prophet and true restorer of the sacred mysteries, and by the Fathers of the church who knew these secrets of God and Nature. Truth is found in this concord between things natural and divine, because truth is "la conuenance des choses", and in the divine scriptures this truth delights and moves the mind so that one seems to change into another mode of being. This is particularly true of the Psalms of David; in these are celebrated the agreement between the two worlds and the archetypal formal world, and the consonance that was restored to all things by Christ the Messiah, by means of which the created world returns to its most perfect Workman.

To continue my paraphrase: a knowledge of true harmony and of divinity must be attributed to those who have discovered this symbolic conformity in the Holy Scriptures, for who does not perceive that all the prophets were instructed in the true art of poesy? Who does not recognize in Moses, Ezekiel, Daniel, and St John the most exquisite and subtle geometrical measures and numerical proportions? or sweet and full musical "accords" in the hymns of David, the epithalamion of Solomon, and in the connection between the two Testaments, like "vn chant nuptial entier et parfaict"? This is a music superior to that of Orpheus or Amphion, and it is this we must follow and take as our guide. To do so entails organizing one's work by means of the very numbers which create harmony, and Giorgio explains that he has himself preferred an organization in 3 groups of 8, since this creates a harmony in which may be felt the Holy Spirit and the Workman of all things. The division into 8 units creates the perfect diapason: the first group describes the consonance between the Earth and the celestial spheres on the one hand, and on the other the Archetype; the second explains the consonance between all things and Christ their head and the restoration, through Christ, of the harmony that was lost; to the third has been given the theme of the new man who has achieved perfect harmony.

The importance of this argument to Renaissance poetics is obvious: Giorgio relates the ratios which create harmony to the created universe, to divine revelation, and to his own book. As Giorgio explains, the laws of harmony are as much part of poesy as of divinity. As Guy le Fèvre de La Boderie puts it in his preface, Giorgio has written his work musically or rather Mosaically ("faict à la Musaique, ou plustost à la Mosaique"), thus anticipating Andrew Marvell's pun in *Upon Appleton House* on the "light mosaic" in which he reads "Nature's mystic book."[52] This light has musical connotations as in the 1:2 ratio between the 25 stanzas on the history of the house (stanzas 11–35) and the 50 on the estate (stanzas 36–85). Because the units constituting Giorgio's treatise have been put together "musically or Mosaically," all its parts are so well joined together that they seem one. Thus to Guy le Fèvre, pondering the structure of the work he was translating, unity was a matter of imitating the divine plan itself.

Passages of interest to Renaissance poetics are found in Giorgio's preface, his "Pour Parler du Premier Cantique" (6 f.), which relates the textual structure to the theme: because his purpose is to celebrate the harmony of the world, he found it useful to preserve the progress of well-ordered degrees established by the Creator ("le souuerain Archimusee"), and God disposed each separate thing, as well as the whole world taken together, by means of harmonious numbers. He did not withdraw his hand until he had invested his work with the most perfect consonance consummated by the full symphony of the diapason. And in truth by this octave the whole fabric of the world is made perfect, since the supreme Workman arranged it by means of seven degrees of things, hidden by Moses under the veil of the six days, at the end of which he rested on the seventh. And if this seventh day is numbered together with the first when God was still in himself ("lors qu'il estait en soymesme"), we must number it the eighth. And the perfect work arranged in terms of this proper and harmonious sequence of days exists in such a manner that after the seventh it returns to the eighth, which is the same and yet not the same as the first. (This alludes to the octave where the last note returns to the first, but in a higher register.) Similarly the acts of God (i.e. his works in the world of time) will be fully achieved when all things are restored to their first perfection in the perfect octave (i.e. at the end of time as symbolized by the seven "days" that are the seven ages of human history). We ourselves (i.e. Giorgio), following the example of the Workman, will achieve the same harmony by always returning in the last eighth "tone" to the subject-matter of the first. (The book is divided into 3 *Cantiques*, each of which consists of 8 *tones*.) While the first "tone" considers the Workman as the beginning of all things, the eighth considers him as our end, thus closing the circle. The "tones" in between will sing our progress from the first to the last, in which consists all earthly and heavenly contemplation.

The preface to the eighth "Tone" of the last "Cantique" (730–32) fuses the art of music with the art of poetry and both with the divine acts of creation and redemption. The "song" or harmony by means of which God leads his creation towards eternal bliss is an image of Eternity; by his wonderful contrivance God has submitted the machine of the world to the sequential movements of time at the same time that it has been liberated from time. For all elementary things are created by the succession of days and years, and the heavenly spheres, too, move in time or, rather, by moving create time. The Earth nevertheless remains stable eternally, and the heavens do not depart from their essence regardless of the fact that, as the Psalmist writes, they are perishable – an argument which recalls Spenser's Mutability Cantos. In terms of months and days was achieved the sweet harmony of the redemption, and yet this redemption is available always as an eternal fruit. God liberates from the sequence of time those who are attracted to him by the power of a harmony sweeter than that of Orpheus or Amphion, lodging them in those sweet abodes where the numbers themselves (if we are to believe Augustine) will seem openly to resound the praises of the Creator. This is why the heavenly secretaries of the one and the other Testament – Ezekiel and St John – have described these eternal abodes with such great diligence by means of exquisite figures, harmonious measures, and symmetrical divisions, as the Holy Spirit taught them. But their message is so hidden that divine illumination is required before one can proceed in contemplation from the visible to the invisible. St John, reposing on the breast of

Christ as on the mountain of Parnasus between the two hills of the divine and human nature, was illuminated by the divine light and inspired by a divine poetic fury, so that without effort he became poet and prophet of the divine mysteries. Taught by the angel and by Christ, "le chantre suprême", he has given us perfect songs according to the laws of music. He has done this by means of the figure of a city that seems to us like a celestial harp in which is engendered and made perfect the consonance that surpasses all consonances. This figurative city is Christ, since Giorgio describes Christ, too, as a musical instrument. The Son was made the organ of God, as in him are the ideas of all the things that were created; these are arranged in him so that they form as it were the pipes of the organ, and the Holy Spirit is the wind blowing through everything. But the Father is the first and principal mover of all things even in the heavenly city.

Giorgio's frequent resort to arguments taken from Augustine may be illustrated by reference to section III.viii.16, which repeats Augustine's familiar definition of peace as order – the tranquillity of order. When all things are well ordered, peace and tranquillity will follow. The peace of the body is health; the peace of the irrational soul is an appetite that is "ordonné et reposé", and the peace of soul and body is an ordered life and a harmonious union between, and operation of, the one and the other. Finally the peace of the reasonable soul is an ordered knowledge and a consenting choice of the will. From this peace follows our peace with God. To such a person the yoke of Christ is sweet and agreeable, and in such persons is the song which the angels chanted on the birth of the Prince of Peace. Such a person will ascend to the celestial city where, according to Job, there is such concord that it constitutes a vision and enjoyment of peace.

Another example may be taken from I.viii.1, which invokes Augustine's *De ordine* to explain the harmony of the universe and of man – the *musica mundana* and the *musica humana*. After the Fall, man is incapable of perceiving more than a small part of the whole divine pattern, but when regenerated he will trace this harmony everywhere. Giorgio finds biblical evidence concerning this harmony in *Job*, significantly juxtaposed with *Proverbs* (8:27–29). He whom Moses introduced as the Workman balanced the foundations of the earth with such exact measure that "all the sons of God shouted for joy" (*Job* 38 : 7). And, alluding to *Wisdom* 8 : 1, Giorgio adds that it was certainly God who, as St Augustine says, disposed all things "d'vne tres-doulce concorde et de nombres bien forts". According to Pythagoras, musical harmony is a mere shadow of what is in the mind of man and in the works of creation, and it is this higher kind of harmony that Job refers to for example in 41 : 11–12. This passage shows how a paraphrase of a well-known Augustinian text serves to introduce an extended discussion of *Job* in terms of Pythagorean and Platonic number lore, the many quotations from *Job* being rendered by the translator in rhymed couplets.

Giorgio applied his Augustinian aesthetic principles to church architecture in a memorandum on the correct numerical proportions for a planned church,[53] and Giorgio reveals his interest in architecture in the *De harmonia mundi* when he refers to Vitruvius in his discussion of the way in which theatres may reflect the harmony of the universe (III.viii.11). Theatres should be built according to musical proportions so that the audience will hear the voices of the actors quite clearly. The vases or vessels used to amplify the voices are intriguing,[54] but the memorandum is of interest primarily because Giorgio explains how a theatre should be constructed so as to ensure harmony. Even so we must never forget that the consonance of the heavenly Jerusalem is much greater than anything made by man, the greatest harmony of all being afforded by the spectacle of God on his throne surrounded by his angels. Augustine says that David knew this harmony and conveyed it to us in his poems "par vne image mystique de la chose, et par diuers sons raisonnables, et accords bien moderez: et d'vne accordée varieté, representent la coniointe vnité de la Cité supernelle bien ordonnée". The smooth transition from architecture to poetry proves that in poetry, too, it is the structure which matters.

Although Giorgio, like Ficino, goes far beyond Augustine in his systematic application of classical number lore, he clearly believed this lore to be impeccably biblical in origin. His logical point of departure is the traditional typological view of the week of creation: Scripture teaches, and the mathematicians confirm, that the story of creation prophesies events that will occur in the course of time. We must accept Augustine's view that the week is a metaphor stating the order in which everything is arranged; this story is one of several passages in the Bible that cannot be taken literally. Almost all the prophecies, in fact, are metaphorical and speak about one thing in terms of another (I.ii.10). Giorgio carefully explains in the very first sentences of his book (I.i.1) that Moses wrote 310 years before the fall of Troy as St Augustine and Eusebius maintain, while, according to Cicero, Homer and Hesiod wrote 150 years after the sack of Troy, and Orpheus lived 300 years after Moses. Moses, then, was the first, and after him came Hermes Trismegistus as the second, and Plato as the third. Pythagoras conveyed much Mosaic wisdom into the realm of philosophy, just as pagan myth contains garbled versions of the sacred truths. Thus Deucalion's flood is a later version of the true story of the Flood, and what Ovid sings about the origin and construction of this world is similarly indebted to the Hebrews. All of I.ii (14 chapters) is concerned with the relationship between revelation and philosophy, parallels being drawn between *John* 1:1 and Plato's *Timæus*. Giorgio quotes extensively from Augustine's *De Trinitate* IV in his comments on the six days of creation (I.ii.11), which are said to create the diapason, for example through the division into 4 + 2. However, I discuss the *De Trinitate* IV in Chapter II, so suffice it here to draw attention to the way in which Giorgio explains in considerable detail how the Mosaic week of creation finds expression in the Platonic *lambda* formula. Like Plato, Moses shows how God, as Unity and hence as the source of all numbers, transforms multitude into harmonious plenitude through the imposition of number, weight, and measure (I.iii.1–2).

One of Giorgio's most frequently repeated statements is that Christ, as the creative Logos, contains within himself the numbers used to structure the universe (II.i.10). Since all number, weight, and measure must be derived from the Word, Christ was the original teacher of the arts of poetry and music. The heavenly hosts acquired from the Son their knowledge of poetic measures and the art of singing (III.viii.8 accord 4). It was similarly Christ who taught David so that he became "vn harpeur et Psalmiste"; it was Christ who made a legislator of Moses and who taught the Apostles the harmonious "song" of the Gospels. Christ was of course responsible for the harmony between the 10 of the Law and the 4 of the Gospels; indeed, the Law and the Gospels were felt to be musical instruments referred to as "le Psalterion du vieil Testament" and "la harpe Euangelique & la gloire de tous" (III.viii.5; p. 767). Since Christ is Unity, he is like a fountain from which issue all numbers and proportions (II.i.10; p. 352), and since all things were disposed in number, weight, and measure, these existed in Christ before creation (II.i.5; p. 343). The definition of the Deity as Alpha and Omega, the beginning and the end, is responsible for the view that Christ not only joins the middle to the beginning and the end, but is himself the beginning, middle, and end (II.iv.2; p. 442). Giles Fletcher makes the literary relevance quite explicit in *Christ's Victorie, and Triumph* (1610), where he writes that it is Christ who himself has no beginning, yet gives beginning to all things, who must teach the poet how to begin and how to end his poem. Since the poem is a truly splendid example of a composition structured by means of verbal repetitions, numbers, and ratios, the lesson derived from Christ clearly was felt to include the intricate patterns woven by Giles Fletcher through his narrative.[55]

It comes as no surprise to discover that Giorgio claims that the art of poetry should be studied in the Bible (I.viii.19; p. 327). He quotes Jerome to the effect that Pindar and Horace should be compared to David, and he argues that Solomon rightly called his poem a Song of Songs since it summarises the message of the entire Bible concerning the marriage between Christ and the Church, the Old Testament and the New, the letter and the spirit, and the consonance between the archetypal world and the created universe. Jeremiah "aussit discourt en vers tragyque ses lamentations" and, as some affirm, Isaiah too proceeded "par quelque ordre mesuré". But the entire Bible, whether written in prose or verse, is all poetry by virtue of *accents* ("par ses accens") which reflect the movement of the spheres and their consonance. Through envy of these divinely inspired poets and writers, the ancient theologians of the gentiles such as Orpheus, Empedocles, Parmenides, Lucretius, and others were led to imitate them and to try to describe the natural and divine music in numbered verse which would permit the style to agree with the subject-matter ("afin que le style conuint auec le subiect").

This is a very clear statement of the principle of numerical or structural decorum that is the basis for so much biblical exegesis. Regardless of its ostensible form, the Bible is all poetry because certain rhythms are traced through it, rhythms which agree with those of the created universe. It is these truly basic structures which permit the "style" to agree with the subject-matter, and the subject-matter is of course the story of the creation and redemption of man. Giorgio wrote his book in order to explain these structures, but its length should not be taken as an indication that they are difficult to understand or extremely involved. They are, on the contrary, fairly simple, and they are easily grasped because Giorgio repeats his explanations over and over again in various contexts. For this reason it is possible to extract the gist of his argument from a limited number of chapters or, for that matter, from the preface written by the translator.

If one were to compress Giorgio's basic message into a few sentences, one might perhaps say that his first thesis is that the work shows the design of the Workman, and his second that all created things issue out of Unity and return to it by virtue of the order imposed on them. *Design*, then, is the most important aspect of God's works and that in them which creates harmony. And the harmony is retained for as long as due order is kept; by moving in their appointed order, the *res creatae* hymn their great Creator – their order becomes their hymn of praise. The plants and the trees praise God as they produce their fruit, and similarly the mists and exhalations as they rise and fall, but the most perfect praise comes from the angels. To quote verbatim: "Or l'ouurage demonstre le desseing de l'ouurier, lequel desseing estant conduict par vn ordre bien-reglé chante la louange de l'Ouurier mesme, auquel en ouurant il est fait semblable" (I.i.4). In other words: the work shows the design of the Workman, and this design – governed by an excellent order – hymns the praise of this very Workman, to whom it bears a certain resemblance in its operation. In the course of his argument Giorgio refers to the songs of praise in *Daniel* 3 and in Psalm 104, passages that Milton made use of when he composed the morning hymn of praise sung by Adam and Eve (*Paradise Lost* 5.152–208).

Design or order, then, is the true image of the Deity which may be traced everywhere, and design entails the use of numbers and ratios. God as the true Unity contains within himself all numbers as their root or source; all multitude, therefore, comes from the One, and nothing can become one (or unified) unless it acquires unity by participation in the One. All things, imitating the course of numbers, try to return to the One whence they issued. As Proclus puts it: order, beginning with Unity, proceeds to a Multitude, and this ordered Multitude in the end returns to its source (I.i.5).

Giorgio's architectural concept of creation according to a preconceived design constitutes the point of departure for the preface written by the poet Guy le Fèvre de La Boderie. His initial definition of the act of creation recalls Philo Judæus (*De opificio mundi* IV.9 and V.20): Nature teaches us, and art and experience confirm that the workman or architect who desires to build an edifice, whether sacred or profane, public or private, first of all must conceive a model in his mind, "vn dessein et modelle sur le plus bel exemplaire, et la plus parfaicte Idée qu'il puisse imaginer et depeindre au tableau de son Entendement". Giorgio ("our author") did this when he planned his treatise, and the pattern he selected for imitation was that of the universe itself as designed by God and afterwards created by the Word. In so doing, our author imitated "le grand Moyse" or rather Nature itself; like Moses, however, he was not content to grasp its external appearances only, but penetrated into the intelligible world, the supreme Tabernacle or super-celestial Jerusalem. This enabled him to create a literary structure reflecting the order of creation, thus imitating the divine workmanship. The Deity, "vnique et triple" like his creation, stands reflected in the three main divisions of the book, each of which is subdivided into eight. In this manner the various parts are so well joined together that the book becomes like a musical instrument through which sounds the breath of the Holy Spirit.

Guy le Fèvre defends Giorgio's syncretistic approach by advancing the three traditional arguments. All who want to testify to the truth of the Christian faith must maintain the priority of the Hebrew prophets ("l'antiquité, authorité, et primauté de Moyse et des Profetes Hebrieux") compared with whom all other philosophers or authors must be seen as derivative. Then, too, Giorgio took Augustine's advice that one may freely spoil the Egyptians to adorn the temple of the true God (*De doctrina Christiana* II.xl.60), and finally we must remember that St Ambrose believed, as did St Thomas, that the truth wherever found is of the Holy Spirit.

Guy le Fèvre rightly stresses the importance to Giorgio of two biblical images: the Tabernacle and Jacob's ladder, both symbolizing the harmony that man aspires to in vain unless aided by divine grace. This insistence on prevenient grace effectively removes Giorgio and his translator and commentator from the unorthodox position that the ascent may be achieved through man's own efforts. Unless aided by "le grand Esprit harmonieux" every attempt will fail; it is this spirit alone that achieves the reconciliation between Mercy and Justice "et qui comme did Iob, faict la paix aux hauts lieux", harmonizing the angelic orders and the movements of the celestial bodies, and sustaining the "mutation & vicissitude" of the four elements by "discordans accords ou par l'accordée Discorde," to quote Empedocles. The tempering of the relationship between body and soul, the balancing of the 4 humours and the 4 passions (the quaternary of the soul is the tetrachord of the inner man) and of these two in their turn with "la supreme & diuine Tetractyde" (i.e. the God whose name is the *Tetragrammaton* or 4 letters), all this can be the work only of the spirit of God, a spirit of love and union producing the sweet consonance of the virtues and spiritual hymns continually offered by our hearts and mouths in celebration of the source of all harmony. And through their organization these hymns are themselves an expression of the same harmony; they are written "en vers nombreux & harmonisez". This crucial statement is capable of one interpretation only: the text of these hymns must be structurally aligned with the numbers and proportions that express the highest harmony.

These numbers are embodied in the structure of Jacob's ladder. Guy le Fèvre states that in his treatise Giorgio ascends the 4 steps of the ladder of Nature, and afterwards the 4 steps of Jacob's ladder, which symbolize the celestial spheres as well as the 4 elements. The Moon connects with water, the Sun with fire, the other five planets with air, and the sphere of the 12 signs with earth. On the Earth itself all creatures form a ladder at the top of which is God as explained in the Bible, which begins its narrative with the inferior part of the ladder, and then pursues it to its very top in the Heavenly Jerusalem. The angels ascending and descending represent the third, angelic world organized in 9 orders, to which man should be added as a tenth. As the creative Logos, Christ contains within himself all parts of the creation, and as the great mediator he connects the two extremes of the ladder, joining it as a whole to the Deity.

The second preface, written by Nicholas le Fèvre de La Boderie, discusses methods of interpreting texts. Nicholas, too, relates the concept of harmony to the art of poetry, and he does so by viewing metaphor and allegory as a reflection of the correspondence which obtains between various levels of existence. In metaphor and allegory two meanings are conveyed through one vehicle, but this could not be so if it were not for the fact that God joined Heaven to Earth in a marriage union so that, as St Paul explains, what is corporal and perishable points towards what is eternal and immutable and without body (*Romans* 1:20). Although these two aspects of existence seem diametrically opposed, they are related by means of proportion and symmetry, as all will know who are not ignorant of the meaning of Plato's rings, Homer's chain, or Jacob's ladder – all of them symbols "des degrez, de l'ordre & entresuitte de l'Vniuers".

Nicholas le Fèvre calls his epistle a "discourse most useful to understand and expound the Holy Scriptures", and he repeats and reinforces Pico's argument that allegory is possible because of the perfect alignment between various levels of existence, an alignment which entails that the numbers or dimensions circumscribing certain events or things become clues to their inner meaning. In itself this is not a particularly new or startling argument; Hugo of St Victor, for example, had used the structure of the Ark of Noah as a kind of numerical memory house for the whole history of man's creation, redemption, and restoration to glory. What is new is the systematic exposition of the ways in which meaning may be extracted from descriptions not only of the Week of Creation or the Ark of Noah, but of Jacob's ladder, Ezekiel's vision of the chariot, the Tabernacle, the Temple of Solomon, or the Heavenly Jerusalem. Not content with the four traditional levels of meaning attributed to Holy Writ, Nicholas le Fèvre adds allegory depending on symbolic numbers, arithmetic, geometry, the laws of music (or harmony), and astronomy ("la dance & le bal mesuré des corps celestes"). To show how structural exegesis functions he inserts a diagram incorporating the two best-known numerical formulas for the work of creation: the Pythagorean *progressio quaternaria* and Plato's *lambda* numbers, both being reconciled with a system of threes and nines. The diagram suggests a strong indebtedness to writers often referred to by the two translators: Nicholas Cusanus[56] and Dionysius the Areopagite. Although Nicholas le Fèvre advises readers to turn to Nichomachus and Boethius for a systematic exposition of the symbolism invested in numbers, he nevertheless devotes several pages to comments on the meaning of the chief astronomical numbers 7, 9, 12, and 72.

I have considered the one-volume edition of Pico and Giorgio and the prefaces contributed by the translators in some detail because of its undoubted importance. This is a volume which performs the double task of advocating and exemplifying the technique of so organizing a work that its textual structure becomes unified in the same manner as God's creation. It is a work which insists over and over again that metaphor and allegory derive from the structural alignments between various levels of existence, and a work which connects the art of poetry with the numbers and proportions employed by God in his two great works of creation and restoration.

Giorgio's text occasionally includes poetry, and Guy le Fèvre's versions reveal his ability to translate structures as well. Thus the 22 lines in praise of the sacred Word (I.i.8; p.24) have a circular structure; the name of God occurs in the first line in the fourth position from the beginning, and again in the last line in the fourth position from the end. The textual centre at lines 11–12 presents God seated above the heavens on a golden throne, so that this French version of a hymn supposedly written by Orpheus enacts the circularity attributed to the Deity in the contents. The sum total of lines, 22, is the number of letters in the Hebrew alphabet, and glosses on Psalm 119 (Vulgate 118) explain its alphabetical structure as signifying circularity, since, when we reach the end of the alphabet, we begin all over again. It was only to be expected that Guy le Fèvre should have provided pre-planned structures for his own poetry as well, as we may see from his *Encyclie des secrets de l'éternité* (1571), the *Galliade* (1578), and the *Hymnes ecclésiastiques* (1578).[57] The year 1578 was curiously significant, since so many syncretistically slanted treatises and volumes of poetry appeared in that year, or shortly before or afterwards. Guy le Fèvre published two translations of Ficino (*De la Religion Chrestienne* and *Discours de l'honneste amour*) in addition to the works already noted. This is therefore the year when Pico, Giorgio, Ficino, and poetry informed by their ideas, all at once became available in Paris, and this happened on the eve of the composition of Spenser's first major work, published toward the end of 1579.

Another poet–philosopher with pronounced syncretistic leanings – Giordano Bruno – contributed to the same tradition by his presence in London during the early 1580s and by the books he had printed there. But I do not wish to consider Bruno here;[58] it is the turn, instead, of two late sixteenth-century encyclopedic works, one learned and the other decidedly popular, both of which promoted ideas and arguments connected with the tradition outlined here.

3. Pietro Bongo and Pierre de la Primaudaye

Although Pietro Bongo's *Numerorum mysteria* has been referred to in several studies of recent years, the man and his work have seemed strangely obscure. The little we know is nevertheless enough to establish a proper context. Bongo wrote this one book only, but it is a magnificent specimen of its kind, and the kind is of course an encyclopedia of knowledge relating to the symbolic aspects of numbers, compiled for the use of readers of the Bible and preachers. Theological treatises would often include long sections on arithmetic (including number symbolism), just as number lore of various kinds would figure in glosses on *Genesis* and the Apocalypse, or again on Ezekiel's vision of the chariot or the dimensions of the Ark. D. E. Smith's *Rara Arithmetica* (1908) conjectures that the first separately published treatise solely concerned with biblical number symbolism was written by a Frenchman who died in 1543, Jodocus Clichtoveus. Clichtoveus was born in Flanders, educated at the Sorbonne, and became a Canon of Saint-Jean, Chartres, where he died. His book discusses the significance of the numbers 1 to 10 and several larger numbers (including that of the beast, 666), but Bongo's book is far more inclusive and detailed.

Bongo (or Bungus) was born in Bergamo, where he seems to have spent his whole life. He must have been well known there since his family was a noble one, and since he served as Canon in the cathedral of that city, where he died on 24 September 1601. In view of the many editions of his *magnum opus* his fame must have been considerable. The *Dizionario Biografico degli Italiani* (1970) states that it had "una grande diffusione in tutta Europa". Its purpose is clearly stated on the title page: to reconcile Pythagorean and Christian doctrines. No fewer than three editions appeared within the first two years, the first edition being in two parts, which appeared at Bergamo in 1583 and 1584. A second edition of the first part appeared in 1585 (together with the first edition of the second part of 1584). I take it that the Venice edition of 1585 must be the third. Before the Paris edition of 1618, four further editions appeared at Bergamo in 1590, 1591, 1599 and 1614. Eight editions within thirty years is an impressive score, even if we take into account that its status as an authorized handbook puts it in a class by itself. It is therefore abundantly clear that Bongo's *Numerorum mysteria* belongs among the popular authorized handbooks of the Renaissance, and not among its esoterica; in its own way it is just as much of an encyclopedia of the arts and sciences as Martianus Capella's *De nuptilis philologiae et mercurii*, which reached eight editions between 1499 and 1599. The discussion of arithmetic in Capella's seventh book by the way transmits to the Renaissance some of the material appropriated by Bongo as by Clichtoveus. The extent to which material from Pythagoras, the Platonists, and Augustine could be included in works on mathematics may be assessed by reading the first chapter in the *Arithmeticae libri tres* (Strasburg, 1540 and 1545) by Willichius, a professor first of Greek and then of medicine in the University of Frankfurt an der Oder.

But, to revert to Bongo's *Numerorum mysteria*, we observe that its orthodoxy is vouched for by the *imprimatur* of the licensing authority of the Roman Catholic Church. The book is said to contain nothing contrary to true doctrine and is highly recommended as most worthy of being used by preachers and exegetes. Although Bongo seems as much of a syncretist as Giorgio, his use of extra-biblical sources is far more discreet, even in the later expanded editions. It is a measure of its currency that Cornelius à Lapide often would insert a *vide Bongo* when the need arose to explain the symbolism attributed to a biblical number. But Bongo provided more than just a summary of received opinion; he presents all the basic theological arguments associated with numerical concepts, as we may see from the opening paragraph where *number* is defined as the beginning of all rational activity:

> Number is the natural growing beginning of all rational activity. Creatures without mind, like the animals, cannot count. This proves at the same time that number is the beginning of those things that can be rationally apprehended; that everything would perish if numbers were removed is proved by our reason. That reason is number in action means nothing else than that it employs itself and forms everything in its own highest, natural similitude.[59]

These opening lines are an almost verbatim quotation from Nicholas Cusanus' *De coniecturis* I.4, as indicated in a marginal gloss. Bongo usually identifies his sources, and his lack of embarrassment on citing Plato and Pythagoras reveals the strength of the syncretistic position within the ranks of professional theologians. In his preface, for example, Bongo calls on Plato and Pythagoras, Cusanus' *De docta ignorantia* I.11, and the gospels (*Matthew* 7 and *Mark* 7) when he argues that if you remove the knowledge of numbers from a man you remove his reason, that arithmetic is the mother of all sciences, and that without this science one can scarcely hope to understand the gospels where so much is conveyed indirectly to avoid profanation. Christ himself warned us not to cast pearls before swine; Augustine and after him Boethius affirmed that numbers were the principal exemplar in the mind of the Creator, and the latter writes somewhere that no one can philosophize properly who spurns the science of numbers. Bongo adds, like Augustine, that this is a reference not to the kind of numbers that merchants use, but to numbers seen as abstract concepts. Many theologians have stated that Plato, Pythagoras, and all the Greek philosophers received their knowledge from the Hebrews: Origen believed this and so did Augustine and Eusebius. Thus Augustine wrote in his *De civitate Dei* XI that *Numeri ratio contemnenda nequaquum est*, nor is it vainly said in praise of God that he arranged everything in number, weight, and measure. Bongo's final point – that he who understands the *order* of an event will easily perceive its *meaning* – echoes a sentiment often expressed by Augustine and Bonaventura. Although God necessarily proceeds rationally in the work of creation and in disposing the course of human history, to the human mind this divine *ordo* will appear as an enigma the solution of which requires all our mental powers.

That there is such a plan, then, is a *datum*, and also that it is rational in the sense that it is conceived in terms of numbers ensuring the highest harmony. The main outlines of the plan are bold and precise: there is a triple pattern of creation, Fall and restoration, the Fall often serving as a kind of pivot between events that are perfectly balanced. The *aequalitas* thus achieved is a reflection of the Unity which is God.

Bongo's first chapter, "De Unitate," necessarily contains a discussion of the nature of God and the created universe. Just as Unity is the *fons & origo* of numbers, God is the beginning of all things, and man may be drawn towards God by contemplating the principle of Unity. The origin of creatures is not in themselves but in God, and the reason why Satan fell was that he persuaded himself that his power derived from himself and not from God. (This Augustinian view is, of course, basic to Milton's presentation; cf. *Paradise Lost* 5.859–64.) Everything proceeds from, and returns to, divine Unity, God forming as it were the immobile centre for this movement. God is immutable and One in the sense that he never changes, and the just man imitates this stability while the sinner is always mutable and torn by internal division and never in the same place. Unity alone is *sibi constans, sibique æqualis semper, omnino eadem, nulli obnoxia varietati, nullam inuehens alterationem* (p. 18). Unity may serve as a similitude for the created universe. Unlike the universe, Unity has no origin but is its own fountain; it existed eternally before all numbers and it persists in its own unity. We may find Unity where there is no imperfection – as in the equilateral triangle, the square, the pentagon, the pyramid, the cube, the circle, and the sphere. These are bodies that possess *æqualitas* and hence partake of Unity in this respect. God alone possesses Unity in his own nature; the *res creatae* possess it by participation alone.

Unity created the world in its own image and similitude. As Cardinal Cusanus explains, God did not require time: *omnia fecit Deus simul. Dixit enim & facta sunt*. For this reason the 6 days enumerated by Moses must refer to a spiritual meaning, a view shared by St Augustine, Hugo of St Victor, Basil, Dionysius, Bede, Cassiodorus, Albertus Magnus, and St Thomas (p. 23). And the meaning is, of course, that the metaphor of the week reveals the order or pattern of existence, a pattern which also reveals the nature of the Deity. Bongo's definition of the relationship between God and his creation resembles that between form and content in a work of art. Because God is One, the world is one; because God is infinite, he created a circular world; because God is eternal, he created a world which is incorruptible and eternal:

> cum ipse sit Unus, Mundum creauit Vnum; cum ipse sit infinitus, Mundum creauit rotundum; cum ipse sit æternus, Mundum creauit incorruptibilem, & æternum; cum ipse sit immensus, Mundum creauit omnium maximum; cum ipse sit summa vita, Mundum etiam vitalibus seminibus exornauit, ex sese cuncta gignentem. (p. 27)

Language is one of Bongo's examples of unity: language serves to unite people, and before the building of the Tower of Babel the same language was used. The proliferation of languages is a reflection of sin, of man's departure from unity and his fall into multiplicity. But with the coming of Christ there will again be only one language. For this reason loquacity may well be taken as a hieroglyph of duality (i.e. discord), silence of unity, and in this context Bongo refers to Zeno who preserved his silence by biting off his tongue and spitting it in the face of the tyrant who tortured him.[60]

Through the incarnation of Christ, unification and a reconciliation of opposites was achieved. God may be said to have exterminated the cause of evil, recalling the world from Multitude to Unity (p. 38). Through the work of one just man the world has been saved three times: first through Noah, then through Abraham, and finally through Christ. *Ephesians* 2:14 conveys this doctrine by stating that Christ is our peace, "who hath made both one" (p. 39). What happened at the Fall was that a divisive discord arose in the perfect man in whom two substances had been fused. St Thomas characterizes sin as a deviation from the divine order, while Augustine's *De libero arbitrio* defines it as a turning away from an immutable to a mutable good. To avoid sin, therefore, we must cling to the order of Charity so that we prefer nothing to God. If we succeed in this, our divided nature will be made one. Through a sequence of eloquent statements Bongo consistently identifies sin with Multiplicity, regeneration with Unity:

> Vbi igitur peccata sunt, ibi est multitudo; ubi autem Virtus, ibi singularitas, ibi Vnitas ... principium bonorum, coangustatio & aturbis in singularitatem redactio ... Hæc est tota merces, hæc est vita æterna, hæc est sapientia quam Sapientes seculi non cognouerunt, ut ab omni multitudinis imperfectione redigamur in

Vnitatem per copulam indissolubilem cum eo, qui est ipsum Vnum. (p. 41)

To summarize: we shall be saved from the imperfection of Multitude and returned to Unity through an indissoluble union with him who himself is One, and whose seamless coat is a symbol of the sacrament of Unity and the bond of concord.

The second chapter, "De Binario", and the last, "De Multitudine", contain many useful comments on these concepts and their role in the Bible. Passages in Pythagoras, Plato, Cusanus, and the Bible are seen to agree in defining duality as the principle of division; the Binary is the number of discord and confusion and of changing opinions, so that it applies to heretics and idolaters. As Herrick puts it in his poem on "The number of two":

> God hates the Duall Number: being known
> The lucklesse number of division:
> And when He blest each sev'rall Day, whereon
> He did His *curious operation*:
> 'Tis never read there (as Fathers say)
> God blest His work done on the *second day*:
> Wherefore two prayers ought not be said,
> Or by ourselves, or from the Pulpit read.[61]

Multitude represents dissimilitude and inconstancy; everything which is in a state of flux and change – like Proteus – should be referred to this concept. While Unity stands for *consensum ac perfectionem*, Multitude represents *diuisionem & imperfectionem*. To the extent that Multitude recedes from Unity it displays confusion without numerical order: *ab unitate recedit, & habet confusionem sine ordine numerali* (p. 667). To quote Herrick again:

> A multitude of dayes still heaped on
> Seldome brings order, but confusion.[62]

Since my concern here is more with a general vision of the divine order than with number lore as applied to biblical exegesis, Bongo's encyclopedia will be left on its shelf until needed for the elucidation of particular structures. But before I turn to Pierre de la Primaudaye, I wish to add a few comments on the usefulness, to poets, of Bongo's *Numerorum mysteria*. The edition of 1591 concludes with a "Hendecasyllabon" praising the book and defending it against envious detractors: its worth has been fully proved by poets and scholars alike (*Doctiloqui Sophi & Poetæ / Summo iudicio probant libellum*). Bongo may perhaps have had some responsibility for Tasso's pronounced interest in number symbolism. Bongo, like Tasso, belonged to a noble family in Bergamo, and Tasso took the manuscript of his discourses on the heroic poem with him to Bergamo in August 1587 to have it copied. Tasso must surely have been familiar with the treatise written by the Canon of the Cathedral Church of Bergamo, and the fact that Bongo expanded the later editions of his work to include more material from the poets suggests that he may have wished to increase its relevance to the art of poetry. For all we know, it may have been Tasso who encouraged him so to do.

Pierre de la Primaudaye's *The French Academie* is a truly popular encyclopedic Renaissance work full of unacknowledged borrowings from more learned sources. Originally published in French, this book nevertheless became something of a bestseller in England: editions appeared in 1586, 1589, 1594, 1602–05, 1614, and 1618.[63] Marginal references are usually to the Bible, but, although the English translator of Book I, like the author, invites the reader to approve of the contents only in so far as they "may be prooued out of the recordes of holy Scripture", this reverence for the Bible is combined with an Augustinian approval of philosophy. In his preface, the English translator refers directly to Augustine's view that, whenever the philosophers agree with Christian doctrine, "we are not onely not to feare it, but rather to challenge it from them as uniust possessors thereof".[64] The expected reference to *Romans* 1 : 20 crops up in this context: many pagan philosophers acquired a just notion of the Deity by seeking the invisible through the visible, while conversely "many a million of carnall gospellers" (i.e. people who read the gospels in a carnal sense only, without understanding the spiritual message) fall far short even of the pagan moral virtues. On the other hand one must reject as absurd the proposition advanced by Clement of Alexandria (*Stromata* lib. 6) that philosophy was to the Greeks what the Law was to the Jews: a schoolmaster leading them to Christ. One should use philosophy as a mere handmaiden "to serue the Scripture to the more plaine and pure exposition of it".

Primaudaye reveals his syncretistic bias most clearly, perhaps, in the opening chapters of Book III where he discusses the creation of Heaven and Earth. Moses not only prophesies about all the high mysteries of our Christian faith, but unlocks "the treasures of all Philosophy" (III.2). What he writes about creation may be found also in the great philosophers and poets from Plato, Hermes, and Pythagoras to Orpheus and Hesiod, but this agreement is less important than the fact that the truth of his writing is amply confirmed by the testimony of miracles and "by the consent of euery part":

> If one reads the text of *Moses*, all points therin are so replenished with prophecies, and future euents, that there is nothing left out there concerning that which belongeth to the mysteries of diuine and Philosophicall matters, nor of the Messias then to come, nor yet of all whatsoeuer should afterward come to passe, as is euident to those who haue the eyes of their minds illuminated, and who vnderstand the bookes of the law, to see cleane through a great many vailes, vnder which (as was most meet) the prophet did hide so many profound mysteries.
>
> (III.7; p. 654)

Although there is widespread agreement between the Scriptures and philosophy, we must reject whatever philosophers may have added of their own invention, honouring only what they fetched from Hebrew sources. Orpheus, for example, confessed that "he learned out of the tables of *Moses*" all that he had to say of God. Then, too, we must observe one important distinction bearing on style: prophets like Moses and David discuss "the workes of creation" and "the diuine prouidence in them" in a manner which can be understood by all. They speak of the spheres and the heavenly bodies not subtly in the manner of philosophers, "but rather vulgarly; to the ende that the most rude and playnest may vnderstand their Philosophy, replenished with the doctrine of saluation" (p. 714). Their natural philosophy, then, is not only taught so that all may understand; it is also full of "the doctrine of salvation".

Here we have the truly basic characteristic of the philosophy associated with the French academies: a study of the visible world conveys insight into the mystery of salvation. This is the opening argument of chapter III.33, and in what follows a fairly simple but moving lesson is taught of how the providence of God may manifest itself for example in the rising and setting of the sun. As the chapter heading puts it, divine providence "shineth in the commodities of day and night". The works of God "are all obedient," as we may see in the harmonious circle of the 4 elements and their qualities, or in the daily and annual solar cycle; God reduces all discord into concord, all enmity into amity. The many references in the Bible to Christ as sun or light prove that this world is an image of a higher world. Christ is the true Sun of Justice, risen with healing in his wings; his light is to our souls what the light of the physical sun is to our bodies. This is why divine things are compared to light, such as are evil to darkness, the sun being a visible image of God. His wrath, though, may often be represented in the Bible by images of darkness. And when men feel this wrath, it is as if "the whole frame of the world were ouerturned, and as if all creatures should set themselves to warre vpon them and confound them by rushing on them, and running at them" (p. 720). The change between light and darkness, therefore, may be used to represent man under chastisement or in a state of grace and joy, and, when the author goes on to explain how the annual cycle is an image of the life of man, Spenser's *The Shepheardes Calender* (1579) springs to mind as a contemporary poetic presentation of this traditional concept. A passage will illustrate the quality of the writing:

> For as we haue in the cause of nature, one while day, and another while night ... in one season summer, in another winter: now hot, anon colde ... euen so runnes all the course of mans life. For we haue therein the time of ignorance and aduersities, of chastisements, punishments, & vengeance of God, which are the night and time of darkenes to men, & their winter and tempestuous seasons. And so haue we the time of knowledge & vnderstanding of God, and of prosperitie, of grace, of ioie, of felicitie, and of consolation, which are to men like the day and the light, and as the spring-time and sommer. And as the daies & nights are some longer, and some shorter: so the Lord prolongeth or abridgeth the times of grace and of rigour; of his fauour and of his wrath, as he pleaseth and in such measures as he knoweth to be expedient .... (p. 720).

There is more plain piety in Pierre de la Primaudaye than in Giorgio, whose vision of the harmony of the world is far more intellectual. This made Primaudaye's syncretism more acceptable to pious readers, just as these would have relished his greater persuasiveness in relating natural phenomena to divine revelation. Thus the Frenchman explains the harmonious linkage between the elements as an act of obedience to God. Similarly the heavens declare the glory of God because the well-ordered motions of the spheres "doe demonstrate, as with the finger euen to our eies, the great and admirable prouidence of God their Creator". The heavens are "visible words, which speake to the eies", and it is there we may find the best "images to represent God" (III.32; p. 712). Like Giorgio, Primaudaye states that the order of creation constitutes a hymn of praise, which is why the royal prophet can exhort inanimate things to praise God. The passage sounds so piously orthodox that one is surprised when he adds that the Pythagorean notion of intelligence resident in the spheres agrees with the Christian concept of angels (III.27; p. 702). But such syncretistic views are not permitted to dominate the argument; everything is made to emerge from a consideration of the Scriptures, the testimony of philosophy being emphatically subordinated. However, the supposition that Moses teaches profound lessons in natural philosophy is very much in evidence, and an interesting passage praises the classical poets for conveying similar lessons. The most famous poets among the ancients "haue by their writings penetrated into the most profound cabinets of nature, and approached the secrets of diuine thought". For they "sung not iests (as some hold)", but have been acknowledged "of the Sages for great Diuines, who hid the mysteries both of the one and other nature [i.e. earthly and divine] vnder the vaile of fables, and for this cause they are celebrated of such as vnderstand their doctrine". "And *Orpheus* singeth more loftily then human knowledge can extend to, the mysteries of Theologie and of the sacred ceremonies, which hee had learned out of holy letters, as himselfe confesseth" (III.30; pp. 708 f.).

The faithfulness with which Primaudaye follows Augustine's exposition of the Mosaic account of creation is obvious throughout Book III (cf. III.12). Moses wrote both for "the rude and common people" and for "the wise and learned". The learning thus attributed to Moses concerns the harmony between God and his creation, and the harmony between the various levels of existence. God is seen as Unity and his creation as harmoniously organized, since harmony is a reflection of his Unity.

All this is sufficiently familiar, but Primaudaye achieves a more complete synthesis between Christian and classical thought, at the same time that the syncretistic argument occupies a relatively modest part of his treatise. The charge of esotericism can scarcely apply to a book of this kind, written to "profit many", which is why the author has avoided all "obscure words and phrases" and all "subtill, curious and vnprofitable disputations" ("The Forespeach" to Book III). The fact that the syncretistic tradition could be presented even in a work designed for a popular audience helps to explain why it came to influence the poetry of the period so intimately; by the end of the sixteenth century, syncretistic views clearly were so widely disseminated as to seem both orthodox and obvious.

Primaudaye as a matter of course organized his own book numerically. As he explains in the preface to Book IV, "we haue specially chosen the number of seuen, therein to comprehend and bound the diuersitie of all our discourse, because the number is anciently and long since knowne to be full, perfect, vnieuersall, and sufficient, to represent all things in perfection: and for that cause is oftentimes set downe and rehearsed in the holy Scriptures" (p. 864). The architectural metaphor is very much in evidence in his description of the work of creation: "For there is nothing produced by nature, or formed by arte, but first it hath abiding in that which performeth it ... so each worke liueth in the minde of the workeman before he puts it in practise. So had the world perfect beeing, in the thought of God before it was builded ... as Saint *Augustine* very learnedly discourseth". God Almighty, "the vnite from which all number proceedeth, and whereto all multitude referreth it selfe", began by increasing himself in himself, engendering the Son ("his Word, the perfect patterne of the world") and the Holy Ghost. Afterwards he produced "the outward worke of the world" which he did "by a kinde of processe of well ordered degrees, and disposing through admirable workemanship the harmonicall formes of the heauens" (p. 639). It is particularly interesting that the Word is described as "the perfect patterne of the world", one of Giorgio's favourite statements.

The creation by means of well-ordered degrees is more fully explained in the passage setting out the similarity between the biblical account and the accounts of Hermes Trismegistus and Pythagoras. Pythagoras esteemed "that numbers, and their subiect (that is, the measures and apt proportions, called harmonies and consonancies) were the originall of things; not those numbers which merchants vse, but the formall and naturall, the knowledge of which lies onely hidden in such, as haue learned Philosophy & Theology by numbers" (III.11; p. 663). The fact that so many philosophers agree with Moses indicates that they were "illuminated with one selfe-same diuine vnderstanding (as the Platonists call it) or with one selfsame spirit (as our doctors teach)". Holy Writ teaches, "and all Mathematicians confirme", that the story of creation is a prophecy of "the euents that should succeede". This is so because the story of the 6 days is a metaphor for the order imposed, and this order prevails also in the providential design for the history of man.

Primaudaye takes great care to assure his readers that no power must be attributed to the numbers by means of which order is created; as the marginal gloss puts it, the number, weight, and measure is in God. Since it is useful to compare his phrasing with Augustine's in the *De Genesi ad Litteram* and with Milton's in the *De doctrina Christiana* I.7, it is quoted in full:

> Now not onely the Philosophers, but also many great personages, Christians, both Greekes and Latins do testifie vnto us by their writings, that there bee many mysteries in numbers ... And it hath not beene spoken in vaine to the praise of God: [Thou hast ordered all things in number, weight, and measure.] Now hereupon we must note, that the number, waight, and measure, whereby all things haue been numbred, poised and measured, subsist not properly in the things created ... but are doubtless without them ... And foreasmuch as there is nothing, besides all things produced, but God, it is necessary, that in him should consist their number, waight and measure ... And in truth, this frame of the whole world duely proportioned, and balanced by waight, could not sustaine it selfe, if it were not poised by the Creator and Gouernor thereof; who likewise hath the measure by which he moderateth and disposeth all that is conteined therein, in well ordered iustice ... And in him also are the numbers without number, because that all things which are in him, are the same onely God. And as he is the true vnitie, hee containeth in himselfe all number, giuing all things the power to bee numbered. For all multitude ariseth from one, and nothing can be one, making with any others a multitude, if by the participation of the highest one it doth not obtaine the state of vnitie. And to it also all things created (imitating the course of numbers, as the true patterne doth the originall, and the end of Gods workes) endeauour to returne, in such sort as they first proceeded. (III.13; pp. 667 f.)

Milton makes exactly the same point when he writes that matter cannot always have been independent of God, "seeing that it is a passive principle, dependent on the Deity, and subservient to him as in the case of numbers".[65]

The chapters on the structure of the universe incorporate many passages from Pico's *Heptaplus*. Thus III.14 is an unacknowledged version of Pico's second proem, the marginal references, however, being to Eusebius (*De præparat. evang.* 11), Plato's *Phædro*, and biblical passages like *Exodus* 25 : 40 on the Tabernacle as a figure of the three worlds and *Rev.* 4 with its highly structured vision of the Heavenly Jerusalem. Chapter III.15 reproduces the first paragraph from Pico's proem to Book III, while III.5 begins by including a translation of *Heptaplus* III.1 and carries on by drawing heavily on Augustine. Among the passages borrowed from Pico is the important one where allegory is referred back to the triple structure of the world: the three worlds are "girt and buckled with the bands of concord" and "this is the principle from whence springeth & groweth the discipline of allegorical sense". Before one can interpret allegory, therefore, one must know the structure of the created cosmos as intimately as the patriarchs and the prophets.

The discussion of the 4 elements (III.38) illustrates the way in which correspondences are drawn between various spheres or levels of being, and one observes, too, that mathematical formulas or concepts play an important role in establishing these correspondences. Primaudaye is a good source for the truly basic numerical arguments as they affect cosmic structure.[66] Harmony is imposed on the world by means of the number 4, as we may see in the 4 elements, the 4 qualities, the 4 seasons, the 4 kinds of creatures (corporal, vegetable, sensitive, and reasonable), the 4 motions (ascent, descent, progression, and turning round). This is so because 4 is "the roote and beginning of all numbers" – a clear reference to the Pythagorean tradition. Because 4 creates the number 10 (through addition of the four first numbers), the universe is also organized in terms of this number, which denotes a return to Unity. Four is an important cosmic number also because the first four numbers (1, 2, 3, and 4) create "all musicall harmony", so that all in all the Pythagoreans quite correctly affirmed this number to be the cause of all things; when they swore by this number "as by some holy thing", they were, in fact, alluding to "that great fower-lettered name of the Hebrewes from whom they receiued their instructions". Like Giorgio, then, Pierre de la Primaudaye links biblical and classical traditions by deriving the Pythagorean explanation of cosmic structure in terms of numbers from divine revelation in general and from the *Tetragrammaton* in particular. Primaudaye goes on to explain how the number 4 prevails in the sciences of metaphysics, mathematics, physics, moral philosophy and architecture, and in divine revelation, too, since the "soueraigne gouernor" of the world "hath willed, that there should bee fower foundations of the most perfect, eternall, and firm laws of grace, to wit, the fower Euangelists".

Since the secret of unity or harmony is proportion, this is why the number 4 must prevail in the Bible as in the universe. The proportion is set out in Plato's *lambda* formula, too, where the two cubes – 8 and 27 – are harmonized through the mean numbers 12 and 18, so that these four numbers express how the harmony between the elements is secured. In the case of the elements, linkage is created also by means of the two qualities attached to each; one of the two is always passed on to the next:

> So that the fower elements are (as if each one of them had two hands, by which they held one another) as in a round daunce: or else, as if they were conioyned and linked together, as with chaines and buckles. And therefore the water is moist & cold, retaining the moisture as peculiar to it self and in coldnesse participating with the nature of the earth: by the moisture thereof, it is also allied vnto the aire; which also in some measure participateth in heate with the nature of fire ... But aboue all, the Academicks haue inuented a goodly concord between these elements, in their discourses of the quadruple proportion; from which onely their musicall proportions doe proceede ... (III.38; pp. 727 f.)

The similar dance of the days, months, and seasons is set out elsewhere in this third Book, and this entire section recalls Augustine who wrote: "The day and the year both run their courses in a quaternion: the day in hours of morning, noon, evening, and night; the year in the months of spring, summer, autumn, and winter" (*De doctrina Christiana* II.xvi.25–26). Milton invokes this "mystic dance" in Paradise Lost 5. 153–208, in a highly structured passage describing how the works of God praise their creator by moving in their appointed order; in this order quaternions prevail. The elements run "in quaternion" perpetual circle, and, among the quaternions enumerated by Primaudaye, Milton includes the 4 motions and the winds from the 4 quarters of the Earth. What is implicit in Giorgio, Primaudaye makes quite plain: the order depends on obedience to God and in its turn forms "visible words" exhorting to obedience.

Book II of *The French Academie* considers the microcosmos of man, where the pattern of harmony is the same as in the universe at large. The 4 humours ought to display the same harmonious balance as the 4 elements, and so should the 4 passions of fear, hope, grief, and joy. As long as the humours are in "a good, moderate, and proportionate temper ... then is there an equality in all the body" so that life and health are ensured. For there is "the like concord and harmony" between the humours as between "the parts of a good consort of Musicke well tuned", and if man had remained in a state of obedience, he would have been immortal (II.65).

The Augustinian influence is particularly marked in the many chapters urging that man must learn to love God more than the creatures, and that upon this union with God depends whatever harmony or concord man may achieve in his own life. The end of love is unity, which is why Christ achieves unity and Satan disruption, division, and separation (II.50). If the heart burns with love of God, then it will glorify God by the voice, and such will be the "accord and consent" between the heart and the voice that these "will utter nothing but the truth ... Wherefore if mans nature had not been corrupted through sinne ... there would alwayes haue bin a goodly concord and consent betweene the heart and the brain, the voice and the tongue, the reason and the affections" (II.36; p. 448).

As far as free will is concerned, Primaudaye's discourse hovers somewhat uneasily between postlapsarian depravity and Pico's optimistic belief in man's innate powers aided by grace. The last chapter of this Book (II.100) compromises by stating that there are different degrees of freedom in different men. About the prelapsarian condition, however, there is of course complete agreement between Augustine and Primaudaye: man was originally created with free will, this being an important part of the image of God in man. God wanted children, not slaves; hence he required a voluntary obedience and an unforced service. The will was created to enable man to pursue the highest good, but in our fallen condition the will moves away from God, not towards him (cf. Augustine *De libero arbitrio* II.xix–xx). Augustine connects free will with the concept of a harmonious universe, his argument being that the God whom we seek as the highest good manifests himself in the order he has imposed, so that by perceiving this order we are led back to him. In the prelapsarian state man kept turning towards God in love, which meant that the movement of his will was aligned with the movement of the universe and of the angelic hosts. Augustine states, like Milton (*Paradise Lost* IX.782f. and 846), that the first defective movement (*defectivus motus*) occurred with the Fall when man preferred a creature to the creator. The movement of the will becomes defective the moment that it turns towards what is changeable, leaving that which is immutable. This Augustinian argument pervades Book II of *The French Academie*, but while Augustine believed that after the Fall the only movement that the will is capable of is away from God, divine grace being required to rise toward God, Primaudaye echoes Pico's more optimistic assessment. If man joins his will to his reason, all will be well:

> Wherefore if the will of man be ioyned with reason, which is celestiall and diuine, and followeth the same, it will become like vnto it, and shall be able easily to gouerne the sensuall part vnderneath it, to be mistres ouer it, and to compell it to obey. But if the Will despise reason and the counsell thereof, and if instead of mounting vpward towards the noblest part, it descendeth to the sensuall part, and ioyneth itselfe thereunto, then shall the Will be made like to that, and shall serue it in place of commanding it. And by this meanes the Will shall become altogether brutish, whereas contrariwise it might make the sensuall & earthly part as it were celestiall and diuine. (II.100; p. 633).

Both Augustine and Pierre de la Primaudaye show how closely connected the issues of Free Will and obedience are with the view of creation as numbers held in time and space. The spatial numbers spell harmony in the visible universe, while the harmony manifested in the course of human history is a matter of the prearranged disposition of the numbers of time. That Milton, in an epic concerned with Free Will, obedience, and divine providence, should display the same interest in the numbers of time and space can therefore come as no great surprise: the combination was predictable.

4. Philip of Mornay, Marin Mersenne, Peter Sterry, and Père André

A Woorke concerning the trewnesse of the Christian Religion (1587) by Philip of Mornay, Lord of Plessie, proclaims its line of descent from Augustine in the title as well as the contents, while the fact that it was translated by Sir Philip Sidney and Arthur Golding proves the attraction which the Augustinian tradition had for English poets.[67] Chapter 1 applies the lesson of *Romans* 1 : 20 by inferring the nature of the invisible world from what is visible; the harmony of the world compels us to posit a creator: "I pray you from whence commeth this goodly proportion, and this orderly proceeding of things by degrees?"[68] This proportion and order create unity, and by being so linked together that they tend towards one, the *res creatae* prove that the nature of the Deity is Unity. A contemplation of the arts and sciences lead to the same conclusion; these, too, "guyde us to the same unitie" (p. 222).

The syncretistic position defended in ch. 3 favours the biographical explanation, and ch. 6 states that Plato, Hermes, and Pythagoras present the deity as a Trinity because they were indebted to the Hebrew prophets. Thus Pythagoras was instructed in Egypt by one "whom some (miscounting the tyme) thought to be Ezechiel. And *Hermippus* a *Pythagorist* writeth that *Pythagoras* learned many things out of the lawe of *Moyses*".

The definition of the creative Logos fuses biblical and Platonic terms or images, the source being Philo Judæus, who refers to the Son or Word as "the Booke wherein the essences of all things that are in ye whole world are written and printed; the perfect Patterne of the World: the Daysonne that is to be seene but only of the Mynd; the Prince of the Angelles; the Firstborne of God; the Shepheard of his flocke; the chief Hyghpriest of the World ... and the Organe or Instrument whereby God ... created the World". As the Logos, Christ is "the invincible bond of the whole world & of al things therein" (p. 291).

This is only one of many passages which associate Christ with the pattern of the world, a point that must be borne in mind on considering the theory that Milton's "On the Morning of Christ's Nativity" incorporates the structure of the world in its textual form.[69] It will also be useful to remember that it was possible for this most Protestant of French writers to define God and his creation in numerical terms: God is

> most simply one: from whose unitie nevertheless flowe all the diversities which we see in the whole world, like as from a Pricke, proceedeth a Lyne, an outside, and all substantial bodies [i.e. in the manner explained by the *tetractys* formula]. And of unitie or one in nombering, proceedeth even and odde, round and square and all the multiplicities, proportions, and harmonies which we see: ... all these parts, which proceede from one and tend to one, doe make us to beleeve that all proceede from one most single one. (pp. 219 f.)

When confronted with this evidence of the pervasive use of numerical concepts it is no longer possible to restrict their currency to a circle of learned initiates. We must associate it, instead, with the familiar Renaissance concept of order and degree. Until the numerical formulas for the harmony of the world have been mastered, this concept has not been fully explored, but when we study the classical formulas we must remember that these were attributed to Moses and Ezekiel, so that Plato and Pythagoras should be challenged as "unjust possessors" of them. Our own better knowledge must not be permitted to obscure this Renaissance perspective.

Although Marin Mersenne's various treatises on music and musical instruments are purely technical, he refers to the Augustinian tradition from time to time, and his concern to remove from Giorgio's work what could not be accepted by the orthodox indicates his commitment to its basic proposition.

One of the most interesting passages in Mersenne occurs in his "Livre de l'Utilité de l'Harmonie, & des autres parties des Mathematiques" added to his *Traité de l'Harmonie Vniuerselle* (Paris, 1627 and 1636). Mersenne advises preachers to illustrate various doctrinal points by means of mathematics, and if a preacher should desire to move the minds of his listeners to "quelque chose de grand & sublime" (a procedure possible only when addressing men accustomed to elevated thoughts), or again if he should desire to console his own mind, he should read the second and third books of Augustine's *De libero arbitrio*, his *De vera religione*, *De ordine*, and *De beata vita*.[70] Mersenne clearly was strongly attracted by the Augustinian combination of abstract thought with strong emotions, so much so that he felt its power to elevate and hence to comfort the mind.

Book II of Mersenne's *La Vérité des Sciences* (Paris, 1625) begins with two chapters on the relevance of arithmetic to a study of the Bible and the writings of the Fathers of the Church, and especially those who have expressed their views by means of Pythagorean numerical concepts.[71] Biblical exegesis cannot be undertaken without knowledge of this science, and among the exegetes cited are Villapandus on Ezekiel, Giorgio (whose *Problemata* had just been published again in 1622), Petaut and Mersenne's own commentary on *Genesis*. Philosophy can afford to do without such knowledge even less than theology, since Plato explains his basic ideas in terms of Unity, the Binary, and the Ternary. Plato expresses what applies to the soul and body by means of the number 27 [the *lambda* formula is clearly referred to here by means of that last number which is the sum of the other numbers], while 12 refers to the body politic, the heavens, and the whole world.[72] Mersenne believed that Plato's preference for numerical concepts stemmed from his desire to avoid the deceptiveness of mutable phenomena: we may be deceived when we measure things, but never by that which the numbers represent.[73]

Mersenne's attitude to numbers is altogether as intellectual as that of Cardinal Cusanus, to whom he refers his readers for a study of the spiritual lessons which may be taught by means of mathematics. As Mersenne puts it in his "Livre de l'Utilité de l'Harmonie", a knowledge of the sciences is not necessary for a spiritual life, but those who are familiar with them have a tremendous advantage since God accommodates himself to the capacity of those who love him "en esprit & en vérité". All truth is the image of the eternal Truth, which is Christ crucified: to know all sciences, therefore, is in some way to know Christ because Christ contains the treasures of the wisdom and knowledge of God, of which our own knowledge is merely a single ray. As the ancient Fathers of the Church would say, those are Christians who live rationally. A rational life and a Christian life are the same thing, as one must conclude on reading Justin Martyr, who wrote that *Quicumque cum ratione, & verbo vixerunt, Christiani sunt*. The reason that we use is an impression of the divine reason or the external Word; all our knowledge, like all our good actions, must be referred back to Christ as the true source. Augustine provides the final argument when Mersenne adds that all Augustine's learning did not diminish his devotion, but that on the contrary many of his treatises show how much his piety profited from it, and notably his *De libero arbitrio* and *De vera religione*.[74]

La Verité des Sciences II.2 defines Unity as a hieroglyph of the Deity and all that is perfect: it contains all numbers "en puissance" and is their origin and end. Also it represents union as opposed to division, form as opposed to matter, God as opposed to his creatures. The "Livre de l'Utilité de l'Harmonie" applies this argument to the unison in music. The unison is the source and origin of all music, and an image of unity with the Deity. When all voices or "chordes" abandon all their differences and varieties to arrive at equality, this is an image of our return from duality to unity, from imperfection to perfection. As we move from 2 to 1 we move towards Unity away from differences in time and place, and from actions that fail to conform to the will of God. The unity established by Christ according to *John* 14:20 can be explained in musical terms as a progress from the octave to its source in the unison, "source & père de l'octaue, dans laquelle sont contenuës les consonances".[75] This theological approach to musical theory is illustrated also in the *Traitez des Consonances*, which opens with a long discussion of "son" and "unisson" as images of Unity. Unison is defined as the conjunction between, or union of, two or more sounds that are so similar that it is impossible to hear a difference; they seem like one sound. It is the spiritual import of this complete *aequalitas* which accounts for its importance to Mersenne. The perception of unison is an act of the mind and not of mere sense perception; in the world of sense, that pleases which displays variety, but not so in the realm of purely intellectual perception. The intellectual pleasure derived from a perception of *aequalitas* is felt in all the sciences: in algebra, for example, we discover all kinds of equations, and in physics the discovery of equilibrium is a kind of unison, and the whole concern of medicine is to establish balance between the humours. If we mount even higher, we discover an eternal unison in the Deity, whose three persons have the same nature and the same goodness although distinct and separate. This is why all the blessed souls sing in unison so that their song may express this equality: because their state is "très-simple", their songs or chants must be "très-simples". One may achieve a similar effect by letting a piece of music begin and end on a unison, but all consonances tend towards unison. The consonances derive from unison like the line from the point, the numbers from Unity, and the creatures from God.

All music is, in a way, unison, just as all virtues are a form of love; consequently unison and love resemble each other. Just as the consonances derive all that is good or agreeable in them from the unison, all the virtues derive their goodness and excellence from love, as stated by Augustine in ch. 14 of his book on the institutions of the church and in his 52nd epistle. This is the epistle which argues that those who love music are not so unhappy as to deprive themselves of the pleasure experienced from the love of God.

A consideration of the consonances (so Mersenne continues) must begin with the octave, since its ratio of 1:2 proceeds from unity to the binary. On turning from the unison to the octave one performs an act similar to that of a theologian who considers first the divine essence of the Deity and next his attributes. Just as the attributes are nothing but the divine essence considered in various ways, numbers are nothing but unity considered in various ways, and a line is nothing but a consideration of the point as it moves and after it has ceased moving.

Mersenne's treatise of music and musical instruments is almost entirely technical, so that philosophical arguments like these stand out. As Mersenne himself puts it, when the perfect musician knows everything which pertains to harmony, it is reasonable that he should consider everything which the Platonists have written about harmony, the more so since their manner of reasoning was praised by the first Church Fathers.

Since Mersenne represents proper science recognized as such today, it is significant that he should be such a fervent advocate of Augustine's aesthetic principles. He must clearly have felt the force of Augustine's argument that numbers and ratios contain eternal truth.

Gretchen Ludke Finney has singled out the years from 1580 to 1640 in England as the period when the Platonic and Pythagorean theories of music as an image of world harmony experienced an enthusiastic revival,[76] but she errs in attributing an esoteric character to these theories. The failure to recognize the Augustinian and biblical substratum in the thought of John Dee has led to a similar exaggeration of Dee's lack of orthodoxy. Thus Frances Yates quotes from Dee's letter to the Archbishop of Canterbury (published in 1592) without recognizing that this passage is an elaboration of *Romans* 1 : 20.[77] Dee may have been "a mathematician who believed that the divine creation was held together by magical forces" (p. 14), but this particular passage was clearly written in order to prove his religious orthodoxy. K. J. Knoespel's study of Dee's preface to the *Elements* of Euclid (1570) rightly argues that Dee's mathematics has as its central concern "the relationships deduced from proportional statements," and that this interest in proportion was closely connected with rhetorical theory "that guided not only the disposition of an argument, but furthered the construction of modulated, balanced sentences and lines of poetry." However, it is scarcely just to state that "religious revelation previously negotiated through language has begun to shift to mathematics."[78] John Dee was certainly not among the first to study "Philosophy & Theology by numbers" in the manner of Pythagoras, to pick a phrase from *The French Academie* (III,11; p. 663), but Knoespel's view that Dee connected narrative and mathematics deserves serious consideration. Knoespel, too, quotes a passage from Dee without identifying its basis in *Wisdom* 11 : 21 and

Romans 1:20 (p. 38). The passage is a prayer or invocation prefaced to the propositions, and, if it is true that the Preface "offers not simply education but initiation" (p. 38), then the religious orthodoxy displayed in the biblical allusions must be interpreted as a smoke-screen set up to protect the author. It seems to me doubtful, however, that Dee's thought here is tinged by the occult or esoteric. Dee's discovery that the secrets of God's creation may be discovered in proportion seems rational enough and sufficiently Augustinian to warrant inclusion in the tradition outlined in these pages. Knoespel makes an important, although obvious, point when he argues that mathematical symbols, when "read as expressions of metaphysical truth," came to be "imbued with an allegorical authority." He concludes that numerology certainly "is an obvious example of mathematical allegory" (p. 39).

My final examples are taken from the Cambridge Platonists, Peter Sterry, and the Frenchman Yves-Marie André, whose influential *Essai sur le Beau* (Paris, 1741) transmitted Augustine's view of unity in a work of art to the generation of Henry Fielding.

Peter Sterry's *A Discourse of the Will*, posthumously published in 1675, relates Augustine's aesthetic principles to those of Aristotle. It was surely Augustine who prompted Sterry's praise of the skill with which God resolves variety into unity; if God's works are his "poems," then numbers are among their most beautiful images: "The *Ideas* or eternal Images of things in God so seem to shine forth most clearly, with the sweetest and fullest beauties, in abstracted numbers" (p. 27). When Christ, through his act of redemption, created harmony from the discord of sin, he seems to "act a *Divine Masque* to the *Divine Musick* of eternal Love" (p. 212). God reconciles the "most opposed Contrarieties, bindeth up all with an harmonious Order into an *exact Unity*: which conveyeth things down by a gradual descent, then bringeth them up again to the highest point ..., opening the *beginning in the end*, espousing the end to the beginning". This is what Aristotle commended, and this is "that which Jesus Christ pointeth at in himself" because in him are "formed and perfected" all the "Divine contrivances" (p. 179). The enthusiasm with which Sterry praises the "Divine and delightful skill" with which God fuses all "scenes, all forms of darkness and death" into one unified grand design where everything finds its proper place (p. 185) points forward to the Earl of Shaftesbury, while conversely his frequent use of the images of Jacob's ladder and of the Tabernacle represents a carry-over from Giorgio and

Pico. The same is true of his interpretation of Ezekiel's vision of the chariot and of the vision of St John, both of whom are said to envisage Christ as the unifying centre diffusing itself through the whole circle of creation. The vision of the chariot shows how all parts are united with each other and with the whole (p. 225), while Sterry's comment on Jacob's ladder is that it forms a "scale of Divine Harmony and Proportions" (p. 30); its steps reveal the order of creation, but the ladder also is Christ. Christ is "a *mystical Ladder*, reaching through the whole Creation, from the top to the bottom". Since Christ is the creative Logos, containing everything within himself, the steps are all the ranks of the creatures (p. 121). In the *Divine Poem*, or Work, the contrasting dark parts function like scenes of storms and tempests which set off "with a greater heightening, even to an extasy of wonder and delight, the Sweetnesses, the Beauties, the Glories of the Divine Harmony surrounding it", "shining forth with a golden calm and lustre in the midst of it" (p. 160).

Sterry seems more attracted by the beauty of this vision of unity than by its truth or its function as an approach to the Deity, and in this respect he anticipates the attitude of the early eighteenth century as exemplified by Yves-Marie André.

According to the author of the preface contributed to the Amsterdam edition of 1760, Père André's *Essai sur le Beau* is more important than anything written by Francis Hutcheson; or, to be quite precise, this is the opinion of the authors of the *Encyclopédie* as quoted in the preface. Père André was born in 1675 and in his capacity as Jesuit and Professor of Mathematics at Caen he was in a good position to appreciate Augustine's aesthetics. André begins by defining beauty as unity of design: beauty is a matter of the rational perception and appreciation of regularity, order, proportion, and symmetry. In any work of art the parts may be arranged so as to avoid confusion, and this may be done by placing unique or single parts in the middle of such as are double or capable of division, while "les parties égales" must be evenly spaced. Parts that are odd in number must be made to succeed each other in a graded arrangement ("une espèce de gradation reglée"). In short, the arrangement must constitute a whole where nothing is out of place or contrary to the unity of the design. Plato may have discussed beauty in the *Hippias* and the *Phèdre*, but Augustine must be preferred as he has treated the issue "plus en philosophe" (p. 10). And André goes on to explain how Augustine's sublime treatise *De vera religione* elevates the reader from the beauty of visible things to the essential beauty which creates the rules whereby beauty is assessed. After summarizing Augustine's principles, the author concludes that it is unity which constitutes the form and essence of beauty. If one ascends with Augustine to the invisible, essential world, one will obtain some idea of the art of the Creator, and it is this supreme art which forms the model for all the marvels of nature.

Andre's main concern is with the beauty found in the totality of a composition: "quelle est la forme précise du Beau dans le total d'une composition?" Many poets restrict their attention to the individual parts of a composition without considering the whole, so that they create disparate or unrelated beauties; yet despite the "gout libertin de notre siècle" some writers still know how to conceive a design within which they organize their material so that it forms a well-knit sequence ("une suite bien liée"). It is only when a writer can connect the parts into a whole *by means of a preconceived design* that the groundwork itself becomes beautiful. When this is missing, or defective, what one reads will be a poor ode full of beautiful stanzas, a pitiful tragedy where individual scenes may be beautiful, or an insipid speech abounding with beautiful figures. One may perhaps read a page of this sort of composition, but who will trouble to read the whole? "La suite y manque: l'unité y est rompue" (p. 109).

This last example of the influence of Augustine's aesthetics is interesting not only because it proves the surprising longevity of the tradition, but because the author so very plainly has his eye on the arrangement of the parts which constitute a poem, a tragedy, or a speech. The general principle of symmetrical or graded arrangement of parts is unambiguously and emphatically applied to literary compositions, and literary unity is defined as resulting from a preconceived design which invests the whole with highest beauty. Unity, then, is a matter of linking parts that have been arranged according to Augustine's prescription; this is the method which ensures that beauty resides in the totality of a composition.

5. From Theology to Poetics

My survey of the tradition which links poetry with prophecy and both with the harmony of creation should, perhaps, have included more about the Cambridge Platonists and their successors, but such an account is already available in the pages of Martin C. Battestin's *The Providence of Wit. Aspects of Form in Augustan Literature and the Arts* (Oxford, 1974). One of the sources Battestin quotes is a passage from Charles Gildon's *The Complete Art of Poetry* (1718) on the relationship between cosmic and poetic structure. The universe was "by *Art Divine* brought into order, and this *noble poem* of the Universe compleated in *Number* and *Figures*, by the Almighty *Poet* or *Maker*". Battestin himself summarizes the basic principle as follows: "Since, then, an artful design was the formal characteristic of Nature ..., the business of the human artist was to reflect this fact in the symmetry and order of his own form, implying, as a consequence, the larger harmonies of the universe". Strangely enough, though, Battestin believes that this was a specifically Augustan development caused by the need to stem the tide of a neo-Epicurean materialism connected with the philosophy of Hobbes. It was as a conscious counter-offensive that the latitudinarian divines "raised the ideals of Order and Form to a theological principle"; countless sermons, poems, and essays "formulate a system of aesthetics by reference to the inherent order of creation".[79] But the sources collected by Battestin proclaim their indebtedness to the Augustinian tradition even in the very phrasing; and if there is a sense in which the Augustans provided a new slant or emphasis, this may, perhaps, be seen in the *use* they made of this traditional material. Its renewed lease on life must be attributed to the convenient way in which it could be made to support the rational proof of a Deity from the order of his works. The tradition was tailor-made to meet this need. Also the physico-theological enthusiasm so typical of the first half of the eighteenth century helps to explain why a system of poetics based on an imitation of cosmic structure should have retained, and even increased, its popularity.

Since the main emphasis of this study falls on the Renaissance, however, I do not wish to extend my scope too far and so will rest content with this reference to the added documentation afforded by Battestin's book. What I have tried to provide in the preceding pages, is a survey of theological arguments about unified structures which may serve as a supplement to the more familiar Renaissance treatises on the art of poetry and so assist us to interpret these treatises more fully and reliably whenever they touch on ideas that bear on structure. Both Christoforo Landino and Torquato Tasso say in so many words that it is by virtue of its unified structure that a poem constitutes a cosmos, and *Jerusalem Delivered* shows how systematically Tasso applied the principles he proclaims.

Christoforo Landino's treatise "Che Cosa Sia Poesia et Poeta, et della Origine Sua Divina, et Antichissima"[80] forms the preface to his widely disseminated and frequently reprinted edition of Dante's *Commedia* (1481) so that its influence must have been great. Although it is true enough, as André Chastel argues in *Marsile Ficin et l'Art* (Geneva, 1954), that Landino formulates a Platonic system of aesthetics in imitation of his master Ficino, Landino's essay pointedly juxtaposes *Wisdom* 11 : 21 on creation in number, weight, and measure with *Romans* 1 : 20 and so recalls Augustine's *De vera religione*. Landino even includes Augustine's famous image of God as poet: "Et é Iddio sommo poeta, & é il mondo suo poema". It is when Landino explains the similarity between the poet and the prophet that he cites the familiar biblical proof passages. Although the poetic fiction does not belong completely to the world of pure mind, it is nevertheless different from the process of mere making; it resembles creation: "And God is the supreme poet, and the world his poem". The comparison is perfect: just as God orders his creation – that is, the visible and invisible world – in number, measure, and weight, the poets fashion their poems with the numbers of their metres, the measure of long and short syllables, and the weight of their sentences and affections. The reference to *Romans* 1 : 20 is oblique here, but it is made explicit later on when Landino discusses the relationship between the human and the divine in his section on divine fury. No one may become a poet, no matter how learned he may be, unless aroused by a divine fury; great poems are divine gifts, and not the invention of philosophers. By the images provided here on Earth (images that are almost like shadows of heavenly things) we are made to *remember* the divine things we knew before birth. Paul confirms this when he says that the invisible things of God are seen by us by means of those that are visible here. Consequently, human wisdom is an image of the divine wisdom, and the music of our instruments an image of the divine harmony. Thus, on receiving images of musical consonances, the soul is led to contemplate the harmony in the mind of the Deity and in the order of the heavenly bodies. Before birth the soul fed on these harmonies, and while confined to earth it struggles to regain them. The divinely inspired poet will incorporate such harmonies in his verse, and it is this kind of imitation only which Plato called poetry. This is a poetry which is not content to feed the ear with sweet sounds, but describes high and divine things, feeding the soul as it were with celestial ambrosia.

Landino's strong emphasis on the prophetic vision of the poet suggests Hermetic influence but, since Landino identifies Hermes with Moses in his chapter on the origins of poetry, he himself must have thought that he remained well within the framework of divine revelation. We find a similar mixture of Hermetic and Augustinian ideas in George Chapman and Giordano Bruno, but the tendency, unfortunately, has been to stress the Hermetic elements and ignore those that are Augustinian so that the perspective becomes quite wrong.

Sidney's view of the poet is far more conservative; like Augustine he posits, not a divine fury, but the clarified vision of the regenerate. When Sidney remarks that the "skill of the artificer" is shown in the "*idea* or fore-conceit of the work" rather than in the work itself, one cannot of course limit the meaning to structure or pattern, but it would be even more absurd to exclude textual structure from its connotations. Similarly when Sidney speaks of the "planet-like music of poetry", he is surely glancing in the direction of the *ars aeterna* by means of which harmony is created and sustained. Sidney may seem a committed Platonist when he describes David as a "passionate lover of the unspeakable and everlasting beauty to be seen by the eyes of the mind, only cleared by faith", and so no wonder that it has been said that Sidney "rather dazzlingly countered Plato's objection to imitation by using Plato's own doctrine of love, in which one rises from love of a beautiful thing to love of beauty itself".[81] But this is to focus on the *Symposium* rather than the *Timæus*, and to ignore the fact that the Platonic account of creation was reconciled with the Mosaic account; moreover, it is to ignore the command given in *Romans* 1 : 20 to trace the invisible in what is visible. It is entirely Augustinian to say that the poet should imitate, not the external and perishable aspects of reality, but the ideas and forms by means of which everything exists. If this is what a poem does, then it will indeed reflect what Sidney calls the "unconceivable excellencies of God". Augustine's *De vera religione* explains the method. The symmetrical or graded arrangements of parts that invest a work of art with unity, reflect the true and primal Unity capable of being perceived by the mind alone (xxx.55). Unity carries the whole similitude of him who is the cause why things exist that are capable of being unified, and it is this Unity we must try to perceive as we ponder the shows of this world, including those which have been created by artists. Unless we consider them in this manner, they will be as unreal as painted banquets, while conversely they will feed the mind if they make us perceive the Wisdom which orders everything *suaviter*. What spectacle can be more wonderful than that of the incorporeal power that creates and rules our corporeal world? And what more beautiful than its ordering and adorning of this material world (li.100)?

Landino is one of the important sources for the first printed English formal defence of poetry, Richard Wills's *De re poetica*, included in his *Poematum liber* (1573). Wills was acquainted with Gabriel Harvey, was included by Fraunce in his *Arcadian Rhetorike* (1588), and may have been the Willye of Spenser's March and August eclogues.[82] Wills is conveniently explicit about the relevance of proportion to verbal artefacts:

> The origin of metrical form is from God the Almighty Creator, in that He created this universe and whatever is contained in its sphere with a fixed design, as it were by measure [*certa ratione, quasi metro composuit*]; to such an extent that Pythagoras has asserted that there is a harmony in celestial and in earthly things. For how could the universe exist, unless it were governed by a fixed order and established harmony? Again, all the instruments we use are made with certain proportions – that is, by *measure*. If this happens with other things, how much more so with language, which gives expression to all things? (pp. 63 f.)

The focus on harmonious design so clearly shown in this passage is usually accompanied by slighting references to the lower kind of harmony which appeals to the physical senses rather than the mind, and this may be why Wills's early enthusiasm for pattern poems seems to have been a passing phase. Their appeal may have seemed to be to the eye alone.

The strong insistence, in Landino as in Augustine, that poetry should appeal to the mind rather than the ear (*De musica* VI.xiv.47) is reflected by Samuel Daniel. Daniel's *Defence of Ryme* (1603) has seemed curiously illogical since it combines praise of rhyme as a harmony "farre happier than any proportion Antiquitie could euer shew vs" with dispraise of poetic effects whose appeal is only to the ear. It is matter alone "that satisfies the iudiciall", and while we seek "to please our eare, we inthrall our judgement". These statements can be reconciled if Daniel employed rhymes to please the mind rather than the ear, and, as I have shown elsewhere, this is precisely what he did: Daniel wrote a kind of poetry that invites a highly intellectual appreciation of the placing of verbal elements within the line and in rhyme position.[83] The appeal to the ear is intellectualized and so lifted to a higher level when structural patterns are created by repeating identical rhyme words.

As the French poet and philosopher Pontus de Tyard (1521–1605) has argued, rhyme can be used in other ways as well to appeal to the mind.[84] In the dialogue entitled "Le Solitaire Second" (published in 1552, 1555, and 1578 and included in the *Discours Philosophiques* of 1589) Pontus de Tyard calls for an art of poetry where rhymes are conditioned by musical laws ("des loix musicales"). He envisages a kind of musical decorum where rhyme schemes are adjusted to the subject-matter so as to produce certain proportions or consonances such as "les proportions doubles, triples, d'autant & demi, d'autant & tiers". The poet who obeyed such laws would become a "Poëte-musicien" who would show that "la harmonie & les Rimes sont presque d'une mesme essence".[85] This is actually what Tasso did, or says he did, in his arrangement of rhymes in the eight-line stanza he favoured for the *Gerusalemme Liberata*; one reason for its perfection is that it embodies various musical ratios. Tasso is surely thinking of the rhyme scheme when he states that the eight-line stanza "is made up of a double quaternion, thus forming a solid web, or of a quadruple binary, or further of a ternary and a quinary, the first odd numbers".[86] Spenser's stanza in the June eclogue may be considered as a double quaternion, its rhyme scheme being the carefully balanced pattern ababbaba. A modern scholar has related Chaucer's seven-line stanza in *The Parlement of Foules* to the 7 celestial tones on the basis of the observation that its rhyme scheme (ababbcc) embodies the three ratios of the diapason (2:1), the diatessaron (4:3), and the diapente (3:2). It is the relation between quatrain and tercet which creates the diatessaron, the rhymes within the tercet the diapason, while the perfect fifth or diapente is found between *b* rhymes and *a* rhymes, and between *b* rhymes and *c* rhymes.[87]

Stanza patterns is an interesting subject. *The Shepheardes Calender* is marked by great variety, and it is therefore an obtrusive fact that the same stanza form is used in *December* as in *January*, so that the cycle ends as it began, the only difference being one of length. The 26 stanzas of *December* relate to the 13 of *January* as 2:1 a harmonious resolution which suggests that we ought to read Colin's final complaint as evidence of reconciliation between man and God.[88] The repetition, in chiastic sequence, of two, three, and even four identical rhyme words to mark the beginning and the end of a textual structure is a related phenomenon.

The principle of unity through harmony manifests itself in many ways from the earliest times, as Julius Cæsar Scaliger explains in his *Poetices libri septem* (1561). The Psalms prove that poetry existed "from the earliest beginnings of nature itself," and in their odes the Pythagoreans praised the sun, moon, and stars. When fitted together, these odes reflect the proportions of the planets, "which are known to the learned only." In this way divine things form the ideal pattern (*specimen*) for poetry.[89] Scaliger's reference to the Psalms suggests awareness of the tradition of aligning the chanting of the Psalms with various temporal cycles, the shortest being a single 24-hour period. Since the Psalms were believed to contain all of the Bible in abbreviated form, they present all of God's works in space and time. When the Psalms are chanted in daily or weekly cycles, therefore, an alignment is created between the Word and the movement of the spheres. To illustrate this point, I quote from the late eleventh-century *Dominus Vobiscum* by Damianus, who describes this alignment in a passage on the monk in his cell as he reads the cycle of the Psalms:

> He contemplates the course of the stars in heaven, and from his lips descends the well-ordered rhythm of the psalm. One after the other the stars produce the day with their alternating motions; the verses bud forth one after the other on his lips as from a fountain-head (*ex quodam oriente*), and the verses and the stars in heaven move towards their goal with equal motion. The friar performs his service, and the stars complete their mission; the one tends in his soul towards the inaccessible light by way of his chanting, the others reconduct the daylight to the physical eyes. Along different routes the friar and the stars tend toward their goal, and the elements adjust themselves to, or accord with (*subserviendo concordant*), the hymn of the servant of God.[90]

The verses and the stars, then, move with equal motion; if this had been written by Ficino, it would no doubt have been taken as yet another indication of his known tendency to attribute magical power to song. This passage therefore serves as a timely reminder that the piety of the Middle Ages and the Renaissance includes cosmic perspectives which must not be taken to hover on the verge of the occult. The elements of the universe are unified, not because the chant has magic potency, but because the harmony of the universe and of the song are one and the same. Each has its source in the divine unity.

By now it should be less difficult to understand how Spenser came to work the rhythms of space and time into the texture of his *Epithalamion*. Similarly the use sometimes made of cosmic and biblical numbers in private buildings and in churches reflects the same desire for perfect alignment with the harmony whose source is in God. What these structures show is a conscious turning of the will to God.

On the subject of this turning of the will to God no one has written more eloquently or with greater power than Augustine, whose *Confessions* is an epic on man's quest for God and God's for man. As we shall see, the very structure of this spiritual epic proclaims that God is Creator and Redeemer, source and end.

Notes to Chapter I

1. A bilingual text of the *De ordine* (Latin and French) is found in *Ouevres de Saint Augustin*, vol. 4 (Paris, 1948).
2. Roy Battenhouse, "The Doctrine of Man in Calvin and in Renaissance Platonism," *A Journal of the History of Ideas* 9 (1948), 447–71. On Zwingli's syncretism see Christopher Sigwart, *Ulrich Zwingli. Der Character seiner Theologie mit besonderer Rücksicht auf Picus von Mirandola* (Stuttgart und Hamburg, 1855). Zwingli held that, although the Bible presents the adequately expressed divine revelation, it is not the only source for such revelation. Prophecies about Christ were given to *illuminati* in many nations, among them the Sibyls, Plato, and Seneca.
3. Henry Bullinger was a minister in Zürich who assisted the Marian exiles. His influential sermons were published in English translation in 1577, 1584, 1587 and later editions, and "inferior Ministers" not licensed to preach were ordered by the Convocation of the province of Canterbury (held in 1586) to read one of Bullinger's sermons every week. Although intended for a popular audience, they sometimes express syncretistic views. Quotations are from *The Decades* as reprinted by the Parker Society in four volumes (Cambridge, 1849–52) on the basis of the edition of 1587. See Sermon IV.1 (Vol. III, p. 19). Sermon IV.10 (Vol. III, p. 385) lists all the ancient theologians "as Trismegistus, Museus, Orpheus, Homerus, Pindarus ... Plato himself". Then, too, Bullinger quotes liberally from the Augustine of the *De vera religione*, *On Christian Doctrine*, *The City of God*, and the sermons on the Psalms.
4. See below, pp. 75–79.
5. Bullinger, Vol. I, pp. 42 and 46.
6. Quotations from *On Christian Doctrine*, tr. D. W. Robertson (New York, 1958) are identified by reference to book, chapter, and section. For this quotation see IV.vi.9 (p. 123). This and related passages are quoted by Bullinger in Sermon V.6 (Vol. IV, pp. 290–92). See Joseph Anthony Wittreich's discussion of prophetic obscurity and the theory of "reader harassment" or "the trial of the reader" in " 'A Poet amongst Poets': Milton and the Tradition of Prophecy", in *Milton and the Line of Vision*, ed. Wittreich (Madison, Wisconsin, 1975), pp. 105f.

7. *The Confessions*, tr. R. S. Pine-Coffin (Harmondsworth, 1961), p. 344 (13 : 34). The Latin text (as given in the Loeb Classical Edition) reads as follows: "INSPEXIMUS etiam, propter quorum figurationem ista vel tali ordine fieri vel tali ordine scribi voluisti ...".
8. Bonaventura, *Collationes in Hexaemeron. Lateinisch und Deutsch*, tr. Wilhelm Nyssen (Darmstadt, 1964), p. 432 (see Collatio XIV.5). See also Coll. XIV.29 (p. 458) and Coll. XVI.10 (p. 496) where it is urged that the same structure or course is found in Holy Writ and the universe, both being conditioned by the number 7: "Secundum hunc numerum facit Deus currere mundum istum et Scripturam, quae explicat decursum mundi; et secundum hunc numerum tradi debuit et explicari". Both must therefore be expounded or explicated in terms of this number.
9. *Oeuvres de Saint Augustin*, vol. 4 (Paris, 1948), pp. 301–459.
10. Ficino quotes this view in a letter dated 8 September 1479. See Ficino, *Opera Omnia* (Paris, 1641), Vol. 1, pp. 794 f. Familiar literary expressions of this idea are found in Shakespeare's *The Merchant of Venice*, V.i.83–88, and Milton's "At a Solemn Music".
11. *Über den Wortlaut der Genesis*, tr. Carl Johann Perl (Paderborn, 1961–64), I, 224. See also Book IV, ch. 3 (pp. 116 f.) on God's creation of the world in number, weight, and measure.
12. Robert Greville, 2nd Baron Brooke, *The Nature of Truth, 1640* (Gregg International Publishers: Farnborough, 1969), p. 30 (from ch. IV).
13. *De musica* VI.xi.33 (quoted from the Latin–French ed. of Augustine's *Oeuvres*). Compare the Pauline concept of carnal man who becomes spiritual man through Christ. Augustine's argument virtually identifies harmony with Christ, or the other way round.
14. *De vera religione* 1v.113. The quotation is from *Of True Religion*, tr. J. H. S. Burleigh (Chicago, 1964), p. 107. Since this translation is unreliable in many ways, subsequent quotations will be my own translation of the Latin text as printed in *Oeuvres*, vol. 8 (Paris, 1951).
15. *On Free Choice of the Will*, tr. Anna S. Benjamin and L. H. Hackstaff (The Library of Liberal Arts: New York, 1964), p. 113.
16. Calvin, *On the Christian Faith. Selections from the Institutes, Commentaries, and Tracts*, ed. John T. McNeil (The Library of Liberal Arts: New York, 1957), p. 12.
17. Bonaventura, *Itinerarium mentis in Deum, Lateinisch und Deutsch*, tr. Julian Kaup (Munich, 1961), pp. 82–88.
18. *Liber de mente*, tr. Heinrich Cassirer, in Ernst Cassirer, *Individuum und Kosmos in der Philosophie der Renaissance* (Berlin, 1927), pp. 203–302. Relevant passages are found also in the *Idiota de sapientia*, translated into English in 1640 and entitled *The Idiot*. This treatise defines numbers as images of the principles they refer to (p. 102), and the Pythagoreans are said to "speak symbolically and rationally, of the number which proceeds from the divine minde, of which mathematicall number is but the image" (p. 92). For Cusanus' definition of number in the *De coniecturis*, see my account of Pietro Bongo in section 3.
19. *Théologie Platonicienne de l'Immortalité des Ames*, ed. and tr. Raymond Marcel (Paris, 1964), Vol. I, p. 138 and Vol. II, p. 223.
20. *Commentarium in Timæum*, in *Opera* (Paris, 1641), Vol. II, pp. 395–421.
21. *Philebus Commentary*, ed. Michael J. B. Allen (Los Angeles, 1976).
22. Another such image is that of a marriage union – between Adam and Eve and between Christ and his church in Heaven.
23. André Chastel, *Marsile Ficin et l'art* (Geneva, 1954), p. 99.
24. I wish to thank Valerie Smith of Oxford University for having provided translations into English of some of the more important parts of the commentary.

25. Landino's preface to his frequently reprinted edition of Dante is an essay on the nature of poetry and the poet and their divine origin ("Che Cosa Sia Poesia et Poeta, et della Origine Sua Divina, et Antichissima"). I have used the edition published at Venice in 1564, and for a translation into English I am indebted to a work in manuscript by my colleague Roy T. Eriksen.
26. *Weight* is rendered as weighty sentences and affections, so that it is made to bear on the contents.
27. See below, pp. 203–5.
28. Giorgio Petrocchi, "Preface," in Tasso, *Il Mondo Creato* (Florence, 1951), p. xi.
29. John Donne, *Essays in Divinity*, ed. Evelyn Simpson (Oxford, 1952), p. 10. Although Donne's interest in symbolic numbers recalls Augustine (see, for example, *The City of God* XV.xx), C. A. Patrides has classified it as occult in his article on "The Numerological Approach to Cosmic Order during the English Renaissance," *Isis* 49 (1958) 397.
30. Quotations are from Pico, *On the Dignity of Man, On Being and the One, Heptaplus* (The Library of Liberal Arts: New York, 1965).
31. Raymond B. Waddington, "The Sun at the Center: Structure as Meaning in Pico della Mirandola's *Heptaplus*," *Journal of Medieval and Renaissance Studies* 3 (1973), 69–86.
32. See below, p. 51.
33. For the importance of the number 8 in biblical exegesis, see Chapter III.
34. I reproduce this interesting drawing in *The Hidden Sense* (Oslo, 1963), p. 47, and so does S. K. Heninger Jr in *The Cosmographical Glass* (San Marino, 1977), p. 93, where its many details are ably elucidated. However, Heninger does not seem aware of Nicholas le Fèvre's indebtedness to Nicolas Cusanus' similar drawing.
35. The best account of the belief in a *prisca theologia* is the one provided by D. P. Walker in *The Ancient Theology. Studies in Christian Platonism from the Fifteenth to the Eighteenth Century* (London, 1972).
36. Relevant information can be found in Anne Lake Prescott, *French Poets and the English Renaissance* (New Haven and London, 1978). Thus we are told that Gabriel Harvey had "high praise for Pico" (pp. 94 f.).
37. James E. Phillips, "Daniel Rogers: A Neo-Latin Link between the Pléiade and Sidney's 'Areopagus'," *Neo-Latin Poetry of the Sixteenth and Seventeenth Centuries* (The Wm Andrews Clark Memorial Library: Los Angeles, 1965), 5–28.
38. Francis Yates, *The French Academies of the Sixteenth Century* (London 1947), *Giordano Bruno and the Hermetic Philosophy* (London, 1964).
39. D. P. Walker, *The Ancient Theology* (London, 1972), lists the various Renaissance editions of texts attributed to Hermes Trismegistus. Sir Walter Ralegh praises "that Ægyptian Hermes" in ch. 2 of *A History of the World* (1614), and in 1635 David Person stated that Hermes and Plato were indebted to Moses (*Varieties*, p. 65), and Robert Fludd was of the same opinion (*Mosaicall Philosophy*, Latin ed. 1638, English version 1659, p. 42). Casaubon's *Exercitationes* (London, 1614) exposed the falseness of the belief in the extreme antiquity of the Hermetic dialogues, but this did not affect their reputation. After his retirement from active service under Cromwell, Thomas Lord Fairfax devoted his leisure hours to making an English translation of part of the commentary published at Bourdeaux in 1579 by François de Foix, bishop and nobleman. The manuscript volume is in the British Library.
40. Frances Yates, *Theatre of the World* (London, 1969), pp. 12 and 17. However, clearer discriminations are made in her more recent book, *The Occult Philosophy in the Elizabethan Age* (London, 1979), where a chapter on Giorgio (pp. 29–36) stresses his Christian piety. She observes that "in a curious way Christian Cabala could support evangelical reform; there is even a kind of Erasmianism

implicit in Giorgio's outlook" (p. 34). However, she has failed to register the authoritative study listed in note 41.
41. J.-F. Maillard, "Le 'De Harmonia Mundi' de George de Venise," *Revue de l'Histoire des Religions* 179 (1971), 181–203. Maillard concludes that Giorgio's ideas are entirely traditional, and that his only claim to originality must be based on the presentation of his material.
42. Pietro Bongo, *Numerorum mysteria* (1591), p. 51 (see the chapter "De Unitate").
43. Désirée Hirst, *Hidden Riches. Traditional Symbolism from the Renaissance to Blake* (London, 1964), p. 117.
44. Alexander Gill, *The Sacred Philosophie of the Holy Scriptures* (1635), p. 101.
45. See below, section 3.
46. Simon Goulart. *A Learned Summary Upon the famous Poeme of William of Saluste Lord of Bartas*, tr. David Lodge (London, 1621), p. 248.
47. See Maillard, "Le 'De Harmonia Mundi' ".
48. It was surely the desire to avoid a similar accusation that made Pierre de la Primaudaye and his English translators play down the role of non-biblical sources in the encylopedic treatise *The French Academie* (1618).
49. The Dutch or Flemish Jesuit Cornelius à Lapide (1567–1637) wrote voluminous commentaries on many biblical books, in which he summarizes all the great authorities. His appeal extended beyond the Catholic camp; Robert Greville, *The Nature of Truth* (London, 1640), p. 143, quotes him with approval.
50. James E. Phillips, "Spenser's Syncretistic Religious Imagery," *ELH – A Journal of English Literary History* 36 (1969), 110–29.
51. Giorgio's Symposium-like picture of the disciple resting on the breast of Christ may have caused Spenser to refer to Christ on Mount Olivet as "For euer with a flowring girlond crownd".
52. Andrew Marvell, "Upon Appleton House", lines 581–82.
53. Reproduced by Rudolf Wittkower in *Architectural Principles in the Age of Humanism* (London, 1949).
54. See Frances Yates, *Theatre of the World*, pp. 121 f.
55. See my study of "Golden Phrases: the Poetics of Giles Fletcher", *Studies in Philology* 88 (1991), 169–200.
56. The works of Cusanus have been published in Latin and German by the Felix Meiner Verlag, but the *De conjecturis* can also be found in the *Philosophische Bibliothek*, Neue Folge, vol. 268 (Hamburg, 1971). This edition reproduces the diagram in an appended table, and the relevant passage in Cusanus' text is numbered I.xiii.64–69.
57. On Guy le Fèvre see the following studies: Henry Hornik, "Guy Lefèvre de la Boderie's *La Galliade* and Renaissance Syncretism," *Modern Language Notes* 76 (1961), 735–42, and Françoise Joukovsky, *Orphée et Ses Disciples dans la Poésie Française et Neo-Latine du XVIe Siècle* (Geneva, 1970). I cannot recommend François Secret, *L'ésoterisme de Guy le Fèvre de la Boderie* (Geneva, 1969), who often discovers indebtedness to Guillaume Postel where a reference to Augustine would have been advisable. Augustine was one of many who believed that truth, wheresoever found, must be from God, but Secret associates this belief with Postel (see p. 51).
Of his pre-planned structures suffice it to mention that for his "circular" poem, *La Galliade ou de la révolution des arts et des sciences*, he chose the circular number 5 (5 is circular because it reproduces itself in the last digit when multiplied with itself). In the *Hymnes ecclésiastiques* we find a sonnet "Du grand Quaternaie" which lists 4 related items in each of the 13 first lines, while the last states that these quaternions constitute our earthly pavilion placed on 4 corners. It is likely that the 52 items listed (i.e. 4×13) refer to the quaternion of the year, just as the sum total of 14 lines (i.e. $10+4$) expresses the quaternion ($10=4$). An

analysis of numerical and verbal patterns in the poetry of Guy le Fèvre would no doubt yield further interesting examples.
58. I touch on Bruno in my essay "'In ordine di ruota': Circular Structure in 'The unfortunate Lover' and *Upon Appleton House*," *Tercentenary Essays in Honor of Andrew Marvell*, ed. Kenneth Friedenreich (Hamden, Conn., 1977), pp. 245–67. The essay suggests that Bruno's *De gli heroici furori* (1585) and his philosophy of love have affinities with Augustine's thought. For a study of the connection between Bruno and Marlowe, see Roy T. Eriksen, *The Forme of Faustus Fortunes. A Study of the Tragedie of Doctor Faustus* (Oslo, 1987), especially Ch. II.
59. My translation, as throughout this section on Bongo. I have used the 1591 edition, whose title explains that Pythagorean number symbolism agrees with the Scriptures: *Numerorum mysteria, opus maximarium rerum doctrina et copia repertum, in quo mirus in primis, idemque perpetuus Arithmeticae Pythagoricae cum Divinae Paginae numeris consensus, multiplici ratione probatur.* The passage translated is found on p. 1.
60. P. 63. Bongo's argument seems relevant to the conclusion of Kyd's *The Spanish Tragedy*, where the play performed in different languages is a means of revenge, while the survivor bites off his tongue to preserve silence. The languages may represent the confusion of multitude, and silence the sacred unity that ensures renewal.
61. Herrick, *Poetical Works*, ed. F. W. Moorman (Oxford, 1915), p. 397.
62. Herrick, "His Meditation upon Death," p. 392.
63. The edition of 1586 contains the first book only. The first edition to contain all four books appeared in 1618. Book I is concerned with society, Book II with man, Book III with the world, and Book IV with "Christian Philosophie, instructing the true and onely meanes to eternall life."
64. My quotations are from the 1618 edition.
65. Milton, *De doctrina Christiana*, Columbia edition, vol. 15, pp. 18 f. In the Latin text the phrase *qvamvis ut numero* is added to the preceding phrase and not related to that which follows. My quotation follows the Latin syntax.
66. Heninger, *The Cosmographical Glass*, ch. 4, discusses Primaudaye's use of Pythagorean ideas. I had discovered Primaudaye's indebtedness to Pico before Heninger's book appeared.
67. Prescott, *French Poets and the English Renaissance*, p. 225, associates Mornay's syncretism with occultist tendencies. It is odd that it is so hard to get rid of this misconception.
68. Quoted from Sir Philip Sidney, *The Prose Works*, ed. Albert Feuillerat (Cambridge, 1962), Vol. III, p. 205.
69. See my analysis of Milton's ode in "Elaborate Song: Conceptual Structure in Milton's 'On the Morning of Christ's Nativity'," in *Fair Forms*, ed. M.-S. Røstvig (Cambridge, 1975), pp. 54–84 and 206–12. A 27-stanza passage in Giles Fletcher's *Christs Victorie, and Triumph* (1610) has a similar textual structure; see my article on "Golden Phrases: The Poetics of Giles Fletcher," 193–97.
70. I quote from the facsimile edition of the *Harmonie Universelle* published by the Centre National de la Recherche Scientifique (Paris, 1965). See vol. 3, pp. 14 and 23 (separate pagination).
71. *La Vérité des Sciences, 1625* (facs. ed., Friedrich Frommann Verlag, 1969), p. 233.
72. Ibid., p. 236.
73. Ibid., pp. 252 f.
74. "Livre de l'Utilité," p. 23.
75. Ibid., p. 37.
76. Gretchen Ludke Finney, "Music: a Book of Knowledge in Renaissance England," *Studies in the Renaissance* 6 (1959), 36–63.
77. Frances Yates, *Theatre of the World*, pp. 13–14.

78. Kenneth J. Knoespel, "The Narrative Matter of Mathematics: John Dee's Preface to the *Elements* of Euclid of Megara (1570)", "*Philological Quarterly* 66 (1987), p. 39.
79. Martin C. Battestin, *The Providence of Wit* (Oxford, 1974), pp. 284, 52, and 32.
80. As stated in note 25, my quotations are from a manuscript translation into English by Roy T. Eriksen. For information about Landino, see Bernhard Weinberg, *A History of Literary Criticism in the Italian Renaissance* (Chicago, 1961), Vol. I, pp. 79–81. Weinberg touches only on Landino's concern with allegory.
81. J. S. Lawry, *Sidney's Two Arcadias. Pattern and Proceeding* (Ithaca and London, 1972), p. 10.
82. A. D. S. Fowler, preface to Richard Wills, *De Re Poetica* (Oxford, 1958). On Wills's interest in pattern poems, see the preface, p. 13.
83. Røstvig, "A Frame of Words: on the Craftsmanship of Samuel Daniel," *English Studies* 60 (1979), 122–37; see also Røstvig, "'Figures and Numbers': On the Poetics of George Chapman," *Dikt og Idé*, ed. Sverre Dahl (Oslo, 1981), 88–104.
84. On Tyard, see Kathleen M. Hall, *Pontus de Tyard and His Discours Philosophiques* (Oxford, 1963). Tyard's poems (1549 and 1573) are available in a modern edition: *Les Erreurs Amoureuses*, ed. McClellan (Geneva, 1967).
85. *Discours Philosophiques* (1589), f. 128 verso.
86. For explanation and comment, see below, pp. 104–5.
87. David Chamberlain, "The Music of the Spheres and *The Parlement of Foules*," *The Chaucer Review* 5 (1970–71), 32–56 and esp. 48–51. The author believes that the relevant source for Chaucer's use of number symbolism is probably Macrobius' *Somnium Scipionis*. This is certainly likely; Tasso, too, refers to Macrobius several times.
88. See my essay on "*The Shepheardes Calender* – a Structural Analysis," *Renaissance and Modern Studies* XIII (1969), 49–75, esp. 58 f.: "in *December* Colin is given the grace to review his life dispassionately and honestly and to turn all his thoughts and his love towards God. Repentance is a sign of grace, and the repentance shown by Colin is perfect in every respect... The tree of his life may be blasted, but it has become engrafted into the Tree of Life which is Christ – our beginning and our end."
89. Giulio Cesare della Scala [Scaliger], *Poetices libri septem* (1561), sig. a^{iii}recto. A facsimile edition was published in 1964 by the Fromann Verlag. I am indebted to Roy T. Eriksen for the location of this passage and for the translation.
90. S. Petri Damiani, *Liber qui apellatur "Dominus Vobiscum"*, Migne, *Patrologia latina* 145 (1867), col. 248. On Damianus see Eugenio Garin, *Medioevo e Rinascimento* (1961), pp. 50 f. I am again indebted to Roy T. Eriksen for the location of this passage and for the translation. It can be added that the Pindaric odes were chanted by dancers moving in agreement with cosmic patterns, and that Milton lets the angels in Heaven move in a dance resembling that of the planets.
The idea of an alignment between cosmic structure and architecture is ancient. See R. L. Gordon, "The Sacred Geography of a *mithraeum*: the Example of sette sfere," *Journal of Mithraic Studies* 1 (1976), 119–65.

Chapter II

Fitly Framed Together
Augustine's *Confessions*

> ... Jesus Christ himself being the chief corner stone, in whom all the building fitly framed together groweth unto an holy temple in the Lord.
>
> *Ephesians* 2 : 20–21

Augustine's treatise *On the Trinity* is a good point of departure because in it Augustine discusses the works of creation and re-creation in terms indebted to the Pythagorean and Platonic concept of world harmony, and because Augustine himself explains the textual structures he selected for his book. Augustine's theology is, in fact, as "musical" as Plato's philosophy. Augustine recommends a knowledge of music as well as of numbers in the *De doctrina Christiana* II.xvi.26; students of the Bible must be familiar with both. The example he cites is strangely enigmatic: the number mentioned in connection with the building of the Temple, 46 years, "somehow has a musical sound" so that when applied to "the structure of the Lord's body" it causes heretics to confess that Christ did indeed assume a real body when he became incarnate. The enigma is solved on consulting a passage on the Temple in *On the Trinity*, where he discusses the issue more fully (IV.v.9). The point is that the Temple and Christ's body are based on the number 6, which contains the ratio of the diapason (2 : 1). When 46 (so Augustine argues) is multiplied by 6 (the number of man, created on the sixth day), the resulting number 276 equals 9 months and 6 days, and Christ was conceived on 25 March and born on 25 December. It is clearly the number 6 that is relevant, since Augustine has already explained in a preceding passage (IV.iv.7) that it contains the ratio of single to double. This ratio is provided by the ternary number, "since one added to two makes three; but the whole which these make reaches to the senary, for one and two and three make six."[1]

Augustine's concern with the ratio of the diapason manifests itself throughout Book IV; his whole thinking about the scheme of redemption is informed by it. The subject of Book IV is the reconciliation of opposites whereby harmony is ensured, and in the course of his exposition it occurs to Augustine that the idea he has in mind is called *armonia* by the Greek philosophers, so that his discussion of the antithesis between discord and concord, Satan the mediator of death and Christ the mediator of life, is based on the classical idea of the reconciliation between the 4 elements (IV.ii.4). It will be remembered that each element has two qualities, and that it is linked to another element by one of these: coldness links water and earth, dryness links earth and fire, heat links fire and air, and moisture links air and water. This is the structure Augustine makes use of in his account of the scheme of redemption, where opposites again are compelled to form a circle or quaternion. Man, who by nature is "not God" and who has been made "not righteous" by sin, must be purified by a God who descends to earth to become a righteous man: "For the sinner answers not to the righteous, but man answers to man. By joining therefore to us the likeness of His humanity, He took away the unlikeness of our unrighteousness; and by being made partaker of our mortality, He made us partakers of His divinity" (IV.ii.4). Christ's "single" answers to our "double", and "this answerableness, or suitableness, or concord, or consonance ... whereby one is to two, is of great weight in all ... co-adaptation of the creature", and it is at this point that Augustine suddenly remembers that the word he needs is the Greek word for harmony.

The pattern Augustine has in mind appears more clearly from the Latin text, where the phrasing is more compressed. Just as fire is opposed to water and earth to air, Augustine opposes God and "not God" (man), Christ who mediates life and Satan who mediates death. The link between Christ and Satan is that each has suffered a single death: Satan of the soul when he turned his back on God, and Christ of the body when he was crucified. Man may experience two deaths – in body and soul – and so will require two resurrections, but Satan "certainly has not been able to apply a single resurrection" (IV.xiii.17). To quote S. K. Heninger's comment on the quaternion of the elements: the "outward thrust" that tends to disrupt the system has its source in "primordial hate", but is counterbalanced by the "concordancy, which tends to keep the system intact – what Empedocles described as primordial love".[2] Augustine's argument and his very terms make the act of redemption a perfect analogue to the act of creation, so that the rhythm of single to double governs and unifies the entire spatial and temporal construct.³ Christ's single death "answers to our double", and Christ's resurrection wrought two for us. Satan's single death leads to his second death when he is dissolved together with the world at the end of time. Even Satan, then, is part of the harmonious world model, and so Augustine justly praises God's wisdom, which reaches from one end to the other, "mightily and sweetly ordering all things" (*Wisdom* 8 : 1).

In his *lambda* formula Plato gave mathematical expression to the idea that the 4 elements are harmonized by means of the same ratio: the last two numbers, 8 and 27, are reconciled by the mean numbers 12 and 18, since 8 relates to 12 as 12 to 18 and as 18 to 27. For every step, one half of the first number is added so that the same ratio prevails between all four numbers. Augustine's thinking is reflected in a medieval illuminated manuscript where a picture shows Christ seated and surrounded by 4 medallions containing the numbers 8, 12, 18, and 27.⁴

Augustine discovers the ratio 2 : 1 also in the number of hours that Christ suffered death: "But from the evening of the burial to the dawn of the resurrection are thirty-six hours, which is six squared. And this is referred to that ratio of the single to the double, wherein there is the greatest consonance of co-adaptation. For twelve added to twenty-four suits the ratio of single added to a double" (IV.vi.19).

Book IV seems to have central accent, since its three central chapters (IV.x–xii) draw contrasts and parallels between Christ and Satan as mediators respectively of life and death. The one offers a true sacrifice and is honoured by true rites, the other is a false mediator who "applies his one death to work out our double death". But God, who mightily and sweetly orders all things, made use of Satan to bring about the salvation of the faithful, and so Satan becomes part of the "connected order of the ages". Such parallels and antitheses prevail even in the microcosmos of individual sentences. Thus "the spirit leaves the body against its will, because it left God willingly; so that, whereas the spirit left God because it would, it leaves the body although it would not" (IV.xiii.16). These verbal patterns are of the same kind as the larger structures traced through the schemes of creation and re-creation.

Augustine himself explains the structure of the 15 books into which he divided his treatise: briefly put, it has central accent and recessed symmetry, while the linear reading yields a division into groups of 1 and 3. The comments are located in Book XV. Book I shows the unity and equality of the Trinity from holy Scripture, while the next 3 books handle the subject more carefully. The second group of 3 books (V–VII) devotes itself to questions concerning substance and essence, and in Book VIII those who have understanding begin, "however feebly, to discern the Trinity, to wit, one that loves, and that which is loved, and love". Such a first vision of the Deity is placed at the textual centre also of the *Confessions*, in Book 7, but in both cases the light proves too strong to sustain, and so "we turned back *in the midst* of the course we had begun and planned" (*De Trinitate* XV.vi.10; my emphasis). In Books IX–XIV the author dwells "upon the consideration of the creature, which we are, that we might be able to understand and behold the invisible things of God by those things which are made" (XV.vi.10). These 6 books are divided into 3 on the image of God in the outer man and 3 on this image as introduced into the mind from without, as the gift of God. There is a "trinity of the outer man" and a "trinity in the mind itself". Book XV finally ascends to the top (like the 15th step to the Temple and the 15th Psalm of Ascent) and attempts to see the Trinity as it is in itself and not just as reflected in the mirror of creation, whether physical or spiritual. In the trinity of man's memory, understanding, and love (or will) the nature of God is finally made fully apparent; in this image the eternal and unchangeable nature "can be recollected, beheld, desired", and man should "refer the whole of his life to the remembering, seeing, loving that highest Trinity, in order that he may recollect, contemplate, be delighted by it" (XV.xx.39). We observe how the idea of the Trinity shapes these 3 groups of 3 verbs, a technique which calls to mind the poems on Trinity Sunday by George Herbert and Henry Vaughan. As we shall see in the next chapter, Cassiodorus composed even more elaborate triple patterns in his *Expositio Psalmorum*, so that he followed in Augustine's footsteps also in this respect.

    Number symbolism, then, figures in the form as well as in the contents of Augustine's treatise, and the sequence of 1–3–3–1–3–3–1 books is a neat expression of its concern with the three who are one. The balanced pattern is conspicuous, and so is the linkage between the books in which the Trinity is envisaged directly–Books VIII and XV. Augustine's sustained concern, in Book IV, with the idea of harmony as expressed especially in the ratio 2:1 owes a great deal to Plato and Pythagoras, but their mathematical thinking is completely Christianized. The Christianization is so perfect that it is with some surprise that Augustine suddenly remembers that the idea he is concerned with expressing is called *armonia* by the Greek philosophers.

The content of Augustine's treatise, and especially of Book IV, is a necessary preamble to any discussion of Augustine's structural strategies as manifested in his great spiritual epic. In the *Confessions*, events and topoi are consciously located within the body of the text so as to form the symmetrical and graded arrangements that unify God's works in space and time. Augustine ordered his text as sweetly as God's Providence did the course of his life; this perfect agreement is perhaps his strongest affirmation of faith. Its nonverbal character invests it with a higher kind of reality and a higher kind of beauty than words can ever hope to reach.

1. The Pre-Planned Poem

Augustine wrote the *Confessions* to provide a Christian epic capable of replacing Homer and Virgil, whose pernicious fables he denounces so roundly.[5] His success is evident from the influence his epic exerted on later generations; but for Augustine, neither Milton nor Defoe could have written as they did. One aspect of his success, however, has not been appreciated in twentieth-century criticism: Augustine supplied a structural model showing how to unify a work consisting of many parts. Our reading experience may seem to contradict this statement, since the 13 books are sharply divided between 9 books on Augustine's life and 4 on the nature of man and the work of creation. Moreover, these last 4 books equal the autobiography in length, so that they appear like a separate work without much connection with the rest. However, we must believe that this curious arrangement in one way or another is part of a general design, since the text itself so often speaks about the superior kind of beauty which consists in establishing a proper relationship between parts. Thus book 4 argues that unity exists when parts are joined together by "a most orderly conjuncture" (*ordinatissimo conventu*). The parts, when separately considered, may be beautiful, but when everything is seen as one unified whole it becomes good and beautiful in a superior way, and this is why God said, when he reviewed everything he had made, that it was *very good*. When "aptly fitted into the whole", a part derives its beauty from it (4 : 13; and cf. 7 : 13). My analysis will show that Augustine's compositional technique proves that being aptly fitted into the whole means being part of a complex system of linkage that serves to unify the autobiography and the work as a whole. Central accent and recessed symmetry are found in the first 9 books as well as in the work as a whole, and these symmetries coexist with two kinds of arrangement in the ratio 2 : 1, as explained later on in this chapter. Order is a key concept in Augustine's thought; virtue is nothing but the "due ordering of love" (*The City of God* 15 : 22), and Augustine discovers order in his own apparently aimless wanderings or *errores*; everything has been directed, in secret, by the hand of God (*Confessions* 5 : 9). The discovery of this secret ordering of his life fills Augustine with delight, and this intense delight is stressed also in *The City of God* when he writes that the numbers which create harmony, although hidden today, will be perceived in the end, and that a delight in their rational beauty will "inflame the hearts of all rational beings in praise of their great Creator" (22 : 30).

The linkages that establish the desired textual structures are based on parallels and antitheses, and in *The City of God* Augustine attributes a major role to the function of antitheses in God's ordered arrangement of his works – his *pulcherrium carmen*. As he puts it, the course of history is "an exquisite poem enhanced by what might be called antitheses", and these are "among the most elegant ornaments of style. In Latin they might be called *opposita*, or, more accurately, *contraposita*." In the same way the beauty of the world is built up by "a kind of rhetoric, not of words but of things, which employs this kind of contrast of opposites" (11 : 18). Words or events, then, may be placed antithetically over against each other, thus enhancing the beauty of the *carmen* by establishing the links which unify the parts so that they become a whole. Among the opposites that adorn the *Confessions* are good and evil, a barren and a fruitful soil, leaving Monica behind on the beach and being left by her on the beach, turning away from God and returning, seeking God in the outside world and finding him in the world within, admiring the style but not the contents and admiring the contents but not the style, being dead in soul or alive, free or enslaved, seeking true or false (or vain) knowledge, ascending or descending. In book 1 Augustine as a child learns to read, but in the end what he learns to read is the scroll of the universe (Book 13).

Although scholars have registered Augustine's aesthetic principles, they have failed to see how they are applied. Robert J. O'Connell believes that Augustine was much too sensible to apply his aesthetic principles to his own composition; his artistic imagination "subtly gives the lie to theory. His mesmerizing art could scarcely have existed were his theory of art, and of symbolism generally an apt account of its uncanny alchemy". Augustine's "incomparable poetic imagination" must necessarily work "at depths profounder than all conscious planning".[6] O'Connell not only applies Romantic criteria strengthened by a strong bias in favour of the subconscious, but at the same time makes Augustine more of a Platonist than he actually is. Thus he will have it that Augustine thought of the Scriptures as "obscuring our direct vision of the divine splendour". He bases this argument on Augustine's reflections, in book 13, on divine revelation in the Bible and in the book of the creatures. This is O'Connell's account of these reflections:

> It [the universe] is stretched over us like a skin, mantling the entire lower world into which our fall into mortal bodies has plunged us. Thus, it separates our terrestrial world from the spiritual celestial realm, or ... it acts as a layer of cloud drawn between our gaze and the radiance of those higher realms. Augustine pleads with God to clear away that cloud from our eyes; his keenest wish is directly to "behold God's face" as do those "supercelestial peoples" who "have no need to gaze up to this firmament" which permits only the feeble, indirect vision of God's "word" that comes by "reading". (p. 108)

Yes and no, but mostly no. Augustine did not conceive of God's work of creation in these negative terms, and the creation of man was certainly not merely a Platonic fall into mortal bodies. The whole weight of Augustine's argument here is on the efficacy of the Scriptures, and we "read" the universe as we do the Scriptures: both point to their great Creator through their order, hence the frequency with which Augustine refers to *Romans* 1:20 and the passages from the *Book of Wisdom*. Both are scrolls that must be studied, and both are powerful (not feeble) shields of protection against our fallen nature. Both show the hand of Providence working to ensure our redemption. The cloudiness is not in the Scriptures or the firmament, but in the eyes that attempt to read them, and hence Augustine prays for clarity of vision: "Let us look, o Lord, upon the heavens the work of thy fingers; clear our eyes of that mist with which thou hast overcast them" (13:15). This is what happens in book 7 at the textual centre, where Augustine records how his "bedimmed eyesight" gradually "began more and more to be cleared" (7:8), and it is actually in this connection that he pauses to consider what the books of the Platonists cannot offer – the mystery of the incarnation when "thy Word was made flesh, and dwelt among men" (7 : 8 and 7 : 21). And what Augustine sees by means of his clarified inner vision is that the whole is better than a part, even if it be Heaven itself. Although "those superior things were better than these inferior things", yet "all things together" are "better than those superior by themselves" (7 : 13). This important argument, then, which connects the middle and the end (i.e. books 7 and 13) effectively refutes O'Connell's attempt to Platonize Augustine's thought about God's two books of revelation. The cloudiness of our vision is simply a consequence of our failure to proceed from physical to inner vision, a point of major concern also in Quarles's *Emblemes*, as we shall see. The *Confessions* is, in fact, an account of the progress from the one to the other, where the point of transition is at the centre in book 7.

When we approach the *Confessions*, therefore, let us try to clear our own eyes of the mist stemming from anachronistic assumptions concerning the true nature of Augustine's art, and let us begin with a preliminary brief survey of some major structures as shown in Diagrams II.1, II.2 and II.3.

As my analysis will show, the symmetrical structure of the autobiography is perfectly integrated with the overall symmetry enclosing all 13 books. Thus we see from Diagram II.2 that the topos of learning to read connects not only books 1 and 9, but also 1 and 13: Augustine reads idle fables and must "weep" for Dido as a boy in school; he learns to read anew and to shed proper tears when he is re-born in book 9, and finally, in book 13, he reads the "scroll" of the universe. This topos, therefore, has been placed so as to unify both the biography and the work as a whole. The final act of reading is taken to the highest possible level in terms of spiritual insights.

As we see from Diagram II.3, one topos may be logically connected with another, as in the case of *eloquence* and *knowledge as food*, where the second functions virtually as a comment on the former: since the eloquence of Faustus is all style and no substance, it provides no food for the mind. These topoi unify both the autobiography and the work as a whole, but in the work as a whole the emphasis is different and the message more trenchant: God and Christ are at the centre in book 7, where God is said to be food for adults, while Christ (the Word) kindly stoops to suckle our spiritual infancy, but when we reach the end we are sternly reminded of Paul's message that we must not remain infants – we must grow so as to be able to receive solid food.

In both structures, linear progression is perfectly integrated with

Diagram II.1 *The Confessions*, The Interlocking Symmetrical Structures

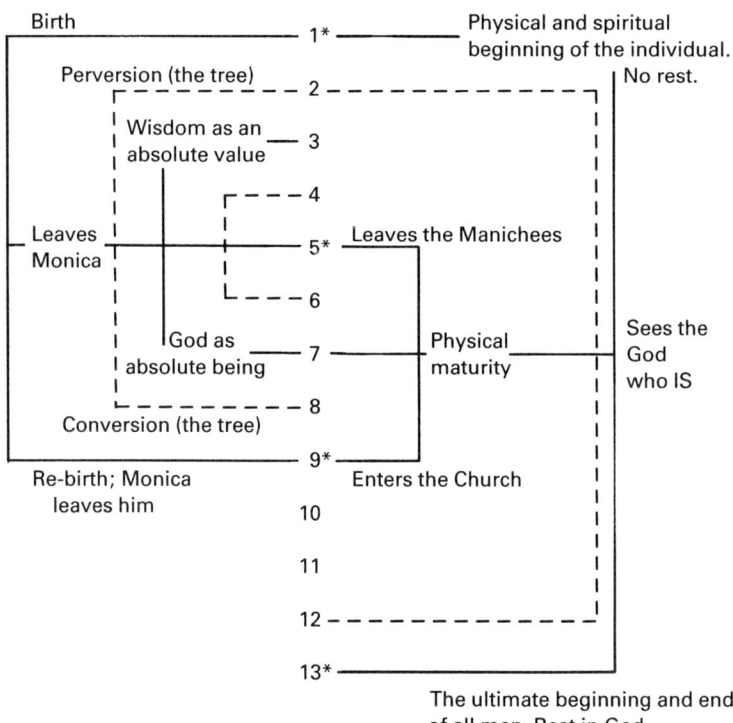

Asterisks mark introductory invocations. To permit the main outlines to appear more clearly, only a few links have been suggested.

spatial form. In the autobiography, the progression from weeping for Dido to weeping on reading the Psalms is logical and psychologically convincing while at the same time the points of emphasis in the balanced pattern draw our attention to a fine series of paradoxical parallels and antitheses. It is a neat point that Augustine professes to take no interest in Cicero's style – what Cicero taught him was a serious love of wisdom; at the same time he despises the Scriptures for their style (book 3). Ambrose is featured at the centre (book 5): Augustine attends his sermons to study the style for which he is so famous, but he has nothing but contempt for the contents. However, since style and contents are one, the truth gradually penetrates, and so for the first time be begins to understand and so to cherish the Scriptures (book 7).

Diagram II.2 *The Confessions*, The Topos of Eloquence

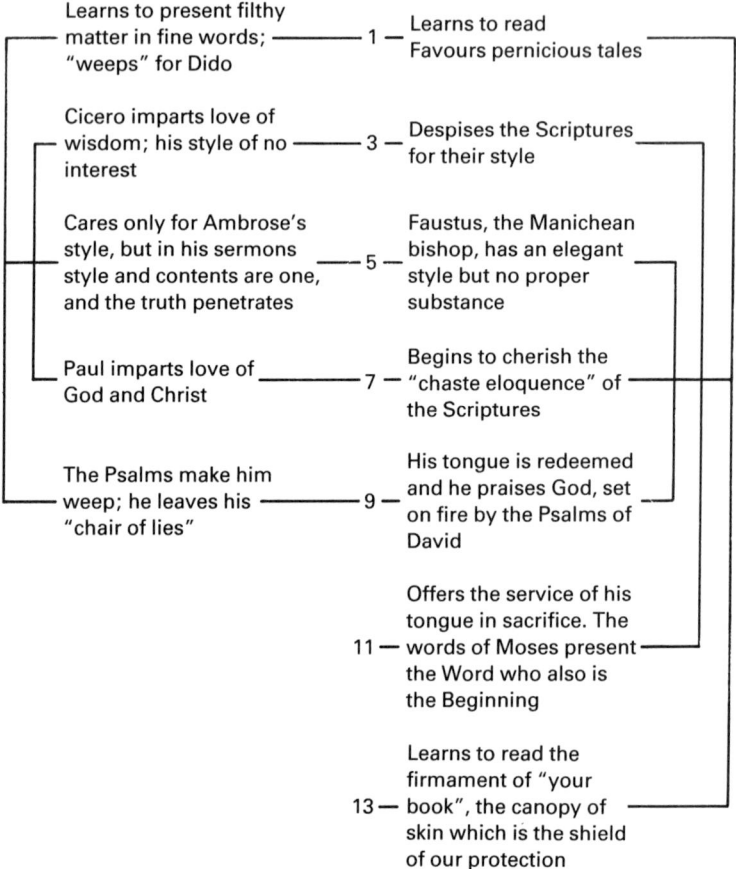

There is considerable overlapping between the two structures, so much so that one may consider them as integrated. The main difference is that it is only the total structure which takes us to the highest form of eloquence in the "canopy of skins" which is both the Bible and the universe.

Diagram II.3 *The Confessions*, The Related Topoi of Eloquence and Knowledge as Food

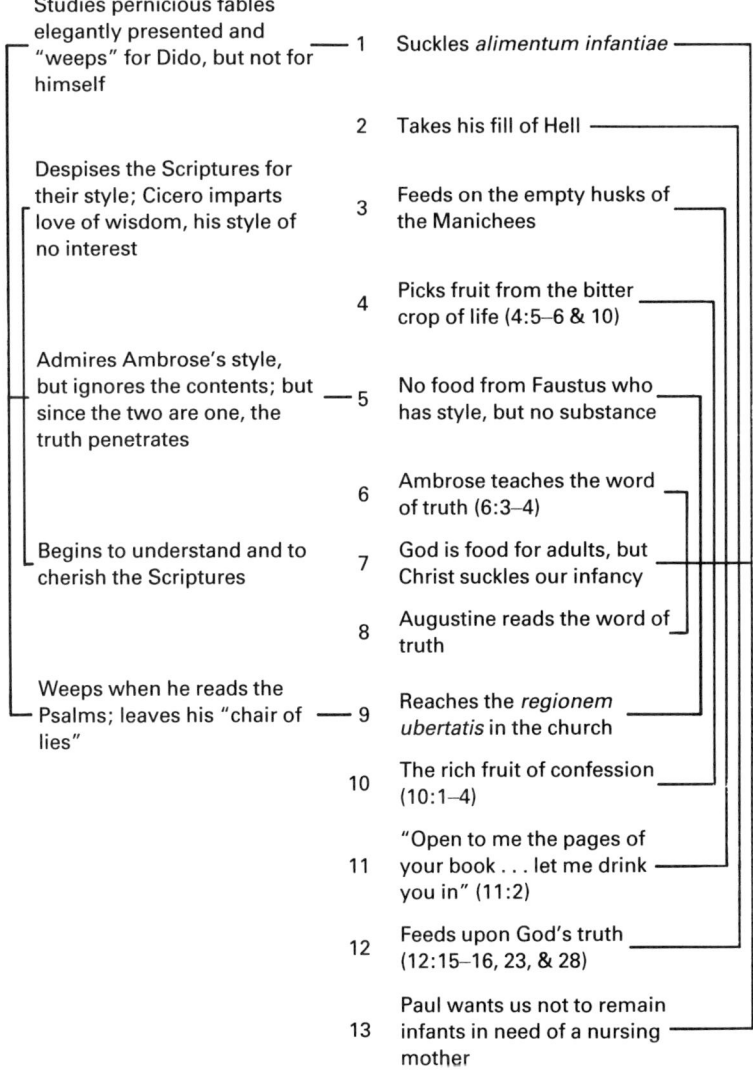

The linear progression from falsehood to truth and from being starved to being properly fed is supplemented by the spatial pattern. The truth begins to penetrate when Augustine listens to sermons where style and contents are one, and by book 9 the "tears" shed for Dido have been exchanged for tears that come from the heart. In the larger pattern of the 13 books God and Christ are at the centre as givers of food in the word of truth, and in book 13 Augustine repeats Paul's statement on the necessity of growing from "milk" to "solid food".

Even the placing of invocations is made to support both structures (see Diagram II.1), located as they are in books 1, 5, 9 and 13 – a neat and effective structural stratagem.

Brief though it is, the survey of the two interlocked symmetries in Diagram II.1 conveys some of the basic themes and events. The birth in book 1 in due course leads to re-birth in book 9. Augustine leaves Monica behind when he embarks secretly for Rome, and in book 9 it is Monica who leaves him behind when she dies at the mouth of the Tiber. The perversion of all values in book 2 (symbolized by the theft of inedible fruit) finds its antithesis in book 8 when the conversion occurs under the tree in the garden. The turning-point when he leaves the Manichees to become a catechumen (book 5) is flanked by his discovery of wisdom as an absolute value (book 3) and of God as absolute being (book 7).

The overall structure encompassing the whole work universalizes the particular. We begin with the beginning of an individual as an integrated physical and spiritual being, and we conclude with reflections on the ultimate beginning and end of all things, and over against the absence of rest in the former is placed the perfect rest in God envisaged when we reach the end. At the point of balance in book 7 Augustine reaches maturity and has his first vision of the God who IS, and this crucial event is flanked by his rejection of the Manichees and his baptism.

After this bird's eye view of a few of the symmetries, we may now proceed more slowly and in greater detail, beginning with the nine books of the autobiography.

2. The Autobiography (Books 1–9)

A number of parallels and antitheses connect the beginning and the end. Book 1 relates how he was born and subsequently learnt to speak and to read and write, and in book 9 he is transferred from his physical to his spiritual mother, the Church, and is re-born in the baptismal waters (9 : 3). When he resigns his "chair of lies", his very tongue is redeemed, and he must learn all over again to speak and to read; what he reads this time, though, is the sacred song of David and not the perverse fiction concerned with the immoral acts of pagan deities. What his eyes now read his soul understands and feeds on. This juxtaposition of a physical and a spiritual birth is pinpointed when he writes about Monica that "In the flesh she brought me to birth in this world: in her heart she brought me to birth in your eternal light" (9 : 8; Penguin tr.).

We lose a lot if we read book 9 without relating it to book 1, perhaps permitting ourselves to be engrossed by the account of the death of Monica and Augustine's passionate response to this sudden loss. Unless we see the links we shall fail to get the emphasis right, and Augustine's emphasis is on the lifting of the level of his narrative from the literal or physical to the spiritual, as in the Bible, where the Temple built by Solomon is replaced later on by man as the living temple of God. A literary example is the Paradise which is replaced by a paradise within, happier far. This lifting to a higher level also recalls the transition from types to antitypes. The linkage required to establish the symmetrical structure therefore is made to depend on a transposition into a higher key or pitch. When a poet reproduces this process, his words are made to point beyond themselves through the order in which they are disposed, like the objects that constitute the created universe.[7]

Diagram II.4 surveys the main themes and events, and book 5 presents itself as a true point of balance. Augustine hovers between the physical and the spiritual, the Manichees and the Christian Church, and during a dangerous illness he is between life and death. Since his soul died when it became subject to sin in book 1, a physical death would have sealed his fate for ever. Monica herself is balanced between the first and the second Eve (see below), while on her deathbed in book 9 she has become the true handmaid of the Lord. The general movement, therefore, is from the physical to the spiritual, from evil to good, from error to truth, from perversion to conversion, and from death to life. The evil which is a perversion of the will is shown in book 2, defined in book 5, and overcome in book 8. Finally, the death of the soul in book 1 (accompanied by absence of rest) is annulled by his spiritual re-birth and the enjoyment of perfect rest in book 9.

It should be noted that the death of Augustine's friend, although recorded in book 4, actually took place before he moved to Carthage, as noted in book 3; the placing of the theme of friendship in book 4, therefore, is more important than the observation of mere chronology.

As Diagram II.2 shows, the topoi which connect the beginning, middle, and end have to do with birth and death, sin, grief, and re-birth with attendant joy; tears are shed, or not shed, for the right or the wrong reason, they may come as punishment for carnal affections or in contrition for one's own sins or those of another (Monica in book 9), or they may be tears of joy and love, as when Augustine reads the Psalms of David. The *in bono / in malo* distinction, therefore, is very much in evidence.[8]

88 CONFIGURATIONS

Diagram II.4 *The Confessions*, Books 1–9

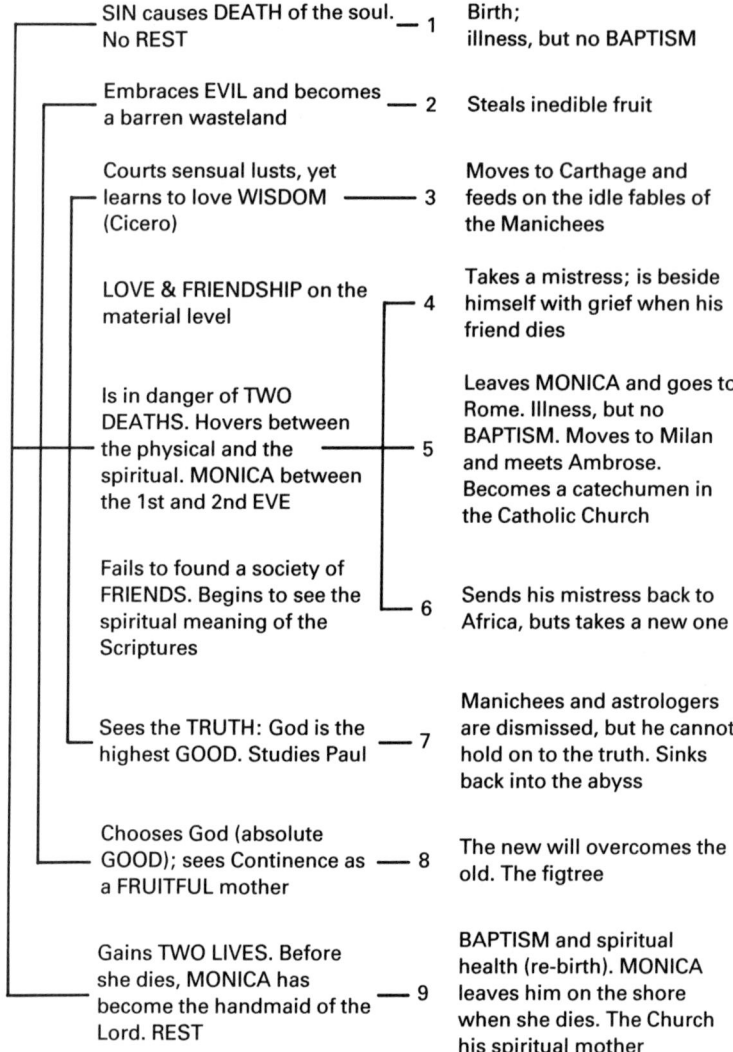

Book 5 is a decisive turning-point when Augustine hovers between life and death, and between a material and a spiritual concept of God; Monica in her turn is presented as hovering between the first and the second Eve. Up to book 5, everything is dominated by the physical world, while the spiritual aspect prevails after book 5. The climactic event is Augustine's spiritual re-birth and his transfer to his spiritual mother (the Church) in book 9.

Let us pursue the topos of giving birth spiritually. It is noted already in book 1 that Monica is "deeply anxious" and "in greater labour to ensure my eternal salvation than she had been at my birth" (1 : 11; Penguin tr.), and we meet this topos again in book 5 when Augustine cruelly leaves Monica behind on the shore as he sets out for Rome. He wants words to express the anguish with which she "was now in labour of me in the spirit", an anguish so much greater "than she had been at her childbearing in the flesh" (5 : 9). When the re-birth takes place in book 9, we read that Monica "had brought forth me: both in her flesh ... and in her heart too, that I might be born again to the eternal light" (9 : 8). This topos, therefore, has been placed so as to set up a firm link between the beginning, middle, and end.

To this double birth or life answers the double death which occupies Augustine's mind in book 5, thus providing a fine example of the figure of antithesis or *contrapositum*. On his arrival in Rome he observes that he was "welcomed with the rod of bodily sickness, and I was even ready to go to hell" (5 : 9). In book 1, too, Augustine had experienced a dangerous illness, but while he desires baptism in book 1 (but does not get it), he does not desire it in book 5. But in book 9, when he has been cured of his spiritual sickness, he desires baptism and is indeed baptized. The topos of baptism, therefore, strengthens the linkage between books 1, 5, and 9. We notice the skill with which Augustine varies this topos.

The tears that Monica weeps for her son are taken *in malo* as well as *in bono*. Monica falls into a passion of sorrow when she discovers that her son has left her behind; her 'carnal desires' cause grief:

> through the strength of mine own desires, thou didst hurry me away, that thou mightest at once put an end to those same desires: and that her carnal affection towards me might be justly punished by the scourge of sorrows ... therefore did she weep and lament; proving herself by those tortures to be guilty of what Eve left behind her; with sorrow seeking what she had brought forth in sorrow.

This grief on the part of Monica has made Andrew Fichter draw a comparison between Monica and Dido.[9] Dido too, was left on shore, weeping for her faithless Aeneas (*Aeneid*, book 4), but the comparison has limited validity. Monica resembles Dido only to the extent that she is "guilty of what Eve left behind her", to wit her carnal affection for her son. Augustine refers to Dido in book 1 as he records how he was compelled, as a schoolboy, "to bewail dead Dido, because she killed herself for love; when in the meantime (wretch that I was) I with dry eyes endured myself dying towards thee, O God my Life!" (1:13). Monica certainly acts like Dido when her son leaves for Rome (5:8), but two passages align her with Juno, the queen of heaven. The first is Augustine's report on his days in school when he had to express Juno's anger and sorrow "that she could not keep off the Trojan King [Aeneas] from going into Italy" (1:17). The second is even more important; this is the flashback narrative of Monica's married life in book 9, where her husband is presented as "very hot and choleric" (9:9) and fond of women. But she "so discreetly endured the wronging of her bed" that no quarrel ever arose. This calls to mind Augustine's having to read about a Jupiter "sometimes thundering, and sometimes adulterating" (1:16). Since her husband is so very much like Jupiter, Monica clearly resembles Juno as well as Dido, at the same time that she is Mary queen of heaven and the second Eve. As she is abandoned on the shore, then, Monica is shown in antithetical roles: she is full of "carnal affection" for a beloved son, and at the same time she is presented as the faithful handmaid of the Lord who "was now in labour of me in the spirit" (5:8–9). But by book 9 Monica has shed her carnal affections and is solely the handmaid of the Lord. She no longer even favours her son at the expense of his friends. On the contrary, before she became ill she took such care of the group of men (including Augustine) "as if she had been the mother to us all" (9:11). But even more important is her attitude to her own death. It had always been her desire to be buried next to her husband, but on her deathbed in Ostia at the mouth of the Tiber this "empty conceit" was removed from her. Since nothing is far from God (*nihil longe est deo*)[10] it does not matter where her body is placed, in Africa or in Italy (9:11). She has been released from her purely human affection for her husband as well as for her son. On this occasion it is Augustine who feels the powerful pull of human love so that he sheds copious tears in secret.

The subject of eloquence is yet another link between books 1, 5, and 9 (see Diagram II.2). It is introduced in a negative context as part of the "hellish torrent" of human custom that the young Augustine is plunged into. The change occurs in book 5. He attends the sermons of Ambrose merely in order to study his rhetoric, but to his surprise he finds that the contents "which I neglected, stole in upon my mind; for I knew not how to part them [i.e. style and contents]" (5:14). After his conversion, he abandons his "chair of lies" and withdraws the service of his tongue "from those marts of lip-labour: that young students ... should no longer buy at my mouth the engines for their own madness" (9:2). Instead he is moved to tears by the Psalms and hymns of the Church.

The web that connects the beginning, middle, and end has been tightly woven. Parallels and antitheses have been deployed to illustrate the contrast between truth and falsehood, the spiritual and the carnal, and the progress from one state to another. We observe Monica's progress from being a mixture of the first and second Eve in book 5, to being altogether the handmaid of the Lord in book 9, while her husband, who has behaved like the Jupiter described in 1:16, in the end is brought to embrace the Christian faith (9:9). Monica's patience and humility, and the silence she preserves when he is choleric, mirror the patient silence of God as Augustine pursues his errors (1:18). Monica's silence is accompanied by listening: she goes to church twice a day, not to indulge in gossip but that "she might hear thee speaking to her in thy sermons" (5:9). The idea of silence and speech is prominently featured in what is surely intended as a climactic episode in book 9. This is when Augustine and Monica silence the "tumults of the flesh" and try to imagine how all created things similarly could be silenced so that they could "hear him whom we love in these creatures", but himself alone, without them (9:10).

Some of the linkages create submerged epic similes: Monica is like Dido, or again like Juno, just as her husband is like the Jupiter presented in the idle fables of the poets. And just as Monica relates to the first and the second Eve, Augustine relates to the first and the second Adam. Monica relates to the second Eve in her capacity as the handmaid of the Lord, and in her bringing forth spiritual life in her son. And as he is baptized in book 9, Augustine passes from the hellish torrents of this world (cf. books 1 and 5) to the waters of grace that restore the image of God in man. But the old Adam remains with him; as his mother dies, his very soul is wounded "by having that sweet and most dear custom of living with her thus suddenly broken off". Augustine reflects that God in this way impressed upon him "how strong is the bond of all custom, even upon that soul which now feeds upon no deceiving word" (9:12). This constitutes an exact parallel to Monica's passion when she is left behind in Africa, "for she much doted on my company" (5:8). But Augustine also repeats the shedding of pious tears by Monica for her son's spiritual death ("Couldst thou despise ... those tears of hers, with which she begged ... the salvation of her son's soul only?"

5 : 9). And so, after her death, Augustine sheds such tears "as flow from a broken spirit, out of a serious consideration of the danger of every soul that dieth in Adam" (9 : 13). We remember how Augustine attributes filthiness to the water he crossed to reach Rome, yet that very water took him to "the water of thy Grace" (5 : 8), that is, to the long-delayed baptism as described in book 9. His journey may have been prompted by sinful thoughts (symbolized by the salt and bitter sea), but divine Providence working silently took him in the right direction without his being aware of it. Water figures again after Monica's death. In an attempt to alleviate his grief he visits the public baths, but "after I had bathed, I was the same man I was before". The bitterness of his sorrow "could not be sweat out of my heart" (9 : 12).

This presentation of the relationship between mother and son makes a general point. No matter how sincere our love of God may be, this love will coexist with purely human affections. However, through the grace of God the all-too-human ties may be broken to permit the growth in us of the second Eve and the second Adam.

It seems to me that to a large extent the impression we receive of psychological complexity and profundity is the consequence of Augustine's conscious use of antithetical and parallel situations, concepts, or topoi. We may, perhaps, fail to observe the precision with which they are located within the body of the text, but their impact is certainly registered. It is precisely because Augustine's art functions at such a highly conscious level that it becomes "mesmerizing", to use O'Connell's term.

The fusion between classical and biblical allusions is another cause of pleasing complexity, as we have seen: Monica is cast in the role not just of Dido or Juno, but even more so perhaps of the first and the second Eve, just as Augustine is as much the prodigal son as he is Aeneas. This is entirely in keeping with Augustine's statement that, instead of attributing men's faults to the gods, he had rather that Homer had "derived divine excellencies upon us" (1 : 16). If we fail to pay due attention to the biblical allusions, we may easily be led to agree with Andrew Fichter, who believes that Monica plays the parts of both Dido and Venus, the mother of Aeneas, which makes him conclude that Monica is "both the advocate and opponent of Roman destiny". And this in its turn makes him attribute to Augustine a belief in the "meaninglessness of epic choice", especially since both "urge the hero in the direction of the city of man".[11] But how can this be true, since the climactic moment is the moment of choice at the end of book 8, after the prolonged struggle between the two wills? And Augustine himself underlines the way in which the hand of Providence works through his own choices. Without his own knowledge, the sea voyage from Carthage to Italy takes him from "the waters of the sea, then full of execrable filthiness", to "the water of thy Grace" (5 : 8) and certainly not to the city of man. This centrally placed topos echoes the apostrophe to the "hellish torrent of this world" in book 1, where the torrent beating on the rocks is the false eloquence of the schools and the torrent of human custom that tumbles the sons of Eve "into that huge and hideous ocean, which they very hardly pass, who are shipped upon the Tree" (1 : 16). Here we see an almost drowned son of Eve enacting the role of an almost drowning Ulysses *en route* for Ithaca, or "the water of thy Grace".

Books 1, 5 and 9 have introductory invocatory chapters. When Augustine calls on his God he uses the verb *invocare* with great frequency: "Thee will I seek, O Lord, calling upon thee", and he calls by virtue of the faith "which thou hast given me, which thou hast inspired into me; even by the humanity of thy Son, and by the ministry of thy preachers" (1 : 1). To be *inspired*, then, means being given faith by Christ and by those who preach the Gospel. Although "when I invoke him, I call him into myself", this does not mean that God can be *contained* by anything, though he fills all things. God is "all everywhere, and nothing contains thee wholly" (*ubique totus es*; 1 : 2–3). This is the first emphatic statement of the *ubique* topos; since God is everywhere, no one is ever far from him, as Monica affirms on her deathbed in book 9. The topos is repeated in 5 : 2, the second of the two invocatory chapters prefixed to this book. Little do the unjust know that "thou art everywhere, whom no place encompasses, and that thou alone art ever near". The *ubique* topos, then, connects the invocatory chapters of books 1 and 5. In books 1 and 9 the invocatory chapters are linked by means of another topos: the praise of God who enters our heart as our salvation. The repeated phrase "I am thy Salvation" is a clear verbal link (1 : 5 and 9 : 1).

The quest for truth or knowledge finds expression in several related topoi, one being intoxication in a good and a bad sense. The two are juxtaposed in book 1, where God inebriates the heart (1 : 5) whereas the "sellers of grammar" are "intoxicated teachers" who fill their pupils with a "wine of error" (1 : 16). Augustine's climactic experience of error is described in book 5 at the textual centre. When the eagerly awaited, supposedly learned Manichean Faustus arrives, he not only has no true knowledge; he falsifies the truth and claims to be fully possessed of the Holy Spirit (5:5). Thus Augustine is compelled to confront his own "shameful errors" (5:6), and, as book 5 ends, he resolves to abandon the Manichees and to become a catechumen in the Catholic Church (5:14). However, the issue is undecided. At this mid-point in the story the scales are evenly poised: "For although the Catholic party seemed to me not to be overthrown, yet it appeared not to be altogether victorious" (5:14). However, truth ousts error by book 9, and Augustine envisages his friend Nebridius after death as laying "his spiritual mouth unto thy fountain ... Nor do I yet think he is so inebriated with it, as to forget me" (9:3). A return to the negative version is apparently called for so as to connect with book 1 in this respect, too, and so Augustine introduces the flashback narrative of how his mother as a young woman was prevented from becoming addicted to wine. This linkage between "intoxicated" teachers and their "wine of error" and the potential wine-bibber Monica functions as a submerged satirical epic simile illustrating the terrible power of custom.

But the new-born baby of course drinks milk, and, since knowledge is as food,[12] feeding becomes a metaphor for acquiring knowledge (see Diagram II.3). And knowledge may be useless, vain, false, or true as the case may be. The constant hovering between food and intellectual or spiritual knowledge becomes semi-allegorical in a way which enriches the narrative, especially when the many linkages are observed. Milk is good, whether in the form of *consolationes lactis humani* (1:6) or the milk of Paradise in *monte incaseato, monte tuo, monte uberi* ("in that mountain of spices, thine own mountain, that fruitful mountain"; 9:3). In their mental ascent to the Deity, Augustine and Monica reach the *regionem ubertatis* ("that region of never-wasting plenty") where Israel is fed with the "food of truth" (9:10), but at the textual centre in book 5 Faustus conspicuously fails to provide anything like the truth. The "trash" of the Manichees remains trash, however well phrased: "nothing ought to seem to be truly spoken, because eloquently set off; nor false therefore, because delivered with an untunable pronunciation. Again, nor therefore true, because roughly delivered; nor therefore false, because graced in the speaking: but it fares with wisdom and folly, as it doth with wholesome and unwholesome diet" (5:6). This is sound doctrine, and the mature Augustine comments satirically on his own training in rhetoric as a young man when a perfect delivery was all that mattered (1:18), and no one cared if the matter was filthy if it were well phrased and delivered (1 : 16). In book 3, however, Augustine begins to love wisdom for its own sake by reading Cicero, and paradoxically enough he cares not at all for the style, only for the matter. Conversely he scorns the Scriptures for the simplicity of their style: "For my swelling pride soared above the temper of their style, nor was my sharp wit able to pierce into their sense" (3 : 4–5). This is when he is captivated by the Manichees "in whose mouth were the very snares of the Devil"; their empty fictions and corporeal fantasies "were the dishes wherein to me, hunger-starved for thee, they served up the sun and the moon". "Yet because I thought them to be thee, I fell to and fed" (3:6). The Manichees, then, represent error and lies tricked out in fancy words: "Such empty husks as these was I fed with, yet not a whit nourished" (3:6). In the last chapters of book 5 Augustine goes to church in Milan to listen to the sermons of Ambrose, but only to test his eloquence; for the contents he has nothing but scorn. But on this occasion truth and eloquence are conjoined, and the meaning he tries to ignore "found its way into my mind together with his words, which I admired so much. I could not keep the two apart, and while I was all ears to seize upon his eloquence, I also began to sense the truth of what he said, though only gradually" (5 : 14; Penguin tr.). As he concludes the book Augustine records his firm decision to abandon the Manichees and be a catechumen in the Catholic Church (5 : 14).

Within the structure formed by books 1–9, book 3 balances book 7. In book 3, Cicero enabled Augustine to take the first important step when he learns to love wisdom for its own sake; in book 7, Plato first, and then Paul, take him up to the point when he is ready for conversion. At this point the relationship between style and contents has been replaced by the related issue of the connection between the spiritual and the corporeal, and the breakthrough to the truth occurs when Augustine turns his attention to the world within: "Into myself I went" (*intravi*; 7 : 10). After his physical *errores* or wanderings from Carthage to Rome and Milan comes this climactic moment when he returns to himself and discovers "the unchangeable light of the Lord" within his own mind. The opening words of book 3, *Veni Karthaginem*, neatly balance the phrase with which 7 : 10 begins: *intravi in intima mea, duce te ... intravi et vidi* ("I entered even into my own inwards, thou being my Leader ... Into myself I went [and I saw]"). But the God he seeks, and for a moment glimpses, proclaims that He is the food of grown men (*cibus sum grandium*; 7 : 10), and, incapable of holding on to this experience, Augustine sinks back again into the abyss. This leads logically on to the chapter where the incarnation is praised: "For the Word was made flesh, that by thy wisdom ... he might suckle our infancy" (7:18). And, as already mentioned, in book 9 Augustine reaches the *regionem ubertatis*, his Paradise of rest in God within the world of time, where he weeps copiously as he reads the true poetry of the Psalms.

All this shows how the same or related topoi connect books 1, 3, 5, 7 and 9. It remains to consider books 2 and 8, and 4 and 6.

The trees that figure so conspicuously in books 2 and 8 are an obvious link. The pear tree from which Augustine and his friends steal worthless fruit is Augustine's version of the forbidden tree, while the theft itself serves to define the nature of evil. Since the fruit cannot be eaten, the theft represents the choice of evil for its own sake. Evil has become their good through a perversion of the will, as in the case of Milton's Satan. As a consequence the last words of book 2 record how "I became to myself a land of want" (*regio egestatis*). Like Milton's Eve, he "wandered away, too far from your sustaining hand, and created of myself a barren waste" (Penguin tr.). The will has become "perverse and bent to the lowest things, frowardly and weakly setting its love upon thy creature instead of thyself" (2:3). When we reach book 8 the will seems entirely mastered by the enemy: "Because that of a froward will, was a lust made; and a lust ever obeyed, became a custom; and a custom not resisted, brought on a necessity" (8:5). When the conversion finally takes place toward the end of book 8, the tempest within his breast takes Augustine into the garden and he flings himself down under a fig tree. This is probably an allusion to the fig tree that would have been cut down after three years of barrenness, but for the intervention of the gardener who begged for respite; he would dig up the soil and dress it in the hope that it would bear fruit after all (*Luke* 13:6–9). This is the more likely since Augustine calls himself an untilled garden in book 2, "withal undressed by thy tillage, O God, which art the only, true, and good landlord of the field of my heart", and so "the briars of unclean desires grew rank over my head, and there was no hand put to root them out" (2:3). In Augustine's case, too, the barrenness had lasted for three years. When he moved to Milan and became a catechumen he was 30 (6:11), and he states that he was 33 when his mother died. When Monica is said to water the ground daily with her tears, she works like the gardener in the parable. As for the fig tree, Augustine elsewhere interprets it as the condition of flesh or original sin on which Christ has mercy – an interpretation based on the episode when Christ sees Nathaniel under the fig tree. On another occasion (so Augustine writes) Christ cursed the fig tree which had no fruit but leaves only (*Matthew* 21:19), and this tree resembles the Pharisees who had words only, but no fruit. We must therefore be like a good fig tree so that Christ may "see in our flesh the fruit of good works, lest we under His curse wither away". And as Augustine places himself under the fig tree in his garden, the "eyes of God's mercy" are not hindered by its shade.[13] The idea of fruitfulness has already been presented to us in the preceding chapter in the vision of Continence, "not barren at all, but a fruitful mother of children, her joys, by thee her husband, O Lord" (8:11), and in the earlier reference to "the fruitful desert of the wilderness" where the monasteries are located (8:6). In this way the barrenness of sin and error in book 2 is juxtaposed with the fruitfulness of a Christian life in book 8.

Books 4 and 6 are linked by the subject of love and friendship. Augustine takes a mistress, "one found out by wandering lust, utterly void of understanding" (4:3); later on, when a marriage is being negotiated in book 6, he dismisses her, but as the girl in question is too young for marriage, he takes another mistress. His love of his first mistress was real enough, so that his heart was broken and "blood drawn from it" (6:15), which recalls Augustine's acute suffering in book 4 when his dearest friend died. This death is the main event of book 4, and a corresponding major event in book 6 is the attempt to establish a community for himself and his friends where they can live in retirement from the world. But this hope, too, is frustrated. God derides their futile effort, "purposing to give us meat in due season, and to open thy hand, and to fill our souls with thy blessing" (6:14). In both books Augustine observes how he is "tossed up and down with every wind" (4:14), carried this way and that by "winds of uncertainties" (6:11). The true doctrine is given memorable statement in 4:12.

> If bodies then please thee, praise God for them, and turn thy love upon him that made them ... Him let us love, let us love him ... He is within the very heart, but yet hath the heart strayed from him. Turn again to your own heart, O ye transgressors, and cleave fast unto him that made you. Stand with him, and ye shall stand safely ... The good that you love, is from him ... But it shall justly be turned to bitterness ... if he be forsaken for it.

That sin stems from a perverse will is important. Thus the "unlawful pastimes" described in book 2 are prompted by a will "perverse and bent to the lowest things, frowardly and weakly setting its love upon thy creature instead of thyself". In book 8 the will is said to be in chains to the enemy, or, rather, the will is itself the chain that keeps him bound. But this froward will is beginning to encounter a new will: "Thus did my two wills, one new and tother old, that carnal and this spiritual, try masteries within me, and by their disagreeing wasted out my soul" (8:5). This theme leads on to the two sacrifices recorded in books 3 and 7. His immersion in the "frying-pan full of abominable loves" which is Carthage leads to a defiling of the "spring of friendship with the filth of uncleanliness" (3:1). In his pursuit of a "sacrilegious curiosity" to try every sensual pleasure, Augustine enters into "the beguiling service of devils, unto whom I sacrificed mine own vile actions ... I was so bold one day, as thy solemnities were a celebrating, even within the walls of thy Church, to desire and to execute a business, enough to purchase me the very fruits of death" (3:3). In book 7 this vile sacrifice is replaced by that of Christ, and the parallel of course enhances the antithesis. At this point lust has been replaced by vanity as the major sin, but in his ceaseless quest for truth he finally discovers the nature of God and hears His voice speaking to him from afar: "I am the food of strong men, grow apace, and thou shalt feed on me" (7:10). And the humility of Christ is shared by Augustine when he realizes that he must turn to Christ as the Mediator who will "suckle our infancy" (7:18; see also 7:21).

3. The Symmetrical Structure of Books 1–13

At the centre of the *Confessions* as a whole, as at the centre of the *De Trinitate*, is Augustine's first direct encounter with God, albeit at a great distance and for a short time only. This encounter, which takes place when Augustine for the first time turns to the world within, leaves him with the message that God is the food of full-grown men and, since he cannot as yet take such food, he turns to Christ who "suckles our infancy" – a phrase that connects with the account, in book 1, of his birth and infancy. The centre, then, marks the transition from the literal to the spiritual as noted above, and it is fully achieved in book 13 with its Pauline admonition not to remain infants in need of a nursing mother. In a clear parallel to the *intravi* of book 7, Augustine in book 13 conveys the inner meaning of the Mosaic account of creation and the spiritual meaning found in the "scroll" of the universe.

The introductory invocations located in books 1, 5, 9 and 13 have a chiastic pattern: the first and the last focus on the idea of invoking God, while the invocations in between offer sacrifices: a sacrifice of confession (5 : 1) and a sacrifice of praise (9 : 1).

As we shall see, the overall structure is made to reflect Augustine's chief theological concern: the nature of God and the problem of evil. This quest for the truth was impeded, not only by his sins, but perhaps even more so by his inability to think of God except in Manichean terms as a diluted substance encompassing the created universe, "environing and penetrating it, though every way infinite". This makes the presence of evil inexplicable; "seeing God who is good, hath created all these things good ... Whence now is evil?" (7 : 5). The conversion therefore depends directly on the ability to perceive that God, although clearly seen in his creation, himself is invisible and immaterial – hence the crucial role played by *Romans* 1 : 20 in the story of Augustine's life.

Augustine leaves the Manichees as book 5 ends, and, as book 9 begins, he is baptized and becomes a member of "our Catholic mother, the Church". The Manichees may speak truly "of many things concerning the creature", but they change "the glory of the uncorruptible God into an image like to corruptible man, and to birds, and to four-footed beasts, and creeping things: changing thy truth into a lie, and serving the creature more than the Creator" (5 : 3). This is followed by a denunciation of vain knowledge. The most ignorant man "is in better estate than he that can quarter out the heavens and number the stars, and poises the elements, and yet is negligent of thee, who hast made all things in number, weight, and measure" (5 : 4). However, in book 9 the created universe is rightly used when it serves to lead the mind to the Creator (9 : 4 and 10), in strong contrast to those who, like the Manichees, set their hearts on shadows and follow a lie. At the textual centre, therefore, *Romans* 1 : 20 is cited at 7 : 10, 7 : 17 (twice), and 7 : 20. This is the moment when Augustine for the first time enters the world within (*intravi in intima mea*) and sees the "unchangeable light of the Lord" (7 : 10). The first step back to his loving father is his return to himself; once this has been done, he may return to the father on whom he turned his back in book 1:

> For I had struggled far away from thy countenance in the mistiness of my affections. For we neither go nor return, from, or to thee, upon our feet ... nor did that younger brother seek post-horses, or waggons, or ships, or fly away with visible wings ...

that living in a far country he might prodigally waste that portion, which thou hadst given him at his departure. A sweet Father, because thou gavest him his portion: yet far sweeter to the poor wretch returning. (1 : 18)

As book 13 draws to its conclusion, Augustine contrasts the acts of creation and restoration with man's rejection of God: "we were moved to do evil when we forsook thee: but thou O God, One and Good, didst never cease doing good" (13:38). And the turning away from God is identified with the darkness of the abyss from which God created the world ("we had sunk from thee into the darksome Deep"; 13:34), whereas the creation of light, and of the sun and moon and the stars, represents the work of restoration. But after Augustine has had his brief contact with God in book 7, he sinks back again into the abyss, incapable of holding on to what he had experienced. Books 1, 7 and 13, then, are closely linked by means of these related topoi of turning away from and returning, and of ascent to God and descent into the abyss of sin. Between books 5 and 9 the link is partly biographical (he leaves the Manichees in 5, joins the Church in 9) and partly thematic. In book 5 Monica represents both the first and the second Eve, just as Augustine combines the first and the second Adam in book 9. Or, to put it differently, in each case human weakness is offset by divine grace.

Books 3 and 11 have a common concern with the idea of wisdom, and it is Cicero who teaches the young Augustine to love wisdom (book 3). As Augustine explains in the *De libero arbitrio*, the call of wisdom comes independently of a Christian faith: "It is no trifling matter that even before the merit of good works, the soul has received a natural power of judgment by which it prefers wisdom to error and peace to difficulty". Nevertheless, the soul "must beg the Creator for help in its endeavor" (III.xx.191–196).[14] The natural power of judgment, then, must be supplemented by assistance from the Wisdom that is the Word – the Creator and Redeemer – and this is the subject of the first part of book 11. Augustine's spiritual voyage, therefore, takes him from error and falsehood to the Wisdom that disposes everything sweetly – the Wisdom whose Providence leaves the will free to give its assent or not, to strive or to remain slothfully "asleep" amidst the precarious inferior pleasures of this world. Error and difficulty mark the first part of the way, but the first breakthrough into the light of truth comes in book 3 when Augustine learns to love wisdom for its own sake.

Another general movement is from evil to good. Augustine begins his account with two books detailing his sinfulness, and the chapter totals – respectively 20 and 10 – express the harmony of the octave as if to show that we are born into a state where carnal man and sin are in a state of negative harmony. This is harmony *in malo*; evil agrees with our fallen state, and so we make it the object of our choice even when it is meaningless, as in the case of the stolen fruit that is fit only for pigs. The subsequent narrative exists to show how we may regain to know God aright, and so to love him, and this true Wisdom is of course acquired through the Word that was in the beginning. This is why the reading of Cicero is such an important event: it makes him begin to "thirst after the immortality of wisdom" and to long for it "with an incredible heat of spirit":

> How did I burn then, my God, how did I burn to fly from earthly delights towards thee ... For with thee is wisdom. That love of wisdom is in Greek called Philosophy, with which that book inflamed me ... Beware lest any man spoil you through Philosophy and vain deceit after the tradition of men ... and not after Christ. For in him dwelleth all the Fulness of the Godhead bodily. (3 : 4)

But at that time Augustine scorned the Scriptures for "the temper of their style, nor was my sharp wit able to pierce into their sense" (3 : 5), and so he remains in the darkness of the Manichean heresy for nine years (3 : 11).

This, then, is how the concept of wisdom is introduced in book 3, like a tentative motif which is fully developed later on in book 11. In book 11, Augustine petitions God the Father by His son, "in whom are hid all the treasures of wisdom and knowledge" (11 : 2). He does this because it is "by thy Word co-eternal with thyself, [that] thou dost once and forever say all thou sayest; and it is made, whatsoever thou sayest shall be made" (11 : 7). The Word, which is the unalterable truth, is "the bridegroom's voice" which returns us "back to that from whence we are derived. This is therefore the Beginning". We return from error by knowing that we return, "and that we may know, he teaches us; because he is the Beginning and speaketh unto us" (11 : 8). The next chapter is a hymn of praise:

> In this Beginning, O God, hast thou made heaven and earth, namely, in thy Word, in thy Son, in thy Power, in thy Wisdom, in

> thy Truth; ... 'Tis Wisdom, Wisdom's self which thus shines into me; even breaking through my cloudiness ... in the words of thine oracle will I boldly cry out: How wonderful are thy works, O Lord, in wisdom hast thou made them all; and this Wisdom is [the] Beginning. (11 : 9)

The wisdom of God is the light of the mind (*sapientia dei, lux mentium*), and this light breaks through in book 7. At that time, though, Augustine could not hold on to it, but sank back "into the abyss", and so his prayer is that he may hold the light "and so fix it, that it may stand a while". Who can hold fast the heart of man "that it may stand" and so catch a glimpse, within the world of time, of "eternity ever still standing" (11 : 12)? This can happen only when "purified and molten by the fire of thy love"; then "will I stand, and grow hard in thee, my mould, thy truth" (11 : 29–30). The rest of book 11 is concerned with the nature of time, a subject touched on more briefly in 3:7. God's righteousness remains the same, although adjusted to times and places.

We must know our beginning, then, so that we may return to it.

From the subject of wisdom in book 3 we turn, in book 4, to the history of Augustine's great love for his friend and his grief when the friend dies, and to a consideration of beauty. Needless to say, the grief is given memorable expression:

> At the grief of this, my heart was utterly over clouded; and whatsoever I cast mine eyes upon, looked like death unto me. Mine own country was a very prison to me, and my father's house a wonderful unhappiness; and whatsoever I had communicated in with him, wanting him turned to my most cruel torture ... I hated all places for that they had not him. (4 : 4)

When he moves to Carthage, other friends console him, and by their empty pastimes "did we set our souls ablaze, and make but one out of many" (*ex pluribus unum facere*; 4 : 8). This unity is of course very much *in malo*, like the unity Milton lets Satan and his followers boast of in Hell. At this point Augustine inserts a discourse on the difference between human friendship and divine, which leads to a consideration of the relationship between parts and the whole. What we know in the flesh "is but in part: and the whole whereof these are parts, thou knowest not; and yet this little contents thee" (4 : 11). However, we should love not merely the whole, but he who made all (4 : 11). Since Augustine's love so far has been a love of "inferior beauties" (4 : 13), he has in fact experienced a descent *in malo* which can be countered only by him who descended willingly to share our human condition: "Descend again, that you may ascend, and ascend to God. For fallen you are, by ascending against God" (4 : 12). However, "these things I as then knew not, and I fell in love with these inferior beauties, and I was sinking even to the very bottom". This statement leads on to his account of the book he wrote on beauty, a book he dedicated to a famous orator in Rome, Hierius, to earn his praise and favour.

The love of praise figures prominently among the sins analyzed in book 10 (fourth from the end). Can we ever get rid of the desire to be feared or loved by other men? We please ourselves "with being loved and feared, not for thy sake, but in thy stead". Thus the adversary "may make us his own, being made like unto him ... even of him who aspired to advance his throne in the north, that all darkened and befrozen, they might serve him, as he imitates thee in his wry and crooked ways (*ut te perversa et distorta via imitanti tenebrosi frigidique servirent*; 10 : 36). The proud "by an affinity of heart" have "drawn unto themselves the princes of the air, their fellow conspirators in pride; to be deceived by them through the force of magic" (10 : 42). This denunciation of magic or sorcery harks back to the beginning of book 4, where Augustine notes that he refused the services of a sorcerer who promised to make certain that he would win the prize for reciting dramatic verse (4 : 2).

It strikes us at once how the themes or topoi of book 4 are lifted to a much higher key in book 10: instead of the human pride that desires to be feared or praised by others, we are concerned with the pride of Satan, and, instead of a human sorcerer, with the deceptions engendered by the "princes of the air". And the same is true of the theme of love and friendship. In book 10, instead of the love of a friend or a mistress (as in book 4), we are concerned with the love of God. An extended quotation makes explicit the difference between earthly love as described in book 4 and the love of God celebrated in book 10:

> Not out of a doubtful, but with a certain conscience do I love thee, O Lord: thou hast stricken my heart with thy word, and thereupon I loved thee. Yea, also the heaven, and the earth, and all that is in them, behold they bid me on every side that I should love thee; nor cease they to say so to all, to make them inexcusable. [cf. *Romans* 1 : 20–21]

This is the twofold action of the Lord: through the word/Word and through the witness of the created universe. We have no excuse not to know and love God, since the visible creation points directly to him.

Then follows Augustine's perhaps best-known hymn of praise in the *Confessions*:

> What now do I love, whenas I love thee? Not the beauty of any corporal thing; not the order of times, not the brightness of the light which we do behold, so gladsome to our eyes: not the pleasant melodies of songs of all kinds; nor the fragrant smell of flowers, and ointment, and spices; not manna and honey; nor any fair limbs that are so acceptable to fleshly embracements. I love none of these things whenas I love my God: and yet I love a certain kind of light, and a kind of voice, and a kind of fragrance, and a kind of meat, and a kind of embracement, whenas I love my God; who is both the light and the voice, and the sweet smell, and the meat, and the embracement of my inner man: where that light shineth into my soul, which no place can receive; that voice soundeth, which time deprives me not of; and that fragrancy smelleth, which no wind scatters; and that meat tasteth, which eating devours not; and that embracement clingeth to me, which satiety divorceth not. This it is which I love, whenas I love my God. (10 : 6)

Giles Fletcher was to paraphrase this passage in *Christs Victorie, and Triumph* (1610), Part IV, stanzas 40–41, surely knowing that most of his readers would recognize the allusion and so remember its poignant associations. Edward Benlowes, too, was to call on Augustine in some of the most fervent parts of his spiritual epic, *Theophila* (1652), and writers of spiritual emblem books reveal similar indebtedness.

So far I have considered some of the major links between books 3 and 11, 4 and 10 and 5 and 9. It remains to assess the links between books 1 and 13, 2 and 12 and 6 and 8. Also it will be necessary to consider book 7 more closely, since it is the pivot for the overall structure.

Books 1 and 13 and 2 and 12, keep returning to the idea of fruit or reward. Augustine characterizes his study of poetry as "empty vanities" turning him into suitable prey for the fallen angels (1 : 17); indeed, all his pleasure-directed activities lead only to anger and bitterness (1 : 7). Hence the lesson that "every man's inordinate affection shall be his own affliction" (1 : 12). His rewards consist in *dolores, confusiones, errores* (1 : 20). These fruitless pastimes reach a climax in book 2 in the episode of the stolen fruit. From an orchard the young Augustine and his friends stole "huge loadings, not for our own lickerishness, but even to fling to the hogs, though perhaps we ate some of it" (2 : 4). This is the nature of pure evil: the pleasure is taken in the act itself; he "loved nothing but the very theft itself" (2 : 8). And so, as book 2 ends, Augustine draws the sad conclusion that the child so richly endowed at birth had made of himself a barren waste, a *regio egestatis*. This is the prelude to his long-sustained inquiry into the origin of evil: "Who was it that ... ingrafted into my stem this scion of bitterness, seeing I was wholly made up by my most sweet God?" (7 : 3). Books 12 and 13, on the other hand, abound with references to good fruit taken in a spiritual sense. The words used by Moses are seen as a fertile orchard; birds "gladly flock thither; and with cheerful chirpings seek out and pluck off these fruits" (12 : 28). In book 13 the attribute of the dry land created by God is fruitfulness, while bitterness belongs to the salt sea. This is the bitterness of those who have no faith and hence no good works or fruit. But when we love our neighbour and engage in works of mercy, "Then are we like a great tree bearing fruit" (13 : 17; Penguin tr.).

Book 1 abounds with praise for all the gifts God bestows on man. God gives "both life and body to the infant" and furnishes him with senses, limbs, and beautiful shape, thus arming the individual. God alone can do this "from whom all proportion floweth; O thou most beautiful, which fashionest all, and after thine own method disposest all" (1 : 7; cf. *Wisdom* 8 : 1). We observe how these gifts function as the child learns to speak and then to read and write. This is Augustine's version of the epic topos of the arming of the hero, but for a long time he makes such a poor use of his "weapons" that he is enslaved by the basest things. His senses will not permit the eye of his mind to function, and so he denounces *phantasmata mea* – that "fluttering troop of unclean fancies" which beclouds his mind (7 : 1). This all-important issue connects books 1 and 7. His pride plays its part as he runs upon the Lord "with the thick neck of my buckler", but only to be overmatched by "these inferior things" (7 : 7). The feeling of a truly epic conflict is very strong in book 7, especially when related to books 1 and 13. Divine aid is required before the hero can regain his liberty (7 : 8), and once God has cleared his eyes he can see truly and so understand the relationship between himself, God, and the lower creation. This relationship is carefully explained in book 13.

The linkage between books 5 and 9 has already been touched upon, since they are the middle and the end of the autobiographical section (books 1–9). At the end of book 5, Augustine leaves the Manichees, and he is baptized and becomes a member of the Catholic Church as book 9 begins. Moreover, he leaves Monica in book 5, while she leaves him in book 9. However, what is specific to the overall structure is the spiritual import of what happens. In book 5, Augustine is still very much the teacher of rhetoric committed to a worldly career, while in book 9 he can scarcely wait for the opportunity to leave his "chair of lies". One antithesis stands out with great clarity: in book 5, Augustine is still betwixt and between, while in book 9 he not only has achieved proper vision – the major event of book 7 – but is permitted to rest in his vision of God as a member of the universal church. A parallel with a difference is the serious illness Augustine has in book 5 – an illness that nevertheless does not make him desire baptism – and the illness of his friend Verecundus who was received into the Church on his sick-bed before he died (9:3). A second parallel-cum-antithesis is afforded by Nebridius, who became a faithful Catholic after he had "fallen into the same pit of most pernicious error with us, believing the flesh of thy Son's truth to be fantastical". But after his baptism he served the Lord "in perfect chastity and continence", converting his whole family, until called by God to live "in the bosom of Abraham" (9:3). In book 5 Augustine ignores the ever-present danger of sickness and death, but in book 9 it is his two friends who die, but only after having received the baptism Augustine had rejected in book 5. Their examples show how Providence protected Augustine when he fell ill in Rome in a state of mortal sin: "How false therefore the death of his flesh seemed unto me, so true was the death of my soul; and how true the death of his body was, so false was the life of my soul, which did not believe the death of his body" (5:9). Conversely – and this is a beautiful instance of *contrapositum* – there is life in dead bodies when the martyrs Gervasius and Protasius are found and brought to Milan to Ambrose's church. The bodies perform miracles and cause the persecution of the church to cease (9:7).

The topos of rich gifts resounds through books 1, 5, 9 and 13, but at first in a negative key, since man abuses the gifts given to him by the Creator. The rhetoric the young Augustine studies is such an abuse, and even more so the misguided efforts of the Manichees to study the secrets of the universe. Augustine uses his gifts properly for the first time in book 7, at the textual centre, when he turns his attention to the world within. The brief ascent to God in book 7 is a gift, and even more so the re-birth celebrated in book 9 – a re-birth shared by Augustine's friends, so that they are said to rest in God and to envisage Verecundus in Paradise, "that mountain of spices, thine own mountain, that fruitful mountain" (*in monte incaseato, monte tuo, monte uberi*; 9 : 3). And the comments on the story of creation in the last book fuse the two rich gifts – creation and re-creation – by virtue of which men are endowed with the various gifts of the Spirit (13 : 18) and made to bear fruit (13 : 19). Man is transformed by the renewing of his mind (13 : 22).

It is equally in books 1, 7 and 13 that the topos of ascent and descent, or rise and fall, is prominently featured. That book 7 describes the ascent twice is a measure of its importance and of the importance of book 7 itself as a pivotal centre. However, before book 7 is considered, the flanking books 6 and 8 call for attention.

Books 6 and 8 share a narrative feature: each contains several interpolated tales. But significant events, too, function as links. Thus the ironic contrast between the unhappy Augustine, intent on the acquisition of honour and wealth, and the happy drunken beggar (6 : 6) shows that his visions are more false than the intoxication. These are replaced by the true vision of Continence (Augustine's version of the goddesses of classical epic) in 8 : 11, and he is filled with the power of God's word (the true wine) when he reads the passage his eye happened to fall upon: "Not in rioting and drunkenness, not in chambering and wantonness, not in strife and envying: but put ye on the Lord Jesus Christ; and make not provision for the flesh, to fulfil the lusts thereof" (8 : 12). In the first chapter of book 6 Monica foresees the final crisis through which her son would pass from sickness to health, and the transition occurs in the final chapter of book 8. The flashback narrative concerning Alypius (6 : 7) relates how Augustine made him admire the Manichees for their ostentatious continence, "which he supposed to be true and unfeigned". The mature Augustine comments drily on the ease with which we are beguiled by a fair outside, and later on in book 8 he presents his experience of a vision of true continence (8 : 11). She encourages him no longer to be a prisoner of habit and a slave of lust (6 : 12 and 15), but to throw himself on the Lord Jesus Christ, who will not let him fall. The idea of delay resounds through books 6 and 8 as a major theme, but the plunge is finally made, in part as the result of providential guidance and in part by an effort of the will assisted by grace.

The interpolated tales prepare us for this development. The three stories concerned with Alypius analyze the power of the will and the need for providential assistance. By an effort of his will Alypius breaks his habit of visiting the circus, and he is encouraged so to do by listening to Augustine's discourse on an occasion when he happened to illustrate a point by referring to the "Circensian races", both to make his meaning plain and to deride those "whom that madness had enthralled". Augustine comments that God spoke through him without his being aware of it. With a great effort of his will, Alypius got rid of "those filths of the Circensian pastimes", nor did he ever suffer a relapse (6:7). The second story reveals what happens if we trust in our own power alone. Much against his will, but trusting in his power to resist, Alypius was dragged by friends to watch gladiators fight. He closed his eyes to avoid the spectacle, but opened them on hearing the spectators roar as one gladiator fell, "and was struck with a deeper wound in his soul, than the other was in his body". As a consequence he becomes drunk with a bloodthirsty joy from which he recovers only very much later by the strong and merciful hand of God (6:8). The third story concerns a theft in which Alypius seems to be the guilty person and is saved only by the providential appearance of a witness (6:9). The stories illustrate the limits of human endeavour; even in the first case it was God speaking through Augustine who caused Alypius to exercise his will; on the third occasion he was without defence and so the only solution was providential assistance. Finally his misjudged confidence in his own powers of self-control is shown up in the episode of the gladiatorial fights. Our will can take us only part of the way. However, the tale of the sword-fight clearly bears also on the climactic moment in book 8 when Augustine is torn between conflicting wills while Alypius watches spellbound. When we relate the two episodes, a submerged epic simile is perceived: the two wills are like gladiators who fight it out until only one remains alive. The other interpolated tales similarly correspond, *mutatis mutandis*, to the tales in book 8. In these tales the issue is no longer that of man's will or even of God's providence, but of his power to strike and possess the soul and so transform the will. Augustine is made to feel this power as he listens to the story of Victorinus, the great orator who proclaimed his Christian faith publicly (although he could have done it in private; 8:2). Enlightened by the beams that come from God, men "receive power also to become thy sons" (8:4). Another story told by Ponticianus concerned "Anthony the monk of Egypt" and the existence of monasteries, of which Augustine and Alypius were entirely ignorant. This reference to monasteries makes us remember Augustine's futile plan, in book 6, to establish a community where he and his friends could live peacefully together; however, God derided their scheme (6 : 14). In book 8, then, Augustine hears about the presence of monasteries for the first time, although there was one such establishment at Milan itself, directed by Ambrose. The visitor next recounts his own experience, at Trier, of the sudden conversion of two of the Emperor's courtiers – a conversion caused by one of them taking up a book that happened to tell the story of Anthony. "One of them began to read, wonder at it, and to be inflamed with it; and even in the very reading to devise with himself upon the taking such a life upon him". He is suddenly "filled with an holy love" and is "inwardly changed" and "dispossessed of worldly cares" (8 : 6). The visitor begins his discourse after having picked up a book from a table and found it to be the epistles of Paul, his story turns on a providential act of the same kind, and Augustine's internal conflict is resolved when he, too, picks up "the Apostle's book" and reads the exhortation to put on "the Lord Jesus Christ" and "make not provision for the flesh, to fulfil the lusts thereof" (*Romans* 13 : 13). Such is the power of the Word that in a single moment it breaks the chain forged by a perverse will since childhood. This event is prepared for in book 6 when Ambrose is said to "open" the text of the Bible "spiritually" (6 : 4), and in so doing begins to instil the faith which eventually will clear the eyesight of his soul. Another strong link between books 6 and 8 is the theme of delay: Augustine keeps postponing his conversion until "tomorrow" and is tossed in several directions by "the winds of uncertainties" (6 : 11), whereas in book 8 the cause is "mine own iron will". By this time he knows that it is much better "for me to give up myself to thy charity, than to give over myself to mine own sensuality", but the law of sin draws the mind of man and holds it against its will (8 : 5; cf. *Romans* 7 : 22–23). As foreshadowed in the interpolated tales of book 6, the role of God is decisive, yet it by no means invalidates what we may call the hero's epic choice as he exclaims, "How long? How long still 'to-morrow' and 'to-morrow'? Why not now?" (8 : 12).

The role played by divine Providence has troubled some readers. As Andrew Fichter argues, the providential plan for Monica and Augustine unfolds "despite their ignorance of its direction", so that "the difference between the forces governing the Virgilian and

Augustinian worlds seems to be that Augustine's God does not require conscious human compliance". The "seems to be", though, is dropped within the next few lines: "This conception of a divine plan conspiring for what is best for the individual, often despite his immediate wishes, dissipates the urgency of Virgilian epic choice and subverts the sense of finality attached to it".[15] But Calvin himself repeated Augustine's view that God's foreknowledge is no cause, as expounded in his treatise *On Free Choice of the Will* (*De libero arbitrio*). Although not free to turn to God after the Fall, the soul must nevertheless exercise itself: the soul arrives at "truth and peace through zealously seeking and learning, and humbly confessing and praying" (III.xx.199).[16] God justly condemns those who "from the first, refuse to strive for achievement, or those who slip back from a higher state". The ignorance of the soul "arises from the fact that it has not yet the power to know; it will receive this power, however, if it uses well what it has received. Moreover, it has received the power to search diligently and piously *if it wills*" (my emphasis). The soul is "raised to blessedness" in part through "its own power", in part through "the goodness and mercy of Him who is the Source of its being" (III.xxii.221–23). He who wills, then, will be aided. God's foreknowledge "does not prove that we do not will anything voluntarily", and our assent is always called for; it is possible to refuse God's offer of happiness (III.iii.28). The paradox, then, is that, although God has foreknowledge, yet man wills what he wills:

> For when He has foreknowledge of our will, it is going to be the will that He has foreknown . . . So the power is not taken from me by His foreknowledge, the power to will will more certainly be present in me, since God . . . has foreknown that I shall have the power. (III.iii.34–35)

In short, God "foreknows our sins in such a way that our will still remains free in us and lies in our power".

There would be no point in Augustine's record of his long-sustained struggle if his conversion were to be attributed to Providence alone so that his own willed actions have no part to play in the drama of his soul. His "zealously seeking and learning" is the subject of the centrally placed book 7, where Augustine "uses well" what he has received at birth. The subject of book 7 is the decisive movement from blindness to vision, a movement which follows as a consequence of Augustine's conscious turning of his mind from the outside world to the world within. In the opening phase Augustine describes his state in terms that recall Hercules beset by pygmies or the Castle of Alma beset by the "rabble rout"; the attackers are his "unclean fancies" concerning the nature of God and man:

> My heart passionately cried out upon all my phantasms; and with one blow I laid about me to beat away all that fluttering troop of unclean fancies, from the eye of my mind. And lo ... they came in multitudes again about me, they pressed upon my sight, and so beclouded it, that though I thought thee not to be of the shape of a human body, yet was I constrained to imagine thee to be some corporeal substance, taking up vast spaces of place. (7:1)

Reality had to be physical, and "whatsoever was not stretched out over certain spaces ... I thought to be a just nothing" (7:1). Nevertheless, ever since he began to love wisdom for its own sake (in book 3), it was logically enough impossible to think of God as a human body, so that he had at least acquired that much of the true faith.

Chapter 2 exposes the errors of the Manichees, while chapters 3, 5 and 7 grapple with the problem of the origin of evil. Although he realizes that God is incorruptible, so that "corruption does no ways infect our God" (7:4), yet he cannot see truly, since his eyes are turned outward. What he does perceive, however, is that he is placed in a "happy mean" between God and the lower part of creation:

> For to these things was I superior, but inferior to thee: and thou art the true Joy of me thy subject: and thou hast subjected under me those things which thou createdst below me. And this was the happy mean, and the middle region of my safety, where I might remain conformable to thine image, and by serving thee, get the dominion over mine own body. (7:7)

However, it is beyond his power to regain this "happy mean", blinded as he is by a "fluttering troop of unclean fancies" (7:7). At the end of ch. 7, therefore, he has returned to where he was in ch. 1.

A linear reading of chapters 1–7 leaves us with the impression of a see-saw pattern – of confusion rather than order. A spatial reading, though, as set out in Diagram II.5, clarifies the outline of the argument. The 7 chapters display recessed symmetry around chapter 4, where a firm basis is established for further progress. This is

Diagram II.5 *The Confessions*, Book 7, Chapters 1–7

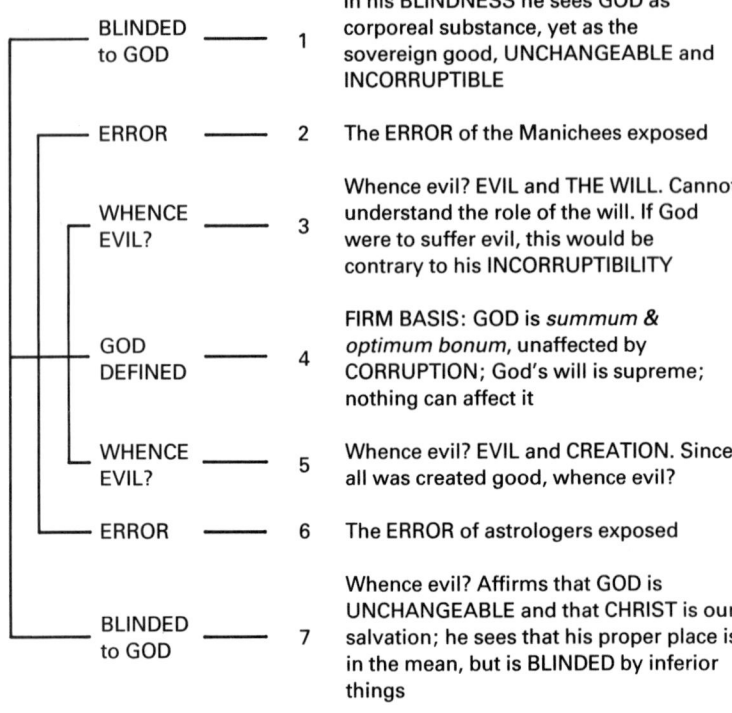

where Augustine defines two of God's attributes correctly: God is without corruption, and his will is supreme. Chapters 2 and 6 expose the fallacy of the Manichees (7:2) and the astrologers (7:6), and both of these chapters are at the centre of triads which flank chapter 4 (see Diagram II.5). Chapters 1 and 3 share the statement that God is the sovereign good, while the link between chapters 5 and 7 is the affirmation of faith in Christ. Yet the fact that the topos of spiritual blindness connects chapters 1 and 7 suggests the necessity of divine intervention.

The intervention is recorded in chapters 8 and 21, that is in the first chapter and the last of the second substructure consisting of 14 chapters (Diagram II.6). By the grace of God blindness yields to true vision (7:8), and in the last chapter God gives the power both to see and to hold and to "keep on the way" that leads to the land of peace (7:21). At the centre, in chapters 7:14–15, we learn what he

THE CONFESSIONS 113

Diagram II.6 *The Confessions*, Book 7, Chapters 8–21

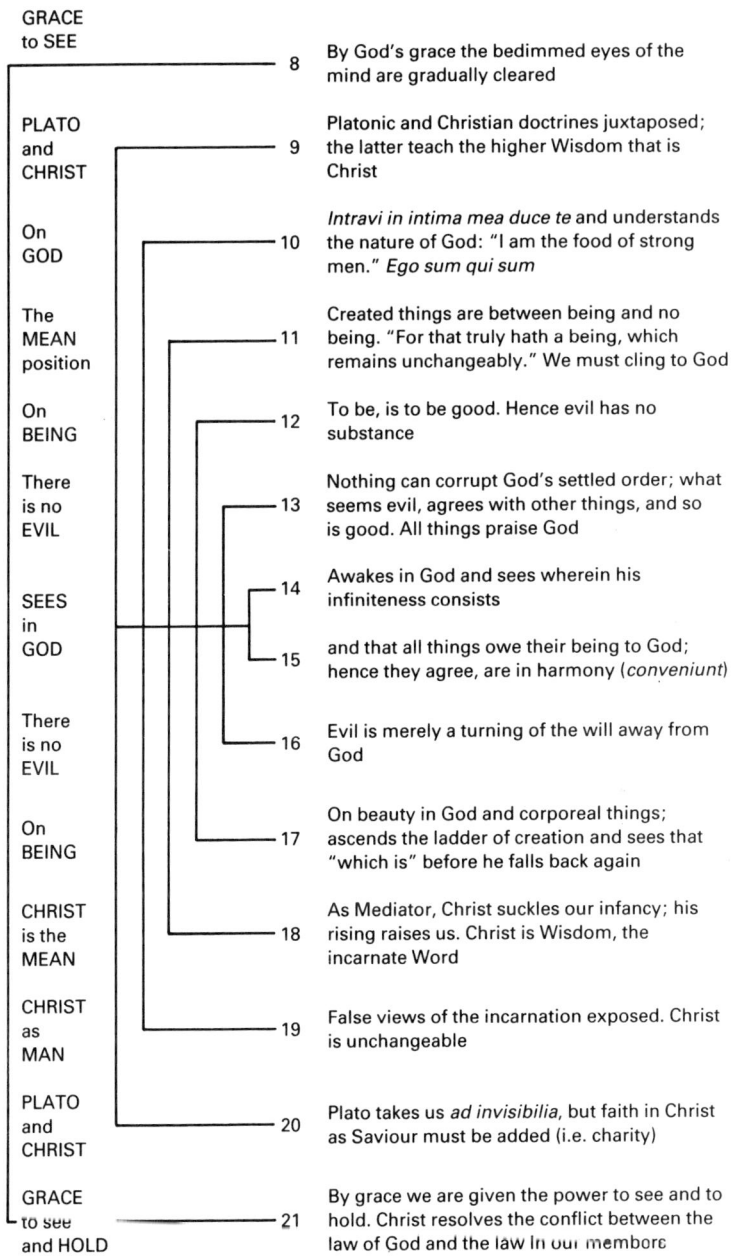

GRACE to SEE	8	By God's grace the bedimmed eyes of the mind are gradually cleared
PLATO and CHRIST	9	Platonic and Christian doctrines juxtaposed; the latter teach the higher Wisdom that is Christ
On GOD	10	*Intravi in intima mea duce te* and understands the nature of God: "I am the food of strong men." *Ego sum qui sum*
The MEAN position	11	Created things are between being and no being. "For that truly hath a being, which remains unchangeably." We must cling to God
On BEING	12	To be, is to be good. Hence evil has no substance
There is no EVIL	13	Nothing can corrupt God's settled order; what seems evil, agrees with other things, and so is good. All things praise God
SEES in GOD	14	Awakes in God and sees wherein his infiniteness consists
	15	and that all things owe their being to God; hence they agree, are in harmony (*conveniunt*)
There is no EVIL	16	Evil is merely a turning of the will away from God
On BEING	17	On beauty in God and corporeal things; ascends the ladder of creation and sees that "which is" before he falls back again
CHRIST is the MEAN	18	As Mediator, Christ suckles our infancy; his rising raises us. Christ is Wisdom, the incarnate Word
CHRIST as MAN	19	False views of the incarnation exposed. Christ is unchangeable
PLATO and CHRIST	20	Plato takes us *ad invisibilia*, but faith in Christ as Saviour must be added (i.e. charity)
GRACE to see and HOLD	21	By grace we are given the power to see and to hold. Christ resolves the conflict between the law of God and the law in our members

sees when he awakes in God: he understands that God is infinite in a way totally different from Manichean doctrines, and that all things are in God and are true in so far as they have being; for this reason they are in harmony (*conveniunt*). The vexing problem of the nature of evil and its cause is finally resolved when he understands that it has no being in itself; it is merely a turning of the will away from God (7 : 13 & 16). To have being is to be good, and all created things constitute a ladder reaching from the lowest to the highest (7 : 12 & 17); on ascending this ladder Augustine finally has "a sight of those invisible things of thee, which are understood by those things which are made" (7 : 17; cf. *Romans* 1 : 20). At the beginning and the end, the role of Christ is stressed, and the points on which Platonic doctrines agree with or fall short of the higher Wisdom that is Christ (7 : 8 and 20).

The symmetrical structure enclosing book 7 as a whole (see Diagram II.7) has a triple centre-piece which defines (1) absolute being, (2) the state between absolute being and no being, and (3) the absence of being. The halfway points at 7 : 5 and 7 : 17 affirm the necessity of clinging to Christ, and other linkages turn on fraud and inadequacy (7 : 2 & 20), truth and falsehood (7 : 6 & 16, and 7 & 15), the incorruptibility of God and the incarnation which raises man to God's incorruptibility (7 : 4 & 18).

Book 7, then, combines overall symmetry with a division into the ratio of the diapason, which expresses the harmony and the agreement of all things as referred to in the contents (7 : 15). This structural *tour de force* underlines the pivotal function of book 7 within the overall symmetrical structure, just as the spatial reading clarifies Augustine's argument concerning the progress from blindness (7 : 1) to seeing (7 : 10–12) and finally to the position of both seeing the truth and holding on to it.

The pivotal function of book 7 is apparent also from the fact that all the main themes of the *Confessions* meet here. All the evil Augustine has suffered is explained and defined here. In itself evil is a perversion of the will when man turns away from God, but man also suffers grievously in order that he may be compelled to return to God. Scourging is part of God's providential scheme for our salvation. We see, too, the various steps which lead to Augustine's conversion: blinded initially by *phantasmata*, his vision is gradually cleared by grace as he struggles to see the truth and to hold on to it. All the errors and frauds he has encountered are exposed, and so are all merely partial truths, such as the teaching of the Platonists. He examines the creation and ascends the scale of being until he sees the God who IS; the theme of beauty is here, and also the idea

THE CONFESSIONS 115

Diagram II.7 *The Confessions*, The Symmetry of Book 7

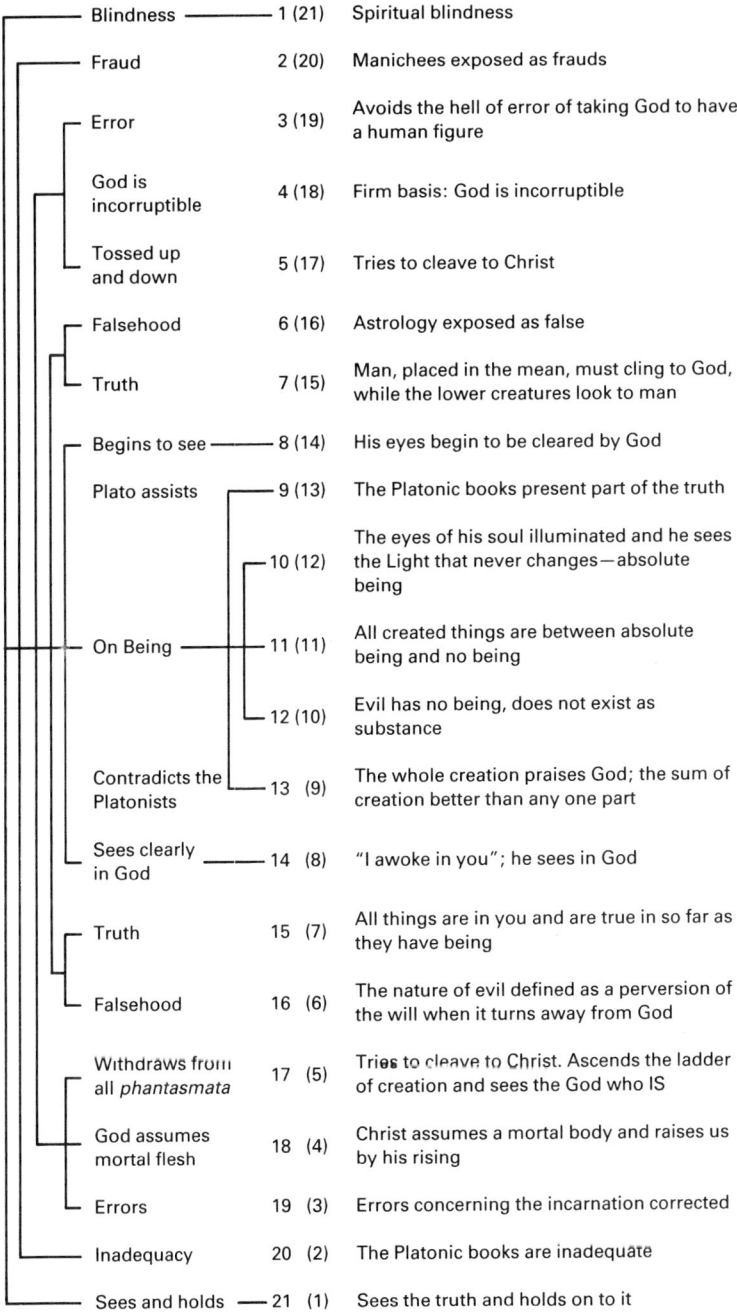

that the beauty of the whole surpasses that of individual parts, though it be Heaven itself (7 : 13). Above all, we find that wonderful fusion between abstract thought and fervent faith in Christ the Redeemer which marks the *Confessions* as a whole. This is Augustine's peculiar grace, and we meet it again in full force in book 13.

4. The Graded Arrangement of Books 1–13

Augustine's superb craftsmanship reveals itself most impressively in his handling of the two graded arrangements.

On surveying the contents, it is seen that books 1–8 present the spiritual autobiography, that book 9 is a transitional point of rest, and that books 10–13 contain reflections on man and God's works of creation and re-creation. The contents, therefore, suggest a division into 8–1–4 books. It seems odd, though, that the highly personal account should be balanced against such impersonal reflections, and another oddity is that the last 4 books equal the length of the first 8. Naturally one queries this curious disproportion in a work so intent on the importance of proportion. The oddity will be resolved, however, if book 9 should prove a pivotal passage between books 1–8 and 10–13, and if the 8 books on the autobiography should somehow be related to the 4 books containing impersonal reflections.

On reading books 1–8, it strikes one that they are arranged in pairs (see Diagram II.8). Books 1–2 tell the story of Augustine's

Diagram II.8 *The Confessions*, Interlocking Graded Arrangements Featuring the Ratio 2:1

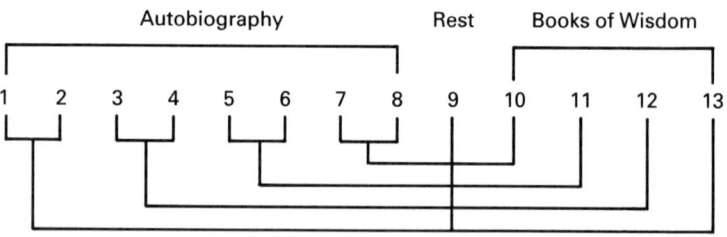

Form and contents alike mark book 9 as a point of transition and of rest. It divides the work into a sequence of 8—1—4 books, thus creating the octave proportion; also it is at the centre of the 2:1 linking between individual books. The 13 chapters of book 9 function as a summary of the 13 books.

birth and early years, terminating with the reflection that he had made of himself a barren wasteland. Books 3–4 begin with the move to Carthage, and focus on love, friendship, and beauty – a love that may be mere lust, but also love of wisdom for its own sake. In books 5–6 the Manichees are discussed and finally dismissed, and Augustine becomes a catechumen in the Catholic Church. The setting is Rome and Milan. Finally, in books 7–8 the basic issues are defined as Augustine turns his attention to his own inner self, and then resolved in his dramatic conversion under the fig tree. Book 9 marks a point of rest, a pause between the painful process of conversion and its rich fruits.

If we juxtapose books 1–2 and 13, 3–4 and 12, and so on, we see that each long book functions as a gloss on the subjects touched on in the two short ones. Whereas the length of the two short books equals the single book, the 2:1 pattern presents Augustine's favourite proportion (see Diagram II.9).

Diagram II.9 *The Confessions*, Some Linking Topoi

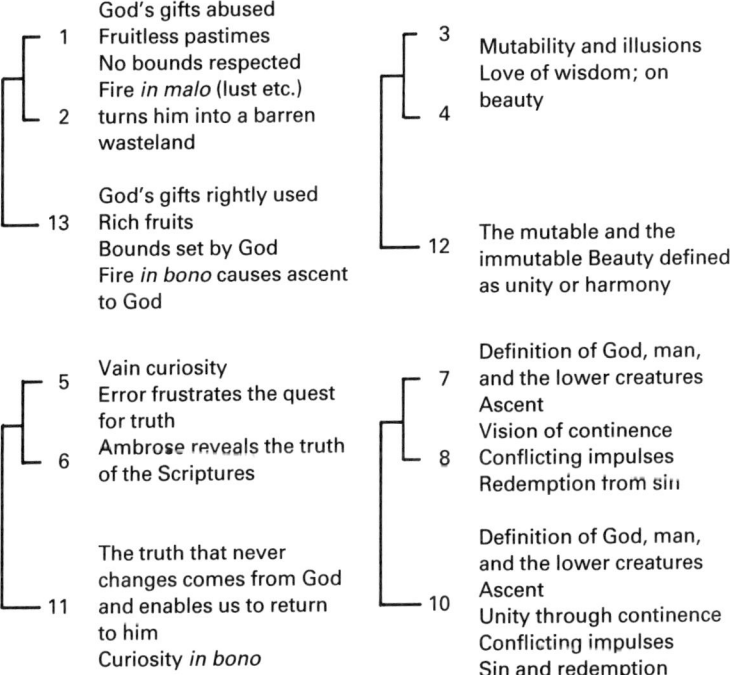

Let us consider the linkages between books 1–2 and 13 in some detail. Book 1 begins with the famous statement about God's work of creation: "For thou hast created us for thyself, and our heart cannot be quieted until it may find repose in thee" (1 : 1), and book 13 concludes with similar praise of the Creator and of the rest He only can provide. Similarly the phrase which concludes book 2 – that he had made of himself a barren waste – recurs early on in book 13 in a passage which places God's *copia* over against man's *egestas*: "This one thing I know, that woe is me except in thee; not only without myself, but within myself: yea, all other plenty besides my God, is mere beggary unto me" (13:8). Against the fire of concupiscence which made him take his fill of Hell (2 : 1) is placed the love of God which burns like a fire: "we glow inwardly with thy fire, with thy good fire, and we go because we go upward to the peace of Jerusalem" (13:9). This ascent through fire is the *in bono* version of the death of Dido that Augustine had to lament in well-turned phrases as a schoolboy (1 : 13). The breaking or keeping of bounds is yet another link: the wilful breaking of all bounds in the enjoyment of "unlawful pastimes" (2 : 2) contrasts strongly with God's setting of proper bounds in the act of creation – God restrains the "wicked desires of men's souls" and sets them "their bounds" (13 : 17). The briars of "unclean desires" which "grew rank over my head" since there was no hand to root them out (2 : 3) recur in 13 : 19 as "bushes of covetousness" that should be pulled up, while the rich young man who could not follow Christ is the "barren earth" (*terra sterilis*). This harks back to the concluding words on the *regio egestatis* in book 2 and to 2 : 3 where Augustine compares himself to the soil that must be cultivated by God, "the only true, and good landlord of the field of my heart".

Perhaps the most important topos is being *fruitful* or *fruitless*. All the pleasures and pastimes pursued in books 1–2 are fruitless, even when the theft of fruit is involved (2 : 4). Almost in exasperation Augustine asks what fruit he had "in these things, of the remembrance whereof I am now ashamed?" (2 : 8). The fruitfulness so often praised in book 13 is connected with trees (cf. 13 : 17 & 25–26). Augustine and his youthful friends certainly wronged a neighbour when they robbed his tree of unripe pears, and, conversely in book 13, doing good to a neighbour when he is the victim of wrong is said to make us seem like a great tree bearing fruit (13 : 17).

The pursuit of *contraposita* must be supplemented by parallels. The fall into sin described with such intensity in books 1–2 is summarized in 13:8; but for God's intervention, his *fiat lux*, the Fall would have been irrevocable:

> Angel flowed downwards, and man's soul flowed downwards; and they pointed to the Deep of the whole spiritual creation which had been in that most darksome bottom, hadst not thou said from the beginning: Let there be light, and there was light ...

The creation of light from darkness, then, signifies the restoration from the fallen state dramatized in books 1–2. The pursuit of false joys engenders the bitterness discussed in book 13 in terms of the salt sea, which contrasts strongly with the dry land from which the living soul is born. The dry earth represents those who have faith to avoid "the love of this world: that so their soul may live unto thee, which was dead while it lived in pleasure; in such pleasures, Lord, as bring death with them ... Be not conformed to this world; contain yourselves from it: the soul lives by avoiding what it dies by affecting" (13 : 21).

Yet another important link is found in the topos of God's gifts to man. When these gifts are abused, disaster follows: the "huge weight of lustful desires presses down into the deep abyss", but "charity raises us up again by thy Spirit which Moved over the waters" (13:7). The gifts with which the child is adorned are listed in the account of his birth and infancy, and book 13 dwells at length on the three great gifts God has given man for his protection: the universe, the Scriptures, and the Word. The firmament is stretched over us like a skin of protection, reminding us of the way in which God dressed man in skins after the Fall, and this "skin" equals the scroll of the Scriptures ("Wherefore hast thou like a Skin stretched out the firmament of thy book, that is to say those words of thine so well agreeing together"; 13 : 15). These two skins function like the shield of Achilles where we may read what we need to know, and the act of reading studied as a child in book 1 is taken to its highest level when we read these two books "to learn thy mercy".

Equally strong links connect books 3–4 and 12, and chief among them is the theme of mutability. Part of this theme is the contrast between truth and illusion, the illusions being the *phantasmata splendida* of the Manichees (3:6) and his love of a very dear friend (4 : 4). The death of this friend turns Augustine's love into bitterness. All love will turn to bitterness if God be forsaken for it (4 : 12), but he did not know it then, and "I fell in love with these inferior beauties, and I was sinking even to the very bottom" (4:13). The positive elements in books 3–4 are his love of wisdom (engendered by Cicero) and his interest in the nature of beauty, on the subject of which he writes a treatise (4:14 et seq.). In book 12 Augustine listens to, and presents, the truth he sought in books 3–4:

> O let truth, the light of my heart, and not mine own darkness, now speak unto me! I fell off into these material things, and became all be-darkened: but yet even thence, even thence came I to love thee. I went astray, and I remembered thee. I heard thy voice behind me calling to me to return; but scarcely could I discern it for the noise of the enemies of peace. And see here I return now, sweating and panting after thy fountain. Let no man forbid me; this will I drink, this will I live. (12:10)

And the most important truth concerns the mutability of all created things, even heaven itself, in contrast to the utter changelessness of God: "Within me I hear the loud voice of Truth telling me that since the Creator is truly eternal, his substance is utterly unchanged in time" and similarly his will (12:15; Penguin tr.). Yet another link is the subject of the nature of beauty which figures so largely in book 4; it recurs in book 12 in the discussion of the imposition of form in the act of creation: form reflects the unity of God, so that beauty must be defined as unity or harmony between parts (12:28).

Augustine's denunciation of the Manichees dominates books 5–6, and especially book 5. Any Christian, even if he "knows not so much as the circles of the north, ... is in better estate than he that can quarter out the heavens and number the stars, ... and yet is negligent of thee, who hast made all things in number, weight, and measure" (5:4). The major concern of book 11 – how time is measured – connects directly with Manichean doctrines concerning the stars and the planets, and nothing can refute these doctrines more effectively than the conclusion that time is measured in our own minds, and not by bodies moving through space (11:27). The Manichees pursue vain knowledge only: "They discourse truly of many things concerning the creature; but the truth, the Architect of the creature, they do not religiously seek after ... They give out themselves to be wise, attributing thy works to their skill" (5:3). The reason why the young Augustine hesitates to condemn the Manichees is that he himself had not as yet ascertained how to compute time and the reason for "the eclipses and wanings of the greater lights" (5:5). When the truth is set forth in book 11,

Augustine modestly attributes it to God. The central fact is that Heaven and Earth proclaim that they have been made "for they are changed and altered from what they were". "They proclaim also, that they made not themselves; but say: Therefore we are, because we are made" (11:4). Time, then, entails change, while the timeless suffers no alteration, and to understand this is to understand the one needful thing, because this is the truth that enables us to return to God.

When he argues that time is measured in the mind, Augustine rejects the external world in favour of the world within, and it is this movement which ensures the return to God: "Let them therefore be turned back, and seek thee ... Let them be turned back; and behold, thou art there in their heart, in the heart of those that confess thee" (5:2). In 11:8 the return is defined as being to our beginning: the "unalterable truth" makes us return "back to that from whence we are derived".

It is in book 6, as he listens to the sermons of Ambrose, that the wisdom conveyed in book 11 begins to dawn on Augustine. Ambrose opens to him the meaning of the Scriptures (6:3–5), and his prayer, in book 11, that "the secrets of thy Word [may be] opened unto me when I knock" shows curiosity *in bono*, in strong contrast to the idle curiosity of the Manichees as described in books 5–6. This curiosity afflicts Alypius as well, when he is tempted to taste those sexual pleasures that Augustine cannot forgo (6:12) and when he opens his eyes to see what had caused the uproar and so instantly becomes drunk with delight in the spectacle of bloodshed (6:8). The warning against idle or vain curiosity that resounds through books 5 and 6 comes to the fore again in book 11 as a major theme. The truth which never changes is found only in God (11:8).

Books 7–8 and 10 share themes that take us to the heart of Augustine's experience: conflicting wills, sin and redemption from sin, a proper understanding of the natures of God, man, and the lower creatures, and ascent to God. The difference between these books is that in book 10 Augustine writes with assured awareness and at length; instead of dramatic experience, there is persuasive exposition. Even the vision of Continence which precedes the conversion at the end of book 8 finds its expository parallel when continence is said to restore us to the unity we lost "by falling apart in the search for a variety of pleasures" (10:29). The dramatic conflict within Augustine's breast (8:10–11) finds its analogue at 10:23 in the reflections on the unhappy state of man, divided as he is against himself ("the flesh lusteth against the spirit, and the spirit against the flesh"); all desire to be happy, but "a happy life is a rejoicing in the truth", and truth is found only in God.

Book 10 begins with a contemplation of the nature of God, man, and the lower creatures, thus connecting directly with the main subject of book 7. All created things proclaim "I am not he, but he made me" (10:6), and by carefully considering all the faculties of man, from the lowest to the highest, the mind gradually ascends toward God. Thus the memory contains not just images conveyed by the senses, but also abstract principles such as "the reasons and innumerable laws of numbers and dimensions; none of which hath been by any sense of the body imprinted in it" (10:12 & 15). The highest faculties, therefore, are in the mind, and it is by reaching out beyond the mind that God may be approached: "See, I am now mounting up by the steps of my soul, towards thee who dwellest above me" (10:17 and cf. 7:17). The rest of book 10 analyzes the various sins that prevent us from achieving this ascent, as already seen in Augustine's own life (books 7–8); also it praises the great mediator who was both victim and victor (10:43 and cf. 7:18).

In book 9 Augustine and his group of friends find rest in a country house owned by Verecundus (9:3–4), while his mother Monica enters into eternal rest (9:8). This emphasis on *rest* makes book 9 a natural centre-piece or pivot which reaches back to the beginning and forward to the end. Since God encompasses everything, and since God alone is at rest, the idea of rest must encompass the *Confessions* by linking books 1, 9 and 13.

Other structural features, too, serve to identify the pivotal function of book 9. Thus each of the 13 chapters bears on the book which has the same ordinal number, at the same time that the 13 chapters have a symmetrical structure (see Diagram II.10). Thus book 9 begins and ends with the idea of the liberation experienced on becoming the servant of God: in chapter 9:1 it is Augustine who has this experience; in chapter 13 Monica. At the centre (9:7), the Church (our spiritual mother) is liberated from persecution. The topos of *weeping* links the middle and the end: in chapter 7 Augustine weeps "at the singing of thy hymns", but it is for Monica and himself that he weeps in chapter 13. The idea of *patience* links chapters 2 and 12, and 5 and 9, and in chapters 5 and 9 the idea of *meekness* is added. *Holy dying* is the subject of chapter 11 as of chapter 3, whereas chapters 4 and 10 celebrate *being set on fire* with love of God and *ascending* to God. Finally Augustine's spiritual *rebirth* links chapters 6 and 8. To see the linkage, then, we must identify the *concepts* dramatized by the events, as in Renaissance

Diagram II.10 *The Confessions*, The Symmetrical Structure of Book 9

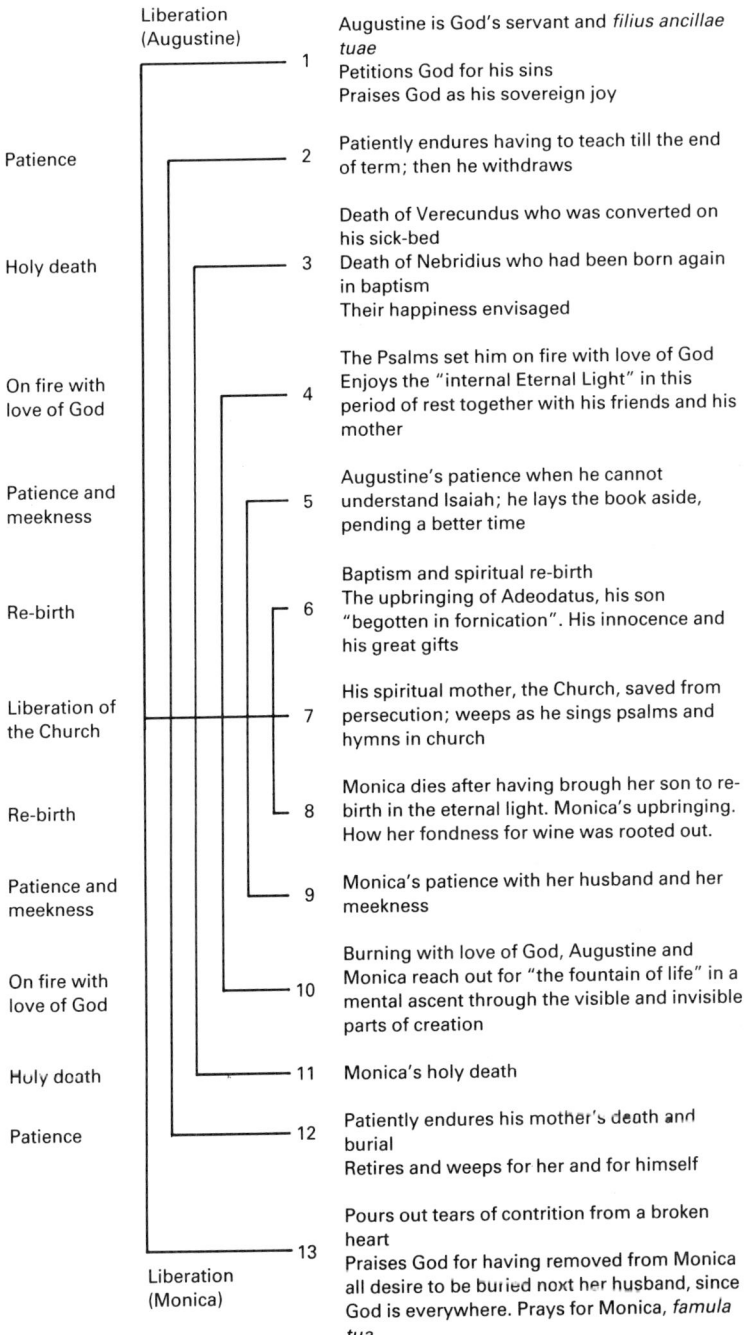

romance epics. As we shall see later on, Augustine's conceptual patterns bear a strong resemblance to the structures created by Tasso and Spenser.

The alignment between the 13 chapters and the 13 books is alone sufficient to identify book 9 as pivotal. When book 1 begins, Augustine presents himself to God and describes his entry into the world from an unknown beginning; at 9 : 1 he again presents himself to the Lord, but this time as his servant and as the son of his handmaid. Book 13 concludes with meditations on our entry into eternal rest, and at 9 : 13 this transition is considered with regard to Monica. Like the *Confessions* as a whole, then, book 9 begins with an entry and concludes with an exit which is the transition from time to eternity. However, more precise echoes are also found. While we are still within the stream of time, the decisive event is the entry of God into our hearts, and this prompts the query in book 1: "Who shall procure for me, that I may repose in thee? Who shall procure thee to enter into my heart; and so to inebriate it, that I may forget my own evils, and embrace thee, my only good?" (1 : 5). In 9 : 1 Augustine praises God for having achieved just this: "Thou hast broken my bonds in sunder ... Yea, what I before feared to lose, was now a joy unto me to forgo ... thou didst cast them out, and instead of them camest in thyself, sweeter than all pleasure, though not to flesh and blood" (9 : 1). It is precisely from the empty vanities of the world (*inania nugarum*; 1 : 17) that Augustine is relieved when book 9 commences; he is relieved of sweet toys, *suavitatibus nugarum*, and of "those biting cares of aspiring, and getting, and weltering in filth" (9 : 1). The sins that beset Augustine in book 2 are annulled "in the holy waters of Baptism" in 9 : 2, and the frustrated feeding on husks in book 3 (the "husks" of the Manichees) is replaced in 9 : 3 by the "inspirations and consolations" that Augustine and his friends receive from God, in whom they find rest.

The links between 9 : 4 and book 4 are particularly impressive, as befits the halfway point between the beginning and the middle. In book 9, chapter 4 Augustine renounces the "school of pride" (*superbiae scholam*); God delivers his tongue, and he dedicates his learning to God and enjoys perfect rest. He rejoices in the Psalms of David and denounces "those fantastical fictions which I once held for truth", and with him is Alypius, "that brother of my love", whom God subdued to the name of Christ. All this recalls book 4, where Augustine is very much a member of the "school of pride": he consults astrologers, gains the wreath in the poetry competition, loves a friend who becomes his "companion in error" (4 : 4), and desires the applause and approval of the Roman orator Hierius for his treatise *De pulchro et apto*. The description of the pain he endures on losing his beloved companion contrasts strongly with his reaction to the death of Nebridius (9:4). Augustine's own comment in book 4 provides the proper perspective: "I lived in misery like every man whose soul is tethered by the love of things that cannot last and then is agonised to lose them" (4:6; Penguin tr.). On the other hand, "blessed is the man that loves thee, and his friend in thee, and his enemy for thee. For he alone loses none that is dear unto him, to whom all are dear, in him that can never be lost" (4:9). Nebridius is a biographical link between book 4 and chapter 9:4. In book 4 he vainly tries to persuade Augustine that astrology is nonsense, and in 9:4 he is part of Augustine's group of friends and co-author of some of the books Augustine was writing. The fact that the death of Nebridius is recorded in 9:3 while his activities are the subject of 9:4 affords yet another example showing how theme prevails at the expense of chronology.

In book 5 Augustine moves first to Rome and then to Milan, and he dismisses the Manichees after his disappointing encounter with the long-awaited Faustus, whose eloquence merely reveals that he has nothing of substance to convey. In 9:5 what he dismisses is his "chair of lies" in order to turn to Ambrose for guidance. This event was prepared for in 5:14 where Ambrose's sermons gradually made him understand the Scriptures and so to respect them. As we learn in book 6, though, his acceptance of the spiritual meaning of the text is accompanied by an inability to conceive of spiritual realities except in a corporeal way, and for this reason his attempt to establish a community of friends fails (6:14). By 9:6 this is no longer so; Alypius even walks barefoot on the frosty soil of Italy to tame his body, and the baptism of Augustine, Alypius, and Adeodati effectively removes them from a carnal to a spiritual mode of life.

The crucial event of book 7 – the miraculous healing, by the grace of God, of Augustine's spiritual blindness (7:8, 7:10 and 7:17) – finds its analogue in the miraculous restoration of the blind man's eyesight in 9:7. In book 8 the story of the conversion of the great orator Victorinus anticipates Augustine's conversion, and so do the conversion and baptism of a man from Augustine's own home town in 9:8. Another parallel between book 8 and chapter 9:8 is found in the vision of Continence and Monica's providential rescue from becoming a wine-bibber, and the theme of course finds its clearest expression in St Paul's injunction to avoid rioting and drunkenness

(8 : 12). As for book 9, the related topoi of patience and meekness (9 : 2, 9 : 5, 9 : 9 and 9 : 12) find their place as a matter of course in 9 : 9, while the theme of ascent to God connects book 10 with chapter 9 : 10.

Before she dies, Monica expresses complete disregard for where she will be buried (9 : 11); her resting-place does not matter since "nothing is far from God". In book 11 God is defined as being outside Time in Eternity (11 : 1), and in Eternity "all is at once present" (11 : 11), which is another way of saying that nothing is far from God.

Death is the most drastic proof of change and mutability, the main subject of book 12, and when Monica dies and is buried (9 : 12) she ceases to be what she has been and begins to be what she never has been (12:6). Death is a "transition from one form to another" as in the act of creation; also it is a transition from the mutable to the immutable and hence highly to be desired. Nevertheless, in the chapter on the burial of Monica, Augustine confesses his inability to rid himself of his carnal affection; he grieves at having "that most sweet and dear custom of living with her thus suddenly broken off" (9 : 12). Since God provided no relief, Augustine states that in this way God impressed upon him the terrible power of custom. In chapter 13, however, the wound is cured and he offers "a far different kind of tears; such as flow from a broken spirit, out of a serious consideration of the danger of every soul that dieth in Adam". He appeals to Christ for intercession for them both, and especially for "this handmaid of thine": "Let none pluck her away from thy protection." Christ's sacrifice is in fact the basic theme of book 13, where Augustine traces the various phases in the scheme of redemption in the Mosaic account of creation (see especially 13 : 12–14). This conflation is traditional, but no one, I believe, has fused the two so completely and in such detail as Augustine.

5. Concluding Remarks

If we are to feel the perfect unity of Augustine's spiritual epic, we must adjust our reading so as to perceive the symmetrical and graded structures. On the whole, it seems to me that the two graded arrangements exert a stronger pull than the symmetrical pattern. Everyone feels the emotional impact of the autobiography, but Augustine did not write his *Confessions* to describe a unique human experience; he consistently lifts the particular to the level of the universal, and it is for this reason that he made use of the two graded arrangements. It is imperative that we should relate books 1–2 to book 13, 3–4 to 12, 5–6 to 11 and 7–8 to 10; unless we do this, we shall fail to see how the particular leads on to the universal. The last four books, therefore, cannot be dismissed without damage to the whole.

Augustine's first structural decision must have been to divide his book into 13 parts (the number of Christ and of the Church), and to let book 9 constitute a pivotal point of rest. This division creates a harmonious balance between the 8 books of the autobiography and the reflections contained in the last 4 books. The harmony is shown in detail in the system of linkage between double and single sets of books (see Diagram II.8). The extraordinary length of books 10–13 therefore is part of the preconceived plan. It is a particularly felicitous feature that the first two books on birth, growth, and decay are paired off against book 13 on the creation and restoration of man. Later on, Milton was to duplicate this pattern when he let the first two books of *Paradise Lost* (the first edition of 1667) be paired off against the last, tenth book on the universal history of man. In this way the fallen state as illustrated by the fallen angels is balanced against the account of postlapsarian life and the scheme of redemption as it unfolds in the course of history from beginning to end. The parallel is so striking that direct influence is likely.

When unity is defined in the terms explained in Chapter I, it must be conceded that the *Confessions* is a highly unified work of art, composed according to the principles that Augustine himself explains. Because they serve to unify, the various textual structures point to God as the source of that which is narrated. Hence, by virtue of the rhythms that pervade it, the *Confessions* bridges the gap between God's *poiemata* and man's.[17] As Marin Mersenne was to put it in the early years of the seventeenth century (perhaps thinking of the *Confessions*), they set the mind on fire and elevate it to the highest things.

Augustine's spiritual epic marks the beginning of a tradition of Christian epics climaxed in the Renaissance by Tasso's *Jerusalem Delivered*, Spenser's *The Faerie Queene*, and Milton's *Paradise Lost*. Tasso's spiritual epic on the deliverance of Jerusalem has the same kind of unity as the *Confessions* (both symmetrical and graded), and another point of similarity is that both epics have an ambiguous hero and heroine. As we have observed, Monica at one point is presented as being now like the fallen Eve and now like the Virgin Mary, the second Eve; she is both the victim of carnal affections and the handmaid of the Lord, until in the end the second

Eve reigns supreme. Much the same is true of Tasso's Armida, just as Rinaldo becomes Christ-like after his spiritual re-birth on Mount Olivet. When Armida in the end surrenders to him, she surrenders to Christ in him, and she does so with the words of the Virgin Mary: "Ecce ancilla tua". Later on, Milton was to explain the relationship in his famous line, "Hee for God only, shee for God in him" (*Paradise Lost* 4.299). In Augustine's epic, though, it is Monica who is "for God only".

Milton must have been a most perceptive reader of the *Confessions*. He chose the same subject (creation, fall, and redemption), and a related genre. *Paradise Lost*, too, is a spiritual epic, the confessional tradition being present in the justification of God's ways to men.[18] Augustine's poetic prose may have played its part in making Milton reject rhyme in favour of blank verse, and he adopted Augustine's textual structures with minor variations. It is virtually impossible to investigate the textual structures of *Paradise Lost* without familiarity with Augustine's aesthetic principles and his application of them in the *Confessions*. One clear structural parallel is that Milton's epic, too, concludes with the prospect of rest. The place of rest sought by Adam and Eve as they leave the Garden is so much more than just a refuge for the pending night; the word *rest* resonates with overtones that Augustine had made familiar. I believe that most readers feel this resonance, although they may not be consciously aware of it; otherwise the concluding lines would lose much of their impact.

Although number symbolism is not absent from the *Confessions*, the symbolic ratios (1 : 1 and 2 : 1) are much more important. I would not go much beyond the observation that the sum total of books, 13, represents Christ and the Church, and that the conversion which ensures eternal life occurs toward the end of book 8. In order to cope with the subject of number symbolism, however, it will be necessary to consider the use of number symbolism in structural exegesis.

Notes to Chapter II

1. *On the Trinity*, tr. Arthur West Haddan (Edinburgh, 1873). *On Christian Doctrine* may be consulted in the translation of D. W. Robertson, Jr (New York, 1958). For *The City of God* and the *Confessions*, all quotations are from the editions published in the Loeb Classical Library, unless otherwise stated. The translation of the *Confessions* is based on that of William Watts (1631). Watts was Rector of St Albans, Wood Street, London, and he made use of an earlier translation by Sir Tobie Matthew (London, 1624) to whom he refers as "the Papist".

2. S. K. Heninger, Jr, *The Cosmographical Glass* (San Marino, 1977), p. 104.
3. One of George Herbert's poems, "Mans medley", playfully relates *single* to *double* in 6 6-line stanzas divided into 4+2. Stanzas 1–4 describe man's happy state: in contrast to the beasts, man has double joys (in this life and hereafter), and he joins two worlds, heaven and earth. However, the last two stanzas contemplate the possibility of a double death: "But as his joyes are double, / So is his trouble. / He hath two winters, other things but one", so that he "of all things fears two deaths alone".
4. See Harry Bober, "In Principio: Creation before Time", *Essays in Honor of Erwin Panofsky*, ed. Millard Meiss (New York, 1961), Vol. I, pp. 13–28. Such highly adorned initials would often contain images of exegetical importance, such as typological links between the Old and the New Testaments. In this particular case Christ is identified as the source of world harmony.
5. It has been said of the early Latin fathers that "in order to gain a full hearing in an age when style as such was well-nigh all-important", they cast their compositions "in the strict forms of literary master-pieces". See Sister Mary Frances McDonald, "Introduction", p. 59 to Augustine's *De Fide Rerum Quae Non Videntur: A Critical Text and Translation* (Washington, DC, 1950) in *Patristic Studies*, vol. 84. On some of the epic features of the *Confessions*, see John O'Meara, "Augustine the Artist and the *Aeneid*", in *Mélanges Offerts à Mademoiselle Christine Nohrmann* (Utrecht/Anvers, 1963), pp. 252–61. Like so many who have studied Augustine's art, O'Meara favours a psychological approach, and this is true also of Andrew Fichter, *Poets Historical. Dynastic Epic in the Renaissance* (New Haven and London, 1982). Fichter's second chapter compares the *Confessions* with the *Aeneid*.
6. Robert J. O'Connell, *Art and the Christian Intelligence in St. Augustine* (Oxford, 1978), p. 93. O'Connell argues fervently in favour of unconscious processes: "Whatever the 'conscious' purposes he may have had for composing the *Confessions*, the forces generated in the process of creation may have burst forth from their initially confining channels; deeper levels of consciousness, obscurer levels of intention may come into play; the result may be a work whose import resonates with, but transcends, and even occasionally defies what was consciously intended" (p. 108).
7. The medieval theory of language posited that a word ("nomen") is a thing or object ("res"); the *res* can be understood only when located correctly within the divine order so that they become part of a system of signs pointing to a spiritual reality. See Walter Haubrichs, *Ordo als Form* (Tübingen, 1968), p. 15. It has been shown that this tendency manifests itself also in 16th-century English poetry; see Anne Ferry, *The Art of Naming* (Chicago and London, 1988).
8. This distinction plays a major role in biblical exegesis as explained in Chapter III; Augustine discusses it in the *De doctrina Christiana* III.xxv.35. The same word or sign may have a good connotation in one context and a negative import in another. This principle applies as a matter of course to numbers as well as words. See Augustine, *On Christian Doctrine*, tr. D. W. Robertson, Jr. pp. 99–100.
9. Andrew Fichter, *Poets Historical* (New Haven and London, 1982), pp. 49 f.
10. This topos inspired Beza's "Emblema II" in *Icones*, 1580, and Milton made good use of it in *Paradise Lost* XI.315–54 (especially lines 349–54).
11. Fichter, *Poets Historical*, p. 50.
12. See Kenneth Burke, *The Rhetoric of Religion* (Boston, 1961), p. 54. *Sapientia* connects with *sapio* (to taste or savour of). Cf. Milton's lines: "But knowledge is as food, and needs no less / Her temperance over appetite, to know / In measure what the mind may well contain (*Paradise Lost* VII.126–128).
13. Augustine, *Expositions on the Book of Psalms*, vol. 1 (Oxford, 1847), pp. 288 f.
14. Augustine, *On Free Choice of the Will*, tr. Anna S. Benjamin and L. H. Hackstaff (New York, 1964), pp. 131 f.
15. Fichter, *Poets Historical*, p. 52.

16. See the edition cited in note 14.
17. The Greek word for "works", as used for example in *Romans* 1 : 20, is *poiemata*. The difference between God's work of creation and poetry disappears when the same word is used for both. When *Ephesians* 2 : 10 describes the Christian as God's *workmanship*, he is quite literally God's poem.
18. On the confessional tradition, see Shirley S. Paolini, *Confessions of Sin and Love in the Middle Ages. Dante's* Commedia and *Augustine's* Confessions (Washington DC, 1982).

Chapter III

Structural Exegesis

> Omnia in mensura, et numero, et pondere disposuisti.
> *Liber sapientiae* 11.21

Like Augustine in the *Confessions*, George Herbert was intensely preoccupied with the relationship between parts and the whole; in "The H. Scriptures II" he bends all his efforts to discover God's patterns, "how all thy lights combine, / And the configurations of their glorie!" The Bible is another universe: if "each verse doth shine", how much more "all the constellations of the storie". Holy Writ declares the glory of God in the same way as the visible creation: in both, lights combine to form constellations and configurations. No wonder, therefore, that the structure of individual poems in Herbert's *The Temple* (1633), and of the collection as a whole, reveals evidence of highest order.[1] Highest order prevails also in Andrew Marvell's "Upon Appleton House", as was only to be expected from a poet who praised Milton's blank verse in *Paradise Lost* for observing number, weight, and measure. The main structure of God's scheme of redemption becomes visible in the structure of Marvell's description of Fairfax's estate.[2] The "light mosaic" is the light that Moses saw by, and the light that we ourselves perceive as we read.

Charles Wolseley (*The Reasonableness of Scripture-Belief*, 1672) felt the appeal of this structural approach so keenly that he based his defence of divine revelation on it. Wolseley urged the time-honoured view that Moses was the originator of all learning, and that the text of the Bible had been preserved intact through the centuries by divine Providence. The integrity of the text is proved by the intricate system of correspondences between all the parts, a system far too difficult for mere human wit to have contrived. The "conjunction of parts" is such that God alone can be held responsible for this extraordinary unity and harmony.[3] Unity of design, then, marks the Bible as a whole and manifests itself most clearly, perhaps, in the pattern of types and antitypes, prophecy and fulfilment. The story of the week of creation is a type of the 7 ages of the world, and this idea recurs in the Book of Revelation in the account of the opening of the 7 seals. The centre is marked by the creation of the sun on the fourth day, an event which foreshadows the arrival of Christ *in medio annorum* as our true *sol iustitiae*. The tree affords another link between the beginning, middle, and end of the biblical narrative: the Tree of Life in the Garden is a prophecy of the Tree of the Cross (located at the centre of space and time), whose fulfilment is seen in the Tree of Life in the midst of the heavenly Jerusalem (*Rev.* 22). No wonder that Pico and Henry Bullinger could say about the Mosaic account that "this is the model, this is the pattern for perfection in a writer", and that "there was no ability wanting in Moses, that was necessary for a most absolute writer".[4] Moses could write as he did because he knew the meaning of the types; God had revealed the course of history to Adam, and the knowledge was handed down secretly from generation to generation. This is of course what happens toward the end of *Paradise Lost*, and Milton expresses a related belief when he lets Jesus say that the Greeks learnt the arts of poetry and music from the Hebrews (*Paradise Regained* IV.334–350). The renowned early seventeenth-century exegete, Cornelius à Lapide, describes Seneca's tragedies as a mere shadow of the tragedy written by Jeremiah, and Theocritus and Virgil modelled their idylls and bucolics on *Canticles*, a *drama sponsale* written in the allegorical mode typical of pastoral.[5] Matthew Poole compared Ezekiel and Homer, stressing the sublimity of Ezekiel's subject-matter, the hidden meaning of his vision, and his figurative mode of writing.[6] Prophets and poets alike wrote *per symbola & ænigmata*, as Cornelius à Lapide puts it in a phrase echoed by Matthew Poole.[7]

The "light mosaic" is far from simple. The Protestant fondness for types and for spiritual interpretations[8] created a complexity comparable to the fourfold method of Scriptural exegesis still practised by Cornelius à Lapide. True, more respectable approaches to biblical exegesis were developed in the Renaissance, but old habits persisted, especially when supported by typological exegesis. The quest for types reached something of a climax in England in the first half of the seventeenth century, which is surely why it marks the poetry of the period so strongly. However, all this is excluded from Arnold Williams' study of commentaries on Genesis from 1527 to 1633 (*The Common Expositor*, 1948). Williams projects a modern bias back into the Renaissance; allegorical exegesis is virtually excluded and even typological exegesis is largely ignored. Benedictus Pererius (circa 1535–1620) is taken to represent the norm because he "advanced the cause of literal interpretation", although he too sometimes "succumbed to allegory".[9] Williams reveals the same bias in his account of Renaissance science. Only the musicologist Marin Mersenne is taken seriously, perhaps because his description of musical instruments is factual. Mersenne's keen interest in Augustine's "musical theology" receives no mention, and the syncretistic bias is connected only with "irresponsible" writers like Pico.

Augustine's *De doctrina Christiana* is a better guide. Augustine explains that biblical exegesis is difficult, since some things are taught openly, while others are conveyed so obscurely that they are as it were "covered with a most dense mist" (II.vi.7). The obscurity may be caused by our own ignorance, or it may serve as a divinely ordained antidote to human pride, or again to "combat disdain", since what is easily discovered may seem worthless. However, the discrepancy between the literal level of a text and its spiritual import may be a very real source of pleasure, just as that which is said figuratively moves and inflames more strongly than that which is said literally.[10] Numbers are among the "signs" that must be read figuratively or in a spiritual sense ("mystically"), and their importance is increased by the fact that they express absolute truth – a truth discovered and not invented by man. Their highly abstract character makes the truths they convey more moving than any other kind of "sign" – and this is of course where modern readers find it difficult to agree. This is therefore the point on which we must readjust our blurred vision of the past: when poets like Spenser and Milton trace highly abstract structural patterns through a text, our perception of the pattern should provoke delight, and we should be moved. Augustine finds it particularly regrettable that an ignorance of numbers may prevent readers of the Bible from seeing its structures and their meaning:

> An ignorance of numbers also causes many things expressed figuratively and mystically in the Scriptures to be misunderstood. Certainly a gifted and frank person cannot avoid wondering about the significance of the fact that Moses, Elias, and the Lord Himself all fasted for forty days. The knot, as it were, of this figurative action cannot be untied without a knowledge and consideration of this number. (II.xvi.25)

The meaning of the event (the three forty-day fasts) must be the same because the number is the same, and the meaning is found on considering the numbers that enter into 40, that is, 4 and 10. And 10 is made by adding 3 and 7 – 3 for the Trinity and 7 for the *res creatae* (because they consist of the 4 of matter and the 3 representing mind). The number 40 therefore means "the knowledge of all things involved in times", 10 representing all things (God as Trinity plus the creation or the number 7) and 4 the temporal cycles (the 4 seasons). But this is not enough: by adding 10 to 40 we get 50 or the mystery of Pentecost, and if we multiply 50 with the number of the Trinity and add the number of the Trinity to the sum, we get 153, which is the number of fishes caught "on the right side" of the boat (*John* 21:6–11). And this miraculous draught of fishes on the command of the risen Lord refers to those who will be saved and therefore placed on the right-hand side. We see, then, how a number used to delimit an event in time explains its spiritual significance. By incorporating the numbers 3, 4, 7 and 10 into the period of fasting, Pentecost, and the miraculous draught of fishes, God is as it were spelling out the pattern of salvation. Numbers and patterns of numbers, as Augustine puts it, function as similitudes in the sacred books.

This kind of numerical exegesis lived on into the Renaissance and beyond, and it must needs be studied today as part of the structurally oriented æsthetics of our Western world. Augustine had no qualms about including Pythagorean and Platonic number lore, and he offers several reasons for so doing. Truth, wherever found, is always from God (II.xviii.28), and Ambrose concluded that Plato and Pythagoras were indebted to the Hebrews (II.xviii.43). Just as logic was not invented by men but "perpetually instituted by God in the reasonable order of things", it is "perfectly clear to the most stupid person that the science of numbers was not instituted by men, but rather investigated and discovered" (II.xxxii.50 and II.xxxviii.56).

What Augustine says about carnal slavery to the letter comes very close to the Puritan bias as exemplified by the sermons of Dr John Everard.[11] His basic text ("For the letter killeth, but the spirit quickeneth"; 2 *Cor.* 3:6) tells us not to remain subject to corporal things. It was because the Jews stubbornly adhered to "signs as things" that they rejected the Lord, but those who accepted the Word were led, not to "a servitude under useful signs, but rather to an exercise of the mind directed toward understanding them spiritually" (*De doctrina Christiana* III.viii.12). This is true Christian liberty. What Augustine says about the Sabbath may have inspired Milton's similar argument:

He who follows the letter takes figurative expressions as though they were literal and does not refer the things signified to anything else. For example, if he hears of the Sabbath, he thinks only of one day out of the seven that are repeated in a continuous cycle; and if he hears of Sacrifice, his thoughts do not go beyond the customary victims of the flocks and fruits of the earth. There is a miserable servitude of spirit in this habit of taking signs for things, so that one is not able to raise the eyes of the mind above things that are corporal and created to drink in eternal light. (III.v.9)

It is this literalism that Milton denounces when he writes about the Sabbath in his own *De doctrina Christiana*. If the seventh day were to be preferred also under the new dispensation, one would have to show what "essential principle of morality is invested in the number seven; and why, when released from the obligation of the Sabbath, we should still be bound to respect a particular number, possessing no inherent virtue or efficacy". Milton will not consider signs as things, nor will he accept slavery even under useful signs, since no sign can have inherent power. The "only moral sabbatical rest which remains for us under the gospel, is spiritual and eternal, pertaining to another life rather than the present". Hence Milton concludes that, if we have been "brought out of a spiritual Egypt, the Sabbath ought to be such as the deliverance, spiritual and evangelical, not bodily and legal".[12] In other words, we must proceed from the number 7 (the sign) to that which it signifies. So far from being a dismissal of number symbolism, therefore, this passage insists on the spiritual meaning of the number 7, in contrast to its literal sense. This view is not in conflict with Milton's insistence on the one plain sense of the biblical text (*De doctrina* I.30); the spiritual meaning of the number 7 is its meaning as a type, and typological exegesis is based on the literal level. Indeed, unless an event or a "sign" is literally true, the type would have no power; it was because Abraham was willing to sacrifice his only son that this event can function as a prophecy of Christ's ultimate sacrifice. We proceed from the letter to the spirit when we proceed from the type to the antitype. The fully achieved process takes us from sabbatical rest to the rest which is eternal.

Yet another important exegetical principle is that the same "sign" may be interpreted in a good and a bad sense (*in bono* or *in malo*), a logical distinction carefully observed by Tasso, Spenser, and Milton. Indeed, the discrimination is necessary to compel us to think logically, as Cassiodorus explains in the preface to his *Expositio Psalmorum*,[13] and in the Renaissance the principle was applied in the exposition of classical myth as well, as Don Cameron Allen has observed.[14] The authoritative source is again Augustine's *De doctrina Christiana*. Augustine warns us that the same "sign" may be possessed of contrary meanings: both the lion and the serpent occur in good and bad contexts (III.xxv.36), so that context must always be consulted. On one occasion a shield may signify the good will of God, but this does not mean that "everywhere we read of a shield raised for defence we should think of nothing except the good will of God" (III.xxvi.37). The Lord himself "used 'leaven' in vituperation when He said, 'Beware of the leaven of the Pharisees', and in praise when He said, 'The kingdom of God ... is like to leaven, which a woman took and hid in three measures of meal, till the whole was leavened'" (III.xxv.35). As we shall see, in Renaissance epics one way of establishing linkage between parts is to take the same "sign" (or topos) in a good and a bad sense, a technique far better than mere repetition. Since numbers too are "signs", the *in bono / in malo* distinction necessarily applies. The number 9 may signify the celestial hierarchies, but may equally well refer to their infernal counterpart; moreover, when considered as falling short of the number 10 of the Law, it represents sin.

As I show in Chapter IX on *Paradise Lost*, we cannot read Milton's text properly without applying this principle. Take the word *bold*: in their confrontation toward the end of book 5 both Abdiel and Satan speak "boldly", but Satan's boldness stems from an obdurate heart, Abdiel's from his firm faith, and so it will not do to confuse the two. And I take it that when Milton describes how water, after its creation, moves "With Serpent errour" (7.302), he is challenging us to see "that it was good" (7.309). Before the Fall, no action and no descriptive term can have evil connotations. This must be so in this particular instance, and it is arguable that it should apply also to Eve's "wanton ringlets" (4.306) as well as to the "mazie error" of the rivers in Paradise (4.239). If the local context is to decide the meaning, neither can be construed *in malo*.

To return to Augustine's consideration of numbers as "signs": such numbers may be present in the text itself, or may be discovered by counting persons, the times that an action is performed, or textual units. Chronology is most important, since such numbers may exist simply in order to convey the symbolic import which explains the nature of the event (III.xxxv.50). Some numbers were so familiar that it was possible to use them in a purely symbolic sense. Thus in the Bible, 7 may mean "time as a whole, whence 'seven times a day I have given praise to thee' means the same thing as 'always his praise shall be in my mouth'" (III.xxxv.51). It was surely the meaning of the number 153 (found in the account of the miraculous draught of fishes) which caused John Colet to provide for this number of scholars in St Paul's school, just as the foundation statutes for Christ's College, Cambridge, stipulated a society of 13 on an analogy with the head and the 12 parts of the body.[15] However, the analogy must also be with Christ as the head of the 12 Apostles, and these in their turn represent the Church. We see, then, how the belief that biblical numbers were highly significant caused men to use numbers in the same way in their own lives. Milton may possibly provide yet another example. When he uses the phrase "ere half my days" in his sonnet on his blindness, he may have had the psalmist's words in mind: "I said, O my God, take me not away in the midst of my days" (*Psalms* 102:24). Bongo takes this to be a reference to the second of the three periods which constitute the life of man (*pueritia, adolescentia vel iuuentus*, and *senectus*), this being the period of perfection.[16]

Although it is true that exegetes often adduce Pythagorean and Platonic number symbolism, the distinction between classical and biblical is of marginal interest. What is important is that numbers were taken to express universal truths. In comments on Ezekiel's vision of the mysterious chariot, the use of Pythagorean number lore is less important than the general idea of harmony; this idea merely happens on this occasion to be conveyed in Pythagorean terms. One is not therefore committed to a Pythagorean cosmology because Christ's harmonizing power is dramatized, or made rhetorically effective, by adducing the "sweetness" of the disposition whereby there are, for example, 4 elements, 4 winds, 4 seasons, and 4 gospels. And the harmony between the Old Testament and the New does not require support from the *tetractys* formula, but it is an eternal truth that the first 4 numbers, when added, make 10, so that 10 contains within itself these 4 numbers as its source, numbers which form the ratios that create the musical consonances. The formula can be used to illustrate how the 10 of the Law points forward to the 4 of the Gospels; with the evangelists the inner meaning of the Law was finally revealed. If one scribbles on a wall that $10 = 4$, this does not have to be a declaration of faith in a Pythagorean cosmos; it can simply be used as a convenient arithmetical formula, possessed of eternal validity, to express the typological relationship between the two Testaments.[17]

Augustine's remark that, if you remove numbers from the world, everything will perish may be applied to his own thought. It is as impossible to remove numbers and ratios from Augustine's æsthetics as from his theology. The two are at one in using the language of numbers to express the unchangeable truth which is highest beauty.

The way in which number symbolism influenced compositional practice is clearly seen in the works of Cassiodorus (480?–575). His *Expositio Psalmorum* develops Augustine's numerical exegesis, and his *Institutions* embodies symbolic numbers in its division into books and chapters, as Cassiodorus himself explains.[18] The *Institutiones* became one of the important school books of the early Middle Ages, and the *Expositio Psalmorum* was just as important, if not more so. It is included in 13 medieval library catalogues, and it was frequently drawn on by theologians such as Bede. It was considered as his *magnum opus* throughout the Middle Ages, and Renaissance editions are numerous.[19] A modern scholar like Leslie Webber Jones writes condescendingly that, although the *Expositio* is "a marvel of erudition", its efforts are largely misdirected. "Our author, for example, maintains ... that the first seventy Psalms represent the Old Testament and the last eighty the New, because we celebrate Christ's resurrection on the eighth day of the week".[20] In the first place this is not a fair summary of Cassiodorus' exegesis, and, secondly, the misdirected efforts nevertheless require close attention if we are to understand the structural principles involved in his analysis of what amounts to a poetic sequence consisting of 150 units.

Cassiodorus' *Institutions, or An Introduction to Divine and Human Readings* is organized in one book on the study of the Bible and another on secular studies. He divided Book I into 33 chapters and Book II into 7 because Christ was 33 years old "when he offered eternal life to a world laid low by sin", while 7 is the number of time and of this world (from the preface to Book II). Cassiodorus cites the example of St Prosper, who wrote three books "of the entire Divine Authority" in 153 chapters, "fish, as it were, which the evangelical nets have dragged from the troubled depths of this life" (I.i.7). The best examples of meaningful textual structures are of course taken from the Bible. Although different editors have chosen different divisions into books, such differences reveal variety rather than contradiction. They do not conflict, but rather "make one another mutually intelligible". Then, too, all of them have observed decorum: "through their divisions [they] have adapted the sacred books to appropriate mysteries" so that they speak with one voice, like the evangelists "in whom the faith in events is uniform and the manner of speaking divergent" (I.xiv.3). Augustine's division into 71 books is especially praiseworthy, since "if to this number you add the unity of the Holy Trinity, there will result a number appropriately and gloriously perfect *in balance*" (I.xiii.2; my emphasis). Cassiodorus offers no comment on the nature of the balance he has in mind, but the modern editor suggests that the number refers to the scholars responsible for the translation known as the Septuagint, 72 in all (later reduced to 70). Again Bongo is of assistance. In his comments on the 72 interpreters he refers to Eusebius and Augustine who aligned this number with that of the disciples who helped to spread the Gospel, and he derives its symbolic import from the 24-hour solar cycle multiplied with the number of the Trinity, the solar cycle being an image or symbol of the illumination provided by the Gospel through him who is our *sol iustitiae*. The textual arrangement into 71 books, then (with Unity added to make 72), reflects the number of translators and the number of disciples and their common concern: to spread the light of divine revelation through the power of the Trinity. The balance, therefore, is between four members: the structure of the text, the number of translators and of disciples, and the "light" of divine revelation. Textual, cosmic, and historical numbers agree to convey the same meaning.

Another organization praised for its symbolic aptness is Jerome's division of the Old Testament into 22 books: this division agrees with the number of letters in the Hebrew alphabet "by which all wisdom is learned" (I.xii.2). When we add the 27 books of the New Testament, we get a sum total of 49:

> Add to this the omnipotent and indivisible Trinity, by which these things were done and on whose account these things were said, and the result without doubt is the number fifty, since after the manner of the year of a jubilee it very compassionately forgives the transgressions and remits the sins of those who are absolutely penitent. (I.xii.2)

To Cassiodorus (as later on to Bonaventura), the words of the Bible are "ordered words" (I.xvi.1), and words full of "parables and dark sayings" (*Psalms* 77:2). And, while the words of God have to display the highest order, "the evil works of the devil are not ordered by weight and measure or number, since, whatever iniquity does, it is always opposed to justice" (II, preface). On the walls of the old cathedrals we may observe this contrast in the depiction of the orderly array of the saints and the grotesque disorder of the damned. Milton makes the point more subtly when the apparent order of the fallen angels is seen to conceal the most gross disorder.

Cassiodorus put Augustine's praise of ordered parts to practical use when he recommended dividing up texts (so far written with precious few divisions to guide the eye of the reader). His recommendation is "to divide a whole composition into members in such a way that these members, *viewed in the light of one's divisions*, become beautiful! For if our body needs to be known through its members, why should a text be left with its parts apparently disordered?" (I.xv.12; my emphasis). It would seem that the theoretical interest taken in textual divisions actually helped to promote better scribal and editorial practices. The beauty inherent in symbolic numbers is transferred to a text when divided so as to produce such numbers.

Book II is divided into 7 parts corresponding to the 7 liberal arts, but Cassiodorus himself assures us that the division has symbolic meaning. Even divisions imposed by the subject-matter, then, can be seen as meaningful. The fourth part or chapter on arithmetic associates Pythagoras with the Bible, since Pythagoras thought that "all things were created by God on the basis of number and measure", and the Bible defines creation in terms of number, weight, and measure (*Wisdom* 11:21). Cassiodorus defines the categories of numbers, such as odd and even numbers and numbers that are triangular, quadrate, pentagonal, and circular. Finally he relates numbers to the Scriptures: the number 1 pertains to the single God, 2 to the Two Testaments, and 3 to the Trinity. Three relates to the Trinity, "not because the Holy Trinity is subject to number, but because it shows the usefulness of number through the power of its majesty". God is one in substance but three in his personal manifestation, "for one reads in the epistle of John: 'And there are three that bear witness: the water, and the blood, and the spirit'". It is enough, then, for three witnesses to be mentioned to conclude that God is a Trinity (cf. 1 *John* 5:8). Cassiodorus similarly relates the number 4 to the gospels because of the reference, in *Ezekiel* 1:5, to "the likeness of four living creatures". The number 5 represents the five books of Moses, 6 the creation of man in the likeness of God, and 7 the Holy Ghost whose gifts are seven. This is how numbers represent a higher spiritual reality, and their power manifests itself in the concluding paragraph where Cassiodorus encourages readers to "gaze upon the celestial virtues" and to try to understand the nature and the works of Christ. His sentences are a living manifestation of this power, as they form groups of 3, whether verbs or nouns or adjectives:

> the Lord Christ, *who has devised* such great and such marvellous works with the aid of providence, *who has arranged* them with his understanding, and *who has perfected* them with his excellence, now *supports them* with the divine Spirit, *holds them* in awe with his power, and *governs them* with his piety – *incomprehensible, ineffable*, and *fully known* to no one except himself. The reader will also perceive that Christ, seated on his majestic throne, *admonishes* the churches through the holy angels, *threatens* the evil with punishment, *promises* rewards to the good, and is venerated in suppliant fashion with the greatest dread by all the *elders*, the *archangels*, and the entire *heavenly host*; and that their particular and sole concern is to celebrate eternally with indefatigable devotion the glory of the Holy Trinity. (Conclusion § 4; my emphases)

We notice that the first two triads present Christ's works in space and time, that the third, central triad states that his nature is "incomprehensible, ineffable, and fully known only to himself", and that the last two triads present him as Christ triumphant, seated on his throne. Larger structures, therefore, find their analogues in the microcosmos of syntactical arrangements.

Milton must have appreciated the argument that connects harmony with *obedience*. Musical science "is diffused through all the acts of our life if we before all else obey the commands of the creator" (II.v.2), and music connects with arithmetic "because music deals, among other things, with the relationship between a simple number and its double" (II.iv.1). Musical rhythms are all-important, "For whatever we say, or whatever inward effect is caused by the beating of our pulse is joined by musical rhythms to the power of harmony". If we "observe the good way of life we are always associated with this excellent science" (II.v.2). This is of course why Eve's footsteps after the Fall falter; the true rhythm has been lost. As we read on in Cassiodorus, Pythagoras is invoked: Pythagoras taught that "this world was founded through the instrumentality of music and can be governed by it. Music also freely permeates religion itself: witness the ten-stringed instrument of the Decalogue" (II.v.2–3). And, I am tempted to add, witness the 10-book epic of *Paradise Lost* (1667). Music is to act in consistence with the ordering of our Creator (II.v.9), which explains the power of music as when Saul was delivered from the unclean spirit by David. Music appeals to the mind by "leading the understanding to heavenly things" (II.v.10).

The importance of the *Institutions* is easily understood today, but the *Expositio Psalmorum* enjoyed a greater popularity and is more directly relevant to Renaissance poetics. If much of it today must be classified as nonsense, it is at least beautiful nonsense; the vision it transmits of the unity of all things is inspiring. In this collection of 150 items, each psalm is supposedly located exactly where it must be to preserve the same order which we find in the Bible as a whole and in the created universe. Cassiodorus, then, sees the Psalms as a structured sequence, which helps to explain the popularity of such sequences in the Renaissance. Sonnet sequences afford one example, structured collections like Herbert's *The Temple* (1633) another.[21]

Cassiodorus takes textual structures for granted and co-ordinates them with structures formed by events, and by aspects of creation or of the heavenly Jerusalem; he weaves them all together if they share the same number. The whole point is this interweaving; everything must be part of a unified whole. As in the examples already cited from the *Institutions*, it is not so much numbers themselves which are important, as the concepts they transmit. The concept of circularity may be present in a number, or in textual structures which connect the beginning and the end. Psalm 145 (Vulg. 144) has an alphabetical composition which in itself expresses circularity, and the concluding exhortation to praise God for ever and ever returns us to the beginning where the same message is conveyed in the same words. Interestingly enough, central accent may be present in verses 11–12 where Yahweh is proclaimed "Kingly and glorious"; all mankind will learn "the majestic glory of your sovereignty" (Jerusalem Bible). The circle is such an important concept because Holy Writ states that God is our Alpha and Omega, our beginning and our end. To say that God is the source of everything is to say that, like the monad, he is the source of all numbers, which is precisely what Cassiodorus says in his comments on Psalm 1. The Psalms issue out of Christ our head and return to him as the sequence ends. Within this overall structure, though, are groups of psalms that form substructures, and individual psalms may have their own structures, like Psalm 119 (Vulg. 118) with its 22 groups of 8 verses. No other commentary on the Psalms pays more attention to textual structures, and no other commentary is equally full and systematic, hence its unusual importance in the Middle Ages and the Renaissance. Cassiodorus therefore is the best single source for the exegetical tradition which is my concern.

It has been said of the celebrated preacher John Smith (1560–1591) that his sermons were written so that his language and his narrative structure enact what the words say: "A sermon by Smith offers its auditors an imitative experience of God's Providential plan for life". "Often, in fact, the importance of an event in Scripture or in life resided, for Smith, in its narrative placement". Smith could end a sermon where he began in order to "imitate the right Christian life of endings that answer beginnings". Smith's "vision of life as a divinely planned poem which the preacher could imitate in his own words"[22] must owe a great deal to exegesis of the kind offered by Cassiodorus and those who followed in his footsteps, like Giorgio and Pietro Bongo.

Beginning, then, with the preface to the *Expositio Psalmorum*, we learn that Cassiodorus divided it into 17 sections because of the sweetness of this number. Equally sweet is the division of the Psalms into 12 groups according to the contents. Divided in this way, the Psalter agrees wonderfully with the number of the 12 Apostles. The sum total of Psalms refers to our redemption from the Flood, which covered the sinful earth for 150 days; the fact that we find the same number in the Psalms proves that they save mankind from its sins. The preface also explains that the same word or thing may be construed *in bono* or *in malo*, and that this teaches us to perceive logical discriminations.

The observation that the 150 psalms should be associated with the Flood occurs also in the comments on Psalm 150 (pp. 1329–32); another observation concerning the *decorus et mirabilis ordo psalmorum* is that their division into 7 and 8 decades proves that they are a summary of both Testaments. Christ's resurrection the eighth day takes us from the 7 of Time to the 8 of Eternity, and, just as the Flood purified the earth from sin in 150 days, so shall we be purified by the 150 psalms. A physical purification, then, is balanced by one that is spiritual, and the parallel makes us aware of the important distinction. Just as the Ark had its dimensions, so do the Psalms. Both must be properly arranged, since the great Creator and Workman of all things made everything in number, weight, and measure. All this is found in the *Conclusio psalmorum*, while the "Expositio" of Psalm 150 explains more at length what this entails. It entails, above all, seeing the Psalms as proceeding from Christ our head as numbers do from the monad, while a return to the beginning is achieved in the last psalm or *carmen*. This *carmen* must have no textual divisions because it returns us to the state of concord and unity enjoyed by all the saints, and because it joins the end of the sequence *ad uirtutem inseparabilis Trinitatis*. Cassiodorus is clearly referring to the subject of the last few psalms when he writes that unity is present in the spiritual marriage union so sweetly sung in the heavenly Jerusalem; the Psalms terminate on a note of sweet grace that somehow looks back to the beginning. Thus the first psalm and the last contain the same syllogism: all spirits praise the Lord; he whom all spirits praise, must be the true God; the Lord therefore is true God (pp. 1326–29). It is right that the end should connect with the beginning (*Decet enim finem respondere principio suo*), because Holy Writ should display harmony (*omnia conuenientia*).

On turning to the commentary on Psalm 1, we read that Christ has been placed at the beginning, since the tree at 1:3 is the Tree of Life, the Cross of our Saviour, from which issue streams of spiritual water (see *John* 4:10). This particular psalm has no heading or title (*titulum*) because nothing must precede him who is the beginning of all things (*princeps omnium rerum*). Because he is unity, simple and perfect and always remaining within himself, the Lord Christ is placed at the beginning of numbers; from this source the multitude of numbers proceed in such a way that they may achieve a return. The Greeks call this unity the monad. Numbers, therefore, must be studied: the Fathers of the Church have said so, and we read in Solomon that God made everything in number, weight, and measure (pp. 27 f., 33 f., and 38 f.). A connection between the beginning and the end is found also in individual psalms where the first verse is repeated at the end (see Psalms 8 and 117); these psalms are defined as circular, and the circular form is said to reflect the nature of God who says of himself that he is Alpha and Omega, the beginning and the end (p. 94).

In Psalms 132 and 150 the absence of division expresses unity, while the division of Psalm 31 into 10 verses is a reference to the Decalogue. The Decalogue is found also in Psalm 14, but in this case it is the content which refers to it. The 10 of the Law represents the 10 chords of the spiritual psaltery, the true *numerus coronalis* won only by him who triumphs over the vices of the world and their author. We see, then, how the tradition of the Roman triumph is transferred to Holy Writ and made subordinate to biblical precedent.

In the commentary on Psalms 1–26, the concluding remarks

(headed "Conclusio psalmi") invariably consider the relationship between the contents of a given psalm and the symbolism of its ordinal number. After Psalm 26 Cassiodorus exhorts the reader to carry on for himself, bearing in mind that the meaning may arise from the number itself or from the parts that compose it (by addition or multiplication). Because God created everything in number, weight, and measure we must believe that he arranged the Psalms in such an order that their "virtue" is declared by their number (p. 242). Pietro Bongo echoes this view when he states that care was taken to make the *gesta* agree with the meaning of the number (*mysteriis numerorum gesta convenire curarunt*; p. 66).

This general principle can be illustrated by citing comments on individual psalms and on groups of psalms. In the first three psalms, a true order has been established: Christ the Lord is described in moral terms in Psalm 1, in Psalm 2 he is seen in his double capacity as human and divine, and in Psalm 3 as resurrected (p. 55). The ordinal number of Psalm 2 consists of two monads, so that it shows how the dual nature of Christ is fused into one (p. 50), while Psalm 3 has been placed in the third position because the ordinal number relates to the Trinity and to the resurrection on the third day. The Pythagorean *quaternarius* is adduced in the comment on Psalm 4. The Pythagoreans praised this number so highly that they considered it sacred, and the number teaches us that the power of the gospels will prevail in the world. The 4 parts of the world will believe in the salvation of the Lord, and the Church will make the whole world *one* (p. 62).

The quest for balanced patterns is shown in the comments on Psalm 6. This is the first Penitential Psalm, and since 6 is a perfect number it is appropriate that this psalm teaches perfect penitence. The number 6 relates to the creation of man on the sixth day, to the incarnation in the sixth age, and to the crucifixion on the sixth day. This balanced pattern depends on the number 6. In the case of Psalm 8, the balance is established by the *ogdoad*, which contains *magnarum rerum sacramenta*: 8 souls entered the Ark of Noah, David was the eighth after Jesse, the circumcision on the eighth day purified the Hebrews, and on the eighth day Christ rose from the dead. To this biblical number symbolism Cassiodorus adds classical ideas: the mathematicians call this number the first cube (2^3), and Pythagoras called it *harmoniam geometricam* because in it are contained all the ratios that produce harmony (i.e. the octave or diapason contains these consonances; pp 94–96). The number 8 as prefixed to Psalm 11 in its heading (*pro octaua*) is taken to refer to our eternal rest (symbolized by the eighth day of the resurrection). Since the world lives within an ever-repeated cycle of seven-day weeks, it cannot attain to this rest, but the prophet prays that the iniquity of this world may be destroyed so that we may in the end arrive at the truth of the future which is promised – and this is the reign which remains imperturbable. This imperturbability is reflected in the number 8 by virtue of the fact that it is the cube of 2, and cubes signify stability.[23]

The principle of the relevance of the ordinal number is extended to a single verse when Cassiodorus remarks that the ninth verse of Psalm 11 (*in circuitu impii ambulant...*) shows how evil men always persue devious paths (*tortuosae viae*) and leave the true road; hence they cannot arrive at the peace of the eighth day, but always keep revolving back again to themselves. The idea of circular return, therefore, is taken *in malo*. The number 9, then, is evil in so far as it goes beyond the number 8 of eternal rest, just as 11 is evil in so far as it goes beyond the just number 10. The number 9 is equally seen as evil in the comment on Psalm 9, which is the first to prophesy the coming of the Antichrist. And the symbolism present in this number is shown also when Cassiodorus remarks that Christ gave up his ghost in the ninth hour (p. 112).

Psalm 10 justly carries the number of the Decalogue because it explains the punishment suffered by heretics and their future pain; however, this number also confirms us in the true faith. Thus the good servant who had been given 10 talents was praised by his master and put in charge of 10 cities, and the Apostles wrote to 10 churches, which signifies the plenitude of sacred doctrine contained in these letters. In other words, at this point the Pythagorean symbolism takes over from the purely biblical symbolism.

Cassiodorus' comment on Psalm 11 touches on rhetoric when he connects the speech of vain men, concerned solely with the phrasing of what they say, with the evil represented by the number 11 (because it transgresses the just number 10). Such men fail to grasp the living truth and instead embrace the lie that leads to death. This psalm, though, conveys the speech of the Lord, and these words liberate men. And Cassiodorus takes 11 *in bono* when he explains that it signifies those who came to the vineyard of the Lord in the 11th hour; this should remind us of the fact that we gain salvation through grace, and not through works. Finally, 11 may signify penitence according to Prosper, who interpreted the 11 curtains in the Tabernacle as a symbol of penitence (pp. 117–22).

The contents show that the ordinal number of Psalm 12 signifies the Law (10) and Christ's charity (the 2 laws). The Hebrew tribes were divided according to this number, and 12 seats are reserved for the judges on Judgment Day. Finally we are reminded that the year is divided into 12 months. Cassiodorus clearly is pleased with these allusions, regardless of the fact that the Apostles, the tribes, and the months are irrelevant to the contents; these associations enhance his enjoyment of this particular psalm. Cassiodorus never hesitates to go beyond the contents in his quest for what might be called enhancing ideas. The meanings derived from the structural placing apparently add to the contents quite legitimately.

Psalm 13 introduces the Church as speaking, and 13 is the number of the Church because it contains the "mystery" of the 5 books of Moses to which must be added the 8 of the resurrection. Then, too, Christ was shown to the world on the 13th day after his birth.

The 5 psalms that have the superscription *oratio* (16, 85, 89, 101, and 141) provoke comments on rhetoric. In these psalms, so it is argued, spiritual things are drawn to our attention by physical similitudes; true *oratio*, though, seeks what is divine and not earthly, since God is the Word. We cannot understand God, since a creature cannot understand its creator, but God is nevertheless the source of all true *oratio*. There is always something like divinity, therefore, in all good *orationes* (pp. 1268 and 1272 f.).

The 22 letters of the Hebrew alphabet express wisdom, so that this is the meaning given to the ordinal number of Psalm 22 (p. 214). The alphabetical composition of Psalms 110, 111 and 118 (Vulgate) indicates praise of the Lord in songs of perfect devotion. Psalms written alphabetically, but with some of the letters missing (as in Psalms 24, 33, 36, and 144), fail to reach perfection.

An "allegory added to the poem" is conspicuous in the comments on Psalm 25 (Vulgate), which admonishes us to flee the company of the wicked and remain faithful to the Lord. Since there were 5 gates leading into the Temple, and since 25 is 5^2, this number tells us that we should purify the body with its 5 "doors" or senses with the water placed within each gate (p. 234).

The division of Psalm 31 into 10 verses makes Cassiodorus think of the Decalogue; in these verses prayer is offered for the forgiveness of sins, and the number of the Decalogue makes us conscious of them and so makes us feel the repentance that leads to forgiveness and rejoicing (pp. 282 f.). Psalm 31 is one of the 7 Penitential Psalms (6, 31, 37, 50, 101, 129, and 142), and there must be 7 to offset those 7 days of the week when we commit our sins. They begin in affliction, but lead to joy; to those intangled in sin they open up the road to salvation, and hence they are *oratori sanctissimi*, instilling hope founded on the promise of the joys of the Lord (p. 1280). Psalm 50, placed at the centre, issues sweetly from the fountain of bitter grief. It is rightly placed in the 50th position, since 50 represents the year of Jubilee (*Lev.* 25:8–17) when all debts were remitted. If we speak this psalm with a pure heart, the remission will apply to us as well. However, the ordinal number relates also to Pentecost and to the coming of the Holy Ghost, an event that signifies remission of sins by annulling the confusion of tongues.

The transition from one number to the next is significant. Thus Psalm 51 is placed after Psalm 50 because it speaks of the Antichrist, the son of iniquity who transgresses the *terminum remissionis* (p. 477). Even more important is the transition from the first 70 to the last 80 psalms, or from 7 to 8; this transition entails a turning away from the world of time to eternity. Similarly the transition from verse 11 to verse 12 in Psalm 90 juxtaposes Satan (verse 11) and Christ (verse 12) during the temptation in the wilderness. Hence those who are committed to this world alone avoid this psalm, which reveals the presumption of Satan and the victory of God. Since 90 is $3 \times 3 \times 10$, it shows how the devil may be overcome by a return to the indivisible, omnipotent Trinity. I take it that it is the number 10 that signifies return, since in it all numbers return to their beginning.

A purely textual structure is made to bear on an event in the life of Christ when Cassiodorus argues that the 5 psalms which predict the coming of the Lord convey the same message as the 5 loaves of bread that fed the multitude – and the message is that Christ is the true bread of life (p. 1058).

Psalm 118 (Vulgate) is a very special case, since it resembles a stanzaic poem by virtue of its 22 groups of 8 lines or verses. It is a special case also because it provided the structural pattern for Nativity hymns, as some exegetes explain. It is of course the meaning attributed to this pattern which made it appropriate for the celebration of the birth of Christ, and Cassiodorus' comment has as its point of departure the fact that this is the third psalm to make use of the whole alphabet and this group of 3 psalms therefore makes known to us the Trinity of perfect faith. In the same way, the 4 psalms that have an incomplete alphabet (24, 33, 36, and 144) agree with the 4 corners of the world and so express the universal character of the Church. As yet they are incomplete, but they are destined to become perfect. The division of Psalm 118 into groups of 8 lines or verses beginning with the same letter signifies the circumcision of the heart (circumcision took place on the eighth day). Also it expresses perfect justice – a classical idea based on the observation that 8 and its multiples divide into equal parts until we reach unity (1+1). This makes Cassiodorus conclude that the chorus of the just speaks throughout the psalm, which means that they speak throughout all of time – all of time being expressed by the structural number 22 by virtue of the fact that it is the sum of the 10 of the Law and the 12 of the Apostles and the New Testament. The just are taken from the beginning of time to its end, but, in order to underline the unity of the Church, only one person is introduced as speaking. Seen in its totality the psalm is a celestial paradise abounding with spiritual apples; its sentences are as many stars – *stellas clarissimas* – shining in highest heaven. The circumstance that Psalm 118 is followed by the 15 Gradual Psalms or Psalms of Ascent reveals that what it proclaims will take place at the end of time when we shall ascend to the heavenly Jerusalem. The meaning of the ordinal number appears from its constituent parts, 100 and 18. The number 100 represents the Ark, which required 100 years to be built, and the Ark is the type of the Church. The number 18 equals the numerical values of the Greek letters *iota* and *eta*, which proves that it contains the names of all the saints and their eternal crown. Cassiodorus fails to explain the basis for this conclusion. Finally it can be added that the fact that all the letters of the alphabet have been used means that the whole psalm becomes circular.

The 15 Psalms of Ascent (Vulg. 119–133) form the most important group of psalms. Just as the 150 psalms summarize both Testaments, the 15 Psalms of Ascent summarize the Psalter: the division into 70+80 is mirrored in the division into 7+8, where 7 represents time (the Old Testament) and 8 eternity (the New Testament) (p. 1171). The centrally placed eighth psalm (Psalm 126) shows us Christ as the cornerstone which always remains stable. The reference here is to 8 as 2^3, and cubes always signify stability. The last 8 psalms supposedly are concerned with the resurrection, and the resurrection of course occurred on the eighth day in Holy Week. Examples of simple numerical decorum abound: the fifth Psalm of Ascent (123) is concerned with the overcoming of the life of the 5 senses; the sixth (124) tells us that he who places his trust in God cannot be moved – he possesses the perfection represented by the number 6; in the ninth (127) the number 9 by means of its *trina triplicatione* (compare Spenser's "trinall triplicities") shows forth magnificence. The 10th (128) leaves what is earthly and draws close to the mansions of glory, as shown in the parable of the Lord who gave rich payment to those who entered his vineyard in the 10th hour. The 11th (129) takes 11 *in bono* as well as *in malo*: we cannot escape from or avoid sin, so that no one can be saved except through grace, but the psalm also presents true penitence. The 12th (130) juxtaposes condemnation of pride (Satan) and praise of humility (Christ), and the number 12 relates to salvation through the 12 of the tribes and of the Apostles. The 13th (131) shows us Christ as the head of the Apostles, as is just (*dignum*), since Christ is *tanquam caput omnium*. The subject of the 14th Psalm of Ascent is the unity of the blessed; they are united in one harmony of love (*caritatis conuenientia*) and for this reason the text can have no divisions. Unity properly precedes the advent to the summit in the last Psalm of Ascent (pp. 1206 and 1209). This last psalm is the third on the love of God, and in this number we recognize the sacred Trinity. The division into 3 verses equally reflects the Trinity, and the plural form of the verb used in verses 1–2 and the singular form used in verse 3 enact a movement from many to one.

Christ, then, is in the midst of the Psalms of Ascent, while in the 15th we are taken to the heavenly Jerusalem where we receive the benediction of the Lord. "Allegory" is added when 15, seen as 3×5, tells us that when the Trinity is applied to the frailty of man's flesh (his 5 senses) we shall be given the final and lasting victory (pp. 1210 and 1212 f.). When Cassiodorus praises the Gradual Psalms, he praises their construction: *gradualium pulcherrimam constructionem*. This divinely inspired poetic sequence reveals its source especially in the many formal details; the presence or absence of divisions convey their message, and so do grammatical tenses, ordinal numbers, the sum total of psalms of a certain kind and their ordinal numbers. Classical number symbolism is freely adduced so that the 8 which signifies eternity derives this meaning not only from the resurrection but also from the fact that it has the stability typical of cubes. There is no conflict between the 4 of the gospels and the 4 of the Pythagorean formula for harmony; the ratios that create harmony are very much in Cassiodorus' thought, most explicitly, perhaps, in his comments on Psalm 1. Christ is the *beatus vir* and the tree described in this psalm, and Christ must be placed at the beginning of the sequence as the fountain whence issue all the psalms like all created things, and they issue in such an order that they may achieve a *return*. The Platonic *lambda* formula is one expression of this order that ensures a return, and 8 expresses the same idea, since in the octave the last note returns to the first (but in a higher key). It is possible and even likely that, when Milton placed his "Ode on the Morning of Christ's Nativity" first in his *Poems* (1645), he too wanted to place Christ first as the true source of his inspiration. *Return* is a key idea in Augustine's *Confessions* as well as in Milton's *Paradise Lost*; the number 10 signifies return (in it all numbers return to the beginning), just as in the octave the last note returns to the first. When Milton based his epic on the number 10, therefore, he chose a structure that expresses the return to God on which all Christians base their hope. Hence his epic exists within a field of tension created by the antithesis between the theme as stated in the title and the harmony expressed by the textual structure. Music therefore permeates not only religion itself as Cassiodorus puts it (*Institutiones* II.v.2–3), but also the epic which celebrates God's ways with man.

What Cassiodorus refers to as the "decorous and wonderful order of the Psalms" (*Explicitus est decorus et mirabilis ordo psalmorum*; p. 1329) became something of an exegetical commonplace; the medieval German bishop Haymo reproduced many of Cassiodorus' structural comments in his treatise *Pia, brevis ac dilucida in omnes Psalmos explanatio* (Freiburg, 1533). As he puts it, the 15 Gradual Psalms represent the virtues by means of which we ascend to the heavenly Jerusalem, and Solomon similarly built 15 steps to the Temple, and these steps prefigure our ascent *ad supernam ciuitatem, quam propheta demonstrat in istis quindecim Psalmis*. And *by means of this number* David and Solomon prophesy that the Old Testament will be fulfilled in the New, since 15 is the sum of 7 and 8, and 7 is of course the number of Time and of the Old Testament, and 8 of Eternity and of the New Testament. The structure conveys yet another important truth in that it tells us that the Law cannot give us the eighth "day" of Eternity with its perfect rest; Christ alone can provide *requiem veram* after we have finished with the 7 days around which the entire world revolves.[24] Such was the strength of the tradition connected with the Psalms of Ascent that it prompted the form as well as the contents of Cardinal Bellarmine's treatise on the ascent to God, a treatise translated into English in 1616 with the title *A Most Learned And Pious Treatise ... framing a Ladder, Wherby Our Mindes May Ascend to God, by the Stepps of his Creatures* (Douay, 1616). Bellarmine divided his book into 15 parts "in resemblance of the fifteene stepps by the which they went vp into the Temple of *Solomon*, and of the fifteene Psalmes which are called Gradualles". A second version was published in London in 1638 entitled *Iacob's Ladder Consisting of fifteene Degrees or*

Ascents to the knowledge of God by Consideration of His Creatures and Attributes, a title which alludes to *Romans* 1:20. The idea of ascent to God, therefore, need not necessarily call for a Neoplatonic context; the Psalms of Ascent will do, and Paul's exhortation to seek God by studying the *res creatae*. As Chapter I made clear, this entails studying their unifying structures.

Psalm 119 (Vulg. 118) proved equally important; its alphabetical structure was interpreted as a literary version of the act of creation through the divine Word. Because the use of the alphabet suggested fullness or completeness, the psalm was taken to present all that was required for the achievement of eternal life. In the early seventeenth century the Jesuit Lorinus summarized patristic interpretations in his *Commentarium In Librum Psalmorum* (Lugduni, 1611–1613). Hilarius stressed the idea of fullness: the psalm contains *omnia viuendi, credendi, & placendi Deo præcepta*, and for this reason Ambrose called this psalm *paradisum pomorum & apothecam Spiritus sancti*. And Lorinus adds that Cassiodorus followed Augustine in admiring this psalm whose perfection was revealed when Augustine saw its structure as that of the tree in the midst of the Garden: *sub similitudine arboris, quæ in medio paradisi erat, Augustino hunc psalmum reuelatum fuisse*. Lorinus refers to Bonaventura, too, but let me quote directly from the *Collationes in Hexaemeron* XVII.12, where Christ is identified both with the tree in Psalm 1 and with the structure of Psalm 119 (118). In the one the tree is described in the contents, while it is found in the textual structure of the other. Bonaventura connects the two on the strength of Augustine's vision of Psalm 119 (118) as a tree with 22 branches each of which had 8 twigs from which issued *guttae dulcissimae*. But the connection is made also on the strength of verbal parallels: Psalm 119 (118) begins *Beati immaculati in via*, and Psalm 1 similarly praises the happiness of the man who absents himself from the wicked – he shall be like a tree (*Beatus vir qui non abiit in consilio impiorum ... Et erit tanquam lignum ...*). We see how interchangeable verbal and structural images are.

This attitude to the text of the Bible presupposes its absolute correctness in every detail, which is the point made by Milton's grammar school teacher, Alexander Gill, in *The Sacred Philosophie Of the Holy Scriptures* (1635). Chapter 34 describes the faithfulness with which the Jews preserved their sacred writings: "with infinite paines and care" they "wall'd in that holy ground, lest beasts should breake into it"; every word, syllable, and letter was reverenced and even counted, and "what verse, what word, syllable, and letter was in the midst of every booke". The tradition of observing the central point in a text therefore must be of considerable antiquity, and the attention given even to individual letters may possibly be the point of departure for the acrostic squares of a Fortunatus and a Hrabanus Maurus as shown below.

The alphabetical composition of Psalm 119 (118) was praised by no less a person than Baptista Spagnuolus Mantuanus (*In omnes Davidicos Psalmos ... commentaria*, 1585), who calls it a *lusum poeticum*, but not a vain one, *sed admirabili obtectum mysterio, ut fere omnia sunt prophetica*. In other words, the purpose of the arrangement is to make everything prophetic, including the formal elements. Francesco Giorgio (*Problemata*, 1536 and 1574) queries the reason for the alphabetical composition sometimes encountered in the Bible (see his Question III.i.26): Aristotle was familiar with it, and the technique prevailed in Latin Nativity hymns, but can it be taken to have a meaning? As one would expect, the answer is in the affirmative, and Cassiodorus may be the source for Giorgio's statement that the alphabetical composition suggests that God is the fountain whence issue all creatures and everything that is good in an ordered sequence, and the letters serve as a key to this divine influx, which penetrates all who listen to the hymn. Giorgio's preface to his *Problemata* – a collection of theological questions and answers – is in part an essay on the art of numerical composition, his argument being that the Holy Ghost, in whom are all numbers, composed the holy books in such an exact manner that those whose minds cling to lower things cannot comprehend it. The absolute authority of the text, therefore, is a *datum*. The original harmony of the world was lost through the Fall, but out of the Fall and the scheme of redemption God created a new consonance, which David well knew and rendered in his music by the power of God. The sub-text here may be *Job* 38, which associates the act of creation with music through the cosmic image of the morning stars singing together and the sons of God shouting for joy. In his own gloss on this passage Thomas Aquinas refers the reader to the Pythagorean theory of the music of the spheres, and he connects this music also with the ninefold angelic hierarchies as expounded by Dionysius the Areopagite. And if we consult his gloss on *Job* 40 we see that he too, like Philo Judæus and St Augustine, associates the week of creation with an ordered numerical sequence; the days represent a sequence and not *temporis successionem*.[25]

Numbers would scarcely have played such a major role in the exposition of the Psalms unless they had been considered of importance to the Bible as a whole. Thus Bede quotes Isidore's view (shared by Augustine) that the *ratio numerorum* illuminates the mystery contained in many parts of the Scriptures, the proof passage being his quotation of *Wisdom* 11:21. Thus the week of creation gives us an ordered progression from 1 to 7, and Bede proceeds to compare it to Plato's account of creation as rendered by Boethius. If we exclude the monad, Plato's *lambda* formula posits 6 steps: out of the creative monad issue matter ($= 2$) and form ($= 3$), and these numbers are then squared and cubed to form a three-dimensional world. And so Bede concludes that the art of numbers is the art of philosophy, and that philosophy is the knowledge of things divine and human.[26]

The circumstance that there are 10 laws and 4 gospels caused many exegetes to seek an explanation in Pythagorean number lore. Cornelius à Lapide (*Commentarii in IV. Evangelia*, 1638) quotes Gregory the Great to the effect that there had to be 4 gospels in order to create a firm structure, since the *Quaternarius* is *numerus solidus et quadratus*, so that it aptly signifies *Evangeliorum solidiatem et perfectionem*. However, even more relevant is the point that the *quaternarius* is the *causa, basis, et fons* of the number 10, which represents everything which is perfect. The 4 rivers of Paradise are a familiar type or prophecy of the Gospels, and the same typological import was attributed to the fourfold alphabet found in *Lamentations*. This book consists of 5 chapters, and chapters 1–4 have an alphabetical composition, like Psalm 119 (118). Because the contents were interpreted as a prophecy of the Passion, the structural numbers 4 and 22 were interpreted accordingly. The 4 alphabetical chapters tell us that Jeremiah's lamentation is for the sins of the whole world, since the world is governed by the number 4 (seasons, humours, and so on). Among those who explain the meaning invested in the form are Cornelius à Lapide and Gasparius Sanctius;[27] both observe that the alphabetical technique is not found in chapter 5, although the number of verses remains the same (22). They fail to remark that the structure is symmetrical, the pattern being one of 22, 22, 66, 22 and 22 verses, but the fact is sufficiently obvious.

A symmetrical division into 5 parts is found also in *Canticles*. Milton remarks in *The Reason of Church-Government* that Origen "rightly judges" that the Scriptures contain a pastoral drama in *The Song of Solomon* or *Canticles*. Cornelius à Lapide (*Commentarii in Canticum Canticorum*, 1637) refers not only to Origen but to St Gregory and others who characterized *Canticles* as a *drama spon-*

sale, sive nuptiale carmen, written as an allegory *stylo comico et bucolico, quem post Salomonem secutus est Theocritus in Idylliis et Virgilius in Bucolicis.* After summarizing various ways of dividing the poem, Cornelius à Lapide decides in favour of 5 acts, each of which describes the progress of the Church from infancy and adolescence to maturity in the third act (*quasi virilem aetatem*); the fourth presents its sad decline (*senectutem*) after Constantine through luxury, ambition, schism, and heresy caused by the pride and avarice of prelates. The fifth and last act, though, shows the renovation and reformation of the Church *ad felicitatem et gloriam aeternam.*[28]

Again we find central accent, since Act III shows the perfect state of the Church, and it is not difficult to find exegetical comments which place Christ *in medio*. Cornelius à Lapide's prefatory remarks on the gospels[29] compare Christ and the Apostles to the sun in the midst of the planets in a manner that recalls Pico's comments, in the *Heptaplus*, on the fourth day of creation. Even more decisive, however, is the common gloss on Ezekiel's vision of the chariot (Ezek. 1 and 10), where the man seated in the midst is Christ. Pico, who connected David's inspiration with that of Moses and both with Plato and Pythagoras, presents "the mystic pageant of Ezekiel" as an example showing how all these (and Christ too) conveyed their doctrine by means of myth, allegory, and mathematical images.[30] Many exegetes consider this vision as a mathematical image. Gregory the Great explains that it shows Christ seated in the middle, so that it anticipates and confirms the vision of St John of the Son of Man placed in the middle of the 7 candlesticks (*Rev.* 1:12–13). The chariot symbolizes the created universe, like the 7 candlesticks, so that both visions reveal the supreme truth that Christ is always in the middle. That the chariot has 4 wheels within wheels proves that the New Testament is contained in the Old, through types, while the 4 winged creatures are a prophecy of the 4 evangelists.[31]

Ezekiel's vision, then, as presented in the splendid frontispiece of Antonius Fernandius' *Commentarii in Visiones Veteris Testamenti* (Lugduni, 1617), shows Christ seated in a triumphal chariot representing all of space and time.[32] The drawing shows the main body of the chariot as a globe studded with stars, and on its top Christ is shown seated and at rest on a throne placed in the middle. The various authoritative interpretations summarized by Fernandius agree that the vision shows Christ triumphant over evil and as ruler of Heaven and Earth. The many occurrences of the number 4 (4 wheels within wheels, 4 winged creatures and 4 faces possessed by each) explain why the vision is connected both with the created universe and with the scheme of redemption. There are 4 winds, 4 seasons, and 4 elements, and since 4 also relates to the 4 corners of the world, this shows that the 4 gospels will be taken to these 4 corners. But the number 4 shows above all that it is Christ the Creator and Redeemer who creates *concentus* and *concordia* through the imposition of this number at all levels of existence, physical and spiritual. This argument is, of course, a clear reference to the Pythagorean formula for harmony. Subsequent comments present Christ as Justice combined with Mercy, and the fact that Christ is seated shows that he alone is at rest. As St Bernard had put it, *tranquillus Deus tranquillat omnia*. For Milton scholars, an even more important gloss concerns the angelic shapes; the gloss, taken from Jerome's commentary on *Job* 25, states that by their free will all the angels turn to God in love and are made as it were immobile because they persist in the truth. Their faces are always turned toward God in contemplation of him, and their fourfold shape (each has 4 faces and 4 wings) makes them a fit symbol of constancy: *forma vero quadrata immobilitatis, et constantiae symbolum est*. Gasparius Sanctius, who published a commentary on *Ezekiel* in 1619, scorns the idea that Pythagoras should have any kind of connection with Ezekiel: they were *not* the same person, nor did the soul of the pagan transmigrate into the body of the prophet. The denial shows that such suggestions must have been made. Sanctius nevertheless goes on to explain the vision in Pythagorean terms: the 4 wheels teach us that nature is made of groups of 4, and it is through this number that unity is imposed upon multitude. Both Fernandius and Sanctius interpret Ezekiel's vision as a revelation of the way in which all creation achieves union with God through *obedience*. Several marginal glosses in Sanctius state that the chariot is a type of obedience, and Fernandius explains that the chariot represents *concordia creaturarum obedientia erga Deum* and the exclusion of all contradiction. And he adds that the vision is a prophecy of the incarnation and hence of the defeat of all evil spirits. The relevance of all this to Milton's *Paradise Lost* will be shown in Chapter IX.

Further exegetical precedents for Christocentric structures are not hard to find; indeed, the argument that *Christus medium tenet* is all-pervasive. The theologian Sardo, writing in 1614, drew up a long list of examples showing Christ in the middle. Thus Christ is the central figure in the Trinity, and Christ was born in the middle of the night in the middle of Palestine, which in its turn is the centre of the world – Jerusalem being the *umbilicus terrae*. Furthermore, Christ was presented in the Temple *in medio doctorum* and crucified in the middle hanging between Earth and Heaven, all of which leads to the conclusion that Christ is *utriusque Testamenti centrum*.[33] In his *Problemata*, Francesco Giorgio pursues the same line of reasoning when he aligns the centre of the heavenly Jerusalem with the centre of the Earth, so that a plumbline dropped from the middle of the heavenly city (where stands the Tree of Life) would hit the roof of the Temple right above the Mercy Seat.[34]

Christ is both centre and circle, his circular nature being defined in *Revelation* 1:8, 1:13, 21:6 and 22:13, where God is said to be Alpha and Omega, the beginning and the end. Relevant comments are found in St Gregory and in Richard St Victor on the Apocalypse,[35] and also in the *De Arcanis Sacræ* (Rome, 1614) by Sardo.[36] When Christ became man he did so in order to complete the circle connecting man and God; the name of God is itself circular in that the three letters composing the name of God (Iod, He and Vau) represent circular numbers; *Et sic Deus est veluti sphæra*.[37] In his capacity as Creator and sustainer of all life, Christ is appropriately viewed as a circle, and, when considered as that toward which all creatures tend, he is the centre. *Apud Mathematicos, centrum est punctum sphæræ, aut orbis medium*; our souls are drawn to this centre, as Augustine writes, and a marginal gloss proclaims that sinners rest in the bosom of Christ *tanquam lineæ in suo centro* (p. 391).

The decided preference, among Renaissance poets, for symmetries created by linkage between parts must owe a great deal to the ingrained habit of tracing such links through redemption history. Its harmony is a matter of *concentus ex dissonis*, to quote from Marcus Vigerius, *Rhetorica Divina* (Nuremberg, 1517) – a work divided into 10 parts forming a *decachord* in imitation of David's 10-stringed instrument, as the author explains in his preface. The division also refers to the 10 days of redemption, beginning with the Annunciation and the Nativity and concluding with the Ascension and Pentecost; on this decachord of 10 days Christ played the new "song", creating out of the disparate voices of the parts *unum concentum*. The English theologian Thomas Becon (*Works*, 1564) found this way of thinking sufficiently appealing to divide one of his own treatises into 10 "chords". The point to remember is that the Fall is not merely annulled by the scheme of redemption, but out of the two is created a musical harmony. Balanced antitheses are traced everywhere. The Fall must have occurred at high noon since this was the hour of the crucifixion. A tree must satisfy the sin committed by means of a tree, and whence death came, life should also come.[38] Marcus Vigerius foregrounds the number 40: the "mystery" of 40 was introduced with the Fall, and Christ spent 40 days in the desert and 40 hours in the grave to annul the 40 days of the Deluge and the 40 years in the wilderness (see "Chorda Octava"). Alexander Ross, *The First Booke Of Questions and Answers upon Genesis* (1620), states that Adam fell the eighth day after his creation so that the Fall was annulled by the resurrection on the eighth day.[39] Cornelius à Lapide as usual summarizes received opinions in his *Commentaria in Pentateuchum Mosis* (1616); thus he refers to Pererius, who believed that 8 days passed between Adam's creation and his Fall, while others argue in favour of 40 days, and others again in favour of 34 since Christ died in his 34th year *et peccatum hoc expiavit* (p. 54). These antithetically poised chronologies were invested with a symbolism derived from the numbers constituting the pattern, and the most common observation is that man was both created and redeemed on the sixth day for reasons connected with the symbolism invested in the number 6.

We see, then, how balanced patterns are created by means of numbers taken to be symbolic, and that the patterns are taken to create harmony from dissonance. The many parallels-cum-contrast between the acts of Satan and those of Christ in *Paradise Lost* reveal a similar way of thinking. If the Creator spends 7 days creating the universe, Satan must undo what has been created by encircling the earth in a web of darkness for 7 24-hour periods. Within the 10-book structure of the first edition these events are perfectly balanced, one being narrated at the end of book 3 and the other at the beginning of book 8. After Satan's "week of uncreation" follows the eighth day of the Fall narrated in book 8, while book 3 tells the story of the Son's acceptance of death and resurrection on the eighth day. The harmonizing power that resolves the dissonance is presented dramatically in the ascent of the Son into the chariot of paternal Deity in the passage located at the mathematical centre by line-count. Spenser, too, balances the Fall against the scheme of salvation in *The Faerie Queene* I. The Fall is represented by Fradubio's metamorphosis into a tree in canto ii, while the redemptive act occurs in canto xi during the battle with the dragon when the balm trickling from the Tree of Life annuls the effect of the Fall. In Tasso's *Gerusalemme Liberata*, the centre-piece is not the ascent of the Son, as in *Paradise Lost*, but the elevation of the host during the celebration of Mass on Mount Olivet (see Chapter V). The expulsion of the Satanic forces occurs with balanced precision in Books IX and XII (the epic contains 20 books).

It is an interesting point that Aristotle's formula for virtue as a mean between extremes was represented as a circle with a centre. As Bongo explains in his chapter on the number 3, the Pythagoreans call this number Justice because it shows how the central unit (the mean) keeps the other two in place, thus curbing the tendency to defect and excess. The mean, then, is a dynamic and not a static state. Bongo adds that all odd numbers have such a mid-point or mean within themselves as a unifying nexus so that they may be envisaged as a circle, and, because the centre in this way mediates between the extremes, the number 3 represents the beginning of all order.[40] In Renaissance epics the textual centre is just such a unifying nexus which reaches out to encompass the whole from beginning to end in a closely knit thematic and formal web. The technique of linking parts equidistant from the centre magnifies the dignity of the centre and presents it as the source of the poem's unity. Spenser's canto on events in the Castle of Medina (*Faerie Queene* II.ii) dramatizes the idea of the dynamic centre which keeps the extremes at bay and compels them to move toward the centre, and the textual structure embodies the idea through its division into a sequence of 30 – 1 – 15 stanzas (see Chapter VI).

The linkage between parts equidistant from the centre also reflects the long-standing tradition of tracing balanced typological patterns through the two Testaments; what linkage can be more important than between type and antitype? Here is a *concentus* without dissonance – a consent where the parallel is more marked than the difference. True, typological exegesis pursues a binary pattern, but the feeling that Christ must always be *in medio* was so all-powerful that it changed the one-to-one pattern into a pattern of odd numbers with Christ as unifying centre. Typological sequences are featured in books like the *Biblia Pauperum* and the *Speculum Humanae Salvationis*, but there are veritable "picture books" in the mosaics of Byzantine churches and in the stained glass of the great medieval cathedrals. The appeal of such sequences was so great that more and more types were invented, and in the late Middle Ages the collection entitled *Pictor in Carmine* lists in all 508 types. This book (which presents verbal descriptions only, not pictures) became current in England, and M. R. James believes that its author may have been English.[41] At the same time that the number of types increased, their character became increasingly literary: a certain theme was read into the particular scene depicted. Thus Moses listening to the advice of his Gentile father-in-law was interpreted as foreshadowing the humility of Christ.

The *Biblia Pauperum* are books that present the biblical text through pictures accompanied by short explanations, and the pictures are structured so as to show Christ in the middle flanked by types. Each book would usually have 40 such triple sequences, no doubt for reasons connected with the symbolism of numbers. In his doctoral dissertation on *The Tradition of Puritan Typology* (University of Missouri, 1968), Thomas M. Davis lists the typological sequences in a late thirteenth-century edition, and from his list I quote six triple sequences:

5. Jacob fleeing his brother	The flight into Egypt	David fleeing from Saul
9. The crossing of the Red Sea	John baptising Christ	The Hebrew spies and the cluster of grapes
18. Melchizedek gives Abraham bread and wine	The last supper	The gathering of manna
25. Abraham prepares to sacrifice Isaac	Christ on the cross	Moses and the brazen serpent
37. Solomon judges between the two mothers	The Last Judgment	David judges Saul's murderer (2 *Sam.* 1)
40. Solomon rewards his bride	The reward of the righteous	The Church as the bride of Christ

Each triple sequence is unified by the central image, which gives meaning to the flanking typical images; thus it is the Last Supper that invests the action of Melchizedek, and similarly the gathering of manna with meaning. The explanatory texts accompanied by appropriate Scriptural quotations helped the reader to understand the images and their relationship.[42] This sequence must have been widely known since it is identical with a sequence found in the tapestries of La Chaise Dieu dating from 1518.[43] Its structure follows Augustine's division of time into three periods: before the Law, under the Law, and under Grace. This structure is found also in a retable at Klosterneuberg near Vienna (dating from 1181), which presents 15 such triple sequences.[44] Artists could vary the pattern so that a real historical event replaced the type, which shows how firmly the type was connected with specific events in salvation history; from salvation history to profane history was but a short step, especially if one posited that the life of nations everywhere was providentially guided. Another variation was to let verbal prophecy replace the representation of an event, and yet another to let one of Christ's parables function as central pivot, for example the parable of the sower. Thus down the centre of one window in Canterbury Cathedral the panes show various steps in the sowing, cultivating, and reaping of grain, each flanked by actions showing a negative and a positive reaction to the message conveyed by Christ in his parable. The seed sown on thorny ground is flanked by the rich who fail to cultivate the life of the seed, and by Daniel, Job, and Noah, who did receive the word of God.

More than two types are often found and, the longer the sequence, the greater the resemblance to the patterns of recessed symmetry so typical of much Renaissance poetry, and especially of epics. A typological cross in the Victoria and Albert Museum presents Christ crucified in the middle with types on each of the four arms, and the centre of the retable at Klosterneuberg has no fewer than 9 typological triads surrounding the crucifixion.[45] Rose windows organize large numbers of images in circles around the centre. In the West window of Notre Dame in Paris, the Virgin and child are at the centre, surrounded by 12 prophets in quatrefoils, and outside this inner circle is a double outer circle consisting of 24 quatrefoils placed over against 24 medallions. The quatrefoils present the virtues and the occupations of the months, the medallions the vices and the signs of the zodiac. The arrangement is such that the virtues confront and dominate the vices: Discord and Rebellion, for example, are paired off against Concord and Obedience. Twelve is the structuring number also of the *Rose Sud* (with an Apocalyptic Christ in Judgment at the centre), while the rose window in the north wall is based on the number 8, expanded to 16 and 32 units. The doubling must be taken to convey the ratio 2:1. At Lyon, the history of the world is aligned with a cosmological structure so that the cathedral is made to contain all of time and space.[46] One scholar – Painton Cowen – relates Pythagorean and Platonic cosmic numbers to the iconography of these great rose windows. Their purpose was to enable the beholder to understand God's order, and "ultimately to become co-creators with the Creator". "From Christian and pagan sources alike they studied the created in order to know the Creator".[47] This study is of course enjoined by *Romans* 1:20. One interesting typological sequence shows the miracle in Cana in the middle, with the 6 pots of water prominently displayed. The images to each side are not proper types; they show, instead, the spiritual significance attributed to the 6 pots. They represent the 6 ages of the world on the one hand, and, on the other, the 6 ages in the life of man (*infantia, pueritia, adolescentia, ivventus, virilitas*, and *senectus*). Normally it is the antitype which reveals the spiritual significance of the types, but in this instance the situation is reversed, and the supposed types actually explain the spiritual meaning of the 6 pots.[48]

The chapel of King's College, Cambridge, is one of the last examples in England of the use of type and antitype sequences in stained glass. The contract for the windows was drawn up in 1526, and its chief demand was that the windows should depict "the old lawe and the new lawe". The design invented to meet this demand is fairly simple. Along each side there are 12 windows, each divided into 4 panels showing two types and two antitypes. The great East window on the crucifixion has a triple structure, two scenes being featured in each pane. (The West window is lost and replaced by nineteenth-century glass.) What we see from a position along the West wall are 12 windows – 2 on the Virgin Mary and 10 on types and antitypes, the triple centre-piece of the East window, then a second set of 10 windows on types and antitypes and 2 on the Virgin Mary. The sum total of types (as of antitypes) is 40, but the number symbolism is less important than the balanced pattern around the scenes showing the crucifixion. Since the types and antitypes have a decided thematic dimension, the resemblance to literary structures becomes marked.

Perhaps the most important structural observation is that Christ always "holds the middle" (*medium tenet*) at the same time that he is also at the beginning and the end, and this is true textually as well as historically. Christ unifies the text of the Bible as he does all of creation and of history. Christ is present at the beginning historically as Creator, textually through the Tree of Life in the midst of the Garden. And Christ is there at the end when he overcomes Antichrist and creates a new Heaven and a new Earth, just as he is present textually in the last chapter of the last book as the tree placed in the midst of the heavenly Jerusalem. The circular form expresses both the nature of the Deity and the pattern of return made possible through Christ. The pattern of time, too, is circular, since time issues out of eternity and returns to it, and Christ again is at the centre since he arrived *in medio annorum*. Moses in a way writes like an epic poet who begins *in medias res*, since his description of what happened in the beginning is a prophecy of what happened *in medio annorum* when the promise given through the Tree of Life was fulfilled in the Tree of the Cross. And both trees were located *in medio terrae*.

Bonaventura is perhaps the theologian who presents this argument most clearly and emphatically in his *Collationes in Hexaemeron*.[49] Bonaventura begins by stating that we must always begin with the middle, which is Christ: *incipiendum est a medio, quod est Christus*. This must be so because Christ holds the middle between God and man in all things. Like Moses and St John – the first and the last exponents of God's wisdom – we must begin with Christ. The entire first *collatio* is devoted to showing the many ways in which Christ is in the middle, the most important example being the Tree of Life in the Garden. It is through this tree that we achieve a return to our origin in God, and it was to secure this return that Christ arrived *in medio annorum, scilicet ut sol* (i.e. as the sun was created on the day which is at the centre of the week of creation). Christ was crucified in the middle hanging between two, and the cross was *in medio terrae*, and the earth itself at the centre of the universe, just as Christ quite literally penetrated to the centre of the earth when he harrowed Hell. If we lose this centre, a return to God will be impossible, our lines instead becoming erratic. Bonaventura finds further examples of Christ being in the middle in *Revelation* 1:13 and chapters 1 and 10 in *Ezekiel* on the vision of the chariot. In *Collationes* XIV and XV Bonaventura traces antithetically balanced structures: the two trees in the Garden are types of Christ and Antichrist, and this opposition prevails throughout history. *Collatio* XIV concludes with a list of 12 types of Christ, and a list of 12 types of Satan introduces *Collatio* XV.

Bonaventura insists that the Scriptures possess organic form. They were not written *ut homo ponit sententiam post sententiam*, they are *ordinatissima* and their order resembles that of Nature: *ordo eius est consimilis ordini naturae in germinatione terrae* (XIV.4–5). This observation must needs refer to Bonaventura's structural analyses, but he provides additional illustration when he goes on to explain that in his capacity as the fruit of the Tree of the Cross, Christ grows from the roots of the patriarchs, the leaves representing the Law, and the flowers the prophecies. Chronological order, too, is carefully preserved in the division of time into a period before the Law, a period under the Law, and a period after it. A fourth period is found in the time after Judgment Day and the resurrection of the dead and the creation of a new Heaven and a new Earth. *Hunc ordinem sequitur Scriptura* (XIV.6). To each of these 4 ages are attributed 3 aspects, and Bonaventura aligns the sum total (12) with the 12 stones on the breastplate of the supreme high priest, and these in their turn are identified with the structure of the universe. This easy transition from chronological to cosmic structure by way of the priestly vestment illustrates the habit of thinking in terms of analogies between various levels of existence, analogies often drawn on the basis of symbolic numbers.

Bonaventura transmitted Augustine's structural vision to the Middle Ages and the Renaissance – a vision of the beauty of the form which shapes the physical event in space, the historical event in time, and the record of these events in Holy Writ. The same form shapes them all, and the structures are, to use one of Cassiodorus' phrases, "appropriately and gloriously perfect in balance".[50] Milton's similar phrase is "the harmonious *Symmetry* of compleat instruction" (*Animadversions*).

It has of course been recognized that this vision resulted in the use of symbolic numbers and ratios in poetry. Old English poetry has been studied from this perspective, and so have poets like Dante, the *Gawain* poet, and Chrétien de Troyes. The emphasis in such studies will vary: sometimes symbolic numbers absorb all the attention, sometimes symmetrical structures or ring composition, and sometimes both. The purpose, too, may vary. Some studies grapple with the problem of compositional method, some show that a work thought to be incoherent and deficient in fact is highly ordered, and some consider the connection between religious poetry and biblical exegesis or the liturgy of the Church. As far as narrative poetry is concerned, the conclusion is often that pattern or design is more important than sequential narrative. Thus the poet of *Genesis A* has been characterized as "indifferent to sequential narrative" because his concern is with a "pattern of contrasts", and *Beowulf* has been seen as part of a tradition that "has as its goal the creation of a pattern or design rather than the naturalistic, chronological depiction of reality".[51] Even Arthurian romances, episodic though they are, have been shown to possess unity through a carefully worked out system of linkage between parts.[52] Although biblical exegesis often is a point of departure in these studies, it is seldom related to the larger perspectives outlined here, nor is Augustine's structural thinking fully understood in all its ramifications, so that it is possible to write about antithesis as a principle of design without adducing Augustine's view of cosmic, biblical, and poetic uses of antithesis.[53]

In the chapter which now follows I present structural analyses of a few selected poems where the connection with biblical exegesis is fairly close; this is particularly true of Maurus' *De laudibus sanctae crucis* and Torquato Tasso's *Sette Giornate del Mondo Creato* (1607). The purpose is to illustrate various kinds of textual structuring, from the simple to the more complex, and to show that, where number symbolism is present, graded and symmetrical arrangements will often be encountered. As we pass from poem to poem, we shall see that the placing of stanzas, verse paragraphs, lines, words, and even single letters may obey the same basic law as God's placing of objects and events in (respectively) the universe and salvation history.

Notes to Chapter III

1. The arrangement of the poems in *The Temple* has been studied by several scholars; the first and most important of these studies is Louis L. Martz's chapter on "George Herbert: The Unity of *The Temple*", in *The Poetry of Meditation* (New Haven, 1954), pp. 280–320. As Earl Miner puts it, "Herbert offers us an example of a poet who integrates lyrics into a collection that, when read sequentially, affords a pleasure and significance not available to one who reads the lyrics separately" (Earl Miner, "Some Issues for Study of Integrated Collections", in *Poems in Their Place*, ed. Neil Fraistat, Chapel Hill and London, 1986, p. 21). Ben Jonson's *The Forrest* affords another example of a structured collection; see Alastair Fowler, "The Silva Tradition in Jonson's *The Forrest*", in *Poetic Traditions of the Renaissance*, ed. Maynard Mack (New Haven, 1981), pp. 163–80.
2. See my analysis of Marvell's poem in *The Sphere History of Literature*, vol. 2 (London, 1986), pp. 234–41. The history of the family (stanzas 11–35) and the description of the estate with its allusions to universal history (stanzas 36–85) relate as 1:2 (25+50 stanzas).
3. "There is in the *totum compositum* of the *Bible* such a peculiar *Oeconomy* relating to the whole, in the conjunction of all the parts, and likewise such an united consent in all the parts when together ... the whole in its connexion is so issued into one great common end, as must needs argue a further and greater design in producing the whole, then what any individual Men could possibly have at several distant Times in writing the particular Parts ... The more *experience* we have of this Book the more we find it at *unity* with it self, and the more we *search* into it the deeper *harmony* still we discover" (Charles Wolseley, *The Reasonableness of Scripture-Belief*, 1672, pp. 238 f).
4. Henry Bullinger, *The Decades, 1587*, reprinted by the Parker Society (Cambridge, 1849–52), Vol. I, pp. 42 and 46.
5. Cornelius à Lapide, *Commentarii in Canticum Canticorum* (Lugduni, 1637), sig. ē4ʳ. *Canticles* is written entirely as an allegory *stylo Comico & Bucolico, quem post Salomonem secutus est Theocritus in Idylliis & Virgilius in Bucolicis*. Solomon in his turn followed the example set by David, since Psalms 44 and 67 (Vulg.) are *simile Drama & Epithalamium Sponsi & Sponsæ*.

6. Matthew Poole, *Synopsis Criticorum aliorumque Sacræ Scripturæ Interpretum* (1669–76), Vol. III, p. 1033.
7. In his *Commentaria in Duodecim Propheta Minores* (Lugduni, 1625), p. 6, Cornelius à Lapide states that the prophets necessarily convey their message *obscuré et ænigmaticé*, but at the same time briefly and concisely in the manner of Pythagoras, Heraclitus, Plato, and the Egyptians, who wrote *per symbola & Ænigmata*. Virgil, too, employed this method. For comments on Jeremiah as the true tragic poet, see his *Commentaria in Ieremiam* (1621), p. 283.
8. See John Everard's posthumously printed sermons, *The Gospel-Treasury Opened* (1659), and the reference to 2 *Corinthians* 3:6 on the title-page ("The letter killeth, but the spirit giveth life"). A few quotations will reveal his bias: "as Christ spake much in Parables, so God doth much in *Allegories*; the Truth is hid under shadows and mysteries, couched and covered within the Letter, as the Woof is hid within the Warp, the Warp only is visible, but 'tis the Woof that holds all together" (p. 13). "You must not think to find the hidden Wisdom of God, floating on the Top of the Letter, but Within is *The Secret Place of the most High*. Gold will not swim, but sinks to the Bottom, and if you would find it, you must *Dive* for it" (p. 358). Whatever was done during the Exodus, "was done in Types and Figures" (II.282). Everard praises the learning of Moses, and attributes Mosaic wisdom to Greek myth; like Moses and like God, the ancient poets used such stories to preserve hidden truths (II.293). That Everard was a radical syncretist appears from his translations of the Hermetic dialogues, the pseudo-Dionysius, and Tauler. On Everard, see Désirée Hirst, *Hidden Riches. Traditional Symbolism from the Renaissance to Blake* (London, 1964).
9. Arnold Williams, *The Common Expositor* (Chapel Hill, 1948), p. 255.
10. Augustine, *On Christian Doctrine*, tr. D. W. Robertson, Jr (New York, 1958). Augustine explains that it is "said of the Church, as she is being praised as a beautiful woman, 'Thy teeth are as flocks of sheep, that are shorn...' [*Canticles* 4:2]", and the image pleases him: "in a strange way, I contemplate the saints more pleasantly when I envisage them as the teeth of the Church cutting off men from their errors ... I recognize them more pleasantly as shorn sheep having put aside the burden of the world like so much fleece" (II.vi.7).
11. Everard, *The Gospel-Treasury Opened*.
12. Milton, *De doctrina Christiana*, quoted from the Columbia edition of the prose works, vol. 17, p. 175.
13. Cassiodorus, *Expositio Psalmorum* (Turnholt, 1958), Corpus Christianorum Series Latina, vols 97–98.
14. Don Cameron Allen, *Mysteriously Meant. The Rediscovery of Pagan Symbolism and Allegorical Interpretation in the Renaissance* (Baltimore, Md, 1970), pp. 172–73 and *passim*.
15. See C. C. Brown, "Henry More's 'Deep Retirement': New Material on the Early Years of the Cambridge Platonists", *Review of English Studies* 20 (1969), 445–54. Sir Thomas More could use numbers symbolically in reference to events in his own life: "Research into More's use of numbers cannot fail to show how elastic our interpretation should be when he tells us in 1515 that 'the Praise of Folly has been reprinted more than 7 times these 7 years' or 'I attended lectures in both Paris and Louvain 7 years ago...'. Such chronological information should be read in the light of other statements, some of them at least half-humorous, involving numbers and especially 7". See the review of M.-S. Røstvig *et al.*, *The Hidden Sense and Other Essays* (Oslo and New York, 1963), in *Moreana*, February 1969, pp. 109 f.
16. Pietro Bongo, *Numerorum mysteria* (Bergomi, 1591), pp. 154 f. (in the chapter "De Numero III"). It is not without interest that in the preceding passage Bongo explains that to lie down belongs to the night, to sit to the morning, while *to stand* is the truly perfect position of mid-day.
17. It will be realized that I disagree with the argument presented by S. K. Heninger,

Jr, concerning the Pythagorean influence on the Renaissance world view. See his book *Touches of Sweet Harmony: Pythagorean Cosmology and Renaissance Poetics* (San Marino, 1974).
18. Cassiodorus, *Expositio Psalmorum* (Turnholt, 1958). The *Institutiones* is available in English translation by Leslie Webber Jones (*An Introduction to Divine and Human Readings*) in the series Sources of Civilization, Vol. XL (New York, 1966).
19. See Adolph Franz, *M. Aurelius Cassiodorus Senator* (Breslau, 1872).
20. See Leslie Webber Jones's preface to *An Introduction to Divine and Human Readings*, p. 20. Jones provides the useful information that there were 15 editions of the *Opera Omnia* between 1500 and 1700, and that the *Expositio Psalmorum* appeared at Basel in 1491 (*editio princeps*), at Venice in 1534, and at Paris in 1519, 1529 and 1579. Cassiodorus' work as an editor reflects his interest in the division of the text: he assembled and edited a text of Jerome's version of the Scriptures (the Vulgate), and "divided the books of the Bible into chapters, provided the chapters with titles, and placed summaries of the chapters at the head of each book" (p. 30). Also he provided the text of the Psalms with punctuation. The almost encyclopedic character of the *Expositio Psalmorum* helps to explain its popularity: it contains "refutations of all the heresies which have ever existed and rudiments of all the sciences which the world has ever seen" (p. 20).
21. Cf. note 1. On sonnet sequences see Thomas P. Roche, *Petrarch and the English Sonnet Sequence* (New York, 1989) and Charlotte Thompson, "Love in an Orderly Universe: a Unification of Spenser's *Amoretti*, 'Anacreonticks', and *Epithalamion*", *Viator* (1985), 277–335, and studies cited there.
22. Walter R. Davis, "Henry Smith: The Preacher as Poet", *English Literary Renaissance* 12 (1982), 30–52. The quotations are from pp. 40, 44, 45 and 52.
23. When Giles Fletcher describes the eternal rest of the saints in the heavenly Jerusalem (*Christs Victorie, and Triumph*, 1610, Part IV), he divides the 50 stanzas so as to permit the cubed numbers 8 and 27 to prevail, together with the 15 of ascent. No other English poet reveals a more profound indebtedness to the tradition represented by Cassiodorus and summarized by Bongo in his encyclopedia. It should be noted that Giles Fletcher often fuses numerical and verbal patternings, so that the latter serve to make explicit the former. See my study of "Golden Phrases: The Poetics of Giles Fletcher", *Studies in Philology* 88 (1991), 169–200. In his *Nativity Ode* Milton borrows a few phrases from Part IV of *Christs Victorie, and Triumph*, and his numerical patterning of the 27 8-line stanzas may owe a debt to Giles Fletcher's textual arrangements. See my forthcoming study "The Craftsmanship of God: Some Structural Contexts for *The Poems of Mr. John Milton, 1645*", in *Heirs of Fame*, eds. David A. Kent and Margo Swiss (Bucknell University Press, 1994).
24. See his comments on the first Gradual Psalm (Vulg. 119).
25. For this commonly accepted view, see John Colet, *Letters to Radulphus* (1876), pp. 23 f.; Augustinus Eugubinus, *Cosmopoeia* (Lugduni, 1535); Jean Bodin, *Universae naturae theatrum* (Lugduni, 1596), pp. 18 f.; Bartholomæus Chassanæus, *Catalogus gloriae mundi* (1617), p. 531; and Benedictus Fernandius, *Commentariorum atque observationum moralium in Genesim* (Lugduni, 1618), col. 106.
26. Bede, "De computo dialogus", *Opera* (1563), col. 111.
27. The dates of their commentaries are respectively 1621 and 1618.
28. Sig. ē4^r and p. 295.
29. Cornelius à Lapide, *Commentarii in IV. Evangelia* (1638).
30. See Pico's preface to *Heptaplus*.
31. Gregory the Great, *Opera* (1674), Vol. I, p. 1174. See also *The Poems of John Milton*, ed. John Carey and Alastair Fowler (London, 1968), p. 763 n. on 6, 749–59.

32. The picture is reproduced on the dust cover.
33. Antiocho Sardo, *De Arcanis Sacrae Vtriusque Theologiæ Scholasticæ* (Rome, 1614), p. 391.
34. Giorgio, *Problemata*, VI.ix.375.
35. Saint Gregory, *Opera* (1674), Vol. I, p. 1174 and Richard S. Victor, *Opera* (1650), ch. 3.
36. Sardo, *De arcanis*, p. 330. When God is defined as Alpha and Omega, the beginning and the end, this means that his nature is circular: *Ipse est circulus*.
37. Ibid., pp. 330–32. The numerical equivalents are 5, 6 and 10. "Numerus namque circularis ille dicitur, qui per se ipsum ductus, in se ipsum semper recurrit" (p. 332).
38. Cornelius à Lapide, *Commentarii in Canticum Canticorum*, p. 489: "ut in ligno satisfieret culpae in ligno commissae; ut Diabolus qui in ligno vincebat, in ligno quoque vinceretur; et unde mors oriebatur, inde vita resurgeret".
39. Alexander Ross, *The First Booke of Questions and Answers upon Genesis* (1620), p. 71. John Swan, *Speculum Mundi* (1635 and 1644), p. 497 of the 1644 ed., writes that "as man was formed the sixth day, and did eat of the tree the sixth hour: so Christ reforming man, and healing the fall, was fastened to the tree the sixth day and the sixth houre".
40. Bongo, *Numerorum Mysteria*: "Impar etiam propter medium, sui ipsius vinculum intra se possidet; & propter centrum, circulare exsistit, & propter comparationem extremorum ad medium, universi ordinis est principium" (p. 96 of the 1591 ed.).
41. M. R. James, "Pictor in Carmine", *Archaeologia* 94 (1951), 141–66.
42. T. M. Davis, *The Tradition of Puritan Typology* (University of Missouri, 1968), pp. 178–82. Davis reproduces the list from a thirteenth-century MS of a *Biblia Pauperum*.
43. Louis Réau, *Iconographie de l'Art Chrétien*, Vol. I (Paris, 1955), pp. 215 f.
44. Ibid., pp. 210 f.
45. Ibid., p. 211.
46. See *Le Vitrail Français* (Paris, 1958), p. 47. The book apparently has no author; it was published "Sous la Haute Direction du Musée des Arts Decoratifs de Paris". See also *Corpus Vitrearum Medii Aevi*, Vol. I (Paris, 1959): *Les Vitreaux de Notre-Dame et de la Sainte-Chapelle de Paris* by Marcel Aubert, Louis Grodecki, Jean Lafond, and Jean Verrier.
47. Painton Cowen, *Rose Windows* (London, 1979), pp. 10 and 14.
48. Bernard Rackham, *The Ancient Glass of Canterbury Cathedral* (London, 1949).
49. Bonaventura, *Collationes in Hexaemeron. Das Sechstagewerk. Lateinisch und Deutsch* (Darmstadt, 1964).
50. Cassiodorus, *Institutiones* I.xiii.2.
51. Peter R. Schroeder, "Stylistic Analogies between Old English Art and Poetry", *Viator* 5 (1974), 185–97; see esp. pp. 189 and 194.
52. See Eugène Vinaver, *The Rise of Romance* (Oxford, 1971) and Norris J. Lacy, *The Craft of Chrétien de Troyes: an Essay on Narrative Art* (Leyden, 1981).
53. Michael R. Kelley, "Antithesis as a Principle of Design in the *Parlement of Foules*", *The Chaucer Review* 14 (1979), 61–73.

Chapter IV

From Exegesis to Composition

> In the beginning God a circle drew.
> Tasso, *Il Mondo Creato*

1. Some Early Latin Poems and Plays

In the *De musica* VI Augustine discovers the ratio 2:1 in the first line of Ambrose's hymn, beginning *Deus, creator omnium*; the ratio is found in the sequence of long and short syllables. The same rhythm, though, is traced by Augustine in the schemes of creation and redemption as we have seen, which means that nothing is too small or too large to be encompassed by God's providential design. In the same way, no poem is too long or too short, just as no textual unit is too large or too small, since even individual letters were used to trace a providential pattern.

The point is illustrated by the pattern poems composed in late Antiquity, for example by Optatianus Porphyrius, whose most famous poem shows the outline of an organ.[1] The letters forming the pipes of the organ increase gradually from 25 to 50, thus forming the ratio of the diapason, as one Renaissance editor points out. Another fourth-century poet, Ausonius, created simple numerical structures in some of his idylls. Idyll 11 is a puzzle on the number 3: the poem lists in riddling fashion some of the occurrences of this number in our daily lives, and the last two lines state that such a poem must needs consist of 3 tens taken 3 times, that is of 90 lines. Idylls 8 and 9 on the coming year have simple calendrical structures: Idyll 8 consists of 52 lines divided into 4 parts by the repetition, at regular intervals, of the first line, and the same kind of repetition divides Idyll 9 into 4+12 lines.[2]

In acrostic squares the unit is the individual letter. The creation of such squares becomes less strange on remembering that Roman script was entirely without word division or punctuation. Word separation has been called "the singular contribution of the early Middle Ages to the evolution of Western written communication".[3] The technique is illustrated in the reproduction of the poem "Ad

Syagrium Augustidunensem" by Venantius Fortunatus.[4] The square consists of 33 lines of 33 letters each, and the accompanying letter explains not only the form itself, but also the sequence of choices leading to the finished form. Since the poem is a gift to ensure the release of a prisoner of war, it had to describe the greatest ransom ever paid – that of Christ to redeem fallen man. The second choice was to fuse the arts of poetry and of painting (the acrostic square clearly represents this fusion), and Fortunatus asks that the poem be painted on a wall. (As we see, acrostic patterns run through the square diagonally, horizontally, and vertically, and these convey their additional messages). The first structural choice was to have as many letters in a line and as many lines as Christ had years when he secured our redemption; the second concerned the acrostic pattern, and the third which letter to place at the centre where the acrostic lines intersect. His choice was the letter M which is at the centre of the alphabet. Fortunatus does not mention the obvious point that this letter, because of its placing, must represent the Redeemer.

The poem begins by describing the creation, fall, and expulsion of man, and the centre-line affirms our eternal damnation under the Law. The second half (lines 18–33) presents the divine counter-movement to secure redemption; the contents, therefore, divide the poem into a sequence of 16 – 1 – 16 lines. The central line on our eternal damnation has at its centre the letter which promises redemption; the condemnation, therefore, is annulled by the unifying centre. The firmness of the square form (33 letters × 33 lines) reflects the firmness of the divine scheme of creation and re-creation, just as the difficulties so triumphantly overcome by the poet (the human artificer) invite comparison with the way in which God brings good out of evil, and reconciles seeming opposites into stable wholes.

Book II of Fortunatus' *Carmina* contains 6 poems on the cross, two of which are acrostic squares, but for these poems Fortunatus did not provide comments on the choice of form. The sum total of lines and letters in these acrostic squares is 35, and it is likely that the number has its traditional meaning of harmony (as the sum of 8 and 27, the last two numbers in the *lambda* formula).[4] The cross restores the harmony that was lost. The acrostic square of *Carmina* II.4

---

* Illustrations in Chapter IV are reproduced from C, Nisard, *Collection des Auteurs Latins* (Paris, 1887) and from Maurus, *Opera Omnia* (Cologne, 1626–27, by permission of the University Library, University of Oslo.

Acrostic Poem by Venantius Fortunatus

```
         AVGVSTIDVNENSISOPVSTIBISOLVOSYAGRI
                        ✠
DIVSAPEXADAMVTFECITDATSOMNIADONEC
AVVLSACOSTAPLASMATAESTEVANECINPAR
FELICESPARITERDIPLOIDELVCISOPERTI
ORECORVSCANTESINTERPIARVRAIVGALES
RIPAEIVCVNDAENARIGRATAAVRAREDIBAT
TVRISDELICIAESATVRABANTVBEREFLATV
VNAFOVEXSAMBOSFLOROSASEDEVOLVPTAS
NOTABOXISREGIOPASCEBATTEMPEBEATOS
ATCVMTAMMAGNOPOLLERENTMAIVSHONORE
TOTAHOMINVMMIREPAREBATTERRADVORVM
OCCVLTVSMENDAXMOXEXERITARMAVENENI
SERPENSELATVSZELATORLARVEVSHOSTIS
ATROXINNOCVOSEVINCENSPELLENOCENTI
CONLISITSVASVQVOSGRATIADIVABEARAT
ETHOMODETERRATVMDENVODECIDITILLVC
REPTANTISQ:DOLOEOOISEXCLVDITVRORTV
HACNATIMORIMVEDAMNATILEGEPARENTVM
ATDEVSEXCELLENSAIEETDELVMINELVMEN
ECAELISOLIODVMMVNERAPROVIDETVLTRO
CASTAECARNERVDIVIVAXINTROIITAGNVS
PRODIITINDESALVSMATVTINIVELVCERNA
INTACTAEPARTVLVXERVITEXCITAMVNDVM
APATREIVREDSHOMODEHINCCARNEVSALVO
VTNOSERIPERETVILISEDETRAHITAVCTOR
OREGISVENALECAPVTQVODDECRVCEFIXIT
TELOVOCEMANVMALFACTVSVERBEREFELLE
ACTVHACSOLVISCAPTIVOSSORTECREATOR
SEROVERADATAESTVITALISEMPTIOMORTE
YMNOSVNDEDEOLOQVORABSOLVENTEREATV
ATVOSAETERNAESVFFVLTILAVDECORONAE
GALLORVMRADIIVOBISQVOFVLGEATETNOX
RVMPITELORAIVGISETSVMITISARMADIEI
IPSAVELIBERTASVOSLIBERATATQ:BEABIT
```

Source: Reproduced from Charles Nisard, ed., *Collection des Auteurs Latins* (Paris, 1887), p. 116, by permission of the University Library, University of Oslo.

again begins with an account of the creation and Fall of man, while a centrally placed three-line contemplation of the crucified Redeemer is followed by praise of the fruit of the cross.

When Hrabanus Maurus (780–856) wrote his cycle of 28 poems on the cross – *De laudibus sanctae crucis* – he (or a medieval editor) added such comprehensive comments on their structure that the work is one of the most important mediaeval sources for the study of pre-planned structures. Such was the fame of this cycle of poems that several editions appeared during the Renaissance. Separate editions were published in 1503, 1605 and 1676, and a joint edition of the poetry of Fortunatus and Hrabanus Maurus appeared in 1617. The text reproduced here is taken from the imposing edition of the *Opera omnia* printed at Cologne in 1626–27. To these publications of individual titles must be added the many collections of Christian verse from the Middle Ages published during the sixteenth and seventeenth centuries, such as the *Hymni Ecclesiastici* (Cologne, 1556, and Paris, 1616) and the *Opera Christiana Poetarum* (Basel, 1564).[5] The poetry considered here therefore is very much present in the Renaissance, as we are led to infer from the fact that the American poet Edward Taylor (a Harvard graduate) on 8 September 1674 sent a love letter to Elizabeth Fitch that makes use of the half-emblematic kind of acrostic poem developed by Hrabanus Maurus.[6] Since no library records exist, we cannot ascertain whether or not one or more copies of Maurus' poem were available at Harvard while Taylor was there, but it seems likely that this would have been the case.

The *Opera omnia* begins with an impressive array of *testimonia* concerning Maurus' achievement, including one by Cardinal Bellarmine and another by John Reuchlin. Maurus is praised as the greatest poet of his age (item 12), and Arnoldus Wion calls the cycle of poems *mirificum* and *artificiosissimum opus*, in which *multa Christianæ fidei mysteria* and *multos mysticos numeros* can be studied as they relate to the sacred cross. As preface to the *De laudibus sanctæ crucis* is reproduced Iacobus Wimphelingius' preface to the 1503 edition, where the reader is exhorted to study these poems with the greatest care so as to acquire a proper love of the sweet tree of the cross and of the crucified Christ. The ingenious patterns, therefore, are supposed to have a strong moving effect.

The purpose of the 28-poem sequence is to show how the cross encompasses and expresses all the numbers of space and time and even eternity itself. Each poem or *Figura* is a complex memory house that calls to mind all the important lessons of our Christian faith. Like the memory houses evolved later on by Hugh of St Victor (such as the Ark of Noah), Maurus' figured poems "are founded in the order of the cosmos and in the frame of salvation history".[7] Their function is to call these orders to mind and to relate them – as Augustine does in the last book of the *Confessions*. Maurus compresses the major structures of both into an object – the cross – and into the poem that presents it. In the well-known country house poems by Ben Jonson and Andrew Marvell the technique is the same: the estate is the memory house, and as we pass from one part to another we are reminded of cosmic, social, and religious structures, at the same time that the poem itself displays some of these structures. We may also think of Spenser's *The Shepheardes Calender* where the 12 months reflect not only the life cycle of an individual, but also national and universal history. In all these cases the particular reflects the universal, and in this process numbers and ratios are important. The way in which this has been done in Spenser's *Epithalamion* is fully recognized today, and it is also fully recognized that this added semantic dimension contributes substantially to the total impact of this splended celebration of Spenser's marriage.[8] What is still missing, though, is an awareness of how this achievement was made possible, and I would argue that Maurus is a key figure in the medieval tradition, and that his patterned poems foreshadow not only the Renaissance emblem, but also the "invisible" structures of the English poems just referred to. But behind Maurus, Fortunatus, and the rest should be seen the Psalms of David, this summary and abridgement of both Testaments and hence of all God's works in space and time.

Maurus (or his medieval editor)[9] provides no comment on the overall structure of the cycle, but assistance is scarcely needed. Figures I–XII consider the work of creation and other important Old Testament subjects, while events in the life of Christ occupy Figures XIII–XXIV, beginning with the Annunciation. The two Testaments, therefore, are represented by two twelves, or 12+12. Figure XXV sounds the Alleluiahs of the heavenly Jerusalem, XXVI and XXVII present the witnesses of the Old Testament (XXVI) and the New (XXVII), and in the last Figure we see the poet himself kneeling in adoration of the cross. Since there are 2 unnumbered prefatory poems, the overall pattern is 2 – 12 – 12 – 4, and the last 4 subdivide into 1 – 2 – 1. The structure, therefore, presents a mixture of *aequalitas*, or the ratio 1:1, and of the ratio 1:2. Alleluiahs and praise frame the testimonies of the two Testaments, and the 2 introductory poems create the same ratio when placed over against the last 4. These introductory poems are adorned with woodcuts showing the poet being introduced to, and kneeling in front of, the Pope as he presents his book of poems. We remember this scene when we look at the last Figure, which shows the poet kneeling in adoration of the cross. Hence the last poem may be said to return us to the beginning.

The guiding concept prompting this overall structure is that these poems present an abridgment of both Testaments, like the Psalms.

Maurus' compositional technique in each individual poem is best grasped by looking at the reproductions included here.[9] Each poem is called a *Figura*, and this term is repeated in the title given to the 1676 edition – *Carmina figurata*. The "figure" refers not merely to the acrostic square, but also to figures within the square, some figurative and others non-figurative. These figures are acrostics that are poems within the body of the poem. However, *Figura* should also be taken in its theological sense: the figures are a concrete manifestation, within the order of the poem, of a divine *ordo* above the world of sense. In Figure XI the form of the cross is created by five rectangles representing the Pentateuch, which means that the figure states that the Mosaic Law is fulfilled in the cross. The visual pattern, therefore, reveals the typological connection between the Law and the Gospels.

Each poem consists of the following parts: the title, the poem printed as an acrostic square, the poem printed in normal fashion, and (on a second page) a prose *Declaratio* explaining the patterns and what they mean. This is the first part. A second part contains prose paraphrases of each poem. In the preface to this second part Maurus explains that he has wished to put as clearly as possible what his poems perforce have expressed more obscurely. Moreover, he has taken Horace's advice to heart and preferred a free paraphrase to a word for word translation; to explain the true sense he has employed, not another language, but another form of locution. The last sentence in the *Declaratio* accompanying Figure XXVIII explains that the sum total of poems had to be 28 to permit the form of the cross to be praised by the equally perfect form of this *numerus perfectus*. (The perfection is a matter of pure mathematics: like 6, 28 equals the sum of its divisors, while other numbers will have parts the sum of which either exceeds or falls short of the number itself. Only a perfect number absorbs all parts into itself in this way).

The shape of the cross appears within each acrostic square in various ways. The simplest pattern consists of single letters running vertically and horizontally through the square; in Figure XXVIII a *tour de force* is achieved since this pattern is a palindrome – a sentence that can be read from right to left, from left to right, from top to bottom and from bottom to top. At the centre is the letter M representing Christ, and the letters A and O are placed at the beginning and the end of each of the 4 arms. The *Explicatio* added to Figure XXVIII draws attention to the fact that the vertical and horizontal lines total 27 letters, no doubt because 27 is the cube of 3 (for the Trinity). These letters signify the beginning, middle, and end (clearly in reference to the placing of the letters A, O and M) so that they express the nature of Christ who comprehends everything within his circle. The cross can also be formed by means of four or five objects placed crosswise: 4 circles, 5 rectangles, 4 large letters, or 4 smaller crosses. The letters that form these shapes convey their own poetic message.

The fusion between biblical and Pythagorean number symbolism is shown with particular clarity in Figure XVIII, "De Mysterio quadragenarij numeri". In this Figure the shape of the cross is created by means of the Pythagorean *progressio quaternaria* from 1 to 4. Each arm is indicated by a sequence of 4, 3, 2 and 1 letters (printed in red and surrounded by boxes), so that the sum total is 40. The poem itself is full of references to the numbers 4, 10 and 40, and the *Declaratio* is virtually a compressed dissertation on them. It begins by explaining that the *quadragenarius numerus* creates the cross, declaring the *mysterij sacramentum* by an arrangement that embodies it. When 4 is divided into a sequence of the 4 first numbers, it reveals the number 10, and this is how the 4 Gospels express the perfection of the Law. That the 4 tens create the cross reveals the majesty of the Law and the Gospels, and that 4 tens are required shows that the 10 of the Law cannot be observed without the 4 of the Gospels. The number 40 expresses our laborious life (the 40 years in the desert as a type of our human existence), which must be guided by Christ if we are to overcome the devil (Pharaoh as a type of the devil); also it puts us in mind of Christ's 40 days of fasting and of the 40 hours when Christ was dead, and again of the 40 days Christ spent on Earth between the Resurrection and the Ascension.

When we begin with the beginning, we see that Maurus places Christ first as our head and as the source whence all things issue, to quote Cassiodorus on Psalm 1. In Figure I it is Christ with out-

Emblematic acrostic square

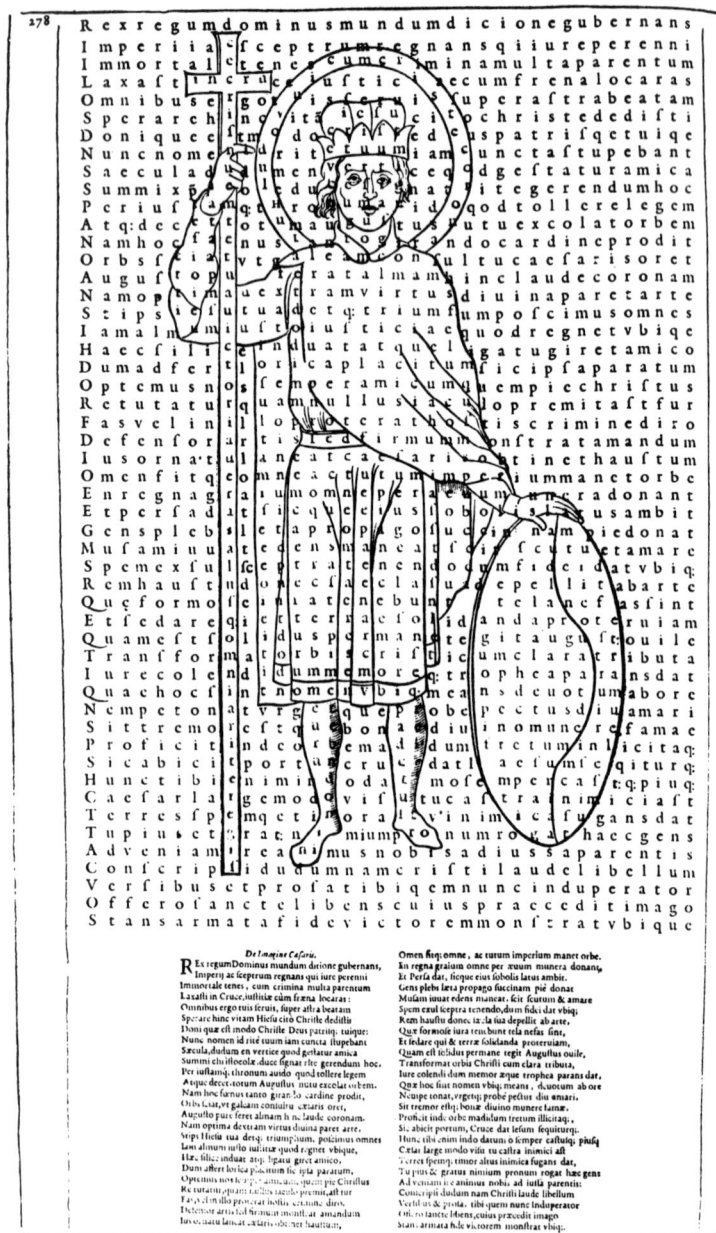

FROM EXEGESIS TO COMPOSITION

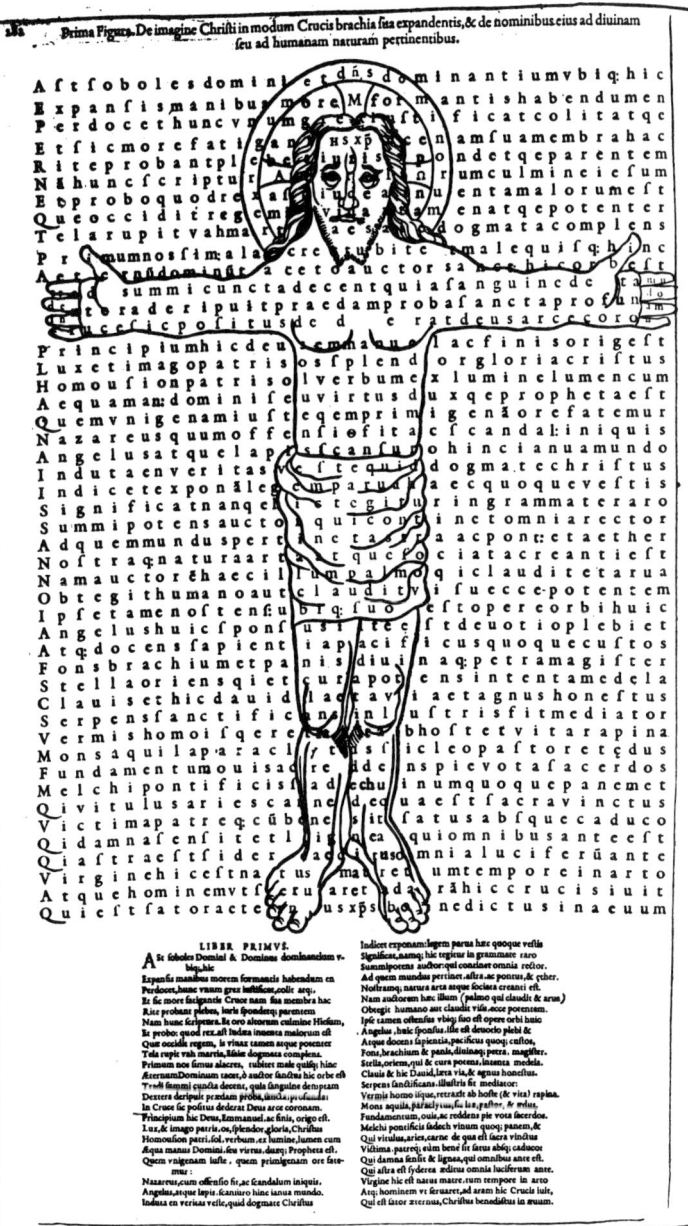

IV. Figura. De Cherubin & Seraphin in Crucem scriptis & significatione eorum.

Cherubin Seraphin de cælo nomen Iesus iam
Exaltate, ignis nam hinc vester famine lucet.
Cum diuina Crucis vera crucis laus, hæc via, vita.
Fructus lucis Christus verus, qui & socia est laus:
Vicit tristia tunc rex, nuncque exultat vbique,
Qui est Seraphin carus: ora fiant celebrando hic
O cælestia monstra multa hac laude supernum:
Vnum est pennarum aram ausu, nam conclamatam
Sacratum atque decus aræ firmant, quoque voto
Edunt, quæ sit virtus, ac bona quæ tribuit rex
Consultu hac Christus re cum conbussit iniqua.
En passus cunctosque fugauit calce potentes:
Et districta rupit excussi clanstra chelydri,
Et veteres actus tersit, dedit ipsa benignus
Quis steterat Adam sons regna Sabaoth in arce:
Quæ ora probant, virtus, & numen, huic ibi ferre
Auxilia in tenebris, in carcere, iussa beatum
In Cruce factorem, confixum in stipite regem:

En thronus hic regis, hæc conciliatio mundi,
Vexillum, framea, sors belli, insigne decorum
Proterit hoc hostes, arma confringit iniqua:
Subleuat atque suos, virtutis præmia donat:
Nam hinc exul ignis scito, quæ tela laterent
Stant Cherubin, hæc quæ aræ assistunt, arcæ quæ
Hic hæc labbara dant signo rite, & satis ora
Sancta ara sapiunt, vna quoque sacra ope fiunt.
Vncta triumphum quæ conatus fercula condunt :
Lætaque distensis ducunt hæc facta beando.
En alis sensim tradunt alma, altaque pandunt
Pennis osque suum Seraphin, vt iam prope tempus
Quo carnalis eat luxus dicant, vitiaque hinc :
Tensa ac brachia saluantis hic officio dant.
Hisque trahi atque vehi celso quæ iudicio ipse hinc
Tum dispensans in tutum leget ipsa probando
Quæ iam nota ante auctu, & cara probauit vbique:
De Cruce non titubant iustorum nuntia vatum.
De Cruce non fallunt istorum signa animantum.

XVIII. Figura. De Mysterio quadragenarij numeri.

```
Pandesalutaremdominovinceatetriumphum
Linguafiguramanuslabiumvoxsyllabasens:
Magnacrucisdominiquemgloriapofcitvbiq;
Sideracelsasuperetquopertingitabyssus
Luxvbipuramanetquotetrasilentianoctis
Perpetuaelatitantvbinoxq;diesq;viciffim
SuccedunteceduntqsibiquotemporecunctusLabiturorbisvbivariabilisindituordoest
Quattuoriftovincirevixsufficitafthaec
Paginadignacrucipraeconiatramitedenas
HafquequadragenasfanctodecallemonadesArteligaresimulplenasquoqueluceserena
MyfticaqasvirtusornatconfecrathonoratTemporisinftantisnumerushicritefigura
Geftatquototachriftofubprincipefancta
EcclefiarabidopiefertcontrariatelahicOpponenshoftibellatrixconfciiapreftans
Virtutumctpugnisvitiafibilauseacuncta
CumfideiscutodomathaecrituhaftaqverboLoricaligatetbeneiuftitiaeintuitalmam
AtqfalutarisgaleamhancinverticegeftatIpfacrucisclarafaciuntinfigniafrontem
FrontisetaduerfaefunduntformofadecoreIncrucefaluatorfaeuumnamvicerathoftem
EiusethocnumerofuadcsertoalmatrahebatExdapibuscunctisieiuniafobriachriftus
StrinxerateripuitqcartodefaucefuperbiRaptorishominemquemcaftrimargiatraxit
InfacinusdiruminimitemiimulattuliriramHuicphilargirialeuisetcenodoxiatrufit
QuemaregnodominusaeternaredemtioiefusSedpreffithoftempraedamfaluauitabipfo
Dapfilisaqthumilismitisetfobriusipfe
Cuiuspugnafaluscuiusvictoriafanctaeft
Cuiusinarcethronusafpect:ininfimacuius
Cruxouatorbishonorcruxefterectiomundi
Cruxmihicarmeneriteriftivictoriaclara
```

LIBER PRIMVS.

Pande salutarem Domino vincente triumphum
Lingua, figura, manus, labium, vox, syllaba, sensus.
Magna Crucis Domini quem gloria poscit vbique,
Sidera celsa super, & quo pertingit abyssus,
Lux vbi pura manet, quo tetra silentia noctis
Perpetuae latitant, vbi noxque diesque viciffim
Succedunt, ceduntque sibi, quo tempore cunctus
Labitur orbis, vbi variabilis inditus ordo est.
Quattuor isto vincire vix sufficit, ast haec
Pagina digna Cruci praeconia tramite denas,
Hasque quadragenas sancto de calle monades
Arte ligare simul plenas quoque luce serena,
Mystica quas virtus ornat, consecrat, honorat.
Temporis inftantis numerus hic rite figuram
Gestat, quo tota Christo sub principe sancta
Ecclesia rabido pie fert contraria tela hic
Opponens hosti bellatrix conficta perstans,
Virtutum & pugnis vitia sibi laus ea cuncta

Cum fidei scuto domat, haec ritu hastaque verbo
Loricam ligat, & bene iustitiae induit almam,
Atque salutaris galeam hanc in vertice gestat.
Ipsa Crucis claram faciunt insignia frontem,
Frontis & aduersae fundunt formosa decorem:
In Cruce Saluator saeuum nam vicerat hostem
Eius, & hoc numero sua deserto alma trahebat
Ex dapibus cunctis ieiunia sobria Christus:
Strinxerat eripuitque atro à fauce superbi
Raptoris hominem, quem caftri margia traxit
In facinus, dirum immitem simul attulit iram.
Huic phylargiria leuis & cenedoxia trusit
Quem à regno Dominus aeterna redemptio Hiesus,
Sed preffit hoftem, praedam saluauit ab ipso.
Dapfilis, atque humilis, mitis, & sobrius ipse,
Cuius pugna salus, cuius victoria sancta est,
Cuius in arce thronus, aspectus in infima, cuius
Crux ouat orbis honor, Crux est erectio mundi:
Crux mihi carmen erit Christi victoria clara.

XXIII. Figura. De numero vicenario & quaternario, deque eius sacramento.

```
Nobiliseceemicat fl os regisnominepictus
Atqenotissignantvictorisfactapotentis
Cornualaetacrucis tr ino sicconditaversu
Q*aenumerantfexinsigniqaterartemonades
Perfectumquedecuso stenduntrebusinesse
Omnib: omnipotensquas condiditatq: redemit
Claradiesillaestqa conditoromniafinxit
Nonminushaeclucetdo ctorqacunctabeauit
Tumbonacunctabon: co npleuitfactacreator
Nuncpiacunctapiuso perabenedixitamator
Quattuorergoplagas l audatfenariusorbis
Sexmicatinnumerisp erfectusprim: etipfeest
Diuiditipfediemtotu mconftringitetipfe
Annimenfifq:biffext ilisatquequadrantis
Hicnumeratoradefta t tollenstemporanutu
Saeculafinecapitet c lauditlimitemundum
Vitamperpetuamtunc regnaetluc'idaducto t
Da fuperaftrapiisd imittensdebitavu ltu
Inde f:e confignansie fuspiapraemia fc is t u
Ex omnimundohisquos t antaddonacorufc a ns
Conduxitfideiluxvi u usetindidithauf tu s
Verusamordecoratiu f tibeatatq:opusalmum
Ergoplagisorbiscon f ignatabomnib: afthic
Adpofitusnumerusen u ndiqepergereplebes
Adcrucisauxiliumpi a numinapofcereiefus
Perfectumq: decusper f ectodogmatedifcant
Perfectaefideiqodf a ctabenignafeqantur
Omnianempedeumveru m haecteftanturvbiqe
Perfectumperfectaq i demformonfadecorum
Quaevertigopolitor n atqaeconditolympus
Quaemareqaetellusq a ecaelicontinetaula
Aftquoquenoshomines inrebusportioparua
Ritecrucemcantufal u antemetvocefonemus
Quibenenosfecitquiq: auxitquiqueredemit
Carmineetincelebr ic r ebroscantem: amores
Quosfatisipfcoperefacroettutaminenobis
Iaminpenditfuafi t i u f fi tostenditamauit
```

LIBER PRIMVS.

Nobilis ecce micat flos regis nomine pictus,
Atque notis fignant victoris facta potentis
Cornua laeta Crucis, trino fic condita verfu:
Quae numerant fex infigni quater arte monades
Perfectumque decus oftendunt rebus ineffe
Omnibus, omnipotens quas condidit atque redemit.
Clara dies illa eft, qua conditor omnia finxit:
Non minus haec lucet doctor qua cuncta beauit.
Tum bona cuncta bonus compleuit facta creator:
Nunc pia cuncta pius opera benedixit amator:
Quattuor ergo plagas laudat fenarius orbis:
Sex micat in numeris perfectus primus & ipfe eft,
Diuidit ipfe diem totum, conftringit & ipfe
Anni menfifque bifextilis atque quadrantis
Hic numerator adeft, attollens tempora nutu.
Saecula fine capit, & claudit limite mundum,
Vitam perpetuam tunc regna & lucida ductor
Dat fuper aftra pijs, dimittens debita, vultu

Inde re confignans Iefus pia præmia, fcis tu
Ex omni mundo his quos tanta ad dona corufcans
Conduxit fidei lux, viuus & indidit hauftus.
Verus amor decorat iufti beat atque opus almum:
Ergo plagis orbis confignat ab omnibus aft hic
Adpofitus numerus en vndique pergere Iefus
Ad Crucis auxilium, pia numina pofcere Iefus
Perfectumque decus perfecto dogmate difcant,
Perfectae fidei quod facta benigna fequantur.
Omnia nempe Deum verum haec teftantur vbique:
Perfectum perfecta quidem, formofa decorum
Quae vertigo poli tornat, quae condit olympus,
Quae mare, quae tellus, quae cæli continet aula:
Aft quoque nos homines in rebus portio parua,
Rite Crucem cantu faluantem & voce fonemus.
Qui bene nos fecit, quique auxit, quique redemit,
Carmine & in celebri crebros cantemus amores,
Quos fatis ipfe opere facro & tutamine nobis
Iam impendit, fuafit, oftendit, iuffit, amauit.

DECLA-

FROM EXEGESIS TO COMPOSITION

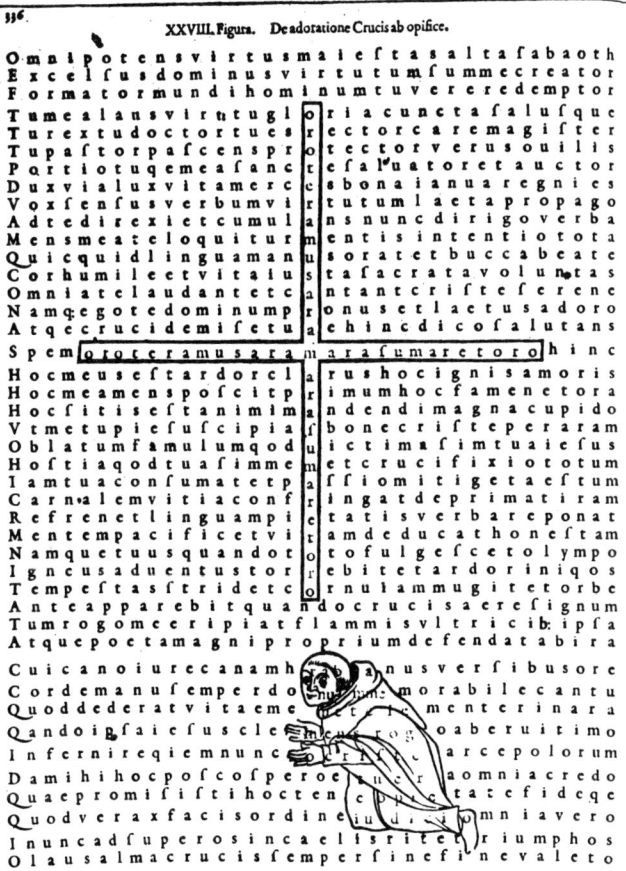

336.   XXVIII. Figura.   De adoratione Crucis ab opifice.

LIBER PRIMVS.

Omnipotens virtus, maiestas alta, Sabaoth
Excelsus Dominus, virtutum summe creator,
Formator mundi: hominum tu vere redemptor.
Tu mea laus, virtus, et gloria cuncta, salusque,
Tu rex, tu doctor, tu es rector, care magister,
Tu pastor pascens, protector verus ouilis.
Portio tuq; mea, sancte saluator & auctor,
Dux, via, lux, vita, merces bona, ianua regni es,
Vox, sensus, verbum, virtutum læta propago.
Ad te direxi, & cumulans nunc dirigo verba:
Mens mea te loquitur, mentis intentio tota,
Quicquid lingua, manus orat & bucca beata
Cor humile, & vita iusta, sacrata voluntas.
Omnia te laudant & cantant, Christe serene.
Namq; ego te Dominum pronus & lætus adoro,
Atq; Cruci demissæ tuæ hinc dico salutans:
Spem oro te ramus aram ara sumar, & oro hinc.
Hoc meus est ardor clarus, hoc ignis amoris,
Hoc mea mens poscit primum, hoc famen & ora,
Hoc sitis est animi, mandendi magna cupido:
Vt me tu pie suscipias bone Christe, per aram

Oblatum famulum, quod victima sim tua Hiesus.
Hostia quod tua sim: memet crucifixio totum
Iam tua consumat: & passio mitiget æstum
Carnalem, vitia confringat, deprimat iram,
Refrenet linguam, pietatis verba reponat.
Mentem pacificet: vitam deducat honestam.
Namque tuus quando toto fulgescet olympo
Igneus aduentus, torrebit & ardor iniquos,
Tempestas stridet, cornu iam mugit & orbe
Ante apparebit quando Crucis aere signum:
Tum rogo me eripiat flammis vltricibus ipsa:
Atq; poetam agni proprium defendat ab ira,
Cui cano: iure canam Hrabanus versibus ore,
Corde, manu, semper domini memorabile cantu:
Quod dederat vitæ memet clementer in ara.
Quando ipsa Hiesus clemens rogo ab eruit imo
Inferni requiem, nunc ô Christe arce polorum
Da mihi, hoc posco, spero, & vera omnia credo,
Quæ promisisti, hoc teneo pietate fideque.
Quod verax facis ordine iudicio omnia vera.
I nunc ad superos, in cælis rite triumphas.
O laus alma Crucis semper sine fine valeto.

stretched arms who forms the shape of the cross, and this placing of Christ in the first position is a clear alignment with the structure of the Psalms. Surrounding the head of Christ are the letters A, M and O, while the letters within the halo form the legend *rex regum et dns* [i.e. *dominus*] *dominorum* (King of kings and Lord of lords). Both the first figure then, and the last, feature the letters that describe Christ as beginning, middle, and end. The Figures that follow consider various aspects of the created universe including the angelic orders. The focus is on the *order* of creation, which is why numbers play such an important role in the argument. Figure II shows a square divided equally into 4, which proves how the 4 arms of the cross govern the 4 parts of the world: the celestial, the earthly, the infernal, and the supercelestial. Then too all created things fall into 4 classes according to whether they have one or more of the following 4 qualities: being, life, sense, and reason. Among the further groups of 4 governed by the cross are the 4 passions, and this fourness of things is the subject also of Figures V, VI and VII. Figure VII shows 4 circles representing all the quaternions of our existence: the 4 elements, the 4 qualities, the 4 seasons, the 4 corners of the Earth, the 4 chief hours of day and night, and so on. This list is so familiar that the *Declaratio* begins by stating that almost no one is ignorant of the significance of the number 4 and of the way in which it reflects the cross. The letters required to form the 4 circles total 36, because its root is the circular number 6, which is well suited to expressing the circularity of the elements and the temporal cycles. All this calls to mind Augustine's statement (*De doctrina Christiana* II.xvi.25) that the day and the year "run their courses in a quaternion", and that these courses, through their circularity, should remind us of Eternity and so make us scorn earthly things. The subject of Figure VIII is the number 12 and its role in time and space as the title indicates: "De mensibus duodecim, de duodecim signis, atque duodecim ventis, & de Apostolorum prædicatione, deque cæteris mysterijs duodenarij numeri, quæ in cruce ostenduntur".

Beginning with Figure XIII the focus shifts to Christ, and the subject of this figure is the number of days Christ spent in the womb. As Maurus explains elsewhere (*De universo* V.i), 13 is the number of Christ because in the New Testament the Acts of the 12 Apostles are followed by the Apocalypse as a 13th, and the Apocalypse reveals Christ fully to us as the one who orders all books and times and sequences. Figure XIV considers the timespan between the Fall and the Passion, and the subjects of the remaining figures are as follows: the 4 evangelists (Figure XV), the 7 gifts of the Holy Ghost (Figure XVI), the 8 beatitudes (Figure XVII), the number 40 (Figure XVIII), the number 50 (Figure XIX), the number 120 (Figure XX), the number 72 (Figure XXI), 'De monogrammate' (Figure XXII), the number 24 (Figure XXIII), and the number 144 (Figure XXIV). Then follow Alleluiahs (Figure XXV), prophetic and apostolic witnesses (Figures XXVI and XXVII), and "De adoratione Crucis ab opifice" (Figure XXVIII).

The fact that numbers connect the two books of revelation – the *liber creaturarum* and the Bible – made them particularly attractive. The comments on the great numbers of Time in Figure IX (in which the cross is formed by means of 4 hexagons with the monad at the centre) recall Augustine's discussion of the number 6 in the *De Trinitate* IV, and this indebtedness is actually acknowledged in the accompanying *Declaratio*. The influence of Augustine, therefore, is well attested.

When, towards the end of his cycle, Maurus contemplates the heavenly Jerusalem, he contemplates the source of all the patterns he has been tracing. Thus Figure XXIII finds the ultimate source of the number 24 in the apocalyptic vision of the 24 elders seated around the throne of the Lamb. And when 144 letters are used to form the cross (Figure XXIV), the commentary observes that they refer to the 144,000 which signify the Church because formed by multiplying 12 with itself and then with 1,000. Since 1,000 is the cube of 10 it signifies the stability of the one true Church. Then too 10 is *numerus quadratus solidus*, which must be a reference to 10 as equalling 4 (i.e. 1 + 2 + 3 + 4).

This must suffice to illustrate how Maurus weaves patterns through time and space by means of symbolic numbers and ratios. His sequence is a meditation on the scheme of redemption as it unfolds itself through structures that explain it. As treated by Maurus, the cross is as much of a "memory house" as the Ark of Noah,[10] and to later ages Maurus and Hugh of St Victor became reliable sources for the study of sacred numbers.[11]

Hrotsvit of Gandersheim (born *circa* 935) is of unusual interest since the structure of her plays (written between the years 963 and 967) is best explicated by referring to Augustine's argument in the *De Trinitate* IV. Hrotsvit's learning as evidenced in these plays has been considered as an unwarranted intrusion; thus Scene One of *Pafnutius* presents a lengthy discussion of ideas about music, which has been condemned as irrelevant display. The scene is about one fourth of the play, and one critic has argued that the Canoness simply tried to make up for her lack of dramatic genius by assuming "ein gelehrtes Mäntelchen".[12] One notices the *von oben herab* attitude in the word *Mäntelchen*. More recent scholarship, though, has appreciated her learning more justly; thus David Chamberlain has proved the direct relevance of Scene One to the dramatic action of *Pafnutius* as to other of her plays. As he himself puts it, the action "shows Pafnutius, in a series of scenes with different 'musical' implications, bringing the discordant sinner Thais back to the norms of concord or *musica humana* that are established in the Prologue" (i.e. Scene One).[13]

Hrotsvit wanted to write plays that would appeal to the learned, as well she might, since Gandersheim was close to the imperial court of Otto I (936–73), and she had easy access to books. She placed her learning entirely in the service of God, her purpose being to inspire love of God through the ideas that inform her plays. These ideas are above all structural; as she phrases it, the more clearly we perceive by what wonderful law God orders everything in number, weight, and measure, the more strongly shall we burn with love of him.[14] This is of course a typically Augustinian sentiment, and a sentiment shared by Maurus, who may have influenced Hrotsvit. As Chamberlain has shown, Hrotsvit's ideas are primarily concerned with musical harmony, so that words like concord, *convenientia, non dissona*, and so forth, figure prominently, and he believes that it is Hrotsvit's achievement to have connected the idea of conversion with the learning acquired from a study of musical theory and mathematics. However, as I have shown, "musical" ideas were assimilated by theologians, and especially by Augustine and Cassiodorus (not to mention Martianus Capella), so that Hrotsvit merely developed what lay ready to hand. Augustine transferred to the scheme of redemption the concept of the harmony between the 4 elements, a harmony which depends on the presence, between two elements, of one shared quality. It is part of Augustine's argument in the *De Trinitate* IV that we can be "tempered together with things eternal" only by means of "things temporal", and that this temperance within the world of time will lead on to a tempering with things eternal. The process of healing must needs have some congruity with the disease, since health and disease are opposites: "For health is at the extreme from disease; but the intermediate process of healing does not lead us to perfect health, unless it has some *congruity with the disease* ... things temporal that are useful take up those that need healing, and pass them on healed, to things eternal"

(IV.xviii.24; my emphasis). It is this process that Hrotsvit dramatizes; her plays show the process whereby concord replaces discord so that a paradise lost becomes a paradise regained. Agreement and opposition are the concepts which determine her choice of characters and the course of the action.

In *Calimachus* Drusiana's preservation of her chastity makes her life preserve its agreement with the life of Christ; chastity is the link that connects them. Hence she commits suicide to escape the embraces of an impassioned lover, and, when her chastity is threatened even after death, it is preserved through divine intervention. We shall miss the play's true dimension unless we realize that the harmonizing power is transmitted through her chastity. Her chastity is irreconcilably opposed to lust, so that, when the two meet, death is the only possible solution. Hrotsvit would at once have recognised that what Spenser presents in the conflict between Mordant, Acrasia, and Amavia (*Faerie Queene* II.i) is the opposition between innocence and lust. We find the same irreconcilable opposition in the interpolated tale of Diana's nymph and Dan Faunus (*Faerie Queene* II.ii.7–10), while events in Medina's Castle (II.ii) show how extremes may be compelled by a unifying centre (Medina) into concord.[15] In *Paradise Lost*, too, the *ill mixture* between good and evil causes the annihilation of what is good.[16] The idea of reconcilable and irreconcilable opposites clearly appealed to many writers in the Middle Ages and the Renaissance, which shows how their thinking was dominated by concepts rather than by psychological analysis. As a consequence, the desire to dramatize a pattern of concepts often prompted their invention of characters and events, and the same desire surely must be seen as largely responsible for making the allegorical mode so popular.

Hrotsvit's *Gallicanus* I is based on the ratio 2:1 in the choice of characters, like *The Faerie Queene* II.ii. Konstantia has embraced a life of perfect chastity, which establishes the necessary concord with Christ; she has done this with the consent of her father, the emperor Konstantin but, when the commander-in-chief requests permission to marry his daughter, the father cannot refuse. This request creates a pattern of irreconcilable opposites, but Konstantia knows how to resolve it: as part of her stratagem she promises to marry, but at the same time sends two of her trusted male associates to accompany the pagan Gallicanus into battle. At the same time she receives into her household his two pagan daughters, her argument being that these exchanges will ensure conformity: she can adjust to his environment and he to hers. Since Christianity is irreconcilably opposed to paganism, we know that such coexistence cannot produce harmony: one of the two opposing forces must be annihilated, and we guess that paganism cannot survive. This is of course what happens; the pagans become Christians, a happy end promised by the 2:1 proportion in these two groups of characters – one male, the other female, one active and the other passive. When the battle goes against Gallicanus he is prevailed upon by his Christian companions to pray to the one true God, and victory is ensured with the aid of heavenly hosts. As a consequence, Gallicanus is converted and he too promises to preserve chastity of life. Meanwhile his two daughters have been converted by Konstantia, and the harmony becomes complete.

The opening scenes of *Abraham* stress the idea of concord: Abraham and his associate Effram are one in relation to each other and to God, and in Scene Two this oneness is extended to include Abraham's niece, Maria, who was one year short of 8 when she became a nun confined to a solitary cell. The subject of the play may be described as the transition from the 7 of Time to the 8 of Eternity, or, in dramatic terms, from worldly pleasures to the joy of receiving a heavenly bridegroom. Maria begins her life as a nun in a solitary cell fairly close to that of her uncle; after 20 years (when she is 27) she is seduced by a man disguised as a monk and subsequently becomes a harlot. This man, then, creates a link with Maria by donning the garb of a monk. When Abraham learns that Maria has left her cell, he sends his friend to discover what has happened, and after two years the friend returns with the sad news that Maria has become a harlot. On hearing this, Abraham aligns himself with the world by donning a knight's clothes, and thus he gains access to Maria so that he can convert her from her vicious life. A shared link then – a worldly apparel – enables Abraham to establish the contact which leads to Maria's return to a solitary cell and eventually to her heavenly bridegroom after a second period of 20 years. During this second 20-year period Maria lives in a small cell without a door, so that her body is covered in the filth possessed by her soul while she was a harlot. Her bodily filth expresses the filth of the world, so that in the course of time her soul may become aligned with the purity of Christ. During her first 20-year stay in her hermitage Maria possessed purity of soul and body; during her two years in the brothel both were filthy, but during the last 20-year period the soul is gradually separated from the filth of the body so that it can regain its lost purity. The balanced chronological pattern $(20-2-20)$ has the divisive diad at the centre, and it is most apt (to use Hrotsvit's favourite phrase) that Maria's stay in the brothel be represented by the number which signifies departure from unity. And it is equally apt that her return to God should occur after 42 years when she is 49. The former is the number of salvation (cf. *Matthew* 1 on the 42 generations), and the latter the cycle of 7×7 years after which all debts are remitted.

The alignment or opposition between outside appearance and inner reality again occupies our attention in *Dulcitius*. When Dulcitius tries to attack three virgins in the room where they are imprisoned, his senses are abused so that he embraces pots and kettles instead and in this way his face, clothes, and hands are made sordid. As the text puts it, it is seemly that his body should have the appearance of one whose mind is possessed by the devil. Even when Dulcitius cleans himself and puts on his most splended costume to seek the emperor, the soldiers still see him as foul and so throw him down the stairs. Regardless, then, of all his attempts to seem pure and noble, his inside condition manifests itself in his external appearance – and what can be more delightful to an audience? When Dulcitius tries to revenge himself on the virgins by ordering them to be stripped naked, this proves physically impossible. Even death cannot disturb their physical appearance, such is the strength of the bond between soul and body, the inside and the outside.

In the edition of her works published in 1501 and adorned with woodcuts by Albrecht Dürer, Conrad Celtis writes in his preface that Hrotsvit may have lived in a barbarous age when the Latin language had become corrupt, but that she was wholly admirable. She is perhaps most admirable when she applies the idea of the harmony of the elements to her dramatic fictions, possibly inspired by Augustine's application of this idea to God's works of creation and re-creation.

Saint Bonaventura (1221–1274) employed textual structures in the *Lignum Vitae* and in the "Laudismus de Sancta Cruce" attributed to him. The former illustrates the connection between textual structures and the art of memory, while the latter provides a most interesting example of recessed symmetry combined with an arrangement in the ratio 2:1.

The *Lignum Vitae* is a prose work arranged so as to assist the memory by associating its various parts with the tree of the cross as drawn on a separate page.[17] The tree is a real tree with 12 branches, each of which has 1 fruit and 4 leaves. Within each leaf is inscribed a phrase that serves as chapter heading, at the same time that these phrases constitute a poem. The *Prologus* explains the mnemonic function; that which is to be remembered is the life, passion, and glorification of Christ – a story taken from the forest of the gospels (*ex sacri Evangelii silva*). The numbers 12 and 4 were probably chosen to permit the numbers associated with the Apostles and the gospels to govern the division into parts. However, even more important, perhaps, is the division into 8+4 books: Books I–VIII are on the life and death of Christ, Books IX–XII on Christ's glorification as eternal king who joins the beginning and the end. The ratio 2:1 expresses this act of joining, since in the octave the last note returns to the first, but in a higher key. The harmony of the octave proportion is actually referred to in the chapter on the resurrection on the day that is both the first and the eighth *in revolutione dierum*.[18]

The "Laudismus de Sancta Cruce"[19] abounds with chiastic arrangements in honour of the cross. "Recordare sanctae crucis" (1:1) is followed by "Sanctae crucis recordare", and examples can be multiplied. Chiastic arrangements include rhyme words: *duce / luce* (stanza 2) recur as *lucem / ducem* (stanza 3). The overall structure combines central accent with a division into the ratio 2:1. Its 39 stanzas[20] are divided into 26 on the joy of the cross and its fruit, and 13 on the grief, while the exclamation in stanza 20 marks it as the joyful centre: "O quam felix permanebis, / Nunc in cruce si studebis". To each side of this centre are groups of 6 stanzas identified as such by rhetorical means: stanzas 14–19 define the cross in lines beginning "Crux est", whereas imperatives prevail in stanzas 21–26.

What this poem shows is that, just as the world is an arrangement of things and events, a poem is an arrangement of words, and that the same kinds of arrangement prevail in both. By virtue of their order they proclaim the glory of God.

2. Torquato Tasso, *Sette Giornate del Mondo Creato* (1607)

Hexaemeral poetry must be expected to reflect the principles of structural exegesis with particular clarity, as is indeed true of Tasso's *Sette Giornate del Mondo Creato*,[21] finished shortly before his death in 1595. Since this is a poem in blank verse, the textual units are cantos, verse paragraphs, and lines.

Direct exposition of the meaning of some important biblical numbers is found in three verse paragraphs in canto 7 ("Day Seven"), but such proof of interest in the subject is scarcely needed.

It would have been impossible for Tasso to write about the work of creation without thinking in terms of symbolic numbers. The extent to which Tasso shaped his text so as to incorporate the numbers and ratios attributed to the biblical account is nevertheless truly remarkable. Appropriate numbers determine the length of many verse paragraphs, or the number of verse paragraphs in a canto or a canto segment; even the unmarked ordinal number of a verse paragraph may be significant. The disposition of the contents creates symmetrical and graded structures, and the repetition of the same topos, without significant modification, helps to identify them.

Much lay ready to hand in the Mosaic account, where the creation of light on the first day connects with the creation of the sun, moon, and stars on the fourth day, both events being interpreted as a prophecy of our redemption through the Son of God. Tasso therefore ensures linkage between the beginning, middle, and end when he placed the topos of light in canto 7 as well, just as he refers to the seventh day of rest in canto 1 (E 1.31–37).[22] Linkage clearly is a major consideration.

Beginning, then, with canto 1 ("Day One"), we observe that the sum total of verse paragraphs is 33, and that the 33rd associates light with Christ triumphant; Christ is the King who rose and "triumphed over darknesses of hell" (E 1.662). The interpretation has Pauline sanction: "For God who commanded the light to shine out of darkness, hath shined in our hearts, to give the light of the knowledge of the glory of God in the face of Jesus Christ" (2 *Cor.* 4:6 AV). The 33 verse paragraphs proclaim this truth numerically in the sum total of paragraphs and in the ordinal number of § 33.

The 33 verse paragraphs have both a symmetrical and a graded structure as shown in Diagram IV.1. After 5 introductory paragraphs, the poem proper begins with the emphatic statement that "The time had come for something to begin" (E 1.223). The 28 paragraphs that follow on the creation of light display a balanced pattern of 1–10–6–10–1 paragraphs, where the framing units are concerned with time. Like 6, 28 is a number of mathematical perfection and hence appropriate for the description of the creation of light that signifies our redemption. The 6 paragraphs at the centre describe the darkness prior to creation, and are flanked by 10 paragraphs on God's eternal art, his *ars aeterna*, and by another group of 10 on the creation of light. As Diagram IV.7 shows, this pattern of 5+28 coexists with a division into 22+11. The sudden transition from darkness to light occurs as we pass from § 22 to § 23, so that the division is clear-cut. The first structural choice must have

Diagram IV.1 *Il Mondo Creato*, Day One (33 verse paragraphs)

Paragraphs	Number of paragraphs		
1–5	5		Introductory
6	1		On time
7–16	10		On God's *ars aeterna* (Segment 1)
17–22	6	28	On the darkness that prevailed (Segment 2)
23–32	10		On the creation of light (Segment 3)
33	1		On time

The canto as a whole divides into the ratio 2:1 as set out below:

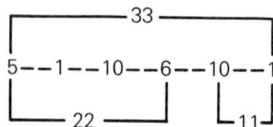

Tasso follows St Paul (2 *Cor*. 4:6) and Augustine (*Confessions* 13) in connecting the creation of light with the redemption.

been to let the canto consist of 33 paragraphs divided into 22+11, and the second to devote the first 5 paragraphs to the introduction and 28 to the work of the first day. These divisions ensured that Christ is present as governing agent (in the number 33) connected with perfection (in the number 28) together with harmony (the ratio 2:1). Since the creation of light had to be reserved for paragraph 23, 10 stanzas on God's *ars aeterna* fill the space before the 6 stanzas on the darkness that prevailed, thus balancing the 10 stanzas on the creation of light.

An additional refinement is that each segment has its own symmetrical structure (see Diagrams IV.2–3). The first (§§ 7–16) actually begins and ends with the image of the circle: "In the beginning God a circle drew" (E 1.254), and God's divine art so mixed the elements that they became "rings of one unbroken chain" (E 1.393–95). The structural number 10 is itself circular (like 6). In the segment on darkness (§§ 17–22) the beginning and the end are joined by the topos of invisibility. The invisibility of the Earth ("Invisibile ancor la nuda terra") finds its spiritual parallel when evil is defined in Augustinian terms (*Confessions* 7) as absence of good (E 1.494 ff.). The third segment (§§ 23–33, Diagram IV.3) features God's eternal light at the beginning and the end, while at the centre

Diagram IV.2(a) *Il Mondo Creato*, Day One, Paragraphs 7–16 (Segment 1)

7	"In the beginning God a circle drew"
8	God's art compared to man's
9	Haphazard works of creation denounced
10	The world is unshakable because created according to the pattern God had in himself
11	The world cannot have two beginnings—one good and one evil
12	Mere matter cannot equal its creator
13	God imposes harmony on the elements
14	Man's childish art contrasted with God's, who made matter and form at once
15	God's craftsmanship praised
16	God balances the elements (in a circular structure)

Diagram IV.2(b) *Il Mondo Creato*, Day One, Paragraphs 17–22 (Segment 2)

17	"Invisibile ancor la nuda terra"
18	The primal dark was *not* an evil power
19	When will the world be freed from evil?
20	Evil cannot proceed from good
21	Evil is *not* a true substance, but lives in our minds
22	Evil is absence of good and hence in a sense invisible

At the centre of each of these two segments is a concern with evil—what it is not and what it is. This is a clear parallel with the *Confessions*.

Diagram IV.3 *Il Mondo Creato*, Day One, Paragraphs 23–32 (Segment 3)

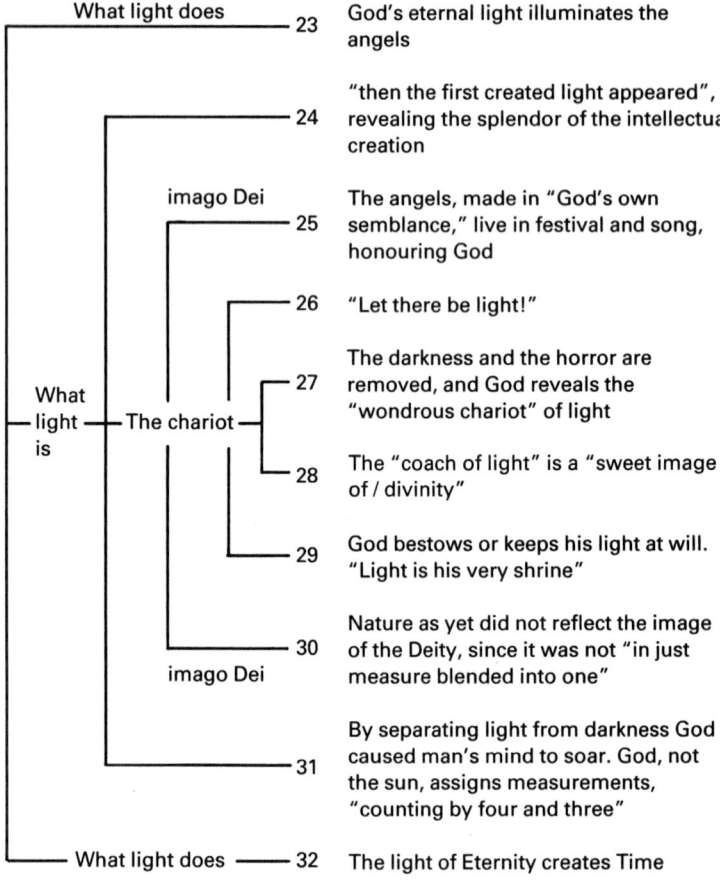

The two paragraphs at the centre share the topos of the coach or chariot of light as a "sweet image of divinity" (compare *Ezekiel* 1 and 10).

Tasso agrees with Augustine when he lets time be measured, not by the movement of heavenly bodies, but by the mind—in this case the light of Eternity. We count "by four and three" when we measure weeks ($3 + 4 = 7$), months ($3 \times 4 = 12$) and seasons.

has been placed the "wondrous chariot" of light which is such a "sweet image of divinity". The chariot of course recalls Ezekiel's vision (*Ezek*. chs 1 and 10) and points forward to Milton's chariot of paternal Deity – the central image of *Paradise Lost*. The first paragraph and the last define what light *does*, but it is the nature of light itself which is defined at the centre. Light illuminates the angels (§ 23) and it creates Time (§ 32), but in itself it is an image of God (like Ezekiel's chariot). Tasso's comments on Time agree with Augustine: Time is measured, not by the movement of heavenly bodies, but in the mind (*Confessions* 11:26–27). On three points, therefore, Tasso agrees with Augustine's *Confessions*: the creation of light is a type of Christ's redemptive act (*Confessions* 13:2), evil must be defined as absence of good (*Confessions* 7:12), and time is measured in the mind (*Confessions* 11:26–27). These parallels between the *Il Mondo Creato* and the *Confessions* reveal the extent to which Augustine's spiritual epic is concerned with a proper understanding of God's work of creation; we cannot understand ourselves without understanding our true origin and end. This is the reason Milton's epic, too, has so many points of affinity with Augustine's.

Day One concludes by referring to the cycle of the week which begins and ends with the day of the Lord – a reference to Easter week, which begins with Palm Sunday and concludes with Easter Sunday as the eighth day of resurrection – which is why Tasso calls the circle of the week an emblem which befits Eternity much better than it does Time (E 1.629 f.). This topos of the eighth day recurs in the last canto in § 8 in connection with the Day of Judgment after which the world will rise in "fairer fashion" and hence it serves to link the first canto and the last.

At the textual centre in canto 4 (Day Four) we meet these very topoi of Judgment Day, Eternity, and rest yet once more, which means that Tasso placed them there to connect the middle with the beginning and the end. The creation of the heavenly bodies provides the excuse: God did not bestow eternal motion on them; when the world comes to an end they will know full rest (E 4.1156–61) as already described in the first paragraph of canto 1 (E 1.31–37). On each occasion Tasso adds an allusion to his experience of life as a time of warfare (E 1.37), which prompts prayer for easeful peace in his own stormy and unsure life (E 4.1216–19), and for release from all the "toilsome movements" of man's "languishing and sickly nature"; "Let this weak aging world have peace at last, / and find its bright eternity in You" (E 7.1100–03).

It would be silly to expect all verse paragraphs to have numerically significant line totals, but particularly important paragraphs certainly do. Thus the first paragraph of canto 1 addressed to the Father, Son, and Holy Ghost totals 77 lines, and so do two paragraphs in canto 7. For an explication we may turn to paragraphs

4, 5 and 6 of canto 7 where we learn that there were 77 generations from Adam to Christ; the 77 lines of the opening paragraph therefore may allude to the generation of the Son within the world of Time. However, also present is the idea of rest combined with forgiveness of sins through the grace of God: the hard Assyrian yoke was broken after 70 years "when the numbers ten and seven fully met", and after the coming of Christ and his gospel a just man may fall "full seven times a day", but "grace uplifts him just as many times". Jesus himself taught Peter the "lofty mystery" of the number 7, "a symbol of forgiveness and of peace", when he told us to forgive, "not seven times, but seventy times seven". These meanings actually prompt much of the substance of the three 77-line paragraphs. The opening paragraph (i.e. 1:1) connects the first day with the seventh, and both with "everlasting, balmy, blessèd rest"; § 7:9 describes how the triumph of Christ brings us to the "bright temple of eternity" where God's own hand will "hang the most triumphant spoils / and trophies of the Cross" (E 7.390–95). In § 7:26 – the last paragraph barring the three-line envoy – the tearful poet offers a prayer for forgiveness and peace from all "toilsome motions": "Let this weak, aging world have peace at last" (E 7.1102). The extended description of the peace of Eternity in § 7:9 is particularly moving; Eternity is a "changeless home where tranquil peace abides / ... unstirred by storm / and pure as sunshine of a steady day / that never will be darkened by its night" (E 7.372–75). "The restless wheel / of fortune ... / will then stand still: and still will also be / our human passions"; all will know peace "in the fixed center of Divinity" (E 7.407–10 and 420).

The poem's first paragraph and the last fuse the beginning and the end of Time. When we begin to read, the world is said to be both ancient and new and "still bright with gold" (E 1.50–55); at the end the poet and the world are equally old and weary, yet the speaker sees himself "like a small child / that keeps all of his ornaments intact / and all his golden radiance still new" (E 7.1071–74). Yet another topos which links these paragraphs is the poet's song and his tears; the poet sees himself as old and full of tears (E 1.39), but through him sounds the music of the Lord: "O Lord, you are the hand, I am the harp" (E 1.64), and it is God's grace which sustains his "uncommon song" (E 1.71–73). In the last paragraph of canto 7 the world sounds its hymn of praise to the Lord, and through his tears and his song the speaker gives himself to God with all his strength (E 7. 1080–83). These links prove Tasso's desire to connect the beginning and the end by means of paragraphs whose line totals provide a numerical expression of what the words say. It is impossible to separate the contents from the form: in the work of composition the two must have been one. The number symbolism provides a biblical dimension and a link with the *ars aeterna* praised throughout the poem, so that it, too, reveals "the greatness of its Maker's wondrous art, / who out of nothing made his master-plan" (E 1.200 f.).

Other paragraphs have a similar numerical dimension. Paragraph 7:16 on the Tree of Life in the Garden totals 33 lines, which serves to identify the tree as a type of Christ. The 8 lines of § 1:8 considers God's eternal art ("l'arte infinita"), and § 7:8 has 28 lines on the eighth day or age, which transfers us from the 7 of Time to the 8 of Eternity. Here the number 28 adds the idea of perfection so appropriate to the vision of the world that will rise in "fairer fashion" and "no more subjected to the change of years" (E 7.365 f.). In the paragraph on evil in canto 1 (I 1.463–73), the number of transgression (11) determines the number of lines, just as the Fall is located in § 11 of canto 7 (I 7.467–503). But 11 occurs *in bono* in the 11-line paragraph (I 7.636–46) on God's "lavish grace". The grace is so lavish that it transgresses all bounds.

Day Seven consists of 27 paragraphs, but the last 2 form a conclusion so that the description of the last day calls for 25 paragraphs subdivided into 9 on the rest of God and 16 on Adam's blissful solitary state before the Fall. The fact that only cubed and squared numbers are used suggests the stability of God's work of creation.

The reason Tasso placed his account of the creation of man in canto 7 is that he defines Adam's condition before the Fall as a state of perfect *repose*. Tasso of course mentions the creation of man in canto 6, but it is in canto 7 that he describes the kind of life led by Adam in the Garden before the creation of Eve. Tasso proceeds from the idea of God's rest to praise of the rest enjoyed by prelapsarian man, the Fall being associated with the creation of woman; she is the cause. The state of innocence when man rested in God foreshadows our final rest in God in Eternity, and for this reason he exhorts us to establish mansions of peace in our souls while here below:

> E 7.437 Let man, though caught in this still fickle race,
> prepare such steady mansions in his soul
> until his naked spirit soars above
> E 7.440 to that sublime, eternal kingdom . . .

From this vision of future bliss Tasso turns to the prelapsarian state, and in so doing he refers to an ancient Hebrew myth according to which plants and trees then enjoyed a higher kind of life more akin to man. While "man lived in freedom and alone, / without his gullible and sinful mate", trees possessed a soul; now "a wood is full of trees but has no soul" (E 7.820–26), while the "magic garden of the Lord / had lofty plants endowed with living soul, / for each of them had speech and sense or mind" (E 7.834–36). Nor is love absent, despite the absence of Eve. Trees extend their leafy arms in love, and the very plants share this hidden yearning, as we may read in canto 5:

> E 5.64 ... there are men who see, and thus admit,
> in awkward trunks and savage bark of trees
> either a bending motion toward themselves
> or an expanse of boughs toward something loved,
> which made one think of leafy arms outstretched
> in secret yearning for some hidden bliss.
> Still others saw, or seemed to see, in plants
> E 5.71 an old, astounded sensitivity.

In this earlier passage Tasso adds that this is an "erroneous belief", perhaps thinking of the Pythagoreans, but in canto 7 he has no such reservations and instead proceeds directly to praise of the "high and awesome wonders of the Lord" (E 7.837).

No one can read these lines without being strongly reminded of Marvell's praise of repose and of the superior kind of love associated with trees and plants in "The Garden". It is unlikely that Marvell's source would have been the Hebrew myth Tasso alludes to; he must have been inspired by Tasso's outrageous praise of Adam's solitary bliss. It would be difficult to find a source which explains Marvell's puzzling ambiguities more satisfactorily than Tasso. I doubt that Marvell took these extravagant ideas at all seriously, although their connection with certain Platonic and Hermetic ideas may have been given serious consideration.[23] The difference between Tasso and Marvell is of course striking: Tasso presents his ideas with almost prosaic plainness, while Marvell's oblique allusions seem invented on purpose to tease and to tantalize.

The balanced pattern of §§ 1–9 is set out in Diagram IV.4. The definitions of God as circle and centre flank this segment, while the idea of divine grace is highlighted in the centrally placed numerical

Diagram IV.4 *Il Mondo Creato*, Day Seven, Paragraphs 1–9

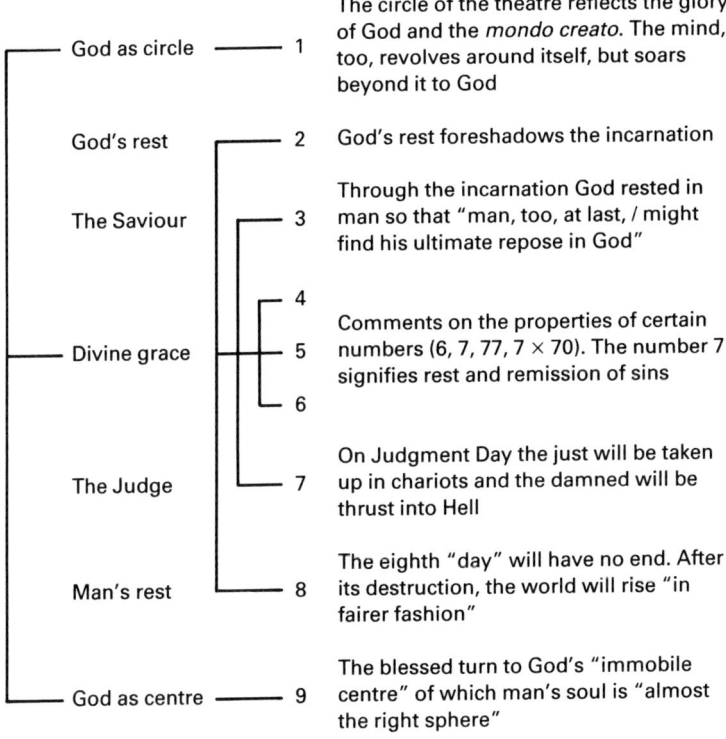

Numerical decorum is observed when the transition from Time to Eternity is described in §§ 7 and 8. At the textual centre the Old Testament meaning of 7 (i.e. 7 × 7) as rest and remission of debts is merged with the New Testament concept of divine mercy.

excursion. To each side of this centre are paragraphs on Christ as Saviour and Judge (3 and 7), and on the rest of God and man (2 and 8). That the transition from Time to Eternity occurs as we proceed from § 7 to § 8 proves the strength of this biblical number symbolism, which inspired Milton as well as Giles Fletcher.[24] When Tasso asks whether a new *fiat lux* will mark the coming of Eternity on the eighth day (E 7.345–47), he connects the end of Time with the beginning.

The segment on man (Diagram 5IV.5) is framed by accounts of the creation of Adam (§§ 10–11) and Eve (§§ 24–25). At the centre

Diagram IV.5 *Il Mondo Creato*, Day Seven, Paragraphs 10–25

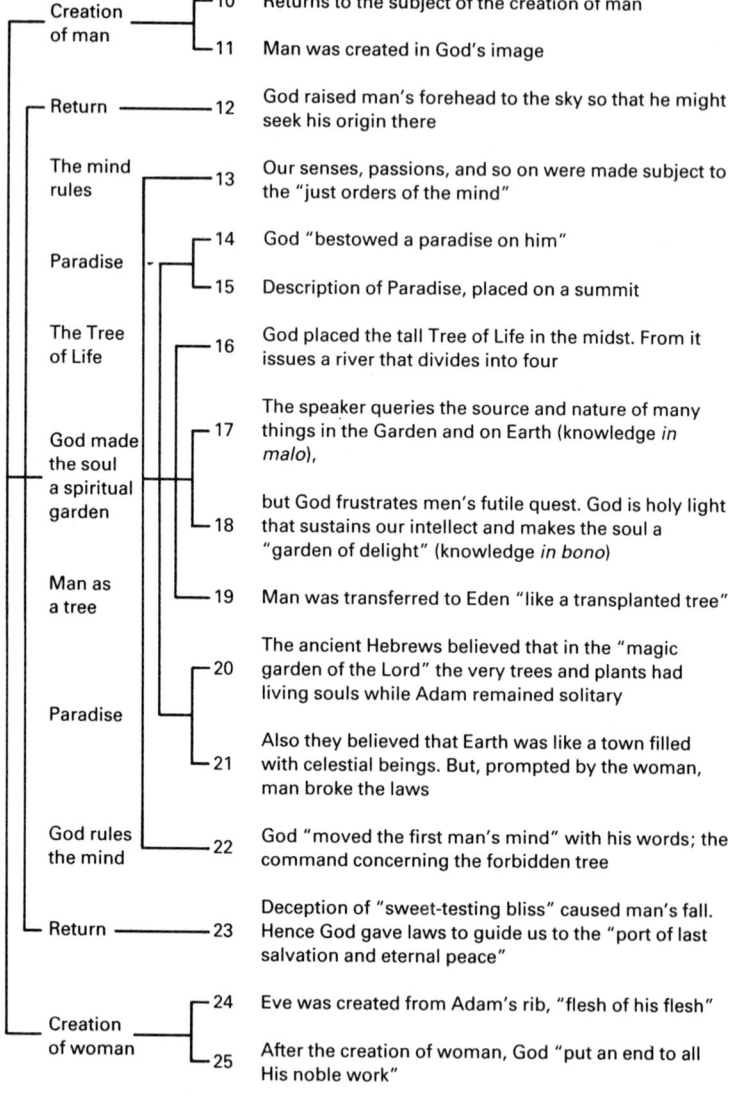

Tasso placed his praise of the mind of man as a "garden of delight", thus anticipating Milton's "Paradise within, happier far". The linkages between paragraphs equidistant from the centre are easily spotted: §§ 12 and 23 share the topos of man's return to his origin, while the proper hierarchical order is stated when the senses are said to be subordinated to the mind (§ 13), and the mind in its turn to God (§ 22). Paradise is described in §§ 14–15 and 20–21, and the topos of the tree links §§ 16 and 19: the Tree of Life is featured in the one, man as a "transplanted tree" in the other. However, this segment may also be seen as consisting of 4 paragraphs on the creation of Adam, 8 on Paradise, and 4 on the interdiction, the Fall, and the creation of Eve in that order. Such a linear arrangement, though, fails to make proper sense; it is only in a spatial reading that the creation of Eve is juxtaposed with the creation of Adam. The spatial structure made it possible to separate the accounts of the creation of Adam and Eve so as to give the responsibility to the woman as the cause of the Fall, while the long passage in between could be devoted to the description of Adam's prelapsarian state of bliss. Although solitary, Adam enjoys the company of angels and the love of trees and plants possessed of living souls. In the two central paragraphs man's misdirected quest for knowledge (which deprives him of rest) is placed over against the light that stems from God and illuminates our intellect.

In a reading of §§ 1–25 as a whole, § 9 stands out as a climactic passage on the tranquil peace and the brightness of Eternity. The blessed move in triumphal procession, wearing their crowns. "The restless wheel of fortune" will "then stand still; and still will also be / our human passions". In "the fixed center of Divinity" all will know peace (E 7.407–20). If we consider § 9 as itself constituting a fixed centre within the sequence of 25 paragraphs, we see that it divides it into 8 – 1 – 16 paragraphs. In other words, § 9 divides the sequence into 8 paragraphs on God's rest and 16 paragraphs on the rest enjoyed by a solitary, prelapsarian Adam; the two are in perfect harmony.

Tasso's Adam is Christ-like, perhaps because he wishes to stress the typological aspect: the first Adam must point forward to the second. Adam is brought into Paradise like "a transplanted tree" (§ 19) in a paragraph linked with § 16 on the planting of the Tree of Life in the midst of the Garden. Adam is king of the whole world, a king who is a "true image of the deathless example", destined to live eternally in the "peace / of the invisible kingdom of the skies" (E 7.115–20; compare E 1.4 f. on the Son). Above all, the prelapsarian state of perfect repose is God-like, as indicated by the location of this description in "Day Seven". With the incarnation, God "wished to rest / in mortal man so that man too, at last, / might find his ultimate repose in God" (E 7.154–56).

Giles Fletcher may have been influenced by Tasso's Augustinian emphasis on rest when he wrote Book IV of *Christs Victorie, and Triumph* (1610), just as his consistent use of symbolic numbers and ratios throughout the four parts may owe a debt to the *Il Mondo Creato*.[25] However, since Tasso employed blank verse, it is reasonable to expect some degree of influence also in *Paradise Lost*. Without being aware of the example set by Tasso, Gunnar Qvarnström discovered that Milton used symbolic numbers to determine the length of some key speeches by God, Adam and Eve. (*The Enchanted Palace*, 1967). The four 23-line speeches by Christ and the one 23-line speech by Eve are noteworthy examples of Milton's use of biblical number symbolism, and Milton could have found a precedent for the use of this particular number in Donne as well as in Giles Fletcher.[26] Although Milton does not seem to have counted his verse paragraphs with the exactness of Torquato Tasso – his blindness was, of course, a natural obstacle – it is possible and even likely that he did so in book 7 of the first edition, as we shall see. In this Book of Rest devoted to the description of the work of creation and its inherent order Milton does seem to have adopted Tasso's structural poetics.

Although technically impressive, Tasso's structural craftsmanship in the *Il Mondo Creato* falls below the standard set in the *Gerusalemme Liberata*, where repetition is never mere repetition, but always repetition-with-a-difference. In the *Gerusalemme Liberata*, the martial topos of the marshalling of troops which connects the beginning, middle, and end is nicely varied so that no repetitiousness is felt, but in the later poem topoi are often repeated without much variation. One of Tasso's better examples is the thrice-repeated simile of the theatre. In 1:17 the invisible, naked Earth is compared to "a new theater with empty seats / and with no actors and no audience" (E 1.403 f.), and we encounter the simile again at 4:2. If we can see "the highest Maker's wonders manifest" in the universe, then "filled are the sections of this theater, / sacred to God, through whose surrounding tiers / his glory's told and sung forevermore" (E 4.75–77). Finally in 7:1 the circular Roman theatre is said to be a fit emblem of the empire of ancient Rome, restored later on by the Church. This empire joined the Earth's two hemispheres, thus creating a great circle where each spectator could see the whole circumference at once. When the mind gazes into God, it may similarly perceive the entire universe in his great light (E 7.39 f.). The simile stands out within the context of the poem, so that the purpose must be to serve as one of several links between the beginning, middle, and end.

It is scarcely fair to Tasso to let these comments on the *Il Mondo Creato* precede the analysis of his great romance epic, but the bare bones of Tasso's hexaemeral structures provide a very useful bridge between exegesis and composition. The diagrams show that the ideas or concepts that function as links between parts pinpoint the main issues; the selected structures enable the poet to articulate his theme, while readers are assisted to grasp the theme when its articulation is perceived. This two-way traffic will be even more important when we approach *Jerusalem Delivered* (1600).

Notes to Chapter IV

1. The text is found in Migne, *Patrologia Latina* 19:429–30.
2. Charles Nisard, ed., *Collection des Auteurs Latins avec la Traduction en Français* (Paris, 1887), and Migne, *Patrologia Latina* 19:895–98.
3. Paul Saenger, 'Silent Reading: Its Impact on Late Medieval Script', *Viator* 13 (1982), p. 377.
4. Nisard, *Collection*, pp. 138–41 and Venanti Fortunati *Opera Poetica*, ed. Fridericus Leo Berolini (Berlin, 1881).
5. See Dominic Baker-Smith, "Donne's 'Litanie'", *Review of English Studies*, 26 (1975), 171–73. John Donne's reference to the poets Ratpertus (died c. 885) and Notker (c. 840–912) in a letter to Sir Henry Goodyear suggests that he had read the last volume of the five-volume collection entitled *Antiquae Lectiones* (Ingolstadt, 1601–08). Baker-Smith points out that the Jesuit Christoph Brouwer (1561–1617) who published a collection of early Christian poetry at Mainz in 1616 was concerned with the preparation of a manuscript copy of Maurus's cycle on the cross from an original at Fulda.
6. Taylor often uses symbolic numbers in his religious verse, for example to condition the number of stanzas in a poem.
7. Grover A. Zinn, Jr., "Hugh of St. Victor and the Art of Memory", *Viator* 5 (1974), p. 233.
8. On Spenser's *Epithalamion*, see Max A. Wickert, "Structure and Ceremony in Spenser's *Epithalamion*", *ELH: A Journal of English Literary History* 35 (1968), 135–57.
9. The issue of the editorial contribution is uncertain, and there is no scholarly edition of Maurus' poems.
10. On the classical art of memory as developed in the Middle Ages and the Renaissance, see Frances Yates, *The Art of Memory* (Chicago, 1966).
11. A Renaissance edition of the works of Hugh of St Victor (reprinted in Migne's *Patrologia Latina*) refers to Maurus, Clichtoveus, and Hugh of St Victor as the great authorities on biblical number symbolism.
12. Helene Homeyer, *Roswitha von Gandersheim: Werke, übertragen und eingeleitet* (Paderborn, 1936), p. 21 as quoted by David Chamberlain, "Musical Learning and Dramatic Action in Hrotsvit's *Pafnutius*", *Studies in Philology* 77:4 (1980), 319 f.

13. Chamberlain, "Musical Learning", p. 321. I had reached similar conclusions concerning Hrotsvit's plays before reading Chamberlain's fine study.
14. "Quanto enim mirabiliori lege deum omnia in numero et mensura et pondere posuisse quis agnoscit, tanto in eius amore ardescit". (Quoted from *Pafnutius* I.21 by Chamberlain, "Musical Learning", p. 322).
15. For a full discussion, see Chapter VI on Spenser.
16. We observe this annihilation for example in book 1 in the description of the subsequent activities on earth of Satan's chieftains, and then in the history of man in book 10. See Chapter IX on *Paradise Lost*. (Book 10 in the 1st edn. corresponds to Books XI–XII in the 2nd edn.).
17. Bonaventura, *Opera Omnia* VIII (Firenze, 1898), pp. 68–87.
18. The eighth day of resurrection was usually conflated with the seventh day of rest; see Jean Daniélou, *The Bible and Liturgy* (Notre Dame, 1956), pp. 262–85 and Thomas D. Hill, "The Typology of the Week and the Numerical Structure of the Old English *Guthlac B*", *Medieval Studies* 37 (1975), 531–36.
19. *Opera Omnia*, VIII, 667–69.
20. The number of the cross is 39; Herrick wrote two 39-line poems on the cross, and one of them is a pattern poem. In both poems a triplet is called for to swell the line total to the desired number.
21. For the English translation see Torquato Tasso, *Creation of the World*, tr. Joseph Tusiani, Medieval and Renaissance Texts and Studies vol. 12 (Binghampton, New York, 1982).
22. A prefixed E signifies that the reference is to the English translation, while a prefixed I refers to the Italian text. The English translation does not observe the line totals of the original, nor is the division into verse paragraphs reliable.
23. I discuss these Platonic and Hermetic ideas in Vol. I of *The Happy Man. Studies in the Metamorphoses of a Classical Ideal* (2nd ed., Oslo and New York, 1962), pp. 152–72. See also my study of "Surprise and Paradox – Perspectives on Marvell's Life and Poetry", in *Andrew Marvell. Poems. A Casebook*, ed. Arthur Pollard (London, 1980), pp. 74–78.
24. Milton begins his *Nativity Ode* with 4 7-line stanzas where we are very much within the world of Time ("This is the month, and this the happy morn"), but changes to 8-line stanzas in the hymn where Eternity (the godhead) enters the world of Time. Giles Fletcher chose an 8-line stanza for *Christs Victorie, and Triumph* (1610), but departs from this stanzaic norm in the last stanza on the inability of mortal words to describe the joys of Eternity. The 7 lines given to this concluding stanza refer to the world of Time; the circle of the week is suggested by verbal repetitions which join line to line and the end to the beginning. For a full discussion, see my essay on Milton's ode in *Fair Forms*, ed. Røstvig (Cambridge, 1975), pp. 54–84 and 206–12, and my study of Milton's *Poems* (1645) in *Heirs of Fame*, eds. David Kent and Margo Swiss (Bucknell University Press, 1994). On Giles Fletcher, see my article on "Golden Phrases: The Poetics of Giles Fletcher", *Studies in Philology* 88:2 (1991), 169–200.
25. For an analysis, see my article on "Golden Phrases", 169–200.
26. On Donne's use of the number 23 see Kate Gartner Frost, *Holy Delight. Typology, Numerology, and Autobiography in Donne's* Devotions Upon Emergent Occasions (Princeton, 1990).

Chapter V

Patterns of Return
Tasso's *Jerusalem Delivered*

> Behold (she says) your handmaid and your thrall,
> My life, my crown, my wealth, use at your pleasure. –
> Thus death her life became, loss prov'd her treasure.
> XX.136

With the publication of Fairfax's translation of the *Gerusalemme Liberata* in 1600 and 1624, Tasso's romance epic entered the mainstream of English poetry. Spenser had drawn heavily on some of Tasso's passages, but Fairfax made the epic available to all in a splendid translation with virtual stanza-by-stanza accuracy. Fairfax preserved Tasso's textual structures with such faithfulness that my analysis will be largely based on his version of the text.

Tasso reveals his bias in favour of textual structures in his discussions of the art of poetry. In his *Discourses on the Heroic Poem* (1594) Tasso states openly that the unity of an epic poem is of the same kind as the unity of God's creation: nothing that we see can be more complex or varied than the world, which "contains in its womb so many diverse things", but it is nevertheless one, and one is the bond that "links its many parts and ties them together in discordant concord". Tasso is at one with Landino when he goes on to state that the poet performs a god-like task when he composes his poem so full of variety of matters, and yet possessed of unity. The next sentence surely bears on the important issue of linkage between parts: all the parts must be "so combined that each concerns the other, and so depends on the other ... that removing any part or changing its place would destroy the whole". My analysis will show that important critical insights are gained by spotting such connections between parts. It is because one episode concerns another and depends on it that "the art of composing a poem resembles the plan of the universe, which is composed of contraries as that of music is. For if it were not multiple it would not be a whole or a plan, as Plotinus says".[1]

Tasso's reference to the plan of the universe recalls Augustine's similar argument about the validity, for artists, of God's *ars aeterna*, and we find direct quotations from Augustine in Tasso's two books *Del Giudizio sovra La Gerusalemme*.[2] The first of these two books concludes with a spirited defence of allegory based on Augustine and Gregory the Great, both of whom (so Tasso writes) held that allegory creates an intellectual structure, "una fabbrica intelletuale, o della mente", which is true of poetry as well as of the Bible. In poetry, too, we should pursue the higher sense, as Saint Augustine suggests when he writes in the *De vera religione* that divine Providence as it were plays with us by means of parables and similitudes. The poet performs a similar function, so that in his work of imitation he becomes semi-divine: "il quale e quasi divino nell' imitazione".[3] This statement virtually eliminates the distinction between creation and imitation: what the poet creates (by imitation) is as true as God's creation. The *De vera religione* figures prominently in the *Libro Secondo* as well, for example in the comments on allegory. The poet and the theologian perform similar functions: both "awaken the mind with images", and originally they were the same person. Like the early poet-priests, the poet should awaken the mind to the reality of the intelligible world rather than the visible one only, and the most powerful images, therefore, relate to the intelligible world.[4] Among the images that relate to the intelligible world we must of course include the structures traced through the text in order to ensure its unity.

Strangely enough, Annabel M. Patterson ignores Augustine in her discussion of Tasso's aesthetic theories (*Hermogenes and the Renaissance*, 1972), although she quotes a passage where Tasso makes use of Augustine's statement that the world is God's poem so that poetry is a divine art:

> it is no marvel that poetry is natural to the human soul, if God himself, by whom we were created, is a poet; and the divine art, by which he made the world, is as it were the art of poetry; and his poem is the Heaven, and the whole world, to which highest and sweetest concord human ears are perhaps deaf and closed.[5]

As we have seen in Chapter I, Tasso maintains that his 8-line stanza possesses this concord. His argument is elaborate:

the eight-line stanza is the best, since the number eight, according to the mathematicians, is the first of the solid or cubic numbers, the ones that have fulness and weight. It is moreover perfect and fittest for action because it is composed of twos, duality being the first moved or *primum mobile*. And the fact that music is composed of odd and even numbers [i.e. the *lambda* formula], of the finite and infinite, constitutes one more reason for the octave's perfection, since it is made up of a double quaternion, thus forming a solid web, or of a quadruple binary, and further of a ternary and a quinary, the first odd numbers.[6]

All the points made here can be found explained at large in Macrobius' *Commentary on the Dream of Scipio*, the popular encyclopedic treatise to which Tasso refers directly in his two books *Del Giudizio Sovra la Gerusalemme*. Macrobius explains Plato's numerical account of creation, and when Tasso writes that an 8-line stanza forms a "solid web" he makes use of Macrobius' favourite metaphor.[7] The division of an 8-line stanza into 2×4, 4×2 or 3+5 may of course be made by means of the rhyme scheme, so that these schemes create the desired musical consonances. Such proportions, however, prevail also in the overall structure of the romance epic, where they serve to make a "solid web" for its 20 books or cantos. In these 20 books overall symmetry combines with a division into triads and tetrads, and with a graded arrangement into 12—2—6 books. My point of departure will be a discussion of the extended centre for the symmetrical pattern.

1. The Extended Centre

So far the concept of a textual centre within a symmetrical structure has been defined in terms of a single line or stanza only, rather than a single episode.[8] It stands to reason, though, that in an epic an episode is a better pivotal point, and my analysis will show that Tasso (like Spenser later on) located such a pivotal episode with mathematical precision in the stanzas that constitute the difference in length between the first and the second half, its function being to tie the whole together as by a knot.

To compute the extended centre is simple enough: Books I–X contain 949 stanzas, whereas 968 is the sum total of stanzas in Books XI–XX. The difference is found in the 19 stanzas that introduce Book XI (949 stanzas precede and follow), and a superficial reading suffices to establish the fact that these stanzas present a self-contained episode relevant to the beginning and the end. The episode is significant: in it, Godfrey decides to set aside a day before the decisive attack in order to celebrate Mass on Mount Olivet. Mass is duly celebrated, and when the "warlike companies" are dismissed they are referred to as *squadre pie* (XI.15:7), a phrase which takes us back to the opening statement of theme: "Canto l'arme pietose". This topos recurs in the last stanza when Godfrey, after the liberation of Jerusalem, hangs up his arms in the Temple, thus dedicating them to God.

Others may seem to have anticipated a minor part of my argument here, but my analysis, although prior, is merely the latest to be published, the postponement being caused by the wish to publish the analysis as part of a complete presentation.[9]

The extended centre is itself symmetrically structured. The key concept in Tasso's description of the celebration of Mass is *order true*: on their way to Mount Olivet the troops move in orderly array and sing hymns "in order true". The pagans on the walls of Jerusalem are amazed to observe "their grave order" and "strange pomp". After the celebration of Mass, all return, "Their order as before, their pomp the same". This episode failed to impress C. P. Brand, who finds such religious passages "cold and unmoving", although inspired by "a love of colour and pageantry". However, the "formal pomp and display" are taken to function negatively: they "destroy the sense of religious devotion".[10] Brand's modern bias reveals itself even more strongly when he is positively angry that Spenser does not permit his readers to enjoy the episode in the Bower of Bliss "without a sense of guilt".[11] If we are to play fair, however, we should rather inquire into the structural function of the episode located at the textual centre; the function may possibly invest it with the desired impact.

The celebration of Mass at XI.1–19 points forward to a passage at the beginning of Book XX, when the Christians command Jerusalem itself while their opponents have taken refuge inside the great tower. The situation parallels the one described in 2 *Maccabees* (cf. 10:18), which may have inspired some of the details in Tasso's narrative.[12] When the Egyptian forces arrive to relieve the besieged, the Christian soldiers wish to engage in battle at once, but Godfrey orders a day of rest (XX.4) as he did at the textual centre. After this day of rest he puts his troops "in good array" (XX.6:2) and, as he does so, his head is encircled by light as by a garland (XX.20). This day of rest echoes the day of rest enjoyed by the Christian forces at XI.1–19, just as Godfrey's sacred appearance

Diagram V.1   *Jerusalem Delivered*, the Topos of Marshalling of Troops

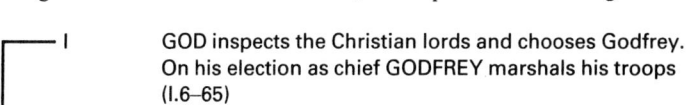

	I	GOD inspects the Christian lords and chooses Godfrey. On his election as chief GODFREY marshals his troops (I.6–65)
	IV	SATAN commands his princes to appear before his throne and then sends his spirits out to cause death and discord among the Christian forces (IV.1–19)
	XI.1–19	The Christian forces march in procession to celebrate Mass on Mount Olivet
	XVII	The pagan forces muster before the king of Egypt (XVII.1–36); EMIREN is nominated leader by the king
	XX	GODFREY puts his forces in good array before the battle and inspects them closely (XX.1–12). EMIREN in the same way musters the pagan forces (XX.21–24)

The martial topos has been deployed so as to create an easily perceived symmetrical structure linking the beginning, middle, and end, and the books that are fourth from the beginning and end.

The linkage between Books IV and XVII is strengthened by the topos of Armida-in-camp: as queen of love, Armida in Book IV conquers most of the Christian champions, and in Book XVII Armida and her troops are the last to parade in front of the king. On both occasions Armida requests champions to support her cause.

repeats and strengthens the earlier description of Godfrey as a good shepherd of his flock (XI.1–3 and 17–19). Yet another link is found in Godfrey's comment on the pagan host as dominated by "strife and discord" (XX.15). In the extended centre this discord manifests itself when the pagans on the walls perform a kind of anti-masque of disorder, possibly in allusion to 2 *Maccabees* 10:34.[13] Book I is largely devoted to Godfrey's marshalling of his forces (I.6–65), a topos that connects the beginning, middle, and end, and in addition Books IV and XVII (see Diagram V.l). In these books, however, the marshalling is done by the opposing forces. In Book IV Satan commands his princes to appear "Before the throne of his infernal seat" (IV.2), whereupon he sends them out with all his fiends to infest the Earth and especially Godfrey's army. In the book which is fourth from the end, the king of Egypt summons his princes and their armies to appear before his throne: there "all the puissant host / Assembled he, and muster'd on the coast" (XVII.2). The linkage with Satan's similar action calls to mind the traditional interpretation of Pharaoh as a type of Satan, and the similarity between the two armies points in the same direction. Satan and his princes are grotesque and ugly, "Mis-shap'd" and "unlike themselves" (a detail picked up by Spenser in his description of the chariot of Night and its horses), and the forces of the king of Egypt contain their quota of the grotesque: thus the "naked folk of Barca" are "unarmed half" (XVII.19), the nomadic Arabians are feminine in voice and appearance (XVII.21), and a "Carpet knight" is described as being unfamiliar with warfare and fired by "fond ambition" (XVII.16). Unlike Godfrey's forces, these have little unity; what inspires them are greed, a total disregard of "law, faith, and truth", love of glory, and rashness (XVII.23). Godfrey's comment, later on, that they are "ill rank'd" and "ill obey'd" is true enough (XX.15–17). Conversely, the choice of Godfrey as the leader is a choice of "virtuous concord" so that "all contentions then began to die" (I.32), and the armada of ships from many countries is "knit / With surest bonds of love and friendship strong" (I.80). What fires these troops is "zeal and faith devout" (XI.2:1). Godfrey is not only virtuous, but sacred as well. Before the final battle Godfrey addresses his troops and draws their attention to the character of the captain of the opposing forces: he is "Ill known, and worse he knows his host", but "I am captain of this chosen crew", and "Each knight obeys my rule, mild, easy, soft; / I know each sword, each dart, each shaft I view" (XX.17–18). Godfrey's yoke, then, is easy and his burden light, like that of the Lord, and the 16-stanza segment on Godfrey's actions as he marshals his troops (XX.6–21) is framed by stanzas that stress his sacred appearance: "Heav'n's gracious favours in his looks appear" (XX.7:3), and a "golden light" surrounds his head as with a halo (XX.20).

The topos of the marshalling of troops, then, includes the idea of order and concord and their opposites, and its finest expression is found in the celebration of Mass as described in the extended centre (see Diagram V.2). The textual structure is simple and effective: 3 groups of 3 stanzas are ranged to each side of a single, central stanza on Mount Olivet. The men move "in triplicati giri" (a phrase not translated by Fairfax), so that the text is arranged so as to imitate the procession. "In triplicati giri" (XI.7:6) therefore is a "self-referring" phrase. During the final attack on the walls later on, Godfrey sees a heavenly host arranged "all by threes" (XVIII.96), and the effect of the textual "triplicities" is to turn Mount Olivet and Godfrey's army into an earthly representation of this spiritual reality; the text itself honours this spiritual reality by adopting the same arrangement.

Diagram V.2 *Jerusalem Delivered*, the Structure of the Extended Centre at XI.1–19

The order of the procession and of the stanzas reflects the order of the celestial hierarchies (arranged all in threes). The first triad and the last function as frames.

The choice of Mount Olivet calls for an explanation: just as the Greeks thought that Delphi was at the centre of the world, the Christian tradition had it that it was Mount Olivet. In book 9 of the *Confessions*, Augustine envisages his dead companion as resting in God's sweet paradise, "in monte incaseato, monte tuo, monte uberi",[14] and later on Spenser was to celebrate Mount Olivet and the Saviour in similar Symposium-like terms (*Faerie Queene* I.x.54). When the host is elevated on Mount Olivet, therefore, this action presages the liberation of Jerusalem: the true centre has been restored. At the centre of the central stanza itself we find the twice-repeated word *monte*:

> monte che da l'olive il nome prende,
> monte per sacra fama al mondo noto.

As Roy T. Eriksen has pointed out, Mount Olivet is described also in the cantos that are third from the beginning and the end, at III.55 and XVIII.15. These stanzas happen (scarcely by chance) to share identical rhyme words in the Italian text: *fronte / monte / monte* (III.55) are repeated as *monte / fronte / fronte* (XVIII.15). The thematic linkage is equally plain:

> The purpose of having a solemn description of Jerusalem and Mount Olivet in the din of Canto 3 is...to prepare us for the ritual cleansing of the Christian army (11.1–19) and of Rinaldo (18.1–17) on top of Mount Olivet...The descriptions of the hill-tops...thus loom above the bustling action of the poem, firmly keeping its protagonists and ourselves aware of their and the poet's higher purpose.[15]

The fact that Mount Olivet is at the centre of Tasso's poem of course means that Christ is at the centre, and that he is there in his benign aspect as merciful redeemer.

There are further links between Books III and XVIII. When Dudon dies in battle, the sacred rites of burial take place (III.66–72), and before battle at XVIII.62 the soldiers receive the eucharist. Then, too, in his valedictory address in Book III Godfrey states his belief that the dead champion will procure "help divine" in the form of "armed angels" (III.70), and this is what happens in Book XVIII.92–96,[16] during the decisive battle for Jerusalem itself. Dudon himself is part of this heavenly host: "with sword and fire" he "Assails and helps to scale the northern port". This union between earthly and heavenly forces proves the reality of the mystical union celebrated on Mount Olivet.

The division into groups of 3 stanzas in the extended centre is clearly indicated. In the first triad, the hermit Peter addresses Godfrey, telling him "in words severe" that Mass must be celebrated before the attack on the walls. Verbal repetition (with chiasmus) links stanzas XI.1 and 3: the phrase that Peter "With words severe thus told his high intent" (1:6) is repeated in the words "Thus spake the hermit grave in words severe" (3:1). The procession is formed and begins to move in the second triad (XI.4–6), the focus being on their order. In "order true" they proceed out of camp into the open fields. Prayers and solemn chants are heard in the third triad (XI.7–9), and in these prayers and chants true order is equally observed: they begin with the Father, the Son, and the Holy Spirit and then proceed methodically via the Virgin Mary and John the Baptist to the Apostles and the saints and martyrs. After the single stanza in honour of the unique event symbolized by Mount Olivet, the fourth triad (XI.11–13) harks back to the third on the prayers and chants that re-echo from surrounding hills and caves. Whereas the third triad refers to the fight between angels and the "blasphemous beast and dragon", the fourth features the antithesis between the "grave order" and "humble song" of the Christians, and the "vile blasphemies" uttered in "hideous yell" by the pagans on the walls (XI.7 and 12–13). The emphasis on *humility* and *order* links the second triad and the fifth (XI.4–6 and 14–16). In the fifth triad the feast of the Eucharist in stanza 14 balances the feast staged in Godfrey's pavilion in stanza 16; the parallel invests Godfrey's feast with religious overtones. Godfrey seems like the good shepherd who prepares a feast for his flock in the sight of the enemy. The sixth triad, like the first, describes events that take place during the hours of the night. In the first triad it is the hermit who intimates the will of God to Godfrey, whereas in the sixth it is Godfrey's will which is proclaimed to the troops. The command is to seek rest, and the transition to action is made in the last two lines of stanza 19 when "trumpets shrill" are sounded to call to arms.

In Fairfax's translation the extended centre is reduced from 19 to 17 stanzas, owing to the omission of one stanza in the second half (XVI.41) and the addition of one in the first (VII.100). Did Fairfax realize that this change entailed shifting the emphasis away from the stanza on Mount Olivet to the preceding stanza? It may seem so, since Fairfax set up a verbal link between them by repeating words from the end of stanza 9 at the beginning of stanza 10:

On these they called, and on all the rout
Of angels, martyrs, and of saints devout.

Singing and saying thus the camp devout
  Spread forth her zealous squadrons broad and wide,
Towards mount Olivet went all this rout.

The repeated rhyme words stand out with startling clarity, and so does the repeated description of the action. This new centre harks back to the centre of the first triad, where *rout* and *devout* again are featured as rhymes. As a consequence of Fairfax's structural revision, then, the emphasis falls on the "camp devout" and on the "rout" of soldiers, angels, and saints rather than on Mount Olivet. The emphasis becomes, as it were, congregational, at the same time that it strengthens the connection with the opening statement of theme: "The sacred armies and the godly knight / That the great sepulchre of Christ did free / I sing".

2. Triads and Tetrads

When we shift the focus from the extended centre to the poem as a whole, the impressive length is made somewhat easier to handle by the circumstance that the action divides it into a twice-repeated sequence of 3—4—3 books. These divisions clarify the thematic development.

Diagram V.3 suggests the overall symmetrical structure and at the same time indicates the division into triads and tetrads. Some symmetries have already been identified, such as the links between the beginning, middle, and end, and between Books III and XVIII, and IV and XVII. A further link should be added because of its precision: it is in the first 8 stanzas of Book III that the crusaders see the walls of Jerusalem for the first time, just as their triumphant entry is achieved in the last 8 stanzas of Book XVIII. The exactness of the balanced pattern reveals the care that Tasso took in the planning of his poem. We observe, too, that in the books that are fourth from the beginning and the end Armida enters the camp of Godfrey (IV) and of the Egyptians and their allies (XVII); in both, she is the queen of love and beauty who reduces champions to mere thralls (IV.96 and XVII.36). An interesting difference accompanies the parallel: on the first occasion Armida is a "sly enchantress" full of deceit, but on the second she is torn between love and hate for Rinaldo, and the fact that she is dressed like Diana suggests a development in the direction of chaste love.

JERUSALEM DELIVERED 213

Diagram V.3 *Jerusalem Delivered*, Overall Symmetry

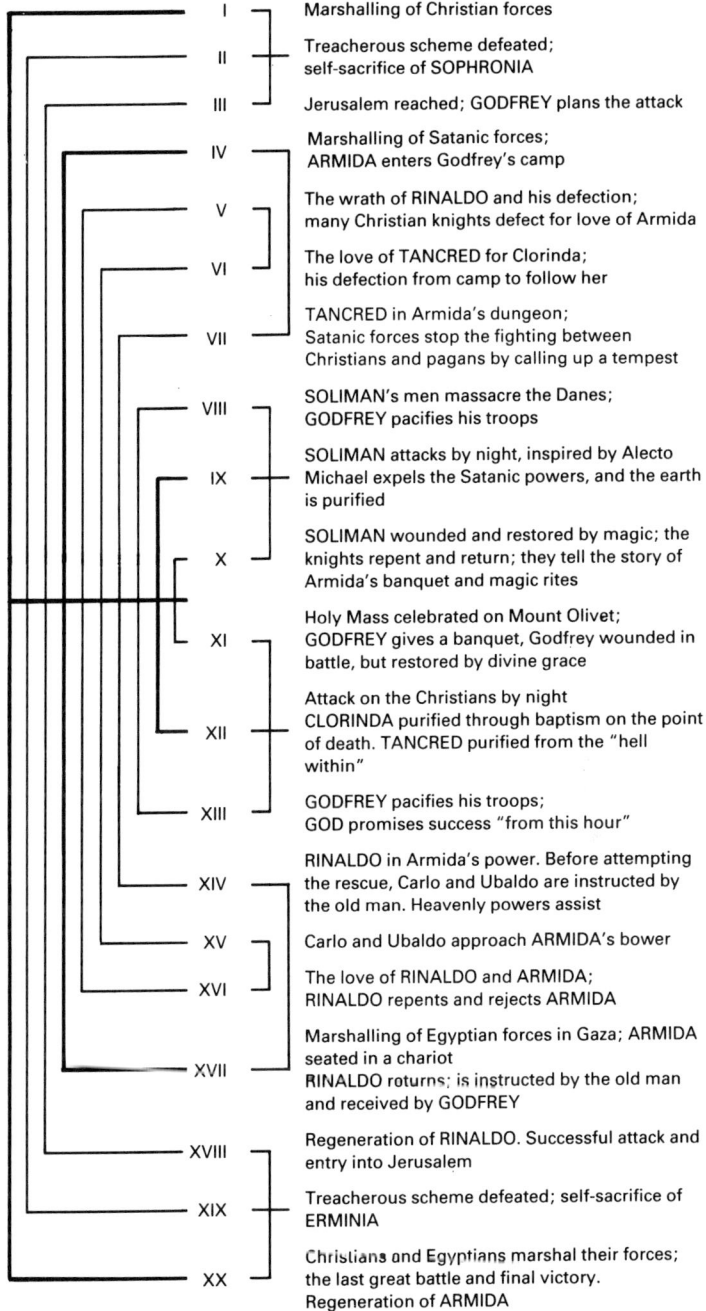

An equally significant parallel-with-a-difference connects Books IX and XII. In both, the Christians are attacked at night, and the action is associated either with Satanic powers (IX) or with the spiritual darkness of Clorinda's paganism and Tancred's despair (XII). Both attacks fail, the one because Michael is sent to expel the powers of darkness, the other because Clorinda is baptized on the point of death, and because Tancred is made to realize that his suffering is the kind of divine chastisement which is proffered grace. The Earth is purified in the one case, in the other the microcosmos of man. The parallel-with-a-difference shows that once the centre has been passed, the action is internalized in a way which recalls the transition from the Old Testament to the New, or from type to antitype. We observe the same kind of transition on comparing the two tetrads (Books IV–VII and XIV–XVII). At the centre of the first is located Tancred's single combat with Argantes, whereas the centre of the second shows Rinaldo enacting the Choice of Hercules between Pleasure (represented by Armida) and Virtue (represented by Carlo and Ubaldo).

Although the division into triads and tetrads is an aspect of the poem's overall symmetry, I shall postpone further comments on that symmetry until the triads and tetrads have been explored.

The First Triad and the Last

Books I–III set the stage. Godfrey is elected leader and musters his troops in Book I, and in Book II we are taken inside Jerusalem where Clorinda, the pagan champion, arrives just in time to save Sophronia and Olindo from death at the stake. This episode is a loose end within the narrative, but within the thematic structure it is highly relevant. The pity felt by Clorinda, and the mercy she exacts from the king, reveal her basic affinity with the Christians whose lives she saves. Sophronia's thematic function is to be the "spotless lamb" who offers up "her blood / To save the rest of Christ's selected fold", but owing to Clorinda's intervention the sacrifice is not consummated. In Book XIX another innocent person offers herself in a sacrifice prompted by love: this is Erminia, the pagan princess who rejects her status to become Tancred's handmaid. When she cuts off her hair to tie up his wounds this is a visual sign that she is his bondslave. (Compare Armida's offer to cut off her hair to serve Rinaldo at XVI.48 in Fairfax, and XVI.49 in the Italian text).

Book III returns to Book I in its renewed roll-call of the Christian champions, this time offered by Erminia to the king as they watch the first combat between Christians and pagans from the walls of Jerusalem. She knows them all, since it was as a prisoner of Godfrey's that she met and fell in love with Tancred. In Book I we are told about Tancred's first fatal meeting with Clorinda when love took him captive (I.46–49), and their second meeting takes place in Book III. During the fighting Tancred seeks out Clorinda and proposes single combat, but when the two withdraw to fight it out Tancred declares his love instead (III.27–28). These two meetings enclose the first triad, and so does the twice-repeated description of the Christian champions. The love of a Christian (Tancred) for a pagan (Clorinda) balances that of a pagan (Erminia) for a Christian (Tancred). Although taken to a heroic level, this love cannot equal the love that prompts Sophronia's willing self-sacrifice at the stake. Her life exemplifies the Christ-like patience and heroic martyrdom later on praised by Milton in *Paradise Lost*.

Love, concord, temperance, and mercy are major concepts in this first triad. The choice of Godfrey as head is a choice of "virtuous concord" (I.35), and concord connects with tempering in Book III when Godfrey restrains his troops "with gentle rein" and guides "their heat" (III.2). When in the end he commands them to cease their fight, Rinaldo bridles his martial wrath and obeys (III.53). (In its proper function, martial wrath must be praiseworthy). These concepts play a decisive role in the last triad as well. Rinaldo's regeneration on Mount Olivet in Book XVIII is an act of divine mercy and an event which is a parallel to, and a pre-condition for, the liberation of the holy city. Rinaldo's re-birth (XVIII.12–16) points forward to that of Armida as she accepts Rinaldo's offer of grace with the words of the Virgin Mary: "Behold (she says) your handmaid" (XX.136:6). Armida accepts Christ when she yields to Rinaldo. In Pauline fashion, the woman is subordinate to the man: Rinaldo receives his grace from God, Armida from Rinaldo, whose eyes are filled with "chaste pity and mild ruth" (XX.134). Thus the conflict in her breast between wrath and love terminates with a victory which represents tempering through divine grace.

Although the thematic emphasis is the same in the last triad as in the first, Books XVIII–XX reveal a marked elevation and internalisation of the main concepts. A fuller understanding of this process, however, depends on our perception of the relationship between the two tetrads—the one a tetrad of defection and the other a tetrad of return.

The Two Tetrads

Books IV–VII are framed by Satanic darkness: the tetrad begins with Satan who commands his princes to appear before his throne, and after his speech to them they issue out to work havoc among the Christian forces. The tetrad concludes with a dark tempest called up by the fiends to prevent the crusaders from gaining the victory. Within this frame of hellish fury are located the unhappy events that turn Books IV–VII into a tetrad of defection.

Each tetrad has its own extended centre, the first at VI.1–53 (188 stanzas precede and follow), and the second at XVI.1–26 (145 stanzas precede and follow). The figures for Fairfax's translation are VI.1–52 and XVI.1–27. Each passage presents a self-contained episode featuring respectively wrath and love. The first presents the single combat between Trancred and Argantes, the second the erotic scene between Armida and Rinaldo in her garden. Each segment has a clear conclusion: the first when the heralds call a stop to the single combat as daylight fails, the second when Armida leaves the garden so that Carlo and Ubaldo can make their sudden appearance.

The sub-centres formed by these passages relate neatly to the extended centre at XI.1–19 in a kind of Aristotelian formula where unbridled wrath and unbridled love are the extremes enclosing the mean represented by God's benign fusion of justice (or wrath) and mercy (or love) in the act of redemption. As we shall see in Chapter VI, Spenser developed this structural technique to advantage in *The Faerie Queene* I and II.

The narrative in the first tetrad is remarkably varied: the focus keeps shifting from one action to another, a pattern of heroic single combats being interwoven with a pattern of defection caused by love. As Diagram V.4 shows, single combats occur at the middle and the end; even Armida's action in Book IV on arriving in Godfrey's camp is a kind of single combat in the form of a series of highly successful amorous encounters. Such is her skill that each knight believes himself to be her favourite. Since love here serves the purpose of war, Venus is the handmaid of Mars; in the second tetrad the roles will be reversed when Rinaldo/Mars is enslaved by Armida/Venus. The pathetic story of Erminia who, dressed in Clorinda's armour, leaves the safety of Jerusalem to seek her beloved Tancred (VI.89–114 and VII.1–22), shows the futility of trying to make war serve the purpose of romantic love. In her way, Erminia is just as rash as the furious Argantes: "Resolved thus, without delay she went, / As her strong passion did her rashly

Diagram V.4   *Jerusalem Delivered*, the First Tetrad

A_1 THE WRATH of SATAN; he addresses his princes and sends his spirits to infest the Earth and oppose Godfrey (IV.1–19)

B_1 ARMIDA, the queen of LOVE, enters Godfrey's camp and engages in "single combats" with Godfrey's champions (IV.20–96)

C_1 THE WRATH of RINALDO compels him to leave the camp (V.1–59)

D_1 For LOVE of ARMIDA many Christian champions leave the camp to follow her (V.60–92)

CENTRE WRATH: Single combat between TANCRED and ARGANTES (VI.1–53)
LOVE: Love of CLORINDA causes TANCRED's fatal pause (VI.26–28)

D_2 For LOVE of TANCRED, ERMINIA leaves Jerusalem (VI.54–113 and VII.1–22)

C_2 For LOVE of CLORINDA, TANCRED leaves the camp (VII.23–49)

B_2 HEAVENLY LOVE protects old RAYMOND in his single combat with ARGANTES (VII.50–98)

A_2 DEVILS shroud all in darkness and stir up a furious tempest to prevent the Christians from gaining the victory (VII.99–127)

The theme of wrath connects the beginning, middle, and end, while the theme of love connects the centre with segments B_1 and B_2. The love that causes Tancred's fatal pause at the centre connects with the defection of Rinaldo (C_1) and of Tancred (C_2). The theme of defection connects D_1 and D_2 as well.

The focus on infernal wrath at the beginning, middle, and end causes Rinaldo's wrath to function as a real fall. Wrath is taken *in bono*, though, when Tancred fights Argantes.

The wrath of Argantes is described so as to align him with Satan. During the single combat, Tancred at first directs his martial wrath to good effect, but in the end "Wrath bore the sway, both art and reason fail" (VI.48:1–2).

guide" (VI.89:1–2); indeed, "her wit and reason both were gone" (90:3), but Providence leads her to a place of refuge in a community of harmless shepherds. Love figures even in the single combat between Tancred and Argantes: overcome by love when he sees Clorinda at a distance, Tancred forgets everything else for a short while, so that Otho steps in instead. Love figures in the second single combat, too, between old Raymond and Argantes, but on this occasion the moving power is heavenly love: Raymond prays to God for aid, and aid is amply given by a guardian angel.

Love, then, whether pretended or too rash and passionate, leads to a series of defections from Godfrey's camp and from Jerusalem. However, the most serious defection is that of Rinaldo, caused by his wrath, just as the most serious threat is posed by the martial wrath of the formidable Argantes. Rinaldo's uncontrolled wrath is provoked by vicious slander prompted by envy. When he plunges his "furious blade" into Gernando's breast, Rinaldo strikes the pose associated with wrath as one of the seven deadly sins. Fairfax underlines the point by using *wrath* as the rhyme word in the first line of stanza V.30 and in the last of stanza 31.

Wrath is of course the key note in the framing passages (A_1 and A_2) on Satan in Hell and on the tempest called up by the fiends to compel the Christians to turn. The wrathful Argantes has striking points of affinity with Satan, as he confronts first Tancred and then old Raymond (VI.23 and VII.52–57). Like Satan, Argantes burns with fury against the Christians, which is why he cannot wait behind the walls of Jerusalem, but must instead issue his challenge to single combat. Hence he takes his stand, "Defying Christ and all his servants true", in pride and presumption "Encelade like, on the Phlegrean strand, / Or that huge giant Jesse's infant slew" (VI.23). References to Enceladus—the giant who dared oppose Jove – connects the beginning and the middle of the first tetrad (IV.15:5 and VI.23), and references to David and Goliath similarly connect the middle and the end (VI.23 and VII.78:1–4). A reference to Enceladus is found also at XV.34, in a passage that balances VI.23 within the overall symmetrical structure. These allusions to classical myth and to the Bible seem consciously located so as to establish the desired textual structures. Enceladus and Goliath are of course opponents of the one true God, and when Argantes waits for his opponent to appear at VII.53–57 his appearance recalls that of Satan at IV.1–7. Both roar like angry bulls (IV.1:8 and VII.55); both are consumed with anger and impatience, and both thunder out their message in a way which instils terror (IV.8 and VII.57:1–4). Satan's speech resembles the thundering noise from Mount Aetna, just as Argantes lets his challenge be proclaimed by a bugle that sounds "Louder than thunder from Olympus' hill" (VII.57:2). Satan's eyes "Two beacons seem, that men to arms assemble" (IV.3–4), and those of Argantes burn "like flaming torches" (VII.113:5). Yet another link between the beginning and the end of

Diagram V.5 *Jerusalem Delivered*, the Extended Centre of the First Tetrad (VI.1–53)

1–14	14 ⎤	Argantes demands action; when this is refused, he requests permission to engage in single combat Permission is granted
15–21	7 ⎦	Godfrey receives the challenge
22–28	7	Argantes and Tancred issue out, but Tancred becomes immobile when he sees Clorinda at a distance
29–35	7 ⎤	Otho engages Argantes, but is thrown to the ground
36–49	14 ⎦	Tancred joins with Argantes
50–53	4	The heralds stop the combat when night falls

The last four stanzas are transitional, so that stanzas 22–28 are at the centre of this segment. Hence Tancred's fatal love of a female pagan champion—a love which immobilizes him—is at the centre of the extended centre.

When Tancred later on becomes imprisoned in the dungeon of Armida's castle, he is truly immobilized.

this tetrad is found in the concluding tempest (VII.116–23), which is anticipated when Satan's trumpet (the precursor of Argantes' bugle) makes a sound like a tempest: "Not half so dreadful noise the tempests cast, / That fall from skies with storms of hail and thunder" (IV.3). We see, then, that not only the main actions but also descriptive details serve to establish the links that mark Books IV–VII as being a symmetrically structured tetrad.

The extended centre of the first tetrad (VI.1–53) has its own poised symmetry, as shown in Diagram V.5. Two segments which lead up to the single combat (14 + 7 stanzas) balance two segments on the combat (7 + 14 stanzas), and in between is a 7-stanza passage on Tancred's momentary *stasis* when he sees Clorinda. The transition at the end requires 4 stanzas. Fairfax comments: "He thinks on Cupid, think on Mars who lust" (VI.28:6), an observation not made by Tasso but invented by Fairfax, surely in order to underline the parallel with the extended centre in the second tetrad, where Mars again is overcome by Venus. Prompted by his love of Clorinda, Tancred leaves the camp and lands in Armida's dungeon (VII.48–49), where his Petrarchan complaint for the loss of his beloved amounts to a spiritual defection. It is this defection which is

Diagram V.6 *Jerusalem Delivered*, Patterns of Verbal Repetition in Book VI, 1–28.

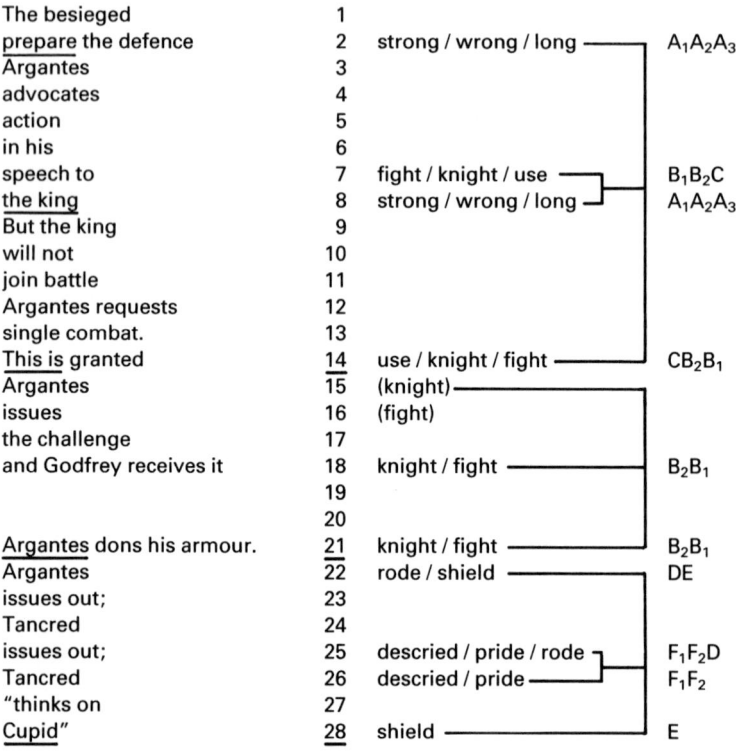

Words in parentheses are words within the line: all other words are placed in rhyme position. A, B, and C rhyme words connect stanzas 2, 7–8, and 14, whereas the B words (knight and fight) carry on the pattern in stanzas 15–21. In the last group of 7 stanzas (22–28) three new rhyme words connect the beginning, middle, and end. For the sake of greater clarity I have excluded substructures.

foreshadowed in his momentary lapse when he fails to engage Argantes/Satan.

    A pattern of repeated identical rhyme words supports the symmetrical structure created by the pattern of actions (see Diagram V.6). Although Tasso on occasion does use rhyme in this fashion, Fairfax's intricate patterning reflects Spenser's craftsmanship, as we shall see in Chapter VI. Spenser developed this technique to a fine point, and Fairfax clearly took his cue from Spenser. This interaction between Tasso, Spenser, and Fairfax proves the latter's awareness of the way in which Tasso and Spenser handle textual

Diagram V.7   *Jerusalem Delivered*, the Second Tetrad (XIV–XVII)

A_1 Godfrey's vision in the night. He sees the true BLISS of Heaven and is told that Rinaldo must return before his mission can be achieved (XIV.1–18)

B_1 Godfrey's vision concludes with the prophecy that Godfrey's line and Rinaldo's will be joined (XIV.19)

C_1 Within the darkness of the womb of the earth, Carlo and Ubaldo are instructed by the old man. He tells them how to resist the lure of PLEASURE and overcome the hazards on the way to Armida's palace (XIV.50–79)

D_1 Carlo and Ubaldo are taken to Armida's island in the Atlantic; they climb the mountain and show firmness under trials; they scorn the allure of false PLEASURE (XV)

Centre   VIRTUE and PLEASURE are confronted when the two knights reach the centre of the maze at the centre of the tetrad, and see Armida and Rinaldo in the garden of love (XVI.1–26/27)

D_2 Rinaldo chooses the path of VIRTUE and firmly rejects the pleas of Armida (XVI.28–67)

C_2 Within the darkness of the night, Rinaldo and the knights see a light which issues from a new armour, next to which they find the old man. He instructs Rinaldo in the choice of VIRTUE (XVII.54–95)

B_2 Rinaldo is told to find inspiration in the noble deeds of his ancestors as depicted on the shield; prophecy of the future greatness of his line (XVII.54–95)

A_2 Return of Rinaldo (XVII.96–97)

The true bliss of Heaven seen by Godfrey in his vision contrasts strongly with the idea of pleasure connected with Armida, and Pleasure is placed antithetically over against Virtue as the two knights watch Armida and Rinaldo.
   Rinaldo's choice of Virtue marks his mental return.

structures, and that he appreciated the skill with which Spenser employs identical rhyme words to indicate his structures.

In the second tetrad (Books XIV–XVII) the action is unified: everything turns on the rescue of Rinaldo and his return to camp. As in the first tetrad, the action forms a pattern of recessed symmetry around an extended centre (XVI.1–26/27; see Diagram V.7). Although darkness serves as a frame for this tetrad, too, the darkness is benign; when Book XIV begins, Godfrey has his important dream vision, and later on the knights Carlo and Ubaldo are taken by the old man into his underground palace, resplendent "With glorious light, though built in night and shade" (XIV.41). There they are given the instruction they need to rescue Rinaldo from the "wanton queen" who holds him captive on her enchanted island. As the tetrad concludes, Rinaldo has been rescued, and walks with Carlo, Ubaldo, and the old man through the darkness of the desert, marching "right against the rising morn" until they reach Godfrey, who starts from his "throne and kingly seat" to receive them with honour (XVII.97).

To this basic pattern should be added a number of significant details. The night when Godfrey has his dream vision is a "gentle night" refreshed with "honey drops of pure and precious dew" (XIV.1), so that sacred connotations are present. In this vision the departed Hugo provides instruction: everything depends on the return of Rinaldo, who sits idle "in love and looseness" (XIV.17). Godfrey's chosen knights will be shown how to proceed so that Rinaldo may be rescued, and "all thy soldiers, wander'd and misgone, / Heav'n may unite again and join in one" (XVIII.7–8). As the duke wakes up, dawn is breaking and hence he "started up; for praise and virtue lie / In toil and travail, sin and shame in bed" (XX.3–4). This is the first statement of a basic theme: Virtue must be our conscious choice, not idle Pleasure. The last occurs at the end of Book XVII, in the old man's discourse to Rinaldo, and he too uses the phrase "toil and travail" (XVII.61:5). Godfrey's messengers, Carlo and Ubaldo, embody this heroic virtue so closely associated with Hercules, whereas Armida of course represents the pleasure that must be rejected. The pleasure-seeking principle is given splendid expression in the song of temptation which lulls Rinaldo asleep so that he becomes Armida's prisoner:

> Ye happy youths, whom April fresh and May
>   Attire in flow'ring green of lusty age,
> For glory vain or virtue's idle ray
>   Do not your tender limbs to toil engage;
> In calm streams fishes, birds in sunshine play,
>   Who followeth pleasure he is only sage;
> So nature saith, yet 'gainst her sacred will
> Why still rebel you, and why strive you still?
>
>   (XIV.62)

Virtue is but "an idle name, / Priz'd by the world 'bove reason all and measure", just as "honour, glory, praise, renown, and fame" are a mere "shade, a dream, a flower, / With each wind blasted, spoil'd with every shower" (XIV.63). In the extended centre of this tetrad the life of man is again presented as a shade, a dream, and a flower in the almost hypnotic song of the rose sung by the wonderful bird in Armida's enchanted garden. Its conclusion, therefore, is the familiar exhortation to "Gather the rose of love while yet thou mayst" (XVI.15).

The two songs of temptation connect the beginning of this tetrad and its extended centre, while linkage with the end is afforded by the old man's message to Rinaldo:

> Not underneath sweet shades and fountains shrill,
>   Among the nymphs, the fairies, leaves and flow'rs;
> But on the steep, the rough and craggy hill
>   Of virtue, stand this bliss, this good of ours;
> By toil and travail, not by sitting still
>   In pleasure's lap, we come to honour's bow'rs:
> Why will you thus in sloth's deep valley lie?
> The royal eagles on high mountains fly:
>
> Nature lifts up thy forehead to the skies,
>   And fills thy heart with high and noble thought,
> That thou to heav'nward aye shouldst lift thine eyes,
>   And purchase fame by deeds well done ...
>   (XVII.61–62)

This gives the lie to the false claims advanced in the two songs: nature does *not* proclaim that he alone is wise who follows pleasure (XIV.62), and when it seems as if "the land, the sea, and heav'n above" in Armida's garden "breath'd out fancy sweet and sigh'd out love" (XVI.16), this is a perverted, artificial environment. It is in the wisdom of the old man that truth can be found: "Nature lifts up thy forehead to the skies".

To repeat: The action of this tetrad begins and ends in darkness, but it is a darkness that encloses light. Godfrey's vision provides spiritual illumination, and the armour which shines in the darkness of the desert surely is the spiritual armour of the soldier of Christ. In the extended centre, spiritual darkness prevails at noon, but true light appears when Rinaldo unexpectedly sees the "glist'ring arms" of the two knights (XVI.27), and when he sees his own reflection in the diamond shield. Finally the old man provides illumination in the darkness of the desert – he presents a true account of the choice each of us has to make, and in the process exposes the illusory character of the pleasure promised by Armida.

The darkness at noon is the darkness of fleshly desires, and the appropriate biblical passage is *Romans* 13:12–14, the very passage which figures so prominently in Augustine's account of his conversion. When Rinaldo, accompanied by Carlo and Ubaldo, at the end of Book XVII marches "right against the rising morn", these verses provide a powerful sub-text:

> The night is far spent, the day is at hand: let us therefore cast off the works of darkness, and let us put on the armour of light. Let us walk honestly, as in the day; not in rioting and drunkenness, not in chambering and wantonness, not in strife and envying. But put ye on the Lord Jesus Christ, and make not provision for the flesh, to fulfil the lusts thereof.

The second tetrad, then, sharply contrasts true and false bliss, true and false rest. The "naked wantons" observed by Carlo and Ubaldo praise the happiness of those who can see "This bliss, this heav'n, this paradise" (XV.62), but, as Godfrey perceives in his dream vision, it is God who is "King of bliss" (XIV.13), and once he has achieved his mission in life Godfrey too will enjoy the ease, repose, and rest of Heaven. The repose of "saints in bliss" is the repose when all desires are fully satisfied in God (XIV.1–8).

Tasso's description of the false bliss in Armida's garden draws heavily on the familiar iconographical tradition of the Choice of Hercules.[17] Renaissance paintings and emblems showing the choice are based on Xenophon's *Memorabilia* (2.1.21–34), according to which Hercules is placed between Virtue and Pleasure. Virtue may have a sword or a shield and spear, and will often have one foot on a stone to suggest the arduousness of her path. Pleasure, on the other hand, may be accompanied by Cupid, and she is often placed next to rich draperies and displays of food. Her chief attributes are her naked breasts. The figure of Hercules is poised so as to suggest a brief leaning towards Pleasure, but it is Virtue who engages his chief attention. This is clearly the source of Tasso's description. Thus Fairfax emphasizes Armida's partial nakedness by repeating the word *breast* in rhyme position at XVI.18:7 and 23:8. Later on Fielding was to dramatize the same iconographical tradition in *Tom Jones*, but Fielding did not let Mrs Waters develop into a Sophia Western figure; he kept the two separate, preferring to discriminate between gross lust (false Pleasure) and true love (Pleasure and Virtue in one). In order to underline the deceptive character of lust, Fielding permitted his Tom Jones/Hercules to become the nicely dressed slave of a far from delectable Lady Bellaston in a parody of the Rinaldo/Armida situation. This second iconographical tradition of Mars enslaved by Venus[18] furnishes the details in the episode when Rinaldo is unexpectedly confronted by Carlo and Ubaldo and compelled to look at himself in the mirror of the diamond shield. In it he sees "all his wanton habit", his balm and perfumes and his sword which "Bewrapt with flow'rs hung idly by his side, / So nicely decked that it seem'd the knight / Wore it for fashion sake, but not for fight" (XVI.30). He is indeed, to quote Ubaldo, "buried in sloth and shame, / A carpet champion for a wanton dame!" (XVI.32)

Although Rinaldo's commitment to Virtue is such that all Armida's pleas are to no avail, the pain each feels at the parting is such that "base love" clearly is in the process of becoming transformed into heroic love. At this point the narrative becomes truly impassioned. Forgetting all her charms and spells, Armida runs after Rinaldo and reaches him "breathless, weary, faint, and weak, / So woe-begone was never nymph or maid; / And yet her beauty's pride grief could not break" (XVI.41:2–4).

> On him she look'd, she gaz'd, but nought she said;
>   She would not, could not, or she durst not speak.
> At her he look'd not, glanc'd not; if he did,
>   Those glances shamefast were, close, secret, hid.
>   (XVI.41:5–8)

Love has become her religion, Rinaldo her saint: "before thy shrine / Alone I pray, thou cruel saint of mine" (XVI.46:7–8). This is surely more than mere Petrarchism, since Armida virtually renounces her faith in the preceding lines, and in the lines that follow she offers to become his bondslave and to cut off her hair in token of her condition. In spite of "death and fate" she will follow him "Through battles fierce where dangers most appear; / Courage I have and strength enough, perchance, / To lead thy courser spare and bear thy lance" (XVI.48:5–8). "I will or bear or be myself thy shield, / And to defend my life will lose mine own!" (XVI.49:1–2). But in Rinaldo's breast "Love enter'd not" to kindle its flame "Which reason late had quench'd", "Yet enter'd pity in the place at least, / (Love's sister, but a chaste and sober dame)" (XVI.51:1–4). True, Armida expresses "bitter Wrath" (XVI.55:8) when Rinaldo rejects her with the words: "Too great your hate was, and your love too hot" and "Call me your soldier and your knight, as far / As Christian faith permits and Asia's war" (XVI.52:8 and 53:7–8). It is left to the narrator to explain Rinaldo's feelings at XVI.60–62. He leaves the coast "with sad and rueful look" and "To land he look'd till land unseen he left". When Armida wakes from her swoon, she swears revenge and leaves for Egypt.

The picture presented of Armida in Book XVII contrasts greatly with her appearance in XVI.1–27, but we see the contrast only if we pay attention to the traditional iconographical features of her appearance. Armida is placed in the last, climactic position in the long procession which files past the king of Egypt; her chariot is drawn by four unicorns, and she is compared to the "new-born phoenix" surrounded by "a host of wond'ring birds" (XVII.34–35). These images suggest not only uniqueness, but chastity and re-birth or regeneration. This positive interpretation is supported by the fact that she is described as having a "gown tuck'd up, and in her hand a bow". This is not the bow of Cupid as described at IV.76; the parallel strengthens the antithesis, since the bow she carries is the attribute of the chaste Diana, who has her gown "tuck'd up". As Edgar Wind explains, a merging of Venus and Diana expresses the union of love and chastity.[19] Diana's bow and arrows were taken to express the *concordia discors* achieved when love is bridled by chastity. The arrows symbolize the passion of love, the bow the restraint which modifies it, and, when Armida attempts suicide towards the end of Book XX, the weapon significantly enough is an arrow. On this occasion, though, the power that restrains it is the strong arm of Rinaldo.

The theme of concord in the first triad and the last acquires a more profound significance when related to the story of Rinaldo and Armida. When Rinaldo is first introduced, it is through the eyes of God, who observes that "To wealth or sovereign power he nought applied / His wits, but to virtue excellent" (I.10:5–6). When the Christian troops are marshalled, Rinaldo is placed in the final, climactic position among the horsemen, and the narrator describes him as "Star of this sphere, the diamond of this ring, / The nest where courage with sweet mercy breeds" (I.58:2–3). The gold ring with a diamond symbolizes beauty adorned by virtue,[20] and the reconciliation between courage and mercy resembles the unity, in God, between justice and mercy. After his experience of unbridled wrath and equally unbridled love, Rinaldo regains the balance he displayed in Books I and III. Rinaldo is not a truant to his cause so much as a champion who must be severely tested before he can fulfil his mission; like Godfrey and Tancred (in Books XI and XII) he, too, must be purified through trial and chastisement. Armida similarly is purified through suffering; her suffering when Rinaldo abandons her on the beach (as Aeneas had his Dido, and Augustine his mother Monica) is so extreme that she faints. The tempering suggested by her appearance in Book XVII becomes clearer still in Book XX. On the field of battle in this last canto Rinaldo ignores Armida, while Armida is torn between conflicting impulses: "Wrath, fury, kindness, in her bosom strove" (XX.64:6), but "love assuag'd her wrath". "Love bridled fury" for "love finds mean, but hatred knows no measure" (XX.62:8, 63:1 and 7). These statements reinforce the impression given by her appearance as Diana in Book XVII, and prepare us for her response to Rinaldo's appeal after the battle has been lost. If we pay attention to the thematic import of all this, it must be conceded that her response has been adequately prepared for, as has Rinaldo's development. Armida's progress corresponds to Rinaldo's. A tempering of the passions precedes regeneration by grace; it does not cause it to happen, but makes it possible to accept. In the last battle Rinaldo is the greatest of the Christian champions whose martial fury none can resist, but, the moment when "none his force withstood", "he assuag'd his fury, calm'd his angry mood" (XX.58:7-8). Within the short span of five stanzas – XX.58 and 63 – Tasso shows us how first Rinaldo, and then Armida *assuage* their fury. In their last confrontation Rinaldo assumes what Paul calls "the ministry of reconciliation" (II *Cor.* 5:20). He comes as an ambassador for Christ, dressed in the "armour of righteousness" and full of "love unfeigned" and "the word of truth" to relieve her from the "bondage of corruption" (II *Cor.*6:6 and *Rom.*8:21).

It has been argued that "the enchantress, Armida, is finally accepted by her former victim, Rinaldo, when she submits herself to him", just as Guyon in *The Faerie Queene* II.xii "may respond to Acrasia only by binding her",[21] but Rinaldo's lineage cannot stem from a bondwoman. Armida's response to Rinaldo in Books XVI and XX requires a New Testament perspective that combines *Luke* 1:38 ("Behold the handmaid of the Lord") with *Galatians* 4:22-31 on the two sons of Abraham, "one by a bondmaid, the other by a freewoman. But he who was of the bondwoman was born after the flesh; but he of the freewoman was by promise". When Rinaldo faces Armida for the last time, he insists that she is to be free and restored to her throne, and that he will serve as her "campione e servo" (XX.134:8). The lineage which Tasso honours in his epic must be legitimate, since Agar represents a Jerusalem in bondage, "but Jerusalem which is above is free, which is the mother of us all".

On turning to the inner triads we shall see that purification through trial is a basic part of their thematic pattern.

The Inner Triads

Whereas the action in Books VIII–X proceeds through a series of disasters to victory over Soliman the Turk and his Arab mercenaries, Books XI–XIII begin promisingly for the Christians but conclude with the disasters of the loss of the wooden tower so necessary for the assault, the loss of water through the terrible drought, and the loss of access to timber when Ismen casts his spell on the grove. This puts a stop to all martial action.

The contrast between despair and a firm faith pervades Books VIII–X, and makes itself felt in Books XI–XIII as well. However, the main theme of Books XI–XIII is purification through trial. Trial is of course the test of faith and a means to increase its strength.

When Book VIII begins, the foul fiend Alecto determines to "Kindle debate" among the Christians, and to "Set all the camp on uproar and at strife" (VIII.3). Disaster strikes, or seems to strike. First a Danish soldier arrives with the news that all the Danish troops have been killed by Soliman and his men, and next a patrol returns with the message that they have seen Rinaldo's battered armour and a headless corpse. During the night the Italian Argillan is tormented by strange visions sent by Alecto; he believes that he sees the dead Rinaldo who proclaims that "Godfrey hath murder'd me by treason vile" (VIII.61:1), and he announces this to the troops, who become enraged. Alecto envenoms their hearts and instils folly, disdain, madness, rancour, ire and thirst to shed blood (VIII.72), but Godfrey's faith is unimpaired. He turns to God and prays that God will "illuminate their dark souls with light divine" and "Repress their rage, by hellish fury bred" (VIII.76). A "sacred heat from heav'n above" makes Godfrey appear "In shape an angel, and a god in speech" (VIII.77–78), and in his speech he tempers justice with mercy, promising the men that Argillan alone will be punished. This quells their senseless rage, and all become "hush'd and still" (VIII.82). The story of the massacre of the Danes at night (VIII.4–45) is a story of disaster bravely met with unshaken faith. The teller of the tale is the only survivor. When the Danish prince receives the report that a mighty host of pagans is near at hand, the men "look pale for dread"; "Only our noble lord was alter'd nought / In look, in face, in gesture, or in thought" (VIII.14:7–8). They are attacked at night and fight until dawn, when only a scant hundred men are still alive. But the prince remains undaunted and "show'd no change", and so this last remnant dies, fully convinced that they have gained the crown of martyrdom. The survivor is rescued by two hermits who raise him virtually from the dead, so that "All whole and sound I leap'd up from the land. / O miracle, sweet, gentle, strange, and true!" (VIII.28). In both disasters, then – the massacre of the Danes and the near-rebellion among Godfrey's troops – a simple, unshaken Christian faith prevails.

In Book IX Soliman suffers a grievous defeat, and when Book X begins he escapes from the field of battle with distempered thoughts. However, he is stopped by the sorcerer Ismen, who cures his wounds and persuades him to return and to enter Jerusalem through a secret passage. When Soliman crosses the battlefield and sees how his men lie dead, he "chang'd his hue for grief and teen" (X.25:4–5), thus pointing the contrast to the imperturbability of the Danish prince and Godfrey. Another contrast is between the miraculous healing of the Danish soldier and Soliman, who is healed when Ismen pours a quintessence into his wounds – a healing by natural magic, not divine grace. On his arrival inside Jerusalem, concealed in a magic mist, Soliman puts an end to the discord between the assembled leaders (the "sad king" and his "nobles sad"; X.34) and puts new heart into them, as Godfrey did to his men in Book VIII.

Book X gives us the true version of what had happened to Rinaldo. Although in chains and guarded by a hundred horsemen, the Christian knights taken captive by Armida are liberated by Rinaldo, who passes on after having discarded his ruined armour and weapons. This account concludes with a splendid prophecy, by the hermit Peter, concerning Rinaldo's future.

The many parallels between Books VIII and X establish the cyclical pattern which turns Books VIII–X into a triad. First Godfrey, and then Soliman, expel discord and despair; the despair in Book VIII follows from the belief that Rinaldo is dead, in Book X from the belief that Soliman is dead. Godfrey's leadership is affirmed in Book VIII, Soliman's in Book X. In defeat the Danish prince has an even mind and a firm faith, but not so Soliman. The greatest antithesis is of course that Godfrey is supported by heavenly powers, while Alecto (the spirit of evil) and the conjuror Ismen support Soliman.

Pivotal though the celebration of Mass certainly is, it does not cause the tide to turn. The Christian forces fail to scale the walls in Book XI, largely as a consequence of Godfrey's untimely pride, for which he is made to suffer. Tancred experiences total despair in Book XII when he discovers that he has killed his beloved Clorinda, and in Book XIII the whole camp suffer agonies in a protracted drought, and again a near-rebellion is quelled by Godfrey. Then, too, the spell cast on the grove by Ismen imposes complete passivity, since no timber can be had for the purpose of building wooden engines of assault. The theme which connects these three books is stated by the hermit Peter when he rebukes Tancred for having become a "heathen damsel's thrall", and for ignoring Heaven's proffered grace:

> To worthy actions and achievements fit
>   For Christian knights He would thee home recall,
> But thou hast left that course, and changed it
>   To make thyself a heathen damsel's thrall:
> But see, thy grief and sorrow's painful fit
>   Is made the rod to scourge thy sins withal;
> Of thine own good thyself the means He makes,
> But thou His mercy, goodness, grace forsakes:
>
> Thou dost refuse of Heav'n the proffer'd grace,
>   And 'gainst it still rebel with sinful ire;
> O wretch! O whither doth thy rage thee chase?
>   Refrain thy grief, bridle thy fond desire;
> At hell's wide gate vain sorrow doth thee place,
>   Sorrow, misfortune's son, despair's foul sire:
> O see thine ill, thy plaint and woe refrain,
> The guides to death, to hell, and endless pain. –
>
> (XII.87–88)

His fear of dying "that second death" causes Tancred to abandon his will to die; "These words of comfort to his heart down went, / And that dark night of sorrow somewhat cleared" (XII.89:1–4). Chastisement, then, is proffered grace, and the hermit's argument recalls *James* 1:2–4 on the trials that should be considered as a happy privilege. These trials put our faith to the test to make us patient, "but patience too is to have its practical results so that you will become fully-developed, complete, with nothing missing" (The Jerusalem Bible). And as we may read in 1 *John* 1:8–10, no one is free from sin, but if we acknowledge our sins, God "will forgive our sins and purify us" (Jer. Bible).

The first to suffer this purification is Godfrey, whose sin is pride masquerading as humility. He dresses for battle like a common footsoldier, and the reason he offers for appearing "half disarm'd" and dressed in "weak defences" (XI.21) is that he has made a vow to this effect, and that God "shall this life defend" (XI.24). When old Raymond sees this, he understands the true reason: "Alas! do you that idle praise expect, / To set first foot this conquer'd wall above?" (XI.22:1-2). Godfrey, however, merely refers to his vow, and his example is followed by "every hardy knight" and his "brethren twain" (XI.25). When a breach is finally made in the wall, Godfrey reveals his true motive in a speech to Sigiere:

> Over these ruins will I passage make,
>   And enter first, the way is eath and low;
> And time requires that by some noble feat
> I should make known my strength and puissance great.
>
> (XI.53:5-8)

The consequence is immediate: "He scant had spoken ... / When on his leg a sudden shaft him hit" (XI.54:1-2). The wound (inflicted by Clorinda) compels him to retire to his tent, and with him departed "the heart / The strength and fortune of the Christian bands" (XI.57). Godfrey meekly endures the pain of the many vain attempts to remove the arrowhead from the wound, and finally faints. This is the moment of true humility. In the end an angel intervenes, and the arrow shoots out of its own accord, and "The leg again wax'd strong, with vigour new" (XI.74). The leech exclaims that some good angel must have been his surgeon, "for here plain tokens are / Of grace divine" (XI.75). Before he joins his troops again, Godfrey puts on proper armour: "A sturdy lance in his right hand he braced, / His shield he took, and on his helmet laced" (XI.75). Although on his return, "armed round about / In trusty plate", the odds are again in his favour, the day is too far advanced and the fighting must cease with the coming of darkness. In this way the crusaders lost, not only the victory, but also the wooden engines so indispensable for an attack on the walls. The great tower "now stood bruised, broken, crack'd, and shivered" as by a sharp storm (XI.83). This loss proves fatal when, in Book XIII, the sorcerer casts a spell on the grove which could have supplied timber for the construction of new engines.

The theme of purification through trial is sustained through Book XII in the story of Tancred and Clorinda, and finds climactic expression in the terrible drought in Book XIII. Men, animals, and the very soil are scorched "with scalding beams" from a merciless sun (XIII.52), and the thematic concern with sin explains this appearance of the dreaded *sol iustitiae*. Again the men rise up against Godfrey, and again he turns to God for aid, his prayer being that God will "ope the springs of grace, and ease this drought" (XIII.70). And again his prayer is answered: rain ends the drought, and all are renewed. In this triad, then, the purification by trial begins with Godfrey (XI), continues with Tancred (XII), and concludes with the whole army (XIII). As we have seen, the process will conclude with the redemption of Rinaldo in the cantos that follow.

We may now leave the subject of the balance between outer triads, tetrads, and inner triads and their own internal symmetries in order to consider the pattern of recessed symmetry formed by individual books.

3. Recessed Symmetry

In a poem consisting of 20 books, plain symmetry demands that Books X and XI should be linked. Such is indeed the case, since the last part of Book X balances the beginning of Book XI by presenting a parody of the sacred rites celebrated by Godfrey and his men. It is Armida who stages the parody in the perverse banquet she provides for the Christian knights who have defected from camp in order to be with her. Armida's ceremony, too, requires 19 stanzas, and the pattern is so exact that linkage is observed between the stanzas that are 13th, 14th and 15th from the end of Book X (X.64–66) and from the beginning of Book XI. Both "banquets" have costly furnishings, and both are accompanied by blasphemies: Armida mumbles "strange and secret things" over a book and a charming rod, and the Christian rites are countered by vile blasphemies yelled by the pagan onlookers. The "communion" provided for the knights who have defected consists in "empoison'd cups" designed to make "each knight himself and God forget" (X.65), and Armida's banquet (X.64–66) entices with rich food, virgins "for husbands able", and "hymns of love" (X.65), as opposed to the sacred hymns sung by Godfrey's men and their sacred food (XI.13–15). To intimidate those who will not be enticed, Armida suddenly turns on her guests "With changed looks where wrath and anger met" and proves her power by causing them to be turned into fish in an evil metamorphosis that parodies the change wrought by regeneration through divine grace. However, all but one refuse to forsake their faith, and so are sent as prisoners to Egypt, but on the road they are rescued and set free by Rinaldo. They return to Godfrey as penitents, full of shame and grief.

The linkage between the beginning of Book X and the end of Book XI is equally strong: at X.14 the sorcerer Ismen cures the wounds of Soliman, just as Godfrey's wound is miraculously healed by an angel in the stanzas that are 12th to 14th from the end (XI.73–75). The parallel makes the antithesis strongly felt. The related topoi of elevation and debasement provide further substantial links. After his secret entry into Jerusalem, Soliman is made the head of the besieged forces within the walls and placed on a throne by the king himself. In Book XI, Godfrey's seeming humility on donning a soldier's garb conceals his ambition to be the first to set foot within the walls; his subsequent humiliation on being wounded is patiently endured, however, and so leads to the miraculous cure that enables him to carry on the battle, yet with so much loss of time that the renewed effort comes too late in the day.

Some of the links between Books IX and XII are obvious, while others are more subtle. In both books the action takes place in darkness, and in both darkness is associated with evil. In Book IX, the fiend Alecto incites Soliman the Turk to attack the Christians at night in their tents, and fiends influence the course of the battle which ensues. However, once the archangel Michael has driven the fiends back into Hell, the victory falls to the Christians. The events of Book XII may at first seem to have little connection with those of Book IX, apart from the spiritual significance of darkness. What happens is that Clorinda, accompanied by Argantes, leaves Jerusalem in secret by night, dressed in black armour; she does this to set fire to the wooden tower on which the success of the siege depends. However, before she leaves, her old eunuch and fosterparent tries to dissuade her, and when this fails he reveals to her that her true parents were Christians and that he has been told in visions that Clorinda must be baptized; if not, she will die (XII.39). Clorinda becomes pensive since she herself has had a similar dream, but she refuses to change her religion and sallies out together with Argantes. Their plan succeeds, but on their return Clorinda is accidentally left outside when the gate is closed. Then follows her fierce encounter with Tancred who pierces her bosom with his sword. On the point of death, a "Spirit of hope, of charity, and faith" enables her to offer prayers and to ask her opponent to save her soul; "baptism I dying crave" (XII.66:3). When Tancred obeys he discovers that it is Clorinda. Thus is the dark veil of paganism lifted from the heroic Clorinda, but darkness descends on Tancred instead, who feels surrounded on all sides by "ugly shades, dark night, and troubled air" (XII.77:3), as in a recurrence of the events of Book IX:

> Madness and death about my bed repair,
>   Hell gapeth wide to swallow up his tent;
> Swift from myself I run, myself I fear,
> Yet still my hell within myself I bear.
>
> (XII.77:5–8)

Rescue comes from the hermit Peter, who admonishes Tancred to accept the chastisement which is proffered grace, and so Tancred bridles his "passion wood", and during the night Clorinda appears to him in a dream and speaks words of comfort. Thus Tancred is purified from the "hell within", just as the Earth is purified from the fiends of Hell in Book IX. The hell within suffers the same extinction as the hell without, and in each case God is the moving power.

At the textual centres of Books IX and XII are located related episodes: in Book XII the combat between Tancred and Clorinda is at the textual centre, that between Godfrey and Soliman in Book IX. In each case the narrator states that the action is worthy of the brightest day: these acts "Which sable night did in dark bosom drown" are worthy of "royal lists and brightest day" (XII.54), and again: "Great deeds they wrought ... / Yet still in darkness (more the ruth) they dwell: / The night their acts her black veil covered under, / Their acts whereat the sun, the world, might wonder" (IX.50).

Book VIII tells the story of the massacre of the Danes and the near-rebellion against Godfrey. Book XIII too has two episodes: Ismen casts his spell on the grove, and a terrible drought saps the strength and the morale of Godfrey's men. As in Book VIII, a near-rebellion is quelled when Godfrey's prayer moves God to extend his grace and relieve those who suffer. The two rebellions provide an obvious link, as does Godfrey's response to this serious threat, which is to turn to God for aid. In Book VIII infernal agents are at work to persuade the soldiers that Godfrey has not only caused the death of Rinaldo, but also appropriated all the spoils and all the honour for himself: "We reaped nought but travail for our toil, / Theirs was the praise, the realms, the gold, the spoil" (VIII.65:7–8). This slander recurs in Book XIII, when Godfrey's humility is presented as mere hypocrisy:

> See, see the man call'd holy, just, and good,
>   That courteous, meek, and humble would be thought,
> Yet never car'd in what distress we stood,
>   ...
> And now he sits at feasts and banquets sweet,
> And mingles waters fresh with wines of Crete.
>
> (XIII.67)

In contrast to Rinaldo, however, Godfrey is not moved by slander. In Book VIII he understands that the rage is caused by "hellish fury" and prays for God to repress it (VIII.76). In Book XIII, though, the situation is much more serious since the scorching sun must represent the dreaded *sol iustitiae* and hence must be a divine analogue to "hellish fury". Godfrey shows the appropriate response to God's avenging justice in his prayer for redemption:

> Father and Lord! if in the deserts waste
>   Thou hadst compassion on thy children dear,
> The craggy rock when Moses cleft and brast,
>   And drew forth flowing streams of water clear,
> Like mercy, Lord, like grace, on us down cast;
>   And though our merits less than theirs appear,
> Thy grace supply that want, for though they be
> Thy first-born sons, thy children yet are we. –
>
> (XIII.71)

Far more is involved here than pacification of angry soldiers; the rain which falls in answer to this prayer becomes the visible sign of inner renewal. What happens to the Earth describes this renewal:

> Earth like the patient was whose lively blood
>   Hath overcome at last some sickness strong,
> Whose feeble limbs had been the bait and food
>   Whereon his strange disease depastur'd long;
> But now restor'd, in health and welfare stood,
>   As sound as erst, as fresh, as fair, as young;
> So that, forgetting all his grief and pain,
> His pleasant robes and crowns he takes again.

> Ceased the rain; the sun began to shine,
>   With fruitful, sweet, benign, and gentle ray,
> Full of strong power and vigour masculine,
>   As be his beams in April or in May.
> O happy zeal! who trusts in help divine
>   The world's afflictions thus can drive away,
> Can storms appease, and times and seasons change,
> And conquer fortune, fate, and dest'ny strange.
>
> (XIII.79–80)

The massacre of the Danes in Book VIII points forward to the defeat experienced by Godfrey's champions and his men in Book XIII when they try to enter the grove on which Ismen has cast his spell. The defeat is a kind of spiritual "massacre", but the parallel is accompanied by a telling antithesis: whereas the Danes die fully convinced of God's grace and trusting in God's power to restore them to life again, those who venture into the grove are routed by deceptive visions. When Godfrey's stoutest champions "attempt the charmed grove" they bring back nothing "but fear and flight" (XIII.31). The last to try is Tancred, who actually succeeds in entering and penetrating to the centre where he finds a cypress "clad in summer's pride". When he tries to cut the tree, blood trickles down, and a lamenting voice cries out that "I was Clorinda; now imprison'd here", confined by magic together with all who have died before the walls, whether pagan or Christian. Tancred will be a murderer "if thou cut one twist" (XIII.43). Tancred realizes that all is mere illusion, yet is powerless to resist and so returns in defeat. The dilemma is resolved when the hermit Peter prophesies the return of Rinaldo, who will succeed where others failed. The drought that follows this spiritual defeat on the part of the Christians is as appropriate a chastisement as Tancred's agony in Book XII. Both aim at purification and restoration.

In Books VII and XIV Tancred and Rinaldo suffer similar fates: each is led astray by a false guide and taken prisoner by Armida. However, whereas Tancred is thrown into Armida's dungeon, Armida falls in love when she sees the sleeping Rinaldo, and takes him to another castle on an island in the Atlantic. A further link between the two books is afforded by the topos of divine protection. In his single combat with Argantes in Book VII, old Raymond is protected by an invisible guardian angel, just as Carlo and Ubaldo in Book XIV are assisted by a "wizard old" who knows how they may counter Armida's charms and spells (XIV.34–35). In contrast to the false guides who led Tancred and Rinaldo astray, the "wizard" is a true guide (VII.27–28 and XIV.55). His *magia naturalis* is stronger than Armida's because placed in the service of God and hence divinely assisted. By virtue of his great skill, the old man is free to range everywhere above or below the surface of the Earth, a circumstance which makes Armida's similar excursions inoffensive as evidence of power over the natural world alone. The power itself, then, is morally indifferent, so that the point to observe is the use that is made of it.

Book XIV begins on a quiet note: "Gentle night" sheds "fleeting balm on hills and dales", and all is peace and quiet (XIV.1). During this peaceful night Godfrey has his dream vision of the bliss of Heaven, and this vision finds its earthly analogue in Book VII, where the unhappy Erminia finds peace and quiet among harmless shepherds in rural solitude and obscurity (VII.1–22).[22] These opening stanzas on the happiness of rural life in Book VII should be contrasted with the concluding stanzas of Book XIV where it is transposed into a false key. The innocent shepherd boys and lasses are replaced by the "virgin bright" who displays her naked beauty as she rises from the stream (XIV.60), and the rejection of the quest for wealth and honour (VII.62–64) is given a hedonistic slant (XIV.62–64). Wisdom tells us to follow pleasure, and nature teaches the same lesson ("This wisdom is, good life, and worldly bliss, / Kind teacheth us, nature commands us this"; 64:7–8). The narrator adds: "Thus sung the spirit false" (XIV.65:1), and Rinaldo is lulled asleep. Seeing this, Armida starts from her ambush, but, as she looks, her wrath dissipates and her foe becomes her beloved. In the neatly balanced passages on rural happiness (VII.1–22) and Armida's seductive voluptuousness (XIV.57–79), the deceptive parallel conceals a strong antithesis. Both seem based on a rational denunciation of the quest for wealth and honour and on praise of peaceful obscurity, but contentment is a true virtue, whereas sensual indulgence is not. What nature offers suffices for the rural dweller, but what nature offers in the song of the "spirit false" is not a healthy diet and simple joys, but the sophisticated play of tender limbs in oblivious idleness. And it is simply not true that *virtue* (like wealth and honour) is "Priz'd by the world 'bove reason all and measure". It is a mere rhetorical trick to contaminate virtue by associating it with the "honour, glory, praise, renown, and fame / That men's proud hearts bewitch with tickling pleasure" (XIV.63). Honour and fame may figure *in malo* or *in bono* depending on the circumstances. At this point Tasso's narrative challenges us to discriminate between goods that may be true, deceptive, or downright false. Since the story of Erminia's vain pursuit of Tancred does not require that she stay among simple shepherds, the episode must have been invented to enable the true values it represents to be played off against the perverted values so seductively proclaimed by the "spirit false" on Armida's island in the river at the end of Book XIV. The exactness of the symmetrical placing suggests as much.

The conflict between love and honour informs Books VI and XV: love prevails in Book VI, honour (or virtue) in Book XV, and again the narrative invites us to draw clear distinctions: love may be worthy or unworthy, of course, but love may also be misdirected and destructive. Love may make the timid rash (as in the case of Erminia), while the bold may forget his honour as Tancred does when stricken motionless on seeing his beloved Clorinda in the distance. During this fatal moment heroic virtue no longer exists. When Carlo and Ubaldo, however, are invited to put off their arms (XV.63), they do nothing of the kind: instead their "armed reason" quenches "fond desire" (XV.66). Poor Erminia's case in Book VI is different: she esteems her honour above life or safety (VI.70), but love makes her thoughts confused (VI.78) so that her psychomachia terminates with the victory of love. When she dons Clorinda's armour and steals out of Jerusalem by night, her "wit and reason both were gone" (VI.90:3).

Book XV is devoted to a single action, the quest for Rinaldo, the man who has forgotten his honour to serve a base love. Carlo and Ubaldo who undertake this quest combine boldness and circumspection, thus ensuring temperance. They listen carefully to the instructions of the old man and then proceed firmly towards their goal, pitting all their strength and art against the threats and seductions of Armida. Their virtue is exemplary; it expels all fear and all temptations to sloth and lust, and they have been taught to understand, and hence to penetrate, her deceit. Erminia comes remarkably close to this virtuous condition when she envisages what she would do to rescue Tancred, if she had the physical strength: (VI.84):

> Love, – fearless, hardy, and audacious love, –
>   Embold'ned had this tender damsel so,
> That where wild beasts and serpents glide and move,
>   Through Afric's deserts durst she ride or go.
>
> (VI.70:1–4)

Wild beasts and serpents are precisely the hazards met by the two knights as they climb the steep mountain on top of which is Armida's castle with its garden at the centre. Erminia's love, therefore, has exactly the same effect as virtue; perfect love has cast out fear. Misguided boldness, though, contrasts with the boldness that is properly informed and directed: in Book VI Erminia leaves the safety of Jerusalem to venture out among hostile Christian forces, and Tancred defects from Godfrey's camp to seek his Clorinda. Both fare badly. But in Book XV Carlo and Ubaldo, who leave the known world to venture into unknown seas beyond the Strait of Gibraltar, meet with success, partly because assisted by an angelic guide in a magic boat, and partly because they have been instructed by the old man so that they are prepared for the hazards that await them. Among them are the temptations to lust and sloth in the last stanzas of Book XV.

Rinaldo and Armida dominate the action of Books V and XVI; Rinaldo's wrath dominates him in Book V, whereas in Book XVI it is his unbridled love of Armida which sways him. The contrast is startling. When Rinaldo leaves Godfrey's camp after having killed Gernando, his appearance outbraves that of Mars himself:

> About his neck his silver shield he flings,
> Down by his side a cutting sword there hung.
> Among this earth's brave lords, and mighty kings,
> Was none so stout, so fierce, so fair, so young.
> God Mars he seem'd descending from his sphere,
> Or one whose looks could make great Mars to fear.
> (V.44:3–8)

When Rinaldo sees himself in the mirror of the shield in Book XVI his transformation is complete; nothing can be more vain or effete:

> Upon the targe his looks amaz'd he bent,
> And therein all his wanton habit spied,
> His civet, balm, and perfumes redolent,
> How from his locks they smok'd and mantle wide;
> His sword, that many a Pagan stout had shent,
> Enwrapt with flow'rs hung idly by his side,
> So nicely decked that it seem'd the knight
> Wore it for fashion sake, but not for fight.
> (XVI.30)

Mars has become enslaved by Venus; Tasso's description is a verbal rendering of this iconographical motif. Related motifs are found in the pictures that adorn the gate leading into Armida's palace: as they pass through, Carlo and Ubaldo see how Hercules sits enslaved among women while Iole is armed with his club (XVI.3), and how the brave Antony flees from battle to seek his beloved (XVI.6). The mirror scene is a scene of cognition; when Rinaldo recognizes what he has become, his shame is extreme:

> Griev'd, shamed, sad, he would have died fain;
> And oft he wish'd the earth or ocean wide
> Would swallow him, and so his errors hide.
>
> (XVI.31:6–8)

Rinaldo's shame soon yields to "fierce disdain, from courage sprung untamed"; he tears his nice attire to shreds and follows the departing knights.

We observe Armida as the all-powerful queen of love at the end of Book V and the beginning of Book XVI in neatly balanced passages of equal length (V.60–85 and XVI.1–26). Among those who resist her allure are Godfrey and Tancred, the latter because "His sails were filled with another wind" (V.65:3). Many knights and champions, however, become "mad with the poison of her secret wiles", nor could "Godfredo's bridle rein them short" (V.71:6–8). The emblematic image of the bridling of the passions is soon followed by another emblem as the "conqueress departs, and with her led / These prisoners whom love would captive keep". The departure is by night, "And as blind Cupid led them, blind they went" (V.79).

Rinaldo's wrath in Book V is not unopposed: Tancred addresses Rinaldo in a persuasive speech calling for temperance (V.46–47), and in Book XVI it is Carlo and Ubaldo who function as agents of a heroic virtue. Rinaldo's reawakened heroic virtue enables him to renounce unbridled love when confronted by a desperate Armida: he "conquer'd his will, his heart ruth soften'd not, / There plaints no issue, love no entrance, got" (XVI.50:6–8). But although love cannot enter, "Yet enter'd pity in the place at least, / (Love's sister, but a chaste and sober dame)" (XVI.51:1–4). Pity moves him almost to tears, but he feigns cheer and addresses her formally, advising her to expel "fond affection":

Truth is, you err'd, and your estate forgot;
Too great your hate was, and your love too hot:

But these are common faults, and faults of kind
　Excus'd by nature, by your sex, and years:
I err'd likewise.
(XVI.52–53)

When Armida sinks into a swoon he weeps and mourns, and takes farewell "with sad and rueful look". Once in the boat, "To land he look'd till land unseen he left" (XVI.60–61).

The process of purification through grief is shared by Armida, whose tearful and angry speeches are prompted by a love ready to endure shame and enslavement. She is no longer a "sly enchantress" who leads men captive, but herself a prisoner of love willing to be jeered at by the camp as "thy thrall and bondslave vile".

... since my lord doth hate
　These locks, why keep I them or hold them dear?
Come cut them off, that to my servile state
　My habit answer may, and all my gear:
I follow thee in spite of death or fate
　Through battles fierce where dangers most appear.
(XVI.48)

This pathetic encounter marks the first, decisive step in the direction of chaste love for both of them.

Armida is an important character also in Books IV and XVII. Book IV introduces Armida as the niece of "false Hidraort", a ruler well acquainted with "all the damned rout / Of Pluto's reign" (IV.20). It is he who sends Armida to the Christian camp to ensnare Godfrey, or to "lead the other lords to deserts waste, / And hold them slaves far from their leader's reach" (IV.25:5–6). Armida herself, therefore, has no direct connection with the "damned rout" described in stanzas 1–19 of this canto; the guilt rests with her uncle, the ruler of Damascus. Armida's mission is successful; with great reluctance Godfrey grants her request for ten champions to support her cause, but his warning to his men to temper the heat which misguides them falls on deaf ears, and Armida is free to wield the arms with which love conquers their "feeble hearts subdued in wanton fights" (IV.96).

As already suggested, the mustering of forces (Satanic and Egyptian) links Books IV and XVII, and Armida's call for champions is another link. In Book XVII Armida appears in the camp of the Egyptians as once she had done in Godfrey's camp, and once again she asks for a champion, this time in order to have Rinaldo killed in battle. Whoever succeeds will become her husband. Darkness taken *in malo* and *in bono* is yet another link: the darkness of Hell (IV.1–19) is antithetically opposed to the benign darkness in which Rinaldo is instructed by the old man and conducted to Godfrey's pavilion (XVII.54–97). In this darkness, too, divine illumination is afforded when the old man relates the prophecy of the hermit Peter concerning Rinaldo's lineage and his future offspring (XVII.86).

Wooden engines of assault are constructed in Book XVIII as in Book III. After he has experienced regeneration on Mount Olivet at the beginning of Book XVIII, Rinaldo breaks the spell cast on the grove by Ismen by cutting down the tree in the midst of the glade at the heart of the forest, regardless of the spurious visions that beset him. Unlike Tancred, he remains unmoved by seeing the semblance of his beloved, even when she seems most impassioned and pitiful:

> Ah! never do me such a spiteful part,
>   To cut my tree, this forest's joy and pride;
> Put up thy sword, else pierce therewith the heart
>   Of thy forsaken and despis'd Armide;
> For through this breast, and through this heart, unkind!
> To this fair tree thy sword shall passage find. –
> (XVIII.34:3–8)

Soft appeals and dire threats are of no avail, and, once the tree is felled, all is peace and quiet, and the wood returns to its former state, "quite void of spirits ill" (XVIII.38:3). Finally, then, new wooden engines of assault may be built. The deliverance of Jerusalem, therefore, depends on a conscious choice of virtue and on a related act of divine regeneration.

Dudon is another link between Books III and XVIII. The death and burial of Dudon in Book III is followed, in Book XVIII, by his appearance among the heavenly hosts at XVIII.95 in order to assist Godfrey and his men to scale the walls. These walls, seen for the first time in the first eight stanzas of Book III, are finally scaled and conquered in the last eight stanzas of Book XVIII.

The link between Books II and XIX is the willing self-sacrifice of the innocent, and another link is found in the treacherous plot. It is as a consequence of King Aladine's treacherous plot against the Christians within Jerusalem that Sophronia assumes the responsibility for the removal of the statue of the Virgin Mary from "Macon's sacred temple". On the advice of Ismen, this statue had been removed from a Christian church to this temple, and on this statue Ismen cast a spell to prevent the Christians from entering Jerusalem. However, the image disappears overnight, whether by mortal hand or by the hand of God, and by way of reprisal the king condemns all the Christians in Jerusalem to death. Sophronia therefore steps forward and professes to be the offender in order to save "the rest of Christ's selected fold" (II.22). Clorinda's timely arrival, however, leads to the pardon of Sophronia and her beloved Olindo who wanted to share her fate. The second half of Book II introduces Argantes, the pagan champion who is one of two ambassadors from the king of Egypt. Argantes is described as wrath incarnate: he is fierce and outrageous, "Scorner of God, scant to himself a friend, / And prick'd his reason on his Weapon's end" (II.59). When Godfrey rejects the offer of peace, Argantes looks "like huge Typhæus loos'd from hell / Again to shake heav'n's everlasting frame", or like him "that built the tower on Shinaar, / Which threat'neth battle 'gainst the morning star" (II.91:5–8). These similes connect Argantes with types of Satan, and later on he is compared to a comet which "In scorn of Phœbus 'midst bright heav'n doth shine" (VII.52:5–6). Argantes, then, is unequivocally associated with Satanic forces. Argantes, introduced in Book II, makes his exit from the epic action with symmetrical precision in Book XIX when he is killed by Tancred in a fierce combat. The episode of Sophronia's self-sacrifice in Book II finds its analogue in Book XIX in Erminia's rescue of Tancred. The combat between Argantes and Tancred that terminates with the death of Argantes occupies the first part of Book XIX, thus balancing the introduction of Argantes in the second part of Book II. Tancred is himself grievously wounded and faints, so that he is taken for dead when Erminia finds him. This is when she cuts off her hair to tie his wounds, thus professing herself to be his "bondslave". Erminia, therefore, performs the action which Armida merely suggests, and she does it as an act of mercy. Before this happens, though, she is instrumental in helping to uncover a treacherous plot against the Christian forces. She recognizes a Christian who has entered the

Egyptian camp in disguise, and she reveals to him the plot to have Godfrey killed in battle by soldiers dressed to seem like Godfrey's own men. The two escape back to Godfrey's camp together, Erminia because she hates her freedom and longs for the prison where she met her beloved Tancred. Bidding her vain modesty and shame farewell (like Armida), she confesses her love for Tancred, and it is on their return to Godfrey that the two come across Tancred's body next to that of Argantes.

> Nought but her veil amid those deserts wide
>   She had to bind his wounds in so great need;
> But love could other bands (though strange) provide,
>   And pity wept for joy to see that deed,
> For with her amber locks, cut off, each wound
> She tied; (O happy man, so cur'd, so bound!)
>
> (XIX.112)

The reader is permitted to share her happiness in a single, pregnant stanza:

> He says – O Vafrine, tell me whence com'st thou,
>   And who this gentle surgeon is disclose. –
> She smil'd, she sigh'd, she look'd she wist not how,
>   She wept, rejoic'd, she blush'd as red as rose: –
> You shall know all (she says); your surgeon now
>   Commands your silence, rest, and soft repose,
> You shall be sound, prepare my guerdon meet. –
> His head then laid she in her bosom sweet.
>
> (XIX.114)

Thus concludes the pathetic story of Erminia, the pagan princess who becomes a Christian through the man she loves. Love made both maidens bold: Sophronia in Book II and Erminia in Book XIX, and both experience a happy resolution despite serious threats and hazards. Like Sophronia, Erminia in a way offers her life for Christ, since she accepts Christianity on relinquishing the freedom which has become imprisonment. One may well suspect that the story of Sophronia was invented to serve as a foil for Erminia; without this story (almost an interpolated tale) the linkage between Books II and XIX would have been imperfect.

The marshalling of troops is the most obvious link between Books I and XX, and closely related to this topos are the ideas of concord and discord. On choosing Godfrey as leader, the Christians move from discord to concord (I.29–32), and in Book XX Godfrey cheers his men before battle by stressing their own concord and the discord which prevails among their enemies. Halfway through this final canto the scales are even, and Godfrey again brings "his squadrons in array, / And either camp well order'd, rang'd, and knit, / Renew'd the furious battle, fight, and fray", the issue being "unresolv'd, and doubtful" (XX.72). The first step toward disaster for the pagans is taken in stanza 73, the first stanza in the second half, when the Soldan, confined within the tower, climbs to the top to survey the battlefield, and so is fired to leave his post to join the fray. Thus the tower is won by the Christians, and Soliman fails to rally the pagan troops sufficiently to win the battle. Armida sees her champions dead or dying, and flees to escape bondage. When the battle is won, Godfrey runs to the temple "And there hung up his arms, and there he bows / His knees, there pray'd, and there perform'd his vows" (XX.144:7–8). Our last glimpse of Godfrey, then, as our first, shows him on his knees, praying (I.14), just as his last action returns us to the opening words: "Canto l'arme pietose". When Godfrey hangs up his arms in the temple they become truly *pietose*.

This study of the symmetrical structure has brought out the main issues in sharp and vivid outline; there can be no doubt that Tasso applied the aesthetic principles he advocates in his *Discourses*.

Andrew Fichter has attempted an analysis of Tasso's symmetries, but with limited success. A chapter on Tasso in Fichter's book on *Poets Historical. Dynastic Epic in the Renaissance* (1982) fails to go beyond a few obvious points. Method and terminology remain largely unexplained, and the presence of an overall symmetrical pattern causes Fichter to state that the pagans have the upper hand in the first half, the Christians in the second, but this is not true as we have seen. Soliman is defeated in Book IX, and the Christians suffer serious setbacks in Books XII and XIII: the loss of the wooden tower and the loss of access to timber impose complete passivity. The true turning-point is indicated by God toward the end of Book XIII: so far everything has gone very badly, but success will follow *from this hour* (XIII.73). This is the moment when God sends "victory like a dew", and lets "the clouds rain it down" (*Isaiah* 45:8). Since the *peripeteia* must be located in Books XIII–XIV it is possible and even likely that these books function as a pivotal centre dividing the epic into a sequence of 12—2—6 books or cantos. The precedent provided by Augustine for such a graded arrangement, and later on followed by Spenser and Milton, makes it a plausible theory.

4. The Graded Arrangement

An analysis of Books XIII and XIV will reveal the extent to which they may be considered as pivotal within a graded arrangement.

It is in Book XIII that we read about the failure of Godfrey's men to break the spell cast on the grove. The grove has always been replete with "natural horror". Its "ugly shade" is like "everlasting night", and when night falls the place is invaded by a horror which fills weak hearts with "sad Terror" (XIII.2–3). To this grove Ismen the sorcerer (once a Christian) compels legions of devils charged with preventing the Christians from obtaining timber. When Rinaldo breaks the spell in Book XVIII, the forest returns to "its wonted state", which is to be "Of horror full, but horror there innate" (XIII.38). In this innate state the forest may well represent unregenerate nature as Fichter believes, but the invasion makes it far worse than unregenerate: the invasion by devils creates an irredeemable state of total corruption. A fallen being may move in one of two directions, total corruption or regeneration, and it will not do to obliterate this vital distinction. Tasso underlines the distinction in the account of the drought, which is the second episode of Book XIII. The drought which causes the second near-rebellion is relieved when Godfrey prays for grace; the rain falls, and all are renewed, spiritually as well as physically. The sun, no longer scorching, emits a "fruitful, sweet, benign, and gentle ray" (XIII.80), and the renewal seems virtually like a resurrection. When Godfrey, in his prayer to God, recalls the moment when Moses struck water from the dry rock, this is an allusion to the best-known Old Testament type pointing forward to the crucifixion when the side of Christ (our rock) was pierced so that blood and water issued out for the salvation of man. The resurrection is alluded to also in the reference to the "virgin primrose and the violet blue" (XIV.1:6); Giles Fletcher may have remembered these lines when he wrote the opening stanzas on the resurrection in Part 4 of *Christs Victorie, and Triumph* (1610).[23]

Tasso takes us, then, from nature unregenerate and nature corrupted by evil spirits to nature restored through Christ by the grace of God. This was as close as he could take his romance material to the core of his religious message. In the episode of the grove, Tasso makes the same point as Milton in *Paradise Lost* when Earth is invaded by Satan, Sin, and Death after the Fall. The trouble with Tasso's devils is that they seem too theatrical; Spenser solved the problem by making do with characters like Archimago, Duessa, dragons, and giants.

The sense of a happy renewal conveyed at the end of Book XIII is carried over into Book XIV when day is succeeded by a "gentle night" which sheds "fleeting balm on hills and dales" with "honey drops of pure and precious dew". During the hours of this night, visions are sent to Godfrey in his sleep; the evil visions of the grove, therefore, are succeeded by Godfrey's vision of the universe and of souls in bliss, and these in their turn are succeeded by the visions experienced by Carlo and Ubaldo within the "hollow womb" of "fertile earth" (XIV.41). Whereas the grove creates darkness at noon, Godfrey sees "glorious shining light" in the middle of the night (XIV.4–9), and this topos of light within darkness is repeated when the old man takes Carlo and Ubaldo to his palace within the earth itself (XIV.41). The old man represents *magia naturalis*; although reared as a pagan he was baptized by the hermit Peter whom he obeys in all things, and he knows that his natural magic is as nothing compared with the wisdom and power of God.

Books XIII–XIV may well be called books of wisdom: we begin with the false wisdom of Ismen and conclude with the old man whose *magia naturalis* is placed in the service of God. In between, the wisdom of God is revealed in the scheme of redemption as manifested in the cessation of the drought and in Godfrey's dream vision. A subordinate topos is found in the maze of the forest in Book XIII, which finds its analogue in Armida's maze-like castle in Book XIV. At its centre is a garden "where many a gin / And net to catch frail hearts false Cupid lays" (XIV.75–76). This maze and its many deadly illusions connect with the maze of the grove and its dread enchantments, at whose centre is the semblance of Armida.

Certain points of similarity are perceived on comparing Books XIII–XIV with book 9 of the *Confessions*, which divides Augustine's narrative into a sequence of 8—1—4 books, as explained in Chapter II. In each case the main action or discourse is suspended, an ascent to God envisaged, and the universe surveyed. Instruction in true and useful knowledge is a main issue, together with "help divine" (XIII.80:5). Chapter IX will show that the same thematic concerns are present in book 7 in the first, 10-book edition of *Paradise Lost* (1667), and that this book serves to divide the epic into a sequence of 6—1—3 books. It would seem, therefore, that we have to do with a tradition according to which material of this kind would be used to create a pivotal section dividing the body of a text in the ratio 2:1.[24]

Before Books XIII–XIV of Tasso's epic can be said to have a pivotal function, links must be present between these books and the beginning and the end. Godfrey's prayer is one such link, since

Godfrey makes his first appearance in Book I while at his morning prayer. This is the moment when the angel of the Lord appears with the message that it is God's will that he become leader of the Christian forces (I.15–17). At the end of Book XIII, Godfrey's prayer for mercy marks the transition from malignant drought to benign fertility, from seeming defeat to the promise of victory. Then too the message given by the angel concerning the will of God (I.15–17) points forward to the similar message conveyed to Godfrey by the dead Hugo (XIV.13–14). Yet another parallel is the panoramic survey enjoyed by God at I.7 and by Godfrey at XIV.4–10; for a moment Godfrey is made to share God's own vision. The theme of re-birth connects Books XIII–XIV with the end: the Earth is re-born when the rain falls at the end of Book XIII and the beginning of Book XIV, and so is Armida when she accepts Godfrey's proffered grace toward the end of Book XX. Armida's action shows what the liberation of Jerusalem means at the human level. The liberation at the end of Book XX connects closely with Godfrey's vision of the heavenly city at the beginning of Book XIV: this is the reality mirrored by the earthly city and by the 12×12 stanzas required to describe the liberation.

The narratives of Books I–XII and XV–XX form identifiable substructures. Books I–XII are unified by the story of Tancred and Clorinda: we hear about Tancred's love in Book I, and the story ends with Clorinda's baptism and death and Tancred's subsequent purification through suffering in Book XII. At the halfway point (at the end of Book VI and the beginning of Book VII), Tancred defects from the Christian camp to seek Clorinda, but only to land in Armida's dungeon instead. The curve of this story, therefore, joins books I–XII. In Books XV–XX it is the relationship between Armida and Rinaldo which holds our attention: each proceeds from carnal love to a love that is chaste (i.e. virtuous and infused with divine grace). Book XV begins with an account of how the "well-instructed knights" ("The Argument", l. 1) climb to the top of Armida's charmed mountain as if in illustration of the ascent up the craggy hill of Virtue, and at the halfway point (at the end of Book XVII and the beginning of Book XVIII) Rinaldo is taught the lesson of the Choice of Hercules. Rinaldo must learn to seek his bliss "on the steep, the rough, and craggy hill / Of virtue" (XVII.61:3–4); he must bridle each secret vice and control his anger, and he must find his inspiration in the glorious deeds of his ancestors as shown in the shield (XVII.64–82). In the opening stanzas of Book XVIII, Rinaldo proceeds from the moral to the spiritual level as he undergoes regeneration through prayer on Mount Olivet, an event that points forward to Armida's acceptance of grace at XX.136, when she yields to Christ in him. Although Rinaldo of course figures in Books I–XII, he does not become an interesting character until he meets Armida as described in the last stanzas of Book XIV, just as Tancred recedes into the background after Book XII. All that remains for him is to meet and overcome Argantes in single combat in Book XIX, and to be so nobly assisted by Erminia in his hour of need. Clorinda dies as the handmaid of the Lord, baptized by the man responsible for her death, and Erminia and Armida become the handmaids of the man they love, thus satisfying romance conventions and Pauline doctrine at the same time. To say that Rinaldo is capable of loving Armida only when she submits to him is to misread the text by ignoring contexts, and the best guide to context is found in the web of parallels and antitheses that unifies Tasso's romance epic.

5. Canto Structure

The structure of individual cantos obeys the same laws as the poem as a whole: a canto may consist of balanced segments, and a segment may itself possess a balanced pattern. Number symbolism can be traced with a fair amount of certainty in stanza totals, as in the case of the 144 stanzas of Book XX, as already remarked. Books IX and XII are of unusual interest in this connection, since each has both a symmetrical and a graded structure based on the biblical numbers 33 and 42. It must be because these books are concerned with deliverance from evil that these numbers of redemption through Christ condition their form. The links between these books, therefore, are structural as well as thematic.

The 99 stanzas of Book IX divide into 66 + 33, since the Satanic forces at work on the field of battle are expelled two-thirds of the way through this canto. The first 66-stanza segment begins with the description of Alecto, the "grisly child of Erebus", who bends all her thoughts against the wisdom of Heaven, whereas in stanza 66 the infernal troop is compelled to leave the Earth and return to Hell. Diagram V.8 shows the pattern of actions, and we observe that central accent cannot be found on the basis of a simple stanza-count. The first 13 stanzas are a separate segment that serves as an introduction; as if to underline this separateness, stanzas 1 and 13 share three identical rhymes: *went / crew / new* are repeated in the sequence *crew / new / went*. With stanza 14 the action proper

Diagram V.8 *Jerusalem Delivered*, the Pattern of Actions in Book IX

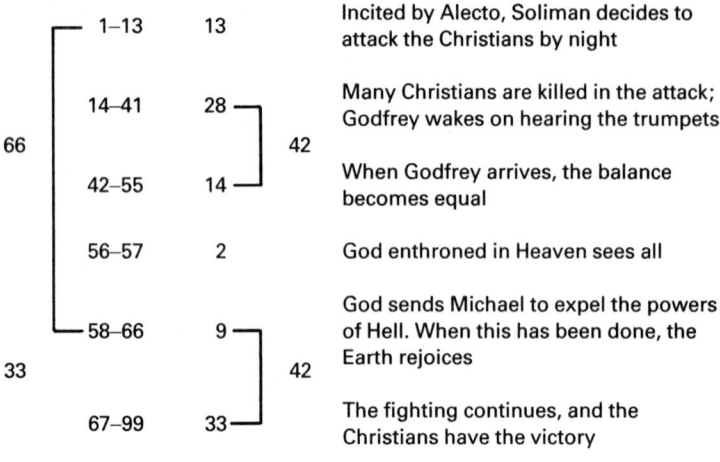

The ratio 2:1 occurs twice: it governs the division into 66 + 33 and the division of segments 2 and 3 into 28 + 14. The numbers and the twice-repeated ratio underline the redemptive character of this canto.

begins, and in this action – an attack by Soliman on the Christians at night – the description of God on his throne is appropriately located *in medio*. From his throne, God surveys the field of battle and sends Michael to expel the fiends. After this has been done Godfrey's men are victorious. We see, then, how complex a canto structure can be: a division into 66—33 coexists with another into 13—42—2—42.

Diagram V.9 shows that Book XII has a similar pattern, since the action divides the 105 stanzas into a sequence of 66—33—6 stanzas. Stanzas 1–66 begin with Clorinda's decision to sally out by night to set fire to the wooden tower, and concludes with her request for baptism when on the point of death. Her death and burial are at the beginning and end of the 33-stanza segment, whereas the last 6 stanzas report the reaction, in Jerusalem, to the report of her death. Each segment has an act of grace at the centre: at XII.29–38 we hear about Clorinda's miraculous escapes from death as an infant, and at XII.85 Tancred is saved from spiritual death by Peter's warning not to spurn the chastisement which is proffered grace. The reader understands too that, when Tancred gave Clorinda her mortal wound, this was equally an act of grace which compelled Clorinda to seek the baptism she had rejected despite her warning visions. The

JERUSALEM DELIVERED   251

Diagram V.9 *Jerusalem Delivered*, Book XII

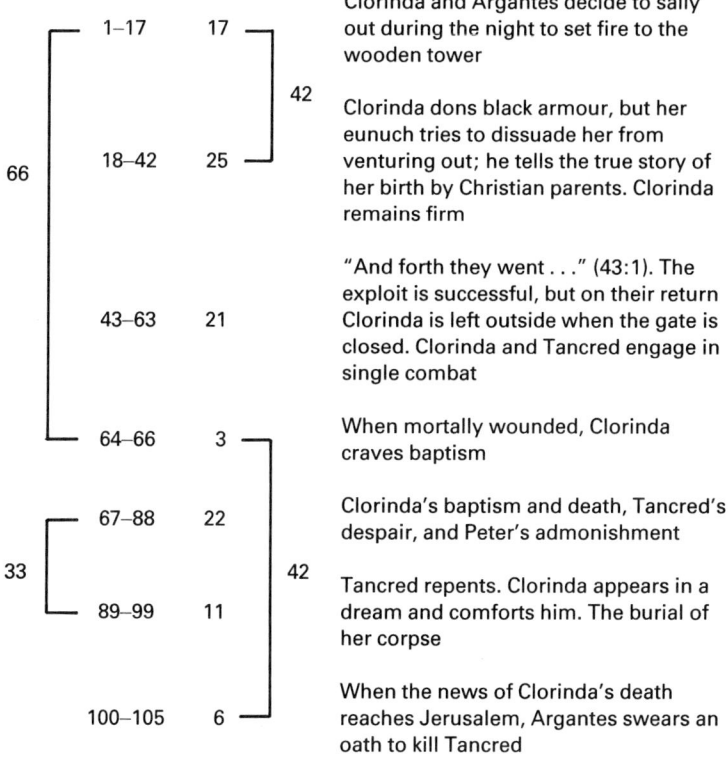

The basic structural numbers 33 and 42 and the ratio 2:1 underline the redemptive character of this canto. Clorinda is redeemed when she is baptized on the point of death, and Tancred is redeemed from his impious despair by the chastisement which is proffered grace.

The ratio 2:1 figures three times: in the overall division into 66 + 33, and in the proportion between 42 and 21, and 22 and 11.

division into 42–21–42 stanzas provides yet another example of a graded canto structure. Stanzas 1–42 present Clorinda's decision to sally out at night, and the eunuch's vain attempt to dissuade her; the nightly exploit requires the next 21 stanzas; while the last 42 are devoted to her baptism and death, Tancred's despair, her burial, and the reception of the news in Jerusalem. At the centre of the canto as a whole is the fierce encounter between Tancred and Clorinda (XII.53).

Diagram V.10 *Jerusalem Delivered*, Book XI

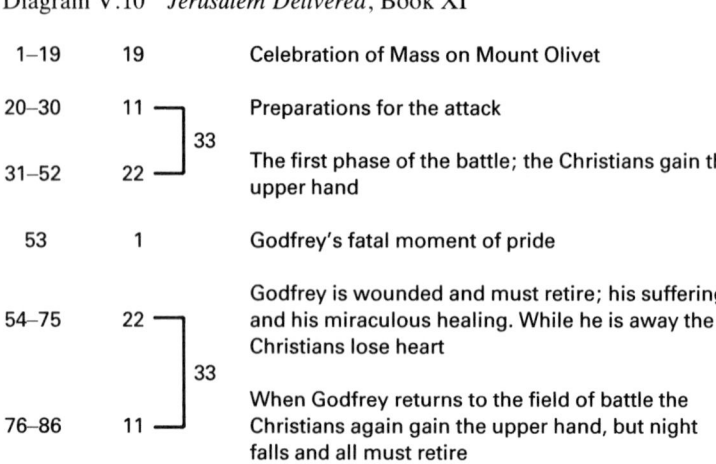

Godfrey's fall from grace is at the centre of the 67 stanzas on the battle, thus dividing them into a sequence of 33—1—33 stanzas. The groups of 33 stanzas in their turn are divided into 11 + 22 and 22 + 11, thus establishing a symmetrical pattern around stanza 53. The structure therefore stresses the gravity of Godfrey's lapse, but the numbers of redemption (33 and the ratios 2:1 and 1:2) are in accord with the process of repentant suffering and final restoration experienced by Godfrey.

The number 33 conditions the structure of Book XI as well (see Diagram V.10); 33 occurs twice, and in each case it is subdivided into 11 and 22. After the introductory stanzas on the celebration of Mass on Mount Olivet follow 67 stanzas (divided into 33—1—33) on the ensuing battle. The single stanza marks Godfrey's fatal moment of personal pride; the lapse from grace, though, is momentary and amply atoned for by the subsequent pain which Godfrey sustains with such admirable meekness and fortitude. When his wound has been miraculously cured Godfrey may return to the battle, but so much time has been lost that daylight fails, and the attack on the walls must be abandoned. Godfrey's momentary pride, therefore, caused him to lose that day's battle for the walls. Since the wooden tower is burnt down in Book XII, there will be no second opportunity until after Rinaldo's return, since he alone can remove the spell from the grove. In this way Tasso shows that no one is free from sin; even Godfrey must suffer chastisement. Old Raymond had roundly denounced his ambition "To set first foot this conquer'd wall above" (XI.22:2), so that he ought to have known

Diagram V.11   *Jerusalem Delivered*, Book XV. The Redemptive Mission

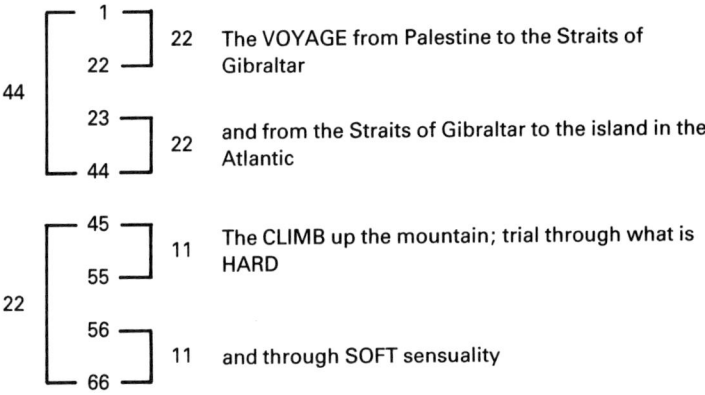

In the two divisions of 44 and 22 stanzas, the halfway points are clearly marked: the passage through the Straits of Gibraltar is the halfway point in the sea voyage, and the 22 stanzas on the climb up the mountain to the palace at the top divides into 11 stanzas on trial through hardships and 11 on the exposure to soft seductions. Not indicated here is the division into 33 + 33 stanzas: at XV.33–34 the travellers are in a halfway position relative to the sun: "At once they saw before the setting sun, / Behind the rising beam of springing day." The overriding concept of a virtuous mean may have prompted these even divisions, which form such perfectly balanced patterns.

better. It may be added that Godfrey's ambition entails attributing to himself what is the Lord's alone: "time requires that by some noble feat / I should make known my strength and puissance great" (XI.53:7–8). All power, however, is from the Lord. By placing Godfrey's lapse from grace at the textual centre Tasso underlines its fatal character.

As is to be expected, the number of redemption plays a crucial role also in Books XV–XVI on the rescue of Rinaldo (see Diagram V.11). Book XV consists of 66 stanzas only, and these 66 stanzas are divided into 44 on the passage, by Carlo and Ubaldo, from Palestine to the island in the Atlantic, and 22 on their ascent up the steep mountain-side. Central accent, however, seems present, since the travellers are said to be between sunset and sunrise at XV.33: "At once they saw before the setting sun, / Behind the rising beam of springing day". The 22-stanza segment on the ascent has an interesting structure. The hard climb is beset with hazards, and ice and snow make them faint with fatigue, but halfway through the

Diagram V.12 *Jerusalem Delivered*, Book XV, 45–66. The Path of Virtue

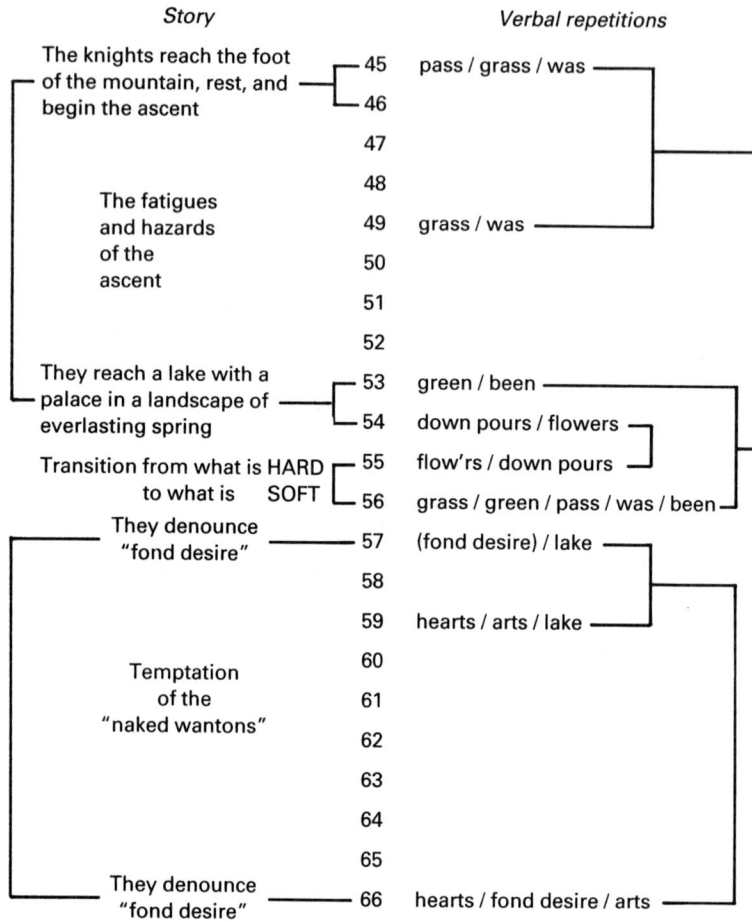

Words placed in parentheses occur within the line; otherwise the repetitions are all in rhyme position. At the textual centre the trials sustained change from what is hard to what is soft and sensual.

segment (at XV.55–56) a transition is made from trial through what is hard to trial by what is soft and alluring. Diagram V.12 shows how the structure is supported by verbal repetitions.

The 75 stanzas of Book XVI were reduced to 74 by Fairfax when he omitted the offending stanza 41, which compares Armida to the sirens (associated with the Fall). Stanzas 1–33 describe Armida and

JERUSALEM DELIVERED   255

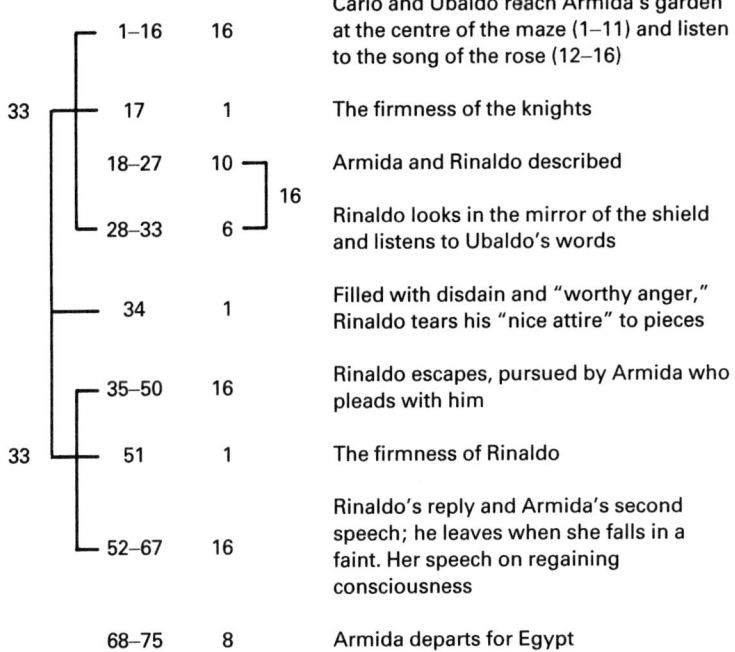

Diagram V.13 *Jerusalem Delivered*, Book XVI. The Choice of Hercules

The centre (XVI.34) and the two halfway points (XVI.17 and 51) mark a firm rejection of Pleasure and an equally firm commitment to Virtue. As in Book XV, the perfect balance may represent the golden mean where Virtue resides, at the same time that the number of redemption (33) suggests its connection with divine grace. (On the connection between virtue and grace, see my discussion of *The Faerie Queene* II in Chapter VI.)

Rinaldo in Armida's enchanted bower of bliss (see Diagram V.13), at the same time that they take the two knights to the garden at the centre of the maze of the palace; there they listen to the song of seduction and observe Armida and Rinaldo in their "wooing fit". Then follows a single stanza (34) where Rinaldo, after having seen himself in the mirror of the shield and understood what he has become, tears his "nice attire" to pieces in a spirit of "worthy anger". Rinaldo's escape and Armida's subsequent return to Egypt require a second group of 33 stanzas (XVI.35–67). At the centre of each group of 33 stanzas (i.e. at XVI.17 and 51 in the Italian text, or 50 in Fairfax) are actions related to the emblematic centre-piece: at stanza 17 Carlo and Ubaldo resist sensual temptations, and at

Diagram V.14 *Jerusalem Delivered*, Book XVIII

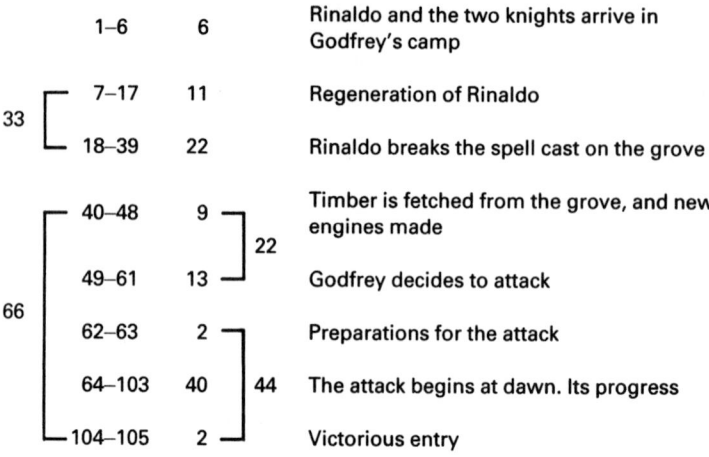

The first 6 stanzas complete the story of the return, and a new movement begins when Rinaldo goes to confession and then undergoes regeneration at dawn on Mount Olivet.

The ratio of 1:2 is found in various ways, first of all in the division into 33 + 66, and then in the subdivision of 33 into 11 + 22, and of 66 into 22 + 44.

Book XII (see Diagram V.9) in the same way consists of 105 stanzas, where the main action requires 99 stanzas.

XVI.50/51 it is Rinaldo who exhibits a similar firmness. Rinaldo's Herculean choice of Virtue at XVI.34 is accounted for simply as an awakening from sleep and idle dreams; no psychological explanation is offered, nor should we expect one: Rinaldo simply enacts the famous Choice of Hercules for which the *reader* has been adequately prepared if he has read and understood the signs provided by the poet.

The structure of Book XVIII is equally conditioned by the number 33. Stanzas 1–6 on Rinaldo's return are followed by 33 on Rinaldo's regeneration on Mount Olivet (22 stanzas) and by his breaking of the spell cast on the grove (11 stanzas; see Diagram V.14). The next 66 stanzas are devoted to the building of new engines of attack, and to the successful attack itself. These 66 stanzas are subdivided into 22 + 44. The ratio of redemption, 2:1, therefore prevails at every point.

My final example is Book XX, whose 144 stanzas reflect the

Diagram V.15   *Jerusalem Delivered*, Book XX. The Final Battle

Stanzas	Count		Description
1–5	5 ⎤		Arrival of Egyptian forces
6–21	16 ⎬ 27		Day breaks and Godfrey puts his host in good array and addresses them
22–27	6 ⎦		Emiren orders the Egyptian troops and addresses them
28–71	44		The two sides engage, Gildippes being the first out among the Christians. At stanza 71 they have sustained "equal loss and equal foil"
72	1		Godfrey again brings his squadrons in good array; the issue is "unresolv'd and doubtful"
73–116	44		The pagans lose; the last of the Christians to die are Gildippes and her husband Edward
117–136	20 ⎤ 27		The story of Armida and Rinaldo concluded
137–143	7 ⎦		Death of Emiren; Altamore yields
144	1		"Thus conquer'd Godfrey..."; Godfrey hangs up his arms in the temple

The battle proper requires 44—1—44 stanzas. Halfway through the first 44-stanza segment (XX.50), the issue is "in even balance," and at stanza 72 it is still unresolved when Godfrey reorganizes his forces. At the halfway point in the second 44-stanza segment (92–93), Soliman has a brief moment of glory, like a thunderbolt, before the victory of the Christians is complete. It is part of the balanced pattern that the first Christian to engage the enemy, the female champion Gildippes, is the last to die (XX.32 and 94–100).

The sum total of stanzas (144) represents the dimensions of the heavenly Jerusalem (12 × 12), thus suggesting the connection between the historical and the spiritual level.

dimensions of the heavenly Jerusalem (*Rev.* 21). As Diagram V.15 shows, the preparation for the battle calls for 27 stanzas, and so does the aftermath, whereas the long-sustained battle itself is at the centre in a sequence of 44—1—44 stanzas. The single stanza at the centre marks the moment when the issue is "unresolv'd and doubtful". These are the main outlines; each of the larger segments contains many substructures in the form of battle episodes.

6. Concluding Remarks

My analysis has shown that central accent is a much more complex phenomenon than has been realized. If we count stanza totals, then the centre of Tasso's romance epic is found in the 19-stanza segment located at the beginning of Book XI, and we have seen that this segment is itself symmetrically arranged around the centre provided by stanza XI.10. However, if one counts cantos rather than stanzas, then the centre is formed by Books X and XI, and more precisely by the end of Book X and the beginning of Book XI. This is true enough since the 19-stanza segment on Armida's perverse banquet at the end of Book X neatly balances the 19-stanza segment on the celebration of Mass which introduces Book XI. We have seen, too, that events at the beginning of Book X have a similar linkage with events at the end of Book XI. What we have, therefore, is *both* an extended centre discovered by counting stanza totals, *and* a symmetrical pattern beginning with the two cantos in the middle, and extending outwards from there until we reach the first canto and the last. Can it be that the fairly simple procedure of pairing books was perceived by most readers, if not by all, whereas the centre by stanza-count called for greater expertise in the art of reading? That the one structure was open, and the other more concealed? For the moment, at least, these questions must remain unanswered pending possible future research. My next chapter, though, will show that Spenser has the more subtle kind of extended centre in Book I of *The Faerie Queene*, whereas Book II has the more obvious kind. Both kinds, therefore, were undoubtedly recognized by poets, if not by all readers.

The issue of centres is further elaborated by the presence of a graded arrangement in the proportion 2:1, as already shown in Augustine's *Confessions*. In *Jerusalem Delivered*, the peripeteia is found at the end of Book XIII and the beginning of Book XIV; it is only after we have passed this pivotal centre that the Christians are successful. Again Spenser will be found to support this practice; it has long been recognized that the action in Books I and II divides each book into a sequence of 8 + 4 cantos. My own analysis will show that this division in Book I is marked by the presence of a pivotal centre based on a counting of stanzas.

The extreme length of Tasso's poem explains why he saw fit to align the symmetrical structure with a division into a twice-repeated sequence of 3—4—3 books. The chief function of this division is to facilitate the survey of the whole and so to clarify the thematic movement. Except for Milton, I know no other poet who adopted this particular structural strategy. The 10-book edition of *Paradise Lost*, however, has a clear division into 3—4—3 books: books 1–3 focus on events in Hell and in Heaven and on Satan's voyage to Earth, books 4–7 on events in the Garden prior to the Fall, and books 8–10 on the aftermath of the Fall and on the universal history of man (see Chapter IX).

Since each tetrad has an extended centre based on stanza-count, the extended centre of the poem as a whole is flanked by similar centres at the halfway points between the beginning and the middle, and the middle and the end. If these centres are truly there, then they ought to show a significant thematic progression. I have shown that this is indeed so: the first presents a picture of unbridled wrath in the combat between Argantes and Tancred, the wrath of Argantes being akin to that of Satan; the third shows a Rinaldo enslaved by Pleasure or false love, whereas the main centre at XI.1–19 displays divine love manifested in the eucharist, that is, in the sacrifice of Christ. The triple pattern resembles Aristotle's formula of a golden mean enclosed by extremes, but the formula has been Christianized. In Christian thought the important reconciliation is between justice and mercy, and we may perhaps see Tasso's pictures of wrath and profane love as perversions of justice and mercy. If wrath is to approximate justice, and if profane love is to approach the divine, then each must be tempered before they can be reconciled – as they are in Rinaldo at the end of the epic narrative. In the course of this narrative, Rinaldo learns to bridle both his wrath and his love, but his own efforts are supplemented by divine grace. Divine grace prompts and supports them. What we see at the centre of the symmetrical structure, therefore, is the tempering agent which is divine grace. It is only when the tempering has been fully achieved that Jerusalem can be delivered: the liberation of Jerusalem is the external manifestation of a spiritual process, just as the Old Testament types are an external or historical manifestation of the spiritual truth fully manifested in the life of Christ.

Like the poem as a whole, individual cantos may have structures that permit a graded arrangement to coexist with simple recessed symmetry. Since a canto may have introductory or concluding segments, however, we cannot look for canto centres merely by counting stanzas; structures must emerge from an analysis of the text itself, and must not be superimposed on a basis of mere counting.

My analysis has been based on a tracing of patterns of actions, and in these patterns traditional topoi together with emblematic situations and descriptions have been shown to be of great value. Whether based on classical myth or on the Bible, such passages seem to have been invented to establish linkage between parts through repetition. The repetition may include key words and phrases (sometimes placed in rhyme position), but I have preferred to reserve a full investigation of such repetitions for my chapter on Spenser.

The repetition of identical rhyme words at the beginning and end of a segment provides evidence of authorial intent, and so do the so-called self-referring passages. Thus Carlo and Ubaldo are said to reach the centre of the maze ("the centre of the inmost hold") at XVI.1, that is, in the first of the 27 stanzas that form the extended centre of the second tetrad, just as Tancred penetrates to the centre of the enchanted grove at the centre of the 80 stanzas that constitute Canto XIII (i.e. in stanzas 38–43). Another event which calls for structural enactment is the triumphal appearance of Armida in the segment on the marshalling of troops before the king of Egypt (XVII.14–53). Armida occupies the two positions associated with triumphal placing: she is last in the procession itself, but the description occurs in the stanzas that are at the centre of the segment (at XVII.33–34). Book XX shows that a whole canto, devoted as it is to the one subject of the final battle, may have a centre which expresses balance: within the 144 stanzas, the centre marks the point where the opposing forces are evenly balanced. These examples show that what we may call the procession of stanzas in a canto possessed a virtually physical reality, so that we must learn to read a segment, a canto, or a whole epic as we would objects in space.

Among the symbolic numbers selected by Tasso to condition his textual structures, 33 and 42 are clear favourites, together with the ratio 2:1. However, he also exploited to the full the evil connotations of the number 19, as shown in Book IV (see Diagram V.16). One may perhaps argue that the celebration of Mass, too, is described in 19 stanzas, but in this case the segment is seen as consisting not of 19 stanzas, but of 3 groups of 3 stanzas located to each side of a unifying single stanza. As we shall see in Chapter VI, Spenser too uses the number 19 for events associated with evil powers. Bongo's comment on this number is unequivocal: its meaning is purely evil. There is nothing of beauty or goodness in this number, which expresses addiction to vice and punishment for it.

Diagram V.16 *Jerusalem Delivered*, Book IV

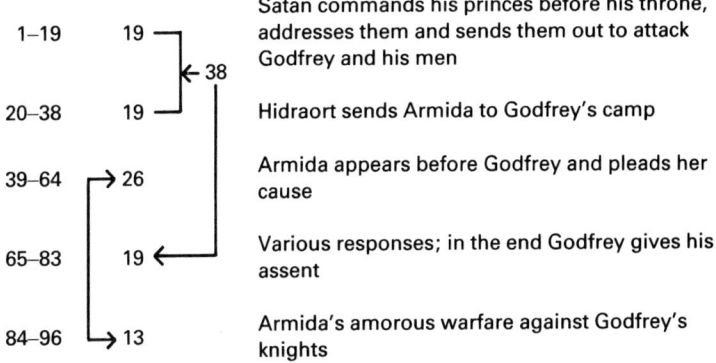

The structure is based on the numbers 19 and 13, both taken *in malo*. The "harmony" of evil is traced in the ratios between 38 and 19, 26 and 13.

Like Spenser and Milton after him, Tasso shows how evil may be countered, expelled, or destroyed. The nature of evil is clearly defined when Hidraort, as associate of the devil, sends his niece Armida to Godfrey's camp in Book IV. Armida is no exponent of evil; she is merely made use of by her uncle, and so she is capable of being purified by suffering and, in the end, of receiving Rinaldo's proffered grace. The Satanic, however, cannot be reconciled or tempered, as we see in Book XVIII when Rinaldo finally reaches the centre of the enchanted grove and cuts down the tree located there. This act of ruthless destruction breaks the evil spell, and Godfrey's men may again fetch timber there for the engines they need to scale the walls of Jerusalem. Unlike Guyon's destruction of the Bower of Bliss (*Faerie Queene* II.xii), this episode cannot be misconstrued; the Satanic element is too obvious. Tasso's forest, though, points forward to Acrasia's Bower of Bliss, Acrasia being Spenser's version of the counterfeit Armida, and not of Armida herself as often assumed. The exposure and defeat of the counterfeit Armida must be complete and relentless, like the exposure and defeat of Spenser's Acrasia. When their charm is resisted, their Satanic character becomes manifest, and the Satanic principle entails death. Because the Satanic principle is contrary to life, it must be purged as a distemper in the way so vividly described by Milton in *Paradise Lost* (see Chapter IX).

I have argued that as we move from the first half of the epic into the second we experience a change similar in kind to the transition from types to the antitype. The linkage between books within the overall symmetrical structure often depends on such parallels-with-a-difference. It is likely that the habit of reading the Bible typologically (which means looking for parallels-with-a-difference) is responsible for this strong tendency to move between a literal and a spiritual level. Thus the lifting of the dark veil of paganism from Clorinda in Book XII is the inner meaning of the expulsion of the Satanic powers from the field of battle in Book IX, just as the physical massacre of the Danes in Book VIII finds a spiritual analogue in the routing of Godfrey's men when they try to enter the enchanted grove in Book XIII. They experience a kind of spiritual massacre. The two near-rebellions provide a further example. The second is part of a spiritual conflict, in contrast to the first, which is caused by deception: the men believe the slanderous rumour about Godfrey inspired by the evil spirit Alecto. The second, however, comes as the consequence of the intolerable heat of a scorching sun, the *sol iustitiae*. On the first, as on the second occasion, Godfrey's prayer resolves the conflict and peace is restored, the difference being that on the second occasion the peace is the consequence of a perfect reconciliation between God and man through divine mercy. In Books VII and XIV the theme of happiness is lifted from its human version (presented in Erminia's stay in happy rural obscurity) to the level of the divine as Godfrey has his vision of the bliss of the saints in Heaven. Events in the second half, then, are intensified by being internalized in a way which recalls Augustine's pregnant phrase, *Intravi, et vidi* (*Confessions* 7:10; see Chapter II). This process of perceiving an elevation from a literal to a spiritual level assists in the understanding of the inner meaning of the epic fable, just as God's plan for the redemption of man stands fully revealed with the coming of the antitype. When the epic ends, therefore, a higher, spiritual concept of heroic virtue and of love has replaced the merely human view, so that when Godfrey hangs up his arms in the temple in the last stanza we know that Christ has entered the living temple which is man, re-making and re-forming him so that he may become a fit inhabitant of the heavenly city.

Notes to Chapter V

1. Tasso, *Discourses on the Heroic Poem*, tr. Mariella Cavalchini and Irene Samuel (Oxford, 1973), p. 78. See also *Discorsi dell' arte poetica*, 1587.
2. Tasso, *Del Giudizio sovra La Gerusalemme*, in *Opere* (Venezia, 1735), Vol. IV.

3. *Del Giudizio, Libro Primo*, p. 335.
4. *Del Giudizio, Libro Secondo*, p. 32. Augustine is referred to in *Libro Primo*, pp. 306, 310 and 330.
5. Annabel M. Patterson, *Hermogenes and the Renaissance* (Princeton, 1972), p. 39.
6. Tasso, *Discourses on the Heroic Poem*, p. 201.
7. Macrobius, *Commentary on the Dream of Scipio*, tr. William Harris Stahl (Records of Civilization, New York, 1952). Macrobius explains that Plato said that the World Soul "was interwoven with those numbers, odd or even, which produce the cube or solid", but not in order to attribute physicality to it. On the contrary, the Soul must have solidity "in order to be able to penetrate the whole world with its animating power and fill the solid body of the universe" (II.ii.14; p. 191). The numbers in Plato's *lambda* formula are listed in II.ii.16, and music pervades the universe because these numbers form the ratios that produce the various consonances. The World Soul must be interwoven with "those numbers which produce musical harmony in order to make harmonious the sounds which it instilled by its quickening impulse. It discovered the source of these sounds in the fabric of its own composition" (II.ii.19). Tasso clearly wants the same harmony-producing ratios to pervade the fabric of his own composition. Macrobius connects the music of the universe with poetry when he writes that "In the hymns to the gods, too, the verses of the strophe and antistrophe used to be set to music, so that the strophe might represent the forward motion of the celestial sphere and the antistrophe the reverse motion of the planetary spheres; these two motions produced nature's first hymn in honor of the Supreme God" (II.iii.5). Compare the argument presented by Damianus (see above, pp. 68 f.). For a more detailed discussion of the number 8, see Macrobius I.v.11–18, and on the perfection of the octave see I.vi.42 and I.xix.20–21.
8. A mathematical centre by line-count has been seen in *Paradise Lost*, 6.762 ("Ascended, at his right hand victory") in the first edition of 1667. See Gunnar Qvarnström, *Dikten och den nya vetenskapen ... With a Summary in English* (Lund, 1961), Ch. V, and pp. 286–88 (the summary), and *The Enchanted Palace. Some Structural Aspects of Paradise Lost* (Stockholm, 1967), Ch. II. The central line is part of a paragraph on Christ's elevation or enthronement (see pp. 56–58). Subsequent discussions have tended to place too great emphasis on the single line to the detriment of Qvarnström's discussion of the enthronement of Christ. The midpoint in canto i of *The Faerie Queene* Book I (ed. 1) has been located at I.vii.12–13, but see my own discussion in Chapter VI on Spenser. See also Michael Baybak, Paul Delany, and A. Kent Hieatt, "Placement 'in the middest' in *The Faerie Queene*", *Papers on Language and Literature* 5 (1969) 227–34, reprinted in A. C. Hamilton, *Essential Articles for the Study of Edmund Spenser* (Hambden, Conn., 1972).

    The reason why it has been possible to locate the centre in a single line or stanza is that an extended centre will itself be symmetrically structured. Thus the stanza on Mount Olivet in XI.10 is pivotal within the extended centre. Since a pivotal centre must connect with the beginning and the end, however, a whole segment is called for, as in Tasso's 19 stanzas.
9. I give a brief summary of some of my structural findings in my essay on "Canto Structure in Tasso and Spenser", *Spenser Studies* 1 (1980), 177–200. A competent brief survey of the symmetrical pattern is found in Roy T. Eriksen, *The Forme of Faustus Fortunes* (Oslo and New Jersey, 1987), pp. 109–15. Andrew Fichter, "Tasso's Epic of Deliverance", *PMLA. Publications of the Modern Language Association of America* 93:2 (1978), 265–74 contains little which is not in my essay, which was published in 1980 after much delay. The book subsequently published by Fichter in 1982 – *Poets Historical. Dynastic Epic in the Renaissance* – incorporates his 1978 essay on Tasso, but the author is incapable of applying an approach through textual structure to Augustine's *Confessions* or

to the other epics he considers. For my discussion of Fichter's comments on Augustine's spiritual epic, see Chapter II.
10. C. P. Brand, *Torquato Tasso* (London, 1965), p. 99.
11. Ibid., p. 234.
12. "Maccabaeus and his men, after making public supplication to God, entreating him to support them, hurled themselves against the Idumaean fortresses. Vigorously pressing home their attack, they seized possession of these vantage points, beating off all who fought on the ramparts ... Nine thousand at least took refuge within two exceptionally strong castles", but these castles are captured (2 *Macc.* 10:16–19, The Jerusalem Bible). The forces subsequently gathered by Timotheus to overcome the Jews resemble the Egyptian forces in Tasso's epic. Again the Jewish forces prostrate themselves before the Lord, begging him to support them: "As the first light of dawn began to spread, the two sides joined battle, the one having as their pledge of success and victory not only their own valour but their recourse to the Lord, the other making their own ardour their mainstay in the fight. When the battle was at its height the enemy saw five magnificent men appear from heaven on horses with golden bridles and put themselves at the head of the Jews". The enemy troops are routed, and Timotheus "fled to a strongly guarded citadel" (2 *Macc.* 10:24–32).
13. Within the fortress, the defenders, "confident in the security of the place, hurled fearful blasphemies and godless insults at them".
14. Augustine, *Confessions*, quoted from the edition published in the Loeb Classical Library, Vol. II, p. 10 (from 9:3).
15. Eriksen, *The Forme of Faustus Fortunes*, p. 111. For a similar example of verbal linkage in Spenser, see my "Canto Structure in Tasso and Spenser", pp. 191–93 on *The Faerie Queene* II.x.9 and II.x.50.
16. Cf. 2 *Macc.* 10:29–30 as cited in note 12.
17. The classical study of this theme in Renaissance art is Erwin Panofsky, *Hercules am Scheidewege* (Leipzig, 1930). For Fielding's use of this motif, see my study of "Tom Jones and the Choice of Hercules", in *Fair Forms*, ed. M.-S. Røstvig (Cambridge, 1975), pp. 147–77 and 222–26. See also G. Karl Galinski, *The Herakles Theme* (Oxford, 1972). Christian versions of the Choice would invoke Matthew 7:13–14.
18. See Edgar Wind, *Pagan Mysteries in the Renaissance* (Harmondsworth, 1967), pp. 89–91.
19. Ibid., pp. 75–80.
20. Gilles Corrozet, *Hecatomgraphie* (1540), sig. Mi^V f.
21. A. C. Hamilton, headnote to *The Faerie Queene* Book Three (London and New York, 1977), p. 163.
22. It is misleading to read this episode in pastoral terms. On the tradition of the happiness of rural obscurity, see my *The Happy Man: Studies in the Metamorphoses of a Classical Ideal*, Vol. I: *1600–1700* (Oslo and New York, 1962).
23. See my study of "Golden Phrases: the Poetics of Giles Fletcher", *Studies in Philology* 88 (1991), 169–200.
24. A biblical analogy may perhaps be found in the Vulgate edition of the Bible, where 19 historical books are followed by 7 "libri didactici" (from *Job* and the *Psalms* to *Ecclesiasticus*), and these again by 18 prophetic books and 2 "Libri Historici Novissimi". In this arrangement of the books of the Old Testament, therefore, the books of wisdom are in the middle. The New Testament consists of the 4 Gospels, the *Acts*, and 21 epistles, in all 26 books. After the books of wisdom, then, follow 46 books. If we were to apply simple mathematics, then the *Canticum Canticorum, Sapientia*, and *Ecclesiasticus* are at the centre of a graded division into 23—3—46 books. There are many numerical arguments about the divisions of the Bible, but I have not come across the argument sketched here. However, let it be added that the table of contents makes the position of the books of wisdom plain to the eye, so that no actual counting need be resorted to.

Part Two
From Spenser to Dryden

Chapter VI

Spenser's "tunefull Diapase"
The Faerie Queene I and II

> For the sweet numbers and melodious measures,
> With which I wont the winged words to tie,
> And make a tunefull Diapase of pleasures,
> Now being let to runne at libertie
> By those which have no skill to rule them right,
> Have now quite lost their naturall delight.
>
> Spenser, *The Teares of the Muses*, lines 547–52

Spenser clearly read his Tasso with keen awareness of his many structural felicities; few could "tie" the "winged words" like Spenser so as to make a "tunefull Diapase of pleasures." As my analysis will show, Spenser's system of linkage is unusually varied and elaborate; the way in which he deploys descriptions, epic similes, and interpolated tales is especially noteworthy, and so is his development of the technique of verbal repetition.

Any impression that unity is not particularly conspicuous in the *Jerusalem Delivered* or *The Faerie Queene* is largely the consequence of a reading habit which fails to connect actions and characters with the concepts they embody, and to honour these concepts as structuring elements. Tasso often lets his narrative depend on thematic development rather than simple causality; it is his preference so to do, and this preference manifests itself (albeit to a much lesser extent) as late as in the fiction of Henry Fielding, where moral issues are so all-important. No one would argue that the episode of Sophronia and Olindo in Book II of the *Jerusalem Delivered* advances the action; on the contrary, it holds it up and so, as some of Tasso's critics have argued, ought to be omitted.[1] However, the episode is a necessary part of Tasso's conceptual framework or grid; he needed it to "tie" his "winged words." I cannot agree with James Nohrnberg that substantial parts of Tasso's story compete with the main action by setting up rival foci of interest; the account of Armida's island is supposed to be a "notorious example", just as the story has no "irreducible plot", since there is no causal connection between Rinaldo's departure and his later return. But the departure is conspicuously a matter of Rinaldo's being a victim first of wrath and then of love, while the cause of his return is his bridling of these passions. The causal connection, therefore, is found at the level of moral action, and it impairs the poem to present the Armida–Rinaldo situation as the polarity between "the truancy of an erotic pastoral, set against the recall to the martial and metropolitan."[2]

The concepts dramatized in *The Faerie Queene* I and II are holiness (or religious re-birth) and temperance, both of which are needed to enable man to become a living temple of the Lord. As in all spiritual epics, it is the world within that matters. In the *Confessions* the decisive moment occurs when Augustine turns the attention to his own inner self and so finds the God he has vainly sought for so long, and a similar turning-point is found in Tasso's epic when Rinaldo enters into himself as he sees himself mirrored in the shield. It is only after he has found his true self in this dramatic situation that he, too, finds his God. Redcrosse knight is a second Rinaldo: his legend is yet another story of defection through wrath and lust, followed by a tetrad of cantos on instruction and purgation leading to final victory. Redcrosse enters into himself, *in malo*, in the Cave of Despair, and *in bono* in the House of Holiness. The hero of the Legend of Temperance does so in the Castle of Alma and when he reads the chronicles in the turret.

Although Redcrosse and Guyon meet many of the same temptations as Rinaldo, Acrasia must not be compared with Armida, nor must Duessa. Unlike Armida they are beyond the reach of redemptive action. There can be no accord between good and evil. Some opposites are capable of reconciliation, but others are not, and the point is to perceive the distinction.

Temperance figures also in Book I; as Augustine explains, temperance and the other cardinal virtues enter into the process whereby carnal man becomes spiritual man.[3] This process is a painful one, and confinement is a major theme. Sin confines, as it does the King and Queen of Eden and their people, but once the dragon has been killed all may issue forth and celebrate the joyous release. In marked contrast to the release described in canto xii, canto i shows us a Morpheus who courts confinement behind locked double gates within the bowels of the earth; his sleep is very much *in malo.* The idea of confinement links cantos ii and xi as well: Fradubio is confined within his wooden walls, Redcrosse within an armour which has become a red-hot instrument of torture through the dragon's fiery breath. This predicament is appropriate punishment for the man who doffed his armour and courted Duessa in the cooling shade in the passage which is part of the extended centre for the book as a whole (see below).

Antitheses structure the narrative of Book I: blindness and vision, truth and deceit, union and division. However, my point of departure will not be such large-scale topomorphs. My analysis of Book I will explore Spenser's structural techniques in detail, and hence I shall begin by considering the structure of a single stanza and a single segment within a canto, and then proceed to an analysis of each of the 12 cantos. This will reveal that the same structural principles prevail at all three levels: in a single stanza, in a segment, and in a canto as a whole. Spenser's use of verbal repetition is particularly interesting, since repetitions serve to verify the structures based on an analysis of the contents. Verbal and numerical structures often coincide with such precision that one must conclude that they are interdependent. Among the structural numbers favoured by Spenser are 19 and 33, as in Tasso. My analysis of the overall structures – symmetrical and graded – will show that it is the rule rather than the exception that where the one structure is found, the other is also present.

The focus in my analysis of Book I, then, will be on Spenser's compositional technique, but the critical relevance of observing this technique ought to be self-evident. My analysis of Book II, however, will subordinate the structural analysis to the critical inquiry, thus putting the cart where it ought to be – behind the horse. If my pursuit of textual structures in Book I should seem relentless, my excuse is that such a thorough study had to be undertaken at one point, and that Book I lends itself to such an investigation, since its interpretation is virtually devoid of important critical cruxes, unlike Book II, where the character of Guyon and the nature of his virtue are a hotly debated issue.

Book I: Canto Structure

In the description of Lucifera enthroned, the repetition of the same or similar words links the beginning, middle, and end:

High above all a cloth of State was spred,
    A   B   C
And a rich throne, as bright as sunny day,

On which there sate most brave embellished

With royall robes and gorgeous array,
                      D   C
A mayden Queene, that shone as *Titans* ray,

In glistring gold, and peerelesse pretious stone:

Yet her bright blazing beautie did assay
      B   A
To dim the brightnesse of her glorious throne,
                              D
As envying her selfe, that too exceeding shone.[4]

(I.iv.8)

Around the "mayden Queene" at the textual centre in line 5 identical or related words are arranged in a pattern of recessed symmetry (A B C D C B A D). The same word (*shone*) connects the middle and the end, while *throne* and *bright* in line 2 recur in line 8 in inverse order. The various repetitions create the rhetorical schemes known as chiasmus (ABC ... CBA), epanados (linking the middle and the end), and epanalepsis (linking the beginning and the end). These verbal schemes correspond to the larger structures I have traced in the *Confessions* and in the *Jerusalem Delivered*, where themes and topoi function like these single words. The difference, therefore, is merely one of scale. Longinus makes an obvious point when he explains that such repetitions stimulate vehement emotion.[5] The emotion stirred in this stanza is one of awe at Lucifera's royal state. To increase the impact, Spenser surrounded this stanza by double frames in the form of two stanzas on the entry into the hall by Duessa and Redcrosse knight (iv.6–7) and two on the brightness of the queen (iv.9–10). Verbal repetition links these five stanzas into one segment; the *b* rhymes of stanza 6 are repeated in the *c* rhymes of stanza 7, just as the *b* rhymes of stanza 9 are repeated in the *b* rhymes of stanza 10. Then, too, whole phrases are repeated: "on every side" occurs at 6 : 5 and 7 : 8, "exceeding shone" at 8 : 9 and 9 : 1, while "fairely for to shyne" (9 : 9) is repeated as "So proud she shyned" (10:1). The ear is virtually cloyed by all this repetition.

In these stanzas the linking is purely verbal, while numerical structures inform the catalogue of trees at I.i.8–9. While it is certainly true that most of the epithets express the usefulness of each tree to society, what are we to make of the maple, then ("seldom inward sound"), or of the "Mirrhe sweete bleeding in the bitter wound"? And the oak is not just the "builder Oake," but also "sole king of forrests all." On considering the arrangement of the list we discover that the seven trees listed in stanza 8 and the thirteen in stanza 9 place a king *in medio*: the oak divides the seven trees into a sequence of 4—1—2, while at the centre of the second we find the King of kings (the "Mirrhe sweete bleeding in the bitter wound") in the midst of the 12 Apostles, nor is Judas absent: the maple's rotten core points to Duessa–Judas, whose skin later on is described as being "as rough, as maple rind" (viii.47:8). Her "secret filth" is the maple's inner rottenness. The forest which is the labyrinth of life clearly does more than house the dragon Error: it accommodates both the earthly and the heavenly king – the one at the heart of a graded arrangement and the other at the centre of a symmetrical pattern. Then, too, the 6 that surround the oak relate to the 12 that surround the myrrh in the proportion which expresses perfect harmony. The forest, then, is presented as an image of the world, and as such it contains both good and evil, yet the promise of harmony is there to all who can "read" the catalogue correctly. Another point of interest is that Spenser saw fit to use both a graded and a symmetrical arrangement, as if to suggest that his orphic song will contain both.[6]

The segment on the story of Satyrane (vi.20–29) is set within a triple frame as shown in Diagram VI.1. Stanzas 17–18–19 and 30–31–32 are linked by simple repetition or repetition-with-a-difference. Cyparisse pined away in anguish for the loss of his hind, but Una's anguish for the loss of her knight prompts decisive action (17 and 32); Una's beauty and her wisdom cause respectively envy and admiration (18 and 31), and Una insists on teaching true, sacred lore (19 and 30). This frame focussed on Una encloses a ten-stanza account of Satyrane, which begins and concludes with his exploits abroad: he has "fild far landes with glorie of his might" (20), and has sought "far abroad for straunge adventures" (29). At the centre are two stanzas on Satyrane's fearlessness (24–25), and, when this topos is repeated at vi.29, the repetition links the middle and the end of

Diagram VI.1 *The Faerie Queene* I, the Story of Satyrane (vi. 17–32)

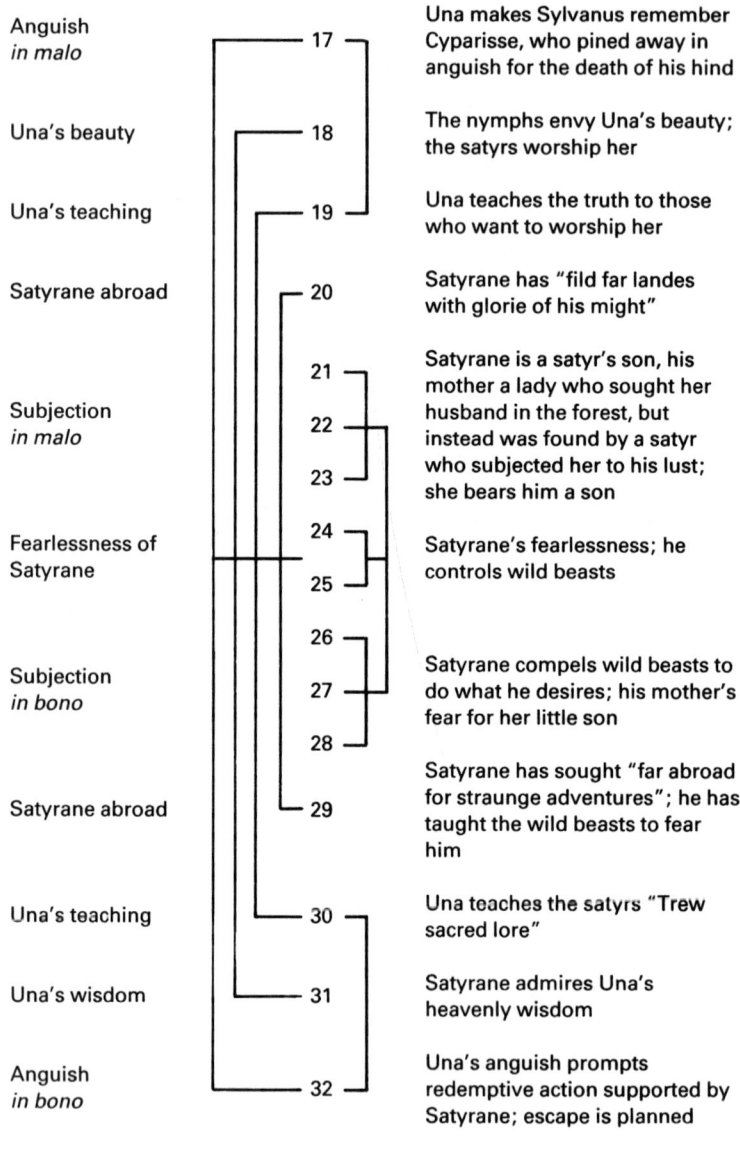

the story. The stanzas in between the beginning, middle, and end share the idea of subjection: Satyrane's mother became subjected to the lust of a satyr (21–23), but subjection is taken *in bono* when Satyrane compels wild beasts to do what he desires (26–28). When ideas are re-stated, the repetition is obvious, and the reason for placing such repetitions with symmetrical precision must be to form the desired pattern. If mere emphasis were the motive, the placing would not be so exact. The most successful kind of repetition depends on taking the same event or concept in a good and a bad sense; one kind of subjection may be good, another bad, and anguish may lead to negative or to positive action. I do not believe that number symbolism is present here, although the ten-stanza sequence may mirror the concern with the law which is Satyrane's role within the allegory. The point of the structure is primarily the poised symmetry, which affects our response to the story.

An equally simple symmetrical structure adorns the segment on Redcrosse's escape from the House of Pride (v.45–53). This passage, though, adds the refinement of patterns of verbal repetition as if to make explicit the presence of the structure created by the contents. The most emphatic repetition is of the rhyme words *Pride* and *spide* (45) in inverse order in the last stanza (53). Diagram VI.2 shows that the episode begins with the dwarf's discovery of the "wretched thrals" in the "dongeon deepe" and of the cause of their grievous plight (45–46), and it concludes with the discovery of the corpses underneath the castle wall (52–53). In between are lists of examples from history of men and women who have been the victims of Pride, but the list is suddenly interrupted at the textual centre in stanza 49 to accommodate yet another passage on the rueful spectacle of the murdered corpses, laid out like so many carcases on a butcher's stall. This image of carcases on a butcher's stall therefore connects the middle and the end, and there can be no other reason for locating the same image in stanzas 49 and 53 than to ensure linkage between the middle and the end, as in the story of Satyrane. The pattern of verbal repetition linking the beginning, middle, and end is shown in Diagram VI.2. Repetitions reach a climax in the concluding stanza, thus ensuring a climax of emotional intensity: the key word *pride* connects the middle and the end ("that great Princesse pride" and "that sad house of *Pride*"), while related words and phrases are arranged symmetrically around line 5. Thus the "corses, like a great Lay-stall" in line 2 balance the "donghill of dead carkases" in line 8, and the absence of "decent funerall" in line 4 is echoed by the "shamefull end" of line 6. The concluding stanza

Diagram VI.2 *The Faerie Queene* I, Segment on Redcrosse's Escape from the House of Pride (v.45–53)

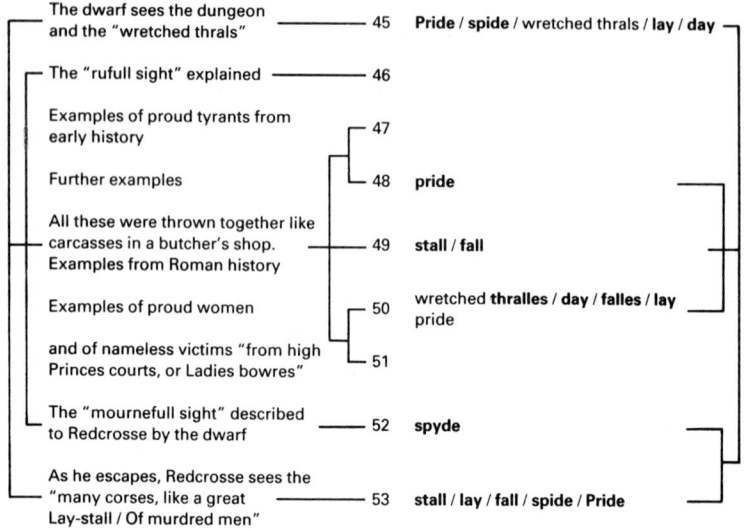

In this and subsequent diagrams, words printed in bold face are in rhyme position.

becomes truly climactic by virtue of these repetitions that create the same kind of balance as in the segment as a whole.

Segments may form balanced patterns within a canto, a technique which Spenser employs far more frequently than Tasso. Another difference is that Spenser's structures are often more complex and yet at the same time more clearly indicated. Spenser is the better craftsman, perhaps because he could profit from Tasso's example. Canto i illustrates the point; as shown in Diagram VI.3 the encounter with the dragon Error and the stay in the false hermitage are events balanced around a central stanza (i.28) in a pattern of 11—16—1—16—11 stanzas. The central stanza presents an emblematic picture of proper action: Redcrosse proceeds purposefully out of the forest, "That path he kept which beaten was most plaine, / Ne ever would to any by-way bend, / But still did follow one unto the end." This is the road *in bono*, in contrast to the path that "beaten seemed most bare" (i.11 : 3). This distinction between the good and the bad road is actually drawn by Cassiodorus in his comments on Psalm 1.[7] It has already been observed that this stanza divides the canto into equal halves,[8] but it must also be seen that the contents

Diagram VI.3   *The Faerie Queene* I, the Events of Canto i

1–11	11	Introduction and entry into the forest, led by delight
12–27	16	The adventure of Error's den
28	1	Emblem of proper action: Redcrosse follows a single path to the end: "So forward on his way (with God to frend) / He passeth forth ..."
29–44	16	They meet the hermit, who offers shelter for the night; he is Archimago, and the magician compels Morpheus to send a false dream to trouble Redcrosse knight
45–55	11	Redcrosse is troubled by wanton dreams; on waking, he sees Una who tries to seduce him. He tempers his wrath and returns to bed

Stanza 28 stands out as an emblematic centre-piece showing proper action. Halfway between the beginning and the middle, at i.14, Redcrosse reveals rashness, while sloth is featured halfway between the middle and the end at i.42 (in the person of Morpheus). This is a triple pattern such as "Aristotle hath devised" (*Letter to Ralegh*).

create a chiastic pattern of 11+16 and 16+11 stanzas, and that contrasting pictures of rashness and sloth have been placed halfway between the beginning and the middle, and the middle and the end at i.14 and 42. At i.14 Redcrosse knight, full of "fire and greedy hardiment," cannot 'for ought be staide," and so he proceeds rashly into Error's den. The opposite posture is struck by Morpheus at i.42, when Archimago's messenger tries to prod the sleeping god into some degree of conscious life, but with little success. At these three points of structural emphasis, therefore, we have related images of rashness, proper action, and sloth in a perfect Aristotelian formula. However, it is not necessary to count stanzas to perceive this triple formula; it is sufficiently obvious that the first episode illustrates rashness and the second sloth. (The topos of sloth recurs at the textual centre of Book I when Redcrosse doffs his armour and drinks of the fountain of feebleness.) It is not Morpheus alone who represents sloth in canto i; when his messenger causes the travellers to be "drownd in deadly sleepe" (36:6), the phrasing connects them with Morpheus, who is said to be "drowned deepe / In drowsie fit" (i.40:8–9). In strong contrast, Una in the false house of holiness in canto iii remains wide awake all night, tired though she is. In canto ii, Fradubio falls an easy victim to Duessa's cruel revenge precisely because he fails to remain on guard after he has seen Duessa in her true shape; he, too, is "drownd in sleepie night" so that she besmears him with "wicked herbes and ointments" and thus bereaves him of all his senses (ii.42). But Redcrosse knight is no easy victim; he stays his hand when confronted by the false Una, yet is still troubled by dreams on returning to his bed:

> That troublous dreame gan freshly tosse his braine,
> With bowres, and beds, and Ladies deare delight:
> But when he saw his labour all was vaine,
> With that misformed spright he backe returnd againe.
> (i. 55 : 6–9)

The rhyme words *braine*, *vaine*, *againe* have already been used in the description of Morpheus at i.42, and on this second occasion we are made to recall the traditional close connection between sloth and lust.

The overlapping between cantos i and ii suggests that they may form a narrative substructure consisting of 100 stanzas, and an analysis of the pattern of actions (see Diagram VI.4) shows that this is indeed so. The authorial comment on Redcrosse knight at ii.12 (the 67th within the sequence) functions as a pivotal passage dividing the two cantos into 33—33—1—33 stanzas:

> But he the knight, whose semblaunt he did beare,
>   The true *Saint George* was wandred far away,
>   Still flying from his thoughts and gealous feare;
>   Will was his guide, and griefe led him astray.

The consequences of this condition are seen in the last stanza of canto ii, where the rhyme words *beare* and *feare* recur in inverse sequence; on this occasion, though, the fear is feigned by Duessa while Redcrosse forgets his own fear:

> Her seeming dead he found with feigned feare,
> ...
> Her up he tooke, too simple and too trew,
>   And oft her kist. At length all passed feare,
> He set her on her steede, and forward forth did beare.

Repeated identical rhyme words play their part in shaping the

Diagram VI.4 *The Faerie Queene* I, the Events of Cantos i–ii

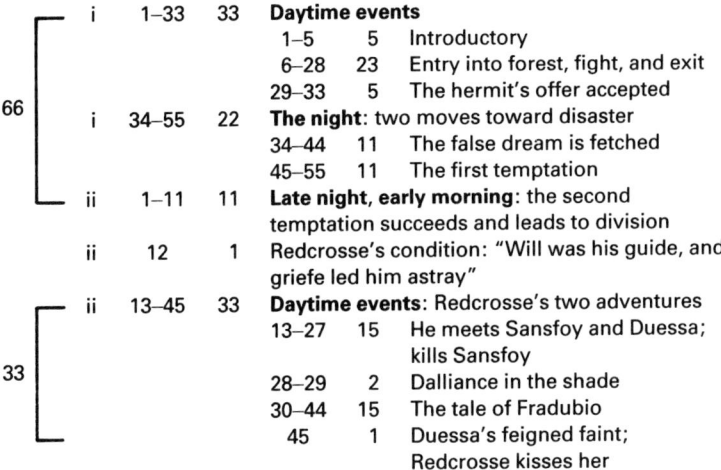

Verbal repetitions link the end of canto i to the beginning of canto ii:

textual structures, as shown in Diagram VI.4 The rhymes *starre, farre, arre* in the first stanza on the action proper (i.7) recur again in ii.1, and the *paine, vaine* of ii.2 and 8 connect with the *vaine, againe, braine* nexus of rhymes in i.42 and 55. When the action overlaps, so apparently do the rhyme words. Another group which ensures overlapping is *spright, sight, night* (i.45, ii.2, ii.3, ii.4, and ii.6). Yet another stylistic feature is the reduction of the rhyme scheme from three to two elements only, as in the last stanza of canto ii, where it strengthens the feeling of terminal climax.

Yet another structural refinement is that the 100-stanza sequence, like canto i, has an Aristotelian progression showing fierceness, temperance, and tameness. At i.17 (at the centre of the first group of 33 stanzas), Redcrosse knight attacks the dragon "As Lyon fierce upon the flying pray," he tempers his wrath at i.50 (at the centre of the second group of 33) when confronted by the false Una, and at ii.29 (at the centre of the third group of 33) he rests his weary limbs, together with Duessa, in the shade which provides protection against the scorching beams of the midday sun (representative of judgment). That the temptation scenes should be divided into 3 groups of 11 stanzas is numerically appropriate; the two moves toward disaster occur in stanzas 34–55, divided into 11 stanzas on the fetching of the false dream and 11 on the failure of the first temptation. In the first 11 stanzas of canto ii, however, the second temptation succeeds, and Redcrosse is led astray. Spenser's use of the number of salvation (33) and of the ratio 2 : 1 in these 100 stanzas creates a structure at odds with the contents: despite the ominous progression from initial victory to final disaster, the textual structure holds out the promise that everything will be put right in the end. God's providence encompasses and annuls the effect of the machinations of the exponents of evil. (We find a similar counterpointing between form and contents in George Herbert's "Deniall.")[9] Finally we notice that balanced structures are found within the larger segments: stanzas i.1–33 divide into 5—23—5, and the last group of 33 stanzas (ii.13–45) into 15—2—15—1. Since the 23 stanzas describe Redcrosse's successful fight with the dragon Error, it is possible that the number 23 has its biblical meaning of vengeance on sinners.

Spenser's structural inventiveness did not abandon him in canto iii on Una, who seeks her "wandring knight" far and wide. Although her condition is one of "wandring woe" (iii.48:8), she endures all with patience and fortitude. The canto is framed by two-stanza laments for Una (see Diagram VI.5), whereas at the textual centre (iii.22–23) she is cursed by Corceca and Abessa. In between are 19-stanza segments, one on Una and the lion in the false house of holiness and another on Archimago's attempt to pose as Redcrosse knight. Like Tasso, then, Spenser resorts to the inauspicious number 19 for episodes where evil is rampant.

Patterns of verbal repetition support these structures (see Diagram VI.6). The canto as a whole is circumscribed by the repetition of the rhyme words *corse* and *forse* (5) repeated in inverse order in stanza 42, and the phrase *full greedie* (placed within the line in

Diagram VI.5 *The Faerie Queene* I, Events in Canto iii

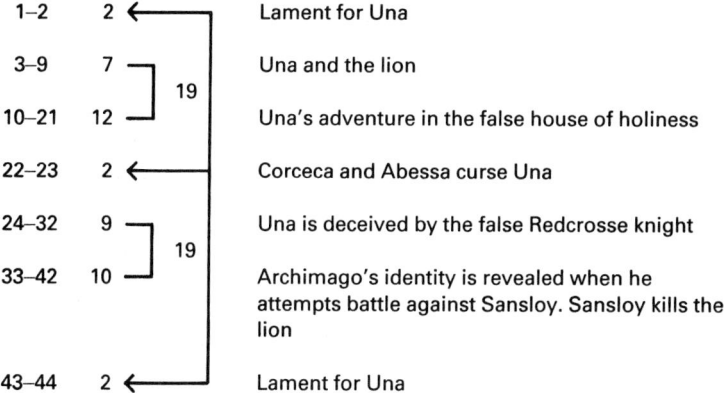

Two stanzas of lament frame this canto, while the "lamenting cry" of Corceca and Abessa at the textual centre presents an infernal analogue of the topos of lament.

stanzas 5 and 41) is another exact repetition. The episode of Una and the lion in the house of Corceca (10–21; see Diagram VI.7) presents a particularly fine example of the use of clusters of identical rhyme words to mark the beginning, middle, and end. The verbal patterns of canto iii are both complex and precise, and it is clearly the lamentable character of the action which calls for such frequent repetitions to engender a maximum of pathos. Halfway between the middle and the end, the false Redcrosse knight engages Sansloy in two stanzas (34–35) where the sudden reversal in Archimago's fortune is mirrored by the repetition of the rhymes *beare, speare, feare* in the order *speare, feare, beare. Fear* is of course a key word in both episodes; Abessa and Corceca quake with fear when Una and the lion force an entry (12), just as the false Redcrosse knight "did faint through feare" on the approach of Sansloy (34). However, the fear which dominates these evil characters is entirely absent from Una's heart: she is "of nought affrayd" (3 : 7). Perfect love casts out fear (1 *John* 4 : 18).

No other canto illustrates Spenser's compositional technique with greater clarity. Although clearly indicated, the patterns are by no means obtrusive; Spenser dresses his structural skeleton so artfully that it is perceived only after close scrutiny. A skilled rhetorician, however, would have fewer problems than the typical twentieth-century reader.

Diagram VI.6 *The Faerie Queene* I, Patterns of Verbal Repetition in Canto iii

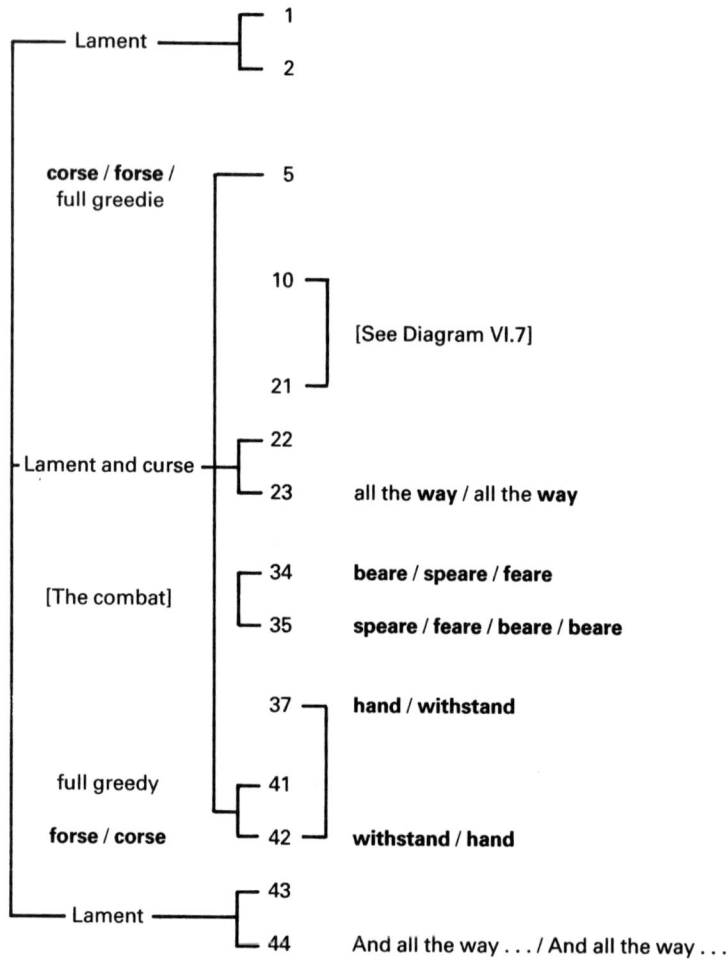

It may be because agreement or concord is so conspicuously lacking in the House of Pride that the structure of canto iv lacks the elegant precision of the preceding canto. Lucifera and her very throne are at odds, each trying to outshine the other, and the six beasts harnessed to her coach are "unequall" (iv.18 : 1 and cf. v.28 on the chariot of Night). The topos of inconstancy, however, connects the beginning, middle, and end: the canto begins with denunciation of inconstancy in love (iv.1 : 7–9), at the centre Lechery personifies inconstancy (26 : 1–2), and as the canto ends

Diagram VI.7 *The Faerie Queene* I, Verbal Structures in iii.10–21

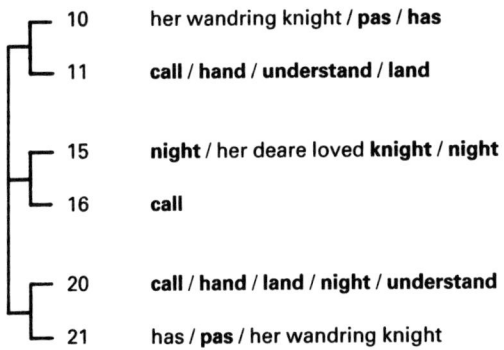

It is remarkable that this pattern includes rhyme words based on no fewer than four different sounds (*pas, call, hand,* and *night*), and that one of them is represented by three words (*hand, understand, land*). The complexity therefore is so great that chance can by no means be held responsible.

Duessa herself fears the "fickle freakes … / Of fortune false, and oddes of armes in field" (50 : 1–2). The most conspicuous structure is the group of 19 stanzas on the pageant of the deadly sins (see Diagram VI.8) located at the centre (15 stanzas precede and

Diagram VI.8 *The Faerie Queene* I, the Events of Canto iv

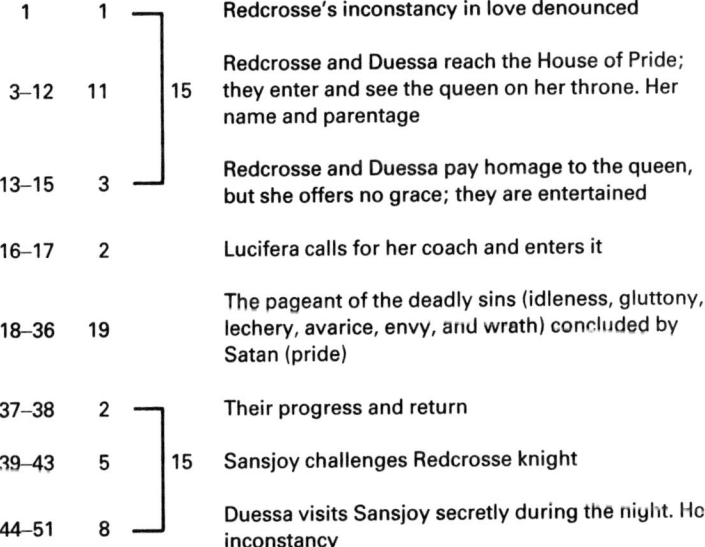

Diagram VI.9 *The Faerie Queene* I, the Events of Canto v

1. The single combat

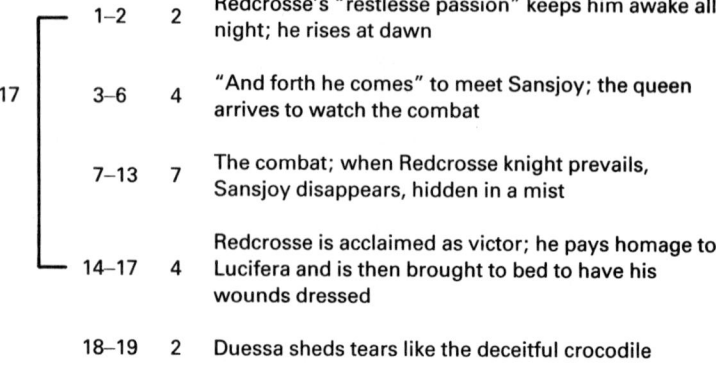

	1–2	2	Redcrosse's "restlesse passion" keeps him awake all night; he rises at dawn
17	3–6	4	"And forth he comes" to meet Sansjoy; the queen arrives to watch the combat
	7–13	7	The combat; when Redcrosse knight prevails, Sansjoy disappears, hidden in a mist
	14–17	4	Redcrosse is acclaimed as victor; he pays homage to Lucifera and is then brought to bed to have his wounds dressed

18–19	2	Duessa sheds tears like the deceitful crocodile

2. Duessa visits the realm of Pluto, while Redcrosse escapes

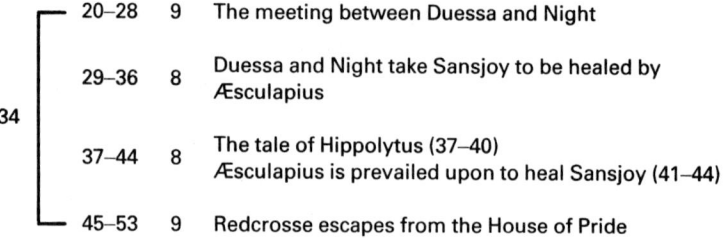

	20–28	9	The meeting between Duessa and Night
	29–36	8	Duessa and Night take Sansjoy to be healed by Æsculapius
34	37–44	8	The tale of Hippolytus (37–40) Æsculapius is prevailed upon to heal Sansjoy (41–44)
	45–53	9	Redcrosse escapes from the House of Pride

Each episode has a balanced pattern at the same time that the ratio 1:2 harmonizes the events of parts 1 and 2 around the pivotal two stanzas on Duessa's crocodile tears.

follow). The canto structure as a whole, though, is not particularly felicitous, and I take it that this is what decorum requires. Numerical decorum however, is present in the 19 stanzas employed to describe the pageant.

In strong contrast, the structure of canto v is highly wrought (see Diagram VI.9). The combat between Redcrosse knight and Sansjoy occupies 17 stanzas (v.1–17), then follow 2 stanzas on Duessa's crocodile tears (18–19), and 2×17 stanzas on Duessa's night-time activities and on Redcrosse's escape from the House of Pride. Duessa's tears, therefore, divide the canto in the ratio 1:2. While in canto iv the structure seems at odds with itself, canto v has the negative kind of harmony (in the ratio 1:2) which stems from Duessa as the offspring of Night. One can also see the canto as

Diagram VI.10 *The Faerie Queene* I, the Events of Cantos vi–vii (100 stanzas)

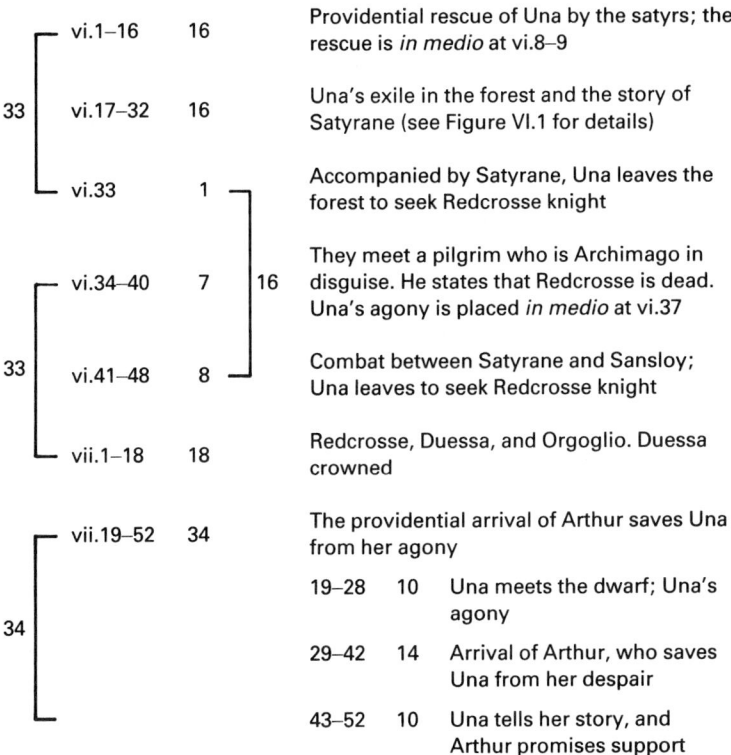

The cycle of 33—33—34 stanzas begins with the providential arrival of the satyrs and concludes with the equally providential arrival of Arthur. Emblematic details in the description of Una at the beginning of Canto vi connect with the description of Arthur in the last part of Canto vii (the veil, the diamond mirror)

consisting of two balanced sequences: one on the combat with Sansjoy (2—4—7—4—2) and another on Duessa's rescue of Sansjoy and Redcrosse's escape (9—8—8—9). In the first sequence the single combat is at the centre in the group of 7 stanzas. The graded arrangement, however, enables us to see Redcrosse's victory as part of an infernal harmony presided over by Duessa.

The central cantos vi and vii shift the focus back again to Una, and the stanza total is 100, as in cantos i–ii. Canto vi is neatly divided into 3×16 stanzas (see Diagram VI.10): 16 stanzas describe Una's providential rescue by the satyrs, another group of 16 stanzas her exile in the forest, and the last group her escape from the forest,

Diagram VI.11 *The Faerie Queene* I, Verbal Structures in Canto vii. 19–52
(10 + 14 + 10 stanzas)

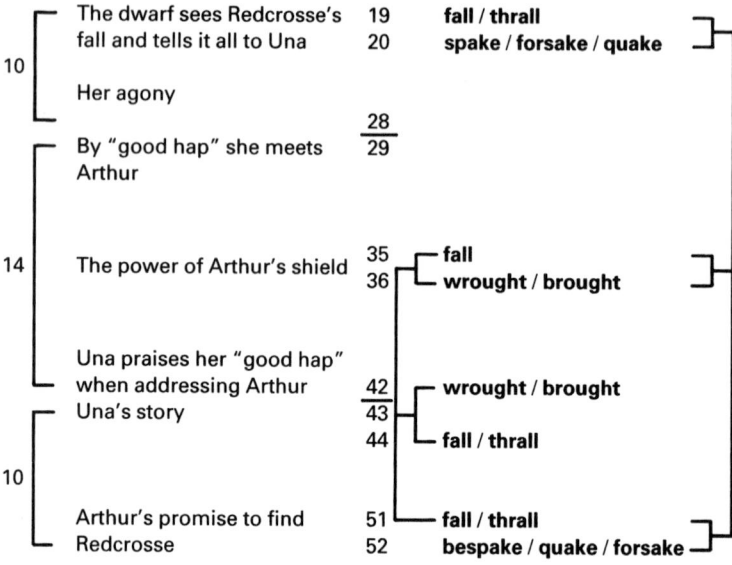

accompanied by Satyrane, their encounter with Archimago with his false tale, and the fight between Satyrane and Sansloy. Una's trials reach their climax with the dwarf's report of Redcrosse's fate in canto vii. Cantos vi–vii invert the pattern of cantos i–ii. While the first two cantos begin in a promising vein only to conclude ominously, in cantos vi–vii an ominous beginning yields to hope with the arrival of Arthur. The Providence which ensured Una's deliverance from Sanslov at the beginning of canto vi, at the end of canto vii sends Arthur to deliver her from despair – a far more cruel enemy. The division of the 100 stanzas into 33—33—34 expresses the theme of deliverance in numerical terms. As exegetes would explain, Christ was 33 when he suffered death, but he was also in his 34th year.

That the last group of 34 stanzas (vii.19–52) constitutes a narrative segment is shown by the verbal repetitions which connect the beginning, middle, and end (see Diagram VI.11). No less than five identical rhyme words connect stanzas 19–20 and 51–52, and one of these is found also at the centre in stanza 35. Again it is a likely explanation that it is the pathetic character of Una's situation which calls for such insistent repetitions. When the segment begins, the

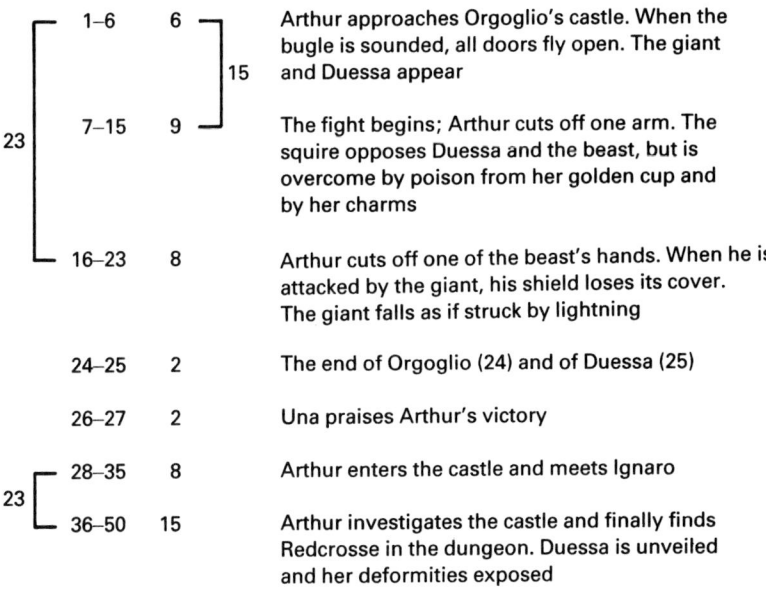

Diagram VI.12   *The Faerie Queene* I, the Events of Canto viii

The division is into two halves of 25 stanzas each, subdivided into 15—8—2 and 2—8—15. The defeat of Orgoglio and Duessa (24–25) and Una's praise of Arthur's victory (26–27) are at the textual centre. Verbal links between stanzas 24–25 include the rhyme scheme (the *a* rhyme in stanza 24 is the *c* rhyme of stanza 25) and the repetition of the rhyme word **pray** in the first line and the last (i.e. at 24:1 and 25:9). The two stanzas on Una's praise (26–27) are similarly linked by means of the rhyme scheme, the *a* rhyme of the first being the *c* rhyme of the second.

In biblical exegesis, the number 23 signifies vengeance on sinners, as Bongo explains in his chapter on this number.

dwarf carries Redcrosse's armour, shield, and spear to Una, who faints three times, and Una faints also after she has told her story to Arthur (20–24 and 52). At the centre (35–36) the account of Merlin's magic art who "Both shield, and sword, and armour all he wrought / For this young Prince" (36:6–7) sets up a link with the beginning. Simple repetition links stanzas 29 and 42, which relate how Una praises her "good hap" in meeting Arthur.

Canto viii has a simple and effective structure (see Diagram VI.12). The action divides the 50 stanzas into a sequence of 15—8—2—2—8—15. The four stanzas at the centre – two on the end of Orgoglio and Duessa and two on Una's praise of the victory – are flanked by the combat with Orgoglio and the discovery of Redcrosse knight in the dungeon of the castle. Halfway through the first half (viii.13) we observe Duessa elevated on the beast, while the debasement of Redcrosse knight is observed halfway through the second half (38). The canto concludes with the debasement of Duessa. By postponing the description of Duessa's punishment until the end of the canto, this topos sets up a link between the middle and the end. The structure highlights the antithesis between fall and retribution (Duessa) and fall and redemption (Redcrosse knight). Justice is the fate meted out to Duessa, while Redcrosse knight is saved by the grace of God. These are the meanings invested in the biblical number 23, which signifies either divine vengeance on sinners, or redemption from sin. As Bongo explains in his chapter on this number, it signifies the joint operation of Justice and Mercy.[10] We may perhaps add that a distinction between action *in bono* and *in malo* may be involved, if we adopt a purely human perspective. (In God, mercy and justice are so much one that they cannot be separated.) Spenser's choice of 23 as his chief structural number therefore reveals considerable subtlety.

For canto ix Spenser again favoured a graded arrangement (see Diagram VI.13). The three stanzas on the exchange of gifts between Redcrosse knight and Arthur at ix.18–20 divide the canto into 17—3—34 stanzas. These gifts signify divine grace as extended in the eucharist and the gospels, and the pivotal function of the idea of grace is shown in the fact that it reaches back to the lovely opening

Diagram VI.13   *The Faerie Queene* I, the Events of Canto ix

1	1	17	Praise of the golden chain that joins virtuous and noble minds
2–17	16		Arthur tells his story
18–20	3		Arthur and Redcrosse exchange gifts and join hands in token of firm union
21–54	34		The adventure of the Cave of Despair; Una counters the appeal to justice with a reminder of the importance of heavenly grace

At the centre of the 34-stanza segment on the Cave of Despair is the first confrontation between Redcrosse knight and Despair (ix.37–38). As if to emphasize their importance, these stanzas are flanked by stanzas that feature the rhyme words **stood** and **flood** in the last two lines.

stanza and forward to the end when Una must remind Redcrosse knight (in the Cave of Despair) of God's saving grace. This grace is the golden chain which pulls sinful man up to Heaven (ix.1).

Grace is stressed even more strongly in canto x on the stay in the House of Holiness, a canto which combines plain symmetry with an arrangement into 1—44—22—1 stanzas. In the symmetrical structure (see Diagram VI.14) Mercy is at the centre, guiding Redcrosse's steps like a careful nurse in the direction of the "narrow way" (x.34–35). We read about this narrow way in the opening stanzas, too, when the travellers are shown a "straight and narrow way" into the house itself (5), just as the very first stanza tells us that it is by grace alone that victory may be gained over spiritual foes.

Diagram VI.14 *The Faerie Queene* I, Symmetrically Placed Topoi in Canto x

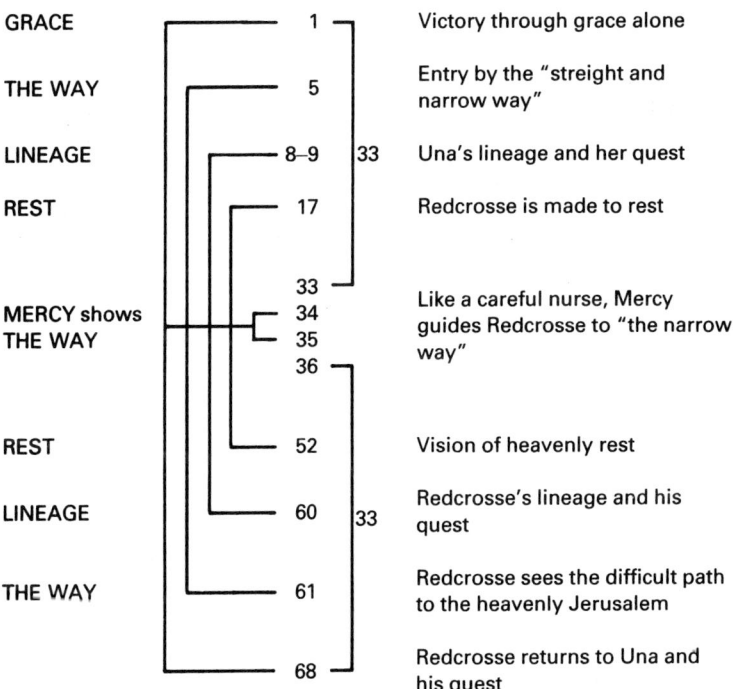

The topos of rest is placed at the two halfway points (x.17 and 52), that of the true lineage and the quest in stanzas 8–9 and 60 (i.e. ninth from the end). The sacred character of the events is brought out numerically by the division into 33—2—33 stanzas. The topos of the narrow way links the beginning, middle, and end.

Finally the topos of the right way recurs at the end when Redcrosse is shown the difficult path to the heavenly Jerusalem (61). The true lineage is revealed at x.8–9 when the lady of the house greets Una as a person sprung from "heavenly race" and dedicated to the redemption of her woeful parents, and in the stanza which is ninth from the end (60) Redcrosse in the same way is identified in terms of his true lineage and his end in life. The lineage serves to remind us of Una's importance; but for Una, Redcrosse would have had no quest, nor would he have been sustained in it. The idea of rest figures at the two halfway points (17 and 52), and in the second half of the canto it is lifted from the physical to the spiritual level. Physical and spiritual rest, then, function as sub-centres flanking the two-stanza centre on the ministrations of Mercy; in other words, by divine mercy Redcrosse's rest in the end will be elevated to eternal rest in God as envisaged by Augustine at the end of the *Confessions*. Number symbolism is discreetly present, since the two central stanzas on Mercy are flanked by 33 stanzas.

The graded arrangement is formed by the events (see Diagram VI.15). After an introductory stanza on the uselessness of "fleshly might" compared with saving grace, 44 stanzas describe Redcrosse's progress from feebleness to the strength of "holy righteousnesse" (x.49 : 9). These stanzas display a balanced pattern of 10—6—12—6—10 stanzas, where the centrally placed 12-stanza segment describes how he is instructed by Fidelia, comforted by Speranza, and supported by Patience, and his wounds cured by Penance and Repentance. The last group of 22 stanzas takes us from practical theology to vision and prophecy, so that the ratio 2 : 1 expresses the harmony between these two aspects of religion.

The fight with the dragon in canto xi spills over into the first 11 stanzas of canto xii, so that it fills 66 stanzas in all (see Diagram VI.16). Events divide these stanzas into 33+33, thus permitting the number of salvation to prevail at the end as it does at the beginning (cantos i–ii) and the middle (cantos vi–vii). The decisive turning-point in the battle with the dragon occurs at the centre in stanzas xi.33–34, when dawn breaks the second day and Una sees her knight rising "brave / Out of the Ocean wave ... So new this new-borne knight to battell new did rise." When Redcrosse rises on the morning of the third day, this occurs halfway through the second sequence of 33 stanzas at xi.51.

The action of canto xii divides its 42 stanzas into 14—7—14—7 stanzas, thus rounding off the story by means of a twice-repeated ratio of 2 : 1 based on the biblical numbers of redemption and

Diagram VI.15 *The Faerie Queene* I, the Pattern of Events in Canto x

Stanzas	Count	Group	Description
1	1		On divine grace that alone gives the victory
2–11	10	⎤	Entry into the House of Holiness; their reception
12–17	6	⎥	Fidelia and Speranza invite them to seek rest
18–29	12	⎬ 44	Redcrosse instructed by Fidelia, comforted by Speranza, and supported by Patience, while Penance and Repentance cure the wounds in his soul
30–35	6	⎥	Charissa schools the knight, and Mercy takes him by the hand
36–45	10	⎦	Redcrosse's stay in the holy hospital with its 7 attendants representing the 7 works of mercy
46–59	14	⎤ 22	Mercy takes Redcrosse to the hermit and the Hill of Contemplation whence he sees the heavenly Jerusalem
60–67	8	⎦	Redcrosse learns his true lineage and true end
68	1		Return to Una and to the quest

The pattern formed by the 44 stanzas is symmetrical: 10—6—12—6—10. All the numbers are the basic biblical numbers of redemption to eternal life. The ratio 2:1 expresses the harmony between theology on the one hand and on the other, vision and prophecy.

creation (see Diagram VI.17). The sum total of 42 stanzas signifies the church under persecution, as explained in the gloss in the Jerusalem Bible on *Daniel* 7:25 and *Revelation* 11:2. To be more precise, it signifies "a temporary time of persecution with a limit set by God's providence". Duessa's letter illustrates the point that the one true church is under persecution while God so permits, and I take it that this is one reason why the episode was invented. The episode of the accusing letter presupposes that Redcrosse knight has failed to explain all that has happened between himself and Duessa, otherwise its dramatic character would be lost. It is to miss the point, therefore, to accuse Redcrosse knight of a lack of honesty; the allegory calls for a continued persecution of Una (the one true church) even after the victory over the dragon, and this is what should chiefly concern us.

Diagram VI.16 *The Faerie Queene* I, Cantos xi and xii.1–11

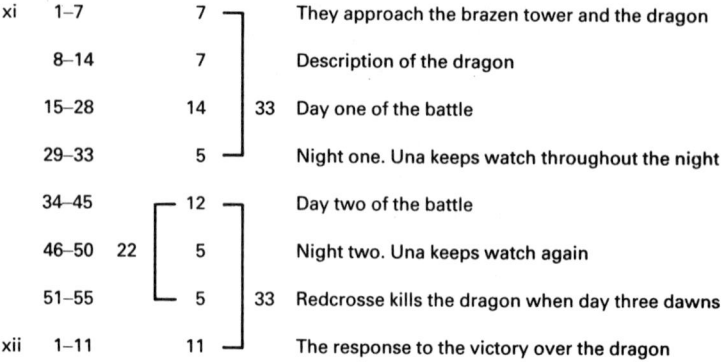

The overlapping between Cantos xi and xii manifests itself in the repetition of identical rhyme words, at the same time that such repetitions also circumscribe stanzas xi.50–55 and xii.1–11 as shown below:

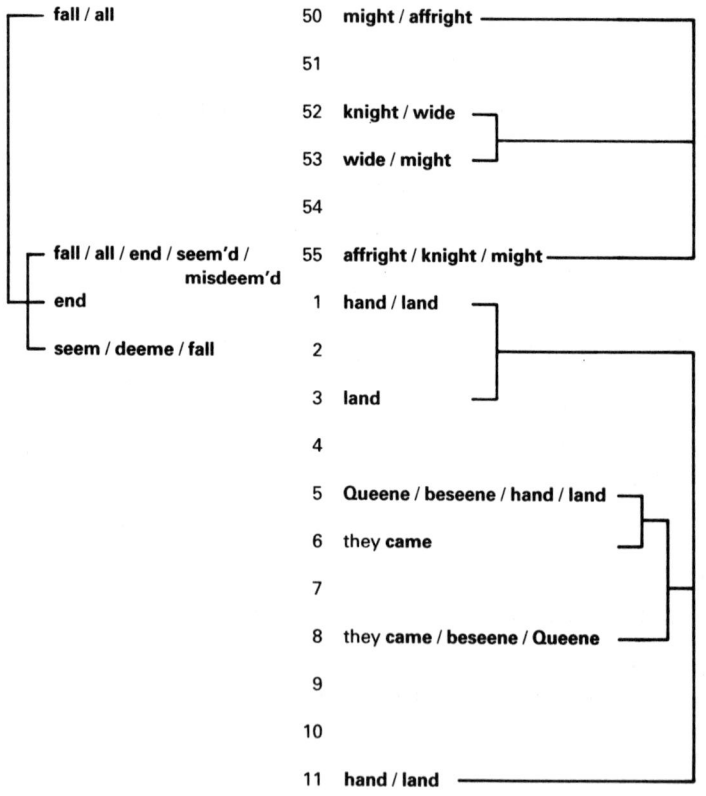

Diagram VI.17 *The Faerie Queene* I, Canto xii

1–14	14	The king and queen and their people issue forth to honour Redcrosse knight and Una. Una *in medio* at xii.7–8
15–21	7	The rich feast begins. Redcrosse tells his story. The king gives him his daughter and his kingdom
22–35	14	The rites are interrupted by a messenger (who is Archimago) from Duessa. Their falsehoods are exposed and he is fettered
36–42	7	The rites are concluded and the betrothal celebrated

This graded arrangement coincides with central accent on the presentation of Una in stanzas linked by the repetition of identical rhyme words:

20	(heire)	
21	heyre / appeare / neare	bedight / sight
22	neare / appeare	
23		sight / dight

The chiastic arrangement should be noted.

A special feature is the linking between the first 7 stanzas and the last 7, as shown below:

	Stanzas:	
Sacred rites	36 ↔ 7	Homage paid to Una
Their hands are joined	37 ↔ 6	Homage to Redcrosse knight
Betrothal ceremony and "sweet Musicke"	38 ↔ 5	Processional ceremony with laurel branches
They hear a "heavenly noyse" as from angels "on hye"	39 ↔ 4	Trumpets sound "on hie"; *musica humana*
A solemn feast proclaimed "throughout the land"	40 ↔ 3	The king "Proclaymed joy and peace through all his state"
Redcrosse returns to the Faerie Queen after killing the "monstrous beast"	41 ↔ 2	The "balefull Beast" seen to be dead
Image of the "feeble bark"	42 ↔ 1	Image of "this wearie vessel"

Linkage between stanzas 3 and 40 is made also through the repetition of the three rhyme words **land**, **understand**, and **hand**.

Extra adornment for the concluding canto is found in the pattern of recessed symmetry which links the first group of 7 stanzas and the last. The canto begins and ends with the image of the "feeble bark" (xii.1) and the "wearie vessel" (42); the death of the monstrous beast links stanzas 2 and 41, the proclamation of a feast stanzas 3 and 40, the idea of music stanzas 4 and 39, and various ceremonial events connect the remaining stanzas (5/38, 6/37, and 7/36). This pattern serves as a frame for the central stanzas (20–23) on the presentation of Una unveiled. A cluster of identical rhyme words adorns these four stanzas.

This survey of canto structures in Book I shows that in Book I Spenser consistently employed a constructivist technique entailing balancing part against part to create symmetrical or graded arrangements, or both at the same time. The pattern of events may sometimes create one structure, while another is formed by concepts or topoi, as in canto x. The segments which constitute a canto may be balanced, and individual segments may have their own carefully worked-out structures. Number symbolism is often present, and the frequent occurrence of the number 33 in Book I is noteworthy, as is the use of 19 and 23 for negative events. Spenser uses numbers like these more frequently than Tasso in the *Gerusalemme Liberata*, but Tasso's *Il Mundo Creato* is of course another matter. Verbal repetitions (including the repetition of clusters of identical rhyme words) are particularly frequent in passages where the action is pathetic or otherwise highly charged emotionally. The presence of such patterns provides a kind of guarantee for the presence of the structures they serve to identify.

2. Book I: The Symmetrical Structure

Like Augustine and Tasso, Spenser was not content to create a simple pattern of recessed symmetry; as in certain cantos, he combined this symmetrical pattern with a graded arrangement in the ratio 2 : 1. Readers have always felt that the action divides the book into 8+4 cantos, at the same time that Redcrosse's dalliance with Duessa by the fountain of feebleness marks the low point in his career, whereas the highest in Duessa's occurs shortly afterwards as she sits enthroned on the beast. We may now identify these structures with greater precision. Like Tasso, Spenser created an extended centre for the symmetrical arrangement in stanzas vii.1.24/25; 296 stanzas precede and follow (see Diagram VI.18). The truly remarkable feature is an extended centre also in the

THE FAERIE QUEENE I AND II 293

Diagram VI.18   *The Faerie Queene* I, Table of Stanza Totals

A The Symmetrical Structure

Cantos i–vi	296 stanzas
Cantos vii–xii	321 (320) stanzas
The extended centre	vii.1–24(25)

The one-stanza difference between the two editions is of no importance since vii.25 is transitional.

The first halfway point	iv.1–8 (i.e. the centre of cantos i–vi)
The second halfway point	x.1–9 (i.e. the centre of cantos vii–xii)

The centre and the flanking halfway points form a logical sequence:

1. iv.1–8   Entry into the House of Pride (elevation that debases)
2. vii.1–24(25)   Debasement of Redcrosse and elevation of Duessa
3. x.1–9   Entry into the House of Holiness (debasement that elevates)

B The Graded Structure

Cantos i–viii	398 stanzas
Cantos ix–xii	218 (219) stanzas
The extended centre	ix.1–19(20)

The first halfway point	v.1–8 (i.e. the centre of cantos i–viii)
The second halfway point	x.44–68 (i.e. the centre of cantos ix–xii)

Again the centre and the flanking halfway points (or sub-centres) form a logical sequence:

1. v.1–8   Redcrosse's vision of false glory in the House of Pride
2. ix.1–19(20)   Arthur's vision of true glory in the Faerie Queen
3. x–44–68   Redcrosse's vision of the heavenly Jerusalem

The logical connection between the three points of structural emphasis confirms the validity of the structural patterns.

graded arrangement: this centre is located at ix.1–19/20; 398 stanzas precede and 199 follow, which means that the ratio 2 : 1 is found even in the stanza totals. To qualify as an extended centre the relevant passage must present a self-contained episode with a pivotal function, as in Tasso's romance epic. This is true of the extended centre in both structures. Each of these two centres is linked not only with the beginning and the end, but with the halfway points as well, as indicated in the Table of stanza totals. Nothing in

Tasso can compare with the complex precision of the two overall structures of Book I, at the same time that Spenser's choice of pivotal themes is more satisfying. The thematic interplay between the two extended centres – one in the symmetrical structure and the other in the graded arrangement – makes the double structure functional: the one features feebleness, the other strength through loving union. Another antithesis is between Duessa (the scarlet whore) and the Faerie Queen, which is the contrast between false and true glory. However, the parallel between the two centres is equally interesting: it is by divine grace that Redcrosse knight is saved from annihilation, just as the gifts exchanged between the two knights signify the grace extended through the gospels and the blood of Christ. As I argue below, the chastisement Redcrosse suffers at the hand of Orgoglio represents proffered grace, so that Redcrosse's fate resembles that of Tasso's Tancred or Rinaldo. The fall and the chastisement which follows lead to his subsequent redemption.

The halfway points play their part in charting Redcrosse's progress; the first describes the entry into the House of Pride (iv.1–8), the second into the House of Holiness (x.1–9). In the one house Redcrosse observes the elevation of Lucifera – an elevation which debases – and in the second the debasement which elevates. We may define the progression in terms of grace: the first halfway point takes Redcrosse knight to a house marked by its total absence; the chastisement that is proffered grace figures at the centre; while the second halfway point introduces Redcrosse into the house where grace is freely bestowed.

In the graded structure, the halfway points and the centre are concerned with false and true visions of glory. At the first halfway point Redcrosse is said to burn with desire for "the eternall brood of glorie excellent," and the combat with Sansjoy seems to promise just such glory (v.1–8). At the centre, Arthur tells the story of his encounter with the embodiment of a glory which is both earthly and heavenly, and at the second halfway point Redcrosse is given his vision of heavenly glory from the top of the Hill of Contemplation (x.44–68). In both structures, then, we begin with a quality which is false and then proceed via a dimly seen vision of the truth to its perfect revelation. The progression resembles an arrangement consisting of a false type, a true type, and the glorious antitype. An analogy may also be felt with Aristotle's thinking; the absence of true peace or glory resembles defect, the glory of the antitype may be seen as excess taken *in bono*, and the point in between – the true type – as a kind of mean. Certainly a kind of mean is struck between Justice and Mercy in Redcrosse's chastisement, and between earthly and heavenly glory in Arthur's encounter with the Faerie Queen.

After these general remarks a more detailed study can be undertaken, beginning with the symmetrical structure.

The extended centre of the symmetrical structure (vii.1–24/25) shows the fall of Redcrosse knight when he doffs his armour and courts Duessa in the shade (1–7). The 11 stanzas on Redcrosse's debasement and Duessa's enthronement on the beast are followed by 7 (or 6) stanzas on Una's agony when she meets the dwarf who carries Redcrosse's armour, shield, and spear. Una's agony is a kind of passion in the course of which she faints three times.

The biblical background for Redcrosse's weakness deserves consideration, beginning with *Isaiah* 40 : 28–31. Young men may "faint and be weary," but they that "wait upon the Lord shall renew their strength; they shall mount up with wings as eagles; they shall run and not be weary; and they shall walk, and not faint" (AV). Later on, in the fight with the dragon, Redcrosse knight will indeed rise up "As Eagle fresh out of the Ocean wave" (xi.34 : 3), but at this point he is found by Duessa "whereas he wearie sate, / To rest him selfe foreby a fountaine side, / Disarmed all of yron-coted Plate" (vii.2:6–8). Sloth quickly leads to lust as Redcrosse is "Pourd out in loosnesse on the grassy grownd" (7 : 2), and this offence to God is presented in mythical terms in the one-stanza tale of the fountain of feebleness. When Orgoglio suddenly appears, Redcrosse is saved from his deadly stroke by "heavenly grace, that him did blesse" (12 : 3). A biblical allusion occurs in the simile which compares Orgoglio's blow to a cannon whose discharge fills the heavens "With thundring noyse, and all the ayre doth choke, / That none can breath, nor see, nor heare at will, / Through smouldry cloud of duskish stincking smoke" (vii.13). This allusion to a volcanic eruption is appropriate, since giants were associated with volcanoes, "and volcanoes were themselves symbols of rebellion or, like the earthquake, of divine judgment."[11] In the Old Testament, Jehovah was connected with earthquakes, lightning, and thunder, as in the description of his appearance, to Moses and the Israelites, on Mount Sinai – a type of judgment day.[12] When Redcrosse knight is saved from the giant's blow by heavenly grace, this rescue tells us that the grace of the gospels intervenes to mitigate the severity of Jehovah's justice. For Protestant readers, therefore, Spenser's central episode is far more satisfying than Tasso's with its celebration of Mass on Mount Olivet. Orgoglio's association with divine punishment is actually made explicit later on in the encounter between Arthur and Orgoglio, when the giant's blow is said to be like that of "almightie *Jove* in wrathfull mood", as he hurls his thunder bolts "Enrold in flames, and smouldring dreriment, / Through riven cloudes" (viii.9). Even more relevant, though, is the context provided by *Hebrews* 12, where the descent of Jehovah on Mount Sinai is contrasted with Mount Sion, the point being precisely the issue of divine chastisement. The chapter begins with the exhortation to "run with patience the race that is set before us." We must endure without becoming "wearied and faint," and what we must endure includes God's chastisement, since God chastises us in order that "we might be partakers of his holiness." Although Redcrosse knight perversely doffs his armour and as it were permits his hands to hang down and his knees to be feeble, and although he becomes a fornicator like Esau (*Hebrews* 12:12 and 16), he is called, not to Mount Sinai but to Mount Sion: "For ye are not come unto the mount that might not be touched, and that burned with fire, nor unto blackness, and darkness, and tempest ... But ye are come unto Mount Sion, and unto the city of the living God, the heavenly Jerusalem, and to an innumerable company of angels" (*Hebrews* 12:18 and 22). These passages make it abundantly clear that Redcrosse knight is chastised with a view to making him a partaker of God's holiness. Like Milton's Satan, Orgoglio is made to serve God's purpose.

In the 1590 text, stanzas vii.12–13 on Redcrosse's escape from the giant's blow and the connected epic simile are exactly at the centre, by stanza-count, of the book as a whole; in the second edition this is true of stanza 13 alone. The advantage of the second edition is that the extended centre (25 stanzas in all) displays perfect balance: the 7 stanzas on Redcrosse's feebleness balance the last 7 on Una's three faints, and in between are 11 stanzas on Redcrosse, Orgoglio, and Duessa. The balanced structure of the extended centre would seem to have been more important to Spenser than the centre within this centre.

The extended centre is of course linked with the beginning and the end. It begins with a warning against deceit which masks in "visour faire" so as to "seem like Truth," which recalls the false Una in canto i, at the same time that it points forward to the attempted last deceit in canto xii. The elevation of Duessa on the beast is the grandest symbol of deceit and falsehood in the Legend of Holiness.

THE FAERIE QUEENE I AND II 297

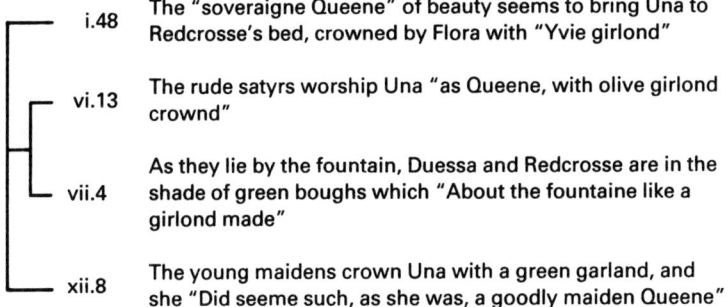

Diagram VI.19 *The Faerie Queene* I, the Topos of Crowning with a Garland

- i.48 — The "soveraigne Queene" of beauty seems to bring Una to Redcrosse's bed, crowned by Flora with "Yvie girlond"
- vi.13 — The rude satyrs worship Una "as Queene, with olive girlond crownd"
- vii.4 — As they lie by the fountain, Duessa and Redcrosse are in the shade of green boughs which "About the fountaine like a girlond made"
- xii.8 — The young maidens crown Una with a green garland, and she "Did seeme such, as she was, a goodly maiden Queene"

The topos of the song of birds provides another link: when the action begins, the travellers joy "to heare the birdes sweet harmony" (i.8:2), and at vii.3 Redcrosse knight listens to the "cherefull birds" that "Do chaunt sweet musick, to delight his mind." On both occasions the music helps to lull the watchful mind asleep, but not so in canto xii where music of various kinds – earthly and heavenly – is very much part of the celebration of the victory and the betrothal.

The impressive topos of crowning with a garland has been placed in cantos i, vi, vii, and xii so as to create perfect symmetry (see Diagram VI.19). The details in the description of the crowning of the false Una at i.48 are as important as in a painting by Botticelli:

And she her selfe of beautie soveraigne Queene,
   Faire *Venus* seemde unto his bed to bring
   Her, whom he waking evermore did weene
   To be the chastest flowre, that ay did spring
   On earthly braunch, the daughter of a king,
   Now a loose Leman to vile service bound:
   And eke the *Graces* seemed all to sing,
   Hymen iö Hymen, dauncing all around,
While freshest *Flora* her with Yvie girlond crownd.

Venus, the queen of earthly beauty and earthly love, *seems* to bring Una to Redcrosse's bed, and the graces *seem* all to sing, while the notoriously unchaste Flora crowns the false Una with ivy, symbol of intemperance. This tableau occupies the eighth position from the end of canto i, and in the eighth position from the beginning of canto xii it is the true Una who is crowned with a garland. After Redcrosse's victory, the maidens run to greet Una, singing a "joyous lay," and the fair virgin appears "As faire *Diana* in fresh sommers day" (xii.7 : 7), and this is when she is crowned:

> Then on her head they set a girland greene,
> And crowned her twixt earnest and twixt game;
> Who in her self-resemblance well beseene,
> Did seeme such, as she was, a goodly maiden Queene.
>
> (xii.8)

Here inner reality corresponds to external appearance: *seeming* and *being* are one. The chaste Diana contrasts strongly with Venus and with Flora, and the garland is an innocent green. A verbal link is afforded by the rhyme word *Queene*, located in the first line of stanza i.48 and in the last of stanza xii.8. The exactness of the placing corresponds to the exactness of the parallel-cum-antithesis. The topos recurs in cantos vi and vii where Una is crowned by the satyrs, who dance round about her much like the graces around the false Una, "And with greene braunches strowing all the ground, / Do worship her, as Queene, with olive girlond cround" (vi.13 : 8–9). To old Sylvanus her identity is very much in doubt:

> Sometimes Dame *Venus* selfe he seemes to see,
> But *Venus* never had so sober mood;
> Sometimes *Diana* he her takes to bee,
> But misseth bow, and shaftes, and buskins to her knee.
>
> (vi.16 : 6–9)

This doubt on the part of Sylvanus suggests the reconciliation between Venus and Diana which signifies chaste love, as in the *Gerusalemme Liberata*. In strong contrast, the love which fires Duessa and Redcrosse knight at vii.4 is as unchaste as the tableau presented at i.48, nor is the garland absent: the "joyous shade" where they take their ease is created by boughs which "About the fountaine like a girlond made."

Topoi located with equal precision are veiling and unveiling, light and darkness, blindness and vision (see Diagram VI.20). Una is introduced as veiled, and she unveils in canto xii after Redcrosse's victory. At vi.4, Sansloy rudely tears off her veil in his assault on her, but Una stoutly resists, her "constant hart" being "As rocke of Diamond stedfast evermore." The veil and the diamond recur in the

Diagram VI.20   *The Faerie Queene* I, Symmetries in the Overall Structure – The Topoi of **Veiling / Unveiling** and of **Darkness / Light**

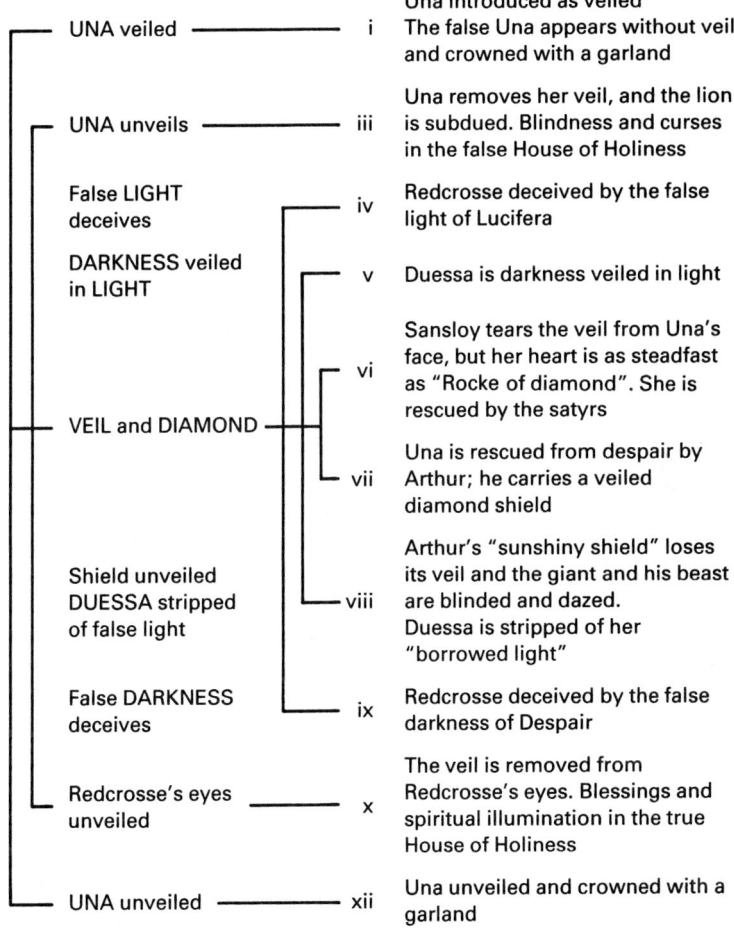

The emblematic veil and diamond bring out the kinship between Arthur and Una; when the shield is unveiled, or Una, the brightness dazzles, and enemies are overcome. Redcrosse is duped, first by false light and then by the false spiritual darkness of Despair; however, when the veil is removed from his eyes, he is given a vision of true glory (the heavenly Jerusalem). The false light of Lucifera is exposed when Redcrosse sees the corpses by the castle wall, and Duessa's true nature is revealed when she is stripped of her "borrowed light."

description of Arthur's veiled shield (vii.33–36), so that Una and Arthur become closely connected. When Una unveils in canto iii, this ensures mastery over the lion, who forgets his rage and kisses her feet in humble submission (iii.5–6), just as in canto x the removal of the veil from Redcrosse's spiritual vision (x.67) promises victory in the fight to come. The vision of heavenly things induces blindness for a while, but this blindness is in strong contrast to the blindness of Corceca (iii.12–14), which expresses her spiritual condition. Falsehood prevails in canto iv: the false light of Lucifera's court blinds Redcrosse knight to the reality of the pageant of the deadly sins, while in canto ix he is blinded by the false darkness of Despair's rhetoric. In this darkness he sees his own sins only too clearly and God's grace not at all. While in canto v Duessa is darkness veiled in deceptive light (v.26), the unveiling of the diamond shield (viii.19–20) decides the battle between Arthur and Orgoglio, at the end of which Duessa stands unveiled (viii.46–49).

Further topoi which unify the 12 cantos through linkage are confinement and sloth, as set out in Diagram VI.21. Confinement and release may be sought or avoided, and each may function in a good or a bad sense, thus ensuring variety. The willing confinement of Morpheus clearly is most perverse, and the sloth he embodies appears later on in the pageant of the deadly sins where Sloth leads the procession, although "Still drownd in sleepe" (iv.18–20). In Archimago's hermitage, disaster strikes during the hours of the night while the travellers are "all drownd in deadly sleepe" (i.36), and Duessa similarly catches Fradubio when "drownd in sleepie night" (ii.42). Finally, at the textual centre, Redcrosse knight doffs his armour and proceeds from sloth to lust as he courts Duessa in the shade. This release from an armour felt as confining is placed antithetically against the triumphant release, in the last canto, of the king and queen of Eden and their folk from confinement in the tower, and this joyous release is also the antithesis of Morpheus's willing confinement within the womb of the earth and behind locked double doors. A subtle parallel is found between cantos iv and ix when Redcrosse, in the Cave of Despair, feels confined by the sins he failed to recognize in the House of Pride, and incapable of bestirring himself. Yet another significant link is between Fradubio within his "wooden wals" (ii.42 : 8) and Redcrosse knight confined within an armour which has become a red-hot instrument of torture from the dragon's fiery breath (xi.26). This is a typical romance *contrapasso*: the knight who once burned with passion for a deceitful Duessa must burn in real earnest within the armour he once

Diagram VI.21 *The Faerie Queene* I, the Related Topoi of Confinement and Sloth

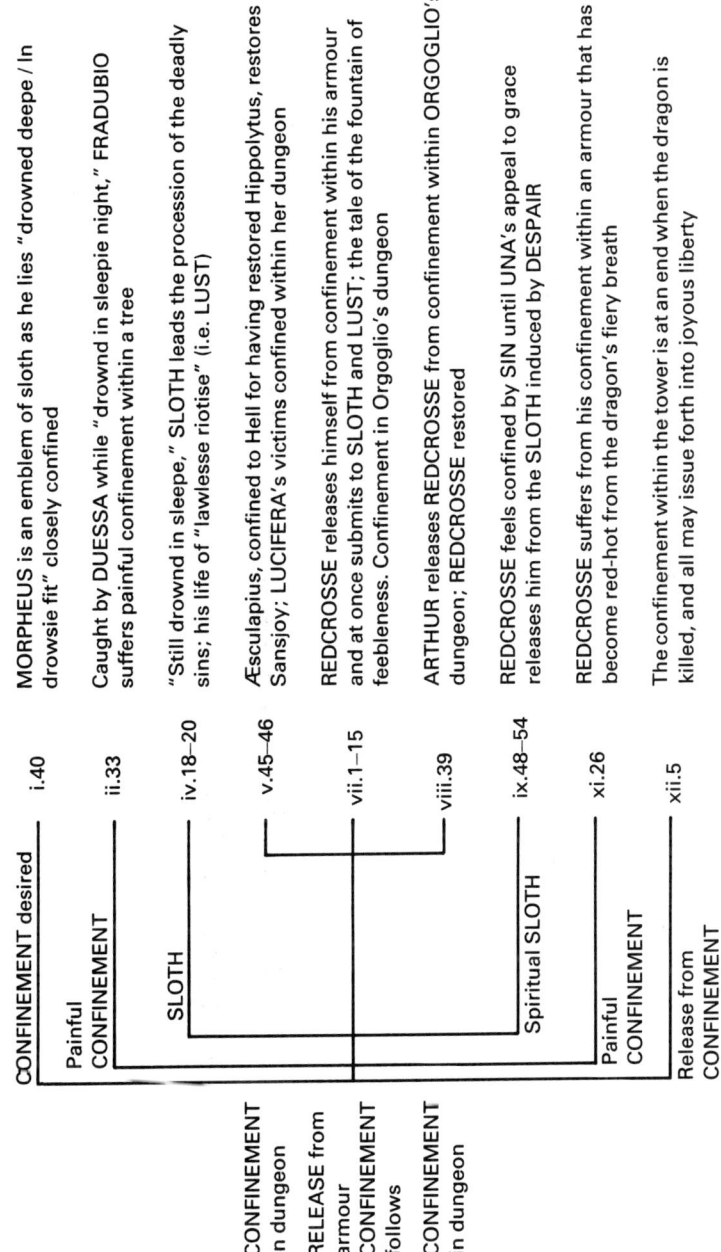

doffed so carelessly. We feel the full import of this torment only when it is linked, first with Fradubio's painful confinement and then with the doffing of the "yron-coted Plate." The "fyrie steele" (xi.27 : 8) functions like Fradubio's "wretched tree" exposed to "cold and heat" (ii.33), but with perfect Christian logic this baneful tree and Redcrosse's related torment are offset not only by the well of living water (ii.43 and xi.29–30), but also by the tree which bestows everlasting life (xi.46). This tree, "Loaden with fruit and apples rosie red," is a just representation of the Tree of Life which is the Tree of the Cross.

Again we observe how systematically Spenser exploits the exegetical principle of construing the same object or event in opposed senses; the context must decide whether the tree and the well and the armour, being crowned with a garland and being confined or released, should have a good or a bad meaning. As Augustine remarks, although on one occasion a shield may be the shield of faith, we must not interpret it as signifying faith whenever we read about a shield (*De doctrina Christiana* III.xxv–xxvi). This familiar exegetical principle enables Spenser to establish links between narrative sections without having to resort to repetition that is too obvious, while at the same time the reader is trained in the art of making logical discriminations.

One is tempted to remark that, in order to write like this, it is at least necessary to think, and that the same necessity perforce imposes itself on the reader. Take, for example, the tale of Hippolytus, restored to life by the art of Æsculapius (v.36–40), who for that reason has been thrust into Hell where he is persuaded to heal Sansjoy (see Diagram VI.21). In canto viii Redcrosse knight, too, has been thrust into a kind of Hell by an offended Deity, but his restoration to life is not through the agency of man's own 'wondrous science" (v.40 : 1) but by the grace of God working through Arthur. However, we may see a parallel between the healing of Hippolytus and the restoration of Redcrosse in the circumstance that the art of man cannot extend beyond the realm of nature. When Redcrosse knight in canto ix is imprisoned and immobilized by Despair's false rhetoric, we understand that his restoration at the end of canto viii remains on the physical level: Arthur may have released him "from bands," and, with the travellers, he may have repaired his "weary powres" and grown strong again (viii.50 and ix.2), but in the Cave of Despair he proves that he is still a frail and feeble "fleshly wight" (ix.53 : 1). Another and more important release awaits him in the true House of Holiness, where his soul will be set free from the

Diagram VI.22 *The Faerie Queene* I, Symmetries Created by Events

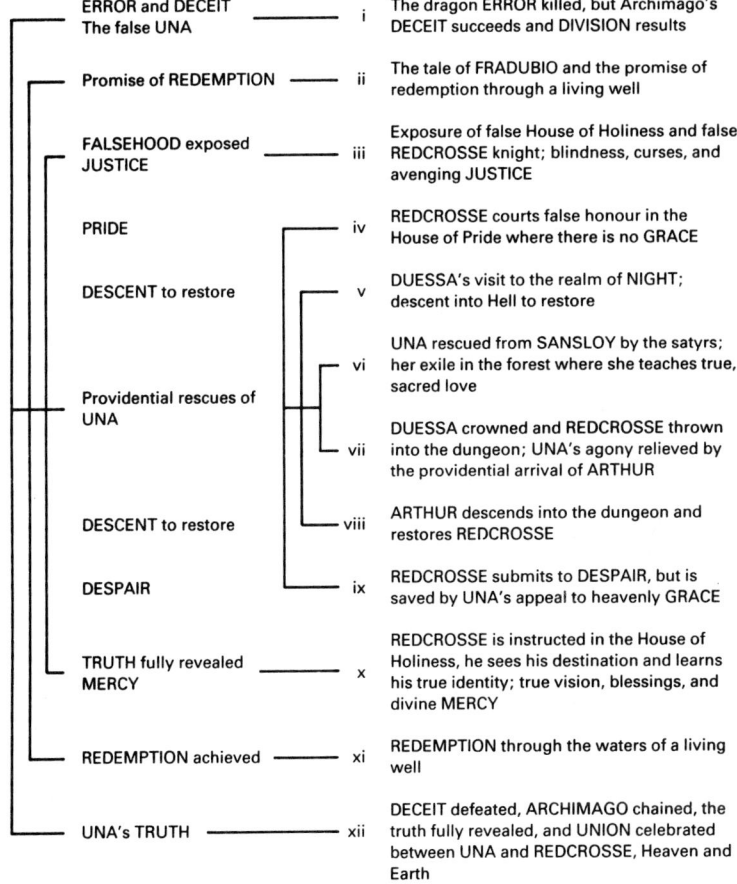

When Redcrosse is preserved from annihilation at the textual centre, this too is a providential rescue through the grace of God.

shackles of sin. But for the interpolated tale of Æsculapius and Hippolytus, the distinction between physical and spiritual restoration, between man's own science and the grace of God, would not have appeared so clearly. The difference between the physical and the spiritual level is also seen in Una's two rescues, one from the rude assault of Sansloy at the beginning of canto vi, and the other at the end of canto vii from her despair. The structure of events, then, coincides with important topomorphs; the story is shaped by the concepts embedded in various actions and descriptions. Thus the connection between pride and despair in cantos iv and ix is part of a pattern of parallels and contrasts, such as the exposure of deceit and falsehood in canto iii and the exposure of the truth about Redcrosse himself in canto x and his vision of ultimate truth from the Hill of Contemplation. The clearest expression of the antithesis between truth and falsehood is found in the perfectly balanced stanzas on the false and the true Una (i.48 and xii.8). The contrast-cum-parallel highlights the beauty of truth, and this is of course the function of the system of linkages: each element in the tightly woven pattern acquires greater beauty and sharper definition when seen as part of a unified pattern.

Emblem sequences like Quarles's *Emblemes* (1635) owe a great deal to Spenser's structural deployment of emblem-like situations. Indeed, in his early biblical paraphrases, Quarles himself shows how such emblem-like passages may inform and guide the direction of the narrative. Some 150 years after Spenser, Henry Fielding based the structure of *Tom Jones* on the Choice of Hercules and similar emblem-like events, as already suggested.

For the structural use of interpolated tales (another romance technique adopted by Fielding), analogues may be found in the Bible, where the parables of Christ function like tales encapsulating the message of the larger narrative. The connection between types and antitypes is another analogue: the progress from a physical to a spiritual level resembles the progress from types to antitypes, and the shift occurs once we have passed through the textual centre of the symmetrical structure. On all these points Spenser resembles Tasso, and so does his application of the Aristotelian triple formula of defect—mean—excess (as in canto i). His Christianisation of this formula appears from canto iv on the court of Lucifera, the extended centre and canto ix on the Cave of Despair. In canto iv Redcrosse fails to react to the spectacle of the deadly sins, in canto ix he is overwhelmed by his own sinfulness, but at the centre he receives the chastisement that is proffered grace. One may also say that in canto iv grace is absent from defect (having been ousted by pride), while excess (of despair) is the cause of its absence in canto ix. God's free gift of grace, his liberality, contrasts strongly with Lucifera's haughty pride, which forbids all acts of grace, and with the despair which believes itself beyond the reach of grace.

Major events, then, plus interpolated tales and emblem-like descriptions of places, characters, and situations, have been arranged within these 12 cantos so as to form perfectly balanced structures. It is clearly impossible to keep Spenser's *invention* separate from his *disposition* of his material; he could not locate the decisive battle with the dragon in canto xi without at the same time locating the tale of Fradubio in canto ii. The tale must have been invented primarily for the purpose of setting up a link with canto xi. Nor could he invent two houses of holiness, one false and the other true, without placing them at the same distance from the beginning and the end. The many details in the description of these houses are complementary; to the curses of the one correspond the blessings of the other, just as the blindness of Corceca finds a parallel-cum-antithesis in Redcrosse's temporary blindness after his vision of the heavenly Jerusalem. The total pattern impresses by its exactness and by the way in which it serves to underline essential thematic concerns.

3. Book I: The Graded Arrangement

It has long been recognized that Book I is divided into 8+4 cantos, and it is now possible to see that this division represents a tradition extending back at least as far as Augustine's *Confessions*. Spenser's structure has much in common with Augustine's; as in the *Confessions*, 8 cantos of *errores* are followed by 4 of instruction and return. The chief difference is that in Spenser the pivotal passage, separating the two movements, consists not in a whole book or canto, but in a self-contained episode (ix.1–19/20; see the Table of Stanza Totals above). There are of course also structural parallels with Tasso's epic, where Books I–XII display a pattern of defection caused by wrath and love, the last example being Tancred's retirement after he discovers that he has killed his beloved Clorinda. The subsequent pattern of return is the subject of Books XV–XX, and the return includes Rinaldo's instruction, his moral choice, his regeneration, and the final battle. The books in between (XIII and XIV) describe a period of enforced inactivity on the part of the Christian forces, but this unhappy *stasis* is broken by divine intervention so that the pattern of return may be initiated. Spenser follows both his predecessors in making his pivotal passage a point of rest; Arthur, Una, and Redcrosse knight take their much-needed rest, and Arthur tells his story, at the end of which they exchange gifts and part to pursue their different quests. Later on, Milton was to let a book of rest – the angelic narrative of book 7 (i.e. Books VII–VIII of the second edition) – divide the 10 books of the first edition into a sequence of 6—1—3 books. All four poets therefore adopt the same pattern.

Before the segment at ix.1–19/20 can be characterized as an extended centre, it must of course have a clear pivotal function, and so it does since its theme is union: union between the virtues and between noble minds (ix.1), between Arthur and the Faerie Queen (ix.13–14), and between Arthur and Redcrosse knight as they join hands and exchange gifts. Arthur "gave a boxe of Diamond sure" containing a few drops of liquor that "any wound could heale incontinent," and Redcrosse's gift is a book "wherein his Saveours testament / Was writ with golden letters," a work "of wondrous grace, and able soules to save" (ix.19). These gifts remind us of Redcrosse's position; he may have been rescued physically from Orgoglio's dungeon, but his spiritual restoration as yet lies in the future. When the two knights join their hands together, 'fast friendship for to bynd, / And love establish each to other trew" (ix.18.6–9), this act sets up a link with the betrothal scene in canto xii, where the old king joins Una and Redcrosse knight and "With his owne two hands the holy knots did knit" (xii.37 : 1). The topos of Redcrosse's quest, re-stated at ix.20 : 2–3, reaches back to the beginning, and yet another link with the beginning is the description of Arthur, which aligns him with Una when first presented; just as Una has been brought up in "every vertuous lore" and is of "Royall linage" (i.5), so Arthur has been trained "in vertuous lore" and is "sonne and heire unto a king" (ix.4–5). Similar verbal parallels link the false Una in canto i and the Faerie Queen: the queen offers "most goodly glee and lovely blandishment" (ix.14:1), just as the false Una proceeds with "gentle blandishment and lovely looke" (i.49 : 1). However, the parallel merely underlines the contrast between love debased and love elevated, and between mere appearance and the truth which is proved by the "pressed gras" (ix.15 : 2). Arthur's brief union with the Faerie Queen rather points forward to the vision of Una unveiled in the central stanzas of canto xii, when she appears "as bright as doth the morning starre appeare / Out of the East, with flaming lockes bedight" (xii.21 : 5–6).

The narrative substructure formed by cantos i–viii begins with the slaying of the dragon Error and concludes with the slaying of Orgoglio, both shrinking to nothing after death. The reunion between Redcrosse knight and Una is the fitting terminal climax, together with the exposure of Duessa for what she truly is. At the centre are the events in the House of Pride (see Diagram VI.23). The elevation of Lucifera in her coach is matched by Duessa's in the chariot of Night, the two being connected like the obverse and

Diagram VI.23 *The Faerie Queene* I, Symmetries in Cantos i–xviii

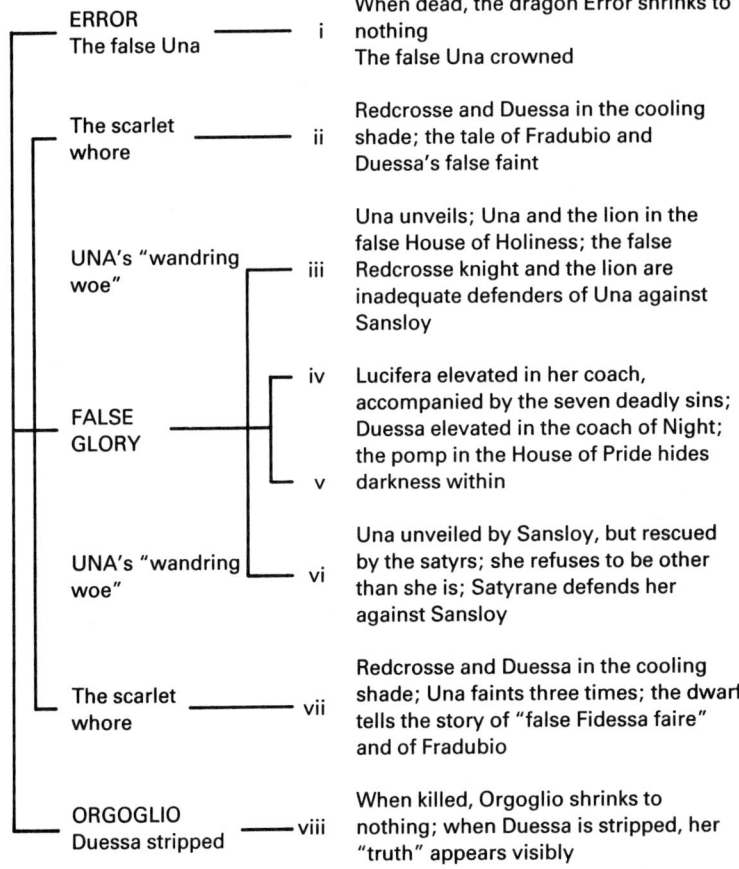

reverse of a coin, or the outside and the inside of an idol. Each is drawn by a team described as "unequall" or "unlich" (iv.18 : 1 and v.28 : 5), and the effect of the deadly sins which accompany Lucifera's golden chair may be observed in Night's "mournefull charet, fild with rusty blood" (v.32 : 2). This antithesis is directly stated in Duessa's speech to Night, "of darknesse Queene" (v.24 : 1):

> I that seem not I, *Duessa* am,
> (Quoth she) how ever now in garments gilt,
> And gorgeous gold arayd I to thee came;
> *Duessa* I, the daughter of Deccipt and Shame.
>
> (v.26 : 6–9).

The falseness of her seeming takes us back to her appearance at i.48, where she seems "of beautie soveraigne Queene," crowned with a garland of ivy by "freshest *Flora*." Flora figures also in the description of Lucifera, who is equally a queen of beauty (iv.8 and 17), which serves to strengthen the connection between the elevation of Lucifera and that of Duessa in the coach of Night. The reality behind Duessa's false appearance is starkly revealed in the last few stanzas of canto viii when she is stripped of her scarlet robe, and her "misshaped parts" and "secret filth" clearly seen:

> Such then (said *Una*) as she seemeth here,
> Such is the face of falshood, such the sight
> Of fowle *Duessa*, when her borrowed light
> Is laid away, and counterfesaunce knowne.
>
> (viii.49 : 3–6)

On this occasion, then, Duessa appears "such as she was" (viii.46 : 6), and when her skin is said to be "as rough, as maple rind" (viii.47 : 8), this detail returns us to the catalogue of trees at the very beginning of the action, when the maple tree is said to be "seldom inward sound" (i.9 : 9).

A verbal link between the beginning and the middle is found when Duessa, in her dialogue with Sansjoy at the end of canto iv, ironically repeats the four rhyme words used in the description of Redcrosse knight in the opening stanza (*field*, *yield*, *shield*, *wield*). As the subsequent combat proves, she has every reason to fear the "oddes or armes in field" (iv.50 : 2).

Redcrosse's meeting with Duessa and their courtship in the cooling shade link the end of canto ii and the beginning of canto vii. Duessa's appearance – she is "clad in scarlot red, / Purfled with gold and pearle of rich assay" (ii.13) – anticipates her elevation on the seven-headed beast when she is given "gold and purple pall to weare, / And triple crowne" (vii.16). The same intensification is felt in the description of the courtship between the two, and in the fainting which overtakes Duessa (ii.45) and Una (vii.20–21, 24, and 52). Duessa's faint is feigned, that of Una an agony that flesh cannot sustain. These repetitions-with-intensification make us feel that Redcrosse moves from bad to worse, and that Duessa's falsehood and her treachery reach a climax when she is plainly seen as the scarlet whore, crowned while seated on the seven-headed beast, which tramples on all that is sacred. The dwarf's discourse to Una refers us back to canto ii since he tells all about the "wanton loves of false *Fidessa* faire," and about the "wretched payre transform'd to treen mould" (vii.26). Despite the ominous events of cantos ii and vii, each concludes with a promise of restoration: Fradubio will be restored when "bathed in a living well" (ii.43), just as Una's prolonged agony concludes when she tells her story to Arthur and he gives his firm promise to redeem Redcrosse knight (vii.52).

Cantos iii and vi describe Una's "wandring woe": she is true light surrounded by darkness – the darkness of falsehood and deceit in the false House of Holiness, and the darkness of ignorance among the satyrs in the forest. (This repeats and thus intensifies the idea of the darkness of Error in canto i and the ignorance of Ignaro in canto viii). Appearances are tested and found to be false when first Archimago and then Kirkrapine are unveiled in canto iii, but Una refuses to be what she is not when the satyrs try to worship her as goddess (vi.19 and 31); instead she teaches true doctrine. In both cantos Archimago figures in disguise, and Sansloy too is a major character in both: he fights the false Redcrosse knight in canto iii, while in canto vi it is Satyrane (the exponent of law) who is his opponent, and Sansloy's lawlessness is shown above all in his attitude to Una. The topos of Una unveiled is an even more potent link between these cantos: in canto iii Una's unveiled beauty causes the lion to abate his rage and lick her feet in humble submission, and the same humble submission is shown by the satyrs in canto vi. Verbal repetitions underline the parallel: The lion "kist her wearie feete, / And lickt her lilly hands with fawning tong," and he is "With pittie calmd" when he hears her sad complaint (iii.6 : 1–2 and 8 : 5); in precisely the same way, the satyrs "feele her secret smart" and, "wonne with pitty and unwonted ruth" they "Do kisse her feete, and fawne on her with count'nance faine" (vi.11–12). The similar actions suggest a similar status, and the fact that the unveiled Una commands the obedience of satyrs and savage lion alike proves how much greater grace is than brutal strength, including the strength of a Satyrane.

The linkage between cantos i and viii (the killing of a great monster which then shrinks to nothing) includes the idea of the perversion of what is sacred. The death of the dragon Error is a perversion of the true sacrifice of Christ when we see how her offspring "Flocked all about her bleeding wound, / And sucked up their dying mothers blood, / Making her death their life, and eke her hurt their good" (i.25 : 7–9). In Orgoglio's castle everything is again a perversion of true rites. The richness of the place (its "royall arras and resplendent gold"; viii.35:2) takes us back to the court of Lucifera (canto iv), while Lucifera's dungeon and the rusty blood in the chariot of Night (canto v) find their parallel in the blood from innocent victims (viii.35). Yet another link is found in Una's role as onlooker. On the occasion of each fight Una has watched "from farre" and comes running to greet the victor (i.27 and viii.25).

The symmetrical structure, then, of cantos i–viii is even more precise than in Book I as a whole; the events of these cantos form a clear pattern of recessed symmetry, and the pattern clarifies the thematic thrust of these events.

Cantos ix–xii are Spenser's version of Tasso's tetrad of return. Rest is a key concept: Redcrosse knight is tempted by Despair to seek death as a harbour of rest after weary storms, but by canto xii rest is no longer a temptation. When the king of Eden suggests that they "devize of ease and everlasting rest," Redcrosse soberly replies that "Of ease or rest I may not yet devize" (xii.17–18); in canto ix, though, the temptation is very real and so are the accusations levelled by Despair against Redcrosse knight. In canto xii it is Fidessa/Duessa who acts as the accuser, but her falsehood cannot prevail against Una's truth, just as Una's reminder of the fact that God's grace is stronger than his justice ("Where justice growes, there grows eke greater grace"; ix.53:6) serves to bring Redcrosse knight to his senses in canto ix. Cantos ix–xii, then, are framed by invitations to court rest and by accusations levelled against Redcrosse knight and countered by Una. In between are cantos x–xi on the two phases of regeneration: instruction, purgation, and illumination are followed by the decisive battle, as in Tasso's *Gerusalemme Liberata*. Spenser proves his Protestant bias when he lets the re-birth be fused with the battle, while Rinaldo is made to experience re-birth in prayer on Mount Olivet before he engages in the final battle. However, the shedding of heavenly dew on Rinaldo finds a parallel in Redcrosse's immersion in "A trickling streame of Balme" from the Tree of Life (xi.48).

Although Tasso's structures are often as complex as Spenser's, Spenser handles them with greater skill. The simultaneous presence, in Book I, of symmetrical and graded arrangements is more effective in Spenser, where the two extended centres (vii.1–25 and ix.1–20) are played off against each other, so that the negative import of the one is modified by the positive import of the other, especially when we realize that Orgoglio functions as the scourge of God. The attractiveness of the ratio 2 : 1 is shown by the fact that it is found in individual cantos as well. Spenser, like Tasso, incorporates symbolically significant biblical numbers in many of his structures, but his canto structures are more precise, more clearly defined, and this is partly due to his subtle use of verbal repetitions. The placing, within the body of the text, of similar or identical words and phrases and descriptive details occurs so often that it must be described as a basic technique. The emblematic diamond which connects Una and Arthur (vi.4 : 5 and vii.33 : 5) is one example, the stanzas on the false and true Una another (i.48 and xii.8), and a third the repetition of the rhyme words *shielde, fielde, wield*, and *yield* (i.1 and iv.50). In a spatial or panoramic reading, the distance between such points is reduced or disappears. The technique is most fully exploited within the limits of a single canto, where the canto as a whole, or individual segments, may possess intricate patterns of verbal repetition in which rhyme words play a significant role. Canto I.iii is a good example. No one can possibly maintain that the careful placing of topoi and of words and phrases within these twelve cantos occurs by chance or as the result of subconscious promptings; we must perforce conclude that the *disposition* is an aspect of the *invention*; indeed, that the invented pattern often prompted the episodes that enable the reader to perceive it. Interpolated tales and even epic similes often have a structural function, noteworthy examples being the tale of Fradubio and the simile of the "divelish yron Engin" at vii.13. The simile alerts the reader to spot the juxtaposition of "heavenly grace" (vii.12 : 3) with God's avenging justice; in God, the two are one. It helps, of course, to remember Tancred's similar plight, but *Hebrews* 12 provides what is needed to understand the situation whose central position within the extended centre indicates its importance. The tale of Fradubio illustrates weakness and pain; it is his weakness that makes him fall a prey to Duessa, as a consequence of which he is made to suffer within his "wooden wals" (ii.42 : 8); this weakness is shared by Redcrosse when he doffs his armour, and it is dramatized in the tale of the well of feebleness (vii.5), while Fradubio's painful imprisonment is re-lived by Redcrosse knight during the battle with the dragon (xi.26). Each episode gains added weight from being seen as part of a pattern, and the weight is the weightiness of the moral sentence or lesson. This moral lesson is the flesh which encloses and partly conceals the structural skeleton.

Allegorical narrative, therefore, depends heavily on structural skeletons for its articulation.

These findings are confirmed on studying the structures of Book II, whose very subject calls for a "tempering" of the text in the form of balanced patterns, whether symmetrical or in the ratio 2 : 1.

4. Book II: The Ethical Crux

Let me begin by considering the import of the unrhymed line in the tale of the virgin well, a departure from the established norm which should be recognized as a willed phenomenon. By departing from an established norm a special effect is gained, as when Spenser in the *November* eclogue locates the sun "in *Fishes* haske," which is the zodiacal sign for *Februarie*, and the error is committed to establish linkage between these two eclogues. Another kind of departure occurs when Spenser reduces his 9-line stanza to 8 lines, or when he perversely avoids the word which would have afforded a perfect rhyme in favour of a word which leaves the line unrhymed, as in II.ii.7 : 7. The context will usually provide the explanation. We find an 8-line stanza at I.x.20 where the subject is the power of faith to command, for example the sun to arrest its course; the stanza illustrates the power by arresting its own course. Another 8-line stanza (III.vi.45) presents a list of famous lovers whose lives have been cut short, and the stanza, therefore, is itself cut short. The editor of the 1609 edition emended the stanza by adding a half-line, perhaps to make the cutting off more easily perceived. However, since the stanza catalogues lovers "To whom sweet Poets verse hath given endlesse date" (45 : 8), it is numerically appropriate to use an 8-line stanza, since 8 is the number of Eternity. This symbolism explains why Giles Fletcher created an 8-line stanza for *Christs Victorie, and Triumph* (1610) – a choice purely biblical in its number symbolism and so in contrast to Tasso's attribution, to his favoured 8-line stanza, of the musical consonances (see above, pp. 204 f.). As I have shown elsewhere, Giles Fletcher's poem concludes with a unique 7-line stanza on the limitations imposed by time, so that his shrinking of the stanza from 8 to 7 lines enacts these limitations, 7 being the number of Time as 8 is of Eternity.[13] Milton followed suit in his *Nativity Ode*, where the concern with the world of time in the introduction ("This is the Month, and this the happy morn") is reflected in the 4 7-line stanzas (4 and 7 for the seasons and the weeks). In marked contrast, the hymn honouring the entry of Eternity into the world of Time consists of 27 8-line stanzas.[14] The decorum which governs the use of an unrhymed line is equally simple, as we may see from stanza II.ii.7 on Diana's nymph, who flees from the grasp of the inflamed Dan Faunus: one day,

> As she the woods with bow and shafts did raunge,
> The hartlesse Hind and Robucke to dismay,
> *Dan Faunus* chaunst to meet her by the way,
> And kindling fire at her faire burning eye,
> Inflamed was to follow beauties chace,
> And chaced her, that fast from him did fly;
> As Hind from her, so she fled from her enimy.

As editors have remarked, the rhyme would be perfect if *pray* (i.e. prey) were to replace *chase*, but Spenser's choice is deliberate; the perverse character of the pursuit, and its failure to obtain the desired coupling, stand reflected in the absence of rhyme. An unrhymed line may also express uniqueness. Thus the unrhymed line at II.ii.42 : 6 refers to the annual feast celebrated in honour of the Order of Maidenhead; at II.iii.28 : 7 it occurs in the description of Belphœbe, and a uniquely perverse action – revenge on a seemingly dead body – is the subject of II.viii.29 : 7. Similar examples are found in the poetry of George Chapman, Ben Jonson, and John Dryden. Chapman's *A Hymne to Our Saviour on the Crosse* has two examples,[15] Ben Jonson's epigram to Margaret Radcliffe concludes with an unrhymed line ("Earth, thou hast not such another"; *Epigrams* 40), and Dryden's *Threnodia Augustalis* affords an example where failure to achieve linking is the point.[16] This playful kind of decorum, therefore, is not restricted to the lyric poetry of George Herbert and Henry Vaughan. The technique reflects an attitude to words and lines as objects located in the poem's space; *res* and *verba* obey the same laws. The repetition of identical rhyme words is a related phenomenon.

When we consider the context, Spenser's unrhymed line on the faun who pursues "beauties chace" carries a lot of weight. The tale of Diana's nymph dramatizes a major theme in Book II: some opposites are irreconcilable and ill mixture (*acrasia*) cannot be tolerated. Diana's nymph escapes "ill mixture" by being metamorphosed into a stone from which her tears issue to create a fountain.

The Legend of Temperance, which begins with the annihilation, through the ill mixture in his blood, of Mordant, concludes with the elimination of Acrasia. The capture of Acrasia is Spenser's version of the elimination of evil; as in the description of creation in *Paradise Lost*, that which is adverse to life must be purged off (7.237–39). We ignore this all-important issue if we accuse Guyon of a lack of temperance as he proceeds to destroy a Bower which today has come to seem so attractive to so many. James Thomson took Spenser's point exactly when he wrote *The Castle of Indolence* (1748), where the Knight of Art and Industry sets out to destroy the sinful bower of the "demon Indolence" (II.34).[17] The accompanying bard takes a lenient view of the wizard's environment: "Ah! nought is pure! It cannot be denied / That virtue still some tincture has of vice, / And vice of virtue" (II.38 : 5–7). But, although the knight admits that all flesh is frail, he will not tolerate brutish vice: 'Justice were cruel, weakly to relent; / From Mercy's self she got her sacred glaive" (II.39 : 5–6). Queen Elizabeth's subjects knew only too well that the royal "mercy" could manifest itself in the most cruel measures, since not to root out evil is to be cruel to the good.[18] As the knight of temperance, therefore, Guyon's task is a double one. In the Castle of Medina he opposes and helps to compel the extremes to move in the direction of the mean, but, when confronted by an irreconcilable opposite, his response is rejection (as in the case of Phædria and Mammon) or destruction. Traditional representations of temperance include this martial aspect.[19]

Let me substantiate this argument by submitting a detailed analysis of cantos i and ii.

Canto i contains two separate episodes: the encounter between Guyon and Redcrosse knight, and Guyon's encounter with Amavia (see Diagram VI.24). Both illustrate the theme which is so important in Book I: appearance and reality may agree, or may be in conflict. A character may seem pure and yet hide filth within, or the other way around, as in the case of Ruddymane, whose innocent hands are covered in guilty blood. Some cases remain doubtful (Amavia). Vengeance is a main theme: Guyon mistakenly addresses Redcrosse knight to redress the wrong done to the fair virgin he has supposedly ravished, Acrasia revenges herself on Mordant, and Guyon subsequently swears to exact "dew vengeance" for the deaths of Mordant and Amavia (i.67 : 7).

Each episode displays perfect balance: the first consists of 8—15—8 stanzas, the second of 5—8—2—8—5 stanzas. In between are

Diagram VI.24 *The Faerie Queene* II, the Structure of Events in Canto i

Part 1: Guyon and Redcrosse knight

1–8	8	Archimago plans revenge on Redcrosse knight, and meets Guyon
9–23	15	Duessa poses as a "virgin Cleene" ravished by Redcrosse knight, and Guyon swears revenge
24–31	8	Guyon and Redcrosse prepare to engage, but Guyon halts when he sees the cross on his opponent's shield; the truth is acknowledged, and Archimago flees
32–33	2	The Palmer praises Redcrosse knight's achievement, but he attributes all to God

Part 2: Guyon and Amavia

34–38	5	Guyon travels on, guided by his Palmer; he is stopped by piercing shrieks and a voice that denounces "carelesse heaven" and calls for "sweetest death"
39–45	8	Guyon sees the pitiful spectacle of Mordant dead, Amavia wounded, and the babe covered in blood; he tries to temper her grief
46–47	2	Dialogue between Guyon and Amavia
49–56	8	Amavia's tale and her death
57–61	5	Guyon and the Palmer reflect on death caused by raging passion; they bury the dead, and Guyon swears to exact "dew vengeance"

Stanzas 32–33 divide the canto into two parts, one concerned with the attempt to discredit Redcrosse knight, and the other with the deaths of Mordant and Amavia. Each part is balanced; the first consists of 8—15—8 stanzas, the second of 5—8—2—8—5 stanzas.

2 transitional stanzas (32–33) where Redcrosse attributes all to God. I see no significance in the numbers; the balanced pattern is what matters. What is truly remarkable, though, is that each segment is beautifully patterned, beginning with stanzas i.1–8 on Archimago's scheme to revenge himself on Redcrosse knight. Archimago's whole purpose in life is now said to be to corrupt the

Diagram VI.25 *The Faerie Queene* II, Canto i.1–8

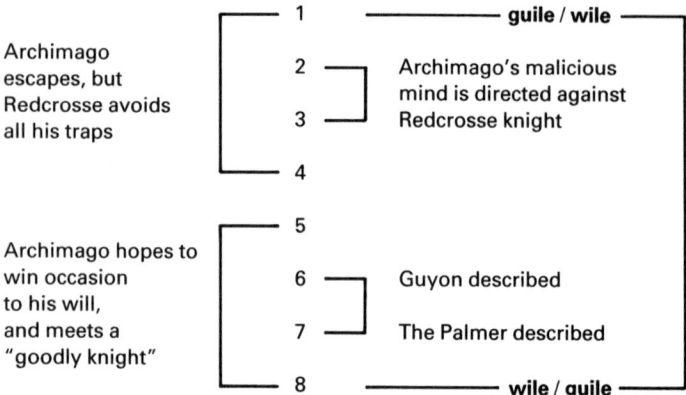

Stanzas on Redcrosse knight (i.1 and 4) enclose those on Archimago (i.2–3), thus as it were nullifying Archimago's stratagems, but the balance is inverted in stanzas 5–8, where the stanzas on Archimago enclose those on Guyon and the Palmer. The segment as a whole is circumscribed by the rhyme words *guile* / *wile* repeated in inverse order.

inner man through sloth and "sensuall delights" induced in deceitful ways (i.23). In other words, Archimago points good knights in the direction of Acrasia's bower, and for this purpose he makes use of Duessa in the first part of the first episode. The stanzas are divided into two groups of 4 (see Diagram VI.25); Archimago is the centre of the first, Guyon and the Palmer of the second, and the whole is circumscribed by the rhyme words *guile* and *wile* repeated in inverse order. The 15-stanza segment on the attempted deceit (Diagram VI.26) has a truly splendid structure created by 5 groups of 3 stanzas. Deceit is featured at the beginning, middle, and end; the triple centre-piece focusses on Duessa's lament for her lost virginity, while the 3 stanzas which precede and follow describe Guyon's attempt to comfort the damsel who has been so cruelly abused by Redcrosse knight. In the first triad (i.9–11) Duessa poses as a "virgin cleene" ravished by "filthy hands," but the truth is revealed by the narrator in the last triad (i.21–23): her appearance is a mere cloak for her "loathly filthinesse." The second triad and the fourth are dominated by Guyon's reaction, which is to swear revenge and to offer words of comfort. The many repetitions engender a feeling of intensity, and the repetition of rhyme words like *torment* and

Diagram VI.26 *The Faerie Queene* II, Canto i.9–23

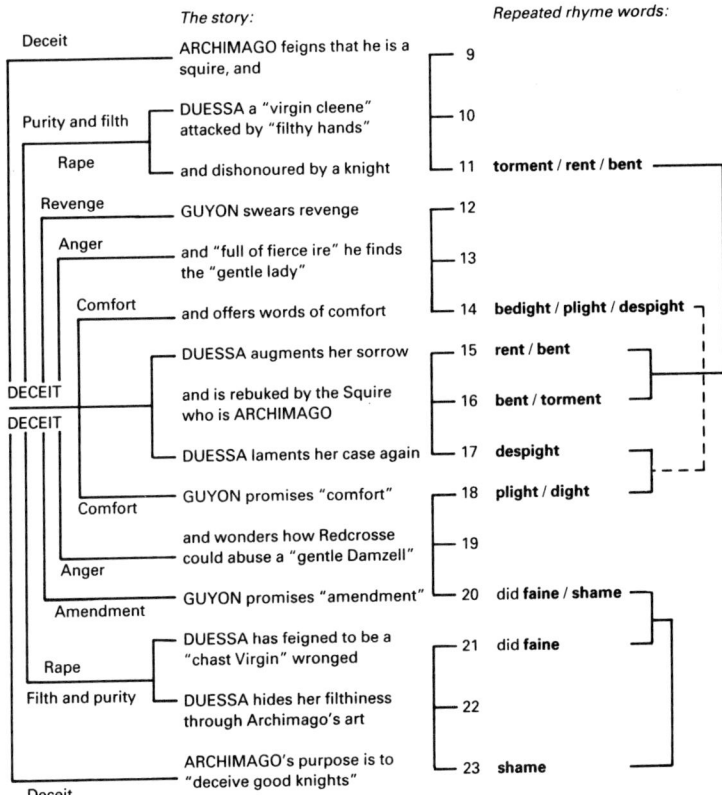

Note the symmetrical arrangement of the characters as indicated by their initials:
A D D / G G G / D A D / G G G / D D A.

despight adds its quota. The symmetrical distribution of the characters (see Diagram VI.26) may be a matter of chance, but Archimago certainly circumscribes the episode and is at its centre as the moving power. However, the segment which follows (see Diagram VI.27) exposes the deceit to the intended victims. The structure pinpoints the antithesis between falsehood and truth. The first three stanzas (i.24–26) present a false guide, a false accusation, and a false opposition between the two knights; at the centre, falsehood suddenly yields to truth when Guyon honours the reality of the cross displayed on his opponent's shield, and when Redcrosse knight

Diagram VI.27   *The Faerie Queene* II, Canto i.24–31

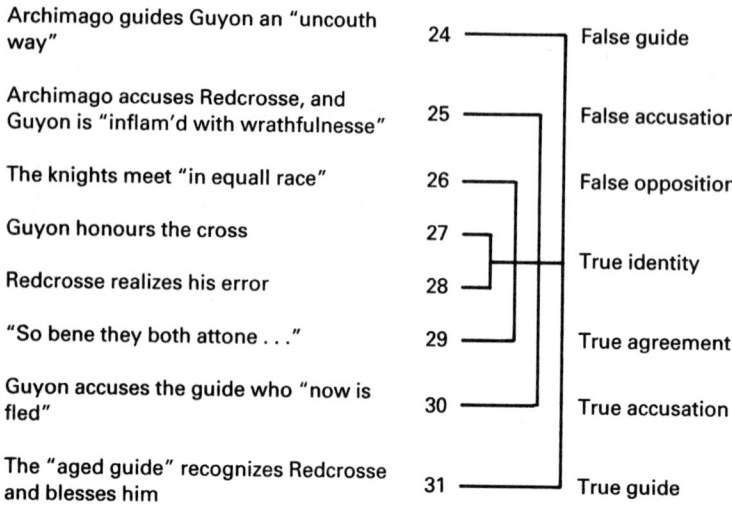

realizes his error on hearing Guyon's speech. In the last three stanzas the same topoi recur, but in inverse order and in positive form: true agreement ousts false opposition, true accusations are made, and a true guide replaces the one who proved so false.

As A. C. Hamilton has remarked, the fact that Guyon refers to "the sacred badge of my Redeemer's death" (27 : 6) places temperance in a Christian context.[20] This is scarcely surprising since it is one of the gifts of the Holy Ghost (*Gal.* 5 : 22–23), and Augustine considers the cardinal virtues in general, and temperance in particular, to be a means of achieving holiness. The virtues temper the movements of the soul through *ordered linking* (*ordinis vinculum*; *De musica* VI.xiv.47), which means that the units which precede the centre should be linked to it in a harmonious order, and so should the units which follow. The objects or units must be joined harmoniously (*concorditer*). The act of tempering, then, may be reflected in the ordered rhythm which governs a soul, redemption history, or a work of human art, and this is surely why Spenser "tempers" his narrative segments so ingeniously, as we also see in the Amavia episode (Diagram VI.28). The experience of the deaths of Mordant and Amavia determines Guyon's actions from that moment: his quest for temperance will entail a ruthless extermination of what Acrasia represents. As in Book I, the choice is between life and death; Acrasia (= ill mixture) cannot be part of any system of

Diagram VI.28 *The Faerie Queene* II, Canto i.34–61

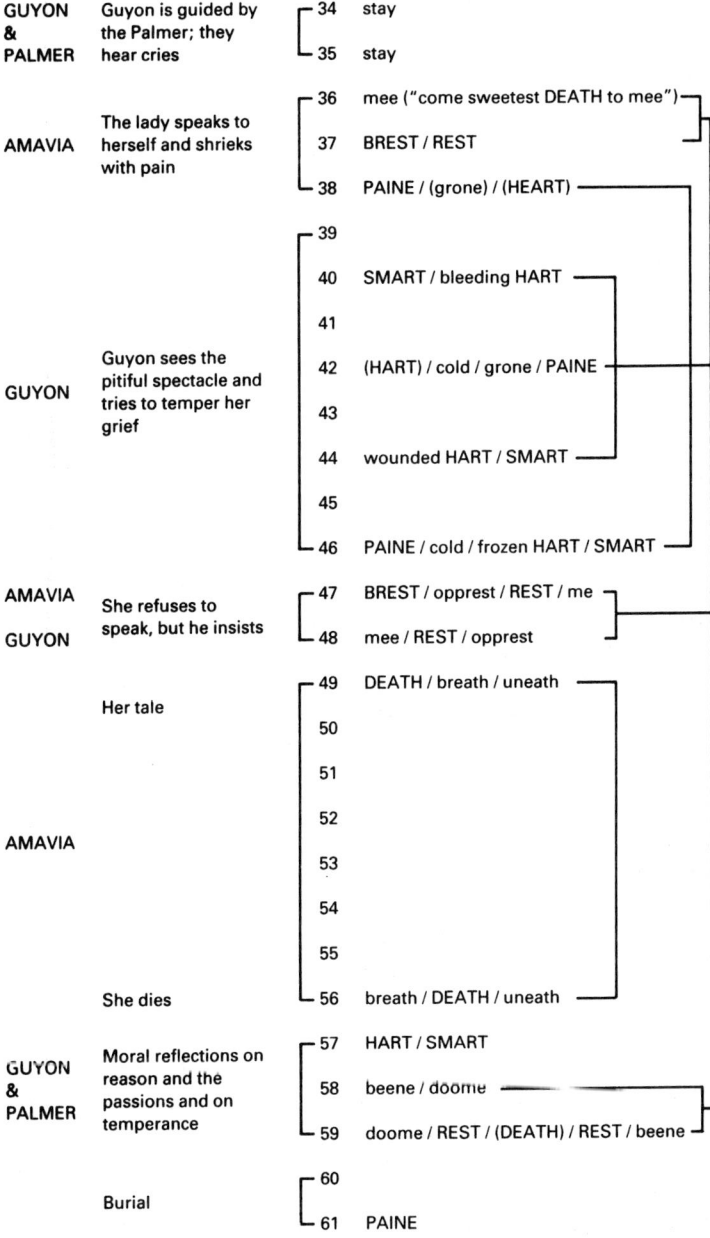

Words in parentheses occur within the line. Particularly important words are in capitals.

harmonious linkage. Whatever "harmony" she may seem to present is as deceitful as the plot woven by Archimago and Duessa to entrap Redcrosse knight and Guyon. The exposure of this plot therefore points forward to the exposure, in the last canto, of Acrasia's deceitful bower, just as the sad fate of Mordant and Amavia proves the mortal effect of Acrasia's cup. As has often been observed, Verdant (II.xii.76–80) is another Mordant.

The pattern of actions in the Amavia episode is perfectly balanced. When the episode begins, Amavia speaks to herself in three stanzas (36–38), and it concludes with a three-stanza dialogue between Guyon and the Palmer on reason and the passions. In between are eight stanzas on the pitiful spectacle seen by Guyon and his reaction to it; this is followed by a dialogue (in two stanzas) between Guyon and Amavia, and the next eight stanzas contain Amavia's narrative, broken off by her death. Reiterated words (mostly in rhyme position) circumscribe the passage: *death*, *brest*, *rest* connect the beginning, middle, and end (see Diagram VI.28), and the passages in between feature the rhyme words *paint*, *smart*, *hart* and *death*, *breath*, *uneath*. *Hart*, *smart*, and *paine* also connect stanzas 38–46 and 57–61. Since death intervenes, Guyon's efforts are fruitless; all he can do is bury the dead and re-dedicate himself to the quest for which he was fetched by the Palmer from the court of the Faerie Queen.

The action of canto i continues in canto ii with the story of Ruddymane and the virgin well, a story which highlights the contrast between purity and filth; the two are incompatible, which causes the death of Mordant (whose blood has become filthy by the potion from Acrasia's cup) when he drinks from the well (i.55). Since the blood which covers Ruddymane's hands is contaminated by this filth, the water from the well refuses to dissolve it and the stains remain. The interpolated tale elaborates on this theme as the structure makes abundantly clear. The episode fills nine stanzas (see Diagram VI.29): it begins when Guyon kneels to wash the babe's "guiltie hands from bloudie gore' (ii.3) and it concludes when he lifts the babe up again, as bloody as before (ii.11). The explanation that the "foule offence" may not be "purged with water nor with bath" (ii.4 : 2) is repeated at ii.10 ("From thence it comes, that this babes bloudy hand / May not be clensd with water of this well"); in stanzas 5 and 9 virtue is said to inhere in fountains (every fountain contains "secret vertues," and the virtues of Diana's nymph "in her water byde"), while in the triple centre the lust of Dan Faunus is flanked by the benign fertility of Dame Nature and

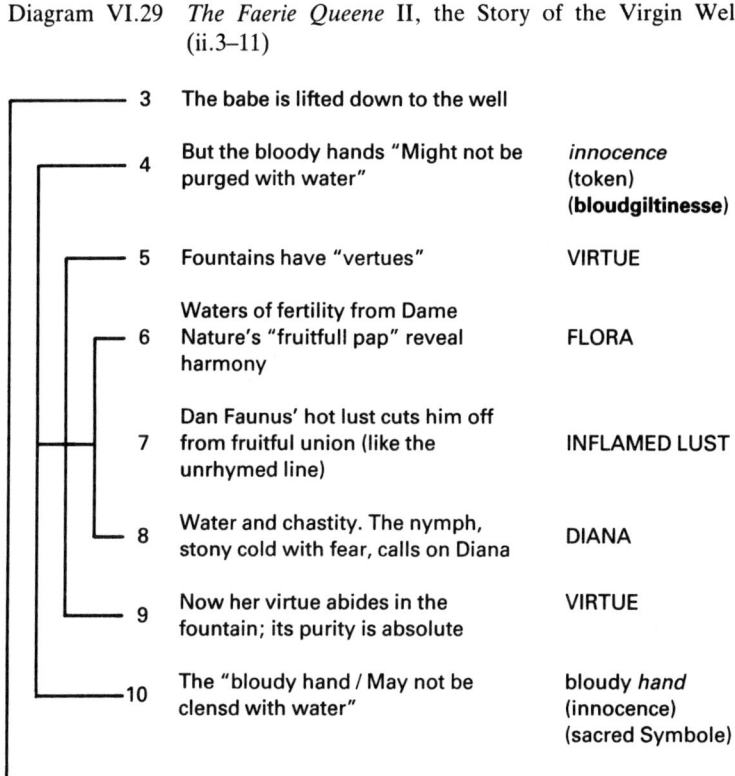

Diagram VI.29 *The Faerie Queene* II, the Story of the Virgin Well (ii.3–11)

by his malignant pursuit. The faun's excessive heat makes impossible the fertility so lovingly described in stanza 6. Dame Nature mediates between hot and cold, moist and dry, but not so Dan Faunus whose excessive lust (his "filth") causes the nymph to feel the coldness of extreme fear. The filthy lust that cuts the faun off from a natural, fruitful union is given structural expression when line ii.7 : 7 is cut off from the perfect harmony of the rhyme scheme. The absence of linkage through rhyme reveals the absence of the tempering on which all life depends; distempered lust leads to death (Mordant) or the metamorphosis which is a kind of annihilation.

The related topoi of filthy water and poisoned cups help to create a pattern of perfect symmetry in Book II as a whole. Thus at the centre in cantos vi and vii we find the muddy water of the Idle Lake, which washes the blood and filth from Pyrochles (vi.42), just as the feculent hands of Pilate (immersed in the river Cocytus) become filthier still the more he tries to wash them (vii.61). In canto xi, the "standing lake" whose water must needs be stagnant readily accepts the body of the strangled Maleger: filth agrees with filth. This agreement points a strong contrast to the absolute refusal of the water of the virgin well to receive the guilty blood on Ruddymane's hands. But for the interpolation of the tale of the virgin well, the issue of agreement and disagreement, or compatibility and incompatibility, would have been much less apparent. This issue strengthens the link between temperance and harmony, and so do the events which take place in the Castle of Medina.

The structure of canto ii is like a set of Chinese boxes where each level displays the ratio 2 : 1 as an expression of the concord that is its subject (see Diagram VI.30). Medina's praise of "lovely concord, and most sacred peace" in stanza 31 divides the canto into a sequence of 30—1—15 stanzas, and when we deduct the framing stanzas ii.1–2 and 46 (note the ratio), the division is into 28—1—14. A more subtle effect is discovered on perceiving that stanzas 3–16 relate to stanzas 39–45, and stanzas 17–30 to stanzas 32–38 (see the compressed diagram) in a twice-repeated pattern of 14 to 7. The theme ensures the linkage. In the first group of 14 stanzas we find the themes of irreconcilable and reconcilable opposites in the tale of the virgin well and the description of the three sisters in the Castle of Medina, while the subject of the last group of 7 stanzas is the Faerie Queen and the fellowship of the Order of Maydenhead (absolute purity), and Guyon's commitment to destroy Acrasia and all her works as irreconcilably opposed to the purity represented by the queen and the Order. The second group of 14 stanzas describes how Guyon keeps his two opponents at bay, while the related group of 7 stanzas shows Medina as she reconciles the opponents and imposes peace. This emphasis on the distinction between reconcilable and irreconcilable opposites moves the idea of the golden mean in the direction of the concord which may, or may not, be established. The effort involved in the act of tempering is great, and the successful outcome of these efforts is shown when the lavish feast of Medina's sisters (16 : 5) is replaced by the feast which is "fairly attempered" so as to please with "meete satietie" (39 : 1–2). Within the overall symmetry of Book II, the feast at the end of canto ii connects with Alma's temperate feast at xi.2, when she prepares a "bounteous banket" for her guests, a banquet "attempred goodly well for health and for delight." Perhaps Milton was to remember this when in

Diagram VI.30 *The Faerie Queene* II, the Structure of Events in Canto ii

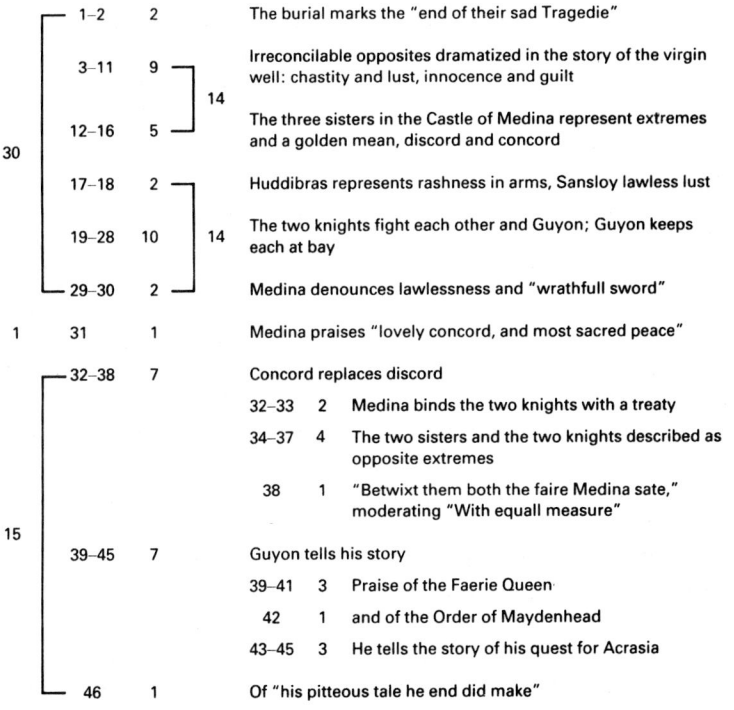

Compressed diagram:

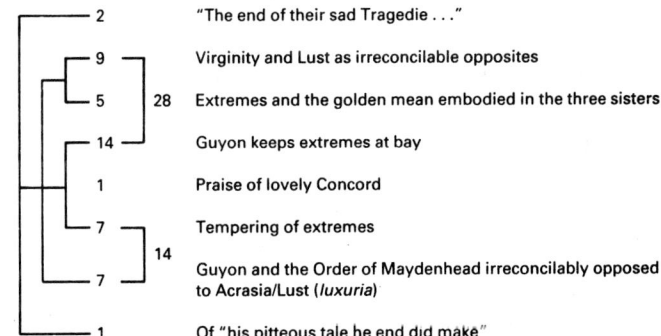

Note the many occurrences of the ratio 2:1 in the overall structure, between segments, within segments, and between the framing stanzas.

Paradise Lost he contrasted the full measure of repasts in the Garden and in Heaven with the greedy "engorging" without restraint as Eve feasts on the fruit from the forbidden tree.

At this point it is time to change the focus; instead of pursuing textual structures systematically, as in Book I, the critical argument will be placed in the foreground so that relevant textual structures will be adduced by way of support. This is of course the way in which a topomorphical method should be applied, but such an application is possible only with an adequate understanding of the basic textual structures normally employed by Spenser in the course of composition. Now that these structures have been mapped, it is possible to address the problem of Spenser's presentation of the Legend of Temperance, on which critical opinions are so sharply divided. Some see Guyon as a self-satisfied prig, unkind to poor Tantalus and pagan in his reliance on his own virtue, while others present him as an almost Christ-like figure. The contexts I shall adduce to illuminate Spenser's argument are (in addition to Aristotle) the sources already presented in Chapter 1. The same syncretistic tradition which helps to account for the structural approach to composition also serves to explain Spenser's view of temperance and the way he presents it. To Augustine should be added Pietro Bongo and Pierre de la Primaudaye, whose best-selling encyclopedia is a better guide to popular thought than Aquinas and the scholastics, or the Elizabethan homilies.

Like Book I, Book II divides into 8+4 cantos whose graded arrangement coexists with an all-encompassing symmetrical structure where cantos vi and vii form the centre. Unlike Book I, Book II has no extended centre of a kind which depends on counting stanzas to ascertain the difference in length between the first half and the second. In Book II Spenser lavished such care on individual cantos that he may have sacrificed this particular structural refinement, or perhaps he simply did not wish to repeat it. The analysis, therefore, must be conducted in terms of cantos. The placing of linked events is remarkably precise: thus, within the overall symmetry, the description of the prostrate Cymochles at the end of canto v balances the description of the prostrate Guyon at the beginning of canto viii, just as, within the structure formed by cantos i–viii, Braggadocchio's attempted rape of Belphœbe at the end of canto iii balances Cymochles' delighted acceptance of Phædria's seduction at the beginning of canto vi. The incompatible couple balance the couple who are only too compatible in their dedication to lust.

As far as Spenser's concept of temperance is concerned, I find it difficult to accept the view, expressed by Ronald Arthur Horton, that "in Book II Sans Loy will appear as the extreme of the concupiscible passions that needs to be balanced by the irascible for the preservation of the virtuous mean."[21] Surely it is each of these that must be tempered. What Spenser's narrative dramatizes is precisely the tempering of wrath and desire; each must find its mean. Temperance and intemperance as explained by Aristotle have this in common, that each is consciously chosen and consistently obeyed; an incontinent person is capable of feeling shame and regret and so of becoming temperate, but not so the intemperate person. Phedon regrets his uncontrolled fury, but Grill abides by his choice and regrets, instead, his metamorphis back into human shape. When the Palmer rebukes Phædria for being "loose and light" (xii.16 : 6), she "turned her bote about, and from them rowed quite" (16 : 9). Since her boat does not need rowing but moves of its own accord, in keeping with her will, the Palmer may have defeated her power, as A. C. Hamilton suggests in his gloss, but the action of rowing may indicate her complete commitment to intemperance in pleasure: she will brook no rebuke or counsel. Horton argues more convincingly when he writes that "unrestraint of the concupiscible and irascible passions prevents them from their natural order and function," and that these perverted extremes are "vicious opposites that must be shunned by proper control. With moderation the opposites are no longer vicious, being no longer perverse, but essential to life and health."[22] But *shunning* is not always enough; expulsion or destruction may be necessary to preserve life, and this is why temperance in iconographical representations can be seen to carry a knife. Wilful intemperance must be cut off.[23] The perverted Garden of Eden in the realm of Proserpine at the end of canto vii is the inner reality of the delightful bower to which Phædria takes Cymochles at the beginning of canto vi, and both are present in the description of Acrasia's bower in canto xii. This recalls Book I where the grisly carriage of Night is the inner reality of Lucifera's golded chariot. As we shall see, the related topoi of fountains, rivers, and waves in the same way draw our attention to the contrast between outward seeming and inner being. He who seeks temperance, therefore, must above all learn to discriminate between false and true goods, and this is how Spenser invites the reader to exercise his judgment, as Guyon does his.

Horton voices what seems a fairly common view when he defines Guyon's virtue by comparing the House of Holiness (I.x) with the

House of Alma (II.ix–x). Each house "provides an inspirational view of the virtue it exemplifies. Red Cross, on the Mount of Contemplation, looks into the future, whereas Guyon, in the turret, surveys the past; for Christian virtue is grounded on faith, and natural virtue on experience. Holiness furthermore has heavenly sanctions, whereas natural virtue has its sufficient justification in the accumulated examples of human history."[24] This is a gross oversimplification. What Guyon studies is the record of Elfin emperors, a record of unparalleled perfection lasting throughout 700 generations, which means that he is fired by a vision of what his virtue aims at. Within the overall symmetrical structure this vision finds its analogue in the person of Belphœbe in canto iii. Belphœbe appears to Braggadocchio, who is a mock version of Guyon, possessed as he is of Guyon's horse, saddle, and spear. It is of course Arthur who studies the *Briton moniments* whose apparently meaningless sequence of peace and war, corruption and honest endeavour, on closer scrutiny reveals a providential pattern pointing to a glorious future. Careful analysis will show that this profane history keeps alluding to events in sacred history, so that faith is very much an issue. As Spenser presents this history, the sacred and the profane merge so that Britain is as much God's chosen nation as Israel. What we see in these historical records, then, are two kinds of temperance or balance: one kept steady throughout the generations and another achieved in the course of time through the grace of God. Cantos I.x and II.x therefore have a great deal in common, including the enraptured vision of the future.

The events in the Castle of Medina dramatize Aristotle's argument concerning the golden mean, but Spenser's Renaissance bias makes him see the mean as a dynamic rather than a static condition. As A. C. Hamilton rightly states in his gloss on II.ii.38, Medina "seeks harmony rather than the mean," and, as we discover on consulting Pietro Bongo, the two are one: to establish the mean is to establish harmony. It has been argued that, since Medina herself is the mean, she cannot seek it,[25] but this is to ignore the writers who transmitted Aristotle to the Renaissance. One such transmission is found in Bongo's chapter on the number 3. Since the Pythagoreans (so Bongo writes) consider the Binary as a confusion of unity, the Triad is the first real number; as such it signifies justice and the sum of perfection when seen as the virtue which is a mean between the vices of defect and excess. The number one is the mean and as it were the centre and spirit (*numen*) which ensures even division and hence a return to itself. Because an odd number always has a single unit at the centre, it possesses within itself its own nexus or bond (*vinculum*), and this is why it exists as a circle where the extremes are pulled to the centre, and this is why the number 3 is the beginning of all order. So far Bongo. We see at once that Spenser presents Medina as such a *vinculum* placed at the centre between her sisters and their lovers: she pulls the extremes towards the centre (i.e. herself), compelling them into union. Although uneasy, this union cannot be deceptive. The currency of this concept of the relationship between the mean and the extremes is shown by the fact that the iconographical representation of the mean is a circle with a centre.[26] Spenser describes Guyon's combat with Huddibras and Sansloy so that it suggests a similar reconciliation: Guyon attacks the two in order to "part their fight" (23 : 8), and in so doing he is said to act like a ship which, breaking the "foaming wave, / Does ride on both their backs, and faire her selfe doth save" (24 : 8–9). In other words, the ship compels the waves into obedient service. The fact that this description is located at the canto centre in stanzas 22–23 indicates its importance. That the mean imposes harmony is suggested by the fact that the episode of the Castle of Medina occupies 35 stanzas, and as the sum of 8 and 27, 35 signifies harmony. More interesting, though, is the way that canto ii as a whole forms a series of 2 : 1 ratios; even the 7 stanzas on the establishing of concord (ii.32–38) divide into 2—4—1, where the ratio occurs twice. Although concord is the main theme, the canto begins and concludes with the lesson that some opposites are irreconcilable: virginity and lust, purity and filth cannot coexist (ii.3–11 and 39–45). As a member of the Order of Maydenhead and sworn to eradicate Acrasia, Guyon is the male version of the principle of virginity as first encountered in Diana's nymph. Guyon relates to the Faerie Queen as the nymph to Diana, and, to include the negative version, as Dan Faunus to Acrasia.

The idea of concord has a significant role in the structure formed by cantos i–viii, and it may function *in malo* as well as *in bono*. The concord between Trompart and Braggadocchio (canto iii) is as negative as the concord between Phædria and Cymochles, or again as Phædria's pacification of Cymochles and Guyon by appealing to the supposedly superior value of pleasure (vi). Friendship between two knights is a topos which links cantos i and viii; In canto i, Redcrosse and Guyon join hands, in canto viii Arthur and Guyon. The persuasion which leads to concord in the House of Medina (ii) can be of no avail in the House of Mammon, where rejection is the only solution (vii); Mammon can be compelled or persuaded no more than the world he rules with such imperious sway. At the centre, though, in cantos iv–v, Guyon does impose peace when he binds Occasion and Furor (iv), and when he overcomes Pyrochles who then accepts his offer of grace (v).

If Guyon is right to reject Mammon's "grace", does he do so for the wrong reason and in the wrong way, with brusque curtness and in a spirit of unpardonable pride? A consideration of Mammon's character takes us part of the way to an answer. Mammon presents himself not only as "God of the world and worldlings" (vii.8 : 1), but also as the source of all good. He is one "That of my plenty poure out unto all, / And unto none my graces do envye" (8 : 3–4). Like Milton's Satan, Mammon ousts God from his true position and places himself there instead, which is why he keeps referring to his "offred grace". If Guyon will "deigne to serve and sew" he will bestow his grace on him freely (vii.9 : 1). A parallel with the temptation of Christ is plain, and so is the fact that Guyon resists and goes on doing so, as indeed he ought to. But does he do so for the wrong reason and for much too long, since he faints the moment he reaches the surface again? Guyon's unworthiness (so it has been argued) is acknowledged by himself when he pays homage to Arthur at the end of canto viii. But how can a knight who recognizes that Mammon's "grace" is a vile and treacherous bait (on purpose laid to make the taker mad) be said to have failed so that he must be cast down and learn to appreciate the grace of God? Are his wisdom and his steadfastness (or fortitude) to count for nought? Surely we are intended to see, with Guyon, that Mammon is placed over against God, the "grace" of the world against the "grace / Of highest God" (viii.1), and that we are to reject the former in no uncertain terms. In fact, the more brusque, the better. *Rejection* is the key term for cantos vi–vii, *annihilation* for cantos i and xii. Acrasia annihilates Mordant, but is in her turn rendered impotent by Guyon and the Palmer. As we have come to expect, the organisation is in terms of concepts, and not of Guyon's supposed development; within the text, development is not at issue, concepts are. It is the reader responding to the text who learns and so develops as he studies Spenser's logical analysis and his careful deployment of parallels and antitheses. Guyon is made to query the source of Mammon's riches simply in order to permit the narrative to display the source for what it is – a wellhead for all that is evil.

The structure of canto vii supports my argument (see Diagrams VI.31–33). Guyon's decisive rejection of wealth in the centrally placed stanzas 33–34 is flanked, at the two halfway points, by his

Diagram VI.31 *The Faerie Queene* II, Canto vii

1–2	2		Guyon left without his guide
3–8	6	⎤	Guyon meets Mammon
9–19	11	⎬ 30	Temptation above ground
20–32	13	⎦	Temptation within the realm of Pluto
33–34	2		Guyon's rejection and the fiend's reaction
35–39	5	⎤	Temptation in the mines
40–50	11	⎬ 30	Temptation in the Palace of Honour
51–64	14	⎦	Temptation in the Garden of Proserpine
65–66	2		Guyon returns to the surface and faints

The division into equal halves stresses the importance of the refusal in stanza 33. That Guyon's refusal in terms of "another blis," "Another happinesse, another end" is given in stanza 33 suggests that the allusion is to what is immortal and hence contrary to what is desired by worldlings. During the first temptation, Guyon presents the familiar account of the happiness of the first age when men lived like angels, and of the subsequent decline after the discovery of gold and silver within the womb of the Earth. Since the Garden of Proserpine is a perverse parody of the original Garden – a parody that turns it into a realm of everlasting death – the last temptation returns to the first, but the parallel merely highlights the difference. This is the end to which the Fall (i.e. the discovery of "Fountaines of gold and silver"; vii.17) ultimately leads.

denunciation of avarice as a "life-devouring fire" (vii.17) and his rejection of "high estate" (vii.50). Each halfway point is the centre of a pattern of recessed symmetry (Diagrams VI.32 and 33). After Guyon's first refusal (vii.10) Mammon enters into a lengthy account of the use of riches, but Guyon rebuts all his assertions, and he does so by means of a Christianized version of the myth of the golden age. During this first stage in the history of man, men were enabled to live like angels by "the Creatours grace," and the Fall is the consequence of the discovery of precious metals (vii.16). Predictably, Mammon scorns the simplicity of the "antique" age and advocates his own grace (vii.18), but Guyon retorts that wealth causes intemperance and moral foulness (vii.15), just as it is often gained through foul unrighteousness and "bloud guiltinesse" or guile (vii.19). The most striking linkage is between vii.11–13 and

Diagram VI.32 *The Faerie Queene* II, Canto vii. Recessed Symmetry around the Centre of the First Half

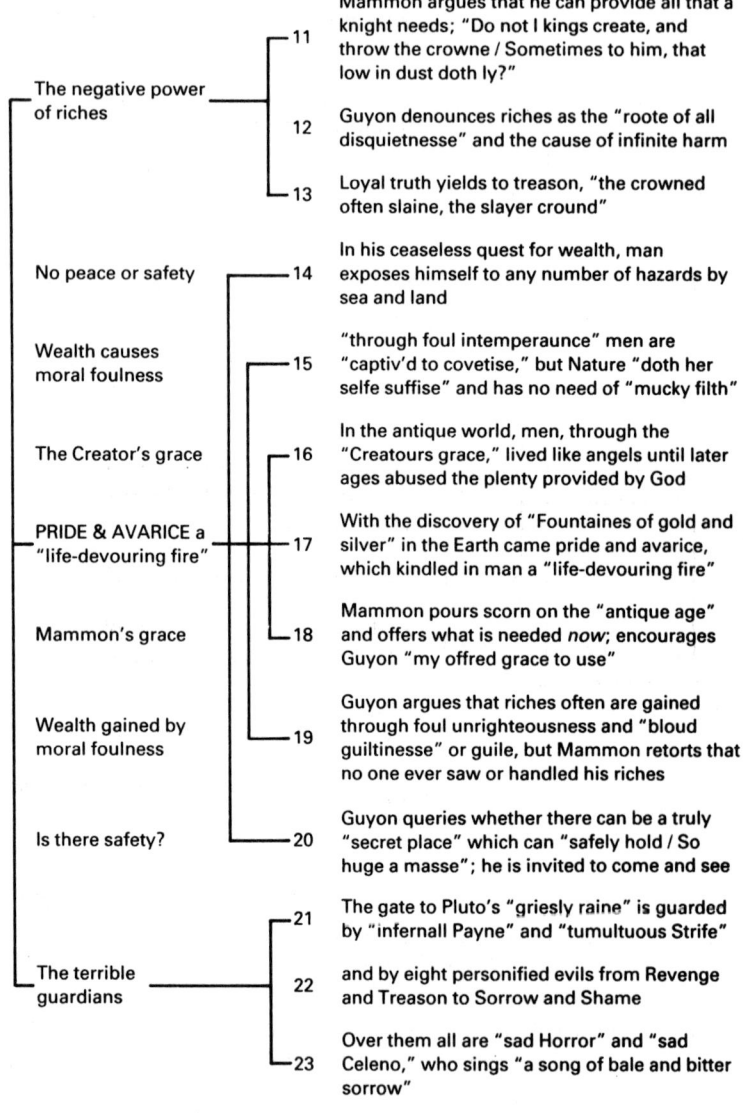

Those who guard the gate represent the negative effect of riches as described in stanzas 11–13. Hence Guyon is made to *see* the truth concerning the effect of riches.

Diagram VI.33 *The Faerie Queene* II, Canto vii. Recessed Symmetry around the Centre of the Second Half

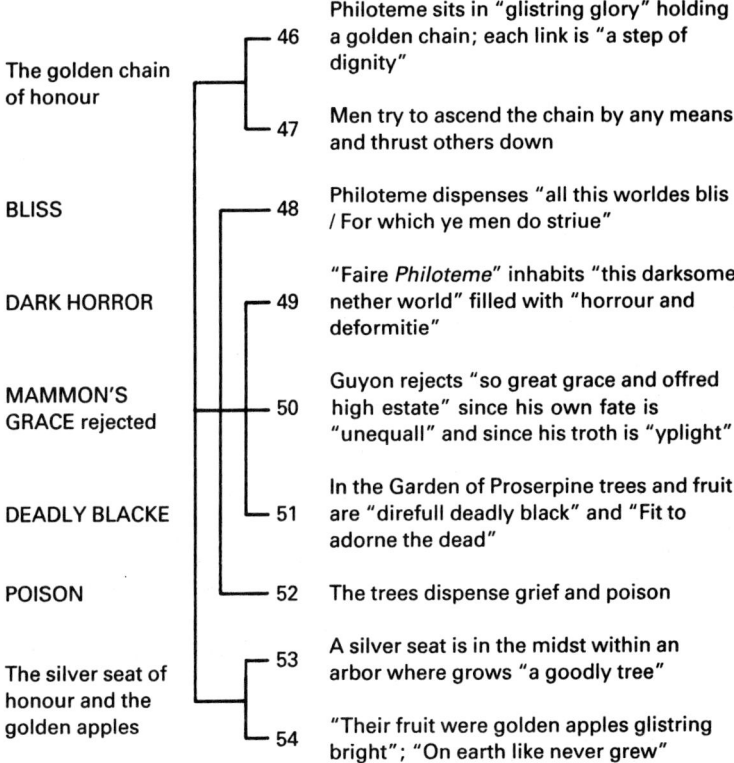

The linkage between stanzas 48 and 52 creates a submerged simile: "this worldes blis" is like poison.

21–23, since in the latter Guyon is made to see the reality of what he has argued in the former. The terrible guardians of the gate to Pluto's "griesly rayne" personify the evils Guyon has described. No wonder, therefore, that he "all the way / Did feed his eyes, and fild his inner thought" (vii.24). What Guyon *sees* confirms what he has *said*. His temperance proves itself through these trials, which call for wisdom, justice, and fortitude. In the pattern of recessed symmetry around stanza 50, the most interesting linkage is between vii.48 and 52, which functions like an epic simile: Philoteme who dispenses "all this worldes blis / For which ye men do strive" (48) is

Diagram VI.34 *The Faerie Queene* II, Cups, Fountains, Waves, and Attendant Filth or Purity

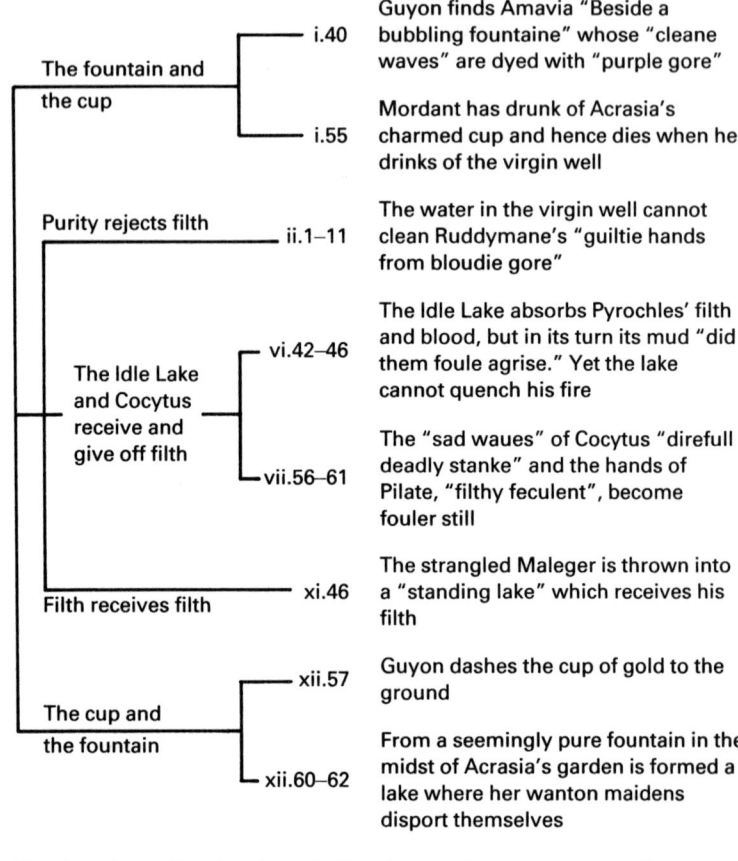

The Satanic quality of gold and silver is brought out when the discovery of "fountaines of gold and silver" within the Earth is associated with the fall from the state of innocence. Mammon's metaphorical fountain connects with the fountain at the centre of Acrasia's garden; each seems attractive and pure, but is life-devouring. They represent a principle of uncreation or undoing. No tempering is possible between purity and filth, nor can the Idle Lake quench Pyrochles' inward fire (vi.42–51); this fire is as life-devouring as Mammon's avarice (vii.17). Both irascible and concupiscible passions, then, are defined in terms of an inner destructive fire. Both the Idle Lake and the river Cocytus give off filth and receive it, as when the lake receives the blood and filth clinging to Pyrochles. In the same way the "standing lake" in Canto xi receives Maleger.

like the trees in the Garden of Proserpine, which dispense grief and poison (52).

The related topoi of fountains and of rivers so prominent in canto vii form a symmetrical pattern in the book as a whole, thus proving their importance (see Diagram VI.34). Mammon proclaims that "Riches, renowme, and principality, / Honour, estate, and all this worldes good / Fro me do flow into an ample flood" (vii.8). In the eighth position from the end, in stanza 59, we find the description of Tantalus (the type of avarice) immersed in the river Cocytus. The juxtaposition of these stanzas sets up yet another submerged epic simile: Mammon's "ample flood" is dark and filthy and an instrument of torment, like the Cocytus. The "Fountaines of gold and silver" (vii.17 : 5) and Mammon's "fountaine of the worldes good" (vii.38 : 6) point forward to the fountain in the midst of Acrasia's garden, "sweet and faire to see" (xii.62 : 1–2), but in reality as foul as the Cocytus (vii.56–57) and the Idle Lake (vi.46). In marked contrast, the "bubbling fountaine" beside which Guyon finds the dying Amavia possesses absolute purity. The cup drunk by Mordant (i.55) contains the poisonous filth which causes his death when mixed with the water he drinks from the well. The tale of the virgin well at the beginning of canto ii, therefore, connects antithetically with the "standing lake" which receives the strangled Maleger towards the end of canto xi. The lake receives Maleger's filth, just as the water of the Idle Lake receives the filth of Pyrochles at the same time that it imparts filth to those who are immersed in it (vi.42–46). In this respect the Idle Lake resembles the river Cocytus, whose water makes the hands of Pilate filthier still (vii.56–61).

In view of this consistent pattern it is difficult to associate the standing lake which receives Maleger, with the waters of baptism. The negative images of water and wine reveal the perverted character of everything connected with Mammon and with Acrasia. Mammon refers to himself as "this worldes blis," and Acrasia's cup is her version of the cup of our salvation. In the same way, the negative fountains and rivers parody the potent images found at the beginning and end of the biblical narrative – the true fountain of bliss waters the Garden of Eden and gives rise to the 4 rivers, which signify, *inter alia*, the 4 cardinal virtues and the 4 gospels (*Gen.* 2 : 10), and in the heavenly Jerusalem the river of life runs through the midst of the city (*Rev.* 22 : 1–2). At the centre of the biblical narrative is Christ (on the Tree of Life) from whose side issue the water and blood of our salvation. Unless we recognize the perverted versions of these images in Spenser's narrative, we shall not fully appreciate the nature of the temptations to which Guyon is exposed. A religious perspective is appropriate since at the heart of the biblical message is the tempering, in God, between Justice and Mercy, and the "tempering" between God and man is part of Spenser's subject in Book II as well as in Book I. Just as Redcrosse knight tempers his wrath (or fails to do so), Guyon possesses some degree of holiness, and he does so by virtue of his virtue. While Tasso lets Rinaldo's regeneration on Mount Olivet be preceded by lessons in ethics and history, Spenser reserves this particular programme for Guyon. Tasso's narrative therefore fuses what Spenser divided between Books I and II of *The Faerie Queene*, a point which encourages us to trace connections between the two books and so attribute to the Legend of Temperance as well some concern with holiness.

James Nohrnberg (*The Analogy of The Faerie Queene*, 1976) has presented a convincing case for linking Books I and VI, II and V, and III and IV in a pattern of recessed symmetry, and temperance and justice certainly have much in common, since the one is concerned with harmony in the individual, and the other with harmony in society. Both are "virtues of experience" and both are "associated with safeguards, like the Palmer and Talus."[27] Certainly Guyon judges justly when he rejects Phædria's advances and Mammon's "offred grace," and when he destroys the Bower of Bliss – these major events that connect the middle and the end of Book II. But it is not enough to think in terms of justice; what Guyon represents in canto xii is God's avenging justice, nor is mercy absent, since the act serves to protect the innocent and to redeem Acrasia's victims. But for this tempering of justice and mercy in God, man would be utterly lost. In the second half of the book, Spenser weaves the concepts of mercy and justice through his narrative as if to insist on their interdependence. At its centre, in cantos ix–x, temperance is the issue, in the flanking cantos viii and xi it is mercy, and in cantos vii and xii justice. In other words, we proceed from justice to mercy to temperance in cantos vii—viii—ix, and in cantos x—xi—xii from temperance to mercy and justice. In canto viii Arthur is the agent of divine grace, whereas in canto xi it is he who stands in need of grace to overcome Maleger. Arthur actually repeats Guyon's pattern: just as Guyon prevails over Mammon in canto vii and is saved by divine grace in canto viii, Arthur prevails over the pagan brothers in canto viii, but is himself saved by grace in canto xi. In Arthur's case, though, no one has felt the need to posit a prior fall.

To justice Guyon adds wisdom (to discriminate) and fortitude (to persist). To quote from Augustine's *De musica* VI, wisdom teaches us what to love, temperance elevates the soul to this love, and in its rejection of the world the soul is assisted by fortitude and justice (VI.xvi.51). These virtues temper the movements of the soul through ordered linking (VI.xiv.47). The opposite of this tempered movement, or *rhythmos* to use Plato's term, is a mutability which ultimately tends towards chaos. This mutability is illustrated when Cymochles veers from lust to wrath and back again to wrath (II.v–vi), and it affects the human condition itself as man sinks to the level of beasts. Like Milton's Satan, Acrasia uncreates. The wandering islands in cantos vi and xii are obvious images of mutability, and in canto vii Mammon creates and uncreates *at libitum* ("The crowned often slaine, the slayer cround"; vii.12). The temptation to be like gods occurs when Mammon suggests that Guyon wed Philoteme; such an attempt to rise in pride beyond the scope of mortals would, in fact, be worse than sticking in the mud with Grill and the "donghill kind" (xii.87).

But how can man become virtuous? This is surely the basic problem, and some readers seem to think that it is enough to study Aristotle. In his early treatise *De libero arbitrio*, Augustine displays a similar optimism: the virtues are within our reach if we apply our free will. The mature Augustine is much more circumspect and realistic; no reader of the *Confessions* is likely to forget the prolonged fight, within himself, of his two wills, or his many warnings against the terrible power of habit. Calvin's position is unambiguous: of himself man can do nothing. When the Psalmist from time to time comforts himself with the assurance of his own righteousness, precisely as Guyon does at vii.2, Calvin invariably refers the righteousness to David's *cause* as given to him by God.[28] Is Guyon's cause, then, righteous? Surely we must say yes, since it was given to him by the Faerie Queen on the request of the Palmer (cf. II.ix.9 and the *Letter to Raleigh*). Calvin's scepticism concerning man's ability to resist the promptings of the flesh was extreme; although David was re-born of God's spirit, "yet knew he how great the stubbornness of the flesh is," so that his only protection was to be "fenced with God's grace." Even so, the faithful "are always tainted with some infirmity."[29] Calvin was so obsessed with this infirmity that he found it necessary to warn against excess even in his comments on Psalm 23 ("Thou shalt prepare a table before me ...").

Spenser steered a course between the optimism of Aristotle and the young Augustine and the pessimism of Calvin, as we realize on considering the nature of the Palmer who accompanies him so faithfully, except for the events narrated in cantos vi–vii. The Palmer speaks most rationally about temperance on sundry occasions in cantos i–v, and we must therefore associate him with right reason. But this cannot be taken to suggest that Guyon is deprived of right reason when he is deprived of his company; he certainly argues rationally enough in his encounter with Mammon. However, if we consider the traditional division of reason into a lower and a higher level (often referred to as discursive and intuitive rational perception, or *ratio mobilis* and *ratio stabilis*), we may perhaps connect the Palmer with the higher level, which provides direct contact with heavenly truth. The image of the star in the opening lines of canto vii suggests as much:

> As Pilot well expert in perilous wave,
>   That to a stedfast starre his course hath bent,
>   When foggy mistes, or cloudy tempests have
>   The faithfull light of that faire lampe yblent,
>   And cover'd heaven with hideous dreriment,
>   Upon his card and compas firmes his eye,
>   The maisters of his long experiment,
>   And to them does the steddy helme apply,
> Bidding his winged vessell fairely forward fly:
>
> So *Guyon* having lost his trusty guide,
>   Late left beyond that *Ydle lake*, proceedes
>   Yet on his way, of none accompanide;
>   And evermore himselfe with comfort feedes,
>   Of his own vertues, and prayse-worthy deedes.
>
> (vii.1–2)

If the Palmer is the "stedfast starre" (*ratio stabilis*), how can we interpret the "card and compas" on which the Pilot "firmes his eye" and so bids his "winged vessell fairely forward fly"? There is no check and no delay; the vessel proceeds as before. The fact that they are man-made instruments of navigation suggests an affinity with discursive or natural reason, and this view is certainly plausible, but something is still missing. An allusion must surely be intended also to Holy Writ where we may find laws and lessons to steer by in our daily lives; these will serve whenever the "stedfast starre" itself is obscured. The Palmer's prophetic vision and his caduceus-like "staffe" prove his close affinity with the divine, while the "card and compas" (the laws contained in the Bible) are more mundane, although derived from what must always be referred to as divine revelation.

In support of this interpretation can be adduced the argument presented by Pierre de la Primaudaye in Book I of *The French Academie* (1586).[30] The very first chapter ("Of Man") distinguishes between man's fallible natural reason and a higher kind derived from the grace of God. This higher reason "by speciall grace from aboue commeth to the elect, accompanieth them, and helpeth them in all their actions" (p. 14). This Christian version of man's *ratio stabilis* suits the function of the Palmer exactly. What is even more interesting, though, is that Primaudaye's attitude to the vexing problem of how one may become virtuous represents an attractive compromise. He states in his preface that he steers a middle course between perfect trust in man's ability to be virtuous, and perfect distrust; faith and virtue are two sides of the same coin, since faith is the cause of virtue and virtuous deeds, but to faith must be added grace from above. The encounter between Redcrosse knight and Guyon in canto i must be taken to indicate that Guyon's virtue is rooted in faith; this is the virtue which sustains him in canto vii, and in canto viii grace is conspicuously added from above.

Much of what Pierre de la Primaudaye has to say about virtue and vice is relevant to Spenser's narrative. It is by the grace of God that fallen man may acquire virtue; God ordained that, despite the Fall, a spark of light should remain in man's spirit, and this spark may move a regenerated Christian to seek the goodness and righteousness he does not possess. This act of grace causes the regenerate to "draw out of the doctrine of holy scriptures" that which may contain and repress his wicked inclinations. In this way he can correct and mend his naturally corrupt manners (p. 18). In other words, this is where Guyon finds his "card and compas." The cardinal virtues adorn the soul of the regenerate; without them everything would be disorder and confusion – as in the rabble rout who besiege the Castle of Alma. When illuminated by wisdom, the soul "bringeth foorth the fruits of loue, ioy, peace, long suffering, gentlenes, goodnes, faith, meekenes, temperancie" (ch. 2, p. 26). A marginal gloss identifies the biblical source as *Galatians* 5 : 22–23. These are no incidental remarks; the many chapters on the various virtues and vices consistently link virtue with faith and divine grace. Then, too, the importance of good habits is stressed, as in Aristotle and Augustine. Ch. 3 on "Diseases and Passions of the body and soule" refers the passions back to pleasure and grief (cf. *FQ* II.i.57), and makes the point that, before the passions "be in force," the mind may strengthen itself against them by the grace of God and "through the discourse of reason." However, man will yield to them if "God strengthen not the soule, and reason the *diuine guide*, accompanie him not" (pp. 29–32; my emphasis). It is precisely because he represents reason, then, that the Palmer is a "diuine guide." Ch. 5 ("Of Vertue") repeats the assertion that "Vertue is the effect of regeneration" (p. 52, marginal gloss). Regeneration in its turn is "by the spirit of God dwelling in us. From religion and pietie towards God comes prudence, and prudence cuts off all excess and defect, moderating between too little and too much" (pp. 52–53). This attribution to prudence of the function which belongs to temperance shows that the two cannot be kept apart: the temperate person acts wisely. Pierre de la Primaudaye produces a truly splendid definition when he writes that "the foundation of all vertue is that *diuine reason*, which floweth into our soules from the free goodnes of our God, and which taketh liuely roote by care, studie, and diligence, when the self-same grace blesseth our labour" (p. 54; my emphasis). In this passage, God's grace and man's own efforts are beautifully integrated without detriment to either side, yet so as to give the primacy to God. No compromise was ever more neatly made. As for the reward of virtue in the life to come, it is of the free mercy of God, as stated in a marginal gloss (p. 56), which expresses the Protestant view with great clarity. Since virtue is founded on the divine reason which flows into our souls as a free gift from God, it follows logically that rewards after death must equally be a free gift. This is where Pierre de la Primaudaye approaches Calvin, or at least nods in his direction. However, Calvin would have denounced the idea that our own care and diligence enter into the process, or that it is at all possible for virtue to become rooted in us. Judging on the basis of the popularity in England of this encyclopedic treatise, the author's *via media* must have appealed to many. The compromise between classical and Christian ideas is made with great tact and with a distinctly Protestant bias.

Temperance is considered in ch. 17, which begins by relating this virtue to the divinely established order of the universe. Temperance is "a well disposed order of things" in contrast to disorder and confusion (p. 179), a definition which explains the events of cantos ii and xi, where the powers of disorder, confusion, and misrule are resisted by Guyon (in the Castle of Medina) and overcome by Arthur (in his battle with Maleger and his troops). Temperance is a knife or a razor to cut off all evil thoughts (p. 183), just as severity is an aspect of clemency (ch. 30, "Of Meeknes, Clemencie, Mildnes, Gentlenes and Humanitie"). Although a noble-minded man must show "gentlenes and clemencie", like God, he must also accompany his gentleness with severity, his clemency with rigour. As Plato says, he must both chastise and pardon, since if too great lenity is shown, "an impunitie of the wicked is bred" (p. 322). "Therefore *Cicero* saith, that it is the property of a noble minded man simply to punish those that are most in fault, & the authors of euill, but to saue the multitude" (p. 323). Acrasia, then, is punished as the author of evil, but her willing victims are restored to human shape and set free. This is a fine example of the way in which this encyclopedist fuses Christian and classical ideas, but the basic concept is the reconciliation between mercy and justice in God, which man must try to imitate by tempering clemency and rigour.

It remains to consider Guyon's satisfaction "with his own virtues, and prayse-worthy deedes". Again Pierre de la Primaudaye assists our critical inquiry. His ch. 31, "Of good and ill Hap", has as its point of departure that happiness can be found only in the possession of a permanent, steadfast good, and that this good is located in the soul alone, never in worldly possessions: the true fountain of felicity is *within*. (Milton would have nodded.) Then follows the decisive statement: this permanent and certain joy grows in strength by his remembrance "of good and vertuous actions proceeding from the soule guided by right knowledge and reason" (pp. 334–36). One's memory of "good and vertuous actions", then, is a source of permanent joy. Hope, too, is involved: hope and the confidence it breeds must support a noble man if he is to persevere (ch. 28, "Of Hope"), since hope depends on the virtue of fortitude (p. 299). The historical example cited is that of Alexander the Great, who trusted, not in his weapons or his soldiers, "but in his owne vertue" (pp. 299–300). To be valid, however, this hope must be "setled and grounded vpon a sure expectation of the helpe and grace of God" (p. 300).

In the structure of cantos i–viii (Diagram VI.35) Spenser weaves a pattern based on the operation of grace and of reason as if to underline their interdependence. The divine grace so strongly present in cantos i and viii functions as a frame for the cantos in between, where rational control and rational rejection of vice are the main concern. And, as we have already had occasion to observe, the concept of concord is part of the pattern; concord is the consequence of grace. When Guyon and Redcrosse knight take leave of each other in canto i, they stand "With right hands plighted,

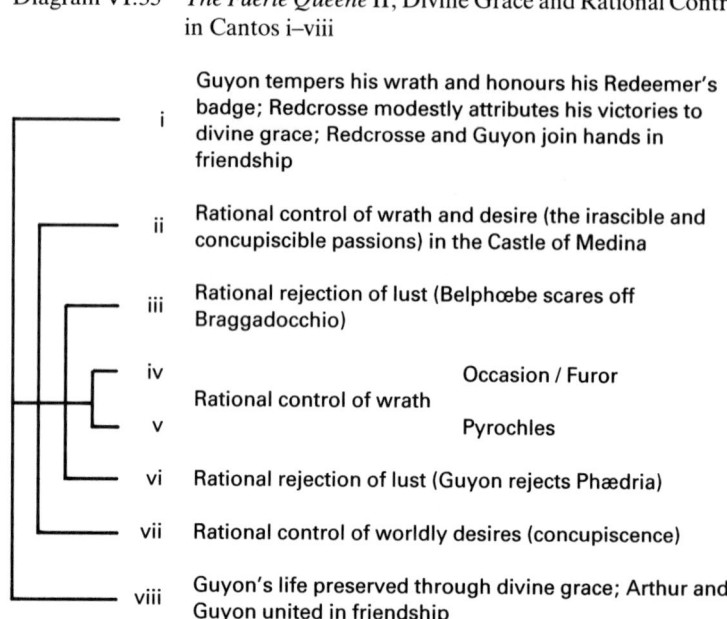

Diagram VI.35 *The Faerie Queene* II, Divine Grace and Rational Control in Cantos i–viii

Grace and reason combine to resist, temper, or reject wrath and lust. Grace frames the action in cantos i and viii, while wrath is featured in cantos iv and v. In cantos iii and vi, unabashed lust is stoutly resisted – male lust in the person of Braggadocchio, female lust in Phædria, a Voluptas character.

pledges of good will" (i.29:1), and a similar happy union is described at the end of canto viii; when Guyon wakes from his trance and learns what has happened, his heart is bathed in affection for Arthur, "the Patrone of his life" (viii.55:4), but when Arthur refuses Guyon's offer of submission the two are united in perfect friendship. If there is grace at the centre, in cantos iv and v, then it must be vested in Guyon, who redeems Phedon in canto iv and overcomes Pyrochles in canto v so that he must beg for mercy. Mercy is readily bestowed, and so are words of advice, but to no avail. The release of Occasion and Furor, on Pyrochles' request, proves his undoing; by canto viii his wrath is so implacable that he rejects Arthur's offer of grace and is content to die.

The topos of wisdom plays an equally important part in these cantos (see Diagram VI.36). Wisdom and folly are systematically contrasted. In canto i Redcrosse knight is sufficiently "wise and warie" by "triall of his former harmes and cares" (i.4) to avoid the

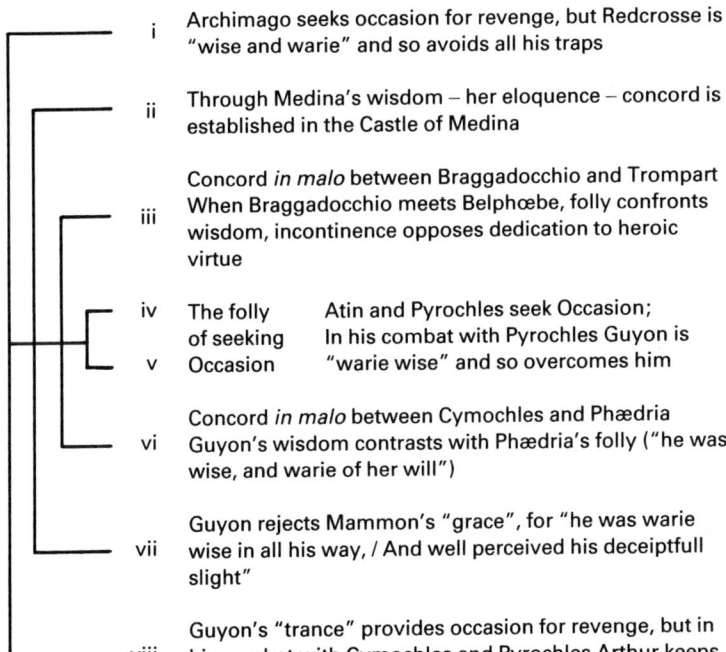

Diagram VI.36 *The Faerie Queene* II, the Topos of Wisdom in Cantos i–viii

i — Archimago seeks occasion for revenge, but Redcrosse is "wise and warie" and so avoids all his traps

ii — Through Medina's wisdom – her eloquence – concord is established in the Castle of Medina

iii — Concord *in malo* between Braggadocchio and Trompart When Braggadocchio meets Belphœbe, folly confronts wisdom, incontinence opposes dedication to heroic virtue

iv — The folly of seeking Occasion — Atin and Pyrochles seek Occasion;
v — In his combat with Pyrochles Guyon is "warie wise" and so overcomes him

vi — Concord *in malo* between Cymochles and Phædria Guyon's wisdom contrasts with Phædria's folly ("he was wise, and warie of her will")

vii — Guyon rejects Mammon's "grace", for "he was warie wise in all his way, / And well perceived his deceiptfull slight"

viii — Guyon's "trance" provides occasion for revenge, but in his combat with Cymochles and Pyrochles Arthur keeps his head and gains the victory

Archimago makes his various appearances with symmetrical precision in cantos i, iii, vi, and viii, always seeking revenge (first on Redcrosse knight and then on Guyon). In contrast to Phedon, who is trapped into the madness of perfect fury, Pyrochles courts disaster by deliberately seeking Occasion and causing her to be set free (iv–v). Pyrochles, therefore, is more culpable and more irrational. Guyon's "trance" later on in canto viii provides the desired occasion for revenge.

Wisdom avoids occasions for wrath or lust, Folly seeks them.

traps set for him by Archimago, and the folly of seeking Occasio/ Fortuna (fortune in her negative aspect)[31] is amply demonstrated in cantos iv–v. Following the sage advice of the Palmer in canto iv, Guyon overcomes Furor by binding Occasion, the root of all strife and discord, and, when Pyrochles attacks him in canto v, Guyon is "warie wise" so that he overcomes his opponent, however furious (v.9). Indeed, it is Pyrochles' uncontrolled fury that is the cause of his defeat in canto v as in canto viii. Just as wisdom is the source of concord, folly may result in false concord, as we see in cantos iii and vi. In canto iii Braggadocchio and Trompart represent concord *in malo*, as do Cymochles and Phædria in canto vi. Moreover, when Cymochles fights Guyon, Phædria's speech on the pleasures of love imposes a concord based on false premises. Medina imposes true concord on her household in canto ii through her wise words, and in canto vii wisdom manifests itself in Guyon's rejection of Mammon's deceit: "he was warie wise in all his way, / And well perceived his deceiptfull slight" (vii.64 : 6–7). Finally, in canto viii Guyon's "trance" provides the occasion so eagerly sought. The connection between Archimago and Occasion is suggested when Archimago is said to have a "faire filed Tong" (i.3 : 6); Guyon puts an iron lock on Occasion's tongue at iv.12 : 9, and, when she is subsequently released, he refuses to listen to her reviling speeches (v.21).

Guyon, so it seems, commands his passions with admirable wisdom, but is he heroic in so doing? With the passing of time it has become increasingly difficult to honour Guyon's virtue as heroic, but the many covert allusions to Hercules, the archetypal hero, suggest a heroic dimension. Like Tasso, Spenser made good use of the famous Choice of Hercules, but other aspects of the myth are equally relevant. An admirable survey is fortunately provided by G. Karl Galinsky's *The Herakles Theme* (1972).[32] It is of course because Hercules came to represent virtue that he became such an obvious archetype for Tasso and Spenser and, later on, for Henry Fielding.[33] Placing the hero between representatives of virtue and vice creates as much dramatic tension as placing Everyman between a good and a bad angel. Rinaldo, Guyon, and Tom Jones lean briefly in the direction of Pleasure/Vice in the persons of Armida, Phædria, and Mrs Waters, but only to embrace the virtue to be found solely in the active pursuit of honour and glory. As Galinsky explains, the myth had "timeless relevance already in antiquity" (p. 185), and medieval and Renaissance writers "simply draped Herakles into the contemporary garb of a knight or nobleman and brought the external features of his exploits up to date" (p. 186). It is typical of the Renaissance to consider the power of Hercules as a moral force and a higher state of virtue; thus Coluccio Salutati (*De laboribus Herculis, ca.* 1406) interprets his slaying of Megara as a triumph of the soul over the flesh, and her three sons "are symbols of irascibility, sensuality, and concupiscence" (p. 197). In Spenser's narrative, Megara is represented by Acrasia, irascibility by Pyrochles, sensuality by Cymochles, Mordant, and Verdant, and consupiscence by Mammon. A number of specific episodes gain considerably by being related to Hercules. Good examples are found in cantos iii and vi, which balance each other within the symmetrical pattern formed by cantos i–viii. In canto vi Phædria succeeds in pacifying Cymochles and Guyon (engaged in fierce combat provoked by Cymochles) by deploring the cruelty of warfare and praising the pleasures of love: "Another warre, and other weapons I / Doe love, where love does give his sweet alarmes, / Without bloudshed" (vi.34). This argument recalls an epic by Silius Italicus where the hero (Scipio) is placed at the crossroads where he must make his choice between Virtue and Vice/Voluptas. The speech of Voluptas is a sustained diatribe against war and all its dangers, and a corresponding praise of the delights of the senses; Phædria, therefore, is a *voluptas* figure to whom Cymochles readily gives his assent. This assent stops the combat between the two knights, and Guyon may subsequently depart in peace. Canto iii presents the speeches of both Virtue and Vice (presumably for the benefit of the reader). Stanzas iii.37–41 on the dialogue between Braggadocchio and Belphœbe present the Choice of Hercules in familiar terms: she praises an active life devoted to honourable pursuits: "Who seekes with painfull toile, shall honor soonest find", but the man who "moulds in idle cell" cannot "Unto her happie mansion attaine." Braggadocchio, though, is all for the pleasures of the "joyous court" where "all delight does raigne"; there "thou maist love, and dearely loved bee, / And swim in pleasure". Braggadocchio's three rhyme words – *is*, *mis*, *blis* – are taken over by Belphœbe in her reply and their sequence inverted to mark the inversion of the argument (iii.39–40).[34]

The presence of Hercules is felt also in cantos iv–v on Occasion and Furor. We spot the connection on learning that the competition between Virtue and Vice could be presented as being between Poverty and Misfortune, that is, Fortuna in her negative aspect. In some medieval pictures the combat is located at a crossroads, thus making the allusion to the Choice of Hercules explicit: a ragged Poverty overcomes a gorgeously arrayed Fortuna and ties her to a post.[35] The moral is simple: the person who chooses virtue places himself beyond the power of fortune, and this is what Guyon does when he ties Occasio/Fortuna to a post (iv.12–13). The choice is referred to again in the passage on Cymochles in Acrasia's bower (v.28–30). The figure of Cymochles, "given all to lust and loose living" (28:3), is contrasted with that of Hercules as obliquely presented in the stanza on the grove on the other side, "full of the stately tree, / That dedicated is t'*Olympicke Jove*, / And to his sonne

Alcides, whenas hee / Gaynd in *Nemea* goodly victoree" (31 : 2–5). There are no goodly victories for Cymochles.

Braggadocchio is yet another Hercules figure. Braggadocchio plays the part of the braggart sham-Hercules of classical comedy, as described by the chorus introducing Aristophanes' *Peace*. The chorus boasts of the author's achievement:

> It was he that indignantly swept from the stage that paltry, ignoble device
> Of a Hercules needy and seedy and greedy, a vagabond sturdy and stout
> Now baking his bread, now swindling instead, now beaten and battered about.[36]

In the *Syleus* by Euripides this sham Hercules intends to violate Syleus' daughter, as Braggadocchio does Belphœbe, and the theft of Guyon's horse and spear resembles the theft of Hercules' lion skin and club by Dionysus in Aristophanes' *Frogs*; Aristophanes exposes his pretentions and his cowardice as Spenser does Braggadocchio's. Even more relevant, perhaps, is the fact that in Menander's *Sham Herakles* it is the *miles gloriosus* figure who has appropriated the lion's skin and the club. As already suggested, the story of Phedon in canto iv alludes to the mad Hercules – *Hercules furens* – as presented for example by Seneca or by Raoul le Fevre in his popular *Recueil des Hystoires de Troyes* (1464; tr. by Caxton in 1484). Hercules listens to lies about his wife's supposed adultery, and in his fury he kills both the accuser and his innocent wife Megara. Phedon has a similar fate. We see, then, how the mad Hercules, the sham Hercules, and the Hercules of the Choice are present in the Legend of Temperance, and in the Palmer's caduceus-like staff we trace the presence of the Gallic Hercules who overcomes all by his wisdom and his rhetorical power.

A sub-text for canto vii may be found in the account of the descent of Hercules into the underworld, and in his fight with Cacus. In book 8 of the *Aeneid*, Virgil describes Cacus, the son of Vulcan, as a thief and a robber and an infernal creature who lives in a cave compared to the entry into hell itself. Fulgentius characterizes Cacus as evil incarnate (as Galinsky explains), and the commentator Servius interpreted Hercules' victory over Cerberus as a victory over earthly lusts and vices, which again fits Mammon's case exactly.[37] One reason for placing Tantalus in hell in the river Cocytus may be that, traditionally, Hercules' *aretē* (virtue) was contrasted with the *kakia* (vice) of Tantalus. This tradition, therefore, explains why Guyon addresses Tantalus in those harsh terms for which he has been blamed. Thus Alastair Fowler speaks of Guyon's "censoriousness towards the suffering Tantalus."[38] In view of these possible allusions to familiar episodes from the Hercules legend, one may argue that, by rejecting Mammon's "grace", Guyon/Hercules overcomes Cacus/Cerberus so that he may return to the surface of the Earth in triumph. We can blame Guyon's exhaustion and his subsequent faint only if we refuse to see his actions in canto vii as a serious test of a valid heroic virtue. If we accept this view of Guyon's virtue, however, we may see Guyon as passing from the protection afforded by virtue (a virtue born from faith) to the direct protection afforded by a merciful God when man can no longer defend his own cause. Even Calvin would not have condemned Guyon: Calvin praises David's virtue and excuses his fainting. (David's virtue is his obedience to the law – including the gospel – in other words, what Spenser refers to as the "card and compas.") David's "inflexible steadfastness in right dealing among so many most grievous temptations" was owing to his always carrying back his mind to "the law of God," and the proof of his virtue is that he "laid hands on himself, and bridled whatsoever he knew to be against God's word." And God's law is never esteemed aright "except we prefer it before all the riches of the world."[39] Calvin's comment on *Psalms* 17:15 comes straight to the point: David sustained his tribulations because he had a good conscience, and this is of course Guyon's case too. Calvin quotes *Isaiah* 3:10, which "exhorts the faithfull to sustain themselves with this persuasion; it shall go well with the righteous." The necessary qualification, though, follows: "And yet he does not ascribe the cause of his welfare to his works." If we were to apply this to Guyon, then the comfort he derives from his praiseworthy deeds would be based on his acknowledgement that his virtue is grounded in faith, so that God is the ultimate cause. This would be in keeping with the interpretation of his "card and compas" as the laws laid down in Holy Writ. Calvin applies the phrase "I shall awake" to David: "For although he was at no time overpowered with stupor, yet it could not be but that after long-continued harassing he lay as it were in a slumber." Spenser was surely no less charitable than Calvin, who goes on to add that this is true of all saints who "by reason of the weakness of the flesh" either "faint for a while, or are terrified, when, as it were, darkness overshadows them."[40] Mammon's long-continued harassing, then, must be expected to take its toll on

Guyon as on David and the saints in general, but God does not forsake us in our hour of need. It is satisfying to think of Guyon as a compromise between Hercules and David, a connection that is the more reasonable since Hercules so often was interpreted as a mythical type of Christ. It is satisfying because it prevents us from seeing temperance as a pedestrian virtue. After canto i, Guyon may have to walk on foot, thus keeping the Palmer company, but his heroic status must not be challenged; Spenser's argument, like Milton's in *Paradise Lost*, is "Not less but more Heroic than the wrauth / Of stern Achilles" (*Paradise Lost* IX.14–15).

In his masque *Pleasure Reconciled to Virtue* (1618), Ben Jonson makes use of the motif of Hercules asleep and surrounded by pygmies who boast that they will steal his club and kill the hero. Like Swift in *Gulliver's Travels*, Spenser may have had this episode in mind when he invented Guyon's faint: for a while the hero is defenceless and at the mercy of moral pygmies. The prostrate Guyon forms a parallel-with-a-difference to the prostrate Cymochles in canto v, as already suggested. Cymochles on his bed of lilies deserves a comment from Calvin, who proceeds from a consideration of those who "indulge themselves in their own drowsiness" to a Christian version of the Choice of Hercules. "For when we are about to take some course of living, we stand as it were in a forked way; yea, rather, in every one of our doings we hang in doubt and are at our wits' end, unless God meet us to shew us the way."[41] The choice made by Cymochles gives him the boldness of the ungodly, whose "drunken carelessness hardens them, and their wilful dulness makes them callous, as it were, in their folly, while forgetting both God and themselves they follow whithersoever lust leads them."[42] Spenser balances the parallels and contrasts between the two; each is dead to the world, Cymochles being "all carelessly displayd" in "secret shadow" on a "sweet bed of lillies softly laid" and "Made drunke with drugs of deare voluptuous receipt" (v.32–34), whereas Guyon lies physically exhausted "in a traunce" on the hard ground (viii.4–5). Both are associated with love: Cymochles is "given all to lust and loose living" (v.28), while the love which encloses Guyon is heavenly and protective (viii.1). His guardian angel is a divine Cupid and a brother of the three graces (viii.6), symbols of divine love.[43] The contrast between the two prostrate knights invites us to reject the one kind of love and to desire the other. Although it is Guyon who seems dead, Atin provokes Cymochles by referring to his master as dead: he is no longer Cymochles, but "*Cymochles* shade" in "Ladies lap entombed" (v.35–36). Atin speaks more truly than he knows: the juxtaposition of the two knights compels us to reconsider the nature of life and death. Cymochles embraces death, but life embraces Guyon.

Even if we believe in Guyon's righteousness, we may nevertheless assume that God is ultimately responsible. As Augustine explains, God "both makes the will of man righteous, and thus prepares it for assistance, and assists it when it is prepared. For the man's righteousness of will precedes many of God's gifts."[44] Guyon's righteousness of will in canto vii precedes the gift of grace in canto viii, and yet the whole work is of God. This is an argument that Calvin could have subscribed to.

Another interesting critical crux is the nature of the educational programme experienced by Arthur and Guyon in the Castle of Alma in cantos ix and x. In canto ix the two knights look into the Mirror of Nature, with its attendant moral lessons, and in canto x into the Mirror of History, whose lessons are no less important. In the same way Milton's Adam was to look in the Mirror of Nature in book 7 of the first edition of *Paradise Lost*, and in the Mirror of History in book 10 (Books VII–VIII and XI–XII of the second edition). Nothing reveals Spenser's structural bias more clearly than his handling of the two chronicles presented in canto x. *Briton moniments* apparently consists of a meaningless pattern of peace and war, rise and fall, where evil prevails, like Maleger and his "rabble rout." However, in the end Maleger, this powerful symbol of death and decay, dies at the hands of Arthur, and the *Briton moniments*, when submitted to a structural analysis, holds out a similar promise of redemption, so that its relationship to the Elfin chronicle is complementary rather than antithetical.[45] *Briton moniments* is the historical analogue to the besieged Castle of Alma, and both are preserved by the grace of God as manifested in the providential pattern of events. The basic textual pattern (see Diagram VI.37) consists of 33+33 stanzas, each group being subdivided into 11+22. The structure, therefore, tells us that this is a story of redemption and not of a decline leading to extinction. The main reason, though, for seeing the history as governed by the hand of God is the system of concords set up between profane and sacred history; various allusions to the great biblical events find their climax in the account of the Nativity (x.50). The beginning of British history is marked by the providential arrival of Brutus, who rescues the country from a state of utter depravity (x.4–14; see Diagram VI.38), and his bestowal of names on the different parts of the country relates him to Adam (*Genesis* 2 : 20). Similarly the story

Diagram VI.37   *The Faerie Queene* II, *Briton moniments* (x.4–69)

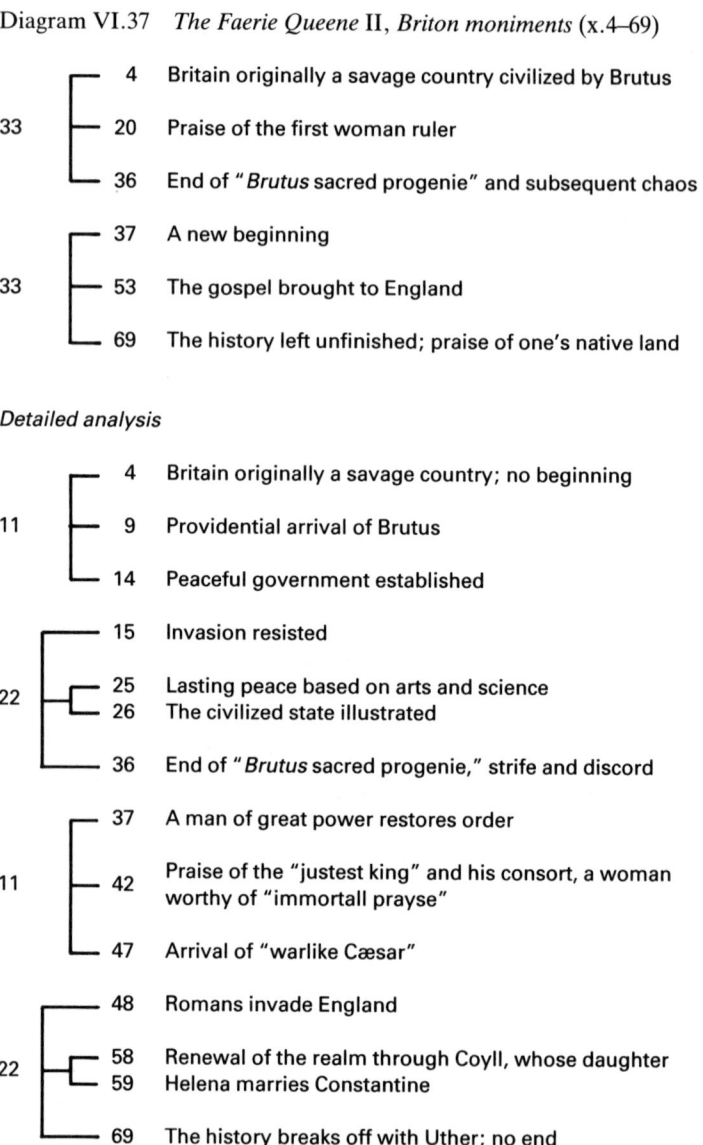

```
        ┌─  4   Britain originally a savage country civilized by Brutus
   33   ├─ 20   Praise of the first woman ruler
        └─ 36   End of "Brutus sacred progenie" and subsequent chaos

        ┌─ 37   A new beginning
   33   ├─ 53   The gospel brought to England
        └─ 69   The history left unfinished; praise of one's native land
```

Detailed analysis

```
        ┌─  4   Britain originally a savage country; no beginning
   11   ├─  9   Providential arrival of Brutus
        └─ 14   Peaceful government established

        ┌─ 15   Invasion resisted
        ├─ 25   Lasting peace based on arts and science
   22   ├─ 26   The civilized state illustrated
        └─ 36   End of "Brutus sacred progenie," strife and discord

        ┌─ 37   A man of great power restores order
   11   ├─ 42   Praise of the "justest king" and his consort, a woman
        │       worthy of "immortall prayse"
        └─ 47   Arrival of "warlike Cæsar"

        ┌─ 48   Romans invade England
        ├─ 58   Renewal of the realm through Coyll, whose daughter
   22   ├─ 59   Helena marries Constantine
        └─ 69   The history breaks off with Uther; no end
```

All the great positive events are located at the centre of a segment: the providential arrival of Brutus (9), the establishment of lasting peace (25–26), praise of the justest king and his consort (42), and the renewal of the realm with Coyll (58–59).

Diagram VI.38   *The Faerie Queene* II, the Arrival of Brutus (x.4–14)

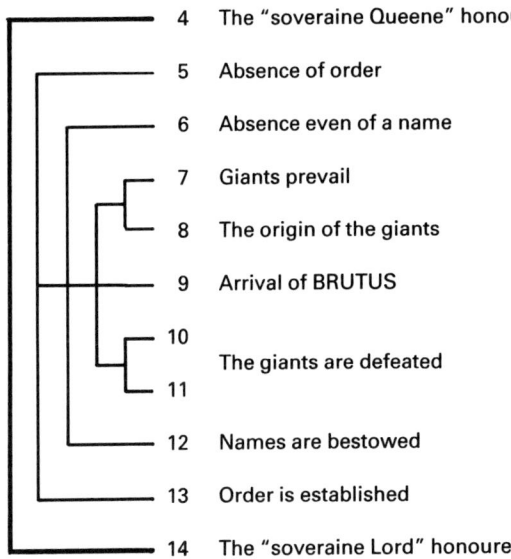

Stanzas 4 and 14 frame the 9-stanza account of the founding of Britain with the arrival of Brutus in stanza 9.

of the giants, the offspring of "feends and filthy sprights" (x.8) recalls *Genesis* 6:4–5).[46] In stanza 15 the attempted invasion is compared to the Flood of Noah, so that the beginning of British history bears a distinct resemblance to the biblical account of the beginning of human history. This story of a promising beginning proceeds, like sacred history, to an end which is as yet unseen, but its nature may be inferred from the structure it displays, based as it is on the number and the ratio of salvation. As my diagram shows, the structure highlights all the positive events: the arrival of Brutus, the establishment of lasting peace based on the arts of civilization, the reign of the "justest king" and his consort, a "woman worthy of immortall prayse," and the renewal of the realm through Coyll, whose daughter marries Constantine. Further concords with sacred history are not far to seek. The "happie father of faire progeny" who has as many children as the year has weeks (x.22), recalls the patriarch Jacob, whose 12 sons were associated with the 12 tribes, the 12 Apostles, the 12 signs of the zodiac, and the 12 months. The king who initiates the second 33-stanza cycle – Donwallo – resembles Moses in his capacity as law-giver: he made "sacred lawes, which some men say / Were unto him reveald in vision" (x.39 : 1–2). The most striking example of concord between sacred and profane history, however, is the textual structure as shown in Diagram VI.39: the division into 33+33 stanzas is aligned with a division into

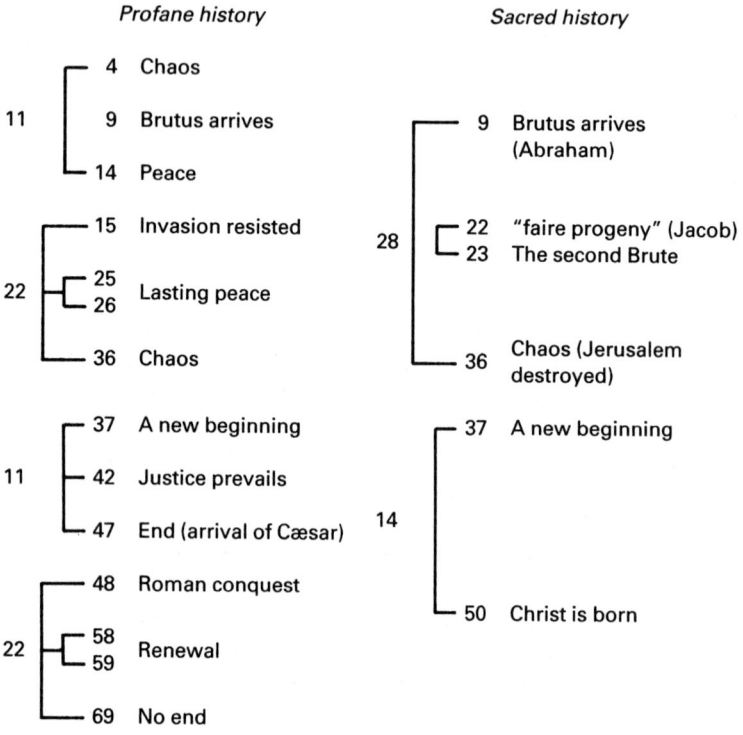

Diagram VI.39 *The Faerie Queene* II, the Concord between Sacred and Profane History (Canto x)

The first structural choice was to let the profane history consist of 66 stanzas divided into 33 + 33, and the second to let the sacred history consist of 42 divided into 28 + 14. Finally, the decisive break in each history – the destruction of all monuments of Brutus and his lineage and the destruction of Jerusalem – had to be located in stanza 36 (i.e. the 33rd position from the beginning). This meant that the beginning of sacred history had to be in stanza 9 on the arrival of Brutus. The description of Brutus and his reign contains allusions to the two great progenitors, Adam and Abraham. The giants were connected with the period before the Flood, an event referred to in stanza 15.

The reference, in the second group of 33 stanzas, to the "thrise eleven descents" from Donwallo (x.45) suggests that the 3 × 11 descents are present in the 3 × 11 stanzas.

28+14. In his opening chapter Matthew lists 3×14 generations from Abraham to Christ, while Luke lists 66 from Adam to Christ (ch.3 : 23–38). If we consider a stanza as marking one generation, and if we see the arrival of Brutus in stanza 9 as an analogue to the arrival of Abraham, then it takes precisely 42 stanza-generations to reach the birth of Christ in stanza 50. If this argument can be credited, then the destruction of Jerusalem (28 stanza-generations after x.9) must occur in stanza 36 (i.e. the 33rd stanza from the beginning of the chronicle), and this is indeed so. Stanza 36 describes the total destruction of Brutus and his line, so that "in the end was left no moniment / Of *Brutus*, nor of Britons glory auncient" (36 : 8–9). The two structures, then – one based on the number 33 and the other on 14 – are perfectly aligned. The symbolic numbers proclaim redemption (33) through the Law and the gospels (10+4). Each structure is marked by the repetition of clusters of identical rhyme words (see Diagram VI.40(a) and VI.40(b)). What these structures do is to assert as a fact that Britain, too, is God's chosen nation, guided by his providence in the direction of the peace which is but another word for the temperate state.

Spenser did not invent this concord between sacred and profane history whereby the profane becomes suffused by the sacred; he could have found it in Dante and in the sources Dante drew on, most notably Joachim of Fiore and his many followers. In a study published in 1980, Marjorie Reeves explains that Dante believed in a "providential purpose in history, focused on the 'Roman people',", and that anyone could see the pattern if he read the signs correctly.[47] In the *Convivio* IV, Dante draws a "parallel or concord between the birth of David, the root from which Jesus sprang, and the birth of Rome in the Advent of Aeneas in Italy, events which he makes contemporary. The divine election of the Roman *Imperium* is manifested in the simultaneous advent of the progenitor of the son of God and of the founder of the holy city, a political actualization to accompany the divine actualization."[48] Spenser makes the same point when he lets the arrival of Brutus to found Britain coincide with the arrival of Abraham, 42 generations prior to the Nativity as described in stanza 50. The connection between stanzas x.9 and x.50 is marked by the repetition of three identical rhyme words repeated in inverse order (*time / crime / slime* repeated as *slime / crime / time*), thus once again proving the care Spenser took to mark the beginning and end of a cycle in this particular way. As the result of "fatall error", Brutus lands in England to redeem the country from its beastly state, and the incarnation is of course

Diagram VI.40   *The Faerie Queene* II, Repetition of Identical Rhyme Words in Canto x

(a) II.x.9–50

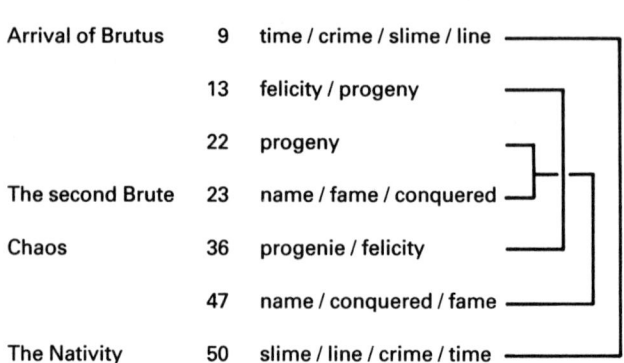

(b) II.x.4–69

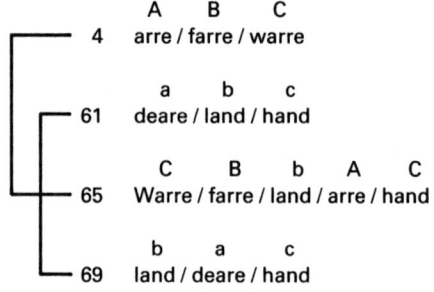

The repetition of clusters of identical rhyme words marks the beginning and the end of each history, the sacred and the profane.

the supreme act of redemption – an act of grace to purge "the guilt of sinful crime" from "wretched *Adams* line." A second link between these stanzas is found in the rhyme word *line*, located in the third position from the beginning and the end of each stanza. At x.9:7 on Brutus' lineage ("old *Assaracs* line"), though, the line is unrhymed, while the description of the birth of Jesus "from wretched *Adams* line" (x.50:3) is marred by no such irregularity in the rhyme scheme. The perfect integration of this particular line of verse illustrates the perfection of that which was born and of the redemption wrought by him, in contrast to the imperfection which must needs be found in the type, that is, in him who descended from "*Assaracs* line", a king associated with the earthly cities of Troy and Rome.

In Spenser's poem it is England rather than Rome which is the empire called into being by the will of God, and Arthur sees it because he reads the signs correctly, and his perception of the pattern leads to a vision of future glory. In Dante and Spenser as in the Old Testament the proper understanding of the past leads to a vision of the future. What the types foreshadow is revealed in perfect clarity with the coming of Christ, the antitype. As Reeves explains, what Dante perceived was "a second 'right moment' in future time which would, in some sense, parallel that first 'right moment' under Augustus." A "limited, but real earthly beatitude" found under "a true Roman rule" is envisaged at the end of the *Convivio*,[49] and a similar vision fires Arthur. What makes the historical prophecies of Joachim of Fiore even more interesting than those of Dante is his strong hostility to the Church of Rome and the papacy. Joachim posited two turning-points within the course of history: the incarnation and, just ahead in time, the full manifestation of the Holy Spirit and, with this manifestation, a spiritual *renovatio*. Joachim of Fiore anticipates Spenser in making his system of concords between sacred and profane history depend on the number 42. Like Augustine's *City of God*, he traces a negative line consisting of 42 generations and a positive line based on the same number. The negative line takes us from Cain to Babylon and from there to Rome as the second Babylon. The positive concord posits an alignment between David and Constantine: "David exalted the first Jerusalem, and forty-two generations later Constantine the Great exalted the New Jerusalem, that is, the Church."[50] Dante showed his high regard for Joachim when he placed him among the blessed spirits (*Paradiso* XII.139–41), and interestingly enough next to Hrabanus Maurus. Dante must clearly have admired them both for the way in which they saw how the great biblical numbers actually shape the course of history, whether sacred or profane.

Spenser seems to have shared the belief in a second "right moment" just ahead in history; it is surely this moment that Arthur foresees when he exclaims "How brutish is it not to understand"; because he himself perceives the true pattern, he is "quite ravisht with delight" (x.69). What we as readers are supposed to understand is probably that the first coming of Arthur (at the point where the record breaks off) heralds his second coming in the reign of

Queen Elizabeth. As Nohrnberg reminds us, Elizabeth was often identified with Arthur and praised as Arthur returned. Also she was compared to Solomon and other Old Testament characters: Hakluyt does this in the Epistle Dedicatory to the *Navigations*, and Foxe in his *Acts and Monuments*.[51] It is a neat device to let Arthur's perception of his own coming constitute a prophecy of the second historical turning-point represented by Gloriana/Elizabeth in whom the sacred and the profane meet and merge to renovate the nation and perhaps the world. We are given to understand what this entails on reading the Elfin chronicle, where a state of perfect harmony is retained and even extended to other territories in the course of 700 generations; as Bongo explains, 700 represents the reign of a just king. Each chronicle, then, reaches the same end, but by different paths: in the one we see through a veil, darkly, in the other face to face. It is worth recalling that the basic principle of typology, as explained by Jean Daniélou, is that there is "an imperfect order which prepares for and prefigures an order of perfection."[52] By setting up concords between profane and sacred history, like Joachim of Fiore, Spenser appropriates for the former the typological power of the latter. Just as Abraham prefigures redemption from the brutish state of sin, so does Brutus who plants the seeds of civilization and of faith. The analogies revealed by typology bestow "as it were the signature of God on his work,"[53] and this signature is seen most clearly in the unified structure which reflects the unity of God. The structure proves that England has taken over the role as God's chosen nation under Elizabeth as divinely appointed ruler – a latter-day Davidic queen.

Spenser offers his homage to Elizabeth directly in stanzas x.1–3, at whose centre he affirms that, although her lineage "from earth it be derived right, / Yet doth it selfe stretch forth to heavens hight, / And all the world with wonder overspred" (x.2 : 4–6, i.e. the exact textual centre of x.1–3). To each side of this passage are descriptions of ascent (of the "lowly verse" to "highest skies") and descent (of the "heavenly lay" to the earthly poet), while the beginning and the end stress the need for adornment: "Who now shall give unto me words and sound, / Equall unto this haughty enterprise?" (x.1 : 1–2). The answer is given in the last few lines: Jove's learned daughters, so he hopes, will impart to him lofty notes "To decke my song withall" (x.3 : 7–8). A circle of perfection, then, joins the lowest and the highest, and this union is the perfect pattern for the tempering which is the subject of Book II.

This structural analysis of Book II, whether of individual cantos or the book as a whole, shows yet again how complex and carefully planned the structures are; their precision is remarkable. We must not rest content, therefore, with vague generalizations of the kind offered, for example, by René Graziani, who argues that "Irascible passions dominate the earlier cantos (while the latter ones are given over to concupiscence: this is the basic thematic structure of the book)."[54] If we list the exponents of these basic passions, we observe that lust is featured at the beginning, middle, and end of the book as a whole, while wrath occupies equivalent positions of emphasis in the graded arrangement (see Diagram VI.41). Amavia's fate holds our attention in the second half of canto i; at the centre, in cantos vi and vii, Phædria and Mammon appeal to man's concupiscence, and Phædria is encountered again in canto xii. However, in this concluding canto it is of course Acrasia bending over Verdant who presents the climactic image of lust. Divided as it is between one episode involving wrath and another involving lust, canto i is the point of departure also for cantos i–viii. Guyon tempers his wrath when he honours the truth of Redcrosse's badge; he redeems Phedon from the madness of his fury in canto iv and overcomes and pacifies Pyrochles in canto v. However, in canto viii Pyrochles is so consumed by wrath that he rejects Arthur's offer of grace. Cantos xi–xii are equally framed by actions prompted by wrath: the "raskall rout" attack Alma's Castle in ix.12–17 (and continue their attack in canto xi) and in canto xii Guyon's righteous wrath is fully displayed as he destroys Acrasia's Bower. Another link too deserves attention: at ix.15 the rabble rout are said to be "idle shades; / For though they bodies seeme, yet substance from them fades." This lack of substance, or of reality, is of course the oustanding characteristic of Acrasia's Bower as well; it presents what Augustine calls "painted banquets" incapable of providing satisfaction.[55]

The basic thematic movement of Book II is from tempering via rejection to expulsion or annihilation (see Diagram VI.42). In canto i Guyon tempers his own wrath and tries to temper Amavia's grief; in canto ii he preserves his patience on discovering the theft of his horse and subsequently he assists Medina in imposing concord on her household. In cantos vi–vii the only proper response to events is rejection: Guyon cannot "overcome" Phædria or Mammon. The world with all its seductiveness will always be there, but once its true nature has been perceived it can be rejected in favour of worthier ends and "another blis."[56] Agents of destruction are another

Diagram VI.41 *The Faerie Queene* II, the Symmetrical and the Graded Structure: Points of Emphasis

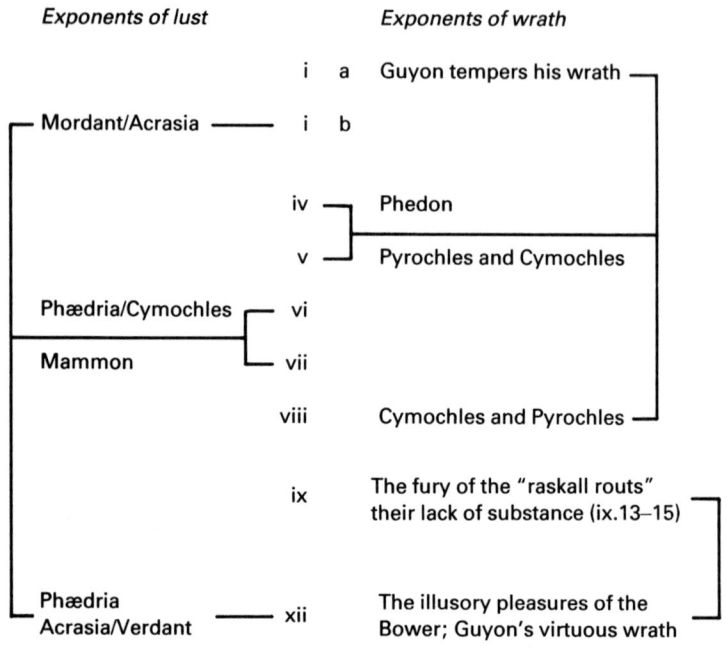

The two episodes of canto i display wrath caused by deceit, and the deaths of Mordant and Amavia caused by Acrasia. Deceit is responsible also for Phedon's wrath (iv), but Pyrochles, having no cause, nevertheless seeks occasion (iv–v) (like Archimago in canto i) and grasps it eagerly when presented in canto viii, through Guyon's "mischaunce". The pattern formed by lust begins with the story of Mordant and Acrasia (i), continues with Phædria and Mammon (vi–vii), and concludes with Phædria, Acrasia, and Verdant (xii). The last four cantos are circumscribed by contrasting pictures of fury: that of the insubstantial, shadow-like "raskall routs" outside the Castle of Alma, and that of Guyon as he destroys the Bower of Bliss with all its deceptive and insubstantial pleasures.

The overall structure places lust at the points of emphasis, the graded arrangement wrath.

matter; these must themselves be destroyed if we are to achieve the temperance which is but another name for peace. As Diagram VI.42 shows, the double centre is framed by cantos featuring intemperance in the persons of Pyrochles and Cymochles; on juxtaposing cantos iv and ix we see the difference between madness and health, while folly and wisdom are contrasted in cantos iii and x.

Diagram VI.42 *The Faerie Queene* II, the Three Phases – Tempering, Rejection, Expulsion

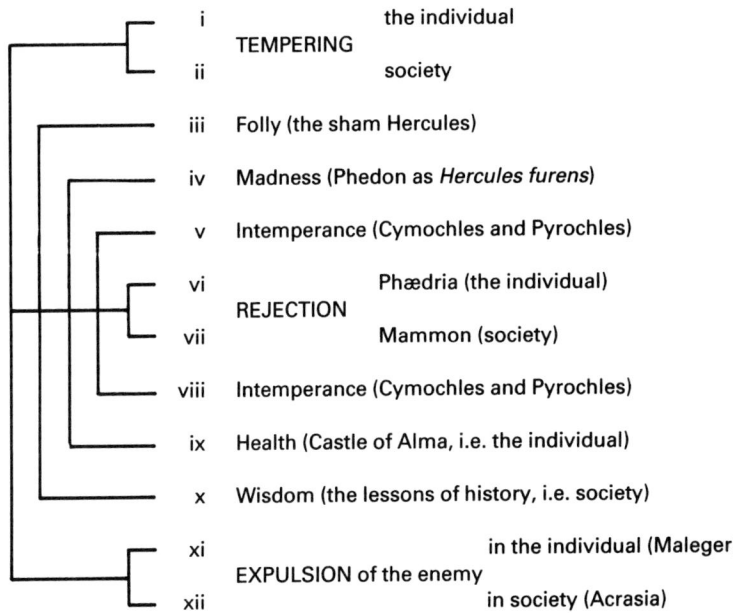

The pattern is consistently one of proceeding from the individual to society (or the family as the basis of society). Guyon tempers his wrath in canto i when he honours the badge on his opponent's shield, and in the Castle of Medina we witness the tempering of extremes in Medina's household. In canto vi Guyon rejects the temptation offered by Phædria, in contrast to Cymochles who accepts it joyfully, while in canto vii the temptations offered by Mammon relate to society (wealth, honour, rank). When Arthur overcomes Maleger in canto xi, it is man's intrinsic enemy who is destroyed (the misrule which leads to death), while the destruction, by Guyon, of the Bower of Bliss is a destruction of that which destroys the family and hence society as a whole.

On each side of the cantos of rejection are displays of intemperance; cantos iv and ix contrast madness and health, just as the folly of Braggadocchio (iii) contrasts with the wisdom sought by Arthur and Guyon in the chronicles of the past and the consequent predictions for the future (x).

The exponent of wrath, Pyrochles, proceeds from folly (canto v) to madness (canto viii) and so to death. Just as the basis of madness is folly, the basis of wisdom (x) is health (ix).

A subtle link between these cantos is discovered on comparing the description of Belphœbe (iii.22–31) with the opening stanzas to the queen in canto x. Just as the queen mediates between Heaven and Earth, so does Belphœbe, whose eyes are "Kindled above at th'heavenly makers light," and whose speech "heavenly musicke seemd to make" (iii.23 : 2 and 24 : 9). Belphœbe in her turn is served by the lower creation: "salvage beastes" are overcome by her, and winds and flowers court her as she rushes through the forest, like Botticelli's Primavera wrapped in "fresh leaves and blossomes" (iii.29–30). Like the "soveraine Queene" (x.3 : 9) Belphœbe tempers Heaven and Earth, thus ensuring their consonance. In Belphœbe temperance manifests itself in her advocacy of heroic virtue rather than pleasure-seeking sloth; as a consequence, virtue is given a partly heavenly and partly heroic ambience. Her perfection finds its analogue in the perfection of the Elfin emperors and their nation. Since Guyon himself is an Elf, this perfection must be his by nature, which is surely one reason why he experiences no fall, unlike Redcrosse knight.

The structural parallels between Books I and II are no doubt largely responsible for the widespread feeling that Guyon, too, must suffer a fall followed by redemption through grace. To impose such a pattern entails giving a negative interpretation to events prior to canto viii. Thus one reader argues that Guyon leaves "the Palmer behind to board Phædria's 'little Gondelay' (vi.2) on the Idle Lake, although her idle mirth offends him."[57] But the text describes, quite simply, how Guyon enters the boat to be ferried across: "himselfe she tooke a boord, / But the *Blacke Palmer* suffred still to stond," and nothing Guyon can say or do can make her change her mind. It is impossible for Guyon to leave the boat once he has entered, "For the flit barke, obaying to her mind, / Forth launched quickly, as she did desire" (vi.19–20). In short, this is as neat an act of kidnapping as was ever seen, and the idle mirth is perceived by Guyon only after he has become an unwilling captive. Even the encounter with Furor and Occasion has been given a negative import by arguing that Guyon avoids "a direct confrontation with Furor by binding Occasion, perhaps because such a course is congenial to his natural human preference for a quiet life."[58] But it is useless to attack Furor, as the Palmer explains, since it is his mother who is "the root of all wrath and despight" (iv.10). One tames Furor by removing Occasion. It is Guyon's nature, as an Elf, to be quick and active – Spenser himself explains the etymology (II.x.71 : 1–2). Guyon is no lazy and cowardly braggart, but a true *exemplar virtutis*. Maurice

Evans rightly calls Guyon "one of the great masters of reality" who "sees things as they really are."[59] It is particularly important to see when persons (or the concepts they embody) are empty and vain, or when apparent strength is borrowed from another. Furor has no power of his own, so that he is deflated the moment that the cause (Occasion) is eliminated. In this respect he resembles the rabble rout who are but "idle shades" (ix.15): "For though they bodies seeme, yet substance from them fades." Phædria's mirth is vain and empty, just as the offers of "grace" extended by Mammon are equally lacking in true substance. These offers resemble the golden apples in the garden of Proserpine. He who is beguiled by these false shows is consumed as if by fire, as we learn on reading Guyon's account of the termination of the first, happy age by the discovery of gold and silver: 'then avarice gan through his veines inspire / His greedy flames, and kindled life-devouring fire" (vii.17). Avarice, then, is as much a life-devouring fire as the wrath which consumes Pyrochles at the end of canto vi. Since happiness is the consequence of temperance, and since temperance depends on seeing things truly so as to make the right choices, Guyon must needs be a master of reality. Conversely, this is why Mammon and Acrasia are past masters of the art of deception. Guyon recognizes, and so dismisses, their illusions.

We see things truly when the head is in command of the body. The connection between body and mind (or soul) is reflected in the rhymes of stanzas ix.21 (on the body) and ix.47 (on the head). The bricks in the castle wall are made from "Ægyptian slime, / Whereof King *Nine* whilome built *Babell* towre," while the turret which is the head resembles "that heavenly towre, / That God hath built for his owne blessed bowre." In other words, the body prone to sin and destined to decay nevertheless may be inhabited by heavenly powers. One of these is the man of "infinite remembrance", who recalls the wars of "King *Nine*, / Of old *Assaracus*, and *Inachus* divine" (ix.56). The reference to Assaracus recurs in the stanza on the arrival of Brutus in England; Brutus, "anciently deriv'd / From royall stocke of old *Assaracs* line", redeems the country from its brutish inhabitants, "borne of her own native slime" (x.9). Brutus becomes a new head so that the body may be purified from its filth, and in due course the earthly head is supplanted by Christ, the heavenly king (x.50). Verbal repetitions strengthen the links between stanzas ix.21 and x.9 and 50: the rhyme words *slime* and *time* (ix.21) are repeated as *time* / *slime* (x.9) and *slime* / *time* (x.50). The purpose of these parallels is to make us perceive the analogy: the body relates to its head as the body politic to its head, and the relationship is a true one as long as the head accommodates Christ as our ultimate head. The temperate body and the temperate society depend on the heavenly powers in that turret, which reflects the glory of God's own "bowre". The Christian message is plain and emphatic. But for the providential arrival of Brutus and, 42 stanza-generations later, of the incarnate Lord, the state of original corruption would have prevailed. Conversely, temperance is the consequence of God's providential scheme.

Yet another thematic link is perceived on considering the topos of the *cunning web*. At i.8 Archimago is said to "weave a web of wicked guile," and Acrasia is captured by means of a "subtile net" forged by the Palmer (xii.81). Mammon's cave is covered by Arachne's "cunning web" and "subtile net" (vii.28), and the veil covering Acrasia's body in canto xii constitutes a similar covering: "More subtile web *Arachne* cannot spin" (xii.77:7). Acrasia, then, is connected with Archimago and with Mammon by means of this image: like Archimago, Acrasia has magic power, and her lust is complemented by Mammon's avarice. Both are a life-consuming fire. Other links between cantos vii and xii enable us to understand the relationship between Mammon and Acrasia. Creatures of ill omen are present in both (vii.23 and xii.36), and so are carcases (vii.30 and xii.7), and deceptive beauty "wrought by art and counterfetted shew" (vii.45 and xii.50). In the garden of Proserpine

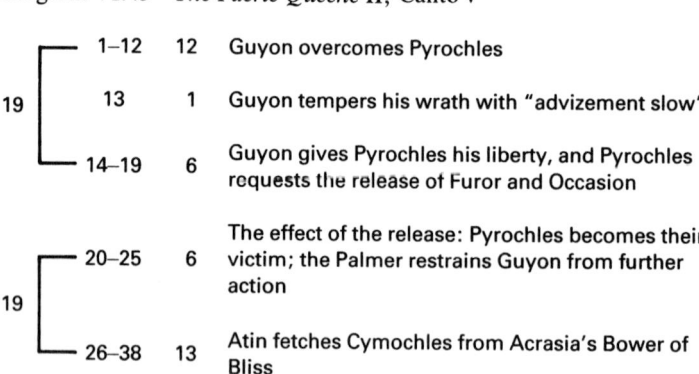

Diagram VI.43   *The Faerie Queene* II, Canto v

Stanzas 1–19 divide into 12—1—6, where stanza 13 is the pivotal stanza on Guyon who tempers his wrath. The ratio 2:1 expresses the harmony established by Guyon.
    The number 19 (twice repeated) again has evil connotations, as in Tasso.

the golden apples are counterfeit (vii.53–54), and so is the fruit of "burnisht gold" in Acrasia's Bower (xii.55 : 1–2).

Symbolic numbers and ratios assist the interpretation in Book II as much as in Book I, or even more so. Canto v on the temptation to wrath (see Diagram VI.43) may be divided into 13—6—6—13 stanzas, or into 19—19, so that the number of evil (19) occurs twice. This unpropitious number occurs in canto xii as well, where the descriptions of the Bower and of its destruction occupy 19 stanzas each (xii.50–68 and 69–87). Canto vi on the temptation to lust and sloth divides into 25—1—25 stanzas (see Diagram VI.44), where the pivotal 26th stanza describes how Guyon tempers "fond desire". At each halfway point are contrasting pictures: Cymochles enjoys "carelesse ease" at vi.13, and at vi.39 an enraged Atin showers abuse on Guyon, who nevertheless retains his composure (vi.40). Temperance, then, is at the centre, flanked by extremes of sloth and wrath. This almost emblematic sequence recalls the similar structure of canto i in Book I. The structural number 25 may be taken to represent the number of the 5 senses squared to indicate firmness of addiction to the world of sense. The action of the last group of 25 stanzas subdivides into 11—3—11 (see Diagram VI.44), so that the episodes of Cymochles on Phædria's island (vi.27–37) and of the

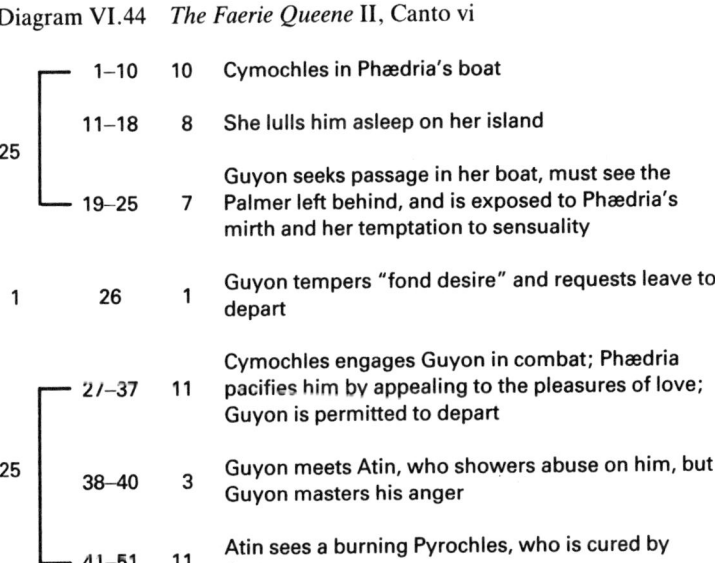

Diagram VI.44   *The Faerie Queene* II, Canto vi

		1–10	10	Cymochles in Phædria's boat
25		11–18	8	She lulls him asleep on her island
		19–25	7	Guyon seeks passage in her boat, must see the Palmer left behind, and is exposed to Phædria's mirth and her temptation to sensuality
1		26	1	Guyon tempers "fond desire" and requests leave to depart
		27–37	11	Cymochles engages Guyon in combat; Phædria pacifies him by appealing to the pleasures of love; Guyon is permitted to depart
25		38–40	3	Guyon meets Atin, who showers abuse on him, but Guyon masters his anger
		41–51	11	Atin sees a burning Pyrochles, who is cured by Archimago

burning Pyrochles (vi.41–51) are based on the number of transgression; the action of going beyond, or exceeding, is rendered by means of the number 11. In strong contrast, the structure of canto xi features the number of redemption; its 49 stanzas divide into 16 on the attack by Maleger's forces on the Castle of Alma and 33 on Arthur's fight with Maleger. These 33 stanzas have the decisive turning-point at their centre, where Arthur, assisted by divine grace, breaks his "caitive bands". This event takes place in stanza 33, so that the number of redemption occurs twice.

Throughout Books I and II we have observed how the structural divisions created by the events are supported by verbal repetitions, and especially by groups of identical rhyme words. A final example may be offered from the "Two Cantos of Mutabilitie", where the 18 stanzas on Dan Faunus, who contrives to see Diana naked (VII.vi.38–55), are remarkable for the precision with which identical rhyme words mark the beginning, middle, and end (see Diagram VI.45). Each half of the tale is framed by identical rhymes and this is true also of the tale as a whole. The tale begins with the description of Arlo Hill where Diana bathes in the river; at the textual centre Dan Faunus has the blissful vision which makes him laugh and so reveal his presence; the tale concludes with the curse Diana bestows on the place as she leaves it for ever. It has been observed that in this episode Dan Faunus is a "disorderly manifestation of erotic energy" in strong contrast to Nature's voluntary fertility; his "voyeuristic intrusion on the 'privity' of Diana's godhead re-enacts the disruptive violence of lust in a harmless and therefore comic mode."[60] Dan Faunus, then, repeats the role he acted in the interpolated tale of the virgin well (II.ii.3–11), when his excessive lust caused Diana's nymph to become stony cold with fear. In this earlier tale though, the mode is tragic and not comic. Whether comic or tragic, however, Dan Faunus is clearly affiliated with Acrasia.

This structural bias manifests itself even in such an unlikely place as the dedicatory sonnets prefaced to *The Faerie Queene*. The sixteen unnumbered sonnets are arranged in strict accordance with heraldic rules for precedence,[61] at the same time that they display central accent with recessed symmetry (see Diagram VI.46). Thematic and verbal links connect sonnets 1–2, 8–9, and 15–16. Sonnets 1 and 2 are addressed to men who have carried "the burdein of this kingdom" (1 : 10 and 2 : 4) and managed its "grave affaires" (1 : 5 and 2 : 2). Sonnets 8–9 honour two men who have protected the realm against external and internal enemies; each has a worthy place in the pageant created by the poet (8) and in the favour of the

Diagram VI.45 *The Faerie Queene* VII, Two Cantos of Mutabilitie: The Tale of Dan Faunus (vi.38–55)

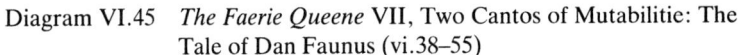

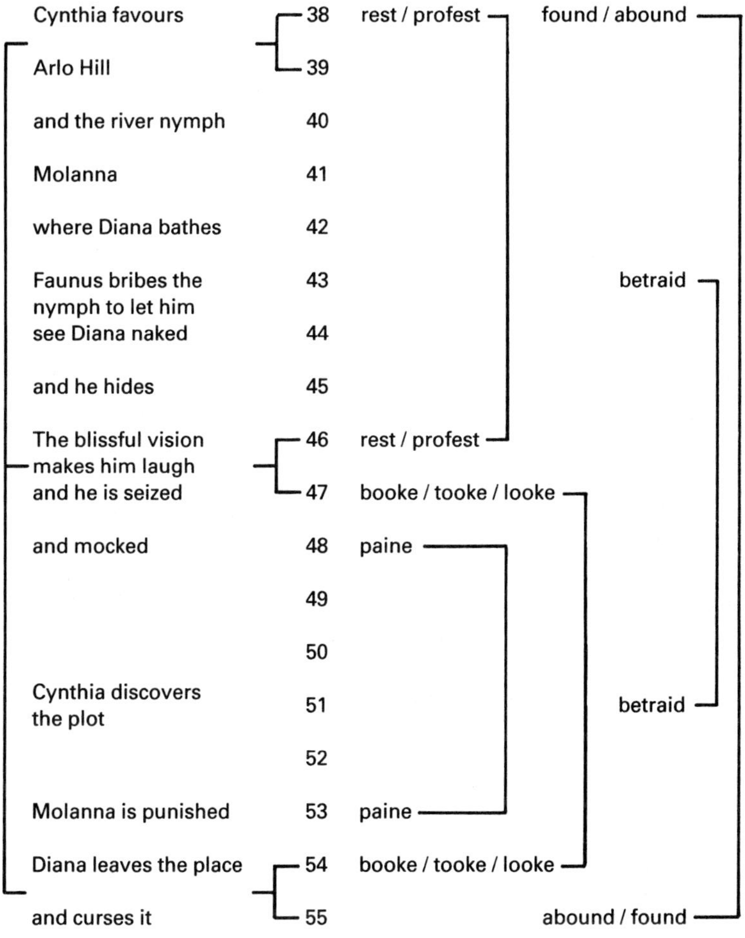

queen (9). The "pageant" concludes with two sonnets addressed to noble ladies, whose function it is to adorn the family and the court with their "heavenly grace" (15 : 12 and 16 : 7). A seventeenth sonnet addressed "To all the gratious and beautifull Ladies in the Court" seems to have been an afterthought, since it is printed after an empty space.

The sonnets in between 1–2, 8–9, and 15–16 focus on the poet's art. Sonnets 3 and 4, and 13 and 14, display an ambiguous attitude to

Diagram VI.46 *The Faerie Queene*, the Structure of the Dedicatory Sonnets

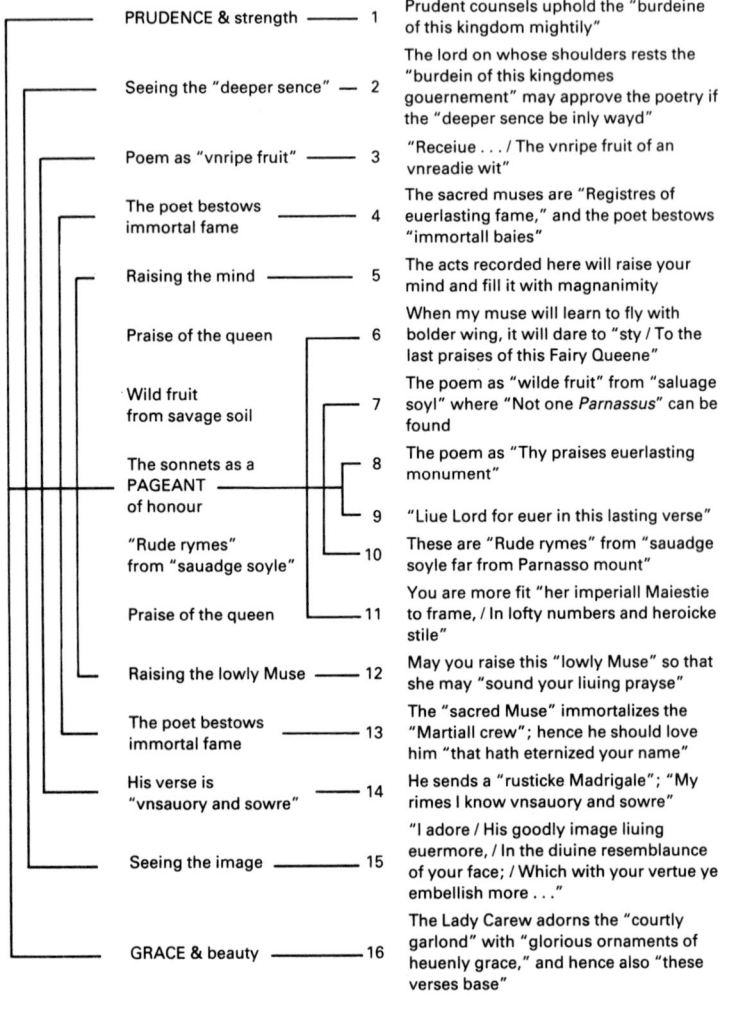

the poet's achievement: on the one hand his verse is "unripe fruit" (3:2), "unsavoury and sowre" (14:8), but on the other hand it may bestow immortality (4 and 13). In sonnets 7 and 10 the rudeness of the verse is again the subject: the poetry is "wilde fruit" from "salvage soyl" (7), and "Rude rymes" from "savage soyle" (10). In the central sonnets, however, the poem affords an "everlasting monument" (8 : 12), and the poet exhorts his dedicatee to live "for ever in this lasting verse" (9 : 13). The topos of elevation links sonnets 5–6 and 11–12: the mind and the muse will be elevated, especially when the subject is the Faery Queen (6) and "her imperiall Majestie" (11).

The careful patterning turns the sonnets into a sequence which must be perceived as such to be properly appreciated. The many repetitious statements serve a structural purpose which must be honoured. What seems like a series of compliments to named invididuals, resolves itself into a beautifully arranged pageant in honour of the two queens who are one and the same. The idea of the pageant unifies the dedicatory sonnets as that of the 12 months does *The Shepheardes Calender*, or the 24 hours the *Epithalamion*.

5. Concluding Remarks

The extent to which Spenser's narrative is shaped by pure logic comes as a surprise. Pure logic dictates the choice of concepts and the analysis to which they are submitted, but the fact that they are so fully dramatized has served to obscure the logical framework. Accustomed as we are to believing that the structure follows the thought, it is difficult to adjust to the idea that the thought follows a preconceived structure. Yet it cannot be doubted that Books I and II of *The Faerie Queene*, like Tasso's epic, are based on a conceptual grid, and that our understanding of the allegory is substantially assisted by a study of this grid. Many of Spenser's structures have much in common with Aristotle's triple formula of defect—mean—excess; some render it with great exactness, as in the case of canto I.i, where rashness, proper action, and sloth are featured at the points of structural emphasis. Other structures may have more purely Christian connotations at the same time that the triple formula is distinctly present. A pivotal centre which reaches back to the beginning and forward to the end in a way functions like the central unit in the number 3, which constantly pulls the flanking extremes toward itself, like Medina between her two sisters and their knights in canto II.ii. In this way a circle is formed around the centre, and this circle-with-a-centre is the iconographical symbol of the golden mean. In much the same way beginnings and ends (and points equidistant from them) are pulled to the centre, which is like a knot that ties the whole fabric together. No wonder, therefore, that Spenser seems to have begun Book VII with cantos vi and vii (the Mutability cantos), since this is where we may find the source of the book's unity.

Those who are repelled by the idea of preconceived structures ought to consider how complex and pliable they are; my survey of textual structures in Book I illustrates this point, and so do the intricate patterns of some of the cantos in Book II. The main source of complexity is no doubt the coexistence of arrangements in the ratios 1 : 1 (symmetry) and 2 : 1. The double focus provided by the double structure is a basic aesthetic requirement: it prevents structural monotony, and it multiplies the points of structural emphasis. It must not be forgotten that this technique of playing off one structure against the other is present from the very beginning, as witnessed by Augustine's *Confessions* and the Latin rhymed poem on the cross attributed to Bonaventura. One interesting variation consists in placing a textual unit as a pivotal centre, as in the division of the 13 books of the *Confessions* into a sequence of 8—1—4 books. This formula is essential when the number of units is even; thus Tasso's 20 books divide into 12—2—6, while Spenser's canto II.ii divides into 30—1—15 stanzas. It is a structural *tour de force* that Spenser in Book I of *The Faerie Queene* created extended centres for both structures – the symmetrical and the graded arrangement – so that they can be computed mathematically by counting the number of stanzas. Tasso did this in the symmetrical structure of the *Jerusalem Delivered*, but not in the graded arrangement. The halfway points between a beginning and the middle and between the middle and the end also may be ascertained in the same way, as we have seen. In fact, it is often these halfway points that, together with the centre, form the thematic triple progression which is so poetically effective. The principle is applied not only to a whole book, but to individual cantos as well (cf. I.i).

The pliability caused by the complexity and by the presence of so many options facilitates revisions of a finished text, at the same time that it becomes possible to compose in piecemeal fashion rather than in a straight sequence. The larger the scale of the poem, the more useful the principle, and for a blind poet it would have been indispensable. Indeed, a preconceived pattern encourages piecemeal composition; the alignment between the Fradubio episode and the account of Redcrosse's combat with the dragon bespeaks a similar alignment in the process of composing, and the same is true of the cantos on the false and the true House of Holiness (I.iii and x); the many parallels and contrasts suggest a comparative compositional procedure, if not a simultaneous one. Such a procedure makes it possible for widely spaced stanzas to echo each other, as in the case of the two crowning episodes at I.i.48 and xii.8, one of the false Una and the other of Una herself after Redcrosse's victory. Since linkage, then, is such a basic compositional technique, it must also be a basic reading technique. Spotting the links is often a matter of seeing the spirit rather than the letter, or ascending from a situation or episode to the concepts it dramatizes. Such a process is of course mandatory in passages of a clearly emblematic kind, like the two crownings just referred to, but a semi-emblematic character is felt on many occasions; hence the pictorial character of so much of Spenser's poetry. In short: the best way to reach an understanding of Spenser's allegory is to perceive the conceptual grid or pattern which informs it. Renaissance allegory, it would seem, owes a great deal – perhaps its very existence – to the compositional method analyzed in these pages.

Notes to Chapter VI

1. James Nohrnberg. *The Analogy of The Faerie Queene* (Princeton, NJ, 1976), p. 22 refers to "Tasso's reluctance to drop this piece, despite advice to do so," and concludes that this fact "indicates that it may not be purely episodic after all."
2. Ibid., p. 21.
3. Augustine, *De musica* VI.xv.50–xvi.54. Temperance protects against the falls that depend on our free will.
4. Quotations are from Edmund Spenser, *The Faerie Queene*, ed. A. C. Hamilton (London, 1977). I have normalized the spelling of i/j and u/v.
5. Longinus, *On the Sublime*, tr. W. Hamilton Fyfe (London, 1927), 22.1.193, as cited by Roy T. Eriksen, *The Forme of Faustus Fortunes* (Oslo and New Jersey, 1987), pp. 208 f.
6. Anne Ferry, *The Art of Naming* (Chicago and London, 1988), pp. 148–50, discusses Spenser's catalogue of trees, but without seeing its relevance to the action: Spenser "makes no effort to associate the names imposed on nature with the characters' particular perspective, although poems of this period are often designed to reflect such reciprocity between the inward state of the observer and the landscape." But the connection is there in the trees that represent the earthly and the heavenly king and the betrayer Judas–Duessa. One may perhaps say, though, that the perspective is more that of the reader than of the characters. The potential harmony between the earthly and the heavenly realms points forward to the betrothal ceremony in canto xii. H. N. Davies adds the further pertinent comment in a written communication to me: "But the most dramatic give-away in the arrangement of the text is surely that each stanza ends with an ill-boding tree. The signal at the end of stanza 8 is ignored blindly. The journey into the 'shadie grove' (*very* shady) continues unchecked, and at the end of stanza 9 the warning is sounded again in the choice of the final item. Once again the signal is ignored. They are 'led with delight' through the catalogue (and through the wood) and pay no regard to the highlighting of the two trees that indicate danger. They rush ahead paying no attention to stanza division – i.e. inattention to *form* is rashness, and inattentive reading makes the reader share the thoughtlessness of the Redcrosse Knight and Una. Thus a lesson in prudence

is also a lesson in *reading*. We need to 'read' the text with its structural markers as they need to 'read' the wood."
7. Cassiodorus, *Expositio Psalmorum*, Corpus Christianorum Series Latina (Turnholt, 1958), p. 38.
8. Mark Rose, *Spenser's Art* (Cambridge, Mass., 1975), p. 14, as cited by A. C. Hamilton in the footnote on i.28 in his edition of *The Faerie Queene*.
9. On "Deniall" see below pp. 403 f.
10. Gunnar Qvarnström cites Bongo to this effect in his study of *The Enchanted Palace. Some Structural Aspects of Paradise Lost* (Stockholm, 1967), pp. 106–07. Bongo bases his exposition on commentaries on *Exodus* 32:28 and 1 *Corinthians* 10:8. Qvarnström argues that this symbolism applies to Christ's four symmetrically placed 23-line speeches on respectively Mercy, Justice, Justice, and Mercy. Reviewers, although struck by the aptness of the symbolism, could not accept this argument, since there was no precedent for such a usage. It is now possible to see that there is ample precedent in Spenser and also in Giles Fletcher. See my essay on "Golden Phrases: the Poetics of Giles Fletcher," *Studies in Philology* 88 (1991), 169–200.
11. Douglas Brooks-Davies, *Spenser's Faerie Queene. A Critical Commentary on Books I and II* (Manchester, 1977), pp. 71–72. Brooks-Davies lists classical and biblical passages on giants and other aspects of this episode. However, *Exodus* 19:16 and *Psalms* 18:7–8 and 18:13–14 ought to be included.
12. Iconographical representations of Mount Sinai wrapped in fire and smoke show that it is a type of Judgment Day, with which it is usually juxtaposed.
13. See my study of "Elaborate Song: Conceptual Structure in Milton's On the Morning of Christ's Nativity'," in *Fair Forms: Essays in English Literature from Spenser to Jane Austen*, ed. M.-S. Røstvig (Cambridge, 1975), especially pp. 61–62.
14. Ibid., pp. 62–63.
15. One unrhymed line (113) denounces those members of the Church who live in "ease and sensualitie", and the failure to achieve linkage through rhyme reflects their failure to be proper members. They cut themselves off from the Church by their intemperance. The second unrhymed line admits that we "die (as much as can immortall creature)." Man's immortality makes him unique among all created beings, and the lack of rhyme therefore expresses this uniqueness. See my essay on " 'Figures and Numbers': On the Poetics of George Chapman," in *Dikt og Idé*, ed. Sverre Dahl (Oslo: Institute of Germanic Studies in the University of Oslo, 1981), pp. 88–104.
16. Line 114 is unrhymed ("Once more the fleeting Soul came back") to express the failure of the "fleeting Soul" to achieve a proper integration with the body. The sound of the last word – *back* – is so emphatic that the absence of rhyme, even within the loose Pindaric form, becomes obtrusive.
17. Quotations are from James Thomson, *The Complete Poetical Works* (London: Oxford University Press, 1951).
18. See James E. Phillips, "Renaissance Concepts of Justice and the Structure of *The Faerie Queene*, Book V," *The Huntington Library Quarterly* 33 (1970), 103–20. Queen Elizabeth's punitive actions were described as acts of Mercy.
19. On the militant aspect of temperance, see Joan Warchol Rossi, "*Briton Moniments*: Spenser's Definition of Temperance in History," *English Literary Renaissance* 15 (1985), 42–58. In iconographical representations of Temperance she may be seen to carry a burning iron in one hand and a bowl of water in the other. Warchol Rossi refers to an earlier study by Peter D. Stambler, "The Development of Guyon's Christian Temperance, "*English Literary Renaissance* 7 (1977), 51–89, where temperance and violence are reconciled, and she herself concludes that "Both Guyon and Arthur are engaged in active and violent quests whose goal is the destruction, not merely the avoidance, of evil" (p. 46). The "destruction of evil is the first task of Temperance/Governance" (p. 49).

20. See Hamilton's gloss on this stanza, and see the article in *The Spenser Encyclopedia*, ed. A. C. Hamilton (Toronto, 1990) on "Guyon" and on Book II.
21. Ronald Arthur Horton, *The Unity of The Faerie Queene* (Athens, Ga., 1978), p. 68.
22. Ibid., pp. 100–101.
23. Pierre de la Primaudaye describes Temperance as carrying a knife; see below.
24. Horton, *The Unity of The Faerie Queene*, pp. 68 f.
25. See Oliver Steele, "Review Article: Recent Editions of the *Faerie Queene*," *Philological Quarterly* 59 (1980), 284–85.
26. See Francis Quarles, *Hierogliphikes of the Life of Man* (1637), Emblem 12.
27. Nohrnberg, *The Analogy of the Faerie Queene*, p. 287.
28. John Calvin, *Commentary on the Psalms* (London, 1965), Vol. I, p. 133 (on Psalm 11 : 7) and p. 143 (on Psalm 13 : 4). On the connection between righteousness and grace, see p. 308 on Psalm 26 : 6 ("some think that in these words David avouches the uprightness which he had used among men. But I think rather that he sets forth God's grace").
29. Ibid., pp. 230–31 and 249.
30. Peter de la Primaudaye, *The French Academie (1586)* (Hildesheim and New York: Georg Olms Verlag, 1972). The date of the French edition is 1580.
31. See David W. Burchmore, "The Medieval Sources of Spenser's Occasion Episode," *Spenser Studies* II (1981), 93–120. Occasion's specific attributes are those of Misfortune: "Spenser's Occasion is one *aspect* of Fortune, just as Impotence and Impatience are aspects of Occasion: she represents those specific instances of misfortune which give rise to wrath and despair" (p. 103). Burchmore cites Guyon's description of Fortune in canto ix (Fortune seldom "yields to vertue aide, / But in her way throwes mischiefe and mischaunce"; ix.8), and concludes that Occasion is "the personification of this kind of adverse fortune" and a cause of Phedon's affliction (p. 104). Stanza II.ix.8 therefore provides a link with the description of Occasion in canto iv.
32. G. Karl Galinsky, *The Herakles Theme. The Adaptations of the Hero in Literature from Homer to the Twentieth Century* (Oxford, 1972).
33. See my study of "*Tom Jones* and the Choice of Hercules" in *Fair Forms. Essays in English Literature from Spenser to Jane Austen*, ed. M.-S. Røstvig (Cambridge: D. S. Brewer Ltd., 1975), pp. 147–77 and 222–26.
34. In his description of Rosamond's vacillation between the claims of pleasure or honour (*The Complaint of Rosamond*, 1592), Samuel Daniel sets up an elaborate pattern of such verbal repetitions in inverse order. See my essay on "A Frame of Words: On the Craftsmanship of Samuel Daniel," *English Studies* 60 (1979), 122–37.
35. Burchmore, "Medieval Sources," p. 112 (Figure 5).
36. Galinsky, *The Herakles Theme*, p. 86.
37. Ibid., p. 190.
38. Alastair Fowler, *Spenser and the Numbers of Time* (London, 1964), p. 114.
39. Calvin, *Commentary on the Psalms*, Vol. I, pp. 200–01 (on *Psalms* 18 : 22) and p. 226 (on Psalm 19 : 10).
40. Ibid., pp. 183–84.
41. Ibid., p. 293 (on Psalm 25 : 15).
42. Ibid., p. 55 (on Psalm 4 : 4).
43. On the graces, see Edgar Wind, *Pagan Mysteries in the Renaissance* (Harmondsworth, 1967).
44. Augustine, *The Enchiridion on Faith, Hope and Love* (Chicago: Henry Regnery Company, 1966), section xxxii, p. 40.
45. My analysis of canto II.x was published in my essay on "Canto Structure in Tasso and Spenser," *Spenser Studies* I (1980), 177–200.
46. The details of Spenser's description of the giants are traditional; see, for example, Berosius, *Antiquitatum libri quinque, cum commentariis Joannis Annii*

Viterbensis (Antwerp, 1545). The tradition is discussed by Jean Céard, "La querelle des géants et la jeunesse du monde," *Journal of Medieval and Renaissance Studies* 8 (1978), 37–76.
47. Marjorie Reeves. "Dante and the Prophetic View of History," in *The World of Dante*, ed. Cecil Grayson (Oxford: The Clarendon Press, 1980), pp. 44–60.
48. Ibid., pp. 48 f.
49. Ibid., p. 49.
50. Ibid., p. 56.
51. Nohrnberg, *The Analogy of The Faerie Queene*, pp. 52 f.
52. Jean Daniélou, *From Shadows to Reality* (London: Burns & Oates, 1960), p. 31.
53. Ibid., p. 30.
54. René Graziani, in *The Spenser Encyclopedia*, p. 264, col. 2.
55. Augustine, *Of True Religion*, tr. J. H. S. Burleigh (Chicago: Henry Regnery Company, 1964), p. 95 (section li.100).
56. The rejection has been characterised as imperfect because on the "wrong footing" since Guyon has not "called out to God from the depths." The whole adventure "turns out inconclusively in the sense that his opponent is not defeated, thus precipitating the crisis of his faint which opens the door to an outrageous assault" (Graziani, *The Spenser Encyclopedia*, p. 266, col. 3, and p. 263, col. 2). Since Mammon is but another name for Satan, it is unreasonable to expect Guyon to defeat him.
57. Maurice Evans, "Guyon," *The Spenser Encyclopedia*, p. 343, col. 3.
58. Ibid., p. 343, col. 3.
59. Ibid., p. 344, col. 3.
60. David L. Miller, "Spenser's Vocation, Spenser's Career," *ELH. A Journal of English Literary History* 50 (1983), 221–22.
61. See Carol A. Stillman, "Politics, Precedence, and the Order of the Dedicatory Sonnets in *The Faerie Queene*," *Spenser Studies* 5 (1984), 132–48. Stillman concludes that the omission of seven sonnets from the first issue of the first edition "was due to some minor oversight of the printer, the poet, or an intermediary. The mistake was soon discovered and rectified by inserting the missing dedications in strict accordance with the heraldic rules for precedence" (p.,146). My analysis supports this conclusion.

Chapter VII

The Religious Sequence
Francis Quarles, *Emblemes* (1635)

> We must flie like Eagles, and our Rhimes
> Must mount to Heav'n ...
> Quarles, "The Invocation"

Quarles's *Emblemes* follow the Bible by beginning with the Fall and Satan's usurpation of power, and concluding with visions of the heavenly bridegroom and the heavenly Jerusalem. Does this mean that Quarles aimed at securing for his collection the structures attributed to the Bible or, perhaps even more so, to the Psalms in their capacity as a summary of the Bible? The fact that the 75 emblems relate to the 150 Psalms in the ratio 1 : 2 is highly suggestive. Our reading experience, however, seems to contradict any such supposition. Hence Barbara K. Lewalski has argued that Quarles's Catholic sources may show the Jesuit stages through purgation to illumination and unity, but that Quarles's Protestant bias forbade any kind of precise structuring. To the Protestant, "the spiritual life is not an ordered progress from penitence to contemplative ecstasy, but a much more uneven, uneasy and essentially episodic sequence of trials, temptations, failures, successes, and backslidings, until the end of life crowns all."[1] Such a statement ignores the strong Protestant emphasis on the role of Providence, manifested as much in the life of the individual as in the universal history of man. When George Herbert wrote his 38-stanza poem on "Providence", his point of departure is *Wisdom* 8 : 1, paraphrased with exactness::

> O Sacred Providence, who from end to end
> Strongly and sweetly movest, shall I write,
> And not of thee, through whom my fingers bend
> To hold my quill? shall they not do thee right?
>
> (ll. 1–4)

Nothing escapes God's command or permission:

> Nothing escapes them both; all must appeare,
> And be dispos'd, and dress'd, and tun'd by thee,
> Who sweetly temper'st all.[2]

(ll. 37–39)

As I show in Chapter VIII, Herbert accordingly "disposed" his own stanzas "sweetly" from "end to end" so as to reflect God's benevolent "tuning", and it is reasonable to relate the Protestant fondness for acrostics and similar witty devices to their faith in Providence. A strong rebuttal of Lewalski's view has come from K. J. Höltgen, who has shown that it is impossible to distinguish between Protestant and Roman Catholic religious emblems.[3] Ignoring, then, the unrewarding issue of Protestant versus Roman Catholic forms of piety in religious emblems, I propose instead to study the poems in order to assess the extent to which they possess structures associated with biblical exegesis and with Augustine.

As described in the *Confessions*, Augustine's life may be a record of sin and transgression, repentance and backsliding, but no one can see it as a meaningless see-saw pattern. Indeed, as seen in Chapter II Augustine's references to the hand of Providence are as many self-referring passages indicating the presence of pre-planned structures. Like his Catholic sources, Quarles was strongly influenced by the *Confessions*, nor can the Augustinian concept of an *ars aeterna* have been unknown to him. The prominence given to Augustine in both camps explains how it was possible for Protestants to ignore a distinction which otherwise assumed such importance.

The many quotations from the Bible favour the Psalms: no fewer than 21 emblems have mottoes that are direct quotations, and among the patristic sources cited are commentaries on the Psalms by Ambrose, Gregory, Augustine, and Cassiodorus. One emblem poem (III.xii) simply paraphrases the contents of the quotation from Augustine's comments on Psalm 30, but as a rule the connection is more oblique: a patristic passage may for example function as comment on the emblem poem (V.xv). As many as 34 emblems have quotations from Augustine, the most frequently cited works being the *Soliloquies* (nine), the sermons on the Psalms (six), and the *Confessions* (four).

The contents of Quarles's poems testify to his close reading of the *Confessions*, and particularly of the two books on Augustine's conversion, books 7 and 8. It is in these two books that Augustine finally achieves his transition from the world of Time (the number 7) to Eternity (the number 8), as in Psalms 7 and 8 of the Psalms of Ascent. Quarles's Emblem II.xiii echoes Augustine in its dramatisation of the reluctance with which worldly joys are dismissed, even after their empty and deceitful character has been understood. The speaker first denounces and renounces the world, but then regrets his decision and postpones his farewell. This is in effect Augustine's stand as he prays for chastity, "but not today" (*Conf.* 8:7). Augustine records how the most trifling things caused him to postpone his decision again and again: "they plucked softly at this fleshly garment, and spoke softly in mine ears: Canst thou thus part with us? And shall we no more accompany thee from this time for ever? ... Thinkst thou to be ever able to live without all that?" This is the whole subject of Emblem II.xiii, where the decision to bid the world farewell is undercut by equally seductive whispers: "For ever? O, to part so long? never / Meet more? Another year, and then for ever."[4] This is a question not so much of backsliding – although it is certainly that – as of dramatizing the slow growth of the new will until the fleshly will no longer exists. The struggle between the two occupies all of Quarles's Book IV, beginning with IV.i, and this struggle is of course the main issue of the *Confessions*, and especially of book 8.

Another theme which may create an impression of aimless recurrence is that of tears and grief. Its importance is indicated by the fact that Quarles places it at the beginning, middle, and end of Book III, and one reason for this repetition must be the need to establish this linkage. What we have, therefore, is not so much mere repetition (a "see-saw pattern") as a firm structural frame. We must take care to see this theme as marking the most important phase in the process of regeneration: God scourges the sinner, and this scourging is proffered grace, but to the sinner the pain seems intolerable. Hence he complains. When the sinner weeps, though, the victory is within sight, so that "the prayer for tears" is a prayer for re-birth.[5] The theme therefore defines a spiritual progress. Augustine explains how his own spiritual eyesight was gradually cleared by the "smart eye-salve of mine own wholesome dolours" (*Conf.* 7:8), and the closer he comes to his complete conversion, the worse his condition becomes: "My wonted unsettledness of mind grew more and more upon me; and I daily sent up sighs unto thee" (8:6). Feelings of grief keep increasing: "With what scourges of condemning sentences lashed I not mine own soul, to make it follow me, endeavouring now to go after thee! And it drew back, it refused, but gave no reason to excuse its refusal by" (8:7). This grief is the necessary prelude to the complete conversion of the will to God, and unless we bear this in mind we may see mere backsliding where, in fact, great spiritual progress is being made. When Quarles lets the affliction lead to complaint, the complaint is rebuked: man is "scourg'd for not repenting" (III.iv; the Epitaph). Augustine's account of his troubled heart finds its analogue in Emblem IV.xi. When the speaker seeks his bed after a fruitless quest, his rest is "poyson'd with th'extremes of grief and fear," but a sudden resolution occurs when, like Augustine, he turns from the outside world to the world within: looking down into his "troubled breast, / The Magazine of wounds, I found him there" (cf. *Conf.* 7:10; *intravi et vidi*). The final statement – that "Heav'n's form's a troubled heart" – must strongly modify our response to the expression of grief: the greater the grief, the closer to God. This very theme is repeated in the next emblem (IV.xii), but with a significant change in emphasis: spiritual progress is shown by devoting more lines to the positive aspect. The quest is equally long, fruitless, and painful, and, when the speaker again throws himself on his bed, his eyes overflow with tears, and tears are a sign of regeneration according to "The Farewell" ("With flouds of tears baptize / And drench these dry, these unregen'rate eyes"). As a consequence, "He that was sought, unfound, was found unsought." The last two stanzas dwell on the union consequent upon the finding. Quarles reverts to the theme of lamentation in IV.xv, but we must look to the Epigram for a proper evaluation: groans and tears are "Harmonious raptures in th'Almightie's ears." The Babylonian captivity which causes the exile to refuse to sing is an exile from Heaven and the state of innocence and hence proof of the exile's total commitment to what was lost. This it is which constitutes harmonious raptures, and this total commitment is a fitting prelude to Book V with its celebration of the union between God and man.

Reflections like these modify and even contradict our first impression of a see-saw pattern, and the contradiction is strengthened on considering the structure of individual books and of the work as a whole. Paradoxically enough, a spatial or panoramic reading is called for to perceive the linear progression.

The overall pattern can be sketched very briefly (see Diagram VII.1). We begin by observing the Fall and its consequence – the entry into the world of Sin and Death and discord even among the elements. In Emblem III.viii (the textual centre) the speaker desires to be dissolved in tears, as if in response to the statement, in

THE RELIGIOUS SEQUENCE 375

Diagram VII.1 *Emblemes*, Overall Structure

```
                    Title-page engraving shows a heart being crowned
        I.i         Eve accepts the fruit, and the soul turns away from
                    God
        I.ii        Enter Sin and Death
        I.iii       The sweets of Earth are "in fruition sowre"

        III.i       Grief and tears
        III.vi      Pleading for mercy: confession of guilt
        III.vii     The path is lost, but Christ is the light, the way,
                    and the life
        III.viii    Grief and tears. The speaker desires to be
                    dissolved
        III.ix      Snares are everywhere, but the soul seeks "thy
                    safe forrest"
        III.x       Pleading for mercy: confession of guilt
        III.xv      Grief and tears

        V.xiii      Everlasting joys preferred
        V.xiv       Exit Sin and Death
        V.xv        Return to God; the soul dissolves in the fire of
                    divine love
                    "The Farewell": a baptism of tears leads to the crown of life
```

"The Farewell", that dry eyes are unregenerate. At the end, Sin and Death are expelled, and the soul confronts its maker in an encounter marked by divine love. As the diagram shows, this overall pattern has been worked out with considerable care, and the placing of the topos of grief and tears in III.i, III.viii, and III.xv invests this sign of regeneration with appropriate emphasis. The system of linkage explains why the expulsion of Sin and Death and the vision of the heavenly Jerusalem should be placed in the penultimate position rather than as concluding climax; this placing ensures perfect balance between the entry of Sin and Death in I.ii and their exit in V.xiv. As we shall see, Milton too arranges the movements of Sin and Death so that they form part of a pattern of recessed symmetry, thus proving that even Satan and his minions are part of God's providential pattern.

In order to see the overall pattern more clearly, it is advisable to analyze individual books first.

Book I (see Diagram VII.2) has three main themes: the world's falsehood and deception, the absence of true weights and measures, and the overwhelming presence of rampant, bold-faced sin. These are arranged symmetrically around Emblem I.viii, which epitom-

Diagram VII.2 *Emblemes*, Book I. Deception, Confusion, and Discord

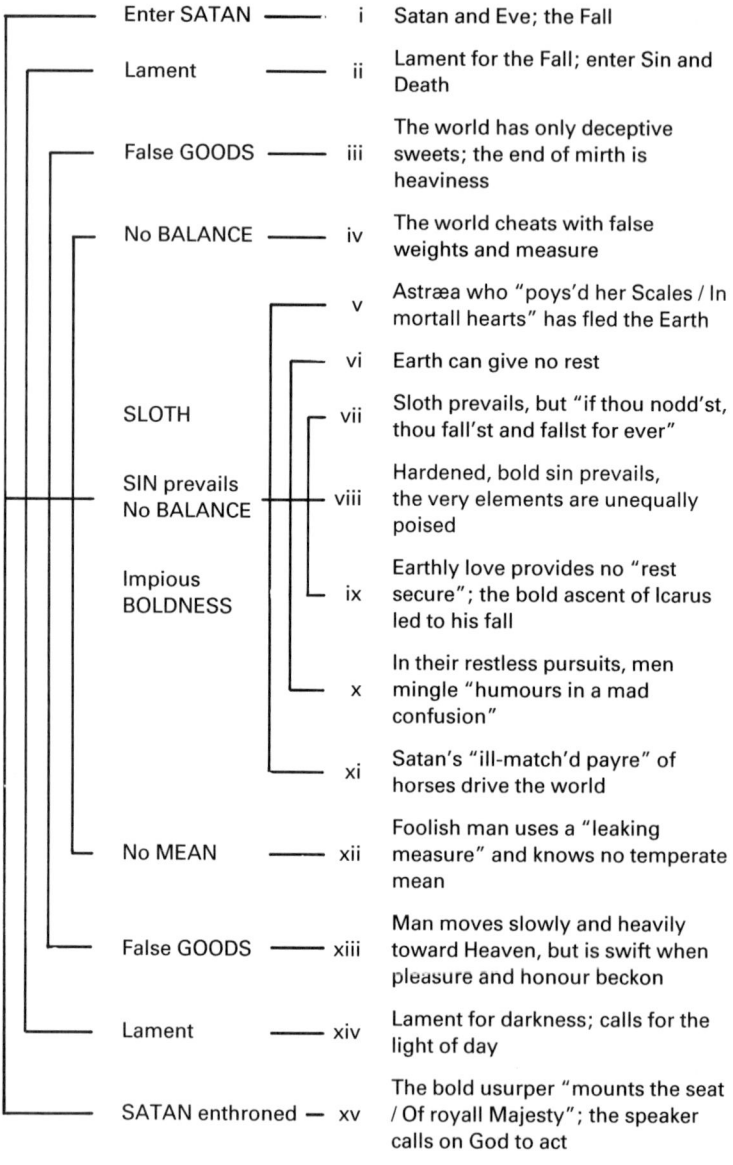

izes these themes in its vignettes of the seven deadly sins and its denunciation of "bold-fac'd Mortalles" who "Can sinne and smile, and make a sport of crimes, / Transgresse of custome, and rebell in ease." Through the "unequall poysing / Of ill-weigh'd Elements" all are distempered. The absence of proper balance is the theme also of Emblems iv/xii and v/xi so that, paradoxically enough, Book I is perfectly balanced by the recurrence of the topos of imbalance and absence of due weights and measure. As the quotation from Psalm 62:9 puts it, when "laid in the ballance, [the world] is altogether lighter then vanitie"; the "bold Impostour" has cheated man with his "false weights and measure, / Proclaiming bad for good" (I.iv), and the consequences are observed in I.xii. Foolish man is "never fill'd", but takes a surfeit where he should but taste: "Who strains beyond a mean draws in and gulps disease." Emblems I.v and xi share, in their biblical quotations, the topos of the "fashion of this world" which passes away, governed as it is by the "Prince of the aire". Just Astræa, who "poys'd her Scales / In mortall hearts," has fled the Earth (I.v), and in I.xi "this mad-brain world" is hurried on by Satan's "ill-match'd payre" of horses – a description which recalls Spenser's "yron wagon" of Night, whose "twyfold" team is an emblem of discord ("of which two blacke as pitch, / And two were browne, yet each to each unlich"; *Faerie Queene* I.v.28). Imbalance is featured in I.iii and xiii as well: the deceptive lightness of mirth ends in heaviness (I.iii), and extremes of swiftness and sloth mark man's progress (I.xiii). These extremes are shown also in the emblems that flank the centre (I.vii and ix). In the one, lustful sloth pays his idle vows at the shrine of Morpheus, and in the other the "brave sparks" disdain "to take their flight, / But on th'Icarian wings of babbling fame." This energy, however, is quickly spent and amounts to nothing.

The reign of sin as described in the centrally placed emblem harks back to the beginning (when Satan persuades Eve to taste the apple) and points forward to the end when he mounts "the seat / Of royall Majestie". An additional link between the middle and the end is found in the reference to God as the angry Thunderer: the hardened sinner respects neither the Thunderer nor his thunder (I.viii), but, when Satan ascends the throne, the speaker invites the great Thunderer to descend and punish the usurper: "Redresse, redresse our wrongs" (I.xv).

The pattern of harmonious balance makes a neat point: however imbalanced the world may be after the Fall, it is nevertheless part of

Diagram VII.3 *Emblemes*, Book II. The Great Antitheses

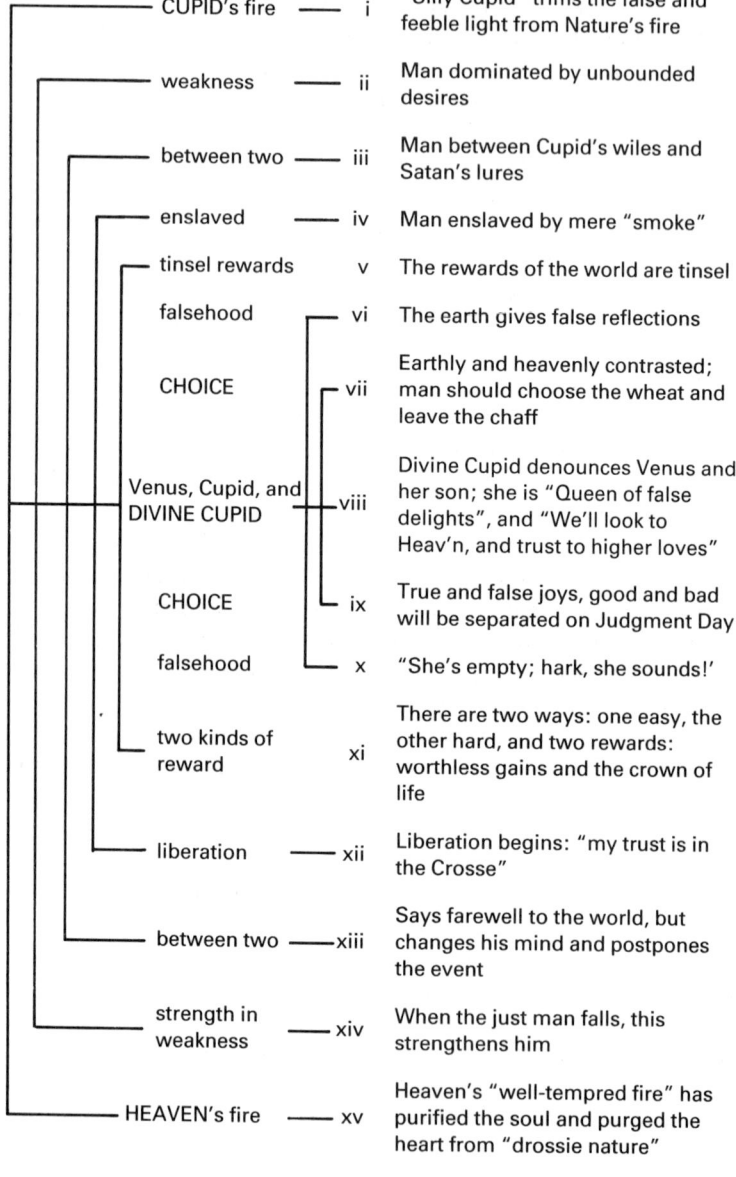

God's preordained plan. As Augustine pointed out in the *De libero arbitrio* (III.xi.113), God made all natures, whether good or bad: "He did not make them so that they might sin, but so that they might adorn the universe whether they will to sin or whether they do not so will." The balanced pattern, then, proves the power of the omnipotent Deity in the very book which shows Satan as triumphant ruler of a diseased world.

From this diseased world we turn, in Book II, to an examination of binary opposites. To false joys is opposed true felicity, to distemper Heaven's "well-temp'red fire" (see Diagram VII.3). The number of division dominates. Man is placed between Cupid's wiles and Satan's lures and torn between two wills (II.iii and xiii); he must distinguish between worthless gains and the crown of life, and must choose between the easy way and the hard one (II.v and xi). Man is a willing slave of a world of deception, but a process of liberation begins with the proclamation of allegiance to the cross (II.iv and xii). Choice is the basic theme: man must choose the grain and leave the chaff, just as on Judgment Day the good and the bad will be separated (II.vii and ix).

Emblems II.i, II.viii, and II.xv summarize the movement of Book II from silly Cupid's false and feeble light of Nature, by way of Divine Cupid's denunciation of Venus and Cupid (mere natural man), to the well-tempered fire of Heaven which purifies heart and soul. Against the negative movement of Book I, then, Book II opposes a true upward movement from natural to heavenly love. The spectacle of a Cupid who cries without knowing why or what he wants is a fitting centre-piece which is given added emphasis by being placed between emblems on the necessity of making a wise choice and bearing in mind God's choice between the true and the false, the good and the bad on Judgment Day. We must not be like silly Cupid who does not even know what he wants, despite all the fuss he makes.

At the beginning, middle, and end of Book III are grief and tears (see Diagram VII.4), and frank acknowledgements of guilt and inadequacy (III.v and xi) are supplemented by prayers for mercy (iv and xii). Emblems on redemption through Christ are encountered for the first time, so that Book III marks the decisive turning-point in the soul's career. A new-found humility is expressed in emblems showing man as fallen ("Remember I am clay"; III.v) and as a ship about to founder unless God lend strength and direction (III.xi). Equally humble is the confession of mortal sickness to Christ the

Diagram VII.4 *Emblemes*, Book III. Penitential Tears

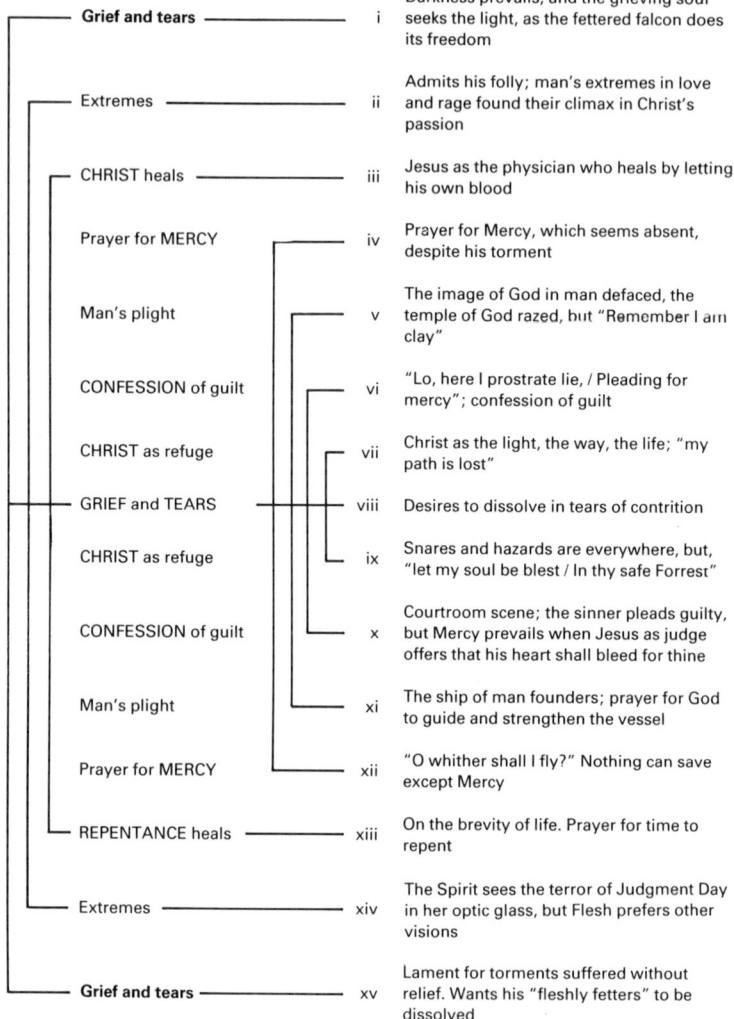

physician (III.iii) and the prayer for time in which to repent (III.xiii). And the open confession of guilt in III.vi ("Lo, here I prostrate lie, / Pleading for mercy") is climaxed in the courtroom scene in III.x where the sinner, though he pleads guilty, is saved by the judge who offers to atone on behalf of man. The prayer for mercy resounds in III.iv and xii as well. Confidence is placed in Christ; when the path is lost, Christ is the light, the way, and the life (III.vii), and, though snares and hazards are everywhere, a safe place of rest may be found in "thy Forrest" (III.ix). The topos of being enslaved enters into the framing emblems: III.i compares the grieving soul to a fettered falcon, and in III.xv the fetters are identified as those of the flesh. This topos introduces the important idea of yearning for God and desiring to be translated to Heaven, which will prevail after Emblem IV.vi.

Book IV (see Diagram VII.5) turns to the issue of the two wills which so occupied Augustine in his account of his own conversion. Emblem IV.i states the nature of the conflict in familiar Pauline terms: "I know what's good and yet make choice of ill," but when we reach Emblem IV.xv one will only prevails – to leave the Babylonian exile and return home. The Babylonian exile is a type of our fallen existence, and so logically enough the grief felt by those in exile is "Harmonious raptures in th'Almightie's ears" as stated in the Epigram. The progress in between these emblems is a painful one, but God is sought as guide through the labyrinth (IV.ii) and as shade of protection against the fiery Sun of Justice (IV.xiv; compare Psalm 90 : 1–4). To reject the "fruits of earth's imployment" is futile "When I resolve to keep the old man still" (IV.v), but in IV.xi Christ has replaced the old man within the troubled breast. The cross affords a link between IV.vi and x. Just as in the former the speaker wishes to nail his lustful thoughts to the cross (as Haman was hanged on the gallows he had erected for Mordecai, Esther's father), so in the latter Christ is sought and found on the cross: "If thou refuse to share a bed with me, / We'll never part, I'll share a crosse with thee." Emblems IV.vii and ix show a beautifully balanced inversion: in the one the soul is in the arms of Christ, and in the other the infant Jesus is in the arms of the Virgin Mary. This arrangement reflects a half literary and half iconographical tradition which juxtaposes Jesus in the arms of Mary with Mary's soul in the arms of Christ (the so-called Dormition scene).[6] The topos of crowning links the two emblem poems: Christ crowns the soul, but as infant he must exchange his "Crowne of glory for a crown of thorn." The erotic language of IV.vii is echoed in the last lines of IV.ix ("seal that granted pardon with a kisse"), and the two poems begin with identical phrases: "Come, come my dear" and "Come, come my blessed Infant". The linkage therefore is unusually strong.

Diagram VII.5 *Emblemes*, Book IV. The Impotent Will

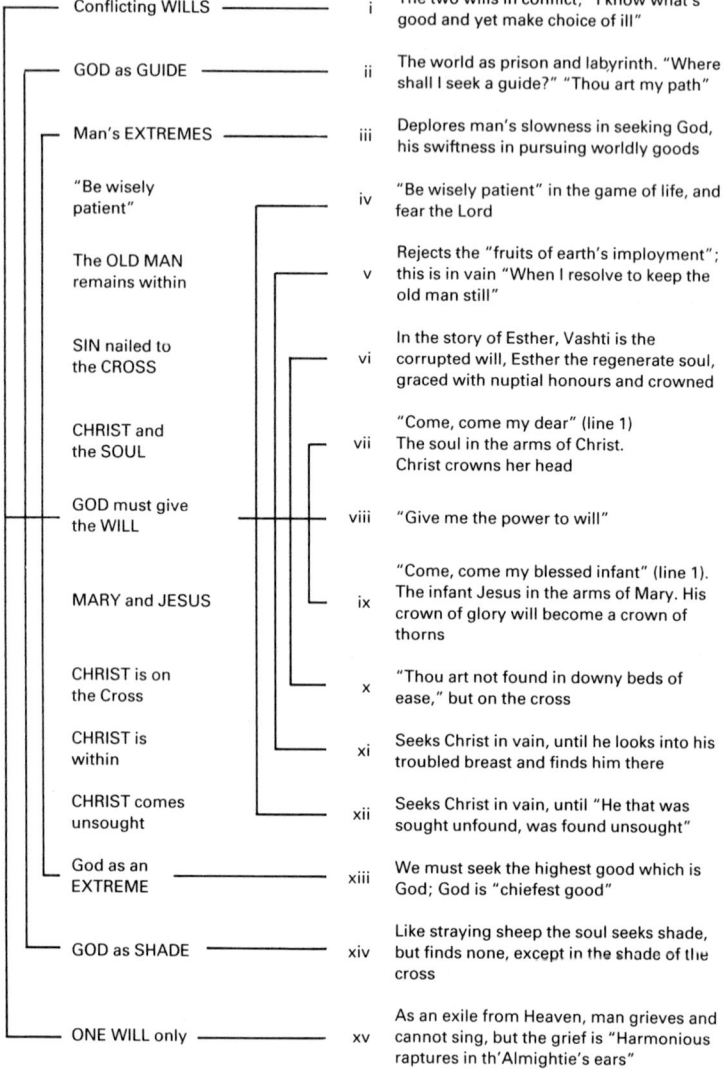

The temperature increases drastically in Book V, in which images of fire prevail, most notably in Emblems V.1 and V.xv (Diagram VII.6). The panting breast is "scorch'd with flames" caused by a "flaming dart, / Shot from his eye" (V.i); in V.viii Jesus presents himself as a suitor, and when the sequence ends the soul yearns for, but recoils from, God's consuming fire. This "conjunction and alienation" (see V.viii, the quotation from Nazianzen) has already figured in Emblem V.viii, where man is encouraged to abandon "the body of this death", the base suitor for his favour. The Epigram puts the case most pithily:

What need that house be dawb'd with flesh and bloud?
Hang'd round with silks and gold? repair'd with food?
Cost idly spent! That cost doth but prolong
Thy thraldome. Fool, thou mak'st thy jail too strong.

We must remember this exhortation when we read Emblem V.xv where the soul seeks the beloved, only to recoil from too fierce flames: "Turn, turn thy face, thy fires are too consuming." This complaint is referred to, however, as the "frantick language of my foolish fear," and when the soul asks: "What, shall we part without a mutuall kisse," this phrase may well be an allusion to the *mors osculi* – death through a kiss.[7] If so, the flesh has indeed become dead, as stated in the last line of Emblem V.viii. Nothing less could conclude the process described in the preceding emblem poems.

The linkage between the remaining poems often depends on a progression from cause to effect; languishing for love (V.ii) leads on to seeing Heaven open (V.xiv), and mutual love between the soul and Christ (V.iii) causes a desire to be released from the fetters of the Earth and feed on joys above (V.xiii). In the same way, love of God (V.iv) prompts the wish to see God face to face (V.xii). Simple parallels, though, connect V.vii and ix, and V.v and xi; the first set expresses a desire to be dissolved, to leave the body behind and ascend, while the second set affirms Christ's healing power: the fires of "thy sweet voyce" (V.v) and of Heaven (V.xi) are a "balsam" to cure the wounds inflicted by lust.

The structures traced through individual books enable us to see how the five books in their turn form a logical pattern: Book 1 presents sin rampant, Book II the conflict between "drossie nature" and the values of Heaven, Book III the harmony of grief, confession of sins, and salvation through Christ, Book IV the conflict between

Diagram VII.6 *Emblemes*, Book V. Consumed by Love

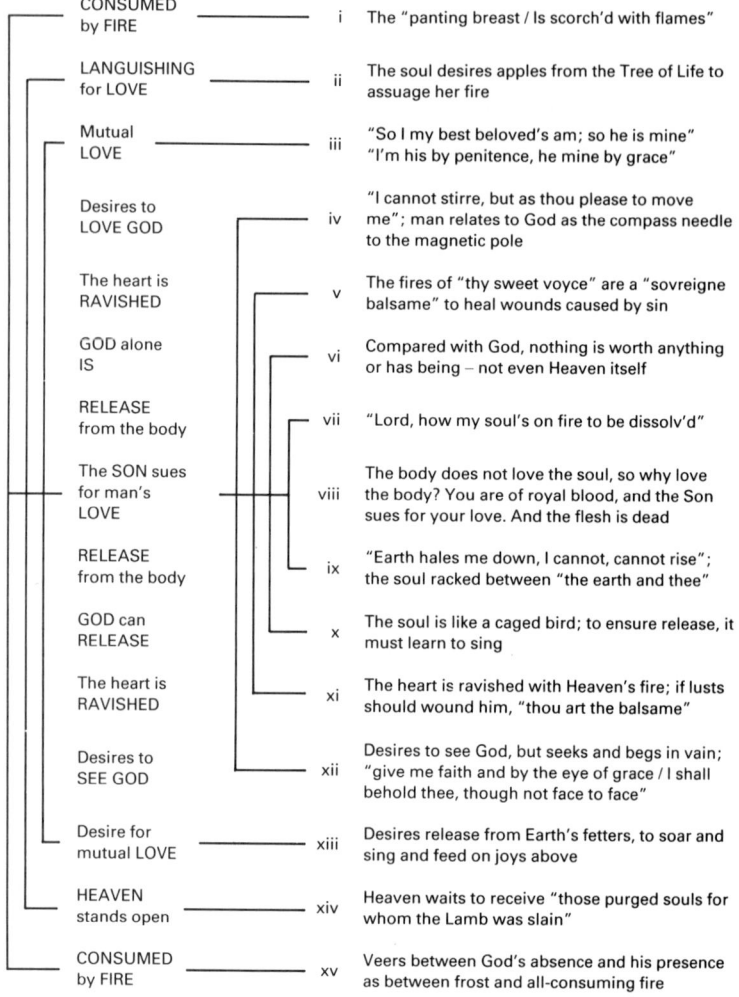

the two wills, and Book V the love that leads to a return to God. Books I and V, therefore, contrast false and true love, Books II and IV the conflict between Earth and Heaven, the old man and the new, while Book III is the decisive turning-point. The parallel between Books II and IV accommodates a significant difference:

Book II appeals to the understanding, Book IV to the will. One may perceive the contrast between earthly or worldly joys and those that are heavenly, but the perception is no guarantee that man will choose the highest good. After the Fall, man's will is no longer governed by his reason, so that the will associated with the new man must grow in strength gradually, assisted by divine grace (the scourging of the sinner is proffered grace), until it finally prevails.

It remains to consider the possibility that the 75 emblems may be arranged as 50 + 25, in order to provide the ratio of the diapason, and Diagrams VII.7 and 8 present the evidence in favour of this supposition. It is most apt (as Hrotsvit would have put it) that the subject of the first emblem poem – the eating of the fatal fruit – is the subject also of the emblem poem placed in the 50th position (IV.v), where the fruits of earth are said to "destroy us in th'enjoyment". In the second emblem, a distempered world fears the Lord; God's voice affrights like thunder, and the antithesis is presented in the 49th (IV.iv), which exhorts us to "Be wisely temp'rate" and to fear the Lord (fear *in bono*). The antithesis between true and false is pointed also in emblems 3, 24–25, and 48 (I.iii, II.x–xi, and IV.iii). The world's dainties are "in fruition sowre" (I.iii), the world is "vain and void," full of deceit (II.x), the only road which leads to the Crown of Life is the hard one (II.xi), and false treasure, honour, and pleasure are dismissed in favour of those that are true (IV.iii). The two central emblems on the vanity of the world and the wisdom of taking the hard road (25–26; II.x–xi) are flanked by poems on *choice*. On Judgment Day, God separates good and bad, true and false, and makes his choice accordingly (24; II.ix), and the world is roundly dismissed in favour of the cross (27; II.xii). What we have, therefore, is a clearly outlined centre consisting of four emblems, and a frame consisting of 3 + 3 emblems. These emblems show the thematic progression with great clarity: the structure highlights the contrast between bad (I.i–iii) and good (IV.iii–v), and the necessity of making our choice accordingly (II.ix–xii). In other words, the reader is placed in the position of the Christian Hercules so popular in the Renaissance, as we have seen in the chapters on Tasso and Spenser. He must penetrate the mask put on by Pleasure to deceive, and instead choose the rugged path of Virtue.

In emblems 51–75 the centre-piece is Emblem V.iii on the union between Christ and the soul: "So I my best-beloved's am; so he is mine." Emblems 51–53 (IV.vi–viii) present the life of the Christian on earth, emblems 73–75 (V.xiii–xv) the desire for Heaven and the

Diagram VII.7 *Emblemes*. The Framing Structure of Emblems 1–50

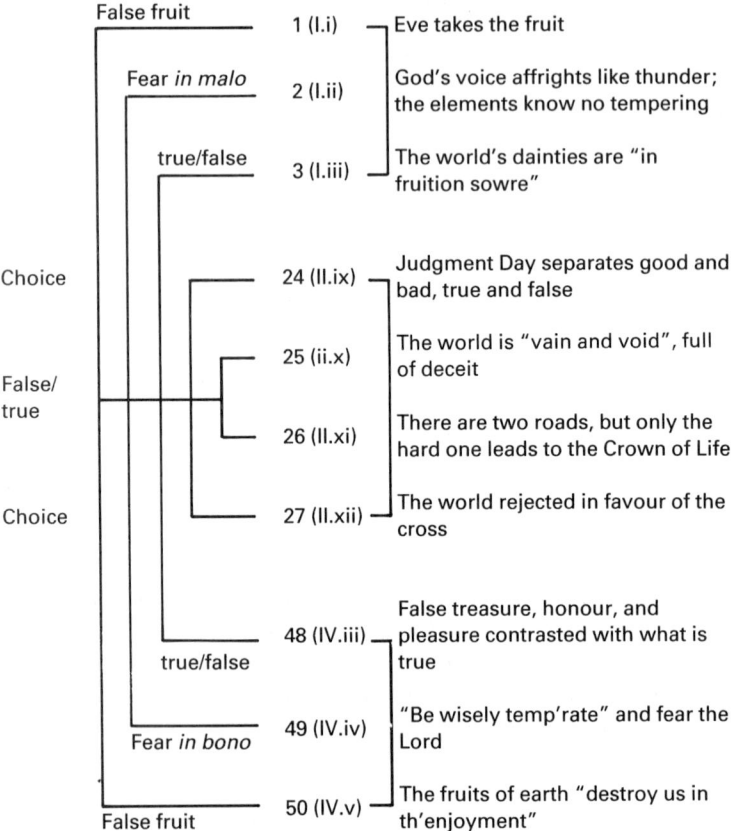

The focus is on the distinction between true and false and on the necessity of making a wise choice between them.

entry. What we see through the veil of allegory in the story of Esther – the soul as holy object of divine love – is experienced face to face in the end, and a similar unveiling occurs when we proceed from Emblem IV.vii to V.xiv: in the former the rural cottage reflects the glory of the heavenly Jerusalem through the presence of Christ, while in the latter Heaven itself stands open. In the same way the desire for a new will and a new life (IV.viii) is transformed into desire for everlasting pleasures in the kingdom of Heaven (V.xiii). The reader proceeds, then, from learning to discriminate between

Diagram VII.8   *Emblemes*, The Framing Structure of Emblems 51–75

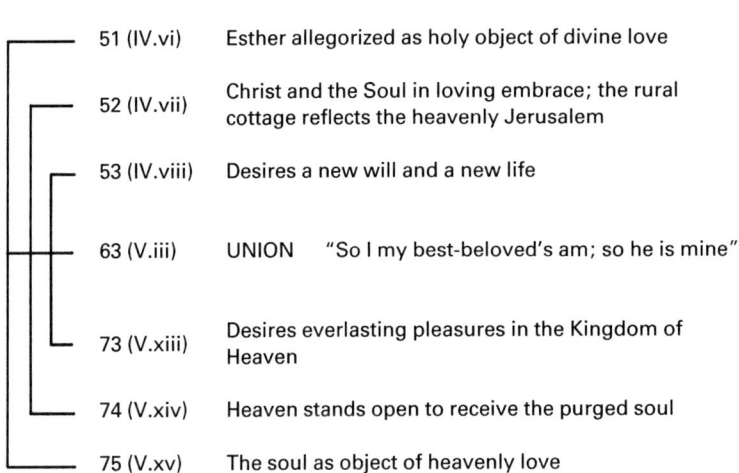

51 (IV.vi)		Esther allegorized as holy object of divine love
52 (IV.vii)		Christ and the Soul in loving embrace; the rural cottage reflects the heavenly Jerusalem
53 (IV.viii)		Desires a new will and a new life
63 (V.iii)	UNION	"So I my best-beloved's am; so he is mine"
73 (V.xiii)		Desires everlasting pleasures in the Kingdom of Heaven
74 (V.xiv)		Heaven stands open to receive the purged soul
75 (V.xv)		The soul as object of heavenly love

Christ's love makes a new choice possible, and so union is restored between God and man.

false and true, good and bad, to choosing the path of virtue in this life, and finally Heaven itself. Learning to accept scourging as proffered grace is perhaps the hardest lesson of all; grace is of course the key concept – however much man may seek Christ, in the end it is Christ who finds him. Christ is found, unsought. Tasso's Tancred, too, must learn to accept scourging, and so must Spenser's Redcrosse knight. All are purified as if by fire.

The fact that these 75 emblem poems, when studied topomorphically, present the great Christian truths about our human existence and the path to eternal life, affords persuasive evidence of the usefulness of adopting a spatial reading. It is satisfying to experience that Quarles's emblem sequence makes good sense when read spatially, at the same time that an appreciation of the design is a source of aesthetic delight. However, the response ought to be more than purely aesthetic: we ought to see that the human artefact, by virtue of its design, owes its being to God's *ars aeterna*.

Coming as he did after Spenser and the Spenserians, Quarles could command techniques that enabled him to exploit to advantage the poetic gift he undoubtedly possessed. His emblem poems, therefore, could be appreciated by sophisticated readers as well as by the more simple-minded, which helps to explain why his book of emblems became such an unparalleled success. Disappointment is certain if we read the sequence serially, expecting a phychologically plausible development. Contemporary readers would have looked for the pattern of God's grace: every Christian is part of the design whereby the fatal fruit is annulled by the fruit of the Tree of the Cross, and the copious shedding of tears at the textual centre (III.viii) proves that the true fruit has been offered and accepted. The initial turning away from God and the consequent fall into the discord of sin (Books I–II) lead on to the slow and painful process of understanding the deceitful nature of the world's joys, so that ultimately the hard and narrow path is chosen, at the end of which is found the Crown of Life. Distinguishing between true and false, melting in tears, and being given the will to embrace the cross are the major phases. However much we may seek Christ, it is always he who finds us; it is his love which enables us to respond in love.

Contemporary readers must have admired the way in which Quarles organized the sequence so that these major themes emerge. True, in Books III–V Quarles made use of Hugo's plates with no omissions and few alterations, but in Books I–II many changes were made in the plates taken from the *Typus Mundi*, and ten emblems are of his own devising as based on a number of different sources.[8] These changes must have been made to create the structures identified in my diagrams, their purpose being to dramatize important concepts. The drama is in the interaction between them – between the hard-faced, open sin revealed in Book I, for example, and the contrite and humble heart shown in Book III, and especially in Emblems III.i, III.viii, and III.xv. Quarles's vigorous verse invests these concepts with so much flesh and blood, however, that modern readers look for a story and are disappointed when it fails to emerge from the accustomed linear reading.

The structure of individual poems is rarely as exact as the overall structure of individual books or of the work as a whole, but interesting structures are certainly there. Book III, for example, which marks the dramatic turning-point, consists entirely of poems in couplets, except for 3 poems in triplets rhyming *aaa*. It is reasonable to consider the form as expressive: by means of the power of the Trinity man is lifted above mere worldly concerns (represented by the couplets). Giles Fletcher, too, invests couplets with a negative import when he lets the song of temptation in Book II of *Christs Victorie, and Triumph* (1610) be written in couplets.[9] The number of ascent featured in the five groups of 15 emblems is found also in Emblem IV.xiii, whose 15 triplets address the soul, exhorting it to mount so as to reach "Heav'n's eternall joyes." (A similar ladder of ascent is found in Book IV, stanzas 1–15, of Giles Fletcher's poem.) The rhetorical patterning divides these triplets into 10+5 (see Diagram VII.9), where the ratio of the diapason reflects the harmony found in God, our "chiefest Good." Music is

Diagram VII.9   *Emblemes*, Emblem IV.xiii

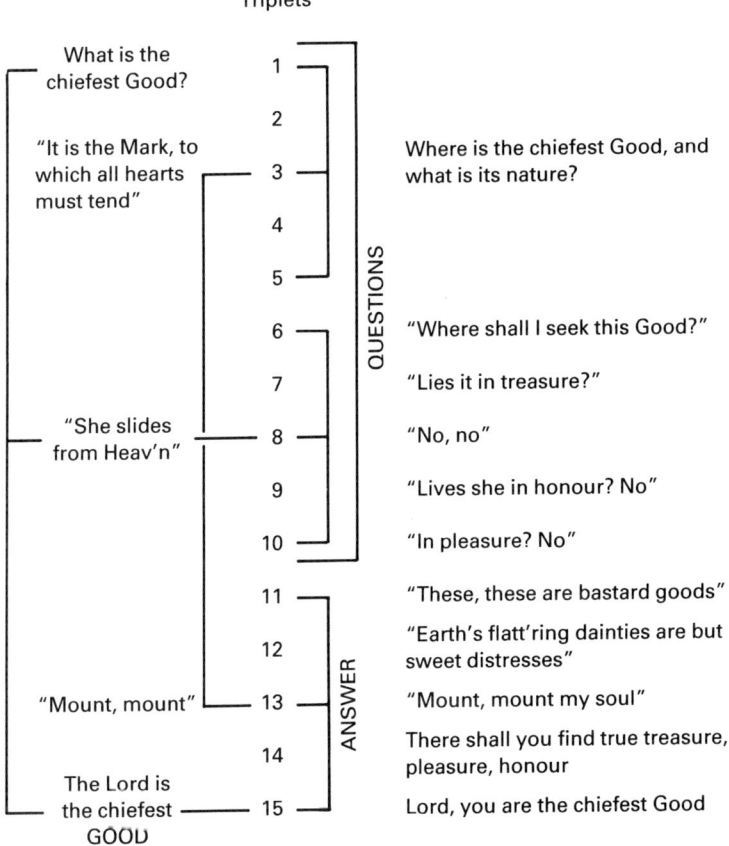

Stanzas 1–10 present a sustained series of questions, while affirmations and imperatives mark the last 5 stanzas. The question posed in stanza 1 is answered in stanza 15, and, between these framing stanzas, stanzas 3, 8, and 13 (the centres of each group of 5) create a symmetrical structure based on the important positive statements. The graded arrangement therefore coexists with a symmetrical pattern, but the 2:1 division carries more weight because more clearly marked.

Diagram VII.10 *Emblemes*. Emblem IV.xv

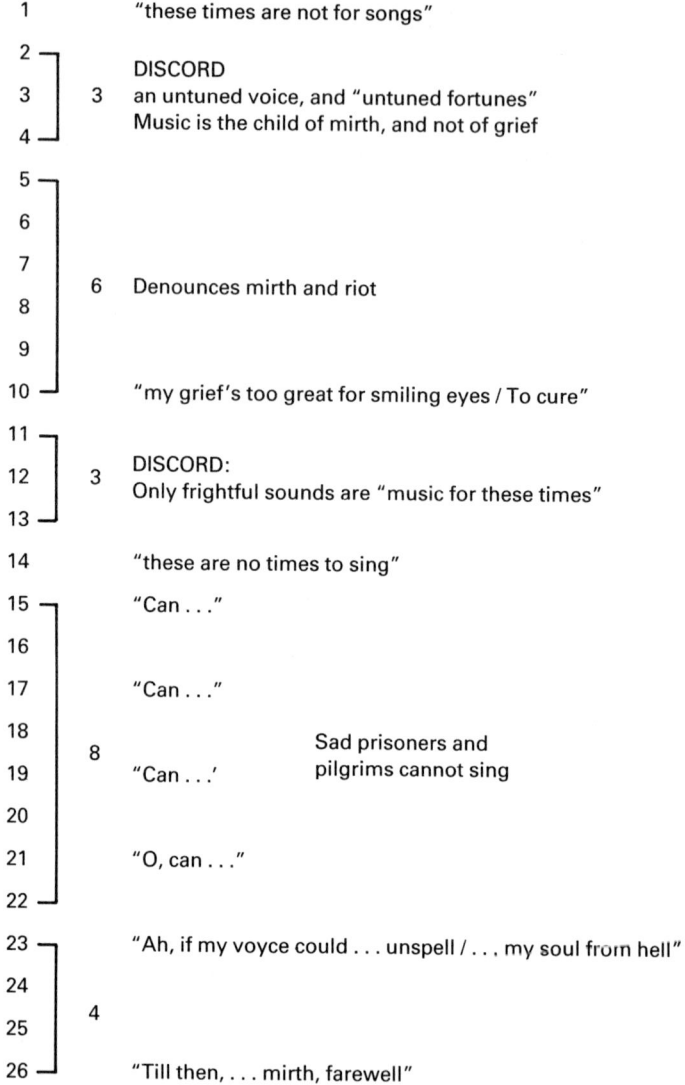

The rejection of music and of song is refuted by the harmonious structure, where symmetry combines with divisions that form the ratio 2:1. The structure, therefore, confirms the statement in the Epigram that "grones and tears" are "Harmonious raptures in th'Almightie's ears."

the subject of Emblem IV.xv, where it is rejected by the speaker as unsuited to the times: "Urge me no more: this airy mirth belongs / To better times; these times are not for songs" (lines 1–2). As shown in Diagram VII.10, this opening couplet is followed by 12 (divided into 3+6+3) on the grief which makes song impossible, and this thematic movement is rounded off with a variation of the first couplet: "These are no times to touch the merry string / Of *Orpheus*: no, these are no times to sing." Then follows a second group of 12 couplets – divided into 8+4 – where a series of questions is followed by a conditional clause: "Ah, if my voyce could, *Orpheus*-like, unspell / My poore *Eurydice*, my soul, from hell / ... O then my breast / Should warble airs, whose rhapsodies should feast / The ears of Seraphims ... " The presence, though, of *aequalitas* (in the structure 1—12—1—12) and of the ratio 2 : 1 (in the division into 3—6—3 and 8—4) belies the contents. The discord called for as appropriate for sad prisoners and pilgrims finds a structural counterpoint in highest harmony, and the Epigram explains why: "grones and tears" are "Harmonious raptures in th'Almightie's ears." As we have seen, a similar counterpointing occurs in *The Faerie Queene* I, i–ii, where the account of Redcrosse's defection is framed by numbers of redemption. An even closer analogue is found in George Herbert's "Deniall", where the grief expressed in the contents is offset by perfect harmony in the verbal texture: repetitions of the same or related words and phrases establish a pattern of perfect symmetry.[10] God's providential patterning supports us even in our moments of greatest grief; or perhaps I should say especially in those moments.

Quarles's basic pattern consists of two movements, one negative and one positive, so arranged that the climactic last stanza in the first forms the centre for the poem as a whole. Thus the 5 stanzas of the concluding poem, "The Farewell", begin with two stanzas on Christ's redemptive death and a third on the grief from which may spring "a Heav'n of love and wonder." This third stanza is a thematic as well as a formal climax; stanzas 1–2 stress the impossibility of comprehending the love which prompted Christ's redemptive action, while stanza 3 states the imperative need for tears. Belief will needs prompt grief: grief will refine the love, and love will refresh the grief in a positive circle. The use of imperatives and the careful balancing of words and phrases within this stanza identify it as a pivotal centre for the poem as a whole (see Diagram VII.11). The theme of tears in this final poem harks back to the

Diagram VII.11 *Emblemes*. "The Farewell", Stanza 3

centrally placed emblem (III.viii), so that its thematic relevance is great. Lines 1–2 and 11–12 form a frame for the 8 lines in between on the prayer for divine action. God must "break this fleshly rock in sunder" so that from it "May spring a Heav'n of love and wonder." This positive message is at the heart of this symmetrically structured central stanza. Stanzas 4–5 are linked in form and content: each proceeds with questions and answers concerning the "crown of Glory" (4:1) or the "crown of life" (5:12), and each concludes with the rhyme words *strife* and *life*. The last two lines of the last stanza summarize the process of regeneration: "The gift is thine; we strive, thou crown'st our strife; / Thou giv'st us Faith; and Faith, a crown of life."

We find similar structures in Emblems II.vii, II.iii, and V.ix (see Diagrams VII.12–14); in Emblem II.xii the first stanza and the last are linked by the repetition of identical rhyme words (see Diagram VII.15), and the same is true of stanzas 1 and 5, and 2 and 4 in Emblem IV.xiv (see Diagram VII.16). The same concept (change) taken *in bono* and *in malo* helps to structure Emblem IV.ix on Mary

Diagram VII.12 *Emblemes*. Emblem II.vii. The Corn and the Chaff

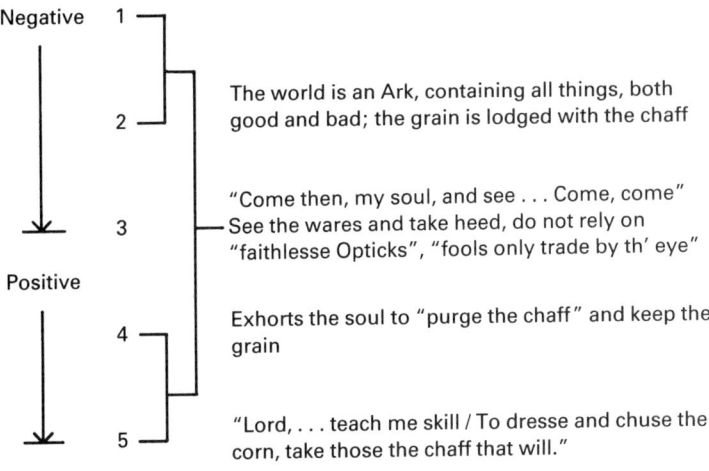

Stanzas 1–2 describe the world as a heap of unwinnowed grain, an Ark where we find things "pure and grosse". "This furnisht Ark" presents the greedy eye with all that "earth can give, or Heav'n can add." The strong imperatives addressed to the soul in stanza 3 mark the climactic last moment in this initial movement. Stanzas 4–5 give sage advice and offer a prayer for the skill "To dresse and chuse the corn".

and the infant Jesus (see Diagram VII.17), while the symmetrical pattern of Emblem IV.v is based on the repetition of the same concept (see Diagram VII.18). The wanton desires (stanzas 1 and 7), the deception (2 and 6), and the mutability (3 and 5) which afflict all who indulge in "the fruits of earth's imployment" point to the centrally placed concept of *extremes* as their cause. In Emblems IV.viii and II.ix, a pivotal stanza divides the stanzaic sequence into the ratio 2:1 (see Diagrams VII.19 and 20). In each, the pivotal stanza invites us to *see* – "See how my sin-bemangled body lies," and "Se, how the latter Trumpet's dreadful blast / Affrights stout *Mars* his trembling son!" Giles Fletcher, too, made use of such a dramatic exhortation to mark the stanza he placed at the centre of Book III of *Christs Victorie, and Triumph*: "See where the author of all life is dying" (III.34).[11] As Chapter VI on Spenser has shown, various rhetorical devices often accompany his structures and so help to identify them. Thus the narrator's lament for Una's "wandring woe" frames the action of *The Faerie Queene* I.iii, and patterns of verbal repetition adorn the structures of Giles Fletcher as well.

Diagram VII.13   *Emblemes*. Emblem II.iii. Man between Two Bawds

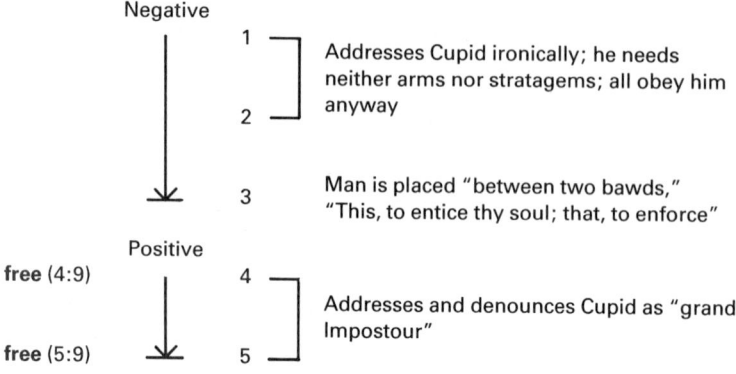

The climactic third stanza has a balanced pattern around the central, fifth line, thus illustrating man's position between two "bawds", one who is a "line" to compel, the other a "lure" to entice:

                        A   B
This, to entice thy soul; that, to enforce:

Way-laid by both, how canst thou stand secure?
          B   A
That draws, this wooes thee to th' eternall curse.
                                 (3:4–6)

Quarles therefore follows in their footsteps; he could study their technique and profit from it.

Quarles's non-stanzaic verse too may create the ratio 2 : 1, as we see in "The Invocation", whose two paragraphs of respectively 16 and 8 couplets express the two meanings invested in the ratio – ascent and song. The octave signifies ascent, since in it the last note returns to the first, but in a higher key; the double octave, as in the number 15, signifies ascent from Earth to Heaven – a most appropriate meaning for Quarles's groups of 15 emblems.[12] The opening lines of "The Invocation" command the soul to expel all vulgar thoughts and screw up "thy sublime Theorboe four notes higher / And higher yet," so that the choir of seraphim may join in "And make thy consort more than halfe divine." The wing that makes ascent possible also provides a tool for the poet: "Snatch thee a quill from the spread Eagle's wing, / And, like the morning Lark, mount up and sing" (lines 11–12). A third meaning attributed to this ratio – that reason should govern the emotions in the proportion 2 : 1 – is

Diagram VII.14   *Emblemes*. Emblem IV.ix. God's Power

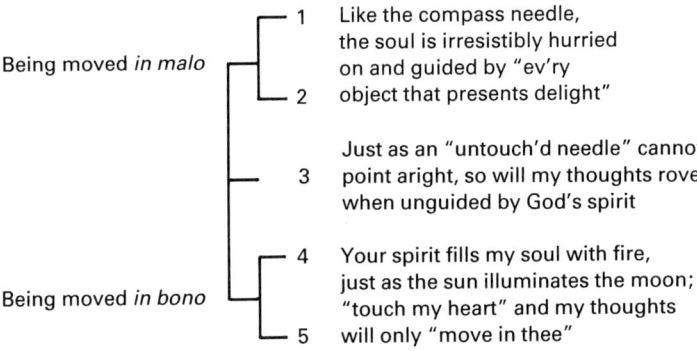

The key mage of the compass needle (used negatively in stanzas 1–2) is turned in a positive direction in stanza 3, and the positive message is given in the prayer of stanzas 4–5. Stanzas 2 and 4 are linked by the rhymes *delight / night* repeated in inverse order as *night / delight*. Stanza 3 is balanced around the rhyme words *move* (3:1) and *love / move me / love me* (3 : 8–10), and is linked to stanza 5 by the rhyme words *love me* and *move in thee*.

Diagram VII.15   *Emblemes*. Emblem II.xii. Discriminating between Lower and Higher

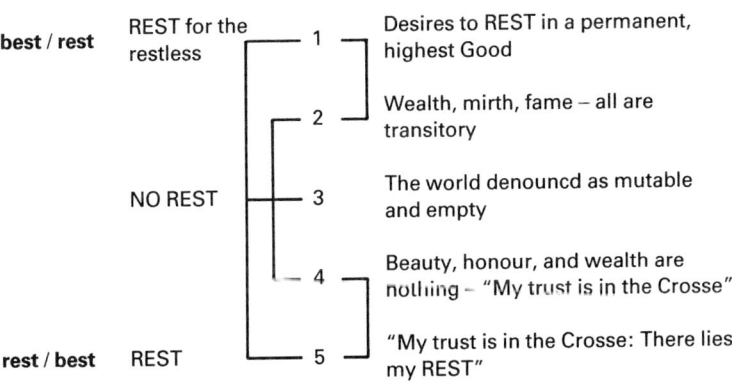

Stanzas 1 and 5 (linked by shared rhymes) are a positive frame for the negative analysis of the world in stanzas 2–4

Diagram VII.16 *Emblemes.* Emblem IV.xiv. Christ as Refuge against the Burning Eye of Vengeance

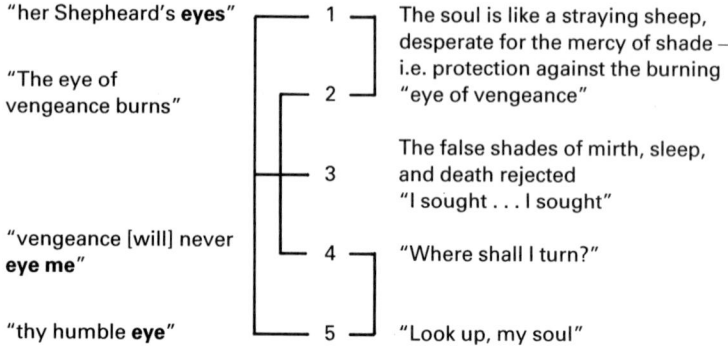

An initial negative movement is climaxed in stanza 3 with the rejection of false "shades". A positive movement follows, beginning with questions in stanza 4 and concluded with answers in imperative form in stanza 5. Christ's godhead "are the flames that fry me" (4:3), but his manhood – his mortal flesh on the cross – provides protection "betwixt those beams and thee" (5:9).

Some verbal repetitions are indicated on the left.

Diagram VII.17 *Emblemes.* Emblem IV.ix. Mary and the Infant Jesus

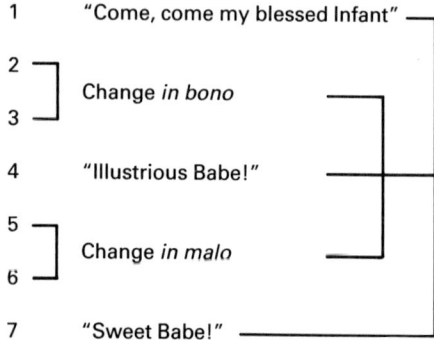

The direct address to the Babe is a rhetorical link between stanzas 1, 4, and 7; the stanzas in between (2–3 and 5–6) consider, first, the positive change Herod would have experienced if he had known the child's true parentage, and then the cruel change in store for the child when he must exchange his Crown of Glory for a crown of thorns. The topos of *arms* links the beginning and the middle: the Babe will be safe in "my sacred arms" (1:2), and he is a "rich armful" who was "so late embrac'd / In thy great Father's arms, and now in mine!" (stanza 4).

Diagram VII.18 *Emblemes*. Emblem IV.v. The Fruits of Earth's Employment

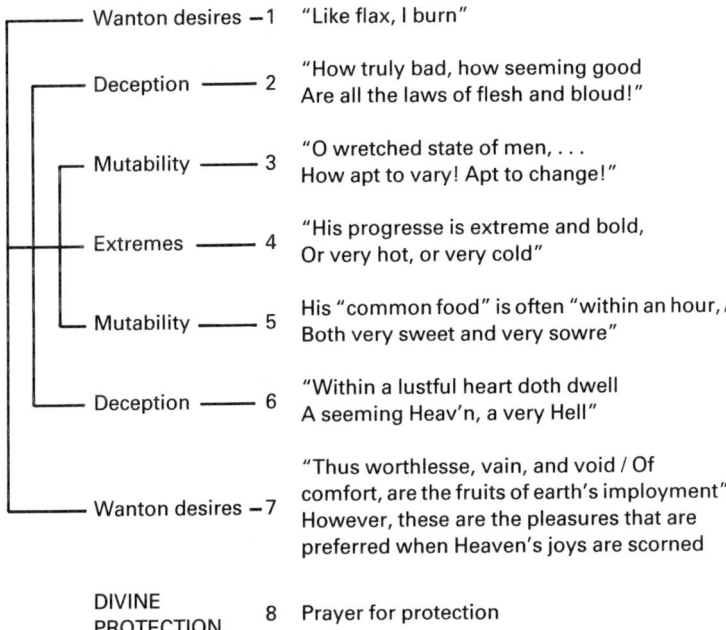

The negative pattern of stanzas 1–7 is negated by the concluding eighth stanza with its prayer for divine protection. The balanced pattern may perhaps illustrate the vicious circle created by man's destructive desires: they make us burn like flax (1) and are a fruit that destroys in the eating (7). Our goods are deceptive (2 and 6) and we ourselves are at the mercy of incessant change: nothing that seems good remains so (3 and 5), and we vacillate between the extremes of hot and cold (4). However, stanza 8 reverses the position by calling on God: "Lord, close the casement, whilst I stand / Behind the curtain of thy hand."

introduced at the textual centre (24–25), when the soul is told to let reason curb the passions. In short, we must "flie like Eagles, and our Rhimes / Must mount to Heav'n (31–32). The second paragraph reaches an even higher pitch in the prayer that Christ's power, his "current", will flow through the "slender conduit of my Quill" and in the end bestow upon him the crown of glory. The poem prefixed to Book III (thus marking its central position) has the same length and the same division into 16+8 couplets, although the division is not marked by a paragraph. Ascent is again a main theme: the last 8 couplets are dominated syntactically by "what if" constructions and

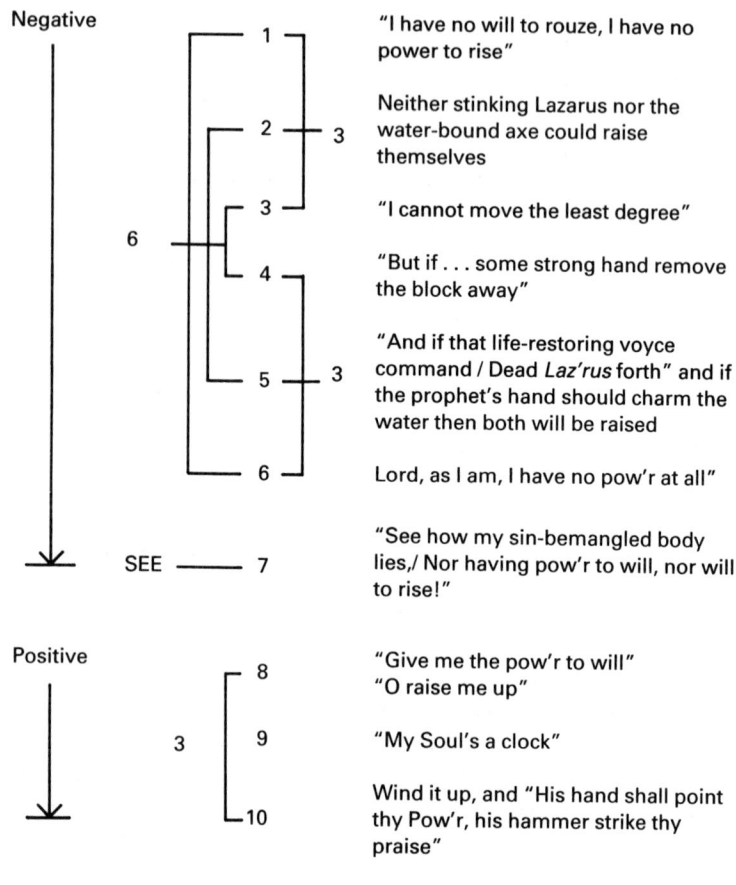

Diagram VII.19 *Emblemes*. Emblem IV.viii. Man's Impotence and the Power of God

Stanza 7 is the pivot which divides the poem into a sequence of 6—1—3 stanzas. Stanzas 1–6 divide into 3 on man's inability to raise himself, and 3 on biblical examples of God's power to raise. The last 3 stanzas present the prayer to God to wind the clock of man "with thy soul-moving keyes" and so enable it to function.

by reiterated commands to "Dart up thy soul in grones," "Dart up thy soul in vowes," "Dart up thy soul in sighes," and "Shoot up the bosome shafts of thy desire ... And they will hit."

It is arguable that emblem poems patterned like these are, in fact, similar to concrete pattern poems. Emblem 8 in John Hall's *Emblems with Elegant Figures* (1658) shows souls ascending to Heaven on a ladder of light, while the poem itself presents the same

THE RELIGIOUS SEQUENCE 399

Diagram VII.20 *Emblemes*. Emblem II.ix. Judgment Day

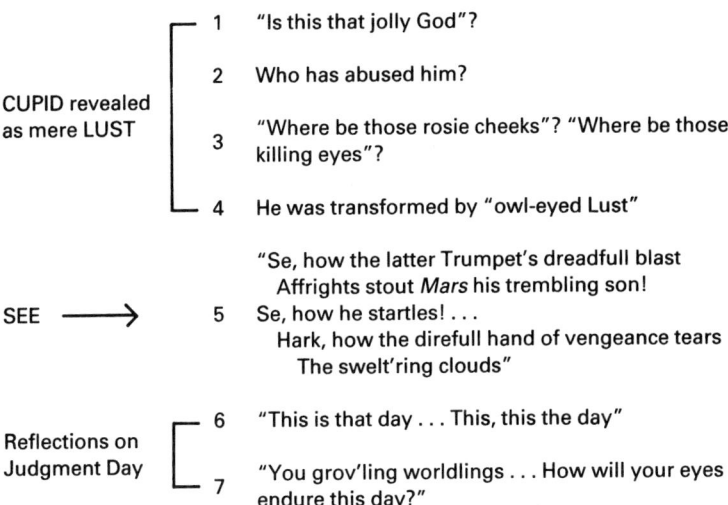

The evocation of Judgment Day (as if present) functions as the pivot which divides the poem into the sequence 4—1—2 stanzas. A negative harmony exists between Cupid (Lust) and the "grov'ling worldings."

"picture" in the textual structure, consisting as it does of 15 3-line stanzas divided into 10 on vain curiosity and 5 on true wisdom. The idea of ascent, therefore, is present in the sum total of stanzas and in the ratio 2 : 1 formed by the contents. Emblem XII in Quarles's *Hierogliphikes* (1638) presents the picture of a vase or urn, and the same shape is found in each stanza, whose lines increase and decrease to form the desired outline, and also to embody the idea of time which hurries us on to an inevitable decline. The rhyme scheme (*a b c d e e d c b a a*) enacts the circle of time, while the number of lines in each stanza (11) expresses our going beyond our prime, or our transgressing through excess (cf. stanza 4). The 9 lines of the concluding fifth stanza (rhyming *a b c d d c b a a*) express our falling short of the desired end. Man's feeble light can "but only rise, / And blaze awhile, and then away."

A ring with a diamond stone (i.e. beauty adorned by virtue) is found in Gilles Corrozet's *Hecatomgraphie* (1540).[13] The ring is found in the circular rhyme scheme (*a a b a a b* repeated as *b b a b b a*) and in the two occurrences of the ratio 2 : 1 – in the division between dimeters and tetrameters, and between the 8 dimeters and the 4 tetrameters. The ratio may also express the harmony created when virtue is added to beauty. Later on Tasso was to describe Rinaldo as the "Diamond of this ring" (*Jerusalem Delivered* I.58:1–2). Emblematic images are frequent in Renaissance epics, where they often mark points of structural interest. Although Quarles does not include an emblem on the Choice of Hercules, the idea of *choice* is virtually omnipresent in his collection. George Wither presents the religious version of the choice in the splendid title-page of his *Emblemes* (1635), where two peaks represent the two ways. Wither presents the classical version in Emblem XXII, where he abandons couplets in favour of crossed rhymes at the same time that he divides the 30 lines into 20+10. Lines 1–20 present a narrative of his entry into the world at 18 when he meets Virtue and Vice sitting "at the highest" at "*Englands greatest Rendevouz.*" The last 10 lines contain his discovery of grim death as the companion of Vice whose beauty is a mere mask put on to deceive, and his prayer for grace "for evermore to view / Her Vglinesse" and set his affection on "Faire VERTVE."

The ghostly presence of emblem pictures is sometimes felt in shorter Renaissance poems such as Andrew Marvell's "The Coronet." The relevant picture is provided by Beza's *Icones* (1580). Emblema XXVIII shows a hand from above wielding a sword to cut asunder a wreath around which are twined the intertwined bodies of Satan and his emissaries (the Pope, bishops, and monks). Beza's Latin poem explains that Satan has brought his followers from darkest Hell, armed by the wrath of the just God to destroy the world. However, Christ pities the bitter fate of man and so he destroys Satan with the sword of the Word. Marvell's poem itself forms a wreath or circle by means of verbal repetitions which connect the beginning and the end: "head have crowned" and "May crown thy feet, that could not crown thy head". Three quatrains with enclosed rhymes describe the speaker's desire to weave a "chaplet" for "the King of Glory", but the rhymes are crossed in the fourth quatrain on the sad discovery of the presence of the serpent:

13   Alas, I find the serpent old
        That, twining in his speckled breast,
        About the flowers disguised does fold,
16   With wreaths of fame and interest.

Then follows a couplet which denounces the whole undertaking, and in so doing divides the poem into 16—2—8 lines:

17 Ah, foolish man, that wouldst debase with them,
18 And mortal glory, Heaven's diadem!

The subsequent prayer asks that the "slippery knots" be untied and the "winding snare" disentangled, and the rhyme scheme follows suit: its shape is as it were disentangled in the pattern *a b c a b c*. The discovery of the serpent is at the centre of the overall symmetrical pattern (lines 13–14), but the graded arrangement around the pivotal couplet in lines 17–18 holds out a promise of redemption by him "who only [could] the serpent tame." We see, then, how the rhyme scheme at every point supports the structures indicated in the contents. Numerical decorum may be present in the 4 quatrains on the worldly attempts to weave a "chaplet" and in the 8 lines presenting the prayer, but the ratio 2 : 1 is more important because of the promise it conveys of harmony restored. Then, too, the ratio expresses the circular movement characteristic of a coronet. Verbal repetitions, the rhyme scheme, the ratio 2 : 1, and numerically significant line totals combine to express in their own way what the words say, and also sometimes to add an extra semantic dimension. The tradition of the emblem sequence clearly encouraged the tendency to let purely formal elements add their quota of meaning to a poem. In this way the line of distinction between emblem picture and emblem poem becomes blurred in those cases when a poem's textual structure presents its own "pictures".

Notes to Chapter VII

1. Barbara K. Lewalski, "Emblems and the Religious Lyric: George Herbert and Protestant Emblematics, "*Hebrew University Studies in Literature* 6 (1978), 38. See also her book on *Protestant Poetics and the Seventeenth-Century Religious Lyric* (Princeton, 1979).
2. Quoted from George Herbert, *Works*, ed. F. E. Hutchinson (Oxford, 1941), pp. 116–17.
3. Karl Josef Höltgen, *Aspects of the Emblem*, Problemata Semiotica 2 (Kassel, 1986), pp. 53–65.
4. Augustine is quoted from the Loeb Classical Edition, while all quotations from Quarles are from Alexander B. Grosart, ed., *The Complete Works in Prose and Verse*, vol. 3 (Hildesheim, 1971).
5. In the Middle Ages, Masses could be offered for the gift of tears; see Sarah Appleton Weber, *Theology and Poetry in the Middle English Lyric* (Columbus, Ohio, 1969), p. 10.
6. See the interesting study by Henry Maguire of *Art and Eloquence in Byzantium* (Princeton, 1981). Paired paintings show "Mary holding the infant with the Hand of God holding the souls of the righteous," and another juxtaposition is of the death of the Virgin with the infancy of Christ, which "became as much a convention in Byzantine art as in literature" (pp. 57 and 60). The Virgin may be shown cradling her child across her body, while Christ cradles his mother's soul

in a similar posture (p. 61). In one set of paintings the "soul appears to *sit* in Christ's arms, and thus to echo the pose of Christ sitting in the arms of his mother." The sitting soul and the sitting child form a "visual pun" (p. 62).
7. On the *mors osculi*, see Nicolas J. Perella, *The Kiss, Sacred and Profane* (Berkeley and Loss Angeles, 1969), pp. 76 f. and 180 f.
8. Höltgen, *Aspects of the Emblem*, pp. 52 f.
9. See my essay on "Golden Phrases: The Poetics of Giles Fletcher," *Studies in Philology* 88 (1991), 169–200.
10. For an analysis of this poem, see Chapter VIII, pp. 403 f.
11. Røstvig, "Golden Phrases," p. 184.
12. The lower octave "should be associated with the created world of time, and the upper, spiritual octave with the supernatural world of eternity" (H. Neville Davies, "Laid Artfully together: Stanzaic Design in Milton's 'On the Morning of Christ's Nativity'," in *Fair Forms*, ed. M.-S. Røstvig, Cambridge, 1975, p. 92).
13. Gilles Corrozet, *Hecatomgraphie* (1540), sig. M_i^v-M_{ii}^r.

Chapter VIII

The Religious Lyric

> ...all must appeare,
> And be dispos'd, and dress'd, and tun'd by thee,
> Who sweetly temper'st all. If we could heare
> Thy skill and art, what musick would it be!
> George Herbert, "Providence"

1. George Herbert

Students of expressive form have found a fertile field in the poetry of George Herbert, but Herbert's range of formal devices is more comprehensive than has been suspected. Herbert's rhyme schemes, for example, deserve more attention, like his placing of words and phrases within a text, and symbolic numbers and ratios are just as relevant. Herbert's most subtle stratagem is to let a textual structure contradict what the words say, instead of functioning as mere accompaniment or elaboration. "Deniall"[1] is a good example (see Diagram VIII.1). While the words express the feeling of being cut

Diagram VIII.1 Herbert, "Deniall"

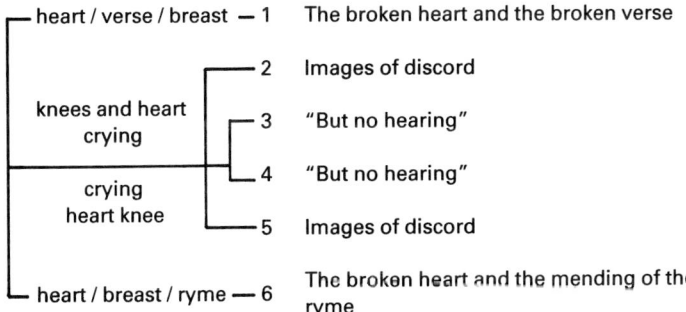

The balanced pattern of repeated themes and words creates an image of providential order, which refutes the denial expressed in the central stanzas. The mending of the rhyme in the last stanza, therefore, is part of a larger positive movement created by the disposition of words and images within the poem's space.

off from God ("But no hearing"), the verbal and thematic symmetries constitute a powerful affirmation of faith in the God who may be closest to us when we feel most isolated. The structure therefore becomes an utterance in its own right; the design becomes a sign which must be read.

The almost physical character of words is seen most clearly in pattern poems representing objects like altars or wings, but this character is revealed in other ways too. "Content", for example, invites us to share the vision which sees the poem as words disposed in space. In these 9 4-line stanzas, the familiar classical theme of the happiness of the contented mind quite unexpectedly is given a cosmic dimension: the contented mind "doth span the world, and hang content / From either pole unto the centre" (5 : 1–2), and the 9 stanzas (for the spheres?) and the 4-line stanzas (for the quaternions of the world?) form a verbal universe where the word "centre" is at the textual centre at the end of line 18. The recessed symmetry created by the contents (see Diagram VIII.2) expresses the harmony represented by the contented soul. Just as Augustine found the God he had sought for so long once he looked into his own breast, the contented mind, by keeping within its own bounds, gains access to the whole universe. To reach this state of perfection, all

Diagram VIII.2   Herbert, "Content"

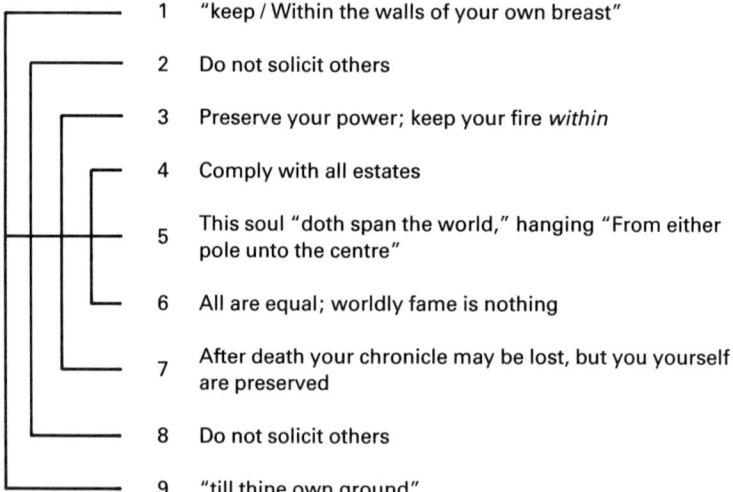

1	"keep / Within the walls of your own breast"
2	Do not solicit others
3	Preserve your power; keep your fire *within*
4	Comply with all estates
5	This soul "doth span the world," hanging "From either pole unto the centre"
6	All are equal; worldly fame is nothing
7	After death your chronicle may be lost, but you yourself are preserved
8	Do not solicit others
9	"till thine own ground"

The keeping within its own bounds makes the soul span the whole universe.

evil impulses from within or without must be firmly rejected (stanzas 2–3 and 7–8). A synoptic or panoramic reading, then, makes us see the 9 stanzas as a poetic cosmos where the contented mind is at the centre, reaching back to stanza 1 and forward to stanza 9. The cosmic image at the centre, therefore, is self-referring in the sense that it explains the alignment between Herbert's poem and God's, by virtue of which outer and inner space coincide.

The subject of "Providence" invites textual enactment: God's providence reconciles the One and the Many, as in the classical formulas for the harmony of creation. God's works, therefore, are music: "If we could heare / Thy skill and art, what musick would it be!" (lines 39–40; stanza 10 : 3–4). God's wisdom "reacheth from one end to another mightily: and sweetly doth she order all things," as the Wise Man puts it (*Wisdom* 8 : 1), and Herbert refers to this familiar passage no less than three times in the course of the 10 stanzas that function as preamble to the praise. The opening lines present a close paraphrase:

O Sacred Providence, who from end to end
Strongly and sweetly movest, shall I write,
And not of thee, through whom my fingers bend
To hold my quill? shall they not do thee right?

Stanzas 8 and 10 repeat the crucial words: "We all acknowledge both thy power and love ... Who dost so strongly and so sweetly move" (ll. 29–31), and "all must appeare, / And be dispos'd, and dress'd, and tun'd by thee / Who sweetly temper'st all" (ll. 37–39). These obvious repetitions serve to indicate the textual structure whereby Herbert "tunes" his own lines in the substructure indicated in Diagram VIII.3. Stanzas 1–6 relate God's art of creating and man's art of praise; in stanza 7 the poem is solemnly presented as a sacrifice of praise, whereas stanzas 8–10 revert to the idea of God's art of creation, where the lines on God's "music" provide a fitting climax. In this sequence of 6—1—3 stanzas the harmony of the diapason is sounded, as in the 6—1—3 stanzas of Spenser's "Prothalamion"[2] and the 6—1—3 books of the first edition of *Paradise Lost* (See Chapter IX).

The 28 stanzas presenting the praise (stanzas 11–38) are unified by a pattern of recessed symmetry as shown in Diagram VIII.4. This balanced pattern expresses God's own art of balancing and reconciling, dividing and uniting, an art which tends to obscure the distinction between the One and the Many, God and his creation. At the

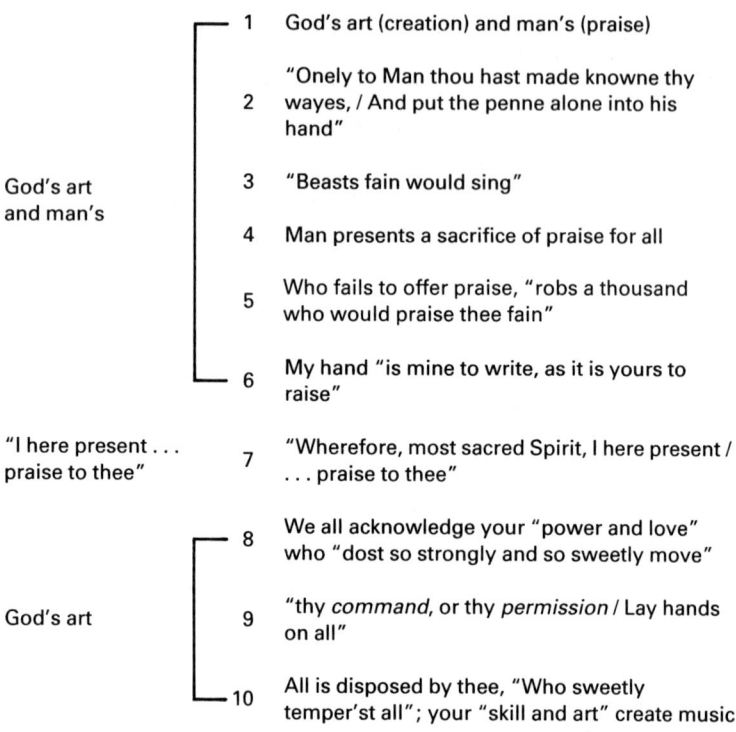

Diagram VIII.3 Herbert, "Providence", Stanzas 1–10

God's art and man's
- 1 — God's art (creation) and man's (praise)
- 2 — "Onely to Man thou hast made knowne thy wayes, / And put the penne alone into his hand"
- 3 — "Beasts fain would sing"
- 4 — Man presents a sacrifice of praise for all
- 5 — Who fails to offer praise, "robs a thousand who would praise thee fain"
- 6 — My hand "is mine to write, as it is yours to raise"

"I here present... praise to thee"
- 7 — "Wherefore, most sacred Spirit, I here present / ... praise to thee"

God's art
- 8 — We all acknowledge your "power and love" who "dost so strongly and so sweetly move"
- 9 — "thy *command*, or thy *permission* / Lay hands on all"
- 10 — All is disposed by thee, "Who sweetly temper'st all"; your "skill and art" create music

Stanza 7 functions as a pivot which divides the sequence into 6—1—3 stanzas, thus creating the ratio of the diapason as an expression of God's tempering or "tuning" of the creation.

Stanzas 8–10 are framed by references to *Wisdom* 8:1, and the whole sequence is introduced by a fairly exact rendering of this verse.

The sum total of stanzas in this segment (10) may relate to the Pythagorean *tetractys* formula and its musical ratios.

centre of this second substructure is located praise of the admirable fullness and goodness of creation: the seas which seem to stop the traveller, actually speed his progress, the winds serve the sailor (ll. 89–92; stanza 23), and "as thy house is full, so I adore / Thy curious art in marshalling thy goods" (ll. 93–94; stanza 24). The phrase "marshalling thy goods" may perhaps be self-referring, since Herbert has marshalled his stanzas with equal care. The balanced fullness praised in stanzas 13–15 recurs as a theme in stanzas 32–34, and the idea which links stanzas 16–18 and 29–31 concerns the

Diagram VIII.4 Herbert, "Providence", Stanzas 11–38

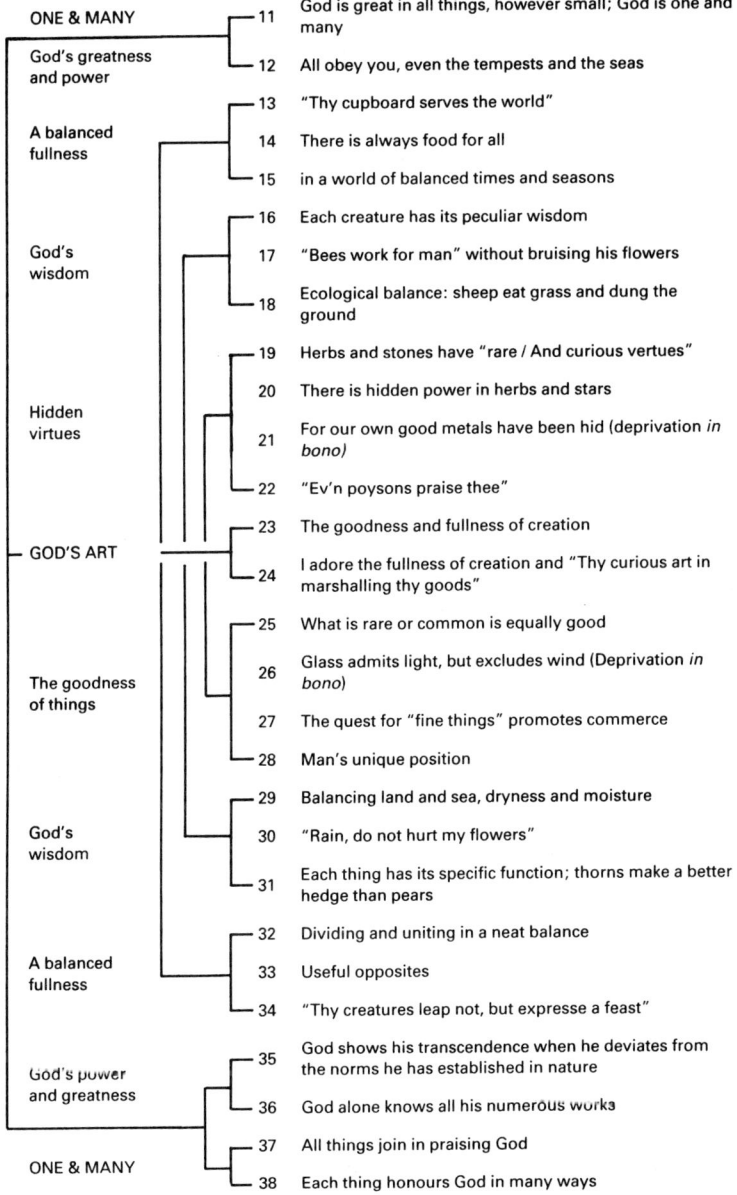

divine wisdom reflected in the creation. A specific link between stanzas 17 and 30 is the reference to flowers: bees that fetch their honey from flowers do not bruise them (stanza 17), and in the same spirit the speaker exhorts the rain to be gentle: "Rain, do not hurt my flowers; but gently spend / Your hony drops" (ll. 117–18; stanza 30 : 1–2). The verbal echo is plain. The linkage between stanzas 21 and 26 is more subtle; here the absence of certain things or qualities is seen as a good: it was good that God hid precious metals in the ground, since the quest for gold so often results in death (stanza 21), and in the same way glass is praised for admitting light, but excluding wind, wool and fur provide warmth without weight, and so on (stanza 26). What we do not have, then, is for our own good. The goodness of things, though, is not always seen, and some virtues are rare (stanzas 19–20), just as man's position in creation is unique (stanza 28). The quest for rare and fine things becomes good when it promotes commerce between nations (stanza 27). One is struck by the logical comprehensiveness of the praise of the goodness of God's creation – "Ev'n poysons praise thee" – and where poisons are found, the antidote is close at hand (stanza 22). The balanced fullness of creation is illustrated in various ways in stanzas 13–15 and 32–34, the most subtle example being the mutual aid provided by opposites: "Most herbs that grow in brooks, are hot and dry," and "Cold fruits warm kernells help against the winde" (ll. 129–30; stanza 33 : 1–2). (F. E. Hutchinson takes "warm kernells" to be the subject, and "Cold fruits" the object.) It is noteworthy that the ideas expressed in the first two stanzas of the praise (ll. 41–48; stanzas 11–12), when repeated at the end, require 4 stanzas (ll. 137–152; stanzas 35–38). Their subject is the God who combines the One and the Many (stanzas 11 and 37–38), and God's greatness and power (stanzas 12 and 35–36). One wonders why Herbert was content to let stanzas 37 and 38 make the same statement twice:

> All things that are, though they have sev'rall wayes,
> Yet in their being joyn with one advise
> To honour thee ...

> Each thing that is, although in use and name
> It go for one, hath many wayes in store
> To honour thee ...

In his edition of Herbert's works, F. E. Hutchinson observes that

"Palmer detects that this verse [i.e. stanza 38] is an alternative for the preceding, the author perhaps having not decided which of the two to retain. This is possible, although there is no indication in the MS. that the verses are alternative." However, the stanzas are complementary: the one proceeds from the Many to the One, the other from the One to the Many, both movements being needed to express the order of creation as disposed by the God who is both One and Many: "Thou art in all things one, in each thing many: / For thou art infinite in one and all" (ll. 43–44; stanza 11 : 3–4). The circle of creation is enacted structurally in the ratio 1 : 2 (twice repeated) formed by the framing stanzas.

The two parts of respectively 10 and 28 stanzas are unified by means of an overall symmetrical pattern as set out in Diagram VIII.5. The beginning and the end are linked by means of the theme of praise, and the linkage is supported by the repetition of the rhyme words *wayes* and *praise* in the stanzas that are second from

Diagram VIII.5   Herbert, "Providence". Overall Symmetry

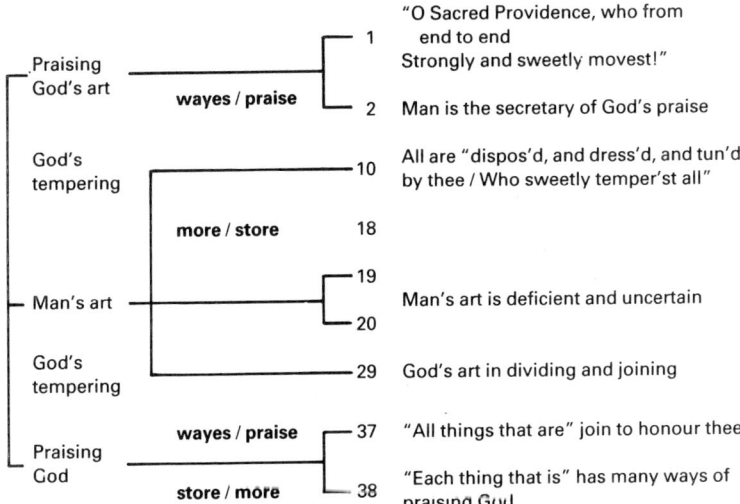

Identical sets of rhyme words connect the beginning, middle, and end. Stanzas 19–20 hark back to the beginning by expressing the wish for a miraculous root to "give expressions," so that all aspects of creation may be adequately described and praised. The tempering described in stanza 29 consists in moderating between land and sea after they have been separated: rivers water the soil, and rain from above.

the beginning and the end. The theme recurs at the centre in stanzas 19–20 (ll. 73–80), but modified so as to express the poverty and uncertainty of the praise offered by man: "O that thy care / Would show a root, that gives expressions!" (ll. 75–76). There is no certainty in the art professed by man, unlike that of God. The opposites created by man ("plagues and plenty, peace and warres") are "much surer than our art is sure."

We see, then, that, just as God reveals his art and skill in his arrangement of things, the poet responds by ordering his praise in a similar way; his "signs" imitate those of God. In this particular poem, blindness to the presence of these textual structures may result in a serious misapprehension of the contents. Thus John R. Mulder believes that the persona finds Providence a "riddling affair," a case of either/or: "Every aspect of the visible world is an instance of Either/Or: Power or Love, command or permission, threat or promise."[3] But the "inventory" does not separate into two categories, nor are they in conflict. God's power is not separated from his love, his strength from his sweetness; in God the two must needs be one, like his mercy and his justice. Also, the analysis of God's scheme must include those occasions when God magisterially chooses to deviate from the pattern he has established (stanza 35, ll. 137–140); nothing can prove more clearly the absoluteness of God's power. (The poet too may deviate from *his* established norm by leaving a line unrhymed, as in "Deniall.") When Mulder remarks that this stanza merely represents an almost comical surrender of "the attempt to circumscribe God's design,"[4] the surrender is instead on the critic's part who fails to circumscribe Herbert's design. The persona does not vacillate between fear and hope as Mulder will have it, nor is he a "*faux naif* who substitutes himself for Christ."[5] Christ is indeed the high priest of man, but man is just as undoubtedly the high priest of the lower creation who offers up praise for all. Man is "Secretarie of thy praise" (l. 8).

Number symbolism may be present in the 4-line stanzas, since 4 is so very much the number by means of which God disposes everything – "times and seasons" (l. 57), the 4 elements and their 4 qualities (hot, cold, moist, and dry (cf. ll. 129–32), the winds that blow from the 4 quarters (ll. 89–92), the 4 kinds of surface: hard or soft, rough or smooth (ll. 121–24), and 4 levels of being: stones, herbs, beasts, and men (*passim*). Later on Milton was to praise the divinely established order in a similar way in the morning hymn offered by Adam and Eve at sunrise in book 5 of *Paradise Lost*.[6] Herbert may have chosen to divide his poem into 10 + 28 stanzas because 28 is the second number of mathematical perfection. Like 6, it equals the sum of its aliquot parts; nothing is left over when you add these parts, and nothing is missing. Its fullness, therefore, is perfect, and this is why it may represent the fullness of God's creation.

I believe it can be safely argued that it is impossible to do justice to this poem without considering its structural images; besides, the textual structures enable us to understand the contents more fully, since the contents are based on a numerical conception of creation as a progress from the One to the Many and back again to the One by means of the harmonious order which is divine Providence. No one would call Herbert a philosophically minded poet, and the presence in this poem of philosophical concepts like the One and the Many shows how very much they had become part of the way of thinking about God's creation. In these lines by Herbert, therefore, the syncretistic tradition outlined in my first chapter finds one of its clearest expressions.

"Mans medley" assumes familiarity with Augustine's argument concerning the presence, in the works of creation and redemption, of the relationship between single and double in the proportion 1 : 2:[7] through Christ's single death (in body alone) man may gain a double life, now and hereafter. Satan presents the evil version: through his one death (in soul, when he turned his back on God), Satan may procure a double death for man. Herbert uses this familiar idea in an unexpected way: man's doubleness is one of joys – man feels the joy common to all creatures, but to this joy is added the joy of a life "hereafter". Stanzas 1–4 of this 6-stanza poem describe how man makes two one by joining Earth and Heaven, whereas stanzas 5–6 explain how man's doubleness may entail "double paines" or the possibility of two deaths. This thematic division into 4 + 2 stanzas presents the ratio of double to single, and we may perhaps see the same ratio in the rhyme scheme, which consists of a couplet and a quatrain. The 36 lines of the 6 6-line stanzas may be glossed by adducing Augustine's reflections on this number, "which is six squared. And this is referred to that ratio of the single to the double ... For twelve added to twenty-four suits the ratio of single added to double, and makes thirty-six" (*De Trinitate* IV.vi.10). It has been stated that Herbert's poem could have ended after the fourth stanza, since "it has come to a coherent position on the question with which it began." However, "Herbert was not comfortable with the position he had taken"; affliction "seems to him more central than joy to the human condition ... The uses of adversity, not the delights of life, are Herbert's theme."[8] This psychological observation is beside the point; logic demands that both possibilities be presented so that the triumphant conclusion may be reached:

> Yet ev'n the greatest griefs
>   May be reliefs,
> Could he but take them right, and in their wayes.
>   Happie is he, whose heart
>   Hath found the art
> To turn his double pains to double praise.

Herbert's poem shows how completely Augustine's argument in book 4 of the *De Trinitate* had become the common property, if not of all Christians, then certainly of Christian poets.

The 13 6-line stanzas on "Home" describe the desire to leave Earth and come to Heaven through him who left Heaven to come to Earth. Stanzas 1–4 set the stage: when man was lost, the Son was the only help, "and must he leave that nest, / That hive of sweetnesse" to redeem those "who would not at a feast / Leave one poore apple for thy love?" (ll. 19–22). The answer is given in stanza 5: "He did, he came" (l. 25), and the remaining 8 stanzas express the speaker's desire to leave the world whose harvests are worth nothing: "We talk of harvests; there are no such things, / But when we leave our corn and hay" (ll. 55–56). The contents, then, divide the 13 stanzas (13 = Christ as the head of the 12 Apostles) into 4—1—8 stanzas, thus expressing the harmony restored by Christ, and the return to God in a higher key, as in the octave.

In "Divinitie" the symmetrical structure is of the simplest kind, based as it is on a series of antitheses (see Diagram VIII.6); this structural simplicity reflects the speaker's rejection of the kind of divinity where "Reason triumphs, and faith lies by," and his corresponding praise of Christ's doctrine, which was as "cleare as heav'n." Stanzas 1 and 7 denounce man-made guides ("Faith needs no staffe of flesh"; 7 : 3); stanzas 2 and 6 oppose reason and faith, stanzas 3 and 5 the wisdom of Christ (stanza 3) and man's foolish wisdom (stanza 5). The central stanza provides the central message: "But all the doctrine, which he taught and gave, / Was cleare as heav'n, from whence it came." It is interesting that Herbert should have considered simple symmetry as an appropriate form for praise of the simplicity of Christ's doctrine.

Diagram VIII.6 Herbert, "Divinitie"

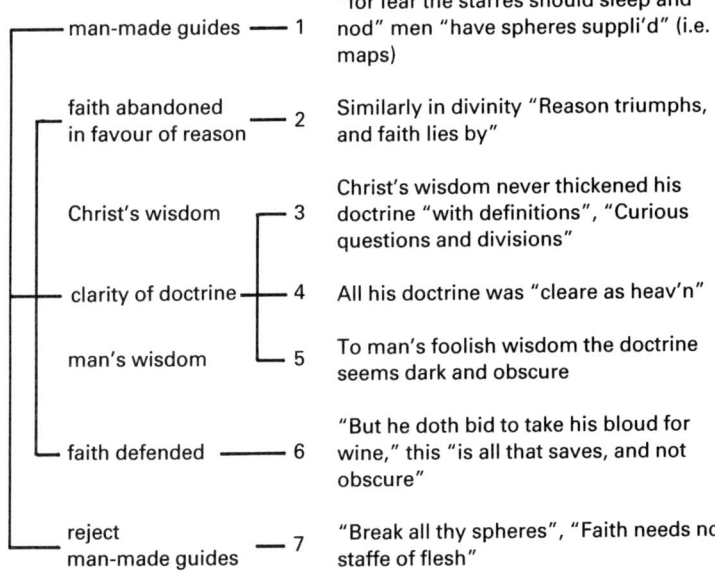

Antitheses provide most of the links, but a parallel links stanzas 1 and 7: like the clod "Which knows his way without a guide" (1:4), faith "needs no staffe of flesh, but stoutly can / To heav'n alone both go, and leade" (7:3–4).

The symmetrical structure of "Sunday" (9 7-line stanzas) is equally simple (see Diagram VIII.7); on this occasion parallels provide the links between stanzas. However, other structural features provide complexity, at the same time that the images are more striking. The numbers of time are present in the 7-line stanza with its 52 syllables, but the most interesting structural phenomenon is the verbal link between stanzas 7 and 8:

As Sampson bore the doores away,	**away**
Christs hands, though nail'd, wrought our salvation,	
And did unhinge that day.	**that day**
The brightnesse of that day	**that day**
We sullied by our foul offence:	
Wherefore that robe we cast away,	**away**
Having a new at his expence.	

Diagram VIII.7 Herbert, "Sunday"

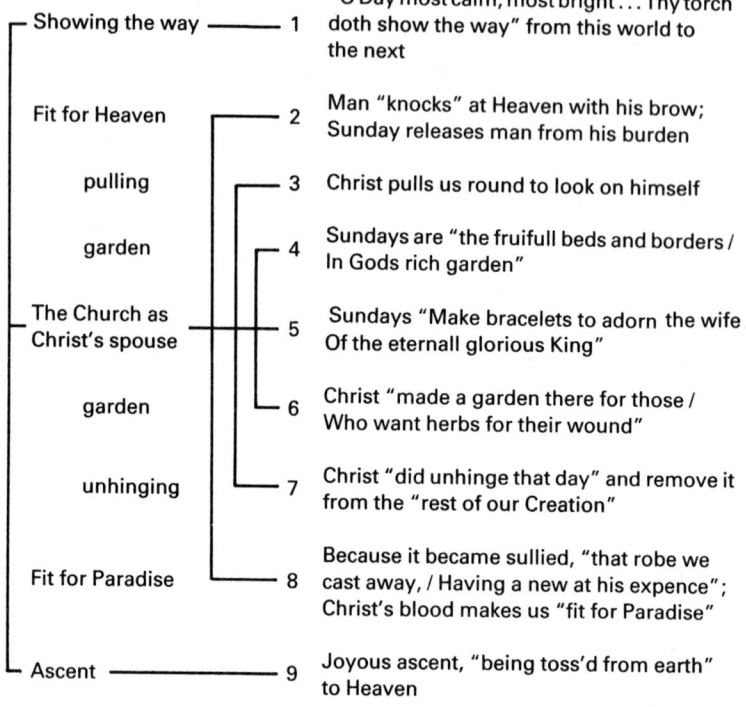

Stanzas 1 and 9 present Sunday as the day which shows the way from this world to union with God in the next, and at the centre is the vision of the union between Christ and the Church (i.e. all Christians). Burdens are cast away in stanza 2 and the old robe in stanza 8, thus making man "fit for Paradise" (8:7). Everything depends on the actions of Christ: Christ pulls man around to look at himself (stz. 3), and in much the same way he "unhinges" the day of rest (stz. 7) in order to transfer it to the eighth day of the Resurrection. The transition from the 7 of this life to the 8 of Eternity is indicated by the rhymes which link stanzas 7 and 8.

The linkage fuses the seventh and the eighth stanza, just as the Resurrection on the eighth day in Easter Week is the seventh as well; in the fusion between the two is expressed the transition from the world of Time (represented by 7) to that of Eternity (represented by 8). This argument is familiar in biblical exegesis as we have seen, and especially in comments on the seventh and eighth Psalms of Ascent. That the whole effect depends upon our observing the use of identical rhymes in inverse order is an indication of the importance Herbert attached to rhymes as to verbal repetition in general. He expects his readers to notice this sort of thing, and on this occasion it is equally important to observe that the linkage is between stanzas 7 and 8 in a poem on Sunday. The linkage through shared rhymes serves to verify the symbolism invested in the ordinal numbers of these stanzas; the image of the "unhinging" of that day can be explained only in these numerical terms. Other verbal images call for similar comments. The image, in stanza 4, that Sundays "the pillars are, / On which Heav'ns palace arched lies" may be glossed by citing one of Bongo's comments on the number 7: Bongo cites Augustine to the effect that 7 represents the perfection of the Church; based on the 7 pillars of wisdom, the Church returns Multitude to Unity.[9] This perfection of the Church is the subject of the next stanza – the centrally placed stanza 5 – on Christ's spouse ("the wife / Of the eternall glorious King"). The Church is the spouse. Finally the traditional structural view of the week of creation (as a circle consisting of 6 circles with a seventh in the middle), explains the curious statement in stanza 2 that man "knocks" at Heaven with his brow:

> The other days and thou
> Make up one man; whose face thou art,
> Knocking at heaven with thy brow.

In his chapter on the number 6, Bongo has a drawing of the 6 circles with the seventh in the middle (containing the word *Quies*) and Will. Marshall uses it in the engraving which adorns the title-page of John Swan's *Speculum Mundi*:[10] within each of the 6 circles he has placed a picture showing the work of that day. As Bongo explains, the creation of light (i.e. the angelic intelligences) is at the top, and then follow the elements (2), the minerals (3), vegetable life (4), creatures that have sense perception (5), and finally those that have reason (6). In this way, therefore, "The other dayes and thou / Make up one man," and the sixth circle touches the first, connecting man with the angels.

The symmetrical pattern of "Miserie" (13 6-line stanzas) is used to good purpose to underline man's perverse addiction to sin and folly (see Diagram VIII.8). Repetitions bring out the repetitiousness of the folly: "Man is a foolish thing, a foolish thing, / Folly and Sinne play all his game" (1 : 2–3), and again: "But sinne hath fool'd him" (13 : 1). The repetition closes the circle of the poem.

The corruption mars even man's very act of praise as stated in the

Diagram VIII.8 Herbert, "Miserie"

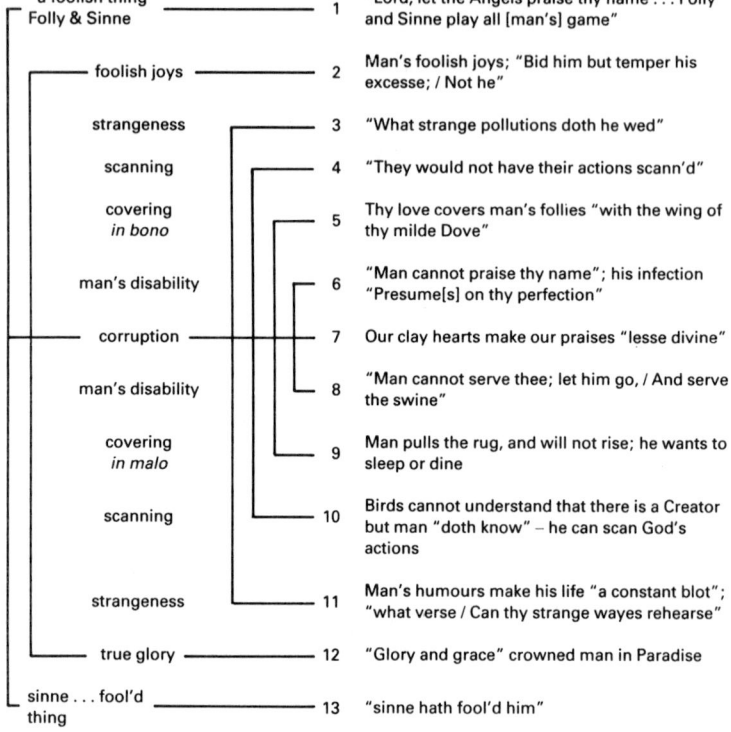

central stanza: 'our clay hearts, ev'n when we crouch [i.e. bend] / To sing thy praises, make them less divine" (7 : 3–4). Such is man's disability that he can neither praise God (stanza 6) nor serve him (stanza 8). Ironical juxtapositions abound: even the best of men will not have their actions scanned, "Nor any sorrow tell them that they sinne" (4 : 3–4), yet man is capable of scanning God's work of creation so that he knows "The spring, whence all things flow" (10 : 5–6). Although God covers man's follies with the wing of his "mild Dove" (5 : 4), yet man obstinately clings to his bed, refusing to have his rug removed; he must "go sleep, or dine" (9 : 7). Man's perversity makes God's love stand out more brightly so that the complaint becomes praise in disguise: God will not suffer those who would, to become his foes – such is his love. The poem, then, dramatizes the contrast between man's folly and the grace of God,

Diagram VIII.9 Herbert, "The Size"

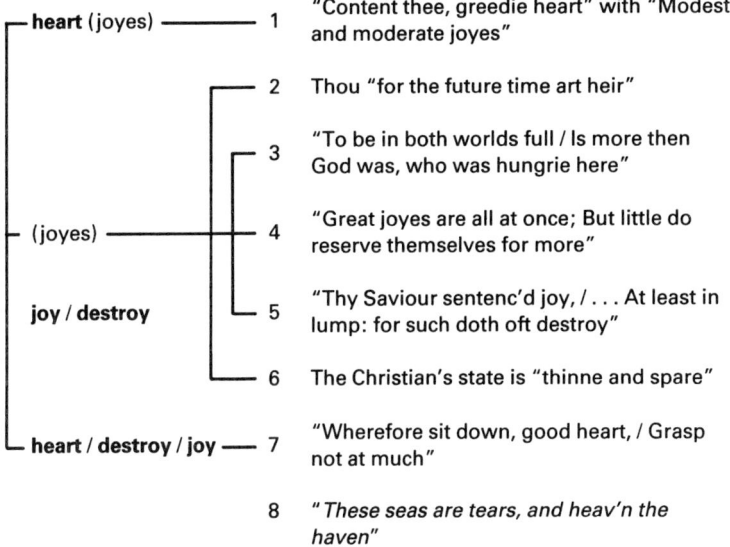

Whereas stanzas 1-3 see the joys of this life in the perspective of life hereafter, stanzas 5-7 underline the destructive aspect of great joys. The prophetic dream narrated in stanza 8 remains outside the symmetrical pattern, as if to mark the distance between a world of seas and the haven found in Heaven alone.

between man's actual condition and the state he desires, and the symmetrical structure serves Herbert's purpose well.

The symmetrical pattern may be varied by letting the last stanza remain outside the pattern, as in "The Size" (see Diagram VIII.9). The theme is contentment: "Content thee, greedie heart" with "Modest and moderate joyes"; if so, you will have "Title to more hereafter" (1 : 1-3). This admonition is repeated in the penultimate seventh stanza: "Wherefore sit down, good heart; / Grasp not at much, for fear thou losest all" (7 : 1-2). At the textual centre in stanza 4 we read that "Great joyes are all at once; / But little do reserve themselves for more." The penultimate stanza, which is the last in the symmetrical pattern, has a curious anomaly or departure from the established norm: whereas the stanzaic norm is 6 lines rhyming *a b a b c c*, stanza 7 has 5 lines only; the fourth line is missing so that line 2 remains unrhymed. This departure from the stanzaic norm expresses the absence of greed: the stanza enacts the reluctance to grasp at much by renouncing a line. As stanza 3 puts it, "To be in both worlds full / Is more then God was, who was hungrie here," and stanza 7, then, reveals an absence of stanzaic fullness. Like the contented man, the stanza reserves itself for more (4 : 1). It is a likely supposition that the 7 stanzas relate to this world, and the eighth stanza to life hereafter. However, the supposition is likely

Diagram VIII.10   Herbert, "Repentance"

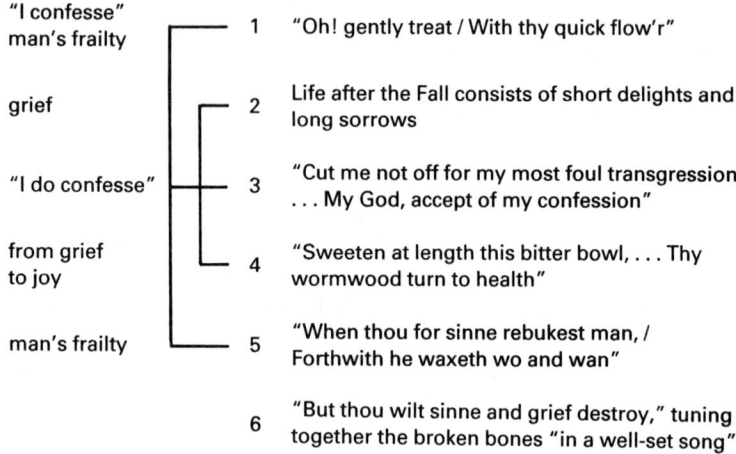

Alternative structure in the ratio 2:1

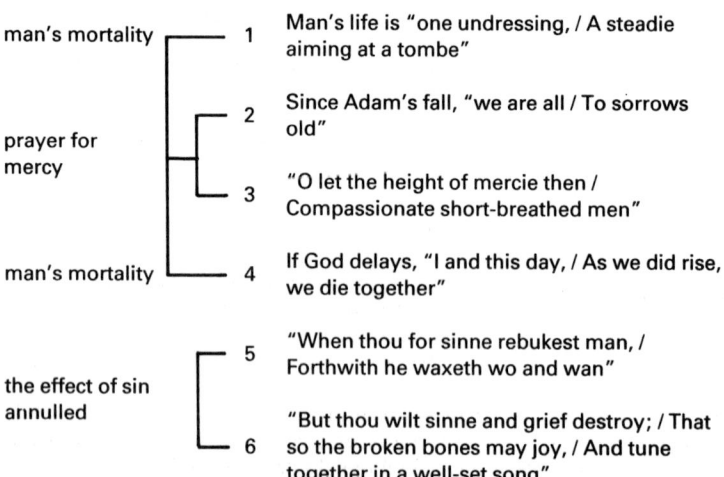

only because the transition from 7 to 8 is so clearly indicated in "Sunday." The "thinne and spare" condition of stanza 7, though, must be considered as intentional.

The 6 6-line stanzas of "Repentance" pursue a similar pattern, and so do the 6 4-line stanzas of "The Familie" (see Diagrams VIII.10 and 11). Simple symmetry encloses the first 5 stanzas, leaving the sixth as a climactic separate utterance. "Repentance" concludes with perfect confidence in God:

> But thou wilt sinne and grief destroy;
> That so the broken bones may joy,
> And tune together in a well-set song,
> Full of his praises,
> Who dead men raises,
> Fractures well cur'd make us more strong.

The music called for in this final stanza may be found in the rhyme scheme (a couplet and a quatrain), but it is more likely that the 6 stanzas have an alternative overall structure where 4 stanzas on man's mortality and 2 on God's redemptive action balance each other, as suggested in Diagram VIII.10.

"Vanitie" provides yet another example of a poem where the last stanza stands apart from the rest; in these 4 stanzas, stanzas 1–3

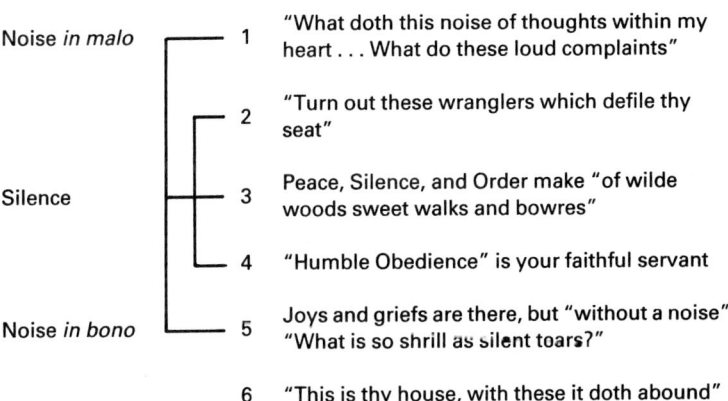

Diagram VIII.11 Herbert, "The Familie"

Within the house of man, riotous inhabitants are expelled (stanzas 1–2); all is transformed (stanza 3), and peaceful inhabitants only admitted (stanzas 4–5). Stanza 6 functions as a coda. The rhyme word *fears* links stanzas 1 and 5.

denounce man's quest for knowledge of the universe (stanza 1), for riches (stanza 2), and for knowledge of the creatures (stanza 3). What is noteworthy is that identical rhyme words connect stanzas 1 and 3, thus marking them as a complete cycle: *minde, doore,* and *before* are repeated in the sequence *minde, before,* and *doore.* The last stanza comments on these quests by pointing out that God only is ignored; man searches everywhere for death, but misses life close at hand. The repetition of no fewer than three identical rhyme words affords a reliable indication of authorial intent.

Rhymes have a similar structural function in the 8 4-line stanzas of "Even-song": the praise of God's love encloses the poem in the

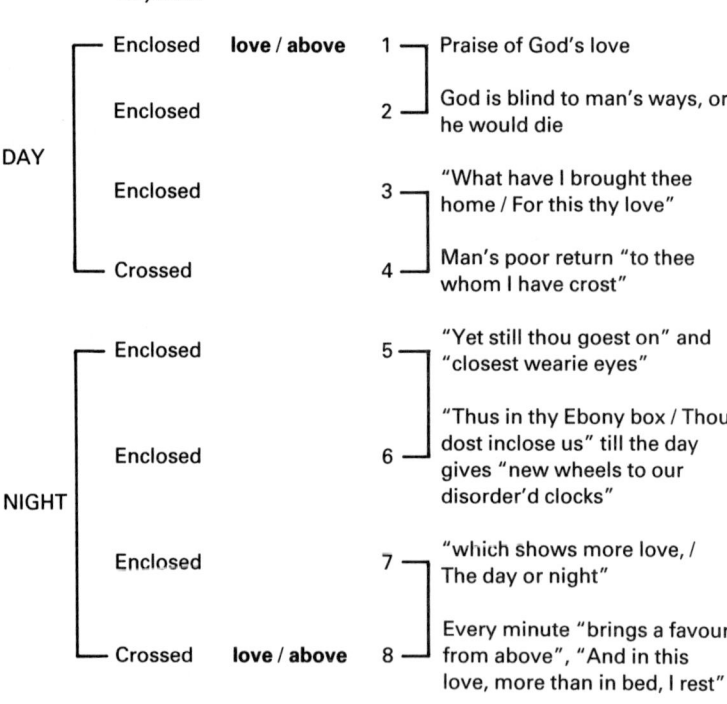

Diagram VIII.12   Herbert, "Even-song"

The 8 stanzas are grouped in pairs thematically as well as formally; the formal linking is a matter of the stanzaic pattern: the second stanza in each pair is virtually a mirror-image of the first. The rhymes *love / above* are repeated in the concluding stanza, which returns us thematically to the first, so that the poem (like man) is enclosed by God's loving care.

first stanza and the last, and so do the rhyme words *love* and *above* (see Diagram VIII.12). The enclosed rhyme scheme points in the same direction, while the admission, in stanza 4, that a poor return is made "to thee whom I have crost" is accompanied by crossed rhymes. The last stanza, too, has crossed rhymes, but in this case the structure functions *in bono*: God as it were "crosses" man by bringing a favour from above every minute. Although the stanzas are linked in pairs formally and thematically, the first edition prints them as separate stanzas, so that the quatrains stand out with the emphasis required for us to perceive Herbert's subtle changes from enclosed to crossed rhymes. We are likely to overlook this phenomenon in F. E. Hutchinson's edition, which gives us 4 8-line stanzas rather than 8 stanzas of 4 lines each.

"Man" is a poem on unity achieved through a harmonious arrangement of parts – within man, between man and the rest of creation (lower and higher), and between man and God. This focus on a proper relationship between parts and the whole prompts the architectural metaphor with which the poem begins and ends: man is a "stately habitation" (1 : 2), a "brave palace" (9 : 2) built by God, and so the poem which defines man in these terms must itself possess the same symmetries and proportions (see Diagram VIII.13). The link between the second and the penultimate stanza is found in the concept of addition: man may be the summary of creation, but "Reason and speech we onely bring" (2 : 4), whereas in stanza 8 it is man who receives the addition: "Man is one world, and hath / Another to attend him" (8 : 5–6). Stanza 3 focusses on the symmetry and proportions by means of which man becomes unified in himself and with the rest of creation, and this theme is repeated, with a variation, in stanza 7 on the beauty of each individual part and on the superior beauty of all things taken together. In stanza 4 man is the knot which ties all together, the lowest and the highest, and this idea recurs in stanza 6, where the idea of descent and ascent points to God as the ultimate *nexus*. At the centre, man is elevated as an *imago Dei* to whom all pay their loving service:

> For us the windes do blow,
> The earth doth rest, heav'n move, and fountains flow.
> Nothing we see, but means our good,
> As our delight, or as our treasure.

The symmetrical pattern, then, is perfect, and each stanza adds its quota of meaningful form based on the arrangement of the rhymes

Diagram VIII.13   Herbert, "Man"

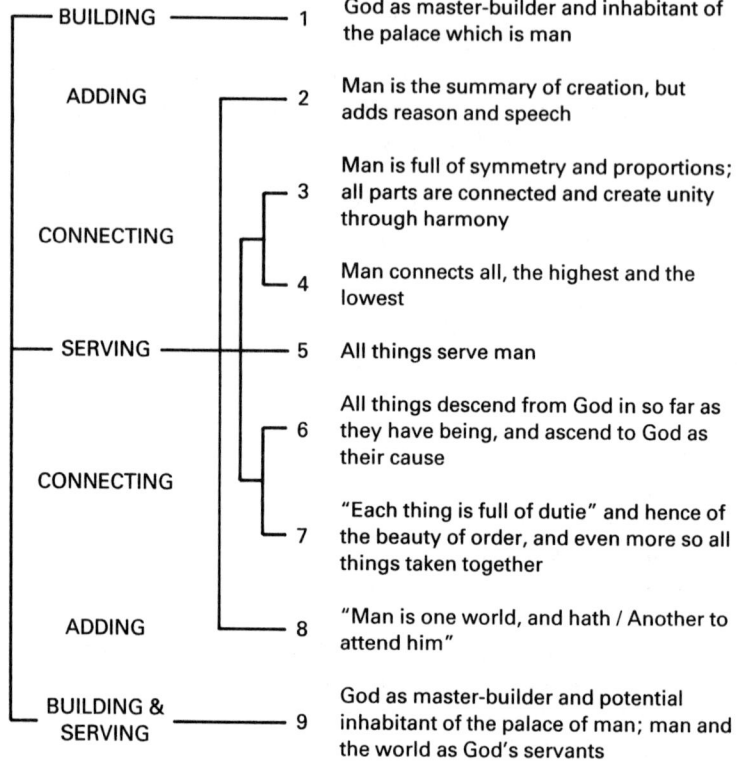

which connect the 6 lines into a whole. Each of the 9 stanzas has its own rhyme scheme, except for stanza 8, which repeats the pattern of stanza 2; in this case, though, a difference is created by means of feminine rhymes. Stanza 1 on the "stately habitation" has a symmetrical scheme (*a b c c b a*), and the other harmony – that of the diapason – is found in stanzas 5 and 9: the one consists of a couplet and a quatrain, the other of a quatrain and a couplet. In the linked stanzas 2 and 8 the scheme is *a b c a b c*, thus presenting the idea of a whole (*a b c*) to which something more is added (*a b c*): in stanza 2, the addition is the reason and the speech which man alone brings; in stanza 8, it is man who is a world to which another is added. I see no specific meaning in the other patterns beyond that of infinite variety, although stanza 4 may suggest the idea of connecting different spheres in life:

THE RELIGIOUS LYRIC

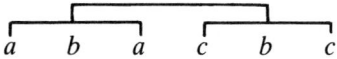

Rhymes have a similar function in the 5 6-line stanzas of "Ungratefulnesse," where the first 4 stanzas have the symmetrical or circular pattern *a b c c b a*, as in the first stanza of "Man." The poem's main conceit is of a box or cabinet. God has two, the Trinity and the Incarnation, and, although the Trinity may be the statelier, "all thy sweets are packt up in the other" (4:1). The rhyme scheme, then, shows how "sweets" are contained within the human frame of the Saviour, as in a cabinet. The rhyme scheme suggests the circle as well – the circle of the return to God through the Redeemer (stanza 1), the jewel or ring of betrothal joining God and his creation (stanza 2), and the return of true vision in death (stanza 3). The last stanza shifts the theme and hence also the rhyme scheme:

But man is close, reserv'd, and dark to thee:	a
When thou demandest but a heart,	b
He cavils instantly.	a
In his poore cabinet of bone	c
Sinnes have their box apart	b
Defrauding thee, who gavest two for one.	c

We can literally *see* how man has two "Boxes" within himself, where one contains the sins he stubbornly refuses to yield up.

The circular form to be expected from "A Wreath" finds expression in various ways, but primarily by letting the first 4 rhyme words be repeated in inverse order in the last 4 lines. Equally striking is the division of the 12 lines into 8 on the giving of the wreath to God and 4 on the simplicity which can alone create a true crown of praise. Such a crown can be offered only by the man to whom the simplicity has been given to know God's ways, "and practise them." The harmony of the diapason, therefore, connects the praise and the life; the two cannot be separated, since it is the life which constitutes the crown of praise. The placing of this poem confirms this impression: the poems which follow are "Death", "Dooms-day", "Judgement", and "Heaven."

It is difficult to consider the possible use of symbolic numbers in poems as short as Herbert's; typically, the convincing examples occur in poems of some length where the subject invites such a use. We are on much safer ground when the analysis shows the presence of symmetrical or graded arrangements, as in "Grief." If we ignore the incomplete last line, the poem consists of 18 pentameters divided into 12 on the eyes which are "too drie for me," and 6 on the verses which are "too fine a thing, too wise / For my rough sorrows." The speaker denounces the lover's grief which "allows him musick and a ryme: / For mine excludes both measure, tune, and time. / Alas my God." "Musick", or the harmony of the 2 : 1 ratio of the diapason, is rejected by permitting an incomplete 19th line. The harmony which nevertheless exists between the too dry eyes and the verses that are too fine, too much a product of preconceived number, weight, and measure, is undoubtedly a harmony which functions *in malo*. The whole idea of a carefully worked-out intricate pattern is roundly dismissed when the speaker exhorts his own verses to "Give up your feet and running to mine eyes" (line 15); the line suggests that normally lines do "run" to the eye, which disposes them according to a preconceived pattern.

A few cases of simple numerical decorum may nevertheless be worth mentioning. Thus the contents of some of Herbert's sonnets show that the form was favoured for the sake of the symbolism invested in its 14 lines. The number 14 represents above all the sum of the Law and the Gospels, the Old and the New Testament, and (more generally) sin and redemption through grace. "Redemption" and the two sonnets on "The H. Scriptures" are convincing examples of an alignment between the contents and the symbolism invested in the sum total of lines. Since "Holy Baptisme (I)" is equally concerned with redemption ("my deare Redeemers pierced side"), the form is again that of the sonnet, but since its companion poem – "H. Baptisme (II)" – has other thematic concerns, its form too differs, consisting as it does of 3 5-line stanzas. The speaker calls for a return to childhood in a spiritual sense: "The growth of flesh is but a blister; / Childhood is health." This idea of a return prompts the circular rhyme scheme (*a b a b a*) and perhaps also the choice of a 5-line stanza, since 5 is a circular number. "The Holdfast" may be offered as a final example: like "Redemption", it takes us from the Old Law to the New, and from man's own efforts to the basic realization that we have nothing, except in Christ: all things, though, are "more ours by being his" (line 13). The dramatic dialogue drives the point home with a logical precision which increases the emotional impact. My argument is strengthened by considering the fact that, when Henry Vaughan addressed the subject of Holy Writ in "H. Scriptures,"[11] he followed Herbert's lead and confined himself to 14 lines. Furthermore, in "The Law and the Gospel" he varied the formula by combining 10 and 4 in 10 4-line stanzas, while "The Passion" has 4 14-line stanzas. Even parts of poems may exhibit the same kind of numerical decorum: when the final section of "The Stone" considers the Law and the Gospel, the line total is 14, and in "Jacob's Pillow, and Pillar" the last section on the type/antitype relationship equally totals 14 lines: "Thy pillow was but type and shade at best, / But we the substance have, and on him rest."

Vaughan's shaping hand is more obvious than Herbert's, whose art conceals itself more carefully. On turning to Vaughan, therefore, we shall encounter poems whose bold and clear outlines often provide a safe basis for structural analysis; then, too, more of Vaughan's poems have their source of inspiration in structural concepts.

2. Henry Vaughan

Vaughan's poem on "The Jews" shows an overriding concern with the divinely ordained cycles of time in salvation history. The opening lines on the delivery of the Jews ("When the fair year / Of your deliverer comes") allude to the Year of Jubilee after a cycle of 7×7 years; this year, which "is not far" (line 20), is the 50th so that the poem itself stops short when 49 lines have been reached. The first stanza consists of 13 irregular lines, thus identifying the Deliverer as the head of the 12 Apostles as well as of the 12 tribes, whereas the second consists of 24 irregular lines in honour of the cycle of the setting and rising sun:

> And the same Sun which here declines
> And sets, will few hours hence begin
> To rise on you again, and look
> Towards old *Mamre* and *Eshcols* brook.
>
> (lines 28–31)

The sun is of course the Son: God "lov'd the world so, as to give / His onely Son to make it free" (ll. 33–34). The solar 24-hour cycle (as represented in the 24 lines of this stanza) therefore serves as an image of salvation. The last 12 lines consist of 3 regular quatrains, where reference is made both to the tribes ("the *eldest* childe"; l. 42) and to the Apostles ("The *youngest*"; l. 42). However, it may also be the number of time *par excellence*, since the cycle of the 12 months is usually aligned with the tribes and the Apostles and the signs of the zodiac. As the speaker puts it in the last quatrain: "Thy gifts go round / By turns, and timely" (ll. 47–48). This cyclical element, therefore, is very much present in Christian thought as it is in this poem by Henry Vaughan.

Vaughan's "Disorder *and* frailty" combines verbal and numerical signs in complex and pleasing patterns. We see from Vaughan's "Affliction" that he follows Herbert in aligning the lines and the life: if God fashions man in his image, man may fashion a poetic microcosmos of himself. It is in the spirit of Herbert's "The Collar" that the speaker of Vaughan's "Affliction" accuses himself of wildness: "Thou wouldst to weeds, and thistles quite disperse, / And be more wild than is thy verse" (ll. 15–16). Again, when Vaughan's persona, in "Disorder *and* frailty," concludes by praying that God will tune to his will "My heart, my verse", we are reminded of the last lines of Herbert's "Deniall".

"Disorder *and* frailty" consists of 4 15-line stanzas, where the contents divide each stanza into 4 + 11 lines, and this division is supported by the metrical form: 4 tetrameters rhyming *a b a b* are followed by irregular lines with an imperfect rhyme scheme. The last stanza, though, reveals the perfect pattern which unites these 11 lines:

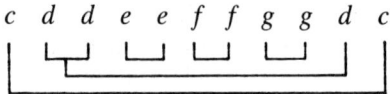

In this perfect pattern the *c* and *d* rhymes encircle the 11 lines, but, in stanzas 1, 2, and 3, lines 5 and 15 are unrhymed, thus breaking the linkage. When these numbers are understood, the stanza pattern is seen to express the contents. The introductory quatrains present the major works of God: creation (1 : 1–4), re-creation through blood and dew (2 : 1–4), the sending of the "Comforter" (3 : 1–4), and the "hatching" of the soul to eternal life (4 : 1–4). In strong contrast, the last 11 lines of stanza 1 focus on man's failure to retain the link with God: "I pine and shrink, / Breaking the link / 'Twixt thee, and me" (1 : 8–10); the rhyme scheme follows suit, and breaks the link. Man's very attempt to ascend is impious and ineffective (stanza 2); his own weak fire expires quickly (stanza 3). Hence the last stanza prays for wings to reach "Up where thou art" (4 : 1–4), and for all perverse and foolish thoughts to be expelled so that the seeds sown in him by God will live and grow, unhampered by sin (4 : 5–15). The quatrains, then, must represent the quaternions of creation and the 4 of the Gospels, whereas man's transgressions are expressed in the groups of 11 lines. But this is not all; the seeds sown by God grow secretly within the poem's space in the form of verbal repetitions that link the 4 stanzas. The rhyme word *hour* occurs in stanzas 1 and 2, and the idea of *sleep* connects stanzas 1 and 3: stanza 1 describes man's "dead sleep" as an echo of his state before creation, but in stanza 3 the "sleeping Exhalation" is "wak'd by heat" and thus made to ascend. The sequence of *fire* and *star* is found in stanzas 2, 3, and 4: "Touch'd by thy fire" man aims "at all / Thy stars" (stanza 2); however, "my weak fire" expires, "*Poor, falling Star!*" (stanza 3); the final prayer, though, voices the desire that God will "give wings to my fire" so that it may ascend "Up where thou art, amongst thy tire / Of Stars" (stanza 4). Indeed, the idea of ascent is found throughout. In the act of creation God beckons out man's "brutish soul" "even from the grave / And womb of darknes" (1 : 1–4), but an impious ascent follows: "I threaten heaven, and from my Cell / Of Clay, and frailty break, and bud" (2 : 1–2), but only to be devoured by flies and beaten down by storms. Man's "weak fire" dies in "sickly Expirations" (stanza 3), and so all hope is lodged in the final prayer that God provide the wings for ascent "Up where thou art." The 15-line stanzas therefore express the idea of ascent, as in the 15 Psalms of Ascent, or the 15 steps to the Temple. Indeed, the 4 groups of 15 lines express the poem's overriding concern with Christ as our ladder of redemption, and in view of the musical conceit found in the concluding lines ("tune to thy will / My heart, my verse") it is reasonable to see the poetic "ladder" or scale as a double octave that encompasses the full range. The consistency with which Vaughan exploits symbolic numbers to fashion his poem affords a degree of certainty which is remarkable, and the missing rhyme in stanzas 1–3 and the circular rhyme scheme which encloses the last 11 lines provide additional evidence of authorial intent.

"Retirement (I)" resembles "Disorder *and* frailty" in form and content. Man's innate sinfulness is effectively countered by God: "When thou wouldst fall / My *love-twist* held thee up, my *unseen link*" (2 : 10–11). The transgression, the going "quite astray" (1 : 8) and the roving around, "untam'd" (4 : 1–2), are reflected in the 11-line stanza and in the absence of rhyme for lines 1 : 1, 2 : 1, 3 : 1, and 4 : 1. It is only when we reach the last, fifth stanza that the rhyme scheme becomes perfect. However, God's "unseen link" nevertheless holds the poem together: line 1 : 1 finds its rhyme in line 2 : 1, and line 3 : 1 in line 4 : 1. Additional links are found in the repetition of key words, often placed in rhyme position: the rhymes *day / way* in stanza 1 recur in inverse order in stanza 2; *way* recurs in stanza 3 as well, and *clay* links stanzas 3 and 4. Finally *dust* occurs at 3 : 9

(within the line), at 4 : 9 (once within the line and once in rhyme position), and at 5 : 7 (within the line). Nothing can illustrate more clearly how consciously words are placed within the frame of the 5 stanzas. The "marring" of the poetic cosmos by sin is offset by these "*unseen links*," which show us home and put us in the way (cf. 1 : 11). In this manner the sinful structural number 11 is counterpointed by God's own secret action within man in a way which recalls Vaughan's "Faith," whose 11 quatrains counterpoint faith and "what sin, and death / Put us quite from" (ll. 37–38). Once again, "Faith brings us home" (l. 40).

We find the same theme of descent and ascent – man's wilful descent and God's gracious assistance – in "The Tempest", the chief difference being that the assistance comes to man through God's work of creation. Nature itself is a redeeming agent, if man would but use his eyes and ears. Like Augustine (for example in the *De libero arbitrio*), Vaughan argues that our senses, rightly used, would show us the way home. They do so through their abstract order and by striving upwards, like mists, trees, herbs, and flowers; except for earth, the very elements are refined: "Water's refin'd to *Motion*, Aire to *Light*, / Fire to all three, but man hath no such mirth" (ll. 31–32). "All have their *keyes*, and set *ascents*; but man / Though he knows these, and hath more of his own, / Sleeps at the ladders foot" (ll. 37–39). Man "Sinks to a dead oblivion" although "all / He sees, (like *Pyramids*,) shoot from this ball / And less'ning still grow up invisibly" (ll. 42–44). To explain the image of the pyramid, I would adduce Robert Fludd rather than Thomas Vaughan, because Fludd's graphic representation of creation shows a black cone-like pyramid whose top reaches from Earth into the intellectual sphere, while conversely a pyramid of light reaches down into the centre of the Earth. The dark cone is the physical creation, while the white cone which thrusts downward represents the world of pure mind,[12] and, since they intersect, as one diminishes the other increases. Since the theme bears such a strong resemblance to "Disorder *and* frailty" it is reasonable that Vaughan chose the same symbolic numbers; however, instead of 4 15-line stanzas he chose 15 4–line stanzas, where the number 4 must refer to the 4 elements that constitute our physical world. However, musical connotations are present, too, since Vaughan speaks of "keyes, and set ascents" (l. 37). A third, perhaps even more important symbolism relates the number 4 to the ladder of creation: this ladder consists of things that have being (stones), growth (plants), sense (animals), and reason (man). In the drawing included in the *Liber de sapiente* by Charles de Bouelles (Paris, 1510), the lowest level is represented by a human figure, which hugs itself in a squat position, clearly asleep and so placed on a par with the stone. This man has reduced himself to a state of mere being in "a rake's progress to annihilation," to quote S. K. Heninger.[13] Both 4 and 15, then, are numbers of ascent selected by Vaughan to express his theme. Further number symbolism may be present in the sum total of lines (60), which may represent man's "short hour" (l. 50), just as "ev'ry hour" shows man to himself, or "something he should see" (ll. 1–2). However, unlike the basic theme of ascent, these possibly self-referring passages are too casual to carry much weight. A point in their favour, though, is that they occur at the beginning and the end.

The simplest way in which the ratio of the diapason can be created is shown in "Joy," whose 30 lines divide into 10 on the false harmony of this world and 20 on the sighs that *"make Joy sure"* (l. 30). In the same way, "The Morning-watch" divides into 22 + 11 lines as an expression of "The great *Chime* / And *Symphony* of nature" (ll. 17–18) and of the "vocall joyes / Whose *Eccho is* Heav'ns blisse" (ll. 21–22). In the 8 stanzas of "Providence" the ratio is present in its division into 2 + 4 + 2 stanzas (see Diagram VIII.14), altogether a very simple pattern compared with Herbert's poem on the same

Diagram VIII.14 Vaughan, "Providence"

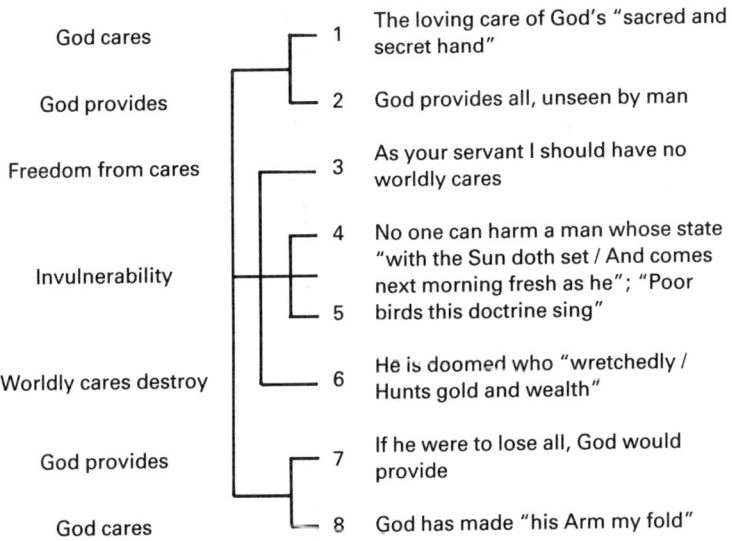

subject. Vaughan's lines on "Praise" (so heavily indebted to Herbert) divide formally into 8 quatrains and 4 6-line stanzas, thus providing yet another simple expression of the harmony which is its subject.

Compared with Herbert's structures, those of Vaughan are more easily perceived and the concern with number symbolism more pronounced. Even Vaughan's symmetrical structures are plainer, as in "The Constellation." The subject is praise of the *order* and

Diagram VIII.15   Vaughan, "The Constellation"

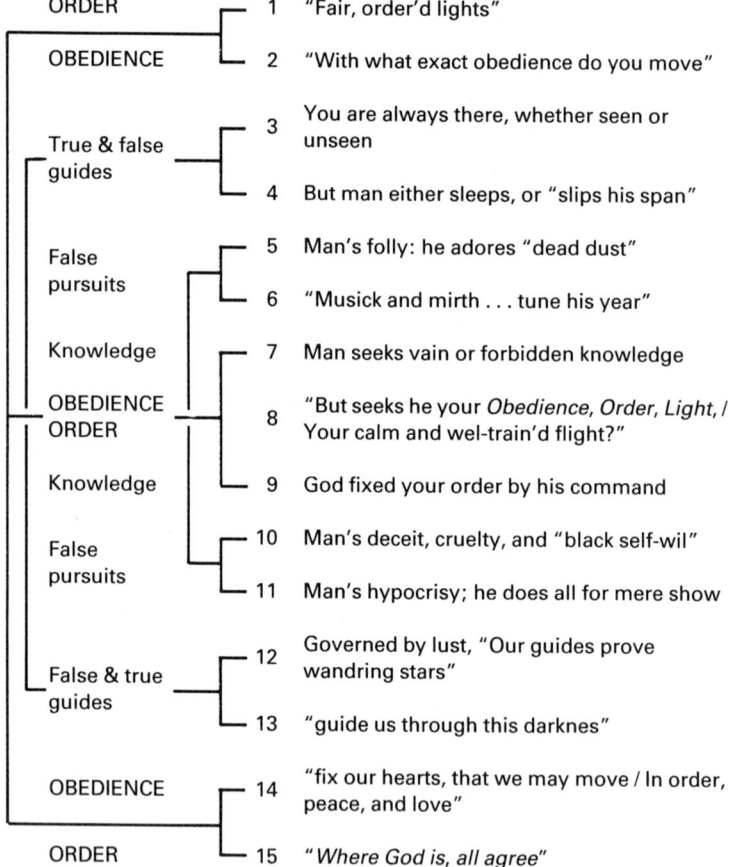

The true position stated in stanza 8 is flanked by stanzas on knowledge taken *in malo* and *in bono*.

Like the stars in the constellation, the stanzas are marshalled in perfect order.

obedience represented by the constellation, and these key words serve to connect the beginning, middle, and end (see Diagram VIII.15). The linkage between stanzas in between these points is equally simple. An added refinement, though, is that the 15 stanzas may represent a double octave signifying the harmony expressed by those who move, like the stars, "In order, peace, and love" (l. 54). "Ascension-Hymn" and "The Agreement" have equally simple symmetries (see Diagrams VIII.16 and 17). "Faith" has a more complex structure (see Diagram VIII.18). At the centre of its 11 quatrains – in quatrains 4–8 – is presented the story of the transition from veils and shadows to glorious day, so that faith itself is the subject primarily of quatrains 1–3 and 9–11. Faith reaches all (1–3), and faith "brings us home" (9–11).

In the first edition of the *Silex Scintillans* (1650), three poems located within pages 39–45 consist of 3 numbered 8-line stanzas; these are "The Storm", "Church-Service", and "Chearfulness". In "Chearfulness" the rhyme scheme assists our comprehension of the meaning invested in the formal arrangement: the first line and the last are joined by rhyme, thus forming the circle of the octave, and

Diagram VIII.16   Vaughan, "Ascension-Hymn"

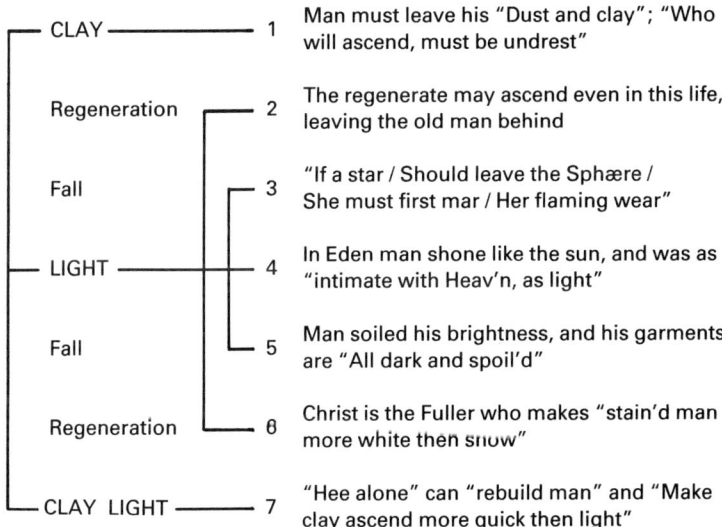

It is possible that the 7 6-line stanzas may represent creation and the subsequent re-creation, since the focus is on these ideas rather than on the ascent as such.

Diagram VIII.17 Vaughan, "The Agreement"

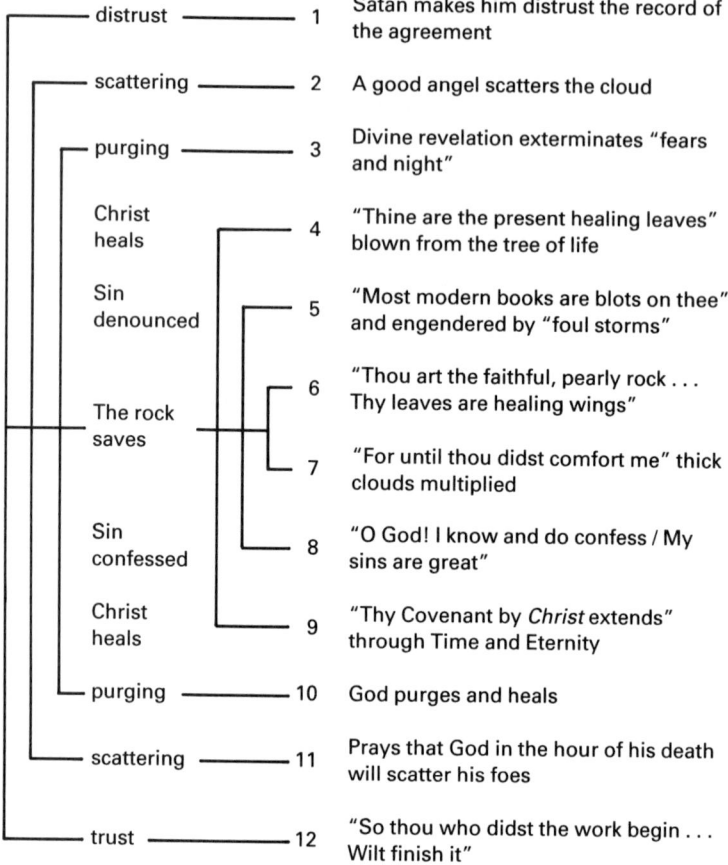

in between are 3 couplets (*a b b c c d d a*). The contents divide the poem into 2 stanzas on the surpassing joy of experiencing "thy least breath" (1 : 3), and a third which presents a prayer:

> O that I were all Soul! that thou
>   Wouldst make each part
> Of this poor, sinfull frame pure heart!
>   Then would I drown
>   My single one,
>   And to thy praise
>   A Consort raise
> Of *Hallelujahs* here below.

Diagram VIII.18 Vaughan, "Faith"

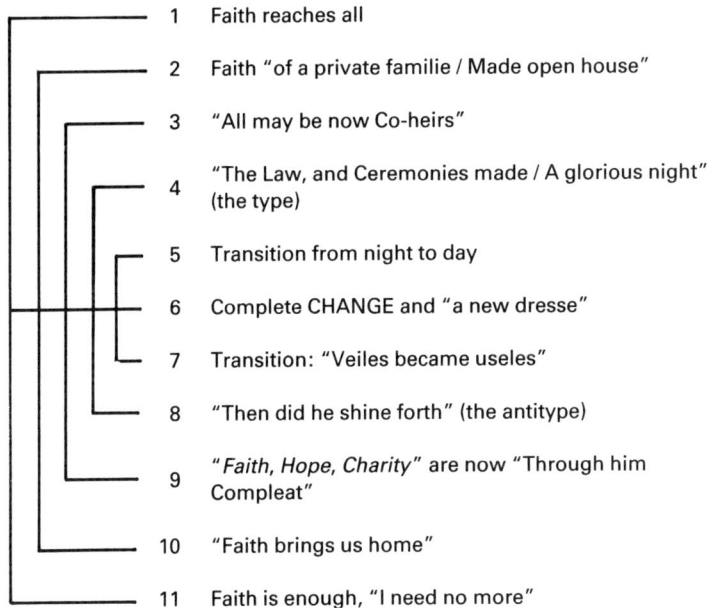

It is this "Consort" which finds expression both in the "octave" of each 8-line stanza and in the division into 2 + 1 stanzas. Milton makes a similar point in "At a solemn Musick" (*Poems*, 1645), where 8 lines (ll. 9–16) are circumscribed by rhyme in the first line and the last (or ll. 9 and 16), while 3 couplets are placed in between, as in Vaughan's poem. The contents divide Milton's poem into a sequence of 16, 8, and 4 lines, thus sounding the 2 : 1 ratio of the diapason in this way too. Vaughan may have been struck by this felicitous way of using rhymes and line totals to create what Milton calls the "perfect Diapason."

"Church-Service" is primarily about music; God is "the God of Harmony, and Love" (1 : 1), and the speaker envisages himself standing "in this thy Quire of Souls," propped by "thy hand" (2 : 1–2), so that "stones, and dust, and all of me / Joyntly agree / To cry to thee" (3 : 1–3). In "this Musick" God is exhorted to present "My Sighes, and grones" (3 : 4–8). Although not assisted by the rhyme scheme, the form in this instance, too, clearly is intended to be musical; in this case, therefore, the symbolism depends entirely on the division into 3 groups of 8 lines.

Sighing and weeping are the theme also of "The Storm", whose 3 stanzas are divided into 2 + 1. The rhyme words *bloud* and *floud* in lines 1 and 3 of stanza 1 are repeated at the end of stanza 2, in lines 2:6 and 2:8, thus closing the first circle. After describing the storms that afflict the microcosmos of man, the speaker presents a prayer in the concluding third stanza for the sighs and the tears which will purge and "Both *wash*, and *wing* my soul" (3:8). (It will be remembered that Quarles, too, defines sighs and groans as music in the Almighty's ear.) But for the precedent set by the other poems composed in the same formal pattern, however, it would seem hazardous to propose an interpretation in terms of the harmony of the octave proportion. This proportion of course also expresses the idea of ascent presented in the last line. "The Morning-watch" which follows "The Storm," provides a much more memorable statement of the idea of the harmony between God and his creation, whether birds, beasts, or men:

> Thus all is hurl'd
> In sacred *Hymnes*, and *Order*, The great *Chime*
> And *Symphony* of nature. Prayer is
> The world in tune ...
>
> (lines 16–19)

Despite the absence of divisions in this poem, whose outline resembles that of a ladder, the rhyme scheme establishes groups of 8 lines rhyming *a b a c d d c b*, so that these groups of 8 lines may be taken to represent the octave. The third group, however, consists of 7 lines only, so that line 19 on "The world in tune" remains unrhymed, probably to indicate the uniqueness of what is stated; another possibility is that the line finds its echo in Heaven and not here; its "*Eccho* is heav'ns blisse." Because of the missing line, the sum total of lines is 33 (rather than 34), so that the number identifies Christ as the ladder which joins Heaven and Earth, and hence as the source of the harmony between them.[14]

The poem without a title that follows "Chearfulness" ("Sure, there's a tye of Bodyes!") is divided into two parts, one of 8 lines and another of 16. The first part is in couplets, the second in quatrains. The contents explain why the textual structure insists on harmony: those who are far separated in the body may nevertheless establish concord and act in perfect unity if joined to the harmony of the world-soul.[15] This proposition finds as it were physical expression in the 1:2 ratio between couplets and quatrains, and between the sum total of lines in the two parts. We see, then, how even the choice of rhyme scheme depends on the wish to establish the desired ratio.

A circular rhyme scheme adorns the song in 3 numbered stanzas at the end of "The Search." The subject of the song is the way to find the Lord: he cannot be found "out of Doores" or in "The skinne, and shell of things," nor by racking "old Elements." The concluding couplet provides the true answer: "Search well another world, who studies this, / Travels in Clouds, seeks *Manna*, where none is." The 3 stanzas have respectively 6, 7, and 9 lines, and in stanzas 1 and 2 the first line and the last are linked by rhyme, the pattern being *a b c b c a* and *a b c b c b a*. After the perfect rhyme schemes of stanzas 1 and 2, the imperfection of stanza 3 startles: the opeing line fails to achieve linkage through rhyme. "To rack old Elements" is a statement entirely without linkage to any other line; the structure therefore tells us that "old Elements" cannot connect with the world which alone is worth seeking.

"The Call" has a similar imperfection. Stanzas 2 and 3 show that the stanzaic norm is 10 lines, but the first stanza has one line missing so that one line remains unrhymed. I quote the last 5 lines:

> Awake, awake,
> Some pitty take
> Upon your selves –
> Who never wake to grone, nor weepe,
> Shall be sentenc'd for their sleepe.

The absence of a rhyme for the third line marks the imperfection of those who never wake "to grone, nor weepe". The two unrhymed lines in "Love-sick" equally indicate the imperfection and disorder lamented in the contents.

In "Son-dayes" the numbers of Time and of Eternity are interwoven, since the day of rest is related to our rest in Eternity. Sunday is a day "to seek / Eternity in time" (ll. 4–5), a "Clue that guides through erring hours" (ll. 21–22), and "A taste of Heav'n on earth" (l. 23). The poem consists of 3 numbered groups of 8 lines, so that the number of Eternity is featured together with the number 3, probably for the God who is a Trinity. Numbers of Time are present in the sum total of lines (24) and in the division of each group into clearly distinguished quatrains. In view of the description of Sundays as "the steps by which / We Climb above all ages" (ll. 5–6) and the time when angels descend (l. 15), the number 4 may represent, not just the number of Time, but also the ladder of creation.

All of "The Dawning" is concerned with time: "Ah! what time wilt thou come? when shall that crie, / The *Bridegroom's Comming*! fil the sky?" (ll. 1–2). When "that day, and hour shal come," "Thou'lt find me drest and on my way, / Watching the Break of thy great day" (ll. 45–48). For Vaughan, the appropriate form for such a poem was a division into two parts, each consisting of 12 couplets, thus providing the 24-hour cycle of the great day.

These examples of Vaughan's structural craftsmanship show how often he "theologises by means of numbers", to use Pierre de la Primaudaye's telling phrase. Vaughan's very thought is informed by the structures imposed by God on his works in space and time, so that these structural concepts spill over from the contents to the form. The form therefore relates, not just to an isolated passage, but to the poem as a whole, and this is why the textual structures can be identified so readily. Herbert reveals this way of thinking in his sonnets on redemption and the Holy Scriptures and elsewhere too, but Vaughan's thinking is so much more explicitly numerical or structural; in this particular respect, therefore, the disciple transcended his master. As we shall now see, Thomas Traherne too connects basic religious concepts with symbolic numbers and ratios, and in so doing he can be shown to rely extensively on the Christianized version of the Hermetic dialogues.

3. Thomas Traherne

In the 37 poems in the Dobell Manuscript no fewer than 10 have a stanza total of 7, and five of them are among the first 10 poems. The preference for 7 stanza units is probably a consequence of Traherne's concern with creation, as in the first poem, "The Salutation."[16] The second poem, "Wonder", shifts the attention away from creation in Time to Eternity; after birth, everything seems like Eternity and like Heaven: "How like an Angel came I down! ... The World resembled his *Eternitie*" (1 : 1–5). For this description of a world transfigured by Eternity, Traherne chose 8 8-line stanzas, since 8 is the number of Eternity. Poems 3 and 4 ("Eden" and "Innocence") carry on the description of the beginning of life in the child; the child's innocence reflects the prelapsarian state ("Eden"), and "that which most I Wonder at" is the inward sense of perfect purity: "I felt no Stain, nor Spot of Sin" ("Innocence"; 1 : 1–4). "Eden" consists of 7 7-line stanzas, whereas "Innocence" has 5 groups of 3 quatrains. The numbers 3 and 4 combined make 7, while 5 refers to the physical world of sense so highly praised (cf. ll. 36–40). Poems 5, 6, and 7 ("The Preparative" in 7 stanzas, "The

Instruction" in 4, and "The Vision" in 7) are further elaborations of the related themes of creation and childhood, and climactic praise is presented in poem 8, "The Rapture", written in 4 5-line stanzas. In this opening sequence, then, the numbers 3, 4, 5, 7, and 8 recur, either in the sum total of stanzas or in the stanza structure. While 8 relates to God and to Eternity, the other numbers should be seen as signs for the work of creation which is Traherne's subject. "The Preparative" (in 7 10-line stanzas) provides interesting evidence of Traherne's thinking about the generation of the child in the womb:

> Before I knew my Hands were mine,
> Or that my Sinews did my Members joyn,
> When neither Nostril, Foot, nor Ear,
> As yet was seen, or felt or did appear;
> I was within
> A House I knew not, newly clothd with Skin.
>
> (lines 5–10)

These are not the sensations of a new-born child, as is usually assumed; the crucial statement is that no bodily member "As yet was seen, or felt or did appear," which recalls *Psalms* 39: 13–16 (AV) on creation in the womb: "Thine eyes did see my substance, yet being unperfect; and in thy book all my members were written, which in continuance were fashioned, when as yet there was none of them". A more precise context for Traherne's thinking may be found in *The Commentary on the Dream of Scipio* by Macrobius, one of the most popular handbooks of the Middle Ages and the Renaissance.[17] The number 7 comes in for attention from a purely scientific point of view:

> seven is the number by which man is conceived, developed in the womb, is born, lives and is sustained, and passing through all the stages of life attains old age; his whole life is regulated by it . . . Once the seed has been deposited in the mint where man is coined, nature immediately begins to work her skill upon it so that on the seventh day she causes a sack to form around the embryo.[18]

Macrobius explains that the presence of such a sack or skin was experimentally verified by Hippocrates. In the case of males the shape of the body appears in the seventh hebdomad, in the case of females in the sixth; this is when "the limbs distinctly appear" (VI.65; p. 113). Traherne, then, places the soul in the embryo while within the sack or skin but before the limbs have appeared, and this is why he can write that "Then was my Soul my only All to me, / A Living Endless Ey" (ll. 11–12). He was "all Sight, or Ey. / *Unbodied* and Devoid of Care, / Just as in Heavn the Holy Angels are" (4 : 6–8; my emphasis). The title ("The Preparative") therefore must refer to this early phase when the infant embryo is literally *unbodied*, and not just unaware of having a body. Traherne's definition of the soul in this state as "A Naked Simple Pure Intelligence" (2 : 10) recalls Macrobius, who writes that the soul is all one, like the Deity; it is "endowed with a single nature" and does not permit any division of its singleness, at the same time that it is "free from contamination with anything material" (VI.9; p. 101). As Traherne puts it, he was unfettered by vain affections: "I was as free / As if there were nor Sin, nor Miserie." Nothing could seduce his sense (5 : 6–10).

Macrobius explains at length how the number 7 regulates the life of man from the moment of conception; the parts that make up 7 – 3 and 4 – are the numbers which are capable of holding everything together. The number 3 is held together by one mean term, 4 by two. Macrobius refers in this context to Plato, the "sanctuary of truth itself," who informs us that "those bodies alone are closely held together which have a mean interposed between extremes to create a strong bond" (VI.22; p. 104). Hence the number 7 "possesses a dual power of binding, for both parts of it have inherited the primary links, three with one mean and four with two means. That is why Cicero ... says concerning the number seven, *It is, one might almost say, the key to the universe*" (VI.23 and 34; pp. 104 and 106). No wonder, therefore, that Traherne so often uses the numbers 3, 4, and 7 for structural purposes. When Traherne concludes "The Preparative" with a reference to the golden mean ("An Empty and a Quick Intelligence / Acquainted with the Golden Mean"; 7 : 4–5) we are not invited to praise moderation in all things. A poet so committed to divine excess cannot be thinking in these terms; his allusion to the golden mean calls for the Platonic context adduced by Macrobius.

In his chapter on the number 7, Bongo summarizes what Macrobius has to say about it, but adds purely Christian ideas. Bongo explains that the septenarius expresses the nature of the invisible Artificer and the visible world: the ternary represents the Deity as a Trinity, and the quaternarius the creatures. The artificer sanctifies his creatures and joins them to himself with a bond of love (*charitatis nexu*).[19] The number 7 therefore tells us that the earthly participates in the divine so that purification proceeds from the septenarius,[20] and this is why the dove was sent out from the Ark on the seventh day. The Sabbath or the seventh day signifies *light* as well as *rest* (as in Tasso's *Il Mondo Creato*). Bongo refers to Cassiodorus' comments on Psalm 7 according to which this number admonishes us to consider our eternal rest. The gifts of the Holy Ghost are 7, and in this number 3 represents the Trinity and 4 the Gospels; we should praise God 7 times a day every day of the week, and when 7 is multiplied by 10 the resulting number expresses our redemption, as with the return of the Jews from Babylon.[21]

The best way to approach such a list of meanings is to consider the way in which cosmic and biblical symbolism is fused in the number 7, and to realize that the meaning which most concerns us (or Traherne) has to do with the close union between man and God – a union experienced most fully by the infant in the womb and by the newly born child. Thus the number turns our attention to God as our source or fountain and our end. This is the subject of "The Vision" (poem 7) whose 7 8-line stanzas convey a vision of the unity of all things in man, and of man's union with God. This is the poem in which the theme of *order* is presented for the first time: "Order the Beauty even of Beauty is, / It is the Rule of Bliss, / The very Life and Form and Caus of Pleasure" (2 : 1–3). The *ordering* and *conjoining* of all things is the main point: "Who all things finds conjoynd in Him alone, / Sees and Enjoys the Holy one" (7 : 7–8). Man is the end of all God's labours, and we contemplate the fountain (God) best in the end (man):

> To see the *Fountain* is a Blessed Thing,
>   It is to see the King
> Of Glory face to face: But yet the End,
>   The Glorious Wondrous End is more;
> And yet the fountain there we Comprehend,
>   The Spring we there adore,
> For in the End the Fountain best is Shewn,
>   As by Effects the Caus is Known.
>   (stanza 6)

The order which is "the Beauty even of Beauty" is the fusion between the fountain and the end, and the fusion occurs when the fountain is shown and adored in the end which is man. This vision is greater than seeing the fountain in itself alone, although this is to "see the King / Of Glory face to face." The startling change in the accustomed priorities enables the true order to emerge in a radical reinterpretation of *Romans* 1 : 20 which takes us to the heart of Traherne's message as a poet. This fusion may be mirrored in the

Diagram VIII.19   Traherne, "The Vision" (Poem 7)

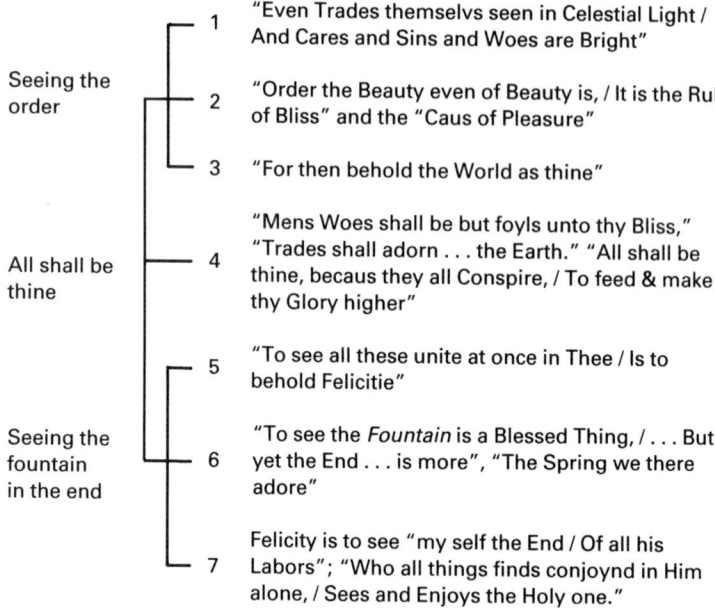

Verbal repetitions connect the beginning, middle, and end: the *Trades* and *Woes* of stanza 1 recur in stanza 4 in inverse order, just as stanzas 4 and 7 are linked by the idea of *conspiring together*, or *conjoining*. The nature of the order praised in stanza 2 emerges in stanza 6.

structural numbers 7 and 8, for the structure of these 7 8-line stanzas consists of a triad, a single stanza, and a triad (see Diagram VIII.19). Central accent falls on the statement that "All shall be thine," while the triads proceed from seeing the order which is the beauty of beauty to understanding that this order consists in perceiving the presence of the fountain in the end. And, in addition, the last triad honours the triad of love, the giving, receiving, and returning, which is represented as "From One, to One, in one to see *All Things*" (7:1).

"Innocence" (poem 4) shows how verbal repetition establishes linkage; one would not expect a poet with Traherne's reputation for ecstatic expression to use such a technique, but his outpourings are nevertheless often guided by functional repetition (see Diagram VIII.20). The poem has 5 numbered units, each of which consists of 3 spaced quatrains. Multiple verbal repetition links the beginning

Diagram VIII.20 Traherne, "Innocence" (Poem 4)

Stanza 1	quatrain 1		"**within** / I felt no Stain, nor Spot of Sin"
	quatrain 2		"No Darkness . . . No Guilt" "all **within** was Pure and **Bright**"
	quatrain 3		"The very Night to me was **Bright**, / "Twas Summer in December"
Stanza 2	quatrain 1		My soul did "flie / All Objects that do feed the **Eye**"
	quatrain 2		
	quatrain 3		That which takes objects "from the **Ey** / Of others, offerd them to me"
Stanza 3	quatrain 1		"My Soul did **kneel** / In Admiration **all the Day**"
	quatrain 2		
	quatrain 3		"For this I **daily kneel**"
Stanza 4	quatrain 1		"Whether it be that Nature is so **pure** / . . . or that **sure** / God did by Miracle the Guilt remove"
	quatrain 2		I may have found this happiness "one **Day**"
	quatrain 3		"I a World of true Delight / Did then and to this **Day** do see"
Stanza 5	quatrain 1		"the Gate of Heav'n, that **Day** / The anchient Light of Eden did convey / Into my Soul"
	quatrain 2		"my Ravisht Sense / Was entertaind in Paradise"
	quatrain 3		"An Antepast of Heaven **sure**! . . . **Within**, without me, all was **pure**"

The emphasis on what is *within* links stanzas 1 and 2 thematically, while stanzas 4 and 5 are linked both thematically and by means of verbal repetition. Finally, the emphasis in the last unit (5:3) on the purity *within* joins the end to the beginning.

and the end of units 1, 2, and 3. *Within* connects quatrains 1 and 2 in the first unit (or stanza), and *bright* quatrains 2 and 3. The *eye* links quatrains 1 and 3 in the second stanza, and *kneeling* the beginning and the end of the third. Finally, the last two stanzas are linked by the repetition of the rhyme words *pure* and *sure* in inverse order. These repetitions establish circular patterns, perhaps to suggest the return to childhood ("I must becom a Child again"; l. 60). The fact that there are 15 quatrains suggests an allusion to the idea of ascent to the gates of Heaven as stated in the first quatrain of the fifth stanza: "That Prospect was the Gate of Heav'n, that Day / The anchient Light of Eden did convey / Into my Soul" (ll. 49–51). The

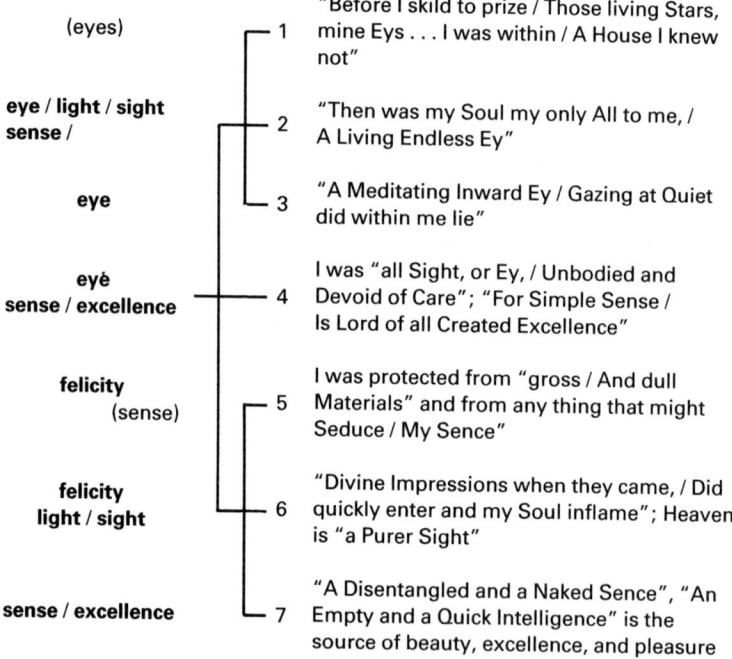

Diagram VIII.21   Traherne, "The Preparative" (Poem 5)

Eye is the key word in stanzas 1–3, *sense* in stanzas 5–7, and in the central stanza the two words combine. The rhyme words *light* and *sight* link stanzas 2 and 6: stanza 2 defines the soul as "A Living Endless Ey" and "an Inward *Sphere of Light* / Or an Interminable Orb of *Sight*," whereas the receptive emptiness is stressed in stanza 6: powers that are pure and empty receive divine impressions at once. Stanzas 3 and 5 connect the inward eye with pure soul, unconnected with "gross / And dull Materials."

prelapsarian state of innocence equals the state of Heaven; and in the same way the gates of Heaven are open to the child.

The 7 stanzas of "The Preparative" (poem 5) combine a symmetrical structure with a division into a triad, a single stanza, and a triad (see Diagram VIII.21). Although poem 1, "The Salutation", arranges its 7 stanzas in similar fashion (see Diagram VIII.22), it does not employ verbal repetition to the same extent as "The Preparative". The 7 stanzas of "The Designe" (poem 19) have a purely symmetrical arrangement where the first stanza and the last share the rhyme words *skies*, *wise*, and *best*. "The Designe" considers God's design in the work of creation, and Traherne's own design stresses the function of truth (see Diagram VIII.23): truth is the daughter of Eternity and his only bride, just as the wisdom of infancy reflects the Wisdom of Eternity (see stanzas 1 and 7, and 2 and 6). At the centre, in stanza 4, Truth is personified as "The Great Queen of Bliss" who draws the soul irresistibly.

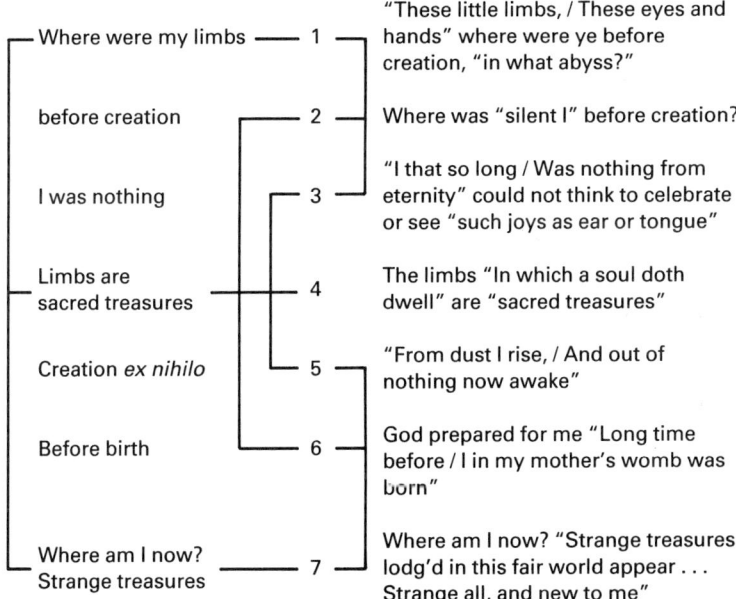

Diagram VIII.22   Traherne, "The Salutation" (Poem 1)

Traherne's concern is with physical creation – of the world and of the individual.

Diagram VIII.23 Traherne, "The Designe" (Poem 19)

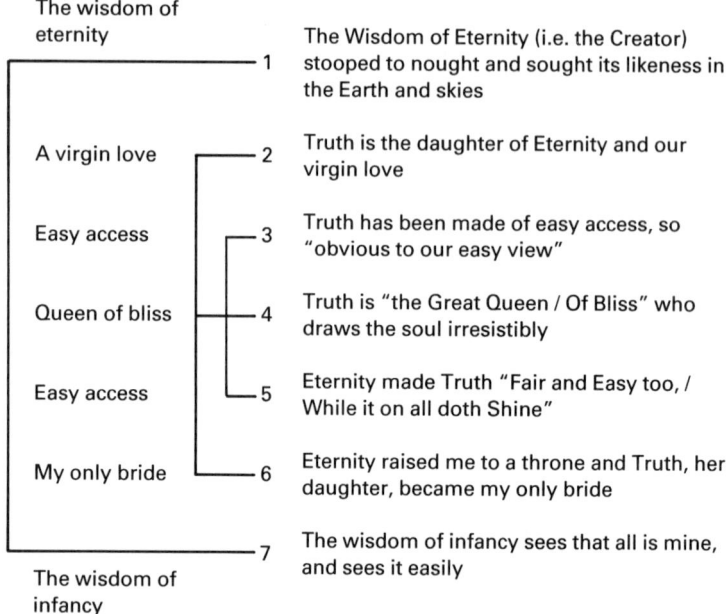

The framing stanzas juxtapose the wisdom of the Creator and the wisdom of the infant, and so virtually identify the latter with the former.

The framing stanzas are linked by the repetition of the rhyme words *skies / wise / best*.

A simple, but effective symmetrical pattern unifies the 7 stanzas of "Eden" (poem 3; see Diagram VIII.24); such is its simplicity that it may be considered as the archetypal pattern for a short poem with an odd number of stanzas. The structural simplicity pleases because it reflects the simplicity which is its subject.

"The Improvment" (poem 9) has the same subject as Herbert's "Providence" and hence makes the same allusion to the Creator who disposes everything sweetly. The difference, though, is marked: when Traherne praises the art with which God creates and governs all things, the whole point is that this order ensures happiness for man, and that the order is there because it is God's bliss to seek "His Creatures Happiness as well as His: / For that in Truth he seeks, and thats *his Bliss*" (9 : 5–6). The universe exalts man when it is "conjoynd in one" (5 : 5), and this is why the poem begins with the forceful assertion that "'Tis more to recollect, then

Diagram VIII.24 Traherne, "Eden" (Poem 3)

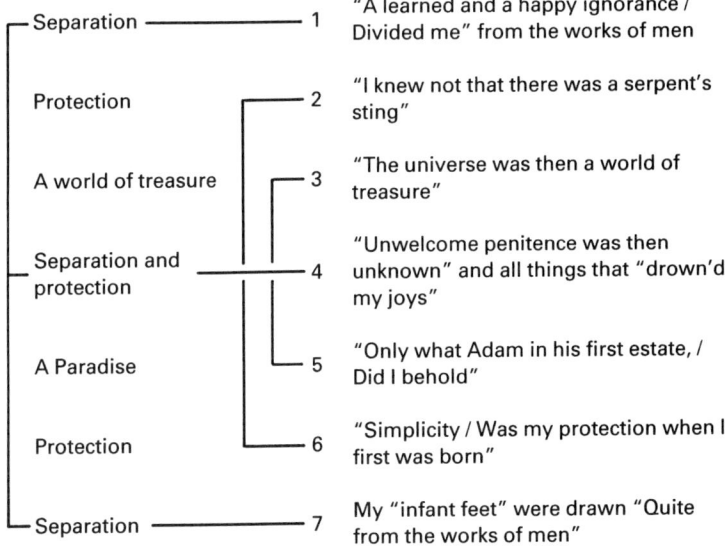

make" (1 : 1). To *recollect* means to gather together, or order. All things are joined in one, for one, to be enjoyed by one, who will then return praise to his great Maker. We recognize Augustine's argument as presented, for example, in the *Confessions*, when we read that God is "more *Divine* / In making evry Thing a Gift to one / Then in the Parts of all his *Spacious Throne*" (7 : 4–6). (The whole is always greater and more beautiful than a single part, though it be Heaven itself, as Augustine puts it.) The 14 6-line stanzas illustrate this unity in their perfect symmetrical structure (see Diagram VIII.25); this structure, however, coexists with a symmetrical arrangement of stanzas 1–7 and 8–14 (see Diagram VIII.26), a division which may be taken to represent the two separate actions of *making* and *disposing*. To quote from stanza 7, to bring all things to bear on man "Is far more *Great* then to Creat them there / Where now they stand; His *Wisdom* more doth shine / In that, his *Might* and *Goodness* more appear, / In recollection" (7 : 1–4). By considering the acts of creating and ordering as two separate steps it becomes possible for Traherne to put the emphasis on the latter.

As we are beginning to realize, poetic collections ever since Antiquity have frequently had their own internal structures; Ben Jonson's *The Forrest* and Herbert's *The Temple* are good

Diagram VIII.25 Traherne, "The Improvment" (Poem 9). Overall Symmetry

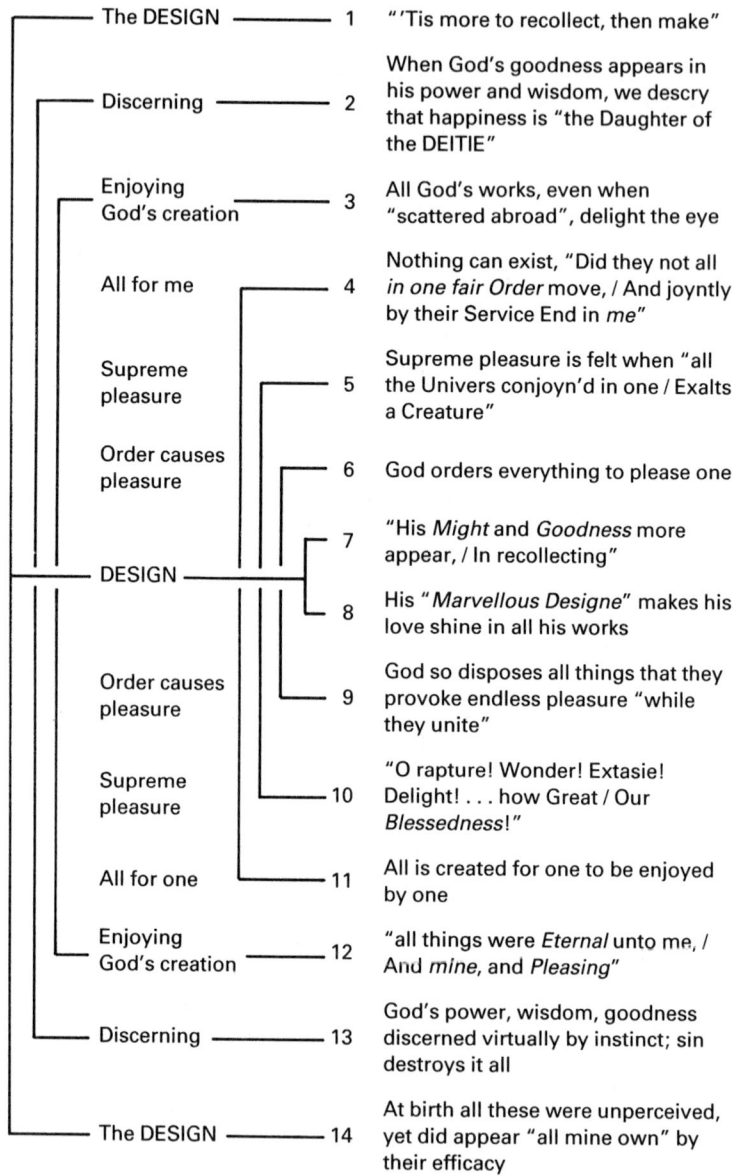

Diagram VIII.26 Traherne, "The Improvment". The Symmetry of Stanzas 1–7 and 8–14

Ordering	1	"'Tis more to recollect, then make"
Happiness	2	God's goodness as seen in his power and wisdom makes us descry the happiness "Which is the Daughter of the DEITIE"
Scattered	3	"all his Works . . . / Even scattered abroad *delight* the Eye"
"in one fair order"	4	Nothing can be unless "they all *in one fair Order* move"
Conjoined	5	All "shine in the utmost Height" when "all the Univers conjoynd in one / Exalts a Creature"
Pleasing	6	When God pleases one man "With all the *Powers* of the Highest Sphere"
Ordering	7	this is greater than to create them; God's power, wisdom, goodness appear in his recollecting or ordering of them
Efficacy of the design	8	The "*Marvellous Designe*" of "that Great Architect" shows how his "Lov doth shine / In all his Works"
Order causes pleasure	9	God so disposes all things that they provide endless pleasure "while they unite"
Exaltation	10	"how Great / Our *Blessedness*!"
Efficacy of the design	11	Almighty power and eternal wisdom "Produce a Creature" who must return a sacrifice of endless praise
Exaltation	12	"All things were *Eternal* unto me"
Sin destroys	13	At first we discerned by instinct what later on "our Care and Sin destroys"
Efficacy of the design	14	At birth all "were unperceivd", yet by their efficacy they appeared "all mine own"

Diagram VIII.27 Traherne, The Last Nine Poems in the Dobell MS

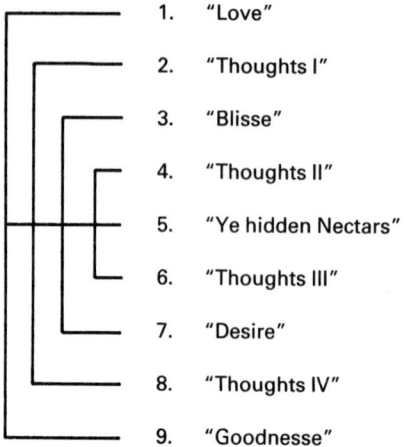

examples.[22] The editor of the Penguin edition of Traherne's *Selected Poems and Prose* (1991) follows this general trend when he suggests that Traherne may have taken special care to provide a meaningful arrangement for the last nine poems in the Dobell MS.[23] From Diagram VIII.27 we observe that the 4 poems on "Thoughts" are spaced regularly throughout this sequence; moreover, on reading poems 1, 5, and 9 we discover the presence of identical images and themes. "Ye hidden Nectars" strikes the main theme, strongly supported by "Love" and "Goodnesse", and its form (4 10-line stanzas) recurs in "Love".

"Ye hidden Nectars" offers ecstatic praise to the "hidden Nectars, which my GOD doth drink," juxtaposing them with the "Images of Joy that in me Dwell" (1 : 1 and 5); these images of joy are "the rich Ideas which within me live", "that do bring and Give / All Joys" (2 : 5 and 7–8). They excel "all Substances" (1 : 7) because derived from the divine essence. "Love" equally begins with an apostrophe to the hidden nectars: "O Nectar! O Delicious Stream! / O ravishing and only Pleasure!" (1 : 1–2). The classical allusion is further elaborated in the lines on the joys which shower down from Heaven so that "Jove beyond the Fiction doth appear / Once more in Golden Rain to come, / To Danae's Pleasing Fruitfull Womb" (3 : 7–10). All this is echoed in the last 2 stanzas of "Goodnesse", which repeat the classical images of nectar and ambrosia: God's goodness extends "beyond the Ends / Of Heaven and Earth" (4 : 7–

8) and "Multiplies / Above the Skies" (4 : 9–10), and hence "The Soft and Swelling Grapes that on their Vines / Receiv the Lively Warmth that Shines / Upon them, ripen there for me" (5 : 1–3), and the "rich Affections" of all things "do like previous Seas / Of Nectar and Ambrosia pleas" (6 : 1–2). It must be conceded that poems 1, 5, and 9 are so closely linked that they may appropriately be considered as the beginning, middle, and end of a sequence.

Can it be shown that a similar linkage exists between "Thoughts I" and "Thoughts IV"? While the beginning, middle, and end of the sequence focus on God's love, which, when received, elevates man to the divine, "Thoughts I" and "Thoughts IV" present the mind as omnipresent and hence God-like: thoughts "Can Enter Ages, Present be / In Any Kingdom" ("Thoughts I"; 6 : 7–8), and this omnipresence is equally the subject of "Thoughts IV":

His Glory Endless is and doth Surround
And fill all Worlds, without or End or Bound.
What hinders then, but we in heav'n may be
Even here on Earth did we but rightly see?
(lines 33–36)

God's omnipresence finds a temple within the mind (ll. 87–88), and lies in us (l. 89).

"Blisse" and "Desire" are logically connected: no bliss without desire; desire is "Ambassador of Bliss" ("Desire"; 5 : 2). Both poems draw a sharp distinction between true bliss, which is "To do as Adam did," and "those Superficial Toys / Which in the Garden once were hid" ("Blisse"; 1 : 1–6). Those who feed on these foolish toys merely increase their wants ("Blisse"; 2 : 4–6). "Desire" posits a "restlesse longing Heavenly Avarice, / That never could be satisfied, / That did incessantly a Paradice / Unknown suggest" (1 : 8–11). The 5 13-line stanzas have a circular pattern (supported by the circular number 5), which suggests the circle of desire and fulfilment, the desire being the manifestation of "A love with which into the World I came, / An Inward Hidden Heavenly Love" (1 : 4–5). The circular pattern is indicated by the fact that the first two lines and the last two share the rhyme words *fire* and *desire* as an expression of their thematic concern with the desire which is "An Eager Thirst, a burning Ardent fire" (1 : 2), and a "sacred Thirst" leading to "Heavenly Pleasures" stemming from desire as heat does from fire (5 : 1 and 11–13). The stanza at the centre also has a circular pattern, like Eve's praise of Adam in *Paradise Lost* IV.641–

56, as Alan Bradford has observed.[24] Even the lovely objects of sight remembered from the Eden of childhood cannot please because they are physical objects that cannot satisfy the thirst of the soul; the list of objects is presented in the first 7 lines and then repeated in inverse order in the last 6 lines, and the repetition includes the rhyme words *Streams* and *Beams* repeated in inverse order. In short, then, man is born into the world filled with "An Inward Hidden Heavenly Love" (1:5), which prompts a desire which can be satisfied by no physical object, however lovely, but only by "Heavenly Pleasures" (5:11). Whatever pleasures are at God's right hand, "must, before I am Divine, / In full Proprietie be mine" (4.11–13). This is Traherne's impassioned version of the love which is given, received, and returned in the circle enacted by the poem's structure. By partaking fully in this circle of love man becomes divine.

It remains to consider the complementary poems "Thoughts II" and "Thoughts III." The one is concerned with God's works, the other with those of man, but in each case the emphasis is on spiritual creation. The "Spiritual World within" is "nearer far of Kin / To God, then that which first he made" ("Thoughts II"; 4:7–9); indeed, in "A Delicate and Tender Thought / The Quintessence is found of all he Wrought" (1:1–2). God prizes it more than "All the Skies" since it makes us like seraphim in our souls (2:10–12). "Thoughts III" puts this proposition even more boldly: "By Thoughts alone the Soul is made Divine" (l. 6). Thoughts are the spring of everything – "Beauty, Order, Peace," and "all the new Jerusalem" (ll. 9–12). Thoughts, like God, include everything within themselves, "All Worlds, all Excellences, Sences, Graces, / Joys, Pleasures, Creatures, and the Angels Faces" (ll. 71–72).

The symmetrical pattern formed by these 9 poems is in part responsible for the feeling of repetitiousness experienced on reading them, but once the pattern is perceived the thematic structure is clarified. As in individual poems, the repetition is functional and not just the result of an artless outpouring of free associations. Traherne therefore is more of a conscious artist than has been perceived; he is an exponent of the syncretistic tradition outlined in these pages, and within this tradition the Christianized version of the Hermetic dialogues often exerted a powerful influence, as we may see from Traherne's thought. Traherne virtually reduces redemption to a matter of the supremacy of pure mind over matter or body, as in his poems on thought, at the same time that such a supremacy makes man a sharer in God's divinity even in this life. Traherne's several quotations from Pico's *Oration on the Dignity of Man* in his Fourth Century (§§ 74–77) prove his interest in a thinker whose own thought was influenced by these dialogues, as shown in the direct quotation from Hermes embedded in the passages cited by Traherne. Additional evidence is found in the extracts from the Hermetic dialogues in Traherne's Commonplace Book and the *Christian Ethicks*.[25]

The contents of Traherne's poetry and prose, then, and his structurally oriented poetics should be related to the Hermetic dialogues, as a short survey will indicate. This will be based on Dr John Everard's translation, published posthumously in 1650 and 1657, and on the voluminous commentary by François de Foix, published in French in 1579 and in Latin in 1630.[26]

Traherne's favourite theme of felicity owes a great deal to Pico and to the Hermetic dialogues to which Pico was so heavily indebted. Part 7 of Pico's *Heptaplus* ("Of the Felicity which is Eternal Life") defines the repose of the seventh day as felicity, and felicity in its turn as "the return of each thing to its beginning." Just as God is the beginning of all things, he is "the end, rest, and absolute felicity of all things." For this reason, a circular motion is "the most express image of the true felicity, through which a creature returns to the beginning from which it proceeded." Thus we are brought back to Unity from the imperfection of Multiplicity "by an indissoluble bond with him who is himself the One."[27] Traherne's frequent use of symmetrical or circular structures should be taken to have these appropriate connotations. Contemplating God's works aright is the key to felicity; we should see God through his creation, where he appears through their *order*: 'Let us therfore survey their Order, and see by that whether we cannot Discern their Governer" (*Centuries* I.22, ll. 23–25). The allusion to *Romans* 1 : 20 is plain. The main thrust of Traherne's prose and verse is to lead us from the world without to the world within. He intensifies Augustine's *intravi et vidi*; not only do we discover God when we turn to this world within, but we become like God. Whereas Augustine deplores how he became depraved by sin as a small child, Traherne deplores his loss of his original perception of the divine essence present in all things. Such thoughts were "blotted out" in him, but later recalled by divine grace (*Centuries* III.7 and III.1). This is how the Hermetic influence manifests itself; it is fused with, but goes beyond, the Christian tradition. Where Traherne echoes Augustine most clearly is in his account of the depravity incurred as he grew older: opinion and custom lead the child away from God (*Centuries* III.8–9 and *Confessions* 1:16). The corruption may be derived from Adam, but it reaches the child through his environment: "I was quickly tainted and fell by others" (*Centuries* III.8, ll. 20–21). Traherne's sorry state resembles Augustine's "I lived among Shadows, like a Prodigal Son feeding upon Husks with Swine. A Comfortless Wilderness full of Thorns and Troubles the World was, or wors: a Waste Place covered with Idleness and Play, and Shops and Markets and Taverns" (*Centuries* III.4, ll. 2–6). Augustine too compared himself to the Prodigal Son, fed on the husks of the Manichees (*Confessions* 1:18 and 5:3–7), just as he concludes book 2 with the memorable description of the way in which he had turned himself into a barren waste land, a *regio egestatis*. Finally both are moved by the Psalms of David, both are set on fire with love of God (*Centuries* III.38 and *Confessions* 9:4), and both denounce vain learning and idle curiosity (*Centuries* III. 40–41 and *Confessions* 1:13).

To this basis in orthodox religious thought, then, must be added a considerable indebtedness to the Hermetic dialogues as filtered through the minds of Renaissance commentators.

The opening paragraphs of the First Century present some of Traherne's main ideas. Meditation in a state of repose leads to God, which means that God "hath chosen the Ways of Eas and Repose, by which you should ascend ... Yet shall the End be so Glorious, that Angels durst not hope for so Great a One till they had seen it" (*Centuries* I.4, ll. 4–15). The key that opens the door to this ascent is to see the divine essence in all things (I.13), as explained in the Hermetic dialogue entitled "The Key." This dialogue is Ch. X in the translation-cum-commentary by François de Foix and Book IV in Everard's translation. The dialogue explains the effect of seeing God: the vision does not blind, but illuminates the soul, and those who are capable of enjoying it "do many times fall asleep from the Body, into this most fair and Beauteous Vision" (Everard, p. 51). Silence is the pre-condition and the appropriate response, together with a suspension of sense perception. The knowledge draws the soul from the body, "*and changeth it wholly into the Essence of God. For it is possible for the soul, O Son, to be deified while yet it lodgeth in the Body of Man, if it contemplate the beauty of Good*" (IV.17–19; Everard, pp. 51 f.). Traherne's companion poems on "Dumnesse" and "Silence" (poems 11 and 12 in the Dobell MS.) transmit these very ideas:

> A World of innocence as then was mine,
> In which the Joys of Paradice did shine
> And while I was not here I was in Heaven,
> Not resting one, but evry Day in Seven.
>
> ...
>
> A vast and Infinit Capacitie,
> Did make my Bosom like the Deitie,
> In Whose Mysterious and Celestial Mind
> All Ages and all Worlds together shind.
>
> ...
>
> The World was more in me, then I in it.
> The King of Glory in my Soul did sit.
>   ("Silence," ll. 47–50, 75–78, 81–82)

The Hermetic dialogue continues with further reflections on childhood. The soul mediates between mind and body, and in the child it is as yet untainted; the growing body, however, distracts the soul and engenders forgetfulness, "and Forgetfulnesse is Evilnesse" (Everard, pp. 60–61). The comment offered by de Foix is that Hermes here predicts the necessity of being re-born, as Christ told Nicodemus; in the child the soul dwells constantly in the divine essence, and hence it is pure and far removed from all error (de Foix, Ch. X, section 15; pp. 376–81). Ch. XIII on regeneration reverts to the subject of the child and of re-birth; re-birth is the product of contemplation: God approaches him who calls upon him in truth, and, with the knowledge of God, joy enters. Conversely, concupiscence makes man lose his proper pleasure, repose, felicity, honour, and glory, and the loss is not for a lifetime only, but for all eternity (XIII.8). This is clearly the context for Traherne's thought, whether in the *Centuries* or the poems. Thus the opening sequence of poems in the Dobell MS. (copied out by the poet himself, not his brother) begins with descriptions of the infant eye and the child's state of innocence (poems 1–5), carries on by denouncing the flesh ("The Instruction"; poem 6), and then proceeds to the ecstatic vision (poems 7–10) and the importance of silence (poems 11–12). The very sequence is suggestive.

The strong hostility to the world of matter and of the senses appears most clearly in the dialogue entitled *Pimander*, but this hostility is greatly modified by the view that the divine essence is present in all things, and that a contemplation of this essence not only takes us to God, but makes us divine (de Foix, Ch. III.4; pp.

141–43). The purging of the senses is described in terms of an expulsion of the 12 vices (associated with the signs of the zodiac) by the 10 virtues (associated with the monad). Unless driven out, the vices turn the body into a prison. If the virtues prevail, man recognizes his own divine essence and finds this essence everywhere. This means that the regenerate person sees all material things in their *form*, which the worldly person never perceives. On considering the form of things, the regenerate discovers God's presence in them; their form issues directly from the divine essence, and by virtue of this essence he shares in the life of all created things (XIII.10). Man forgets his proper nature and condition, but the Holy Spirit causes him to remember it, which he is then free to reject or accept. By the grace of God, then, and by an act of the will man may receive a spiritual vision of this memory, and the vision causes him to issue out of himself and so become an immortal body. It is the abuse of the senses, not their proper use, that is evil (p. 603).

The most dramatic manifestation of the total change caused by the process of regeneration occurs when the divine powers in man sing the praises of God. The Hermetic dialogues therefore provide strong support for the view that poetry may be divinely inspired. Significantly, de Foix associates this hymn of praise with the Psalms of David. In the dialogue itself, Tat begs Hermes to sing the hymn he is reputed to have sung when Tat was born; he refers to it as "la priere des puissances, que tu disois en l'octonaire", and de Foix explains that the ancients discovered that God accepted prayers presented in the form of hymns or chants. Thus David and other prophets used "cantiques" diversified by numbers, measures, rhymes, and other devices. Just as Hermes sings his "chant de nombre octonaire", David wrote Psalm 119, which consists of as many groups of 8 lines as there are letters in the Hebrew alphabet; both Hermes and David, therefore, praise and exalt God "par cest octonaire" (XIII.15; p. 614). By associating the Hermetic "song of the number 8" with Psalm 119, de Foix effectively removes from it all taint of magic or the occult. When proceeding in this "tres belle maniere", the bodily tabernacle is as it were dissolved and the inner man released from the 12 "miserables vengences" and purged. The song or hymn therefore is an important phase in the process of regeneration, and there can be little doubt that Traherne from time to time had such a purpose in mind; his ecstatic lines call for such a context, and so does the form in which they are composed. The reader is expected to respond to them in the way that Tat responds to the "chant de nombre octonaire" sung by his father: the chant takes him beyond himself so that he feels a change in his own nature. The chant, which is the work of the Holy Spirit, praises God as creator and as the eye of the mind – what Traherne calls our third eye (cf. "Sight"). To avoid blasphemy, it has been kept secret from the vulgar, and the doctrine must be received in secret and in silence until it can be revealed to all. It is the 10 divine virtues that sing in him, and St Paul refers to this verbal sacrifice as a reasonable service, while St Peter calls it "laict d'intelligence" (p. 620).

To illustrate the characteristic tone of the dialogues – their frequent recourse to repetition, for example, and to lists, precisely like Traherne – I quote a few passages on seeing God in the creatures and on the mind's God-like omnipresence. The translator is John Everard:

> Increase thy self unto an immeasurable greatness, leaping beyond every Body, and transcending all Time, become Eternity, and thou shalt understand God ...
> Become higher then all heighth, lower then all depths, comprehend in thy self, the qualities of all the Creatures ... and conceive likewise, that thou canst at once be every where in the Sea, in the Earth.
> Thou shalt at once understand thy self, not yet begotten in the Womb, young, old, to be dead, the things after death, and all these together; as also, times, places, deeds, qualities, quantities, or else thou canst not yet understand God.
> ...
> For it is the greatest evil, not to know God.
> But to be able to know, and to will, and to hope, is the straight way, and divine way, proper to the Good, and it will every where meet thee, plain and easie ...
> For there is nothing which is not the image of God.
> And yet thou sayest, God is invisible: but be advised, for who is more manifest, then He.
> For therefore hath he made all things, that thou by all things mayest see him.
> This is the Good of God, this is his Vertue, to appear, and to be seen in all things.[28]

De Foix connects this argument with the parable of the talents: man must not plead inability to understand God; God demands of each that he should employ those virtues and powers with which he has been endowed. Everything depends on man's willing to use the means of salvation offered to him. True, carnal man cannot perceive God through his senses, but he who has knowledge of God may be transported by means of them. This man may prudently employ his reason, his knowledge, and his intelligence – the virtues of the Holy Ghost – to consider the *cause* which produces the effects perceived by the senses. However, it is only his mind which can recognize the divine essence in all things, since the mind is the image of this essence.

It is startling to discover how closely Traherne follows the Christianized version of the Hermetic dialogues as expounded by de Foix. Since we know that Thomas, Lord Fairfax after his early retirement busied himself with translating this commentary into English,[29] its appeal to the serious-minded was clearly considerable. It would be foolish to say that Traherne's prose and verse present paraphrases of the Hermetic dialogues as expounded for example by de Foix, but Traherne's main ideas together with his style of writing certainly recall many of the crucial passages.

Traherne's favourite image of the soul or mind as an ocean, river, or fountain invites comparison with the Hermetic concept of the mind as a basin, as in the title of Ludovico Lazzarelli's *Crater Hermetis* (1505; French tr. 1549).[30] Lazzarelli's dialogue summarizes what the Hermetic dialogues have to say about regeneration, and attributes divine inspiration to the poet's song; the muses were sent to man to provide assistance, and Lazzarelli himself chants "le cantique de diuine contemplation." His interlocutor (the king) reacts to it by feeling "presque rauy & transporté hors de moy mesme" so that he states it must have been inspired, not by the muses, but by "la puissance & maiesté du verbe de Dieu" (pp. 146^v–147^r). A related passage on the "rauissmēt & extase de Lazarel" (152^r et seq.) refers the ecstasy back to his contemplation of the sovereign and supreme felicity of the soul. Many names are given to what he enjoys in this state: "les delices & voluptez de Paradise", the heavenly city, the kingdom of Israel, the age of gold, the repose of the Sabbath, and the supper of the Lamb. This, then, is the experience of him who plunges into the basin of the mind. François de Foix says much the same in his commentary on the fourth dialogue (i.e. in his Ch. IV). Wisdom is the basin of the divine mind, and he who plunges into it partakes of the divine wisdom by means of which he sees and contemplates God. To reach "ce seul & unique Dieu" he must pass through all the heavens and the circuit of the stars, mounting higher than the angelic hierarchies. After the vision, he will despise all that the world can offer. Only he can plunge into the basin of the divine mind who loves God so that he is embraced and transported by the divine. In this fashion he is elevated above all numbers in order to contemplate the true Unity which is the source of number.

In the chapter which follows (Ch. V), de Foix makes the familiar point that it is the *order* of all created things which declares who has made them, and the same point is made in Ch. I, sections 7-8, where Hermes, on looking into the mind of Pimander (i.e. God), sees the archetypal pattern according to which everything was made. This was the pattern revealed to David and Solomon after which the Temple was built, as Giorgio had already explained in his *De harmonia mundi*, and it is likely that de Foix was influenced by Giorgio on this point.

Traherne expresses his own feeling of kinship with David in various ways. The autobiographical Third Century, for example, devotes the last third to David as the Psalmist, thus suggesting that harmony prevails between his own life and the Psalms that he praises. Psalm 119 comes in for special mention:

> In the 119th Psalm, like an Enamord Person, and a Man ravished in Spirit with Joy and pleasure he treateth upon Divine Laws, and over and over again maketh Mention of their Beauty and Perfection. By all which we may see what inward life we ought to lead with God in the Temple.
> (*Centuries* III.92; ll. 24-28).

Traherne's poem on David is in a way a "chant de nombre octonaire", written as it is in 8 10-line stanzas. By attributing an ecstatic vision to David, as supposedly expressed in the Psalms, Traherne felt that his own vision was given the highest possible sanction:

> When I saw those Objects celebrated in His Psalm which GOD and Nature had proposed to me, and which I thought chance only presented to my view: you cannot imagine how unspeakably I was delighted, to see so Glorious a Person, so Great a Prince, so Divine a Sage ... rejoycing in the same things, meditating on the same and Praising GOD for the same. For by this I perceived we were led by one Spirit: and that following the clew of Nature into this Labyrinth I was brought into the midst of Celestial Joys.
> (*Centuries* III : 70)

Thus speaks the religious poet, fired by the syncretistic vision of the Unity of all things in God. The vision is not esoteric, let alone of an occult character; Traherne merely expresses in ecstatic terms what earlier religious poets had made familiar in more sober ways.

As he wrote *Paradise Lost*, Milton too may be said to have followed the "clew of Nature" when he let the perfection of the prelapsarian universe mirror a state of obedience based on love of the great Creator. Despite the imperfection which entered with the Fall, the perfection reflected in the epic's textual structures promises a happy end, much as the symmetries of Herbert's "Deniall" contradict the speaker's lament for a lost state of joy.

Notes to Chapter VIII

1. Quotations are from *The Works of George Herbert*, ed. F. E. Hutchinson (Oxford, 1941).
2. On the *Prothalamion*, see Roy T. Eriksen, "Spenser's Mannerist Manoeuvres: *Prothalamion* (1596)," *Studies in Philology* 91 (1993), 143–75.
3. John R. Mulder, "*The Temple* as Picture," in *Too Rich to Clothe the Sunne. Essays on George Herbert*, ed. Claude J. Summers and Ted-Larry Pebworth (Pittsburgh, 1980), pp. 3–14.
4. Ibid., p. 4.
5. Ibid., p. 6.
6. See below, pp. 470–73.
7. See above, pp. 76 f.
8. Richard Strier, "George Herbert and the World," *Journal of Medieval and Renaissance Studies* 11 : 2 (1981), p. 221.
9. Pietro Bongo, *Numerorum mysteria* (Bergamo, 1591).
10. John Swan, *Speculum Mundi* (2nd edn, Cambridge, 1644).
11. All quotations are from *The Works of Henry Vaughan*, ed. L. C. Martin (Oxford, 1914). See also Henry Vaughan, *Poetry and Selected Prose*, ed. L. C. Martin (London, 1963).
12. One of Fludd's drawings of the intersecting cones or pyramids is reproduced in S. K. Heninger, *The Cosmographical Glass* (San Marino, 1977), p. 28. I quote Heninger's comment: "Formality decreases as it descends from God until it diminishes to zero at the surface of the Earth, thereby tracing out a 'formal pyramid.' Conversely, in the other direction a 'material pyramid' (as Fludd identifies it in the text) stretches up from Earth until it diminishes to zero at the presence of God."
13. Ibid., p. 163. Heninger reproduces Rouelles' drawing of the 4 steps up and down the levels of being.
14. For an analysis of "The Morning-watch," see H. Neville Davies, "Laid Artfully together: Stanzaic Design in Milton's 'On the Morning of Christ's Nativity,'" in *Fair Forms*, ed. M.-S. Røstvig (Cambridge, 1975), pp. 112–15.
15. See A. J. M. Smith, "Some Relations between Henry Vaughan and Thomas Vaughan," *Papers of the Michigan Academy of Science, Arts, and Letters*, XVIII (1933), 551–61, as quoted by Alan Rudrum, in Henry Vaughan, *The Complete Poems* (Harmondsworth, 1976), p. 555.
16. All quotations are from Thomas Traherne, *Centuries, Poems, and Thanksgivings*, ed. H. M. Margoliouth (Oxford, 1958).
17. No fewer than 36 printed editions appeared between 1472 and 1670. For an English translation, see Macrobius, *Commentary on the Dream of Scipio*, tr.

William Harris Stahl, Records of Civilization, Sources and Studies, Vol. XLVIII (New York and London, 1952).
18. Macrobius, *Commentary*, p. 112 (Ch. VI, sections 62–63).
19. Bongo, *Numerorum mysteria*, p. 303.
20. Ibid., p. 318.
21. Ibid., pp. 310–11.
22. See the essays contained in *Poems in Their Place. The Intertextuality and Order of Poetic Collections*, ed. Neil Fraistat (Chapel Hill, NC, and London; 1986).
23. For this editorial comment, see Thomas Traherne, *Selected Poems and Prose*, ed. Alan Bradford (London, 1991), pp. 343–44.
24. Ibid., p. 343.
25. See Carol L. Marks, "Thomas Traherne and Hermes Trismegistus," *Renaissance News*, XIX:2 (Summer 1966), 118–31. In his notebook, Thomas Traherne copied out the first part of Ficino's "Argumentum" prefaced to his translation. See also the discussion of Traherne in Robert Ellrodt, *Les Poètes métaphysique anglais* (Paris, 1960).
26. On François de Foix, duke of Candale and bishop of Aire, see Jean Dagens, "Le Commentaire du Pimander de François de Candale," *Mélanges offerts à Daniel Mornet* (Paris, 1951), pp. 21–26. The complete titles of the translations and commentaries are as follows: Hermes Mercuris Trismegistus, *His Divine Pymander, In Seventeen Books*, By that learned Divine Dr. Everard (London, 1657), and François de Foix, *Le Pimandre De Mercure Trismegiste De La Philosophie Chrestienne, Cognoissance du verbe diuin, & de l'excellence des oeuures de Dieu* (Bordeaux, 1579).
27. Pico, *On the Dignity of Man, On Being and the One, and Heptaplus*, tr. Douglas Carmichael (New York: The Bobbs-Merrill Co., 1965), pp. 147–53.
28. Everard, Ch. X.
29. The incomplete translation, in manuscript, is in the British Library.
30. Quotations are from the French edition of 1549.

Chapter IX

John Milton, *Paradise lost. A Poem Written in Ten Books* (1667)

> ... mazes intricate,
> Eccentric, intervolv'd, yet regular
> Then most, when most irregular they seem:
> And in thir motions harmonie Divine
> So smooths her charming tones, that Gods own ear
> Listens delighted.
> *Paradise lost* 5.622–27

The advantages of the 12-book edition of *Paradise Lost* (1674) have seemed so obvious that little attention has been paid to the structures of the 10 books of the first edition of 1667. On considering edition 2, we see at once that Christ is at the centre where he ought to be, triumphing over Satan in Book VI and creating a universe in Book VII (Roman numerals identify books in edition 2, Arabic those in edition 1). These events connect so closely with the beginning and the end that they are recognized as being pivotal: the Satan who "ruins" from Heaven as we begin to read, began his fall at the end of Book VI, just as the week of creation in Book VII points forward to the scheme of redemption as it unfolds in the course of the "week" of human history in Books XI–XII. All this is so satisfying that we applaud Milton's division of books 7 and 10 into two so as to achieve the 12 books that an epic ought to have. Christ triumphant is surely the only possible centre-piece; who can prefer the Abdiel episode at the end of book 5 and the beginning of book 6? Why, then, did Milton locate this episode at the textual centre in his original conception? We may as well ask why Spenser placed the fall of Redcrosse knight at the centre of the symmetrical structure of Book I of *The Faerie Queene*: as we have seen, Spenser plays off this negative centre against a positive centre which divides the book into 8 + 4 cantos. Could it be that Milton too felt that plain symmetry was much too simple, unless counterpointed by a 2 : 1 division? It is difficult to believe that Milton would have been less structurally ambitious than Augustine, Tasso, Spenser, Quarles, and Dryden. Certainly the textual structures that may be traced in the *Poems* (1645) – in individual poems and in the collection as a whole – suggest perfect awareness of the effects that may be achieved in this way.[1] In the same way, my analysis of the structures of the 10-book edition will show that Milton's epic is part of the structural tradition explored in this study, and that Milton's original design combined symmetry with a graded arrangement. The contents suggest a division into 6—1—3 books; the books which precede and follow book 7 are complete narrative cycles: books 1–6 form one cycle, books 8–10 another. Events that occur before the Fall, then, are balanced against the Fall and the subsequent universal history of man to the end of time. Then, too, book 7 is so very much a book of rest after the tumult of book 6, although the rest is marked by intense intellectual activity leading to the acquisition of wisdom. This structure recalls Augustine's division of the *Confessions* into 8—1—4 books, where book 9 similarly combines physical rest (after the climactic victory at the end of book 8) with meditation on, and contemplation of, the highest things. The pivotal books which mark the turning-point in the action of *Jerusalem Delivered* (books 13–14) equally combine rest (i.e. enforced inactivity) with divine grace, heavenly visions, and divine wisdom imparted by the old man to the knights who are to rescue Rinaldo. Finally Spenser too lets the division of Book I into 8 + 4 cantos be marked by a pivotal passage at the beginning of canto ix, where much-needed physical rest is accompanied by the account of Arthur's vision of the Faerie Queen, and concluded by an exchange of gifts between Arthur and Redcrosse knight, gifts that represent divine grace and wisdom. Milton therefore is the fourth we know to have adopted this pattern when he let book 7 (= VII–VIII) constitute a book of wisdom which describes the works of God and their true order.

The graded arrangement into 6—1—3 books coexists with a symmetrical structure centred around the end of book 5 and the beginning of book 6, and it is this symmetrical structure which is the basic pattern. As in the *Confessions*, however, a third possibility presents itself on considering the narrative structure of each book. It is seen at once that books 7 and 10 are excessively long, like the last four books of the *Confessions*, and that the narrative divides each into two fairly equal halves. Book 7 presents the account of creation first, and then the ensuing dialogue between Adam and Raphael, while book 10 is divided between visions and prophetic narrative. Although of normal length, book 3, too, has a bipartite structure: the first half describes the Council in Heaven, the second Satan's voyage to the Earth. These three books, therefore, are unique in having a built-in narrative doubleness. True, the last third of book 5 leaves the Garden to focus instead on events in Heaven, but, as we shall see, this passage, together with the first part of book 6, functions as the pivotal centre for the symmetrical pattern. In strong contrast, other books are arranged in groups of two: this is so in books 1–2 on events in Hell, 4–5 on Adam and Eve in the Garden, and 8–9 on the Fall and its immediate aftermath. These divisions into single books with a double structure and groups of two books recall the graded arrangement of individual books in the *Confessions*; indeed, books 1–2 and 10 bear a strong resemblance to books 1–2 and 13 of the *Confessions*. Both epics begin with a descent into Hell and conclude with redemption history. The narrative doubleness of book 3 and its concern with the redemption which will annul the effect of the Fall make it an appropriate point of balance for books 8–9 (= IX–X), just as books 4–5 share with book 7 (= VII–VIII) the theme of the divinely established order. This arrangement leaves book 6 as a pivotal centre supplementing book 7 (the centre of the overall division into 6—1—3 books). In the two graded arrangements of the first edition, therefore, books 6 and 7 are the pivotal centres, which goes far to explain why it was possible to rearrange the structure in the second edition. The second edition merely makes more visible what was already there in the two graded arrangements of the first edition.

The three structures are set out in Diagram IX.1 with greater clarity than can be provided by words. The theory that there are two graded arrangements as in Augustine's *Confessions* (see Diagram IX.2 for a comparison) is supported by the complementary character of books 6 and 7: the one features divine Justice, the other divine Mercy. Justice calls for the expulsion and punishment of the apostate angels, while Mercy prompts the work of creation, which foreshadows redemption history. The Abdiel episode echoes these themes in a minor key: Satan spurns the concept of a benign creation, instead insisting that the angels are "self-begot, self-rais'd," and on his return to the loyal angels Abdiel strikes the first blow against Satan, thus foreshadowing the last blow dealt by Christ at the end of time.

It may perhaps be felt that the graded arrangement of individual books complicates the structure to the point of confusion, but this is not so, as one realizes on comparing it with the symmetrical structure. All that it entails is a simple enlargement of the basic

Diagram IX.1 *Paradise Lost*, 1667. The Structures of the 10 Books

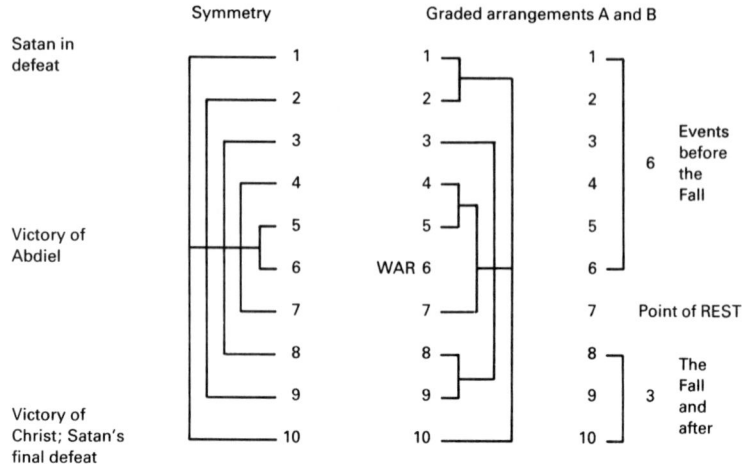

Unlike Augustine, Milton has aligned graded arrangement A with the plain overall symmetrical pattern by inverting the 2:1 formula so that book 3 is paired off against books 8–9. We see this more clearly on considering each of the three sets of three books separately:

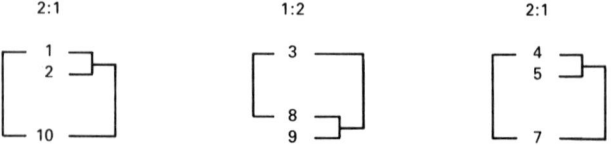

The symmetrical linkages are shown on the left side. This partial alignment with the symmetrical structure makes the graded arrangement function like an expansion of the former. After the division of books 7 and 10, the following linkages are retained: books 1 and 10 (= XII), 2 and 10 (= XI), 3 and 9 (= X), and 5 and 7 (= VIII).

symmetry. If book 1 balances book 10 within the symmetrical pattern, then within the graded arrangement it is books 1–2 that balance book 10; book 2 is merely added. If book 3 balances book 8, then book 9 is added to book 8, and, finally, if book 4 balances book 7, then book 5 is added to book 4. The addition of the extra book creates a pleasing irregularity which is then most regular when most irregular it seems. One felicitous consequence is a strengthening of the unifying pattern: it is virtually impossible to separate parts in the way invited by Spenser's narrative technique: everything coheres to a much higher degree. The symmetrical structure as

Diagram IX.2 The *Confessions* and *Paradise Lost* Compared

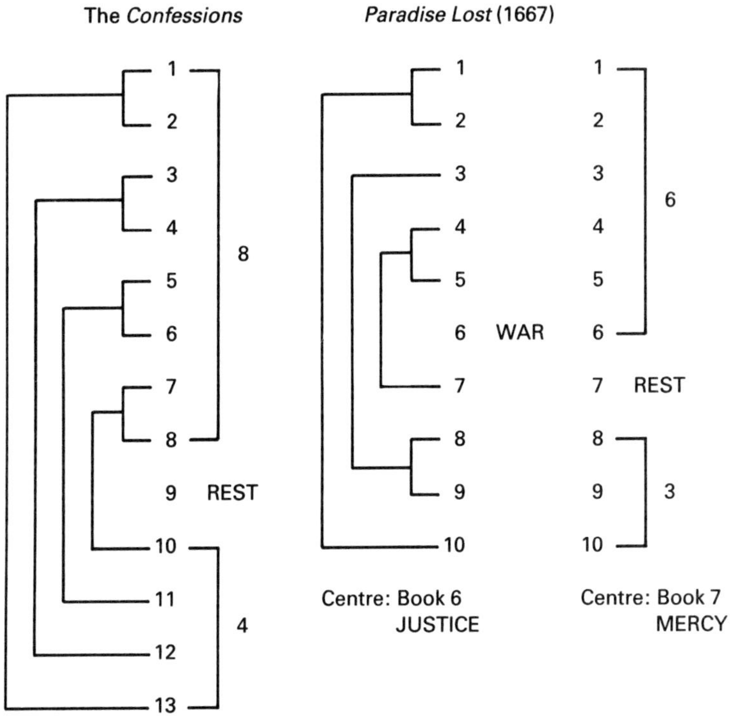

```
       The Confessions              Paradise Lost (1667)

     ┌──┌─ 1                       ┌──┌─ 1              ┌─ 1 ┐
     │  └─ 2                       │  └─ 2              │  2 │
     │  ┌─ 3                       │     3              │  3 │
     │  └─ 4                       │  ┌─ 4              │  4 │  6
     │        8                    │  │                 │  5 │
     │  ┌─ 5                       │  └─ 5              │    │
     │  └─ 6                       │     6   WAR        │  6 ┘
     │  ┌─ 7                       │     7              │  7   REST
     │  └─ 8 ┘                     │  ┌─ 8              │  8 ┐
     │    9    REST                │  └─ 9              │  9 │  3
     │   10 ┐                      └───  10             │ 10 ┘
     │   11 │                     Centre: Book 6       Centre: Book 7
     │      │  4                      JUSTICE              MERCY
     │   12 │
     └── 13 ┘
```

Books 7 and 10 of *PL*, like books 10–13 of the *Confessions*, are twice the normal length, at the same time that they have a bipartite structure. Although of normal length, book 3 too has a bipartite structure. The linkage is precise in that book 1 relates primarily to the second half of book 10, book 2 to the first half. Book 4 (where Eve looks in the mirror of the lake) connects with the second half of book 7 (where Adam looks in the mirror of the universe). In the same way the second half of book 3 (on Satan's mission) connects with his successful temptation of Eve in book 8 (= IX), while the first half on the Council in Heaven connects with book 9 (= X) where Adam and Eve are given the grace to repent and turn to God for mercy.

In book 7 (= VII–VIII) the week of creation points forward to the "week" of history and the scheme of redemption, specifically foreshadowed in the creation of the sun on the fourth day. Hence books 6 and 7 may be said to present God's punitive and benign aspects, or his Justice and his Mercy.

enlarged by the graded arrangement creates a thematic and verbal density unequalled by any other Renaissance epic. As in Ezekiel's chariot, there are wheels within wheels, yet one spirit rules them all.

Thematic analysis lends further support to the theory that groups of books should be seen to form triads divided into the ratio 2 : 1 or 1 : 2. The outer triad (books 1–2 and 10) is dominated by images of sickness and decay and the presence of irreconcilable extremes. In sharp contrast, the inner triad (books 4–5 and 7) foregrounds the state of harmony which is a state of health and attendant joy. The triad in between (books 3 and 8–9) shows the progress from health to sickness and the first step back again to health as Adam and Eve humble themselves before God at the end of book 9 (= X). This return to God through an act of prevenient grace takes us back to the Council in Heaven and God's solemn declaration that man shall find grace.

The three triads enable us to see the extent to which Milton's epic is affected by the confessional mode. The mode manifests itself in the justification of God's ways in the second triad, and again in the uncovering of the state of sickness in the outer triad. By uncovering this sickness in book 10 – a sickness which reflects the state of the fallen angels in books 1–2 – the epic assists in the task of renovation and regeneration whereby we may "regain to know God aright", to use Milton's phrase in *On Education*. Sadly, we must begin by getting to know the faces of sin. In the inner triad, health is shown to be the consequence of a proper balance between man and God, man and woman, and man and creation. Various images of balance constantly draw our attention to this important concept. The extremes which cause discord find their logical place in the outer triad; in the inner triad, bounds are established and observed; in the outer, all bounds are transgressed, thus making the import of the great interdiction dramatically effective. Balance results when all parts of creation occupy their proper position and perform their proper function, which is why Adam and Eve begin their lives with a divinely assisted act of cognition as described in books 4 and 7. The process of cognition is further assisted when Raphael in book 5 describes the great ladder of creation issuing out of, and returning to, God. Books 4–5 and 7, then, are books of wisdom where the reader is made to share the cognitive process, moving with Adam and Eve from the particular (in books 4–5) to the universal (in book 7). While book 7 presents the balanced pattern of the universe and the balanced relationship between man and woman, books 4–5 invite us to consider specific details which reflect the larger harmonies of creation. Even the most physical and apparently trivial of actions, such as eating and drinking, are related to the realm of mind through their abstract patterns. As readers of the *Confessions* will know, this way of thinking is most Augustinian. It is the *pattern* we are invited to appreciate when Eve provides "Taste after taste upheld with kindliest change" (5.336), just as the fruit is "of all kinds" in that they range from "Rough, or smooth rin'd" to "bearded husk, or shell" (3.341–42).[2] Rough and smooth, soft and hard surfaces are part of the harmonious quaternions praised in the morning hymn at the beginning of book 5. The pattern is the spiritual kernel of truth within the physical world which enables us to ascend from the visible to the invisible in keeping with *Romans* 1:20, Augustine's favourite Scriptural passage. The ascent from the visible to the invisible is made explicit in the descriptions which show how Earth is the shadow of Heaven. The "circling row / Of goodliest Trees" and the tree in the midst (4.146–47 and 195) reflect the angelic hosts arranged "all in Circles" and in "Orbes of circuit", "Orb within Orb" around the Father, who is seated "amidst" (5.594–98 and 631). The fall of angels and of men causes a descent into grossness, whereas ascent up the ladder of creation (book 5) or the ladder of love (book 7) leads to increasing degrees of spirituality. However, the triad on redemption and the Fall (books 3 and 8–9) makes us see how love outweighs fiendish hate as Christ offers to atone for man; Christ shows that his very nature is love when in book 9 he comes to pass sentence on Adam and Eve. He comes as mild judge and intercessor, and he clothes their nakedness, thus foreshadowing that act of redemption which covers man in an imputed righteousness.

This brief sketch of the main textual structures will serve as a guide through the analysis which now follows.

The best argument in favour of there being a graded arrangement of individual books has still to be presented. This argument removes the proposition from what is possible to what is likely and even a virtual certainty. A possibility of indebtedness to the *Confessions* may be dismissed, but one cannot dismiss the fact that the 12-book recension has a symmetrical structure, and that the graded arrangement of individual books provides the only satisfactory explanation of the presence of symmetries in both editions (see Diagrams IX.3 and IX.4). The explanation satisfies by its simplicity. When Milton changed the structure from 10 to 12 books he provided incontrovertible proof of the presence, in the first edition, of the graded arrangement I have just identified. The critical dilemma posed by

Diagram IX.3 *Paradise Lost.* The 2:1 Structure of Edn 1 as Basis for the Symmetrical Structure of Edn 2

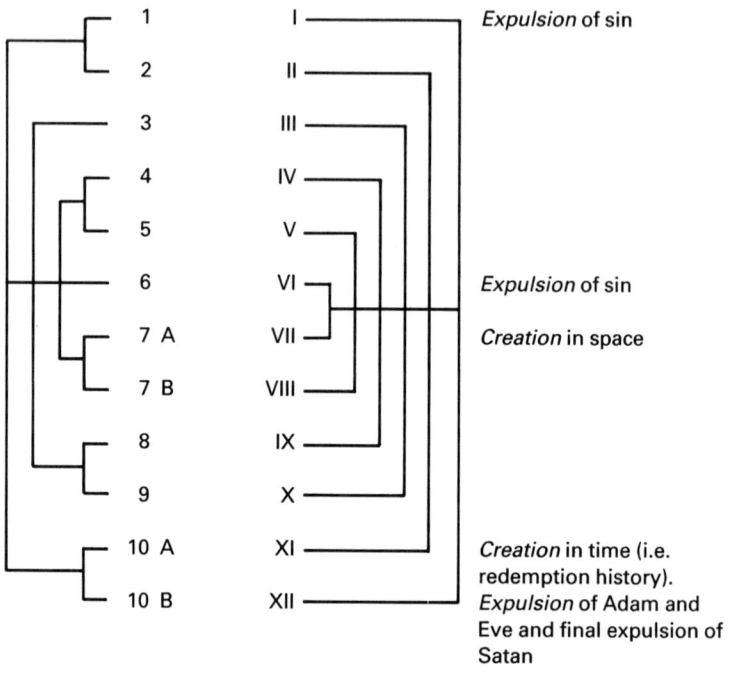

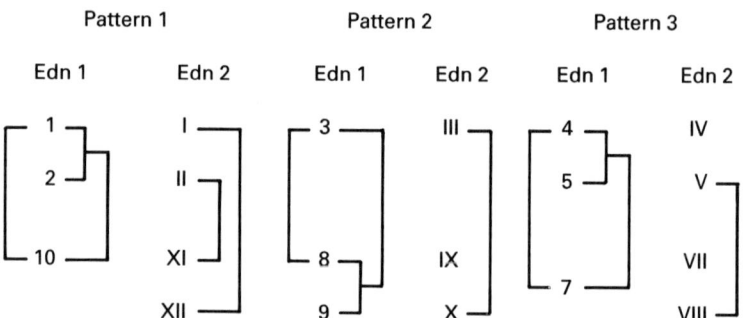

By separating each pattern in the graded structure of edn 1, we see more clearly how the symmetrical structure of edn 2 relates to the two structures of edn 1.

Diagram IX.4 *Paradise Lost.* Symmetries Carried over into Edn 2 from the Graded Arrangement of Edn 1

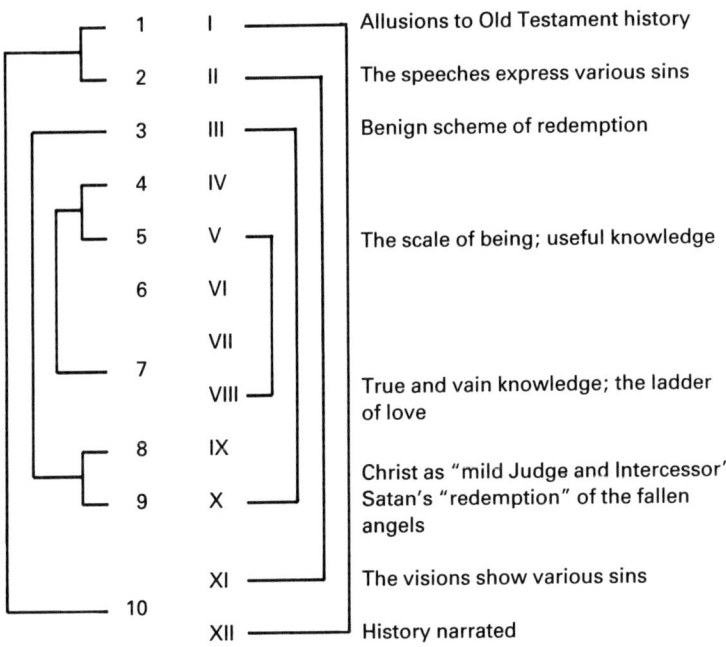

There is no foundation in edn 1 for a linkage between Books IV and IX; such linkage must be found primarily in Satan's activities directed against Adam and Eve. With the breaking up of the inner triad (books 4–5 and 7) the impact of the theme of order and harmony is greatly reduced.

It is seen that enough of a balanced pattern remains to ensure unity through symmetry. On the other hand, in edn 2 passages that obviously ought to be part of a balanced scheme no longer are so. Thus Christ's willing acceptance of incarnation (book 3) no longer balances Satan's reluctant incarnation in the serpent (book 8/IX), just as Eve's story of her first awakening (book 4) no longer balances Adam's (book 7/VIII). Nor are the activities of the infernal Trinity (books 2 and 9/X) part of the providential pattern, or Satan's two enthronements in Hell (books 2 and 9/X).

the presence of symmetries in the second edition can find no other resolution. We may well ponder the reason for the change from relative structural complexity to the simplicity of plain symmetry, but in the absence of biographical evidence all must remain conjectural. Could it be that some readers did not go beyond mere symmetry, and that they considered it as so important that nothing ought to obscure it? If we stick to the text itself we see that the change entailed losses that Milton could not have accepted with a light heart, so that he must have permitted the revision very much against his own inclination.

Let us consider the losses. There is little loss at the beginning and the end. If books 1–2 balance book 10 (= XI–XII), then the balance is retained between book 1 and the second half of book 10 (= XII), and between book 2 and the first half (= XI). The only loss is that we can no longer see books 1–2 as balanced by all of book 10. In the second triad, the linkage is retained between books 3 and X (= 9), but the link between books 3 and IX (= 8) is lost. It is certainly a distinct loss not to be able to see the Fall in book 8 (= IX) as balanced by the scheme of redemption as presented in book 3; instead the linkage is with book 4, a structural reorientation which causes the figure of Satan to loom larger than it would otherwise have done. In the inner triad (books 4–5 and 7), the link is broken between book 4 and the second half of book 7 (= VIII), and between book 5 and the first half (= VII), and we can no longer see all of books 4 and 5 as linked with all of book 7 (= VII–VIII). The only surviving link is between book 5 and the second half of book 7 (= VIII). The saddest consequence of the revision is that, with the breaking up of the inner triad, its main theme – harmony as based on obedience to true order – loses much of its power. In short, the revision resulted in a weakening of the positive themes and a strengthening of those that are negative. This brief comment on the losses sustained will become more meaningful when the structures of the first edition have been explored; only then will the shift in thematic emphasis be clearly felt.

The analysis will not focus on textual structures, as in the case of Book I of *The Faerie Queene*. It should not be too much to expect that references to, for example, books 3 and 8 will be recognized as bearing on the symmetrical structure, and references to books 3 and 8–9 on its expanded version. If the structures are to be subordinated to the general exposition, their identification must often be taken for granted. My first subject, however, is the numerical thinking manifested in the contents rather than the form.

1. Theologizing by Means of Numbers

Lack of familiarity with the tradition of "philosophizing and theologizing by means of numbers" has prevented recognition of this aspect of Milton's thought. One of the passages which make it manifest is the morning hymn of praise at the beginning of book 5, a hymn based on *Daniel* 3 : 52–90 and Psalm 104 on the wonders of God's creation. Giorgio juxtaposes these biblical passages in his *De harmonia mundi* (1525; or the *L'Harmonie du Monde*, 1578) since both show how the work reveals the design of the Workman, and that it is this design, governed by such an excellent order, which hymns the praise of the Workman (I.i.4; p. 16). It is of course this order which is the whole subject of Giorgio's treatise, and for this reason Giorgio repeatedly emphasizes Ezekiel's vision of the mysterious chariot: the chariot, too, expresses the divine order (see, for example, III.viii.6 : 3). The popularity of this interpretation among orthodox theologians was indicated in Chapter III. If we accept this "common gloss of theologians", it follows that the closest possible link exists between the morning hymn of praise at the beginning of book 5 and the description of the chariot of paternal Deity at the end of book 6. The benign aspect of God's providential order, then, is presented at the beginning of book 5, its punitive aspect at the end of book 6. In other words, God shows his mercy in the work of creation, his justice in the expulsion of the fallen angels.

A closer study of the morning hymn and the chariot of paternal Deity reveals many interesting details. Christ's decisive ascent into the chariot takes place when "the third sacred Morn began to shine / Dawning through Heav'n":

<pre>
6.749   forth rush'd with whirlwind sound
         The Chariot of Paternal Deitie,
         Flashing thick flames, Wheele within Wheele undrawn,
         It self instinct with Spirit, but convoyd
         By four Cherubic shapes, four Faces each
         Had wondrous, as with Starrs thir bodies all
6.755   And Wings were set with Eyes, with Eyes the Wheels
         Of Beril, and careering Fires between;
         Over thir heads a chrystal Firmament,
         Whereon a Saphir Throne, inlaid with pure
         Amber, and colours of the showrie Arch.
6.760   Hee in Celestial Panoplie all armd
         Of radiant *Urim*, work divinely wrought,
         Ascended, at his right hand Victorie
6.763   Sate Eagle-wing'd...
</pre>

The wheels within wheels and the groups of 4 express the harmony of creation in space and time, from the 4 elements and the 4 rivers of Eden to the 4 gospels taken to the 4 corners of the Earth. Enthroned in the chariot, Christ represents the unifying power whereby all of existence is kept in a state of harmony through obedience freely given; hence the chariot was interpreted as a *typus obedientiæ*.³ The morning hymn functions virtually as a gloss on this triumphant scene. In it, all creation, from the angels to the elements, hymns the Creator by moving in appointed order; as in the chariot, this order finds expression above all in circular quaternions. No better example can be found of Milton's numerical or structural way of thinking than his juxtaposition, within the overall symmetry, of the morning hymn of praise and the chariot of paternal Deity. The two gather into themselves all the images of harmony with which the epic abounds, especially in the inner triad (books 4–5 and 7). The hymn is offered at sunrise (the point of balance between night and day), as the sun appears "With wheels yet hov'ring o're the Ocean brim" (5.149), an image surely intended to provoke associations with the Son and the chariot, and so to alert us to the inner connection between them. Both define obedience as a constant turning to God in love, and as long as the wills of Adam and Eve similarly keep turning to God they too are part of the universal harmony.

Since the epic turns on "Mans first Disobedience" it is of course necessary to understand what it entails. The idea of obedience tends to strike a jarring note today. Merritt Y. Hughes asserted that Milton was uncomfortable with it: "it must be acknowledged that Milton's use of the word and concept of obedience is too vague to be very helpful to defenders of his architectonic powers and of the unity of *Paradise Lost*. Milton never defined it. Indeed, the very word disappears after the prologue to Book IX, because Milton had come to understand its inadequacy".⁴ Milton, however, could not have foreseen that his images of harmony and the related image of the chariot of paternal Deity would no longer be appreciated by later centuries; this is where he defines his term, nor is it difficult to grasp once it has been explained. Its import, though, has been obscured also because the structural revision in the second edition severed the link between the two passages.

Ezekiel's vision, so faithfully followed by Milton, invites interpretation in terms of obedience: the 4 "living creatures" go "whither the spirit was to go"; "whithersoever the spirit was to go, they went" (*Ezek*. 1 : 12 and 1 : 21–22). Obedience, then, creates perfect union through love freely given, and the harmonizing power stems from Christ, seated in the midst. The quaternions express this harmony, and for this reason the morning hymn of praise is itself a continued series of circular movements. All creatures are exhorted to "extoll / Him first, him last, him midst, and without end" (5.164–65); the syntactical ambiguity aligns the praise with the circle which reflects the nature of God. This image of the circle spills over, as it were, from the contents to the form; it conditions both, thus creating the kind of structural decorum so often attributed to the biblical narrative. The movement (*rhythmos*) of praise begins with the angels who "circle his Throne rejoycing" (5.163), and it continues with the course of the sun and the moon and the stars, and in the rising and falling movement of dew and rain. The very elements "in quaternion run / Perpetual Circle" (5.181–82), the wind blows from 4 quarters, and the creatures have 4 kinds of movement: flying, swimming, walking, and creeping. Like the chariot, the prelapsarian universe is a *typus obedientiæ*, and all of creation is part of the *rhythmos* of the diapason, as already expressed by Milton in "At a solemn Musick" (*Poems*, 1645).

On moving beyond the hymn to what follows, we observe that life in the Garden is described in the same way as possessed of rational order. The narrative focusses on sense perception to such an extent that even God is referred to in terms of seeing and hearing: "Gods own ear / Listens delighted", and God is "th'Eternal eye" (5.708 and 626–27). We are taken as it were on a conducted tour of the "five watchful Senses" (5.104) in the course of which we are made to see how they function. It is possible for a single sense to form its own circle of perfection, as when taste after taste is "upheld with kindliest change" (5.336), or when various fruits are described in terms of how they seem to the touch ("Rough, or smooth rin'd, or bearded husk, or shell"; 5.342). This is Spenser's Castle of Alma with a difference. Sense perception is the privilege even of angels, who "contain / Within them every lower facultie / Of sense, whereby they hear, see, smell, touch, taste" and "corporeal to incorporeal turn" (5.409–13). The point of all this is that, by observing the ordered operation of the senses, the mind is led to God as the source of all rational order. The angels turn from dancing to "sweet repast" (5.630), and from "this refection sweet" (5.636) to "Melodious Hymns" (5.653) or to sleep, "Fannd with coole Winds" (5.652), and the sense of smell is satisfied when night is said to be "ambrosial" (5.639). In between the peaceful scenes in Eden and in Heaven the two momentous warnings are given, Raphael's to man and God's to the assembled angels: obedience is a matter of firm union with the One, and the state of harmony depends directly on this union. Disobedience violates that relationship: "him who disobeyes, / Mee disobeyes, breaks union, and ... falls / Into utter darkness" (5.611–14). All the circles, from those formed by the angels in Heaven and the celestial bodies to those of the elements and the senses and each individual sense, express the harmony which depends on this union. The union in its turn depends on love freely given to the Creator who pours out his gifts with such a bounteous hand.

Our understanding of this connection between sense perception, ordered movement, and free will may be deepened and clarified on consulting Augustine's treatise on free will, the *De libero arbitrio*.[5] Augustine too connects his discussion of free will with the order of the created universe and the faculties of man, including his senses. Augustine anticipates Milton when he presents sense perception and the human faculties in general so that we are compelled to admire their numerical order and so ascend the ladder of creation to God. As Augustine points out, Providence has seen to it that the source of our greatest temptation – the world of sense perception – may function as a means of our redemption. This is surely why Milton describes the sensuous aspect of life in such a way that its rational order obtrudes itself upon our awareness: the order is the best element in God's bounty, since it leads the mind back to God himself as its source. Augustine refers to this order as "number":

> Wherever you turn, wisdom speaks to you through the imprint it has stamped upon its works. When you begin to slip toward outward things, wisdom calls you back, by means of their very forms, so that when something delights you in body and entices you through the bodily senses, you may see that it has number and ask whence it comes ...
>
> Look at the sky, the earth, and the sea, and at whatever in them shines from above or crawls, flies, or swims below. These have form because they have number. Take away these forms and there will be nothing. Whence are these except from number? Indeed, they exist only insofar as they have number.
> (II.xvi.163–64)

Augustine goes on to say that "In art, the makers of all bodily forms have numbers by which they organize their works", and when such works are communicated they "delight the inner judge who gazes upwards upon numbers" (II.xvi.165). We see how close the connection is between seeing rational order in the world and transferring the same order to a work of art. Once we perceive that a rational order is praised in the morning hymn and expressed in the chariot of paternal Deity, it becomes less strange to discover a similar order in the textual structure of the epic itself.

Augustine's discussion of order is the preface to his discussion of free will. Like Milton later on, Augustine explains that God's foreknowledge does not compel events to take place; God foreknows without being the cause of what he foreknows (III.iv.39 and cf. *Paradise Lost* 3.98–119). With free will, a fall away from God becomes a real possibility, but the presence of evil cannot affect the providential order, nor mar its beauty. God made all natures, even those who will sin, but he made them "so that they might adorn the universe whether they will to sin or whether they do not so will" (III.xl.113–14). This is possible because God's punishment "places natures in their right order". Conformity is beauty, as when a slave who has been caught in some offense has to clean the sewer. The slave "adorns the sewer even by his disgrace" so that the offense and the cleaning of the sewer "are joined and reduced to a kind of unity", and this principle applies to the universe as well (III.ix.96–99). This is one of the ideas Hrotsvit made use of in her plays, and it is equally valid for *Paradise Lost*, where the beauty of the divine order is shown in the agreement between the fallen angels and the universe of death that they inhabit. Here impure is joined to impure, extreme to extreme, evil to evil. In other words, like is joined to like in a negative harmony, or a harmony *in malo*. The consequence of joining good and evil is revealed to Adam in the visions shown in the first half of book 10: the good men who are united to corrupt women instantly become corrupt. This is the human version of what happened in Heaven at the end of book 5, when Satan's corruption infects one-third of the angelic host. Yet another example is the contamination of the Israelites, as narrated in book 1, when idolatrous temples and shrines are placed next to the temples and the shrines of the one true God. What is evil, then, must be purged off, as in Book II of *The Faerie Queene*. Evil rightly belongs within a frame of evil, as in Milton's Hell.[6]

We witness the movement of the will away from God when Satan collects his forces in the north at the end of book 5. As Augustine remarks, Satan delights in his own power, in a perverted imitation of God (III.xxv.262). Satan, then, does not see that he is in love with a reflection – that when he loves his own power and glory he loves that of God as reflected in himself. Unlike Eve, though, he does not listen to the voice of truth when it addresses him through Abdiel. He will recognize and honour no source other than himself;

he is "self-begot, self-rais'd" (5.857). Again, Augustine's *De libero arbitrio* provides relevant comment: "Nothing can give itself form, since nothing can give to itself what it does not have" (II.xvii.172). Augustine calls the form which comes from God, Providence.

Since "the will is moved to action by what can be seen", everything depends on what is seen and how it is seen; the spirit "is affected by higher and lower perceptions". The rational mind selects what it wills, and "by virtue of its selection achieves misery or blessedness. In the Garden of Eden, for example, the command of God was visible in the higher goods; the suggestion of the serpent through the lower" (III.xxv.255–57). Milton makes these higher goods visible even in the lower goods through the *form* which is impressed upon them. This form is characterized above all by circular patterns, as already explained, and the circular pattern is extended to include the form of the morning hymn of praise. Thus the hymn begins and ends with the idea of goodness: "These are thy glorious works, Parent of good" (5.153), and "Hail universal Lord, be bounteous still, / To give us onely good" (5.205–06). The hymn consists of 7 lines apostrophizing the Creator and 49 lines presenting the encouragement to praise (5.153–59 and 160–208). We may perhaps see the number of the week of creation featured in these numbers (i.e. 7 and 7×7). The 49 lines of the praise begin and conclude with vocal praise by angels and men, and in between are ranged all the other parts of creation whose praise consists of their order. That the "prompt eloquence" of Adam and Eve in this way reveals the same structures as the universe proves that its source is in the wisdom of God.

Proof of Milton's numerical way of thinking is found when Adam defines the nature of God numerically: God is "through all numbers absolute, though One" in contrast to man who is "in unitie defective, which requires / Collateral love, and deerest amitie" (7.1058–63). Augustine puts it more briefly: "tu solus es, quia solus simpliciter es" (*Confessions* 13:3). God, then, is the source of numbers at the same time that he is above number, weight, and measure. A fall from God is a fall from Unity into the chaos of Multiplicity, and Multiplicity is by definition devoid of the harmonious ratios which ensure participation in, and return to, Unity. When Milton in book 1 stresses the physical hugeness and the large numbers of the fallen angels, we should associate these aspects with the idea of Multitude as defined for example by Pietro Bongo in his chapter on Multitude in the *Numerorum mysteria* (1591). The fall of angels as of men entails physical grossness: "Purest at first, now gross by sinning grown" (6.661). Conversely, the prospect held out to Adam is of an ascent away from physicality so that "perhaps / Your bodies may at last turn all to Spirit, / Improv'd by tract of time, and wingd ascend / Ethereal, as wee" (5.496–99). However, such are the consequences of the Fall for man as well that he must be purged "As a distemper, gross to aire as gross" (10.53). The immeasurable distance between God and Satan appears in a detail taken from their respective enthronements: while Satan is "High on a Throne of Royal State" (2.1), the Almighty Father is "High Thron'd above all highth" (3.58). No one who understands what the contrast reveals can possibly feel that Satan cuts the more impressive figure. As Augustine explains in the *Confessions*, the perversion of the truth ought to turn us to the truth itself. Pride imitates high-spiritedness, but God alone is "the highest over all"; ambition seeks honour and reputation, "whereas thou art to be honoured above all things, and glorious for evermore". In this way, "all awkwardly imitate thee ... and yet by thus imitating thee, do they declare thee to be the Creator of all the whole frame of Nature" (*Confessions* 2:6). However, Satan will make no conscious or open admission; on the contrary he defies the idea that he has been created, instead insisting that the angels are "self-begot, self-rais'd / By our own quick'ning power, when fatal course / Had circl'd his full Orbe" (5.857–89). Satan speaks as if to illustrate Bongo's statement, in his chapter "De Unitate", that to fall away from Unity entails losing all knowledge of one's true origin, so that it leads to the denial that God is the Creator of all; thus when Lucifer fell he maintained that his power was his own (cf. "Our puissance is our own", *PL* 5.861) and not derived from God, from whom alone all goodness comes as from a fountain. Lucifer, so Bongo continues, was deluded into thinking that it came from himself, but no number can derive from itself, only from unity or the number 1. Who can fail to observe that the creatures do not have their origin in themselves? Bongo cites the warning given in *Deuteronomy* 8:17–18 to the same effect: "Beware of saying in your heart, 'My own strength and the might of my own hand won this power for me.' Remember Yahweh your God: it was he who gave you this strength and won you this power".[7] As Augustine remarks in the *Confessions*, a false unity is loved when God is forsaken out of a personal pride, but God sets us free "if so be we do not lift up against thee the horns of a feigned liberty" (3:8). It is of course such a feigned liberty that Milton's Satan embraces.

Milton reveals his numerical way of thinking very clearly when he lets Christ say on the morning of the third day of the war in Heaven, that "Number to this dayes work is not ordain'd / Nor multitude" (6.809–10), since "Vengeance is his, or whose he sole appoints" (6.808). God, then, is One and the source of all numbers, and hence the One will execute vengeance so that the enemy will discover "which the stronger proves, they all, / Or I alone against them" (6.819–20). A clear numerical bias is revealed also in Milton's theme of the one just man as presented in book 10, as we realize on reading Bongo's chapter on Unity. Bongo too presents an account of redemption history in terms of the one just man. Bongo explains that God recalls man to Unity and away from a multitude of false gods, as when one man, Noah, resisted a multitude of wicked giants. When the world again fell into impious ways after the Flood, God chose one man, Abraham, to make a new beginning, and finally there came one man who was Jesus Christ, whose union with the one God was perfect. Christ is our peace who turned *dualitatem populorum* back to unity (p. 38). Noah, Abraham, and Christ, then, are aligned with God in their singleness; in their single state, their union with God is close or, as in the case of Christ, perfect. It is clearly wrong to associate Milton's choice of this theme with a pessimistic attitude; on the contrary, against revolted multitudes one just man suffices, because God in him suffices. This is why Milton placed the Abdiel episode at the centre of the symmetrical structure of ed. 1; Abdiel's truth prevails over Satan and his fallen multitudes since these, on abandoning God, pursue error and follow lies, having lost all contact with the truth. This theme reaches back to the beginning where the same errors and lies are revealed in the speeches and postures of Satan and his followers, just as Abdiel, as the one just angel, points forward to the various examples of the one just man in redemption history as narrated in book 10. To quote Bongo again, unity leads to *consensum ac perfectionem: multitudo diuisionem & imperfectionem*. In short, multitude is *principium malorum omnium* (p. 667). Interestingly enough, Bongo puts the blame for the Fall on disordered love (*amorem inordinatum*), which causes divisive discordance in man, and division means death, union means life – *Vita presens est vnio; mors, diuisio* (pp. 40 and 49). The physical separation of Adam and Eve should perhaps be related to this view; it prepares us for the spiritual separation consequent upon Eve's "engorging" of the forbidden fruit. When Adam later on chooses to follow Eve, he violates the basic union on which all unions depend, and thus the fall into discord and division becomes an inevitable consequence.

Milton's description of the heavenly city as "undetermined square or round" (2.1048) equally calls for a numerical explication. As Bongo explains, all perfect figures are symbols of unity, and the square and the circle are among them. However, in this case Giorgio's *De harmonia mundi*, or the sources on which he drew, are a likelier source. Giorgio explains that because the heavenly city is four-square it is based on the *quaternarius* which contains the musical consonances, and he attributes a similar symbolism to "le grand Nom de Dieu Quattrelettrée". However, the city is not only "quarrée", but "toutesfois auecque rondeur" (II.viii.3:3; p. 753), and the circularity inheres in the 4 Hebrew letters in the name of God (two of which are identical) whose numerical values are 5, 6 and 10. And 5, 6 and 10 are circular numbers. Both the square and the circle are taken to express the consonance of the diapason, the one because it represents the *quaternarius*, and the other because the last note of the octave returns to the first, thus closing the circle. When the angels circle the throne of God, therefore, and when the *res creatae* move in their appointed circles, they create the perfection of the diapason (III.viii.8:4; p. 776). It is this harmony that expresses their perfect union with the God who is through all numbers absolute, though One.

Milton may have been thinking of Augustine's *De Trinitate* IV when he let God, Christ, Adam, and Eve form a pattern analogous to the quaternion of the elements. In this quaternion, Eve relates to Adam as Adam to Christ and Christ to God; the subordination of the Son to the Father is as plain as that of Eve to Adam, but the subordination is not the point, the harmony is. If we see subordination only, perhaps in irritation with the Pauline doctrine of "Hee for God only, shee for God in him" (4.299), our thinking will resemble that of Satan. At the centre of the symmetrical structure, Abdiel praises God's infinite goodness: we know "How provident he is, how farr from thought / To make us less, bent rather to exalt / Our happie state under one Head more neer / United" (5.825–28). Through God's reign the angelic powers are made, not more obscure, but more illustrious, "since he the Head / One of our number thus reduc't becomes", and "all honour to him done / Returns our own" (5.838–42). However, Satan sees only "Knee-tribute" and "prostration vile" (5.779), an attitude clearly reflected also in books 1–2. After the Fall, man becomes part of an infernal quaternion, since he now relates to Death as Death to Sin and as Sin to Satan. Sin joins man to the deceitful mediator, leading him "into the fellowship of punishment: even of him who aspired to advance his throne in the north, that all darkened and befrozen, they might serve him, as he imitates thee in his wry and crooked ways" (*Confessions* 10 : 36).

The most important idea shared by Milton and Augustine is undoubtedly the divinely established order which alone ensures rest in God; this order is God's Providence. To quote Augustine: "Things a little out of their places become unquiet: put them in their order again and they are quieted" (*minus ordinata inquieta sunt: ordinantur et quiescunt. Confessions* 13:9). The love which seeks its proper object finds its proper place and rests in it. This is why Adam and Eve must be told who their "author" is. As long as Eve loves Adam and Adam loves God, both are at rest in God. In Milton as in Augustine, the restlessness of the fallen angels defines their condition:

> For even in that miserable restlessness of the falling spirits that discovered their own darkness, bared of the garment of thy light, dost thou sufficiently reveal how noble the reasonable creature is which thou hast made; unto which nothing will suffice to give a happy rest, that is in any way inferior unto thyself: and therefore she cannot herself give satisfaction unto herself.
> (*Confessions* 13:8)

This restlessness manifests itself strongly in Adam and Eve after the Fall. After having taken "thir fill of Love and Loves disport" (8.1042), they rise "As from unrest" (8.1052). In the end, though, they find rest, although the dramatic character of the expulsion may cause us to miss the point. The last epic simile on the labourer who is "Homeward returning" (10.1523) carries more weight than has been observed; its function is to suggest not merely the time of day, but an affinity with Adam who from now on will have to eat his bread in the sweat of his face (9.205). The idea of finding a place of rest for Eternity has already been suggested in the passage on Joshua,

10.1201	whom the Gentiles *Jesus* call,
	His Name and Office bearing, who shall quell
	The adversarie Serpent, and bring back
	Through the worlds wilderness long wanderd man
10.1205	Safe to eternal Paradise of rest.

(XII.311–14)

This promise should be remembered when we read the concluding lines:

10.1537 The World was all before them, where to choose
Thir place of rest, and Providence thir guide:
They hand in hand with wandring steps and slow,
10.1540 Through *Eden* took thir solitarie way.

Like "long wanderd man" and like the labourer in the last epic simile, Adam and Eve are homeward returning to "eternal Paradise of rest". As Augustine writes toward the end of the *Confessions*, man shall "Rest in thee in the Sabbath of life everlasting" (13:36). An earlier passage too is appropriate: "Let us now at last, O Lord, return ... We shall not need to fear finding a place to return unto, because we fell headlong from it; for however we have been long absent from thence, yet that house of ours shall not fall down, and that is thy Eternity" (*Confessions* 4 : 16). Both Milton and Augustine may have had *Hebrews* 3.7–4.11 in mind, where the issue is finding a place of rest. The erring Israelites were not permitted to enter their "place of Rest" in the Promised Land (a type of Heaven), and the writer of the epistle applies the lesson to all men: "Let us labour therefore to enter into that rest, lest any man fall after the same example of unbelief" (AV). Other translations (the Jerusalem Bible and the Amplified New Testament) write *disobedience* instead of *unbelief*. Milton's phrase, "Thir place of rest", therefore means so much more than just finding a suitable place for the pending night; the phrase opens up to include their final rest and the final rest of all mankind at the end of time, when all the redeemed shall be "Made one with me [Christ] as I with thee am one" (10.44). Milton's final lines, then, and Augustine's open up the same perspective of a return to final rest in God.

Milton may have chosen to divide his epic into 10 parts because the number 10 expresses this idea of a return to Unity (God) through the harmony created by the first 4 numbers and especially by the harmony of the diapason or the octave proportion. It would be wrong to associate this simple symbolism with Pythagoreanism as such and then refute the idea by saying that Milton was no Pythagorean. The meaning is a matter of mathematical fact whose truth cannot be challenged. Besides, mathematical "signs" are so much more pure than words and connote so much more (cf. Augustine's *De doctrina Christiana*). It is both logically and aesthetically satisfying to see the 10 of the Law as having its source in the 4 of the Gospels, and the harmony of these numbers encompasses space and time. If earlier examples should be called for, suffice it to mention that Marcus Vigerius divided his treatise on divine rhetoric into 10 parts,[8] and that the famous Elizabethan clergyman Thomas Becon (*Workes*, 1564) adopted the same division in one of his treatises to permit it to form a *decachord* in imitation of David's 10-stringed harp. Becon explains it himself in his preface. However, a division into 10 parts was as common as a division into "centuries", so that precedent need not be documented.

Some of Bongo's comments on the number 10 may be cited to recapture the nimbus of meaning which this number once possessed. Basically, the number 10 has the same meaning as the number 1, or Unity, and it signifies a return since in it all numbers return to the unity from which they issued. Since things are like numbers (so Bongo writes), 10 contains all things that can be numbered; also it returns all things to their source, just as water returns to the sea from which it rose. For this reason 10 represents God; the Pythagoreans called it the World because the world is made from it, and Plato agrees, as Ficino explains (the reference is clearly to Ficino's commentary on the *Timaeus*). Just as what is sown in corruption shall rise in incorruption (1 *Cor.* 15), we shall return to the decad which has been reduced by the fall of the apostate angels; man has been added to the 9 angelic orders to supply the missing tenth. Bongo illustrates the number-conscious way of thinking when he relates the life of man to the first 10 digits. Man takes his beginning from earth, but he became separated from unity and divided in himself (= 2) through sin. Hence man calls on the sacred Trinity, and so is taken from the quaternion of the elements to the quaternion of sacred penitence. When purified by this penitence he praises God, and his 5 senses function in the way they should. Strengthened by the spirit of God, he is then transferred to 6, the most perfect of all numbers, and in the number 7 (= the Sabbath) he is transferred to eternal life. In this way man is made to triumph over death (= 8 for the eighth day of the Resurrection). He becomes subject to God and humbled in the number which denotes a lessening of pride (= 9, because 9 falls short of the just number 10), and finally man is added as a tenth to supply the place of the fallen angels. It is possible to apply similar numerical reflections to each of Milton's 10 books. Adam and Eve certainly humble themselves before God at the end of book 9, just as book 10 leads man to an eternal paradise of rest, and the epic begins with two books on the division from Unity (the "ruining" from Heaven) by the fallen angels. Book 3 presents the scheme of redemption as achieved by the Father, the Son, and the Holy Spirit, just as books 4–5 feature the harmonious circles of existence, extending from the quaternion of the elements and the 5 watchful senses to the whole ladder of creation including the angelic hierarchies. As we have seen, a major issue in book 5 is the correct operation of the senses in the Garden and even in Heaven itself. The perfection represented by the Son as he ascends the chariot of paternal Deity in book 6 is appropriately represented by the ordinal number, just as the account of the week of creation is given in the book which carries its number. In book 8 (= IX in edn 2) the text identifies the day of the Fall as the eighth; Satan circles the Earth, always keeping to its dark side, for "The space of seven continu'd Nights", and "On the eighth return'd" (8.63 and 67). This eighth day is the Satanic analogue to Christ's eighth day of the Resurrection; after Satan's 7 days of "uncreation" follows the eighth of his "redemption" of man to eternal death. Like Augustine, therefore, Milton contrasts redemption to life and to death (cf. *De Trinitate* IV); in theological circles in general it was of course *de rigeur* to balance the two events numerically. Some theologians argued that the sixth day of the crucifixion annulled the sixth day of the Fall, since Adam fell the same day that he was created; others favoured the number 40, and Alexander Ross the number 8, like Milton. Such balanced numerical patterns resemble the balanced textual patterns of *Paradise Lost*, as when Christ freely undertakes to become incarnate and to atone for the sins of man in book 3, while in book 8 (third from the end) Satan with extreme reluctance accepts "incarnation" in the serpent in order to ensure the Fall. This balanced pattern is of course lost in the second edition, and so is the balance between Satan's two enthronements in Hell, the one in book 2 and the other in book 9. The providential pattern, therefore, appears much more clearly in the first edition, where book 2 balances book 9, and book 3 balances book 8. The idea of balance is more strongly felt when it finds expression in the textual structure as well.

By virtue of the musical connotations of its symbolism, the number 10 expresses the same idea as the diapason. Milton's contemporary, the learned Jesuit Marin Mersenne, designated the unison as the ultimate musical consonance because in its total refutation of interval it perfectly expresses the unity of the Deity, but Mersenne also argued that, where an interval exists, the $2:1$

ratio comes close to that unity by leading 2 to 1. We may perhaps see the number 2 as leading to the number 1 in *Paradise Lost* when the two books 1–2 lead to the one book 10 on the return to God, just as the two books where unity is threatened (4–5) lead to the one book (7) where it is perfect. Finally, book 3 on the providential scheme is the unit which absorbs into its unity the two books on the Fall (8–9). The balance entails a kind of outweighing, by the one textual unit, of the two. Mersenne observes that the reconciliation between God and man can be stated as a progress from the octave to its source in the unison, origin and father of the octave which contains all the consonances. As we move from 2 to 1, we move from duality to unity, from imperfection to perfection, from actions that fail to conform to the will of God, to Unity.[9] It is relevant, too, to remember that Cassiodorus considers music a symbol of *obedience*,[10] so that the recurrence, in *Paradise Lost*, of the ratio of the unison (in the 1 : 1 relationship of parts within the symmetrical structure) and of the 2 : 1 octave ratio (in the two graded arrangements) expresses the concept of the obedience that was violated. However, we may also see it as an expression of the perfect obedience of the Son, the "one greater Man". In effect, Milton's epic is pervaded by the Christianized version of the Platonic *rhythmos*, and even Satan himself contributes to the harmony he attempts to destroy, so that his prominence becomes a measure of the power which absorbs it. Contemporary readers would not have failed to understand why the title-page reads: *Paradise lost. A Poem Written in Ten Books*. Northrop Frye believes that Milton published the first edition in 10 books "to demonstrate his contempt for tradition, and the second in twelve to illustrate the actual proportions of the poem",[11] but contempt is not involved; how could Milton *not* have incorporated into his poem the structures attributed to divine revelation and to God's providential scheme for man's redemption? Our concern must be to try to ascertain, not whether he did so, but to what extent and in what ways. The division into 10 books must have been one of Milton's first structural choices, if not the very first, since so much depends on it. The choice must have been made with an eye to the richness of the symbolism invested in this number in biblical exegesis. The primary meaning may have been the return, in a higher register, to the harmony that was lost, that is, to a paradise within, happier far.

Since Augustine inevitably must have been one of Milton's chief sources for a numerical or structural way of thinking, it is only to be expected that the structures of the *Confessions* should be echoed in

Paradise Lost. Thus the overall structures, whether symmetrical or graded, are strikingly similar, but more specific structural parallels are equally present. In both epics the first 2 books and the last have the same thematic function: each narrative begins with a descent into Hell and concludes with the promise of redemption and final rest in God. Augustine takes his "fill of Hell" at home and later on in Carthage, that "frying-pan full of abominable loves" (*Confessions* 2:1 and 3:1). In his theft of inedible pears Augustine embraces evil for the sake of evil (2:8), and in the end he has made of himself a barren waste (2:10). Augustine enters into the beguiling service of devils "unto whom I sacrificed mine own vile actions" (3:3), just as the fallen angels in books 1–2 of *Paradise Lost* are said to cause the erring Israelites to pollute the temple of the living God. Pollution is a key concept in both. After the reader has been plunged into Hell, it stands to reason that the contrasting state should be described. Books 3–4 of the *Confessions*, therefore, contrast earthly love (in the form of lust and friendship) with the love of wisdom which leads to love of God, and praise is given to the love which made Christ undertake his redemptive mission (4:12). In book 3 Milton, too, contrasts the love of Christ for man with Satan's hatred, "bent on his prey" (3.441), and in book 4 we observe Satan's lust as he pines for Eve with vain desire (4.511). The thematic curve, then, is the same in both books. The God of both Milton and Augustine is full of derision: God derides Augustine's desire, first for "honours, gains, and wedlock" (6:6), and then for the establishment of a separate community for himself and his friends (6:14). Milton's God similarly derides Satan's efforts to found his own empire and effectively prevents it (5.716–39). In book 7 Augustine struggles to understand the nature of God and his creation and is finally assisted by divine grace, which clears his vision (7:8–10); in book 7 of *Paradise Lost* Raphael is the agent of divine grace who imparts this knowledge to Adam. While Augustine records how God from far off cries to him, "I am that I am" (*Conf.* 7:10), Milton's Adam meets a Creator who says: "Whom thou soughtst I am" (7.953). Both, then, are given divine assistance to know their Creator. Raphael's discourse on the ladder of creation (5.469–512) and on the ladder of love (7.1228–29) has much in common with Augustine's account of an ascent to God which proceeds "by degrees passing from body to the soul" and thence to the reasoning faculties and the understanding so as to reach "that which is" (*Conf.* 7:17). Augustine's books 8–9, like Milton's books 6–7, pass from anguished conflict terminated by victory to a period of peaceful meditation. In Augustine it is the old man (the fallen Adam) who is finally overcome and expelled at the end of book 8; in Milton it is the fallen angels at the end of book 6. In the period of rest which follows in the *Confessions* as in *Paradise Lost*, a main point is the insight that "We created not ourselves, but he that remains to all eternity" (*Conf.* 9 : 10; cf. *PL* 7.914–15).

It is possible that at this point Milton may have looked directly to Augustine, since the querying of the *res creatae* is a theme found in both. I quote Milton first:

> 7.910   Thou Sun, said I, faire Light,
> And thou enlight'ned Earth, so fresh and gay,
> Ye Hills and Dales, ye Rivers, Woods, and Plaines,
> And ye that live and move, fair Creatures, tell,
> Tell, if ye saw, how came I thus, how here?
> Not of my self; by some great Maker then,
> In goodness and in power præeminent;
> Tell me, how may I know him, how adore,
> From whom I have that thus I move and live,
> 7.919   And feel that I am happier then I know.

Augustine puts the same question in book 10:

> And what is this? I asked the earth, and that answered me: I am not it; and whatsoever are in it made the same confession. I asked the sea and the deeps, and the creeping things, and they answered me: We are not thy God, seek above us ... I asked the heavens, the sun and moon and stars: Nor, say they, are we the God whom thou seekest. And I replied ... Answer me concerning my God ... And they cried out with a loud voice: He made us. My questioning with them was my thought, and their answer was their beauty.
>
>   (*Conf.* 10 : 6)

On this particular occasion Milton's general indebtedness to Augustine may be specific.

The many parallels, formal and substantive, between Milton, Augustine, Giorgio, and Bongo show that Milton must be considered as part of the tradition outlined in Chapter I. The very contents of Milton's epic reveal familiarity with this tradition, whether in its more popular or its learned version. Milton's thought, however, must not be separated from the poetic context, as so often happens. In a study of *Paradise Lost* the poetic context must be given absolute priority. Although it may be of considerable interest to identify specific ideas as stemming from Plato or Augustine, such a study does not substantially affect our understanding of the text itself. Then too the syncretistic tradition is so different from pure or strict theology or philosophy (if I may so qualify them) that specific ideas are hard to identify. What the tradition provides is a structural attitude and a structural or numerical terminology, and the presence of both in Milton's text is undeniable.

2. Linking the Beginning, Middle, and End

The preceding pages have already identified several links between the beginning, middle, and end. To these may be added the familiar epic topoi of the marshalling of troops, and of elevations or debasements. When the action begins in book 5, God enthroned proclaims the elevation of the Son, and soon afterwards Satan withdraws to the north to establish his own "Royal seat / High on a Hill, far blazing" (5.753–54), thus opposing his throne to that of God. At the beginning of book 6, the loyal and the apostate angels marshal their forces, and again Satan exalts himself:

6.99   High in the midst exalted as a God
Th'Apostat in his Sun-bright Chariot sate
Idol of Majestie Divine, enclos'd
With Flaming Cherubim, and golden Shields;
6.103   Then lighted from his gorgeous Throne ...

This pattern of one genuine and two sham elevations is completed with a climactic genuine elevation when Christ ascends the chariot of paternal Deity toward the end of book 6. The deception on which the false elevations rest is clearly indicated: Satan is merely a false image or "idol" of God's true majesty, unlike Christ. Christ's "filial Godhead" manifests itself in his perfect humility: in the very moment of his elevation, Christ gives all glory and all power to the Father:

6.730   Scepter and Power, thy giving, I assume,
And gladlier shall resign, when in the end
Thou shalt be All in All, and I in thee
For Ever, and in mee all whom thou lov'st;
But whom thou hat'st, I hate, and can put on
Thy terrors, as I put thy mildness on,
6.736   Image of thee in all things

The confrontation between the false and the true image, therefore, has been placed at the textual centre, thus supplementing the confrontation between Abdiel and Satan. As God puts it, Abdiel has "maintaind / Against revolted multitudes the Cause / Of Truth, in words mightier then they in Armes" (6.30–32). Here as elsewhere, *multitude* has all the pejorative connotations traditionally invested in it as numerical term.

The negative or false image is presented more fully in books 1–2 and 10 (the outer triad). In Hell Satan repeats the arguments already advanced in the dialogue with Abdiel, and again places himself "amidst" and on a throne:

    2.1   High on a Throne of Royal State ...
            Satan exalted sat, by merit rais'd
    2.6   To that bad eminence.

    2.508 Midst came their mighty Paramount, and seemd
            Alone th'Antagonist of Heav'n, nor less
            Then Hells dread Emperour with pomp Supream,
            And God-like imitated State; him round
            A Globe of fierie Seraphim inclos'd
    2.513 With bright imblazonrie ...

Both Satan and Christ are raised by merit; Christ "by right of merit Reigns" (6.43), but the parallel merely enhances the contrast, since "merit" clearly may be taken *in malo*. The elevation after the "great consult" (2.508–13) repeats (or anticipates, if we ignore the epic chronology) all the main features of the elevation just prior to the joining of battle at 6.99–103. In book 2 as well, the elevation occurs prior to a major event – Satan's departure on his "redemptive" mission. Neither elevation, though, can compare in power and majesty with the elevation of Christ in the chariot of paternal Deity just prior to his expulsion of the apostate angels from Heaven, or again with his elevation after having achieved the work of creation in book 7. These true elevations point forward to Christ's victory over Satan, Sin, and Death toward the end of book 10 (= XII). Christ "shall ascend / The Throne hereditarie" (10.1260–61) and "shall ascend / With victorie, triumphing through the aire / Over his foes and thine" (10.1342–43), phrases which hark back to his ascent into the chariot of paternal Deity in book 6: "Hee in Celestial Panoplie all armd / Of radiant *Urim*, work divinely wrought, / Ascended, at his right hand Victorie / Sate Eagle-wing'd" (6.760–

63); and, as Gunnar Qvarnström was the first commentator to observe, line 762 is at the centre of the epic by line-count.[12] Another link between the middle and the end is afforded by Christ's last speech, at the beginning of book 10, which echoes his words at 6.730–36. Speaking to the Father, Christ prays that man, through his intercession, may "live / Before thee reconcil'd", and finally pass from death to life, "where with mee / All my redeemd may dwell in joy and bliss, / Made one with me as I with thee am one" (10.38–44).

Parallels-cum-antithesis connect the description of activities in Hell with those in Heaven. *Change* is a key word: in Heaven all enjoy "change delectable" (5.629) and "Grateful vicissitude" between light and shade (there is no night – this extreme is excluded) and between various activities, all equally delightful:

5.647   Th'angelic throng
        Disperst in Bands and Files thir Camp extend
        By living Streams among the Trees of Life,
5.650   Pavilions numberless, and sudden reard,
        Celestial Tabernacles, where they slept
        Fannd with coole Winds, save those who in thir course
        Melodious Hymns about the sovran Throne
5.654   Alternate all night long.

The angelic dance is surely a "self-referring" passage which bears on Milton's choice of textual structures:

5.620   Mystical dance, which yonder starry Spheare
        Of Planets and of fixt in all her Wheeles
        Resembles nearest, mazes intricate,
        Eccentric, intervolv'd, yet regular
        Then most, when most irregular they seem:
5.625   And in thir motions harmonie Divine
        So smooths her charming tones, that Gods own ear
5.627   Listens delighted.

The harmony of Heaven should be borne in mind when we read books 1–2. We should remember the "change delectable" when Satan laments the "dire change / Hateful to utter" (1.625–26), and when we read about "the bitter change / Of fierce extreams, extreams by change more fierce, / From Beds of raging Fire to starve in Ice / Thir soft Ethereal warmth ... thence hurried back to fire" (2.598–603). The "mazes intricate" of the angelic dance similarly find their negative analogue in the infernal eloquence which leads nowhere, "in wandring mazes lost" (2.561). The discord of Hell is illustrated in the description of the band of explorers who "bend / Four ways thir flying March, along the Banks / Of four infernal Rivers that disgorge / Into the burning Lake thir baleful streame" (2.573–76). These rivers represent the infernal passions of deadly hate, sadness, lamentation, and rage (2.577–81). Unlike the human passions of fear and hope, grief and joy, these passions cannot be harmonized. These rivers, therefore, are malevolent, contrary to the rivers described in books 4 and 7, which express harmony or concord. In the Garden of Eden, a river which runs underneath the mountain on which the garden rests rises as a fresh fountain, "with kindly thirst updrawn", watering the Garden "with many a rill", and "thence united fell / Down the steep glade, and met the neather Flood". This flood, on "emerging from his darksom passage", divides into "four main Streams", which wander through "many a famous Realme". These are the rivers that foreshadow the gospels that will be taken to the 4 corners of the earth. The very movement of these waters is harmonious: they separate only to unite again. The parallel passage in book 7 occurs on the third day of creation when water and dry land are separated: "Wave rowling after Wave, where way they found", either "under ground, or circuit wide, / With Serpent errour wandring, found thir way" (7.298–302). Since all is good, the goodness must include wandering with "Serpent errour"; no foreshadowing of the Fall can be present in the description of God's work of creation. Apparently unpropitious words are clearly taken *in bono*, which makes one wonder whether the same applies to Eve's "wanton ringlets" (4.306). What we can say, though, is that we are made more keenly aware of the consequences of the Fall when we see the words used in such unspoilt and carefree innocence; after the Fall, certain words are bound to be fatally blackened. Moreover, after the Fall, in book 9 (which balances book 2 within the symmetrical structure), Earth resembles Hell rather than Heaven, and the state of man resembles that of the fallen angels as he feels the effect of irreconcilable extremes: Earth is afflicted "with cold and heat / Scarce tollerable" (9.653–54); "Thus began / Outrage from liveless things", and discord "Death introduc'd through fierce antipathie" (9.706–09).

Perhaps the most important theme which connects the beginning, middle, and end is the corruption which infects all when evil is placed next to good. Satan's defection at once contaminates one third of the heavenly hosts, and we observe the same vicious process in the third vision shown to Adam in book 10 (= XI). Because the process is so frightening in its speed, Abdiel's stand becomes a worthy anticipation of the similar stands taken in book 10 by Enoch, Noah, Abraham, and Christ. Each is a just man in a world corrupt.

Although Milton does not seem to have deployed verse paragraphs as systematically as Tasso in *Il Mondo Creato*, he undoubtedly does so on occasion, just as he structured some individual verse paragraphs. Books 1–2 are a case in point, as the extraordinary length of some verse paragraphs indicates: the roll-call of leaders in book 1 totals no less than nine pages, and four pages in book 2 are devoted to the dissolution of the council and the subsequent activities of the fallen angels. The pattern which emerges on considering the paragraph structure is sufficiently precise to suggest conscious intent (see Diagram IX.5). The thematic emphasis falls

Diagram IX.5   *Paradise Lost*. Paragraph Structure in Books 1–2

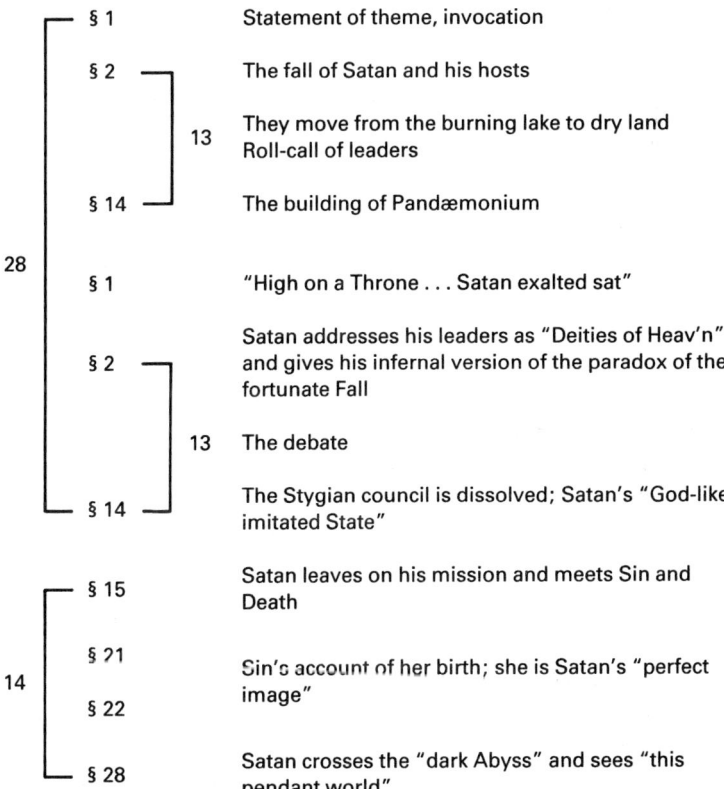

The parody of Hell includes the structures of salvation history.

on the points of structural emphasis, at the same time that the numbers involved parody the divine scheme. Book 1 consists of 14 verse paragraphs and book 2 of 28, thus sounding the ratio of the diapason – as do books 1–2 of Augustine's *Confessions*, which consist of 20 + 10 chapters. Both, therefore, provide a structural expression of a harmony which functions *in malo*. The action which connects books 1 and 2 also divides book 2 into 14 paragraphs on the council in Hell and 14 on Satan's departure on his hazardous enterprise. These numbers recall the 42 (3×14) generations leading to the birth of Christ as listed by Matthew, but in this case the birth is of Sin and Death. Diagram IX.5 shows the substructure formed by the 14 paragraphs of book 1 and §§ 1–14 of book 2. Since the opening statement of theme stands apart from the action, the narrative begins with book 1, § 2 (or § 1 : 2), and its first phase concludes with § 2 : 14. Within these 13 + 14 paragraphs, the centre (at § 2 : 1) shows Satan enthroned, and a similar enthronement scene forms the conclusion in § 2 : 14. The central enthronement at § 2 : 1, therefore, is flanked by 13 verse paragraphs, which recalls Satan's state as the head of 12 fallen "apostles". As symbols, these numbers may not be important; what is more interesting is the structural emphasis given to the two enthronement scenes, which connect with Satan's two similar enthronements at the textual centre (at the end of book 5 and the beginning of book 6). Satan's marshalling of his troops in book 1 logically enough connects with the marshalling of the opposing forces at the textual centre, while the roll-call of leaders and further descriptive details point forward to the history lesson given in book 10 (= XI–XII), as we shall see. Satan's two enthronements in book 2, however, also connect with his enthronement on his triumphant return to Hell in book 9, since book 2 balances book 9 within the overall symmetrical pattern. On this later occasion the triumph is turned into dismal defeat when Satan is punished by being transformed into the serpent, the shape in which he sinned, and with him all his followers. His carefully staged elevation therefore becomes a humiliating debasement. Conversely, when Adam and Eve humble themselves before God at the end of book 9, their humility elevates. The elevation of Christ in the same way is caused by his humility. This beautifully balanced pattern of elevations and debasements, so reminiscent of Tasso and Spenser, did not survive the Caesarean section performed in the second edition; Tasso would have commiserated, and Spenser too.

The first 13 verse paragraphs (§§ 1 : 2–14) form a separate substructure, where Satan's speeches in §§ 3–4 and 12–13 connect the beginning and the end. In these speeches the same ideas recur in the same order, thus ensuring double emphasis. Satan's first speech to his second-in-command begins by stressing the idea of *union* as he invokes their "united thoughts and counsels" (1.88), and his first address to his followers similarly appeals to "the united force of gods". Who could have expected "how such / As stood like these, could ever know repulse" (1.629–30)? This is of course a travesty of the true union shown in Heaven by the "Powers Militant, / That stood for Heav'n, in mighty Quadrate joyn'd / Of Union irresistible" (6.61–63). The "Quadrate" or square form is itself an emblem of irresistible firmness. Satan's second appeal to Beelzebub, as to his legions, is to their own intrinsic power and to fate: "By Fate the strength of Gods / And this Empyreal substance cannot fail", nor can the fallen angels fail to "re-ascend, self-rais'd", and repossess their native seat (1.116–17 and 633–34). Finally Satan advocates war, "eternal Warr / Irrevocable" (1.121–22) and "War, / Open or understood" (1.660–61). In book 2 Satan equally begins his speeches with an affirmation of "union, and firm Faith, and firm accord, / More then can be in Heav'n" (2.36–37), while Moloch's advocacy of open war in the face of total destruction is modified by Satan speaking through Beelzebub. The declaration of war of course points forward to the centre of the symmetrical structure, and so does the appeal to their own intrinsic power. As Satan puts it in his response to Abdiel, the angels are not created; they are "self-begot, self-rais'd / By our own quick'ning power, when fatal course / Had circl'd his full Orbe, the birth mature / Of this our native Heav'n, Ethereal Sons" (5.857–60). At the beginning of book 6 Satan reaffirms this position when he accuses Abdiel of having opposed one third of the angelic hosts, "in Synod met / Thir Deities to assert, who while they feel / Vigour Divine within them, can allow / Omnipotence to none" (6.156–59). "Self-rais'd" is a key term: the fallen angels cannot fail to "re-ascend, self-rais'd" (1.116), and all angels are "self-begot, self-rais'd" (5.857). (In the graded arrangement of the epic as a whole, the work of creation in book 7 is at the centre, thus contradicting Satan's almost Darwinian assumption of a "fatal course" which leads to "the birth mature / Of this our native Heav'n".) Closely related to this idea is the declaration of confidence in the supremacy of the mind. As Satan states to his "Companions deare" (6.419): After their initial defeat during the War in Heaven, nothing is lost as long as "we can preserve / Unhurt our mindes, and understanding sound" (6.443–44). Hence Satan's first boast in book 1 is a reference to his "fixt mind" and his "unconquerable Will" (1.97 and 1.106), just as his "bold Compeer" asserts that "the mind and spirit remains / Invincible, and vigour soon returns" (1.139–40); "Heavenly Essences" cannot perish (1.138–39). This assertion is advanced with even greater confidence in Satan's first speech to the assembled legions:

> 1.250   Hail horrours, hail
> Infernal world, and thou profoundest Hell
> Receive thy new Possessor: One who brings
> A mind not to be chang'd by Place or Time.
> The mind is its own place, and in it self
> Can make a Heav'n of Hell, a Hell of Heav'n.
> 1.256 What matter where, if I be still the same ...

At 4.20, however, the narrator refutes this impious assumption of a changelessness which can be attributed only to the Deity: "within him Hell / He brings, and round about him, nor from Hell / One step no more then from himself can fly / By change of place" (4.20–23). Subsequently Satan makes the same admission: "my self am Hell" (4.75). Satan, then, is unchanged by place or time only in the sense that he always brings Hell within and around himself; this is a kind of omnipresence *in malo*. The true version is given in book 7, where the Father is said to have accompanied the Son (invisibly) and yet to have remained, "such priviledge / Hath Omnipresence" (7.589–90). The last occurrence of this topos is in book 10, as is to be expected. On this occasion it is Adam who is made to understand that place and time are of no significance to God; as Monica was given to understand on her deathbed, God is always equally accessible everywhere. Eve gives memorable expression to the topos in her lament for the loss of Paradise:

> 10.269 Must I thus leave thee Paradise? thus leave
> Thee Native Soile, these happie Walks and Shades,
> Fit haunt of Gods? ...
> How shall I part, and whither wander down
> Into a lower World, to this obscure
> 10.284 And wilde ...

Adam's regret is for the loss of God's presence; whereas Eve grieves to consider that her flowers no longer will benefit from her tender care, Adam looks up to the God who sustains him:

10.315 This most afflicts me, that departing hence
As from his face I shall be hid, deprivd
His blessed count'nance; here I could frequent,
With worship, place by place where he voutsaf'd
10.319 Presence Divine, and to my Sons relate;
. . .
10.328 In yonder nether World where shall I seek
10.329 His bright appearances, or footsteps trace?

Michael, though, provides assurance; God's "Omnipresence fills / Land, Sea, and Aire"; "in Vallie and in Plaine / God is as here, and will be found alike / Present" (10.336–51). The last epic speech is given to Eve, and Eve honours God in Adam when she proclaims her indifference to place:

10.1505   but now lead on;
In mee is no delay; with thee to goe,
Is to stay here; without thee here to stay
Is to go hence unwilling; thou to mee
Art all things under Heav'n, all places thou,
10.1510 Who for my wilful crime art banisht hence.

As God to Adam is "all places", so is Adam to Eve; the harmony is perfect. We see, then, that what began as a misplaced faith in the supremacy of the mind even in Hell itself, as expressed in books 1 and books 5–6, in the end resolves itself into a realization of the supremacy of God, whose omnipresence fills land, sea, and air so that place becomes a matter of indifference. Satan's sham version of the topos points forward to its true version in book 10. Other topoi trace the same curve. To the Satan who proclaims to be "self-begot, self-rais'd" and that his puissance is his own (in books 1 and 5–6) is opposed the realization, in book 10, that Christ is both Creator and Redeemer. Satan's parody of the paradox of the fortunate Fall is another case in point: "From this descent / Celestial vertues rising, will appear / More glorious and more dread then from no fall" (2.14–16). The reader is necessarily aware of the true version as expressed by Adam in book 10 (10.1360–69), and the synoptic reading virtually obliterates the distance between them. As Augustine would have remarked, the fact that Satan is capable of such an imitation shows how highly he honours the truth he abuses.

The fall becomes fortunate because God turns evil into good; Satan's greatest humiliation is that he is compelled to promote the greater good of man:

> 10.1360 O goodness infinite, goodness immense!
> That all this good of evil shall produce,
> And evil turn to good; more wonderful
> Then that which by creation first brought forth
> Light out of darkness! full of doubt I stand,
> Whether I should repent me now of sin
> By mee done and occasiond, or rejoyce
> 10.1367 Much more ...

Adam's speech takes us back to book 1 and to Satan's proclamation that "our sole delight" will be "ever to do ill" (1.159–60):

> 1.162 If then his Providence
> Out of our evil seek to bring forth good,
> Our labour must be to pervert that end,
> 1.165 And out of good still to find means of evil.

The narrator, however, leaves us in no doubt about the outcome; Satan merely heaps damnation on himself while he seeks "Evil to others, and enrag'd might see / How all his malice serv'd but to bring forth / Infinite goodness" (1.215–18). This topos balances not only books 1 and 10, but books 4 and 7 as well. In his soliloquy in book 4, Satan embraces evil: "all Good to me is lost; / Evil be thou my Good" (4.109–10), and in book 7 the chorus of angels states the divine purpose:

> 7.613 Who seekes
> To lessen thee, against his purpose serves
> To manifest the more thy might: his evil
> 7.616 Thou usest, and from thence creat'st more good.

Satan's ambition, then, is to *uncreate*; he is a Redeemer unto death also for himself, as Abdiel realizes in the pivotal, central passage: "Then who created thee lamenting learne, / When who can uncreate thee thou shalt know" (5.891–92). In book 2 Mammon reveals the perversity of Satan's doctrine:

2.257   Our greatness will appear
     Then most conspicuous, when great things of small,
     Useful of hurtful, prosperous of adverse
     We can create, and in what place so e're
     Thrive under evil, and work ease out of pain
2.262 Through labour and endurance.

A related perversity is stated in book 6 when the defeated apostate angels rally, "hope conceiving from despair. / In heav'nly Spirits could such perverseness dwell?" (6.787–88). Similar statements occur in books 1–2: thus Satan encourages Beelzebub to consider "What reinforcement we may gain from Hope, / If not what resolution from despare" (1.190–91), and on his throne Satan is "from despair / Thus high uplifted beyond hope" (2.6–7). Again the positive version is given in book 10: after they have humbled themselves before God, Adam and Eve feel strength from above, "new hope to spring / Out of despaire, joy, but with fear yet linkt" (10.138–39). What Satan presents as indomitable courage is merely a hardened heart, a perverse obstinacy; true strength comes from God after repentance and prayer.

Milton traces a consistent pattern. To know the nature of evil, it suffices to study books 1–2 and 10, while book 7 is sufficient to know good in itself. No good is present in books 1–2, and no evil in book 7. In book 10 we trace the history of both from the beginning to the end of time.

The nature of evil is shown most clearly in the roll-call of Satan's leaders in book 1, in the speeches of book 2, and in the mirror of history as presented in book 10. The function of the roll-call (and of the descriptive similes) and the speeches is in part to establish links with book 10. Thus the same exodus events are referred to in books 1 and 10, and so is the worshipping, by the erring Israelites, of false gods. To these obvious links should be added the observation that the visions shown to Adam in the first half of book 10 (= XI) embody the sins already met in Satan and his leaders in books 1–2. In book 10 these sins are incarnate in man, books 2 and 9 having shown that they are the work of Satan, Sin, and Death, the infernal Trinity. The reason why Milton chose to divide the history into visions and prophetic narrative has often been debated, one important reason being the need to establish a link with the beginning. The reader is to see a pageant of the deadly sins in book 10 as well as in books 1–2, the whole point being the transfer of these sins from Hell to Earth. Like Adam, the reader must recognize their presence in his own life, and a historical narrative, however dramatic, cannot make the direct impact afforded by the visions. These visions are Milton's version of Spenser's pageant of the deadly sins in *The Faerie Queene* (I.iv.16–37). The period from Cain and Abel to the Flood lends itself to an analysis of sin since it is a record of sin rampant and unrestrained.

As already suggested, *ill mixture* is the cause of universal corruption, and book 1 puts this argument in terms of altars and temples. Satan's chief leaders are those who placed their altars and temples right opposite those of the true God:

> 1.381 The chief were those who from the Pit of Hell
> Roaming to seek their prey on earth, durst fix
> Their Seats long after next the Seat of God,
> Their Altars by his Altar, Gods ador'd
> 1.385 Among the Nations round, and durst abide
> *Jehovah* thundring out of *Sion*, thron'd
> Between the Cherubim; yea, often plac'd
> Within his Sanctuary it self their Shrines,
> Abominations; and with cursed things
> His holy Rites, and solemn Feasts profan'd,
> 1.391 And with their darkness durst affront his light.

This juxtaposition recalls Satan's revolt in Heaven when he, too, placed himself in opposition to the throne of God, one throne against another and his "sun-bright chariot" against the chariot of paternal Deity. In book 10 the process is internalized in the third vision, which shows how "just men" whose study was "To worship God aright, and know his works / Not hid" (10.573–75) are corrupted by "A Beavie of fair Women, richly gay / In Gems and wanton dress" (10.578–79). Their wantonness prevails over their piety. *Acrasia*, then, is a main concern in Milton as in Spenser, and so is the attendant concept of purification through expulsion. The expulsion which takes place in books 1 and 6 is repeated in book 10, but in a different key. The archetypal expulsion occurs in the account of creation in book 7. The spirit of God infuses "vital vertue" and "vital warmth", but "downward purg'd / The black tartareous cold infernal dregs / Adverse to life: then founded, then conglob'd / Like things to like" (7.234–40). Like must be joined to like, which is the gist of Adam's argument with God concerning a fit consort, and the idea is present also in the description of angelic love as a "Union of Pure with Pure" (7.1264). It is the impurity of Adam and Eve after the Fall which necessitates their expulsion to a sphere of life which is equally impure. The actions of Satan's chiefs, as told by the narrator, therefore pinpoint a truly basic theme.

References to Old Testament events equally serve to link books 1–2 and 10, especially when we consider that Pharaoh and Nimrod are types of Satan, as the locusts are of the fallen angels (see 1.305–13 and 10.1086–1105 on Pharaoh and his forces, and 1.338–43 and 10.1076–80 on the locusts). The many parallels between the building of Pandæmonium and Nimrod and the Tower of Babel have already been observed,[13] but the parallels between the visions and the events of books 1–2 remain to be explored.

The vision of Cain and Abel corresponds to the description of Moloch, and Moloch is listed first in the roll-call and speaks first during the council in Hell. Cain has a strong affinity with Moloch, "horrid King besmear'd with blood / Of human sacrifice" (1.392–93): as he advocates open war, Moloch embodies the murderous violence manifested in Cain (2.43–105). The second vision shows the "Lazar-house" filled with the groaning victims of excess, debased "under inhuman pains" (10.507–08). Belial – the second to speak and the last in the roll-call – opposes the idea of open war since the consequence will be eternal misery, "Each on his rock transfixt ... / ... or for ever sunk / Under yon boyling Ocean, wrapt in Chains" (2.181–83). His advice, therefore, is to accept the present state, painful though it be; time may in due course make them "to the place conform'd / In temper and in nature" (2.217–18). As described in book 1, Belial epitomizes an excess of lust and violence: "In Courts and Palaces he also Reigns / And in luxurious Cities, where the noyse / Of riot ascends above thir loftiest Towrs" (1.497–99). It is this excess which, in the world of men, fills the "Lazar-house" with its miserable victims in a way which recalls the wretches confined within Lucifera's dungeon in the House of Pride (*FQ* I.v.45–53). The third vision showing the consequence of the ill mixture between the grave men descending from the hills and the wanton women has already been commented on; the fourth shows the offspring "Of those ill-mated Marriages", "Where good with bad were matcht, who of themselves / Abhor to joyn" (10.680–82). The offspring are giants devoted to merciless conquest, "To overcome in Battel, and subdue / Nations, and bring home spoils with infinite / Man-slaughter" (10.687–89); this is what they call glory. The same perverse ambition is revealed in the speech of Beelzebub (prompted by Satan) counselling an attack on "the happy seat / Of som new *Race* call'd *Man*" (2.347–48); they may either "waste his whole Creation, or possess all / As our own" and "Seduce them to our Party" so that their God may "with repenting hand / Abolish his own works" (2.365–70). It is this fourth vision which presents Enoch, the seventh from Adam, "The only righteous in a World perverse, / And therefore hated ... for daring single to be just" (10.696–99). The parallel with Abdiel is strongly felt. The fifth vision harks back to the theme of lust already present in the third vision: the conquerors "change thir course to pleasure, ease, and sloth, / Surfet and lust" (10.790–91), thus expressing the temper of Belial, the last to be mentioned in the roll-call of leaders in book 1. Again the one just man opposes the multitude,

> 10.804   the onely Son of light
> In a dark Age, against example good,
> Against allurement, custom, and a World
> Offended; fearless of reproach and scorn,
> Or violence, hee of thir wicked wayes
> Shall them admonish ...
> ... of God observd
> 10.814   The one just Man alive.

Once more the parallel with Abdiel is strongly felt, as it must be to link the middle and the end. As explained above, the singleness of Abdiel, Enoch, and Noah is a source of strength since it suggests their perfect oneness with God. If they had not been at one with the One they could not have resisted the hostile multitude so fearlessly and so successfully. We should therefore associate them with the Messiah in book 6, who similarly resists and overcomes revolted multitudes. As he puts it, "Number to this dayes work is not ordain'd / Nor multitude"; it will be a matter of showing "which the stronger proves, they all, / Or I alone against them" (6.809–20). Number must be absent, together with multitude, because the victory belongs to the One alone.

3. Linking Books 3 and 8–9

As we have seen, the linkage between the beginning and the middle, and between books 1–2 and 10, is often a matter of the contrast between parody and truth. One good example is Satan's offer to undertake his redemptive mission unaccompanied; the "mighty powers" may "intend at home" while "I abroad / Through all the coasts of dark destruction seek / Deliverance for us all: this enterprize / None shall partake with me" (2.457–66). Satan's insistence on this occasion is a textual, but not a chronological, anticipation of the Son's similar stand on the third day of the War in Heaven. When the third sacred morn dawns, the loyal angels are told to "stand still" while the Messiah disposes of the enemy:

> 6.808 Vengeance is his, or whose he sole appoints;
> Number to this dayes work is not ordain'd
> Nor multitude, stand onely and behold
> Gods indignation on these Godless pourd
> 6.812 By mee.

Since the apostate angels measure all by strength (thus showing their lapse from unity), they must "trie with mee / In Battel which the stronger proves, they all / Or I alone against them" (6.818–21). By placing the *in malo* version first – by positing an evil camouflaged as a seeming good – Milton challenges us to discriminate between good and evil. In books 3 and 8–9 (our concern in this section) the sequence is inverted, as if in obedience to the inversion of the ratio, and we move from what is truly good to what is clearly felt as a bad imitation. The transition from Hell to Heaven in book 3, therefore, is a transition from parody to the truth in all its simplicity, as seen in the contrast between Satan's enthronement at the beginning of book 2 and God's at the beginning of book 3.

The structural relevance of verse paragraphs is seen in the 12 paragraphs on the Council in Heaven (3.1–415). The balanced pattern of the opening invocatory paragraph is shown in Diagram IX.6. *Light* is the subject of the opening and concluding lines, which are additionally linked by means of rhyme. In between these frames are three balanced passages on *song*, where *sacred song* is located at the centre. At this textual centre, balance prevails between "Cleer spring, or shadie Grove, or Sunnie Hill" (3.28). To each side, however, night prevails, either in "*Chaos* and *Eternal Night*" (the subject so far of the poet's song), or in the song of the "wakeful Bird" which "Sings darkling". The description in the central line (3.28) of the place frequented by the Muses recalls Heaven whose "grateful vicissitude" excludes the darkness of night, permitting only a twilight obscurity as in the "shadie Grove" (see 5.642–43 and 6.11–12). In the last 5 lines on inner light the phrase "there plant eyes" is located at the centre of the central line (3.53). The effect of

Diagram IX.6 *Paradise Lost*. Verbal Symmetries in Book 3, Lines 1–55

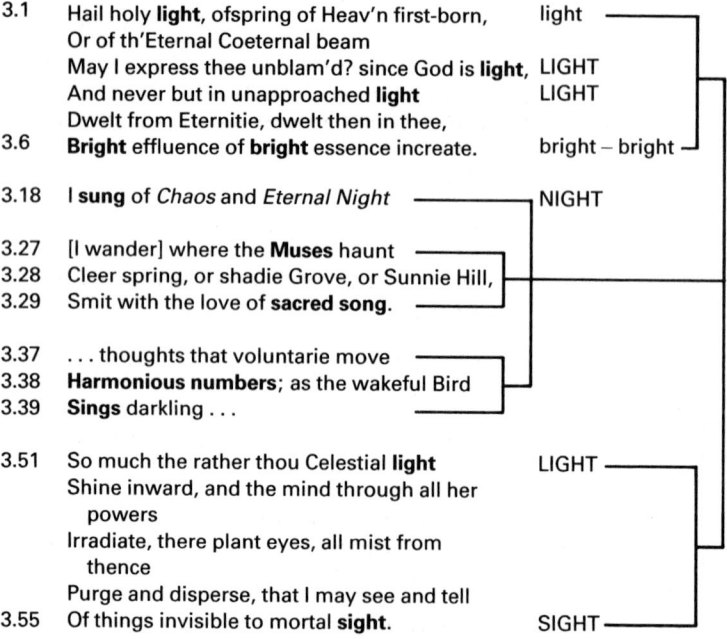

Lines 1–6 and 51–55 are connected not only thematically, but also by means of the repetition, within a line or at its end, of rhymed words. These framing passages on light invite us to conceive of *song* as *light* – as the offspring of the "Celestial light" which shines "inward".

the total structure is to invite us to conceive of *song* as *light*, as the offspring of the "Celestial light" that shines "inward".

Paragraph 12 also combines the ideas of *light* and *song*, so that §§ 1 and 12 function as frames for the Council in Heaven (see Diagram IX.7). A specific verbal link is found in the description of God as a fountain of light (cf. 3.4 and 3.381–82). Paragraphs 2 and 11 are a second frame, describing as they do God enthroned (§ 2) and the loud hosannas which resound through Heaven after the debate has been concluded (§ 11). We observe, then, that the Council in Heaven, like that in Hell, is preceded by an enthronement. The contrast between the two enthronements has already been noted: Satan is within the realm of number, weight, and measure, but the Creator is necessarily above it. The distinction identifies Satan as a created being dependent on the Creator; the distinction is crucial,

Diagram IX.7　*Paradise Lost*. Paragraph Structure in Book 3, Lines 1–415 (the Council in Heaven)

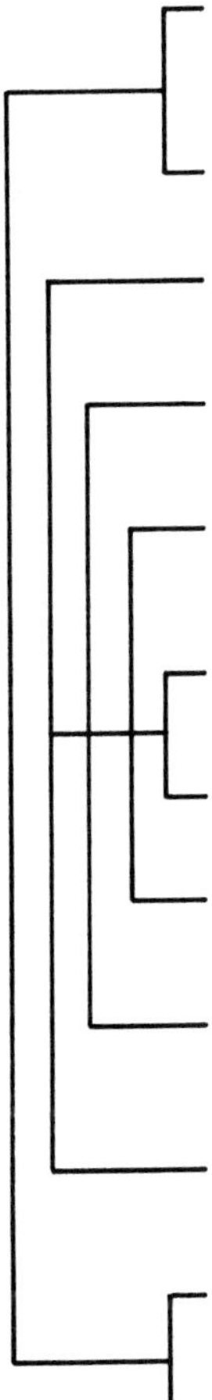

§	
1	"Hail holy light" – "Whose Fountain who shall tell?" God dwells in "unapproached light" "Smit with the love of sacred song" the poet feeds on "thoughts, that voluntarie move / Harmonious numbers"
2	God enthroned surveys all of space and time
3	The Father addresses the Son: man will fall, but man "shall find grace"
4	In the Son's face "Divine compassion visibly appeerd, Love without end"
5	Christ's speech: The adversary shall not fulfil his malice – God will not "abolish [his] Creation"
6	The "great Creatour thus reply'd": man shall not be lost but saved through grace; but who will atone for man? "Die hee or Justice must"
7	"silence was in Heav'n"
8	Christ's speech: "Behold mee then, mee for him, life for life, / I offer"
9	His "meek aspect" "breath'd immortal love / To mortal men"; "Admiration seis'd all Heav'n"
10	The Father praises the Son: redemption will be achieved for man through incarnation, death, and resurrection
11	Loud Hosannas resound through Heaven
12	The angels praise the Father as "Fountain of light" The "brightest Seraphim" must "veil thir eyes"; "Hail Son of God ... thy name / Shall be the copious matter of my Song"

The linkage between §§ 1 and 12, and 4 and 9 can only be a willed phenomenon, in contrast to the sequence of speeches, which must needs alternate.

but we see the difference only when the terms which convey it are understood. As indicated in Diagram IX.8, the 24-line paragraph on God's enthronement has a symmetrical structure. At the beginning, God "from above ... bent down his eye" (3.56–58), and at the end he is again said to behold everything "from his prospect high" (3.77). Rhymes play their part in the system of linkage, and the twice-repeated word *love* at the end of the two central lines may perhaps suggest the perfection of the unison. The happy pair,

Diagram IX.8   *Paradise Lost*. Book 3. God Enthroned (3.56–79)

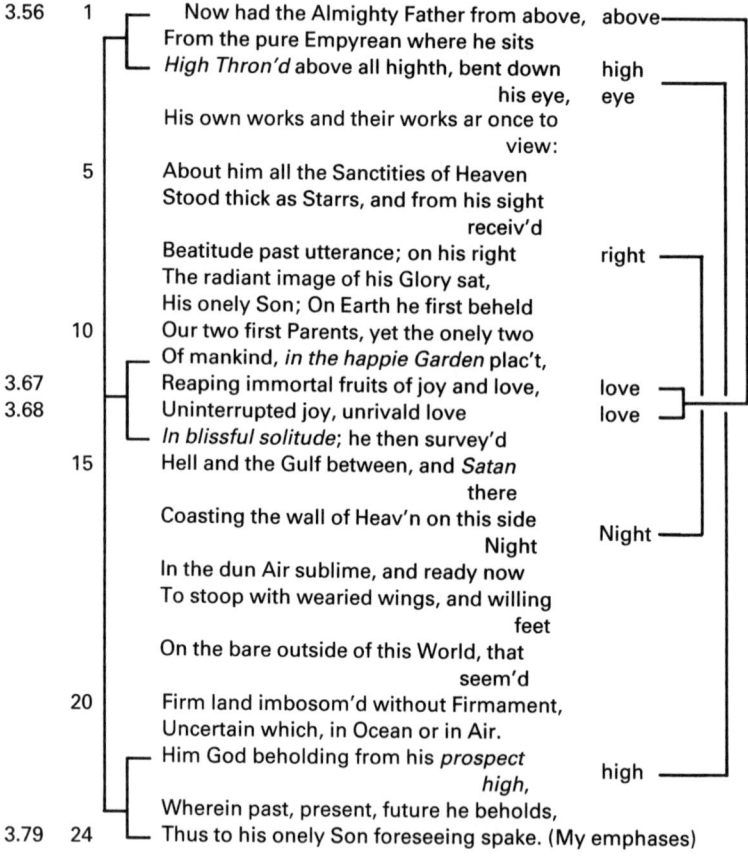

Rhymes connect the beginning and the middle, the third line from the beginning and the end, and lines 7 and 16 (ninth from the end). Since the two lines on love are at the exact centre, Milton must have counted the lines.

described as "Reaping immortal fruits of joy and love, / Uninterrupted joy, unrivald love" (3.67–68), are perfectly at one with the love of God. This first vision of our first parents in book 3 contrasts strongly with the spectacle, in books 8–9, of the eating of the mortal fruit and the subsequent fruitless hours spent in a far from blissful solitude. As Roy T. Eriksen has observed, Milton has placed love at the centre of this paragraph not merely to describe the blissful state of our progenitors, but to show "the principle of divine love at work in the universe".[14]

In the 8 paragraphs on the conflict between Justice and Mercy, the Father comes first, midst, and last, as shown in Diagram IX.7. This is a truly logical placing of the God who is first, midst, and last. The speeches of the Son are of course placed in between those of the Father, but the dialogue form cannot explain the symmetrical placing of similar descriptions of Christ in paragraphs that precede and follow his speeches (i.e. §§ 4 and 9). These descriptions emphasize Christ's love of man: "in his face / Divine compassion visibly appeerd" (3.140–41), and "his meek aspect ... breath'd immortal love / To mortal men" (3.266–68). This symmetrical placing must be by design. The basic issue is stated at the centre: "Die hee or Justice must" (3.210). After the Fall, God's mercy manifests itself in his treatment of the peccant couple:

9.58 Easie it may be seen that I intend
Mercy collegue with Justice, sending thee
Mans Friend, his Mediator, his design'd
Both Ransom and Redeemer voluntarie,
9.62 And destin'd Man himself to judge Man fall'n.

The loving kindness shown as Christ passes judgment (in book 9) proves that he is indeed the mediator whose function he assumes in book 3.

As shown in books 3 and 9 (= X), Christ is the true image of the Father, and for this reason he shares the Father's throne: "on his right / The radiant image of his glory sat, / His only Son" (3.62–64). In book 9, too, the Father unfolds his glory to the right: "on the Son / [he] Blaz'd forth unclouded Deity; he full / Resplendent all his Father manifest / Express'd" (9.63–67). (A similar description is found at the centre of the graded structure; cf. 6.680–82).

A strong link between books 3 and 8 is the argument concerning the necessity of redemption. Christ presents it in book 3: man must not be lost, since he falls circumvented by fraud:

> 3.156 Or shall the Adversarie thus obtain
> His end, and frustrate thine, shall he fulfill
> His malice, and thy goodness bring to naught,
> ... or wilt thou thy self
> Abolish thy Creation, and unmake,
> 3.164 For him, what for thy glorie thou hast made?

Before he accepts the fruit, Adam argues in similar terms. He doubts whether God, "Creator wise", will destroy his prime creatures: "so God shall uncreate, / Be frustrate, do, undo, and labour loose, / Not well conceav'd of God". God will surely not permit it, "least the Adversary / Triumph and say: Fickle their State whom God / Most Favors" (9.939–49). The precise echo shows how truly Adam sees: his reflection is no parody but evidence of an intuitive rational perception which for a moment enables us to see him as a type of the second Adam. Linkage through contrast, though, is more common than linkage through parallels: Adam and Eve are first seen (through the eyes of God) as they enjoy a blissful solitude in unexampled love, and the contrast is marked when Adam in book 8 yearns for a "savage" solitude: "O might I here / In solitude live savage, in some glade / Obscur'd" (8.1085–87). Augustine interprets the desire for darkness (in his comments on *Gen.* 3:8) as a turning away from God to the creatures: God seeks Adam and Eve in the evening, because they had lost the light of truth.[15] Adam's exclamation certainly proves that he has turned away from the truth as from Eve herself. Linkage through parody is found again in Eve's praise of Adam for choosing to share her fate: "O glorious trial of exceeding Love, / Illustrious evidence, example high!" (8.961–62). These words function as a parodic echo of the praise given to the Son in book 3: "O unexampl'd love, / Love no where to be found less then Divine!" (3.410–11). The most noteworthy parody, however, is Satan's when he considers incarnation in book 8; he recoils from the prospect in proud disdain:

> 8.163 O foul descent! that I who erst contended
> With Gods to sit the highest, am now constraind
> Into a Beast, and mixt with bestial slime,
> This essence to incarnate and imbrute,
> 8.167 That to the hight of Deitie aspired.

Christ's offer in book 3 is made in all simplicity and humility:

3.238 Account me man; I for his sake will leave
       Thy bosom, and this glorie next to thee
       Freely put off, and for him lastly die
3.241 Well pleas'd.

As a consequence, God elevates his incarnation:

3.311   because in thee
       Love hath abounded more then Glory abounds,
       Therefore thy Humiliation shall exalt
       With thee thy Manhood also to this Throne;
       Here shalt thou sit incarnate, here shalt Reigne
       Both God and Man, Son both of God and Man,
3.317 Anointed universal King.

On his triumphant return to Hell in book 9, Satan too experiences "incarnation" while seated on his throne, but the involuntary transformation simply debases and humiliates even more than his reluctant entry into the serpent. This punishment which Satan must experience should be contrasted with the repentance felt by Adam and Eve at the end of book 9. God foresees this repentance at the beginning of book 3, when he says that he will

3.188   cleer thir senses dark,
       What may suffice, and soft'n stonie hearts
       To pray, repent, and bring obedience due.
       To prayer, repentance, and obedience due,
       Though but endevord with sincere intent,
3.193 Mine eare shall not be slow, mine eyes not shut.

This is what happens when Adam recalls how God "Cloath'd us unworthie, pitying while he judg'd" (9.1059). Placing his trust in God's grace, he decides to repair to the place where he "judg'd us", and

9.1087   prostrate fall
       Before him reverent, and there confess
       Humbly our faults, and pardon beg, with tears
       Watering the ground, and with our sighs the Air
       Frequenting, sent from hearts contrite, in sign
9.1092 Of sorrow unfeign'd, and humiliation meek.

The subsequent repetition of these lines recalls the virtual repetition of line 3.190 on prayer, repentance, and obedience due, thus setting up a formal or rhetorical link between the beginning of book 3 and the end of book 9. The visual symbol of God's grace is the passage joining Heaven and Earth; this "passage down to th'Earth, a passage wide" (3.528) finds its sad analogue in book 9 in the stupendous bridge which joins Hell and Earth.

An obvious narrative link between books 3 and 9 is that Satan reaches Earth at the end of book 3 (unrecognized by Uriel), whereas he returns to Hell (fully recognized by Sin and Death despite his disguise) at the beginning of book 9. On this occasion Satan's colloquy with Sin and Death sets up a striking contrast with the colloquy in Heaven between the Father and the Son: whereas Christ will reunite Heaven and Earth, Satan's offspring will unite Earth and Hell. Sin and Death proclaim the kingdom of Satan: "here thou shalt Monarch reign" (9.375), while Satan on his part invites them to descend to Paradise, "There dwell & Reign in bliss" (9.398–99). These speeches parody those of the Father and the Son in book 3; Christ's offer to assume mortality will result in his victory over Sin and Death – through his death and resurrection he will overcome his vanquishers (3.250–51), and man will "live in thee transplanted, and from thee / Receive new life" (3.293–94). At "one fling / Of thy victorious Arm, well-pleasing Son, / Both Sin, and Death, and yawning *Grave* at last / Through *Chaos* hurld", shall seal the mouth of Hell for ever (9.633–37). This repetition, in book 9, of the promise given in book 3 helps to counteract the feeling of utter loss experienced on reading about the Fall in book 8. The affinity between Adam and Eve on the one hand and, on the other, Sin and Death, is nevertheless dangerously close, as we see in their respective arguments concerning unity. Adam appeals repeatedly to a "Bond of Nature":

8.913   I feel
       The Link of Nature draw me: Flesh of Flesh,
       Bone of my bone thou art, and from thy State
8.916   Mine never shall be parted, bliss or woe.

8.954   Death is to mee as Life;
       So forcible within my heart I feel
       The Bond of Nature draw me to my owne,
       Mine own in thee, for what thou art is mine;
       Our State cannot be severd, we are one,
8.959   One Flesh, to loose thee were to loose my self.

Sin too speaks of a "sympathie, or som connatural force" which attracts her to the Earth, in company with Death: "Thou my Shade / Inseparable must with mee along: / For Death from Sin no power can separate" (9.246–51). In both cases the attraction is God-given: God calls Sin and Death his "Hell-hounds" sent to lick up the filth produced by "mans polluting Sin" (9.630–31). On the other hand, Adam is drawn to Eve as her "author", just as God is drawn by his love to uphold man despite his fall, but Adam's bond is natural, not divine. The ambiguity, though, enables us to sympathize with Adam's choice, at the same time that we realize that his invocation of this particular bond violates the union upon which all unions depend. However, with the Son's offer to become incarnate and to atone for man, the union between God and man will be restored.

A study of books 3 and 8–9 makes God's infinite mercy apparent at every point, before and after the Fall. This mercy or compassion is Christ's point of departure. The Father is a "Father of Mercy and Grace":

3.401   thou didst *not doome*
So strictly, but much more to pitie encline:
No sooner did thy dear and onely Son
Perceive thee purpos'd *not to doom* frail Man
So strictly, but much more to pitie enclin'd,
He ... offerd himself to die
3.410   For mans offence.

(my emphasis)

The repetition is noteworthy, so that the phrase is remembered when we encounter Adam's similar reflection in book 9. Adam recalls "with what mild / And gracious temper he both heard and judg'd / Without wrauth or reviling" (9.1046–48). "How much more, if we pray him, will his ear / Be open, and his heart *to pitie incline*" (9.1060–61; my emphasis). On this, as on other occasions, Adam echoes Christ so faithfully that it is tempting to see his choice of Eve as bearing some resemblance to Christ's choice of man; after all, marriage symbolizes the union between Christ and his Church. However, the difference is of course striking – Adam does not die for Eve in order to redeem her – but a parallel is nevertheless there almost as an exculpation. Adam is presented so that we can see him as a type of the second Adam – hence the degree of similarity – but, as in all typological exegesis, the difference too must be noted. Like Augustine in the *Confessions*, Milton juxtaposes the first and the second Eve and the first and the second Adam. (Augustine traces both in his mother Monica and in himself, just as Tasso shows how Armida achieves the transition from the first to the second Eve, and Rinaldo from the first to the second Adam). The parallels between Adam and Christ cause the tragic peripeteia of the Fall to contain within itself the promise of a new upward movement, thus inspiring confidence in God's plan for man. At the very moment when the fatal step is being taken, Adam's echo of the words spoken by Christ moderates our grief. The echo proves not just the nature of Adam's understanding, but his perfect faith in God. It is this perfect faith that makes him a type of Christ, and this faith manifests itself abundantly when Adam and Eve return to God in a spirit of humble repentance. By contrast, the faith which Sin and Death have in their infernal Father is a ludicrous parody. The scene showing the fiends in Hell transformed into serpents becomes a parody of a parody when they greedily pluck "The Frutage fair to sight" (9.560–61), for Eve "Greedily ... ingorg'd without restraint, / And knew not eating Death" (8.791–92), just as the serpents, on discovering that the apples contain ashes only, literally eat death. Both scenes parody the first vision we have of Adam and Eve in book 3, where they reap "immortal fruits of joy and love" (3.67). The contrast is drawn at the end of book 8, when their hours become "fruitless" (8.1188). Augustine drew the same contrast in the *Confessions*, between the fruitlessness of the young Augustine's pursuits (including the theft of inedible fruit) and the fair fruitage of the gospels as described in book 13.

The description of God's work of creation at the end of book 3 prompts several parallels and antitheses at the beginning of book 8. Thus the work of creation finds its negative analogue in Satan's week of "uncreation" as he circles the Earth, riding with darkness for "The space of seven continu'd Nights" (8.63). The narrator's description of the universe in book 3 singles out "The golden Sun in splendor likest Heaven" and the stars that

> 3.581   towards his all-chearing Lamp
> Turn swift their various motions, or are turnd
> By his Magnetic beam, that gently warms
> The Univers, and to each inward part
> With gentle penetration, though unseen,
> 3.586 Shoots invisible vertue even to the deep.

To Satan in book 8, Earth seems a "terrestrial Heav'n, danc't round by other Heav'ns / That shine" all for the sake of the Earth:

8.106   In thee concentring all thir precious beams
        Of sacred influence: as God in Heav'n
        Is Center, yet extends to all, so thou
8.109   Centring receav'st from all those Orbs.

Both passages stress the all-pervasive "gentle penetration", and the "invisible vertue" or "beams / Of sacred influence". To Uriel in book 3, Satan pretends to have come in order to praise the "Universal Maker" and "All these his wondrous works, but chiefly Man". God has justly "driven out his Rebell Foes / To deepest Hell, and to repair that loss / Created this new happie Race of Men / To serve him better" (3.676–80). Uriel approves of his desire to "glorifie / The great Work-Maister", for "wonderful indeed are all his works" (3.696 and 702). The parody occurs when Sin and Death meet Satan at the beginning of book 9, and exclaim: "O Parent, these are thy magnific deeds, ... Thou art their Author and prime Architect" (9.354–56), just as the soliloquy at the beginning of book 8 returns to the idea of the creation of man "to repair his numbers thus impair'd" (8.143). Satan's parody also becomes explicit when he glories in the prospect of what he will achieve by himself alone:

8.135   To mee shall be the glorie sole among
        The infernal Powers, in one day to have marr'd
        What he *Almightie* styl'd, six Nights and Days
8.138   Continu'd making.

This topos of "I alone" sets up a link not only with book 3, but also with books 5–6 (the Abdiel episode, and Christ's words "I alone against them").

The description of Limbo (3.444–97) deserves special mention, since it may seem irrelevant to the epic action. Its relevance, though, is understood on relating it to the account of the Fall in book 8. Limbo is peopled by, *inter alia*, those who have courted death for a foolish reason, and this is of course what the Fall is about: Eve first, and then Adam, court death for a very foolish reason. Eve believes that she will achieve "not Death, but Life / Augmented, op'ned Eyes, new Hopes, new Joyes" (8.984–85), and, as the reader knows, this is as realistic as his belief "who to be deemd / A God, leap't fondly into *Ætna* flames, / *Empedocles*, and hee who to enjoy / Plato's *Elysium*, leap'd into the Sea, / *Cleombrotus*" (3.469–73). As in the *Confessions*, the parallel creates a submerged epic simile: Eve is like Empedocles and Leombrotus. A link may also be found between the abortive creations, "monstruous, or unkindly mixt" (3.455–56) which fill Limbo and the equally abortive creations, unkindly mixed, represented by Sin and Death in book 9. A minor detail shows the care with which Milton balances part against part: in book 3 we are told how Satan "windes with ease / Through the pure marble Air his oblique way" (3.562–63), and in book 8 Satan again moves with "tract oblique" (8.510). Obliquity is Satan's hallmark.

In the second edition, the links between books 3 and 9 (= X) were retained, but those between books 3 and 8 (= IX) were lost.

4. Linking Books 4–5 and 7

Rational order is perhaps the most important concept which unifies books 4–5 and 7. We observe the order which creates harmony at all levels of existence, earthly and heavenly, and the narrative highlights the attendant topos of the setting and breaking of bounds. Readers with a Romantic inclination favour Satan as a matter of course, since he will brook no bounds; the apparently static character of a bounded existence makes it singularly unattractive. The dynamic character of prelapsarian existence, though, is undeniable, and the paradox is resolved on recalling that unity with God and the observance of proper bounds are the basis for the dynamic upward movement outlined in the angelic discourse on the ladder of creation in book 5. As long as proper relationships are observed, the individual is in effect drawn upward by God, who permits himself to be shared by his creation. The Fall, whether of angels or of men, therefore consists in replacing this gracious upward movement by a violent, self-based thrust in defiance of all rational order. Milton's use of compounds beginning with *self* shows the importance he attaches to such self-based actions: in addition to "self-begot" and "self-rais'd" (5.857 and 1.634) there are "self-left" (10.93), "self-tempted, self-deprav'd" (3.130), and "self-lost" (7.154). It is this perspective which makes the interdiction all-important. As described in book 7, the act of creation is primarily a setting of bounds which must not be transgressed. Christ takes the golden compasses "to circumscribe / This Universe" (7.226–27):

> 7.228 One foot he center'd, and the other turn'd
> Round through the vast profunditie obscure,
> And said, thus farr extend, thus farr thy bounds,
> 7.231 This be thy just Circumference, O World.

The Creator infuses "vital vertue" (7.236) at the same time that he expels or purges "The black tartareous cold infernal dregs / Adverse to life: then founded, then conglob'd / Like things to like" (7.238–40). In this joining of like things to like is found the principle which explains the fatal character of "ill mixture". If Milton is to be accused of pessimism, then the basis must be this uncompromising belief in the necessarily fatal consequences of "ill mixture". However, when we see this mixture as being between purity and corruption, the argument is more readily accepted. It is impossible to tolerate *corruption*: death is its inevitable consequence, whether in body or in soul. Because he has been tainted by Acrasia's corruption, Spenser's Mordant is literally a giver of death, as is Milton's Satan. In an age when the prevailing tendency is to try to understand and forgive, if not condone, what is evil, the message conveyed by Milton as by Spenser will seem contrary to the principle of charity and to the best interests of society, since all must learn to coexist. When absolute norms are absent, Milton's thought makes no sense. To enter into the world of *Paradise Lost*, therefore, is to accept absolute norms for purity and corruption, and to realize that there is no bargaining with Satan, Sin, and Death. We must, instead, remain within our proper bounds, and in order so to do we must understand the nature of true relationships.

The concept of transgression is dramatized when Satan enters the Garden: "Due entrance he disdaind, and in contempt, / At one slight bound high overleap'd all bound / Of Hill or highest Wall" (4.180–82). When Satan is later confronted by Gabriel, the latter asks: "Why hast thou, *Satan*, broke the bounds prescrib'd / To thy transgressions" (4.879–80 and cf. 4.910). Satan's prime act of transgression is of course described toward the end of book 5, when, raising his standard in the north, he opposes his throne to the throne of God, and rejects Abdiel's statement that the angels are created beings. As presented in the inner triad, Adam and Eve exemplify the observance of proper bounds and the honouring of true relationships, and the basic act of cognition is related in the flashback narratives of their experiences on first awakening to conscious life. In the first edition, as in the *Confessions*, the interpolated tales are given symmetrical placing (in books 4 and 7), a circumstance which increases their significance by underlining their complementary character. There is, of course, a difference: Eve sees her own reflection, Adam that of his great Creator, but both are concerned with an act of cognition assisted by divine intervention. Whereas

Satan will not admit that what he admires in himself is the reflection of God, Eve is taught to honour Adam as her "author", just as Adam's fruitless search for the Creator whose traces he sees everywhere is terminated when the Creator appears and says: "Whom thou soughtst I am ... Author of all this thou seest" (7.953–54). Eve meets her "author" as Adam does his. It is wrong to exaggerate the degree of difference between the two narratives by associating Eve's experience with the Narcissus-myth: it must be borne in mind that, in Renaissance thought, a person looking at himself in a mirror is an emblem of the quest for self-knowledge. It is in fact Satan who enacts the Narcissus-myth as he contemplates the spectacle of the two "Imparadis't in one anothers arms / The happier Eden", while he himself "Still unfulfill'd with pain of longing pines" (4.505–11). Eve would have "pin'd with vain desire" for her own reflection (4.466), and Adam for the reflection of the great Creator, were it not for the divine intervention that enables them to perceive their true place within the scheme of things, and so to enjoy bliss on bliss. Frustrated desire, as in the myth of Narcissus, is the lot only of Satan: the "idol" or false image of majesty divine must for ever pine with vain desire for the true original.

The topos of man as the image of God links books 4 and 7, as many passages testify, and another unifying concept is the union of pure with pure, as between Adam and Eve in book 4 and in the love of angels as described toward the end of book 7 (= VIII). Man's love of God and Eve's of Adam is the subject of the first exchange between Adam and Eve, and Adam's speech conveys the gist of his flashback narrative in book 7 (= VIII), just as Eve's speech is the preamble to her similar account. These are Adam's opening lines:

> 4.411 Sole partner and sole part of all these joyes,
> Dearer thy self then all; needs must the Power
> That made us, and for us this ample World
> Be infinitly good, and of his good
> As liberal and free as infinite,
> That rais'd us from the dust and plac't us here
> 4.417 In all this happiness.

Eve joins in this just homage, but adds acknowledgement of her "happier Lot", which is to enjoy "thee / Preeminent by so much odds" (4.446–47). Eve's perspective here recalls Abdiel's on subordination in Heaven: this subordination is noticed as such by Satan alone, since God is bent "rather to exalt / Our happie state under one Head more neer / United" (5.826–28). Like the angels, Adam and Eve are crowned with glory "since he the Head / One of our number thus reduc't becomes" and "all honour to him done / Returns our own" (5.839–42). Unless we see the connection between Abdiel's speech and Eve's we shall be in danger of adopting Satan's perspective, which discovers only "Knee-tribute" and "prostration vile" (5.779). These reflections redress the balance between Adam and Eve in her favour; Eve's perception of true relationships is as acute in its way as Adam's. Eve's fascination with the mirror of the lake parallels Adam's with the mirror of the universe, and their preoccupation with reflections or images is a logical part of the series of reflections portrayed in the inner triad. Satan, himself a false image of the Deity, pines with vain desire for the true image in Adam and Eve; Eve on her part is in danger of pining with vain desire for a mere reflection of herself, but is assisted to turn to the true image of God in Adam, an image she herself reflects. This image resides above all in his wisdom, "which alone is truly fair" (4.491). When Adam meets the Creator he meets the source of the reflection he sees everywhere, but Christ is himself the perfect image of the Father. As Satan exclaims, it is too much to owe homage to two – "To one and to his image now proclaim'd" (5.781). As we have seen, books 1–2 present Satan as false image, while in book 10 Adam, on seeing the faces of sin in the mirror of history, must recognize their source in himself: he is their "author". Satan and Christ form the great antithesis: Satan, in love with the attributes of God, seeks them in himself, while Christ, although invested with them, attributes them solely to the Father. Through an act of free will, Satan turns his love in the wrong direction and so falls into error, whereas Christ remains in the truth. Hence it is Satan alone who enacts the Narcissus-myth; it is he who loves a shadowy reflection in himself and who stubbornly refuses to recognize it for what it is, although assisted towards the truth by the divine wisdom speaking through Abdiel. While Satan therefore proclaims that the angels are "self-begot" and "self-rais'd", Adam and Eve proclaim their source in the great Creator in whose image they were made. In addition, Eve acknowledges that Adam is her immediate source, her "Author and Disposer" (4.635).

As long as Eve relates to Adam as Adam to Christ and Christ to God, the harmony established by this quaternion ensures ascent.

Ascent through loving union is explicit in God's plan for his creation. Book 5 begins and concludes with false ascents – of Eve in her dream and of Satan in Heaven – but the morning hymn of praise restores wonted calm, and Raphael's discourse on the scale of being puts everything in a proper perspective. Ascent depends on obedience, that is, on love of God. Man may find his body turned all to spirit,

> 5.498   and wingd ascend
> Ethereal, as wee, or may at choice
> Here or in Heav'nly Paradises dwell;
> If ye be found obedient, and retain
> Unalterably firm his love entire
> 5.503   Whose progenie you are.

Love is the basis of the obedience, as shown in the scenes between Adam and Eve in book 4 and again in the discourse on love toward the end of book 7 (= VIII). Adam's reply to Raphael's description of the scale of being contains an allusion to *Romans* 1 : 20, when he praises him for having taught

> 5.508   the way that might direct
> Our knowledge, and the scale of Nature set
> From center to circumference, whereon
> In contemplation of created things
> 5.512   By steps we may ascend to God.

The ascent to God is our prime concern; obedience is the precondition, and love the moving power. The point is repeated in the Father's speech prior to the work of creation in book 7. It is God's will to create a new race of men innumerable in a new world,

> 7.156   there to dwell,
> Not here, till by degrees of merit rais'd
> They open to themselves at length the way
> Up hither, under long obedience tri'd,
> And Earth be chang'd to Heavn, & Heav'n to Earth,
> 7.161   One Kingdom, Joy and Union without end.

And the trial comes through love, as Raphael explains at the end of book 7:

7.1225   In loving thou dost well, in passion not,
Wherein true Love consists not; love refines
The thoughts, and heart enlarges, hath his seat
In Reason, and is judicious, is the scale
By which to heav'nly Love thou maist ascend,
Not sunk in carnal pleasure, for which cause
7.1231   Among the Beasts no Mate for thee was found.

Raphael directs Adam's quest for knowledge, always turning it toward God as his great Creator; other kinds of knowledge are futile and misdirected, as Augustine also came to realize in the *Confessions*. This realization is the basis of the interdiction: in the quest for and ascent to God, knowledge of good alone is required, since God is the greatest good. This is the knowledge within bounds that Adam seeks in book 7; this is useful knowledge, everything else being vain or destructive (cf. 7.825–34). The destructive aspect is revealed in Satan's response to the interdiction in book 4:

4.521   O fair foundation laid whereon to build
Thir ruine! Hence I will excite thir minds
With more desire to know, and to reject
Envious commands, invented with designe
To keep them low whom knowledge might exalt
Equal with Gods; aspiring to be such,
4.527   They taste and die: what likelier can ensue?

Before the Fall, knowledge and love of the Creator is all that is required; after the Fall, knowledge and love of the Redeemer must be added, and, in his praise of the work of redemption, Adam in book 10 connects the basic themes of books 4–5 and 7:

10.1448   Greatly instructed I shall hence depart,
Greatly in peace of thought, and have my fill
Of knowledge, what this vessel can containe;
Beyond which was my folly to aspire.
Henceforth I learne, that to obey is best,
And love with feare the onely God, to walk
As in his presence, ever to observe
His providence, and on him sole depend,
...
Taught this by his example whom I now
10.1464   Acknowledge my Redeemer ever blest.

Another basic theme – ascent – is pitched in a new key by Michael in his comments on the Law. Man is incapable of observing the Law:

> 10.1191 So Law appears imperfet, and but giv'n
> With purpose to resign them in full time
> Up to a better Cov'nant, disciplin'd
> From shadowie Types to Truth, from Flesh to Spirit,
> From imposition of strict Laws, to free
> Acceptance of large Grace, from servil fear
> 10.1197 To filial, works of Law to works of Faith.

The more literal ascent from flesh to spirit as described in book 5, is now replaced by one which is purely spiritual; in the same way, the paradise which will be regained is a paradise within, happier far. The movement to the world within is as marked as in the *Confessions*, where the turning-point occurs with the words *intravi et vidi*. We have observed the same movement also in Tasso and Spenser, but in Milton it is more subtle and more purely biblical.

5. The Structure of Book 7

Book 7, as already observed, is a Book of Wisdom which divides the 10 books in the ratio 2 : 1. The hexaemeral subject is handled so as to connect the concepts of knowledge and love; both must be kept within proper bounds. When book 7 was divided, it became more difficult to recognize how interrelated these concepts are, but, if my analysis of the paragraph structure can be credited (see Diagram IX.9), then the theme of knowledge links the beginning and the middle, and the theme of love the middle and the end. This interaction between knowledge and love in the structure of book 7 was lost when book 7 was divided so as to make Books VII and VIII. In the first edition, however, the two are as closely connected as in Platonic thought.

The textual structure reveals perfect balance. After the invocatory first paragraph there follow 15 paragraphs on the story of creation; and after the quadruple centre in §§ 17–20 there follows a second set of 15 paragraphs on Adam's story of his first awakening, his subsequent dialogue with the Creator, and the coming of Eve. Each group of 15 paragraphs is further subdivided into 5+10 and 10+5 (the ratio of the diapason). Thus 5 paragraphs on knowledge within bounds (§§ 2–6) are followed by 10 on the work of creation: Christ leaves his seat next to the Father in § 7, and returns in

JOHN MILTON 519

Diagram IX.9 *Paradise Lost*. Paragraph Structure of Book 7

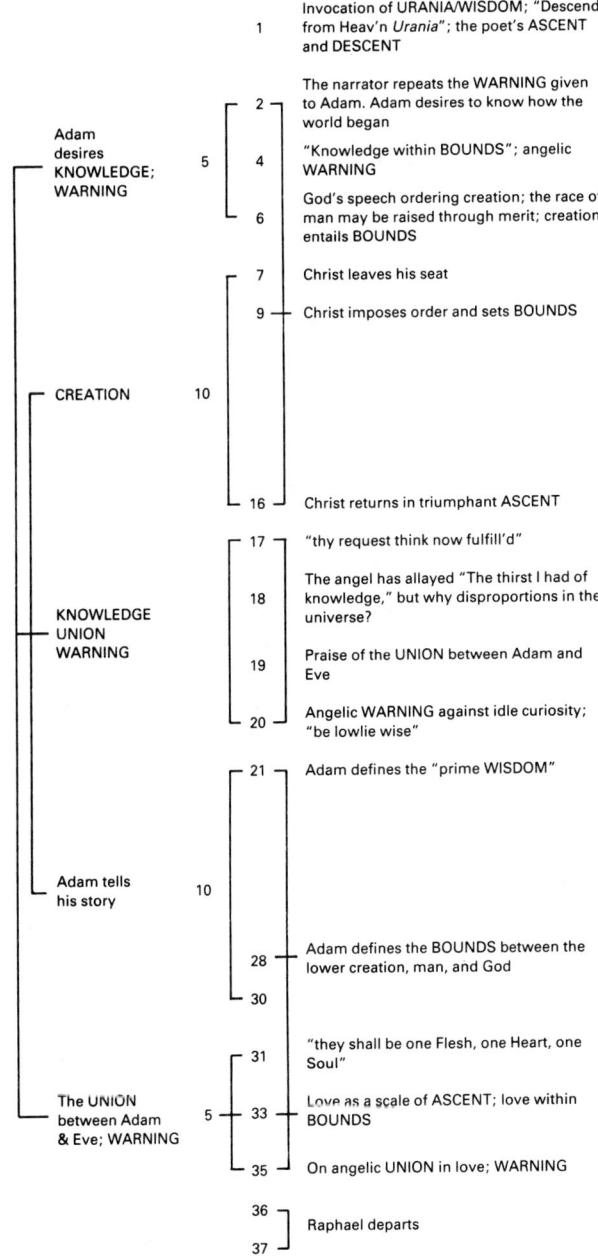

triumph in § 16. This return is a splendid triumphal ascent to the gates of Heaven, and Christ is surrounded by a "glorious Train" of angels singing their hymn of praise. Paragraph 16, the 15th in the sequence, describes the ascent which is a return as well, as in the octave proportion. The paragraph at the centre of the 15 paragraphs (§ 9) shows Christ as he begins his work of creation by setting bounds: "And said, thus farr extend, thus farr thy bounds, / This be thy just Circumference, O World" (7.230–31). At the centre of the 15 paragraphs on Adam's story and the ensuing dialogue on love (§§ 21–35), Adam defines the nature of man as compared with the lower creatures and to God, thus assigning proper bounds. These balanced paragraphs (§§ 9 and 28) share not only the topos of the setting of bounds, but also the principle of joining like to like and avoiding ill mixture. Christ purges the "cold infernal dregs / Adverse to life, then founded, then conglob'd / Like things to like" (7.238–40), and Adam's argument with God turns on the absence of a fit mate. Unlike God, who is "already infinit; / And through all numbers absolute, though One", man is "In unitie defective" and so must "beget / Like of his like" in "Collateral love, and deerest amitie" (7.1057–63). Adam, then, states the basic principle observed in Christ's work of creation. True union occurs only when like is joined to like, and this true union is the subject of § 19 (7.676–702) and again of §§ 31–35, where it is taken to its highest pitch in Raphael's description of angelic love as a "Union of Pure with Pure" (7.1264). This description or definition of true union serves as a foil to the "ill mixture" featured in books 1 and 10.

To avoid ill mixture, bounds must be honoured – the bounds between good and evil and between the Creator and his creatures. The state of harmony depends directly on the due observance of bounds. By distinguishing clearly between the lower creation, man, and God, Adam shows that he possesses the kind of knowledge which is both true and useful, the knowledge which is prime wisdom. This knowledge points forward to the supreme knowledge concerning the Redeemer conveyed by Michael in book 10 (= XII). The contrast with Satan's wilful ignorance is plain.

It has often been recognized that Adam's attitude to Eve, as expressed in the dialogue with Raphael, contains a dangerous element:

> 7.1183   when I approach
> Her loveliness, so absolute shee seems
> And in her self compleat, so well to know

>   Her own, that what she wills to do or say,
>   Seems wisest, vertuosest, discreetest, best;
>   All higher knowledge in her presence falls
>   Degraded, wisdom in discourse with her
> 7.1190 Looses discount'nanc't, and like folly shewes.

In other words, Adam's love may exceed proper bounds; his love of Eve may take him to the same point as Satan's love of himself. After all, Eve is part of himself, flesh of his flesh. Adam's opening remarks on "the prime Wisdom" (§ 21; 7.831) prove that he sees the danger and the futility of trying to know "at large of things remote / From use, obscure and suttle" (7.828–29), but Eve is closer to home. To the angelic warning concerning vain knowledge, therefore (in § 21), is added the warning against passion (§§ 33–35): "In loving thou dost well, in passion not" (7.1225). Love is "the scale / By which to heav'nly Love thou maist ascend, / Not sunk in carnal pleasure" (7.1228–30). The second group of 15 paragraphs, therefore, is as much concerned with ascent as the first.

We see, then, that one of the important lessons taught by book 7 is that the quest for knowledge and for love must be kept within limits which permit God to come first. This is the wisdom praised at the beginning and at the end of book 7 (= VII–VIII), as at its centre. No wonder, therefore, that the first paragraph addresses Wisdom as well as Urania, and that the sisters play "In presence of th'Almighty Father" (7.10–11), thus invoking the theme of divine love as well. Heavenly wisdom and heavenly love are inseparable, just as Adam's love of Eve must be combined with the wisdom to seek God first as the source of all love and wisdom.

Book 7 is truly pivotal in the sense that it presents basic issues which reach back to the beginning and point forward to the end. Books 1–2 show us a Satan alienated from all good through his wilful violation of the bounds set between Creator and created, and when the epic draws to its end Adam praises the "goodness immense" that will produce good from evil, "more wonderful / Then that which by creation first brought forth / Light out of darkness!" (10.1362–63). This interpretation of the creation of light as a type or prophecy of the redemption was so widely known that Milton could depend on it to establish the desired link between books 7 and 10 (= XII). Tasso had used it to good effect in the *Il Mondo Creato*. In the same way, in the act of creation the purging of the cold infernal dregs, adverse to life, sets up a link with the purging of Satan and his hosts from Heaven at the beginning of book 1. Linkage between books 7 and 10 is also established by the theme of true wisdom as combined with love of God:

10.1448   Greatly instructed I shall hence depart,
           Greatly in peace of thought, and have my fill
           Of knowledge, what this vessel can containe;
           Beyond which was my folly to aspire.
           Henceforth I learne, that to obey is best,
10.1453   And love with feare the onely God.

The connection with book 7 could not have been made more plain.

Milton may have been inspired by Augustine to let so much depend on a true definition of the nature of God, man, and the lower creation, since this is the subject which occupies Augustine in book 7 of the *Confessions*. This book, which has both a symmetrical and a graded structure,[16] is a climactic centre within the symmetrical structure of the 13 books. In it Augustine finally perceives the true nature of God and his creation and of evil; this insight is the turning-point in the story of his life.

The most disastrous effect of the division of book 7 in the second edition was to obscure the connection between wisdom and love, the issuing from God in the act of creation and the return to God in love. A related effect was the obscuring of the topos of keeping proper bounds. Knowledge within bounds consists in knowing our origin in God, and, given that knowledge, of loving God first as our source and end. To know the Creator is to experience his abundant love for man; the only knowledge which matters is knowledge of this love. While God's love is as boundless as his brightness is excessive, man's love of woman, and woman's of man, must avoid the excess entailed by "passion", since such excess obscures the love which leads man to higher levels of being. The double focus on wisdom and love appears very clearly in the opening paragraph, where Urania is accompanied by her sister, Wisdom. To divide book 7 is to separate the two.

6. Concluding Remarks

Textual structures are more easily perceived in stanzaic poetry; stanzas are more reliable textual units, though the example set by Tasso's *Il Mondo Creato* shows that verse paragraphs could be used just as systematically and effectively. Tasso, however, was in a position to supervise the printing of his manuscript (as Dryden was, later on), whereas Milton had to leave it to others; hence the line numbering is sometimes wrong, and the division into verse paragraphs may differ between the first and second editions. That such divisions may have structural significance has not been realized by modern editors, but it is a possibility that must be taken into account. As far as I have been able to ascertain, verse paragraphs do not function as consistently in *Paradise Lost* as in the *Il Mondo Creato*, but my analysis of books 1, 2, 3, and 7 supports the view that Milton could on occasion organize his text by means of verse paragraphs. He may have reserved the practice for a few selected books, or he may have been partly defeated by his blindness and the obtuseness of amanuenses. This view is supported by the circumstance that single verse paragraphs may be carefully structured.

The nature of Milton's textual units, therefore, helps to explain why number symbolism does not function as openly in *Paradise Lost* as in *The Faerie Queene* or *Jerusalem Delivered*. Another point is that Milton's use of the required repetitions is more subtle; his parallels are always with a distinct difference, as in his frequent use of parody. The conflict between Satan on the one hand and, on the other, the Father and the Son invites the parody which permits a seeming parallel to reveal the disastrous difference. The reader is constantly challenged to perceive the difference, but modern critics do not always survive the test. A parody, however, even if placed first within the body of the text, cannot invalidate the truth when it finally appears. On the contrary, the sudden perception that the first occasion was mere parody engenders an experience so intense that it may well be referred to as an epiphany. When Adam toward the end of book 10 (= XII) is struck by the paradox of the fortunate Fall, it dawns on us that Satan's version as expressed in book 1 is nothing but an empty boast intended to deceive and so to rally his fallen compeers. Equally lacking in substance is the claim that the angels are "self-begot, self-rais'd"; even Christ was begotten, and man will be born anew in Christ with the coming of the great Redeemer. The narrative needs such foils to set off the truth. To argue, as one critic has done, that Satan has the initiative simply because his actions precede those of God within the linear narrative[17] is to deprive the epic of much of its strength. If this is the consequence of a linear reading, a spatial or synoptic approach is called for as a much-needed corrective. Milton exploited to the full the double vision engendered by parallels-with-a-difference, thus teaching his readers not to be taken in by first impressions.

Interesting examples of numerical structures in *Paradise Lost* have already been documented. Independently of each other, Gunnar Qvarnström and Alastair Fowler ascertained that the chronological scheme consists of 33 days divided into 22 + 11, thus creating the ratio 2:1 of the diapason.[18] Moreover, Qvarnström discovered that some of the epic speeches have numerically significant line totals: Christ has four symmetrically placed speeches totalling 23 lines, and the concern of these speeches is with justice, mercy, mercy, and justice, in this sequence.[19] As Bongo explains, taken *in malo*, 23 signifies vengeance on sinners (i.e. justice), but salvation (i.e. mercy) when it is taken *in bono*.[20] A precedent for this usage is found in a poem Milton knew, Giles Fletcher's *Christs Victorie, and Triumph* (1610),[21] so that Milton can by no means be accused of singularity. As I show elsewhere, Milton's *Nativity Ode* reveals an indebtedness to Giles Fletcher's poem in both phrasing and textual structuring,[22] and it is likely that Giles Fletcher's textual structures inspired some of Milton's in *Paradise Lost* as well. Giles Fletcher, too, uses the number 23 to represent Justice and Mercy. During the debate in Heaven in Part I, an angry personified Justice calls for vengeance on sinners in a speech totalling 23 stanzas, but, in the last 23 stanzas (I.63–85), Mercy's intervention tips the scales in favour of redemption through Christ. Nor must the precedent set by Tasso be forgotten, or John Donne's in his *Devotions Upon Emergent Occasions* (1624). As Kate Frost has shown (*Holy Delight*, 1990), Donne's division of his work into 23 parts has a symbolic import relevant to the interpretation of this spiritual autobiography.[23] A stumbling-block for modern readers has been a widespread ignorance of the sign value of certain numbers and ratios, and of the way in which certain ideas, as expressed in the contents, call for structural enactment. A quarter of a century after Qvarnström's *The Enchanted Palace* (1967), it is finally possible to see how far ahead of his own generation this enterprising scholar was, and to give his work the recognition he himself can no longer receive.

Milton must have appreciated the way in which Giles Fletcher fuses rhetorical and numerical schemes even more insistently than Spenser, and in his own paragraphs on the Council in Heaven the presence of such schemes lifts the speeches of the Father and the Son to a higher stylistic level than those of Satan and his chief leaders. To the examples already cited should be added the Father's 70-line speech (3.274–343 or § 10) on redemption history. The number refers to the Babylonian captivity as a type of all of time, and Diagram IX.10 shows the balanced pattern. The paragraph

Diagram IX.10 *Paradise Lost*. The Father's Speech to the Son (3.274–343)

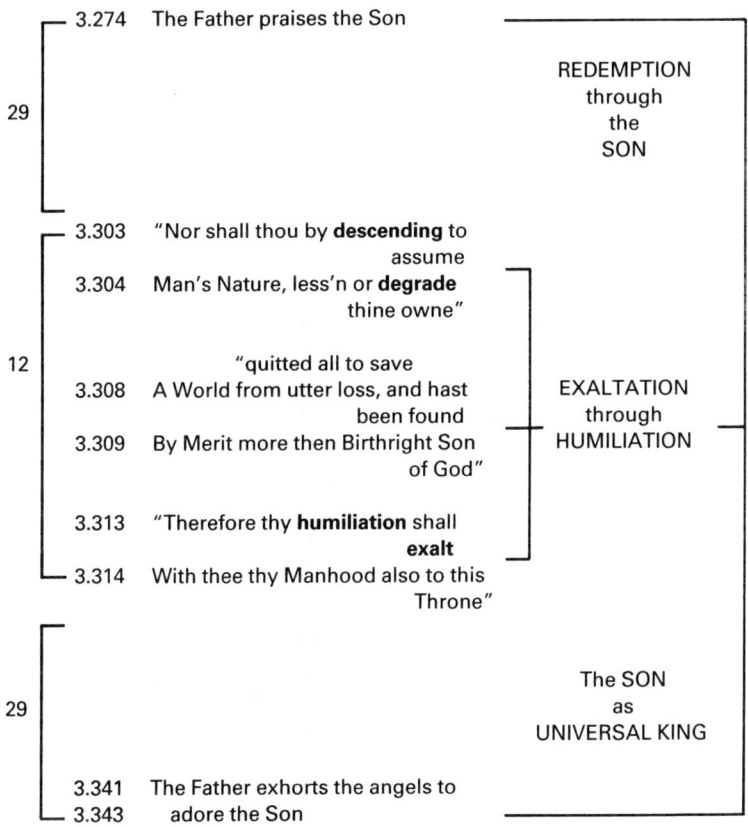

begins with the Father's praise of the Son; at the centre, Christ is said to quit all "to save / A World from utter loss", and at the end the angelic hosts are exhorted to adore the Son. Three lines above and below the centre are found parallel statements on the humiliation which exalts. Within the first part of the speech, a rhetorical scheme joins lines 3.281–301 into a balanced pattern, as shown in Diagram IX.11. The pattern begins and ends with the word *redeeme* at the line-end (3.281 and 3.299); on the last occasion, *redeeme* is framed by "Hellish hate" similarly placed in final position (lines 3.298 and 3.300). The rhetorical schemes repeatedly place positives and negatives in close opposition, as at the centre, where "His crime" is

Diagram IX.11 *Paradise Lost.* Verbal Symmetries in the Father's Speech (3.281–301)

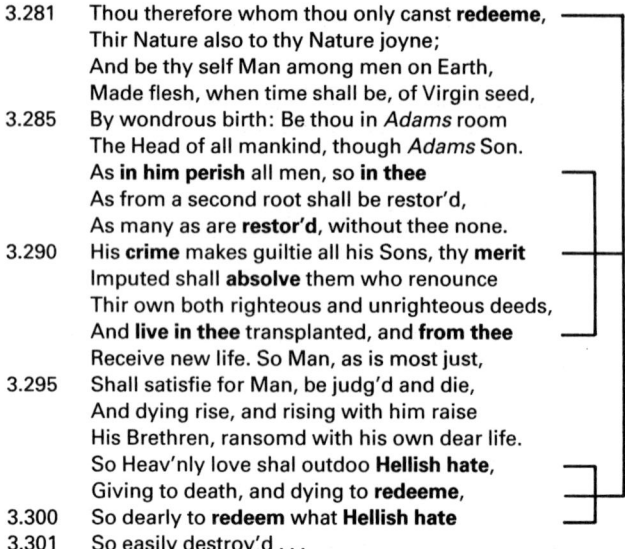

3.281 Thou therefore whom thou only canst **redeeme**,
Thir Nature also to thy Nature joyne;
And be thy self Man among men on Earth,
Made flesh, when time shall be, of Virgin seed,
3.285 By wondrous birth: Be thou in *Adams* room
The Head of all mankind, though *Adams* Son.
As **in him perish** all men, so **in thee**
As from a second root shall be restor'd,
As many as are **restor'd**, without thee none.
3.290 His **crime** makes guiltie all his Sons, thy **merit**
Imputed shall **absolve** them who renounce
Thir own both righteous and unrighteous deeds,
And **live in thee** transplanted, and **from thee**
Receive new life. So Man, as is most just,
3.295 Shall satisfie for Man, be judg'd and die,
And dying rise, and rising with him raise
His Brethren, ransomd with his own dear life.
So Heav'nly love shal outdoo **Hellish hate**,
Giving to death, and dying to **redeeme**,
3.300 So dearly to **redeem** what **Hellish hate**
3.301 So easily destroy'd . . .

The balanced pattern created by the recurrence of the word *redeem* in final position is perfect. The central line states the central message, and to each side, two lines removed, are the chiastically arranged phrases "in him perish" and "live in thee transplanted."

opposed to "thy merit", just as the act of *restoring* and *absolving* is opposed to *making guilty*, so that the two former annul the latter. In the same way, the phrase "in him perish" (placed three lines before the centre) balances "live in thee" (placed three lines after the centre). These balanced parallels and antitheses between words and phrases are a microcosmic version of the balancing of themes and topoi within the epic as a whole. The many repetitions engender a feeling of emotional intensity, just as the antitheses adorn the poem as they do the *carmen* of the universe:

   3.298 So Heav'nly love shall outdoo Hellish hate,
   Giving to death, and dying to redeeme,
   So dearly to redeem what Hellish hate
   3.301 So easily destroy'd.

The chiasmus in line 299 enacts the reversal from death to life and

Diagram IX.12 *Paradise Lost*. Co-ordinated Symmetries in 3.372–415 and in 3.383–415

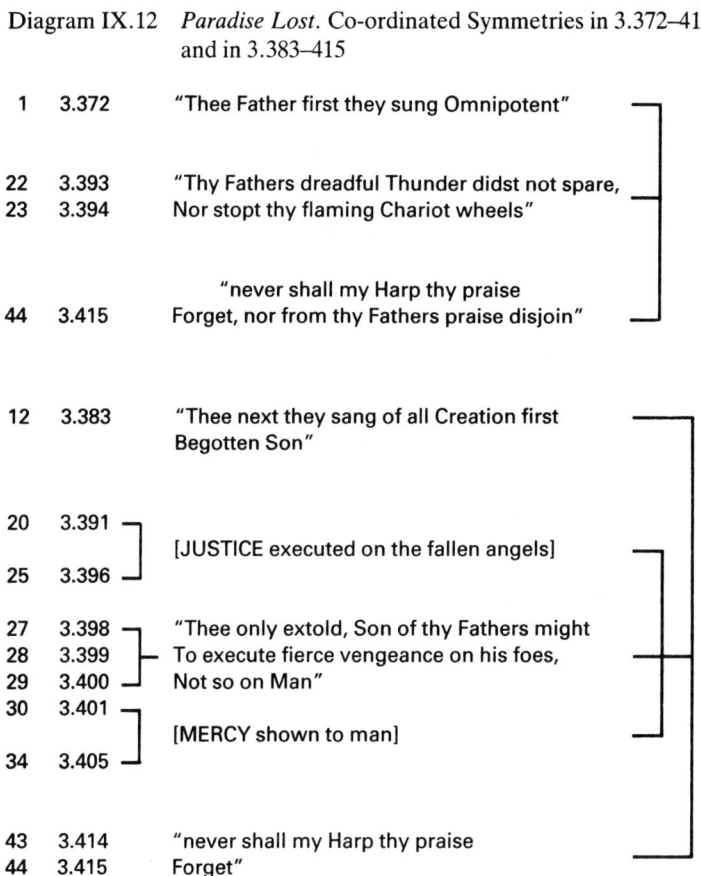

The perfect co-ordination between these symmetrical structures may perhaps be taken to express the union between the Father and the Son.

from hate to love. The last part of the speech (3.315–43) is equally symmetrical, in that it begins and concludes with praise of the Son as universal king; after Judgment Day, though, the Son will lay his regal Sceptre by, "For regal Scepter then no more shall need, / God shall be All in All" (3.34–41). The sense of grandeur conveyed by this 70-line speech is engendered largely by its balanced words and phrases. When read with perfect awareness of its balanced patterns, the impact is enhanced, just as an extra dimension is added on associating the 70 lines with that exile where "Hellish hate" is only too clearly manifested in those who, "when they may, accept not grace" (3.302).

In this 70-line speech, then, numerical decorum combines with rhetorical schemes to elevate the contents. On other occasions, numerical decorum is not accompanied by such elaborate rhetorical schemes, so that the Father's speech is clearly an exceptional case, as indeed it ought to be. Simple numerical decorum is found in the Father's 50-line speech on salvation through grace (3.167–216 or § 6), where 50 represents the Year of Jubilee with its remission of all debts. Another example is the Son's 39 lines on his offer to atone for man (§ 8, or 3.227–65), where 39 is the number of the cross.

The concluding 44-line verse paragraph (3.372–415) is yet another special case. This paragraph has the Father at the beginning, middle, and end, as shown in Diagram IX.12, while at the same time it divides into 11 lines on the Father and 33 on the Son. The number 11 is appropriate for the Father, since 11 taken *in bono* expresses his excess, or going beyond everything we know: God is "dark with excessive bright" (3.380). The 33 lines on the Son (3.383–415) are balanced by the concepts of Justice and Mercy, themselves balanced in the Son as praised at the textual centre (3.398–400). Angelic song in honour of the Son, and the poet's song, frame the 33-line passage. Again, the precision of the balanced patterns is remarkable. Milton's memory clearly was more visual than that of most modern literary critics; blind as he was, he must have *seen* his words and his lines as objects in the poem's space. His *verba* were *res*, as medieval linguistic theory would have it, and this medieval attitude persisted well into the Renaissance.[24]

Giles Fletcher's 15-stanza ladders of ascent[25] find their analogues in Milton's 15-line ladders, as we have seen. Diagram IX.13 shows that the ladder described at 3.540–54[26] is marked by the use of rhymes and by verbal repetition: the rhymes *stair, unaware*, and *faire* connect the beginning, middle, and end. In a poem in blank verse, the use of rhyme functions as powerfully as the absence of rhyme in a stanzaic poem. The picture of Satan perched on the heavenly stairs of gold creates the same incongruous contrast as Satan's abuse of sacred numbers; the numerical "image" amplifies the verbal image. As Augustine reminds us so often, evil is either formlessness or perverse form. True form is observed in Eve's last speech on the promise of redemption: "By mee the Promis'd Seed shall all restore" (10.1514); its appropriate form is manifested in its 14 lines, where 14 is the number of redemption (as the sum of the 10 of the Law and the 4 of the gospels). The number of ascent is encountered again in Michael's 15 lines on Christ's triumphant ascent (10.1342–56). At the beginning and the middle, the ascent is

Diagram IX.13 *Paradise Lost*. Linkage through Rhyme and Verbal Repetition (3.540–554)

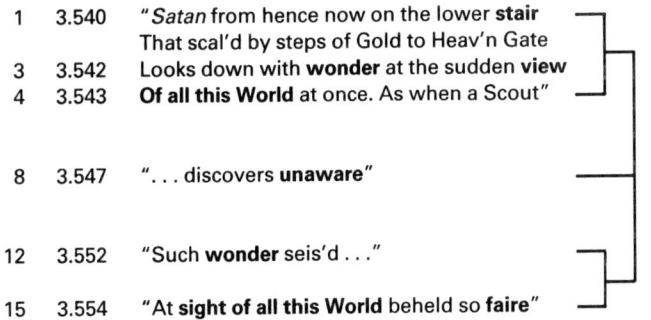

The rhymes *stair*, *unaware*, and *faire* connect the beginning, middle, and end of this 15-line passage on Satan's survey, from the lowest step, of all this world. The phrases "*wonder* at the *view / Of all this World*" and "*wonder . . . at sight of all this World*" respectively follow the first rhyme and precede the last. The repetition of identical phrases strengthens the sense of wonder, and the rhymes serve to identify these 15 lines as a textual structure.

described in physical terms: "he shall ascend / With victorie" (10.1342–43), and he shall be "exalted high / Above all names in Heaven" (10.1348–49). At the end, though, the ascent is unambiguously spiritual: the ascent will be to a "far happier place / Then this of *Eden*, and far happier daies" (10.1355–56).

It seems to me most unlikely that Milton counted lines on all occasions, yet he undoubtedly did so on some. All we can safely say about Milton's use of number symbolism in the structure of verse paragraphs is that it is present on some occasions. On most occasions, though, number symbolism seems quite absent. Why should the last part of book 3 – the part concerned with Satan – consist of 4 paragraphs only? Are we to assume that the 4 paragraphs are a parody of Christ's redemptive mission as described in the 4 gospels? Equally speculative is the notion that the 360 lines on the Council in Heaven (3.56–415) may represent the perfection of the circle, and that the 33 lines in honour of Christ at the textual centre of book 3 are preceded and followed by 327 lines (when the 55-line invocatory first paragraph is omitted). The 327 lines equal $3 \times 100 + 3^3$, so that the number 3 prevails. Such computations seem to me more typical of Tasso and Spenser than of Milton. Thus the 433 lines of Spenser's *Epithalamion* may be seen as 216+1+216, where the central line celebrates the endless character of the matrimonial union ("The which do endlesse matrimony make"), and 216 is the product of 2^3 and 3^3 (8×27), as in Plato's *lambda* formula for the creation of the world. Through the sacred rites, two worlds, each represented by 216, become one, as stated at line 217. Milton may have achieved a similar *tour de force* in book 3, but the case remains uncertain. Numerical structures supported by verbal patternings provide more reliable indications of authorial intent, as do the larger balanced patterns, whether symmetrical or graded, that enclose the epic as a whole. As in Spenser and Tasso, the same structural principle can be seen at work in a short segment (a stanza or a verse paragraph) and in the poem as a whole. The scale may differ, but the principle is the same.

Unlike *Jerusalem Delivered* and *The Faerie Queene, Paradise Lost* does not lend itself to presentation in the form of diagrams; the episodic character of romance epic invites such a procedure, but the tightly woven web of Milton's epic does not. Diagram IX.14 shows the symmetries created by some of the standard topoi, such as the mirror – the mirror of the lake and the mirror of the universe – and the marshalling of troops and enthronements. The marshalling of troops connects the beginning, middle, and end, since the visions shown to Adam in the first part of book 10 (= XI) are a kind of marshalling of the deadly sins, as in the roll-call of Satan's leaders in book 1. Elevations and debasements link books 2 and 9 and the middle. Books 2 and 9 are also linked by the theme of *discord*: after the Fall, the discord evident in the geography of Hell is transferred to Earth and to Adam and Eve. However, when Adam and Eve humble themselves before God at the very end of book 9, their humility is in striking contrast to Satan's pride as he sits enthroned in Hell in the opening lines of book 2. In their humility, Adam and Eve may perhaps be taken to foreshadow the second Adam and the second Eve. Christ's offer to atone for man by becoming incarnate and to suffer the penalty, and Satan's parodic "incarnation" in the serpent, are the most obvious specific link between books 3 and 8, while the anticipation of the Fall and its actual occurrence provide a more general link. A third link is found in Adam's echo of Christ's argument to the Father that the Father ought not to abandon his creation and permit the enemy to triumph. Then too a link is found in the contrast between the "fruitless hours" spent by Adam and Eve after the Fall and our first vision of them in book 3, reaping immortal fruits of joy and love. The harmony of God's creation displayed so fully in books 4 and 7 finds its noblest expression in the morning hymn of praise at the beginning of book 5, and in the

Diagram IX.14 *Paradise Lost*. Some Symmetries in Edn 1

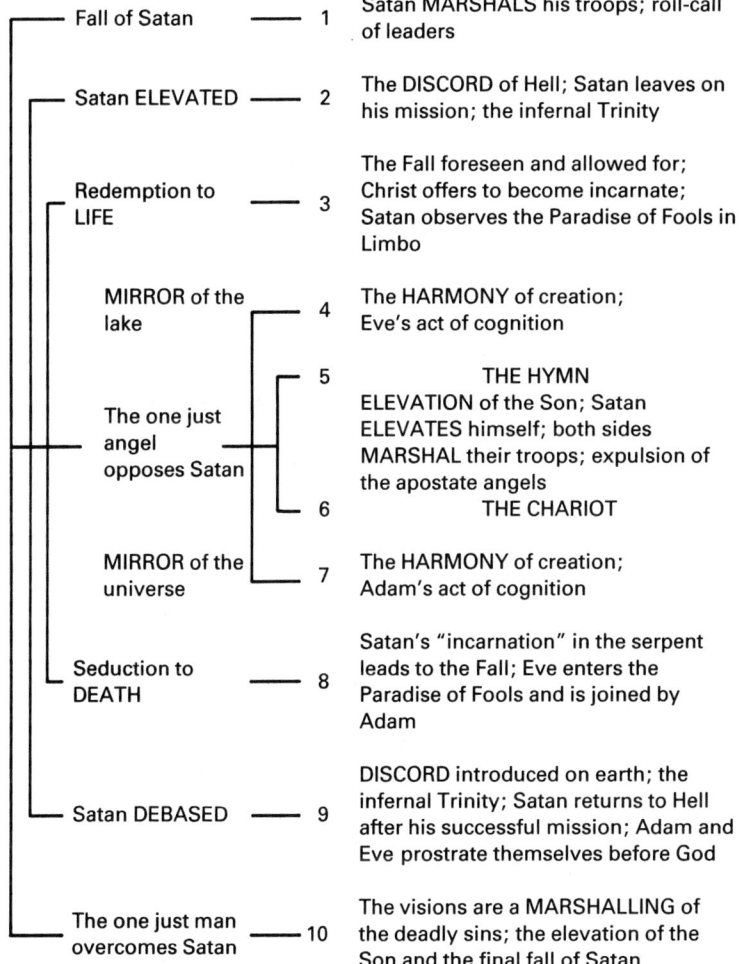

chariot of paternal Deity at the end of book 6. In these closely linked passages, the idea of obedience is fused with the love which subsists between Creator and created; in loving obedience, all of creation turns to its great Creator, drawn up to him through the order which makes creatures share in the Unity from which they take their origin. When the parodic character of Satan's speeches and actions is fully realized, his stature shrinks; nevertheless, since his imitation is of God himself – or of the Son – it is necessarily possessed of some degree of grandeur, perverse though it be. It is a moot point whether Eve's praise of Adam's glorious trial of exceeding love in book 8 is pure parody of the just praise given to Christ in book 3, or whether perhaps we are to feel that Adam's choice reveals some degree of grandeur – that his love of Eve in fact shadows God's love of man. Such parodic passages, so it seems, are never purely negative, since that which is parodied is what is highest and best.

Linked passages often have a logical connection. It is logical that, after the Fall, the sins represented by Satan's leaders should take possession of Adam's offspring, beginning with Cain. It is equally logical that the harmony of Eden (as described in book 4) should stem from the harmony established by Christ in his work of creation (as seen in book 7). Whereas at the textual centre God proclaims the engendering of the Son, Satan's offspring – Sin and Death – are featured in books 2 and 9. In this way the balanced patterns so often traced in exegetical treatises find a balanced placing within the 10-book structure.

In the 12-book structure of the second edition, all these balanced parallels and antitheses disappear, with the exception of the balance between book 1 and the second half of book 10 (= XII). It must be conceded that the loss is considerable. The unifying symmetrical structure of the first edition is powerful as well as aesthetically satisfying, and at the same time the basic thematic concerns are brought out with greater clarity. As already explained, the symmetries of the second edition represent the remnants of the graded arrangement of individual books, an arrangement which functions as an expansion of the basic symmetrical pattern. It is therefore difficult to accept the prevailing view that the 12-book edition is to be unequivocally preferred to the edition in 10 books, and it is to be hoped that the latter will be restored to favour as a superior original conception aimed at a fit audience capable of appreciating its structural felicities and their relevance to a richly satisfying interpretation.

Notes to Chapter IX

1. See my essay on "The Craftsmanship of God: Some Structural Contexts for the *Poems of Mr. John Milton* (1645)" in *Heirs of Fame: Milton and Writers of the English Renaissance*, eds. D. A. Kent and Margo Swiss (Bucknell University Press, forthcoming).

2. All quotations are from the facsimile edition of edn. 1 published by the Scolar Press (Menston, 1968).
3. See above, p. 156.
4. Merritt Y. Hughes, "Beyond Disobedience", in *Approaches to Paradise Lost*, ed. C. A. Patrides (London, 1968), pp. 182 and 191.
5. Quotations are from Augustine, *On Free Choice of the Will*, tr. Anna S. Benjamin and L. H. Hackstaff (New York: The Bobbs-Merrill Company, Inc., 1964).
6. The concept of ill mixture has a biblical basis in 2 *Cor*. 6 : 14–18 on the nature of true fellowship: "Be ye not unequally yoked together with unbelievers: for what fellowship hath righteousness with unrighteousness? And what communion hath light with darkness? And what concord hath Christ with Belial? ... And what agreement hath the temple of God with idols? for ye are the temple of the living God ... Wherefore come out from among them, and be ye separate". Similar passages are found for example in Ps. 106 : 34–39, *Samuel* chs 5–7, and *Ezek*. 37 : 22–23.
7. Pietro Bongo, *Numerorum mysteria* (Bergamo, 1591), pp. 182 and 191.
8. Marcus Vigerius, *Rhetorica Diuina de Oratione Domini Guilermi Parisieñ* (Nuremberg, 1517). The preface to this thoroughly syncretistic treatise explains that its 10 parts form a decachord in imitation of the psalter with 10 strings; from the disparate voices of the separate parts is created *unum concentum*. Also the decachord refers to the 10 days of the scheme of redemption, beginning with the Annunciation and the Nativity, and concluding with the Ascension and Pentecost; on this decachord of the 10 days Christ played the new song. The chapter entitled "Chorda Septima" explains the idea of *concentus ex dissonis* whereby the Fall is balanced and annulled by the act of redemption (cf. f. CXXIX verso).
9. See Marin Mersenne, *La Verité des Sciences*, the "Livre de l'Utilité de l'Harmonie", and *Traitez des Consonances*, as discussed above, Chapter I.
10. Cassiodorus, *Divine and Human Readings*, as discussed above, pp. 141 f.
11. Northrop Frye, *Five Essays on Milton's Epics* (London, 1966), p. 11.
12. Gunnar Qvarnström, *Dikten och den Nya Vetenskapen: Det Astronautiska Motivet: With a Summary in English* (Lund, 1961), see pp. 286–88 (the English summary of Ch. V). Qvarnström gave a more comprehensive account of the textual structures of *Paradise Lost* in *The Enchanted Palace* (Stockholm, 1967); see ch. 2 on the Christocentric structure.
13. See Steven Blakemore, "Pandemonium and Babel: Architectural Hierarchy in *Paradise Lost,*" *Milton Quarterly* 20 (1986), 142–45. Blakemore traces thematic similarities that connect Satan's building of Pandæmonium with Nimrod's building of Babel. Verbal echoes, too, are noted.
14. Roy T. Eriksen, "God Enthroned: Expansion and Continuity in Ariosto, Tasso, and Milton", in *Milton in Italy*, ed. Mario di Cesare (Binghamton, 1991), p. 420.
15. Augustin, *Über den Wortlaut der Genesis*, tr. Karl Johann Perl (Paderborn, 1961), Vol. II, pp. 212 f. For the Latin text, see *De Genesi ad Litteram Libri Duodecim*, XI.xxxiii.43.
16. See above, Chapter II.
17. N. Forsyth, "Full of Doubt I Stand: the Structure of *Paradise Lost*", in *The Structure of Texts*, ed. Udo Fries (Tübingen, 1987), pp. 159–76, argues that Satan has the initiative so that God is left to pick up the pieces.
18. Qvarnström, *The Enchanted Palace*, and Alastair Fowler, "Introduction", *The Poems of John Milton*, eds. John Carey and Alastair Fowler (London, 1968), pp. 440–43.
19. *The Enchanted Palace*, pp. 91–120. Bongo's main conclusion concerning the number 23 is that it expresses the joint operation of Justice and Mercy (p. 107). The speeches are located at III.144, VI.723, VI.801, and XI.22 (see pp. 90–103).
20. Bongo, *Numerorum Mysteria*, pp. 441–43.

21. See my study of "Golden Phrases: The Poetics of Giles Fletcher", *Studies in Philology* 88 (1991), 169–200. The number 23 also signifies the combination between eloquence and salvation; this is so because the number 23, when taken to refer to the 23 letters of the Latin alphabet, signifies *sapientiæ perfectionem* (Bongo, p. 176).
22. Røstvig, "The Craftsmanship of God".
23. Kate Gartner Frost, *Holy Delight. Typology, Numerology, and Autobiography in Donne's* Devotions Upon Emergent Occasions (Princeton, NJ, 1990).
24. The way in which this attitude can be traced in sixteenth-century poetry is explained by Anne Ferry, *The Art of Naming* (Chicago and London, 1988).
25. Røstvig, "Golden Phrases", pp. 181 and 192. The "ladders" are located in stanzas III.1–15 and IV.1–15. Both are subdivided into 5 triads.
26. H. Neville Davies traces various occurrences of the number 15 in the *Nativity Ode* and in *Paradise Lost* in "Laid Artfully together: Stanzaic Design in Milton's 'On the Morning of Christ's Nativity'," in *Fair Forms*, ed. M.-S. Røstvig (Cambridge, 1975), pp. 85–117 and 213–19. See also his essay on "The Structure of Shadwell's *A Song for St. Cecilia's Day, 1690*", in *Silent Poetry*, ed. Alastair Fowler (London, 1970), pp. 209–20 on Milton's 15-line ladders of ascent in *Paradise Lost*.

Chapter X

Dryden and the Art of Praise

> So, she was all a Sweet; whose ev'ry part,
> In due proportion mix'd, proclaim'd the Maker's Art.
> Dryden, *Eleonora*, 1692

Dryden is perhaps the last major English poet to exploit the semantic dimension of symbolic numbers and ratios; his *Song for St. Cecilia's Day, 1678* incorporates symbolic numbers at the same time that the diapason plays a major role in the form as well as the contents.[1] Even better examples are afforded by Dryden's panegyrics, a genre which approximates the epic in dignity.

In order to perceive Dryden's numerical felicities, it is necessary to count metrical units such as couplets and triplets. An early poem like "To His Sacred Majesty, a Panegyrick on His Coronation"[2] consists entirely of heroic couplets, 68 in all. The contents divide the panegyric into a sequence of 33—2—33 couplets, where the two couplets at the centre describe the universal joy attending the event. The first 33 couplets consist of 22 on the restoration and 11 on the coronation ceremony, while the last group consists of 11 couplets on the future happiness envisaged and 22 on the love of the king which has made all discord cease in a reconciliation of opposites. This, then, is the symmetrical pattern:

$$\frac{33}{22-11-2-11-22}\frac{33}{}$$

The number 33 associates Charles with Christ's redemptive action, just as the ratio 2 : 1 expresses the harmony established by Christ in the acts of creation and redemption. The panegyric, then, pays its greatest compliment to the king through its structural images of harmony restored.

The structure is fairly simple, as one would expect from such an early poem, but greater inventiveness became possible once Dryden discovered the structural usefulness of triplets. "The Character of a Good Parson; Imitated from Chaucer, and Inlarg'd" (1700) has a most complex structure, beginning with the 33 lines of the first verse paragraph with its 15 metrical units. These units consist of 12 couplets and 3 triplets. The contents explain why 33 has been combined with 15. If 33 (for the parson's Christ-like character) had been the sole objective, 15 couplets and 1 triplet would have sufficed to obtain 33 lines, but Dryden saw fit to insert as many as 3 triplets, thus achieving a sum total of 15 units. The number 15 relates to the extended passage on ascent through the "music" of his preaching of the Word:

17   With Eloquence innate his Tongue was arm'd;
      Tho' harsh the Precept, yet the Preacher charm'd.
      For, letting down the golden Chain from high,
20   He drew his Audience upward to the Sky:
      And oft, with holy Hymns, he charm'd their Ears:
22   (A Musick more melodious than the Spheres).

The drawing upward calls for the number 15 of ascent, just as the superior kind of music, "more melodious than the Spheres", is represented by the 15 which is the double octave. The parson is one with God in his tempering of the Law and the Gospel, Mercy and Justice:

30   He taught the Gospel rather than the Law:
      And forc'd himself to drive, but lov'd to draw.
      For Fear but freezes Minds; but Love, like Heat,
33   Exhales the Soul sublime, to seek her Native Seat.

In his comments on Dryden's ode "To the Pious Memory Of the Accomplisht Young Lady Mrs Anne Killigrew" (1686), H. Neville Davies points out that "the first sentence of Dryden's poem is of fifteen lines and is about Anne's 'Promotion' from earth to heaven", just as the 15 lines of stanza 4 "deliberately imply, by numerological means, a connexion between Anne and Christ as ladders of redemption".[3] Davies adds that the metrical irregularity of lines 1, 8 and 15 (1 and 8 are tetrameters, 15 a hexameter, and the rest pentameters) set them apart so that they should be seen to correspond to "the three soundings of the musical tonic".[4] In the double octave musical scale represented by the number 15, the lower octave "is associated with the created world of time, and the upper, spiritual octave with the supernatural world of eternity",[5] and Dryden's parson combines them both. His "letting down the golden Chain from high" (line 19), recalls the image, in the ode "On the Death of Mr. Henry Purcell", of the "Heav'nly Quire, who heard his Notes from high, / [and] Let down the Scale of Musick from the Sky" (ll. 23–24). In his paraphrase of Chaucer, then, Dryden based his counting on couplets and triplets, so that his choice of three triplets was conditioned by his wish to incorporate the 15 of ascent and of the double octave into his textual structure. If further examples of the same technique can be found, we must perforce conclude that Dryden's fondness for triplets connects with his fondness for symbolic numbers and ratios.

The number 33 conditions the overall structure as well, since its 67 metrical units (61 couplets and 6 triplets) divide into 33—1—33, as we see from the contents. The central unit expresses the parson's rejection of worldly advancement; he refuses "To chaffer for preferment with his Gold, / Where Bishopricks, and *sine Cures* are sold" (ll. 70–71), and this idea connects the beginning, middle, and end. At the beginning and the end the parson's attitude is shown in the antithesis between appearance and reality, richness and poverty: "Rich was his Soul, though his Attire was poor" (l.5), and the food he provides for souls is equally rich: "He went not, with the Crowd, to see a Shrine, / But fed us by the way with Food divine" (ll. 135–36). Lastly, he needs no foil, "But shines by his own proper Light" (l. 140).

The symmetrical structure coexists with a division into 44—1—22, where Christ's passion is at the centre: "The Crown he wore was of the pointed Thorn: / In Purple he was crucify'd, not born" (ll. 94–95). However, the main structural division is into 50 units on the character sketch and 17 on the narrative of temptation, which functions as a coda, much like the concluding story of Balaam in Pope's *Epistle to Bathurst*. Diagram X.1 sets out the symmetrical structure of the 50 units of the sketch; its balance is precise, as we see from the repetition of identical rhymes and phrases. Thus the penultimate couplet repeats the rhyme words of the second:

```
3    His Eyes diffus'd a venerable Grace,
4    And Charity it self was in his Face.

102  Such was the Saint; who shone with every Grace·
103  Reflecting, Moses-like, his Maker's Face.
```

The rhyme word *poor* circumscribes the mid-section (units 23–27; ll. 48–57), at the same time that it reaches back to the beginning

Diagram X.1 Dryden, "The Character of a Good Parson"

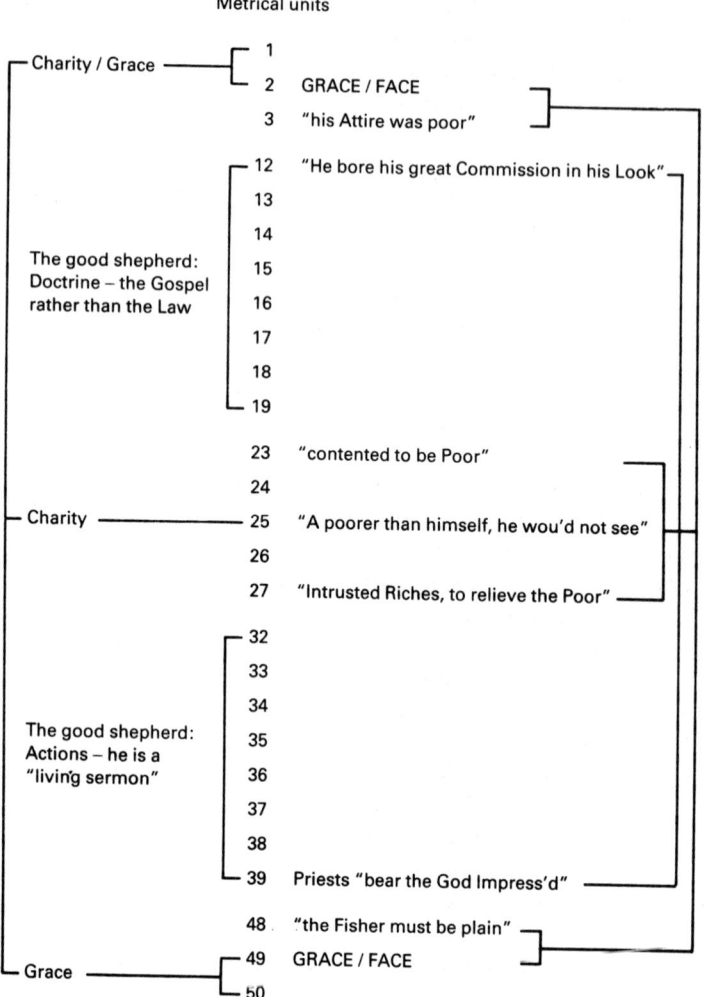

Identical rhyme words circumscribe the sketch (*grace / face*), just as the central section on his charity is balanced by the repetition of the rhyme word *poor*. Related statements connect units 3 and 48, and 12 and 39. The exactness of the placing is remarkable.

("his Attire was poor", l. 4) and forward to the end ("the Fisher must be plain", l. 101). In between are passages on the parson's preaching (units 12–19) and on his life, which is a living sermon (units 32–39). The 50 units of the sketch proclaim remission of sins very much in the parson's own spirit, while the 17 units of the narrative coda may refer to the 10 of the Law and the 7 gifts of the Holy Spirit.

The connection between form and content, then, is admirably close: the various structures express that *tempering* which makes the Parson so Christ-like:

> 25 He bore his great Commission in his Look:
> But sweetly temper'd Awe; and soften'd all he spoke.
> He preach'd the Joys of Heav'n, and Pains of Hell,
> And warn'd the Sinner with becoming Zeal;
> 29 But on Eternal Mercy lov'd to dwell.

The connection between form and content is even closer in *Eleonora: A Panegyrical Poem Dedicated to the Memory of the Late Countess of Abingdon* (1692). In this poem all the main ideas are structural, so that the inspiration must have come from them. Like God, Eleonora possesses Unity and is all One; she balances hoarding and spending in a golden mean which favours bounty, and she reconciles opposites like humility and elevation. From her oneness stems an almost inexhaustible fullness, and her fullness is like that of God's creation: "her 'ev'ry part, / In due proportion mix'd, proclaim'd the Maker's Art" (ll. 158–59). This is the art she passes on to her children, so that to imitate the Creator or Eleanora is all one; she is an equally true pattern, and so is the poem written in her praise. No wonder, therefore, that Dryden states, in his prefatory letter to the Earl of Abingdon, that at first he had "intended to have call'd this Poem, the Pattern", and that he strikes a prophet-like stance when he professes to have prophesied beyond his own natural power.

In the poem itself, Dryden on two occasions introduces the topos of poetic inadequacy: the picture is said to be "lamely drawn" (§ 11, line 142 or 11:142) and to constitute an "imperfect draught" (21:263). Such humble expressions, though, may relate to the elevation of the poem as Eleanora's humility to her elevation, and both to Christ's. However, the poetic reflection is certainly imperfect in the sense that it must fall short of her excellence, since "the true height and bigness of a Star, / Exceeds the Measures of th'Astronomer" (21 : 263–65). This star-like eminence manifests itself in the perfection of the circle: "The Figure was with full Perfection crown'd; / Though not so large an Orb, as truly round" (22 : 272–73). The poem, then, falls short of her excellence, which exceeds all measures, but on the other hand the poem enacts this going beyond all measures in the sum total of lines. The 180 metrical units would have equalled 360 lines (like the 360° of the circle) if all of them had been couplets, but the presence of 17 triplets swells the line total to 377. At the same time, though, one can argue that the 180 units relate to the 360° of the circle as 1 : 2; as reflection of the true pattern, the poem relates harmoniously to the "true orb" of perfection represented by Eleonora.

Our perception of the textual structures is facilitated by Dryden's marginal glosses. Thus the opening paragraph is identified as "The Introduction" and the last two as "Epiphonema: or close of the Poem". The praise, then, is circumscribed by 1+2 paragraphs whose line total (30) equals the number of paragraphs in the poem as a whole. This may be why so much is made of the fact that her record shows "a Blank beyond the thirti'th Page" (25 : 296). She did not live much beyond the 30th year. This kind of decorum was a fairly common practice; Milton, for example, divided his "Epitaph on the Marchioness of Winchester" into 23+14 couplets, so that the 23 couplets on her life and death reflect her age ("Summers three times eight save one").

Diagram X.2 shows that Dryden has placed unity at the centre; the centrally placed § 15 praises the unity between Eleonora and her husband in the line placed at its own textual centre: "One Joy possess'd 'em both, and in one Grief they mourn'd" (15 : 184). The precision of the placing could not be greater. The accent on grief refers us back to the beginning (§ 2) and forward to the end (§ 28). This thematic linking is strengthened by the repetition of the same pair of rhyme words (*heart / part*) in the first couplet of § 2 and in the last of §§ 15 and 28; again the placing cannot be more precise.

If grief is present at the centre of the central paragraph, so is joy, but the main theme here is unity. Eleonora and her husband are one in joy and in grief, and their oneness is of the kind which ought to prevail between subjects and their king, and between man and God. The oneness defines her role as progenitor (§§ 14 and 16), and the oneness has already been elaborated on in §§ 11–13, just as the consequent fertility is the subject of §§ 17–19. Her oneness makes her seem like undistinguished light (§ 11), or like the circle (§ 12), or again like God's work of creation (§ 13). The link between §§ 13 and

DRYDEN AND THE ART OF PRAISE 541

Diagram X.2   Dryden, *Eleonora* (1692)

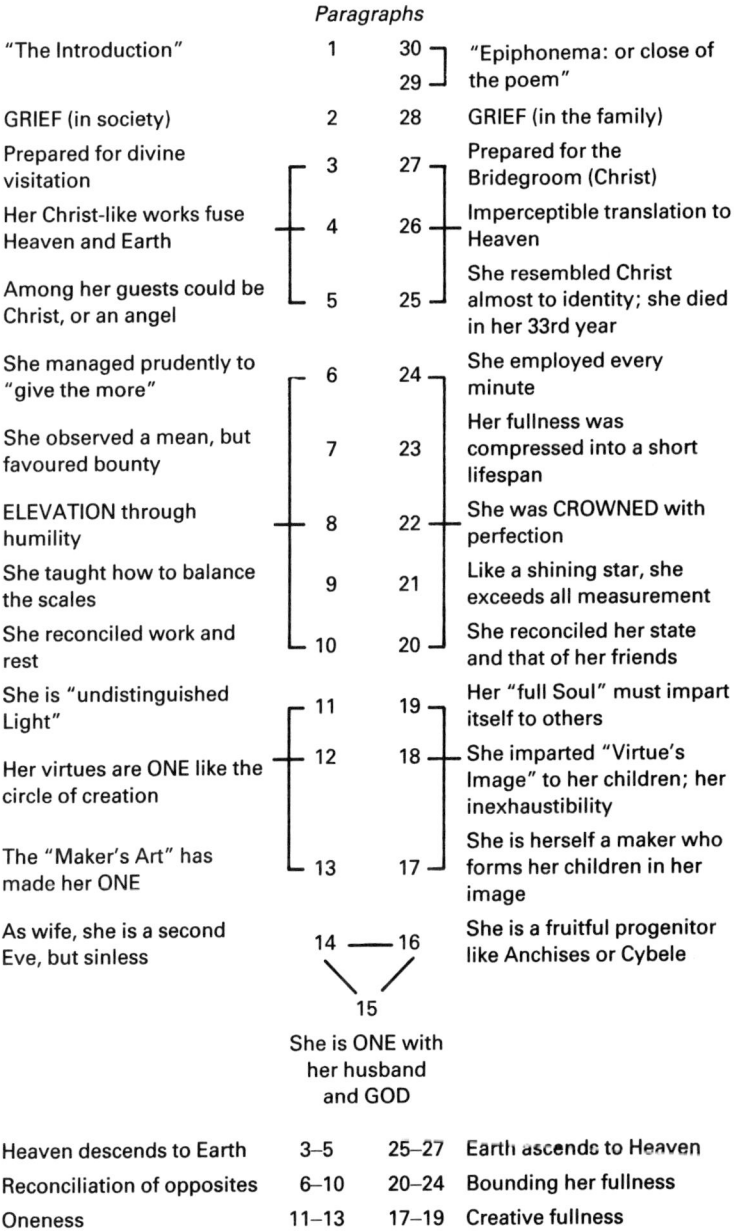

17 is plain: both are concerned with the "Maker's Art". She fashions her children as God fashions her. Her oneness as praised in § 12, is the cause of her fertility as a mother (§ 18), and the same causal relationship connects §§ 11 and 19.

Halfway between the beginning and the middle, and between the middle and the end we find truly climactic images of praise. In the one her virtues are seen to raise "her Fabrick to the Sky" (8 : 89), and in the other she is "with full Perfection crown'd" (22 : 272). These paragraphs are also at the centre of the five paragraphs on her balancing between extremes and the five on her transcendent fullness. In her these opposites are reconciled.

We see, then, how the idea of oneness has implications for the poem itself, whose verse paragraphs are marshalled to each side of the unifying centre in a sustained pattern of one-to-one linkages. This is how unity becomes a matter of "due proportion", and this is why even her virtues must be presented as fused into "one Heroick" which "comprehends 'em all" (12 : 147). This is not another virtue, but simply the unity formed by them all. Its effect is the Christ-like reconciliation between Earth and Heaven described in §§ 3–5 and 25–27; it is this reconciliation which Dryden placed at the beginning and the end, and the marriage union described at the textual centre merges with the idea of the soul's marriage to the heavenly bridegroom as envisaged in § 27 through the reference to the parable of the 5 wise and the 5 foolish virgins. This parable balances the parable of the talents referred to in § 3, where the emphasis favours Justice more than Mercy. Between them, §§ 3 and 27 balance the two kinds of divine visitation: Judgment Day, when we are called to account, and the day of our death, when Christ meets us as the bridegroom.

Let us take a closer look at the paragraphs on balance (§§ 6–10) and excess or transcendent fullness (§§ 20–24). The balancing, which at first is between hoarding and spending, avarice and profusion, subsequently is taken to a higher level when she is said to have reconciled the active and the contemplative life, hours of prayer and hours of charity; the reconciliation is so perfect that "business" could not disturb her prayers, since she "pray'd by deeds" (9 : 115). In this sense "Her ev'ry day was Sabbath" where "works of Mercy were a part of rest" (10 : 116 & 119). This is a perfect reflection of the life of the blessed in the endless day of eternity: they, too, are employed "In Praise alternate, and alternate Pray'r" (10 : 125), and vary between "Sacred Hymns, and Acts of Love" (10 : 121). The approximation is so close as almost to amount to identity. In her life, therefore, Earth and Heaven commingled to such an extent that, when she died, she was received in Heaven familiarly, "As one returning, not as one arriv'd" (10 : 133). This is the most subtle kind of reconciliation achieved by Eleonora, as already suggested, and one which makes her Christ-like – a Copy near the "Original" (25 : 300).

In §§ 17–24 her fullness constantly compels her to go beyond herself, partly in her creative fertility and partly to seek friends who can receive her bounty (cf. § 9: "Then wonder not to see this Soul extend / The bounds, and seek some other self, a Friend"). It is in her nature to exceed all, as a star "Exceeds the Measures of th'Astronomer" (21 : 265), and the line enacts this by swelling the couplet into a triplet. The strict limit imposed upon her brief lifespan makes it seem like a triumph crowded into a single day (§§ 22–23 : 270–85), which in effect creates a kind of balance or reconciliation of opposites.

As Diagram X.3 shows, the paragraphs leading up to, and away from, the triple centre form a pattern of 4+8 and 8+4 units. Paragraphs 2–5 highlight her God-like provision for the poor ("They stood prepar'd to see the Manna fall"; 2 : 21); she cures and feeds them all. Christ himself might be pleased to stay beneath her roof, or "some benighted Angel" might ease his wings there, "seeing Heav'n appear / In its best work of Mercy" (5 : 56–59). This closeness to Heaven and to Christ is the subject also of §§ 25–28. As a consequence of this closeness, her transition from life to death and renewed life is virtually imperceptible: "She vanish'd, we can scarcely say she dy'd" (26 : 305); "Her Soul was whisper'd out, with God's still Voice" (27 : 318). Having discarded her mortal part, she now is "all Intelligence, all Eye" and may look "up to God, or down to us" (28 : 342). From this position she is called on to shed beams of comfort, "as much as mortal Eyes can bear" (28 : 352), just as in § 2 she is portrayed as shedding manna from above on the poor.

In the course of the poem, the focus shifts repeatedly between Earth and Heaven, and it is now possible to see why: the main thrust of the argument is to portray Eleonora as a female analogue to Christ. She resembles Christ not only in her works of mercy, but perhaps even more in her creative fullness. No sooner has she been said to husband her resources in order to give the more, than the thrift of Heaven is commented on: a single light only was provided to create our day, and "his Reflection too supplies the Night" (6 : 77–78). In this way, the difference between Eleonora and the Creator almost disappears. All the attributes noted in Diagram X.3

Diagram X.3 Dryden, *Eleonora* (1692). The Graded Arrangement

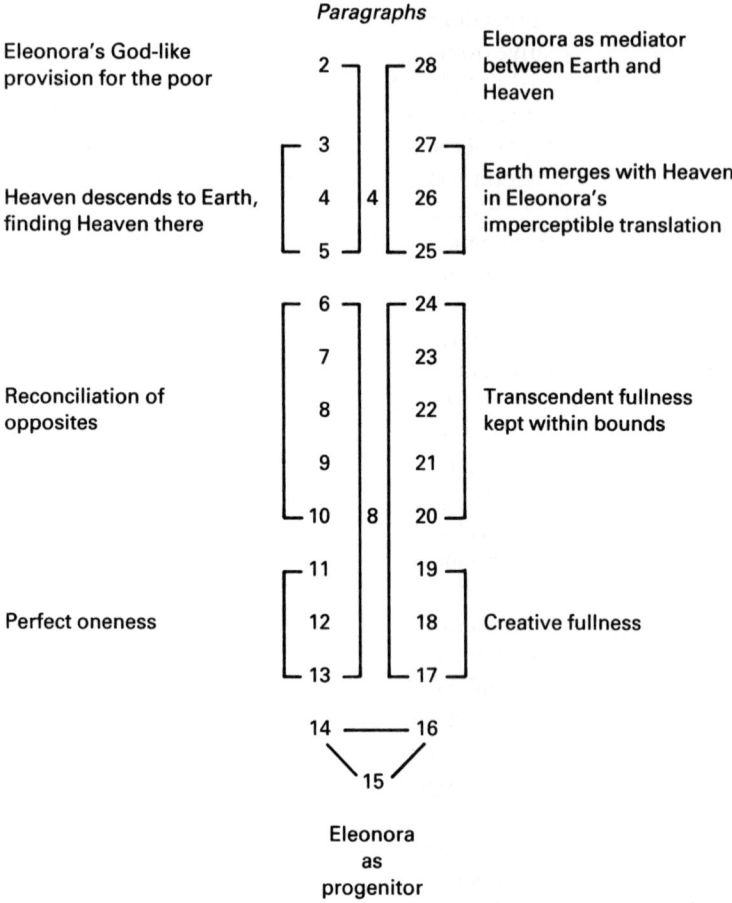

The triple centre-piece on Eleonora as semi-divine progenitor divides the 27 paragraphs of the poem proper into 12 + 12, further sub-divided into 4 + 8 and 8 + 4.

are attributes of Christ as Creator and Redeemer, and the 3 centrally placed paragraphs on her oneness with her husband and her role as progenitor (§§ 14–16) suggest an analogue with the Trinity.

The smoothness of the linear transition from one theme or topos to another is remarkable. The introductory topos of *charity* (§§ 2–5) is retained in §§ 6–10, but combined with the topos of the *golden mean*. This is succeeded by the topos of *oneness* (§§ 11–13), which connects with the preceding topos of *balancing*, through the association with the creative principle according to which everything is "in due proportion mix'd" (13 : 159). The parts are there, but such is their fusion that they are "hidden in the Piece" (12 : 164). In the triple centre the topos of oneness merges with the topos of creative *fullness* (in the progenitors), and this fullness then assumes dominance in §§ 17–19. With § 20 the fullness which has extended Eleonora's bounds becomes wedded to the topos of the transcendence which is *restricted* within narrow bounds (§§ 20–24). By virtue of this transcendent fullness, Eleonora's transition from Earth to Heaven (§§ 25–28) becomes as smooth as the transition from topos to topos within the poem. A comparison with the harmony of the elements obtrudes itself: the topoi function like the qualities which connect the 4 elements in a perfect quaternion or circle; in this way the parts become "hidden in the Piece" which is the poem. When the poem ends, it is the poet who is envisaged as transcending imposed limits: his rage, "Unsafely just", may "break loose on this bad Age" (29 : 368), and impair her portrait: "Take it, while yet 'tis Praise" (29 : 367).

The smoothness of the transitions makes it difficult to divide the poem into linear sequences, but the placing of the topos of poetic inadequacy in §§ 11 and 21 serves to divide it into 3 groups of 10 paragraphs. In this way the perfection represented by the full and complete number 10 is augmented by the 3 of the Trinity as represented in the 3 theological virtues of faith, hope, and charity (cf. 12 : 146–53).

A structural conceit of even greater ingenuity is found in the circumstance that the poem has 3 17-line paragraphs and 17 triplets; this fact could have been dismissed as pure chance, but for its presence in *Britannia Rediviva* (1688), whose 13 triplets are balanced by 3 13-line paragraphs. The symbolism invested in 13 (Christ as head of the 12 Apostles) and 17 (the Law and the gifts of the Holy Ghost) is too familiar to require glossing; commentaries on the Psalms suffice as a source. We have already observed in "The Character of a Good Parson" that Dryden used triplets to achieve certain numerical structures, and this practice is confirmed in *Eleonora* and the *Britannia Rediviva*. Pope's refusal to follow in Dryden's footsteps on this particular point therefore is a rejection of number symbolism. What is surprising is that this rejection came so late, but, when it finally came, it came as one major poet's reaction to another. The end of the seventeenth century therefore saw the end of a tradition with ancient roots.

Dryden's firm commitment to the symbolism of numbers and ratios can be seen from the many further examples that can be adduced from the *Eleonora*. In certain paragraphs, the number of lines or metrical units is significant, one example being § 3 whose 5 couplets and 10 lines state that "Of her Five Talents, other five she made" (3 : 24). Three couplets are used to define the 3 terms of the golden mean (defect, mean, excess) (7 : 83–88), just as 3 metrical units (1 couplet and 2 triplets) and 8 lines define the circle of the 3 theological virtues (12 : 146–53). Eleonora's virtues are one so that "one Heroick comprehends 'em all"; they are "One, as a Constellation is but one", and they are "Ever in Motion":

> 151   now 'tis Faith ascends,
>   Now Hope, now Charity, that upward tends,
> 153 And downwards with diffusive Good, descends.

The 3 virtues agree with the 3 metrical units, and the point that 3 are one is made by each of the triplets, whose 3 lines constitute a single metrical unit. The 8 lines relate to the harmony of the octave, just as the circular movement of the virtues finds its musical expression in the octave, whose last note returns to the first. Paragraph 13 reflects its subject – the "Maker's Art" – in various ways: the "Maker's Art" is proclaimed in line 6 in a paragraph consisting of 6 couplets, and the line consists of 6 feet (13 : 159). It clearly pleased Dryden to work these structural references to the 6 days of creation into his text, and we see why when we read that in Eleonora the parts of wife, mother, and friend were equally mixed:

> 160 No single Virtue we cou'd most commend;
>   Whether the Wife, the Mother, or the Friend;
>   For she was all, in that supreme degree,
> 163 That, as no one prevail'd, so all was she.

These 3 parts that are one recall the numbers 1, 2, and 3 that are one in the number 6, as so often explained in the sources cited in Chapter I. Augustine's comments to this effect in the *De Trinitate* ought to be consulted also because in Book VI he proceeds to explain how the virtues in the mind are so much one that they cannot be separated (VI.iv–vi). Each has its own "several and different meaning", yet cannot be detached from the others. In the same way, the soul in each body is both "whole in the whole, and whole in each several part of it". The Trinitarian implications emerge when Augustine states that each member of the Trinity "are in each, and all in each, and each in all, and all in all, and all are one" (VI.x.11). The conjunction of ideas, then, is the same in Dryden as in Augustine, and in both the numerical argument leads to a reproduction, in the textual structure, of the relevant numbers and ratios.

"To my Honour'd Kinsman, John Driden" (1700) is yet another poem inspired by structural concepts. The point of departure, for example, is Driden's single state, which is highly praised at the expense of matrimony:

21 Minds are so hardly match'd, that ev'n the first,
   Though pair'd by Heaven, in Paradise, were curs'd.
   For Man and Woman, though in one they grow,
24 Yet, first or last, return again to Two.

This argument has nothing to do with man's mortality, as J. Douglas Canfield believes.[6] Dryden's lines make excellent sense when we associate the single state with the God-like state of Unity, and marriage with the diad of division and discord. The allusion is too obvious to be subtle, but it pleases by its wit. The same allusion to these numerical concepts is found in the passage on the "Apothecary-Train". When apothecaries are connected with physicians (as Eve with Adam), ruin results:

105 From Files, a Random-*Recipe* they take,
106 And Many Deaths of One Prescription make.

What can be more lacking in order and decency than this particular proliferation of the One into Many?

The destructive diad, however, may become part of a harmonious whole if pulled into a circle by a unifying centre; this process is represented by the number 3, as Bongo explains.[7] In this number the central unit pulls the two flanking units toward itself, so that they form a circle with a centre, and a circle with a centre is the emblematic representation of the golden mean, as in Quarles's *Hierogliphikes* (1638), Emblem XII. In this emblem picture, the golden mean (a circle with a centre) is opposed to excess (a pig) to each side of the burning candle signifying the life of man. It is arguable that the golden mean is the basic image of Dryden's epistle, and that it finds expression also in the many images of circles. Driden himself is a unifying centre between two; unless he were there to pull them together, excess would be the consequence. The patriot, then, is the unifying nexus, placed between fighting opponents, like Guyon in *The Faerie Queene* II.ii:

> 175   Betwixt the Prince and Parliament we stand;
>   The Barriers of the State on either hand:
>   May neither overflow, for then they drown the Land.
>   When both are full, they feed our bless'd Abode;
> 179   Like those, that water'd once, the Paradise of God.

The 4 rivers that watered Paradise are the type of the 4 gospels (i.e. of their harmony), the 4 elements, and the 4 virtues, and numerical decorum is observed when the passage on the patriot (ll. 171–79) totals 4 metrical units.[8] In short, harmony (= 4) follows when extremes are compelled toward the centre so as to form a circle around it.

The idea of the golden mean meets us already in the opening lines, where Driden is said to enjoy his age as he had his youth; he reconciles contending neighbours (§ 2), his private life with the "Common Good" (§ 8), hoarding health and spending it, the country and the court (§§ 14–15), and the power of Prince and Parliament (§§ 19–21). The golden mean represents above all a state of peace (a unified state), and the resulting plenitude manifests itself in the liberal distribution of gifts, "As Heav'n in Desarts rain'd the Bread of Dew" (7 : 49).

The circle surfaces and becomes explicit in §§ 8–9 (ll. 50–70) on the chase, where it figures as an emblem of the human condition; the hare is the vehicle. The hare "runs the Round",

> 64   And, after all his wand'ring Ways are done,
>   His Circle fills, and ends where he begun,
> 66   Just as the Setting meets the Rising Sun.

The image functions both *in malo* and *in bono*; certainly it may signify the "dreary circularity of history" in which one prince falls as another rises (James II and William),[9] but we cannot rule out its positive significance as a symbol of resurrection to eternal life; the setting sun after all *meets* the "Rising Sun". This is stated in the eighth and last metrical unit of § 8, and the number 8 refers both to the octave as an image of circular return, and to the resurrection to eternal life on the eighth day. This richness of meaning explains why the circling hare may be used as an emblem of human life. Dryden strikes a neat balance between positive and negative versions of the circle in this particular instance, and we encounter further positive and negative versions in the course of the poem, beginning with the circle of love in the opening paragraph ("All who deserve his Love, he makes his own, / And, to be lov'd himself, needs only to be known"). The same kind of circle of love is expressed in the wish, in § 7; "And ever be you bless'd, who live to bless" (l. 45). Negative circles are found when man and woman, briefly joined in one in marriage, "return again to Two" (l. 24), when the fox returns to where he "did the murd'rous Deed" (l. 57), and when princes "chasing, sigh to think themselves are chas'd" (l. 70).

Since the epistle has so much to say about unity and balance, we would expect the presence of unifying, balanced structures in the various divisions of the text. As soon as we consider the structure in terms of paragraphs and metrical units, the pattern becomes plain enough; 99 metrical units (88 couplets and 11 triplets) are divided into 33+66 units, and 9+13 verse paragraphs. The line of division falls where the praise of Driden's happy rural existence ends and the denunciation begins of an age marked by excess: "So liv'd our Sires, e'er Doctors learn'd to kill" (10:71). The fact that these first 33 metrical units on Driden's life consist of 70 lines may be a reference to the "threescore Years and ten" (11:91) to which our lifespan has dwindled, but the most important numerical allusion is of course to the 33 years of Christ's lifespan, which invests the classical idea of the *beatus vir* with a Christian dimension. True, the dimension is there in the reference to the "Bread of Dew" distributed by Driden to his "own *Israel*-Host" (7:49), but the number 33, like the ratio 1:2, sets up an unambiguous comparison with the Creator and Redeemer, as in the case of the Good Parson.

As Diagram X.4 shows, the first third has its own balanced pattern, which begins and concludes with an image of the circle and with statements concerning happiness: "How Bless'd is He" (1:1) balances "But happier he ..." (9:67). The positive circle of love (giving, receiving, returning) in lines 5–6 finds its negative analogue in the princes who, "chasing, sigh to think themselves are chas'd" (9:70). An allusion to the rise and fall of princes and the wheel of fortune may be present here, but the more obvious reference is surely to the *beatus ille* tradition identified in the opening phrase on the blessed life. A gloss may be fetched from Abraham Cowley's

Diagram X.4   Dryden, "To my Honour'd Kinsman", Metrical Units 1–33 (§§ 1–9)

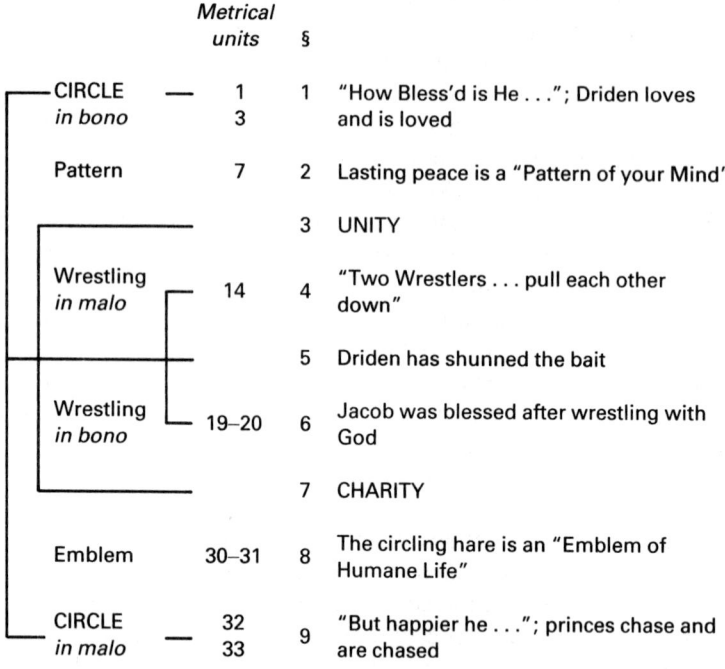

Driden's unity and his charity are divine attributes by virtue of which he composes strife and promotes concord and feeds his own "Israel-Host". His rejection of the married state similarly makes him god-like in his self-sufficiency. Like Jacob, who wrestled with the angel of the Lord throughout the night and in the end compelled God to bless him, Driden has the power to stand.

Essays and Discourses (1668) – this compendium of *beatus ille* arguments and sentiments – where the great man is never at rest and liberty is lost to him: importunate suitors crowd his antechamber and invade his privacy. The great man's misery contrasts strongly with the sweet state of peaceful liberty enjoyed by Driden and even by his "Grandsire" when in prison.

The comparison of Adam and Eve to two wrestlers who "pull each other down" (4 : 30) should be linked with the reference to Jacob in § 6. Heaven "to the Second Son a Blessing brought", and Jacob obtained this blessing from God after having wrestled for a whole night with an angel of the Lord. The function of the comparison with two wrestlers, therefore, is to set up the desired linkage between §§ 4 and 6. The point of the story of Jacob's wrestling is his strength, his ability to stand where others fall.

The three paragraphs which contain the next 22 metrical units (see Diagram X.5) point the antithesis between excess and health. The excess which leads to increased mortality is the subject of §§ 10 and 12. The impious quest for forbidden knowledge is denounced; if man could achieve immortality, "The Doom of Death, pronounc'd by God, were vain" (l. 78). After the advice, in § 11, "to hunt in Fields, for health unbought", we return to the subject of excess and disorder when the "Apothecary-Train" are said to make "Many Deaths of One Prescription" (l. 106).

The last 44 metrical units (see Diagram X.5) are devoted to the subject of balance, reconciliation, and peace in the state, to whose affairs Driden must sacrifice his loved retreat. The role of the patriot, placed as he is between the country and the court, the king and the people, the prince and Parliament, is to mediate between these extremes and compel them to form a harmonious circle around the centre.

The idea of balance, then, balances this last segment as it does the poem as a whole. The great circle of love alluded to in lines 5–6 finds its finest expression in the concluding lines on the soul's return to Heaven, "from whence it came" (l. 208). The picture of Driden's soul is a second topos which connects the beginning and the end. When we begin to read, the lasting peace established by Driden between contending neighbours is said to be a pattern of his mind (ll. 14–16), while in the final paragraph it is the poem which serves as a picture of his soul (ll. 198–99).

The overall symmetrical structure based on the 22 verse paragraphs is shown in Diagram X.6. The existence of symmetrical patterns has long been recognized; thus J. Arnold Levine wrote in 1964 that "Each of John Driden's activities in the first part of the poem has its equivalent in the policies advocated in the second half; the metaphor of the individual as a kind of state could not be more thoroughly exploited".[10] Eleven years later, J. Douglas Canfield listed some of these parallels, but there is no rational order in his list. Paragraphs 10–12 are taken to constitute a centre around which parallels are ranged in no particular sequence.[11] Thus Driden's freedom from cares in the country (2 : 7–16) is opposed to his assumption of them in the city (13 : 117–26), and this antithesis is true enough, of course, but Driden's public activities are the subject of other paragraphs as well, so that the topos has not been defined

Diagram X.5 Dryden, "To my Honour'd Kinsman". Parts 2 and 3 (22 + 44 units)

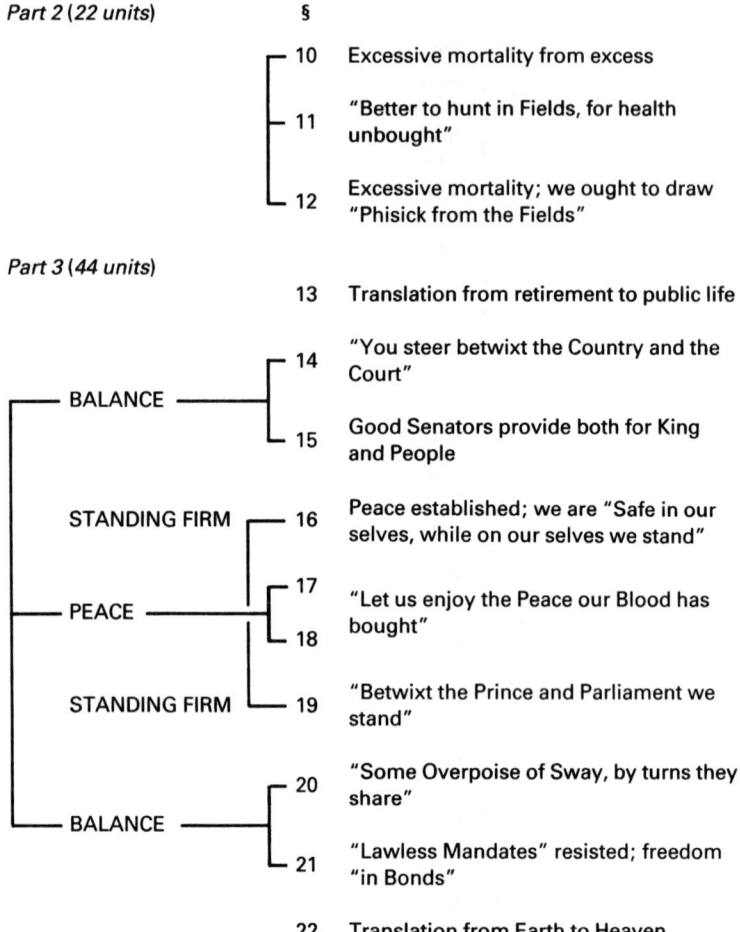

Formula for the overall structure:

$$33 - \underbrace{22 - 44}_{66}$$

The ratio 1:2 occurs twice.

DRYDEN AND THE ART OF PRAISE 553

Diagram X.6 Dryden, "To my Honour'd Kinsman". The Symmetrical Structure

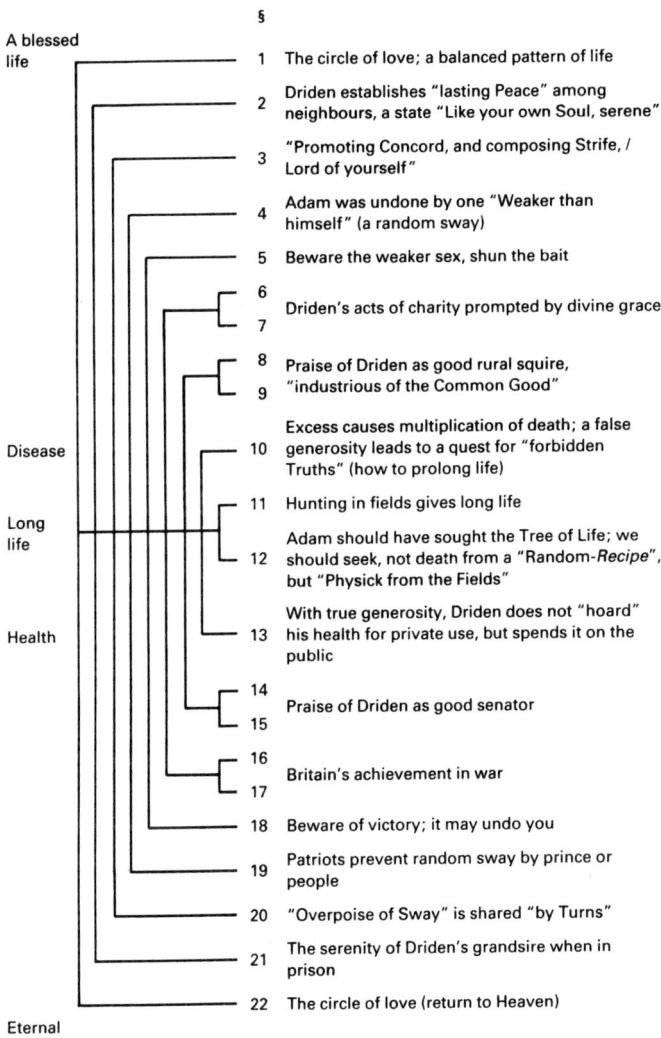

with sufficient precision. As stated above, Driden's private life is featured in the first 9 paragraphs, and his public activities in the last 9. For more specific symmetries we must look for more specific topoi.

The 4 central paragraphs (10 : 71–13 : 126) focus on health and disease, long life and the multiplication of death. The positive message emerges from §§ 11 and 12: long life is found in rural environments; it is "Better to hunt in Fields, for Health unbought" (11 : 92) and to seek "Phisick from the Fields" (12 : 116). The subtext for the phrase "Health unbought" is Horace's *dapes inemptas* in the second epode, rendered by Dryden as "unbought dainties". Man's excessive mortality is the consequence of a life marked by excess. The link between §§ 10 and 13 is found in the idea of generosity taken *in malo* and *in bono*: the mistaken efforts of the "gen'rous Kind" to prolong life by seeking "forbidden Truths" (§ 10) are contrasted with the true generosity of Driden, who spends his "rich Produce" of health on the public instead of hoarding it for his own private use. This health, which is his fortune, is a mental and spiritual state as well. Driden is "industrious of the Common Good" (8 : 53) both as rural dweller (§§ 8–9) and as good senator (§§ 14–15), and his acts of charity in the private sphere (§§ 6–7) form an analogue to Britain's wartime exploits (§§ 16–17). In §§ 2–5 and 18–21 the basic concept is the serenity of mind shown by Driden (§ 2) as by his grandsire in prison (§ 21). It is this serenity which resolves discord into concord (3 : 17), and preserves the single state to preserve unity (§§ 3–5), so that he may become a centre of power like Jacob, similarly graced by Heaven (§ 6). In the public sphere, Albion is presented as such a centre of power (§ 17). In the state, it is possible to balance even an "Overpoise of Sway" by letting it occur "by Turns": the king has more power in times of war, Parliament in times of peace (§ 20). As in § 3, apparent discord is resolved into concord, and Albion, like Driden, is lord of himself. This idea of reconciliation or balance in the course of time incidentally points forward to Pope's main argument in the *Epistle to Bathurst*. As already mentioned, it is the patriot's achievement to compel Prince and Parliament toward the centre; neither is permitted to overflow, or to exercise random sway (§ 19), and this idea takes us back to § 4, where Eve's random straying "from the Fount" (3 : 26) causes Adam to fall: "How cou'd He stand, when put to double Pain" (4 : 27). The "double pain" reflects the unlucky number of division.

To summarize: At the heart of this homage to John Driden is the concept of the unifying centre; this centre not only stands "betwixt", but exercises such a powerful pull that extremes are drawn towards it and reconciled. As in *The Faerie Queene II*, the golden mean is an active, not a passive condition. God may be the source of all harmony, but God works through men like John Driden. This is why the image of the circle is so important; the circle which is an image of God is an emblem of human life as well. Hence the poem connects the beginning and the end in a large circle which encloses the three lesser circles of its major divisions.

Dryden probably chose to divide his poem into 22 paragraphs in order to permit these 22 units to reflect the symbolism invested in the Hebrew alphabet as used in Psalm 119 (Vulg. 118) – circularity and the sum of wisdom. Other possible examples of simple number symbolism are not hard to find. The 33 lines created by the 11 triplets repeat the number found in the division into 33+66 metrical units, and the only 11-line paragraph (21 : 184–94) describes the transgression of the law ("Lawless Mandates") resisted by Driden's grandsire. A paragraph of 11 lines can be created only by means of a triplet, and on this occasion the triplet has no other function. The serenity which is a pattern of Driden's mind is celebrated in 4 metrical units (2 : 7–16), and 4 is of course the number of concord. In § 19 on balance in the state, 4 metrical units are found again. Finally, the 15 lines of the last verse paragraph express the ascent to God envisaged in the concluding triplet. (Again a triplet is called for to obtain the desired number.) However, the most important statement made in structural terms is the twice-repeated division into the ratio 1 : 2; everything the poem says about concord and unity and the closing of the circle is expressed through this ratio. Tasso had already used this structural formula in Book XVIII of the *Jerusalem Delivered*, whose 99 stanzas are divided into 33+66, and the 66 in their turn into 22+44.[12] Dryden therefore comes at the end of a tradition which he was the last to exploit to the full. We shall certainly underestimate his technical achievement – and we may also fail to interpret his thematic concerns correctly – unless we adopt spatial readings of the kind illustrated here. The complexity of Dryden's patterns is a challenge we must be prepared to meet, but the reward is great, since the contents of these poems cannot be properly understood without familiarity with the structural concepts that condition their form.

The contents and the textual structure of Pope's third moral essay, the *Epistle to Bathurst*, invite comparison with Dryden's panegyrics. Pope's concern, like Dryden's, is with the golden mean, and he balances the textual structure just as carefully as Dryden, but

Diagram X.7 Pope, *Moral Essays* iii. To Allen Lord Bathurst. Of the Use of Riches

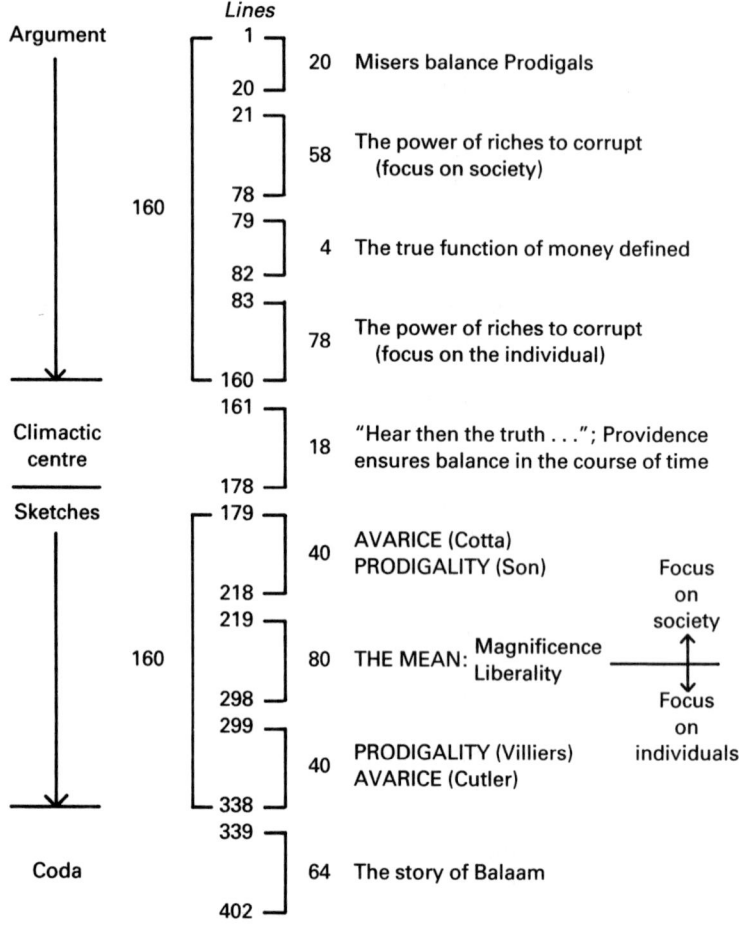

Balaam proceeds from avarice to prodigality, from being a private to being a public figure, thus summarizing the whole argument.

he pays no attention to number symbolism. As Diagram X.7 shows, the poem as a whole is balanced around the positive message in lines 161–78 as a climactic centre which rises to sublimity in the lines on the Creator:

> 166 That POW'R who bids the Ocean ebb and flow,
> Bids seed-time, harvest, equal course maintain,
> Thro' reconcil'd extremes of drought and rain,
> Builds Life on Death, on Change Duration founds,
> 170 And gives th' eternal wheels to know their rounds.[13]

The quaternions, so it seems, still run their perpetual circle, and extremes are still harmonized. In the 160 lines leading up to this centre, the subject is the abuse to which riches lend themselves, and the corruption exercised to acquire wealth, but a positive doctrine is expressed in lines 79–82, in two couplets located at the halfway point. The 160 lines which follow the climactic centre consist of an unbroken sequence of character sketches so carefully balanced that even the line totals support the pattern: the extended passage on Magnificence (Bathurst) and Liberality (the Man of Ross), which totals 80 lines, is the point of balance between the preceding 40 lines on Cotta and his son, and the 40 which follow on the Duke of Buckingham and Cutler. The concluding dramatic character sketch of Balaam (so reminiscent of the last part of Dryden's lines on the Good Parson) functions as a coda which summarizes the sketches that precede. The balance between the 4 negative sketches (an infernal quaternion?) is admirable. The avarice of Cotta and the prodigality of his son balance the prodigality of Villiers and the avarice of Cutler in a chiastic pattern. Then, too, the figures seen in relation to society (Cotta, his son, and Bathurst) balance characters seen in relation to themselves and their end (the Man of Ross, Villiers, and Cutler). Compared with Bathurst, the Man of Ross lives in a restricted sphere, but this is the whole point: he is a man of modest means, yet his liberality is such that it transforms his environment. It is therefore absurd to argue that the modest character of his achievement and the obscurity of his life reveal a sceptical attitude on the part of Pope to the power of virtue. The carefully balanced textual pattern gives the lie to such a theory, and so does Aristotle, who defines the golden mean as it applies both to a person of modest means and to a person of great wealth. The epistle as a whole seems to have been written in the mood described by Dryden in the penultimate paragraph of *Eleonora*: the praise of virtue has been written "in a Clime / Where Vice triumphs, and Vertue is a Crime" (ll. 363–64). Pope, though, seeks comfort in the reflection that, as generation succeeds generation, Providence ensures the desired balance, as manifested in the balanced structure of the epistle itself. But for the structural enactment of this view, it would have been difficult to take Pope seriously.

It is an interesting reflection that the impression of infinite variety created by the epistle as a whole actually depends upon a relatively simple pattern, based, like the world, on 4 elements: hoarding and spending in a private or a public sphere of life. This skeletal structure not only sustains a splendid body, but is largely responsible for its splendour. If Pope could lean on Dryden, he did so with confidence in his own strength, and it is part of this strength that he rejected the dimension afforded by number symbolism; in this respect Dryden took the "Providence of Wit" too far. Pope was content to exploit the circle of the quaternion, and so was Samuel Johnson in *Rasselas* (1759). Johnson based the solution of the quest for happiness on the quaternion of the elements and their qualities, two of which are active and two passive. Our mental attitude to life may in the same way be active or passive, just as we may prefer a private or a public mode of life. The conclusion in which nothing is concluded presents all these possibilities in the 4 choices made:

PEKUAH	NEKAYAH	RASSELAS	IMLAC
passive & apart	apart & active	active & immersed	immersed & passive

Pekuah chooses complete withdrawal, mental as well as physical; Nekayah lives in retirement, but is mentally active (she wants to "learn all sciences" and to "divide her time between the acquisition and communication of wisdom"); Rasselas boldly commits himself to an active life in a public sphere; while Imlac and the astronomer are content to immerse themselves in the stream of life without trying to direct the course. Although the similarity to Pope's epistle and to Dryden's poems of praise is apparent, it is equally clear that Samuel Johnson trots out these 4 choices in a spirit of wry amusement. On this particular point he knew better than to trust to human thinking. However, the fact that he made use of the traditional scheme of the quaternions proves that he could rely on its being recognized; otherwise the effect would be lost. Can his ultimate message be that, whatever choice we make, we are always part of the larger pattern provided by God? If so, we are back again where we started – with Augustine.

Notes to Chapter X

1. See Alastair Fowler and Douglas Brooks, "The Structure of Dryden's *A Song for St Cecilia's Day, 1687*", in *Silent Poetry*, ed. Alastair Fowler (London, 1970), pp. 185–200.
2. I have used the text of the California edition as supplemented by James Kinsley, ed., *The Poems and Fables of John Dryden* (Oxford, 1970).
3. H. Neville Davies, "Laid Artfully together: Stanzaic Design in Milton's 'On the Morning of Christ's Nativity'", in *Fair Forms*, ed. M.-S. Røstvig (Cambridge, 1975), pp. 101 and 103.
4. Ibid., p. 104.
5. Ibid., p. 92.
6. J. Douglas Canfield, "The Image of the Circle in Dryden's 'To My Honour'd Kinsman'," in *Papers on Language and Literature* 11 (1975), pp. 169 f. Canfield argues that the theme of death pervades each of the poem's three sections.
7. See my analysis of *The Faerie Queene* II.ii (the Castle of Medina) in Chapter VI.
8. It has been observed that the reference to the 4 rivers of Paradise entails a reference to the 4 cardinal virtues: see J. Arnold Levine, "John Dryden's Epistle to John Driden," *Journal of English and Germanic Philology* 63 (1964), 467 f.
9. Ibid., p. 471. See also p. 460: "William may play the hunter in the field, in politics, and in war, but he himself is being pursued by Death".
10. Ibid., pp. 457 f.
11. Canfield, "The Image of the Circle", pp. 175 f. David Vieth, "Concept as Metaphor", *Language and Style* 3 (1970), p. 201, sees the structure as concentric.
12. See my Chapter V on Tasso.
13. I have used the text of the Twickenham edition, Vol. III.ii, ed. F. W. Bateson (London, 1951).

Postscript

It is a finding of major importance that a symmetrical structure may coexist with a division in the ratio 2 : 1. One can easily understand the challenge posed by such a double structure: the graded arrangement not only adds a pleasing complexity, but permits two interacting centres. It must have been a distinct advantage for an epic poet to be able to locate a decisive turning-point in the epic action two thirds of the way through the text. This happens in Book I of *The Faerie Queene*, where the release of Redcrosse knight at the end of canto viii heralds the new upward movement which begins with the meeting between Redcrosse and Arthur at the beginning of canto ix, and with their exchange of symbolically significant gifts prior to their separation. If Spenser had been content with the symmetrical structure, the positive movement would have had to be initiated at the mathematical centre; instead, he could place Redcrosse's fall at the beginning of canto vii, reserving the positive *peripeteia* for the beginning of canto ix. Because critical attention has been focussed only on symmetrical structures, it has been assumed that the turning-point in *Jerusalem Delivered* occurs in Book XI.[1] As I have shown, however, Tasso has placed the decisive moment at the end of Book XIII and the beginning of Book XIV, that is, in the books which divide the epic in the sequence 12—2—6 books. The terrible drought described in Book XIII terminates with an act of divine grace prompted by Godfrey's prayer for mercy; the Father's speech on this occasion leaves no room for doubt:

> Mine armies dear till now have suffer'd woe,
>   Distress and danger, hell's infernal pow'r
> Their enemy hath been, the world their foe;
>   But happy be their actions from this hour,
> What they begin to blessed end shall go;
>   I will refresh them with a gentle show'r;
> Rinaldo shall return; th'Egyptian crew
> They shall encounter; conquer, and subdue. –
>
>   (XIII.73)

The subsequent description of the benign fall of rain recalls *Isaiah* 45 : 8, "Send victory like a dew, you heavens, and let the clouds rain it down. Let the earth open for salvation to spring up" (Jerusalem Bible).[2] The danger of an uncritical counting of stanzas is further illustrated when a critic locates the centre in Giles Fletcher's *Christs Victorie, and Triumph* (1610) in a passage on "laughing Bacchus" (II.51), the supporting argument being that references to Bacchus and Ceres should be taken to symbolize the sacraments.[3] The context, though, forbids such an interpretation: it is impossible to associate Bacchus and his "spewing rout" with Christ.

A quest for textual structures can never be a simple matter of counting; the approach must be from within the text itself. Even in individual cantos a centre may often be found only after introductory or framing stanzas have been identified, just as a division in the ratio 2 : 1 or 1 : 2 is a distinct possibility at this level too. Both Tasso and Spenser rely on canto segments to establish balanced canto patterns, whether symmetrical or graded or both, and it is surely this compositional practice which explains the presence of extended centres in some epics. I believe it is wrong to look for a centre in a single line or stanza, whether in Tasso, Spenser, or Milton; the centre is instead a well-defined episode possessed of its own textual structure. This realization makes the idea of textual structuring less mathematical and hence less mechanical. The circumstance that mathematical precision is achieved in some cases (as in Tasso and Spenser) does not mean that it is to be expected in all. Book II of *The Faerie Queene* illustrates the point, since its overall structures do not depend on a counting of stanzas.

The best guide to textual structures is the observation of the recurrence of significant events, descriptions, topoi, or key words and concepts. When traditional topoi such as the marshalling of troops and elevations and debasements keep recurring within the body of a text, the resulting topomorphs provide reliable indications of the author's structural intent. The repetition of identical sets of rhyme words in inverse sequence is a particularly valuable indication. It is a distinct advantage that a poem is of some length, since length permits a sufficient number of the repetitions-with-a-difference (or antitheses-with-a-similarity) on which linkage between parts depends. Even Milton employs traditional topoi to indicate his structures in the first edition of *Paradise Lost*, although his treatment sometimes is such that the topos may be difficult to recognize. It is sufficiently obvious that troops are marshalled in book 1 and at the end of book 5 and the beginning of book 6, but it has not been realized that the series of visions given to Adam in the first half of book 10 (= XI) constitutes a marshalling of the deadly sins as in the roll-call of Satan's leaders in book 1. Yet on this perception depends our understanding of Milton's handling of his narrative: his choice of visions and the fact that they take up so much of the text are explained by the need to provide an earthly analogue to the roll-call. The thematic and structural patterns coincide since it is at the points of structural emphasis that the main themes are made explicit.

Augustine's *Confessions* is an interesting case since its unity depends so entirely on our perception of the conceptual grid which encompasses the 13 books. The autobiography is unified by the linear movement from birth to spiritual re-birth, but books 10–13 have seemed to have little connection with the story of Augustine's life. However, a writer so intent on defining beauty as a joining of parts into a single whole cannot have omitted to give this superior kind of beauty to his own writing. It is impossible to believe that the whole thematic thrust of the *Confessions* should have been denied the structural expression which it calls for. The analysis presented in Chapter II shows that Augustine did indeed apply his aesthetic principles to the composition of his spiritual epic, and that the particular events in Augustine's life should be related to the general concepts featured in the last four books. Augustine's writing – like that of Tasso and Spenser later on – has a conceptual orientation unfamiliar to readers accustomed to looking for psychological rather than logical analysis.

A topomorphical approach entails recognizing the structural connotations of many of the ideas current in the Middle Ages and the Renaissance, and the most important of these are connected with creation and redemption. Dryden's *Eleonora* is a splendid late example of a perfect fusion between theme and form; the fusion is so perfect that it is impossible to distinguish between them. In this particular instance the structural formula seems to have prompted the nature of Dryden's praise, rather than the other way round: it is likely that the textual structure came first in the process of invention, so that the poem itself is a verbalisation of the ideas embedded in the form. This is surely why Dryden at first thought of calling his poem "The Pattern".

In the allegorical poetry of Tasso and Spenser, the conceptual grid enables us to read the allegory without losing contact with the specifics of the narrative. When we observe how the actions of Redcrosse knight in canto i of Book I of *The Faerie Queene* embody, first rashness, then proper action, and finally sloth, the narrative loses little or nothing of its direct appeal: we keep seeing Redcrosse as he engages with the dragon Error, then as he finds his way out of the labyrinth of the forest, and finally as he is beset by deceitful temptations in Archimago's hermitage. His actions retain their validity at the same time that they present the familiar Aristotelian paradigm of extremes enclosing a golden mean. His actions provide delight and insight at the same time, and the insight in its turn enhances the delight. The circumstance that concepts are just as important in Augustine's *Confessions*, Quarles's *Emblemes*, and Dryden's *Eleonora* as in Tasso's and Spenser's romance epics reduces the distance between allegory and other modes. It is a case not so much of allegory invading other poetic precincts, as of the importance of concepts in the thought of all these poets. What my many diagrams have shown is the conceptual structure perceived on ascending from the literal level to what is signified. This hermeneutical ascent resembles the scrutiny of our own thoughts and actions with a view to ascertaining their true character.

Today it goes against the grain to consider as most real that which is most abstract: a system of signs based on concepts and the patterns they form in a text. This built-in reluctance helps to account for the strong resistance to a topomorphical or numerological approach to Renaissance poetry, especially among Milton scholars, to whom psychology seems so much more real than logic. In the Renaissance, however, as in earlier times, symmetries and proportions functioned as powerful signs pointing to a transcendent reality with far greater efficacy than the words themselves. To Traherne as to Augustine, order was the beauty even of beauty itself, and in *Paradise Lost* the angelic dance becomes a metaphor for Milton's own method of composing: the "Mystical dance" forms "mazes intricate, / Eccentric, intervolv'd, yet regular / Then most, when most irregular they seem". Their *motions* create a "harmonie Divine" to which "Gods own ear / Listens delighted" (5.620–27). The text "moves" in the same way, creating similar "music", and in so doing it mirrors God's works in space and time. Augustine's and Bonaventura's advocacy of an *ars aeterna* had many followers, as the examples collected in this study amply testify.

My examples will have shown that textual structures are capable of many variations, and that they may occur in short and long poems alike. In fact, the same structural principles can be seen at work in a single stanza or verse paragraph and in an epic as a whole. When linkage through repetition occurs across what seems a large textual expanse, this circumstance reminds us of the way in which a spatial or synoptic reading obliterates the distance. A topomorphical approach must necessarily influence our very reading technique, teaching us to supplement the linear reading with a reading intent on tracing the relationship between parts. The Augustinian emphasis on such relationships imposes a reading technique adjusted to this perspective.

To consider the subject of number symbolism is in many ways to grasp a nettle rather than to pick a rose, although the possibility of a rose is certainly there. Number symbolism has been traced in most of the poems considered in this study, but it is not necessarily present wherever we find symmetry. This is shown in a poem like George Herbert's "Deniall", where the symmetrical placing of words and phrases does all the work, and similar examples are found in the panegyrics that Samuel Daniel published in 1603, as I show elsewhere.[4] On the other hand, the structure of some poems (or parts of poems) may be entirely a matter of numerical decorum. In these cases the connection between subject and numerical form must be sanctioned by traditional biblical exegesis; otherwise it would be hard to credit. Another point to observe is that the symbolism attributed to a structural number must be sufficiently specific; it will not do to write at large about numbers that are "holy" or "perfect". There is no easy substitute for a first-hand knowledge of Renaissance ways of thinking about numbers; such knowledge can be acquired only by contact with primary sources. Another temptation which must be resisted is to count any kind of unit without regard to the whole; the framework must be the poem as a whole, and the issue must be the connection between the subject of a poem and its overall textual structure. Thus the attempt to relate the subject of a specific stanza in Milton's *Nativity Ode* to the symbolism invested in its ordinal number seems to me mistaken.[5] In George Herbert's "Sunday", it is the presence of verbal links between stanzas 7 and 8 which invites us to see the transition from the one stanza to the other as a transition from Time (= 7) to Eternity (= 8). A similar transition may be seen when Milton's *Nativity Ode* proceeds from 7-line stanzas (in the introduction) to 8-line stanzas (in the hymn). The biblical warrant for such a symbolism is very strong, since Cassiodorus based his comments on the 150 Psalms and the 15 Psalms of Ascent on this transition from 7 to 8. It is therefore a truly basic numerical sign.

Number symbolism is of course at the root of all symmetrical and graded arrangements, since their function is to impose unity on multiplicity, as in the Platonic *lambda* formula, but it calls for tact and experience to perceive whether a poet has gone on from there to base his structures on symbolic numbers. Some poets do, and others do not, or only to a modest extent. The poets who come last in my survey – Milton and Dryden – illustrate the two possibilities. Whereas Milton is more intent on topomorphs than on symbolic numbers (though the latter are by no means absent), Dryden places such numbers in the immediate foreground, exploiting their semantic potential to the full. Spenser pays equal attention to both, and in so doing remains unequalled.

Notes to Postscript

1. "The *Liberata* can be divided into two movements, one initiated by God as he calls on Goffredo ... in canto 1, the other initiated by Goffredo as he personally engages in the first assault on the city in canto 11, the poem's midpoint. Goffredo's action is in many respects an echo of ... the intercession of Christ on man's behalf". Andrew Fichter, *Poets Historical. Dynastic Epic in the Renaissance* (New Haven and London, 1982), p. 139.
2. Cf. the text of the Vulgate: "Rorate caeli, desuper, Et nubes pluant iustum; Aperiatur terra, et germinet Salvatorem". In the Roman Catholic Church this is a key text in the season of Advent.
3. James Bobrick, "The Numerological Structure of Giles Fletcher's *Christs Victorie, and Triumph*", *Tennessee Studies in Literature and Language* 21 (1979), 522–52.
4. M.-S. Røstvig, "A Frame of Words: On the Craftsmanship of Samuel Daniel," *English Studies* 60 (1979), 122–37.
5. See C. W. R. D. Moseley, *Milton. The English Poems of 1645*, Penguin Critical Studies (London, 1992), p. 113. Moseley relates the contents of stanzas 16, 10 and 9 to the symbolism invested in their ordinal numbers.

Appendix

John Keats, *The Eve of St Agnes* (1820)

It may be foolish to look for evidence of pre-planned textual structures in Keats's *The Eve of St. Agnes*, Spenserian though this poem is, since the text as we have it may not be what Keats himself wanted. His publishers and their legal and literary adviser, Richard Woodhouse, imposed minor and major changes much against Keats's own will.[1] Thus two of Keats's manuscript revisions were rejected; he revised stanza 36 to make the erotic character of the lovers' union plain. At the same time he wanted to insert a new stanza between stanzas 6 and 7, the reason being that he wished "to make the *legend* more intelligible, and correspondent with what afterwards takes place".[2] Again, what Keats wished to make "intelligible" was the erotic import, but he was not permitted so to do. The proposed new stanza 7 and the revised stanza 36 (seventh from the end) were rejected out of hand; the former was suppressed and the latter returned to the earlier, more discreet version. If we accept Keats's own judgment, then, and restore the text accordingly, we observe that stanzas 7 and 36 – so exactly balanced within the body of the text – indeed are what Keats called "correspondent". (In what we may call Keats's own version, the poem totals 43 rather than 42 stanzas, and "our" stanza 36 is his stanza 37). The last stanza provides further evidence of Keats's awareness of Spenser's structural felicities and his desire to adopt some of them. Keats revised it so that the three pregnant rhyme words of stanza 1 – *cold / told / old* – are repeated in inverse order, thus closing the narrative circle. Some of Keats's revisions, therefore, show how he tried to create the balanced patterns that are such a conspicuous feature of Spenser's art. The repetition of three identical rhyme words, in inverted sequence, is particularly valuable evidence of intent because so incontrovertible.

If we read Keats's poem as we would a Spenserian canto, we observe that the action has two phases: stanzas 1–14(15) set the

Diagram A.1 Keats, *The Eve of St. Agnes*. The Division into 14 + 28 Stanzas

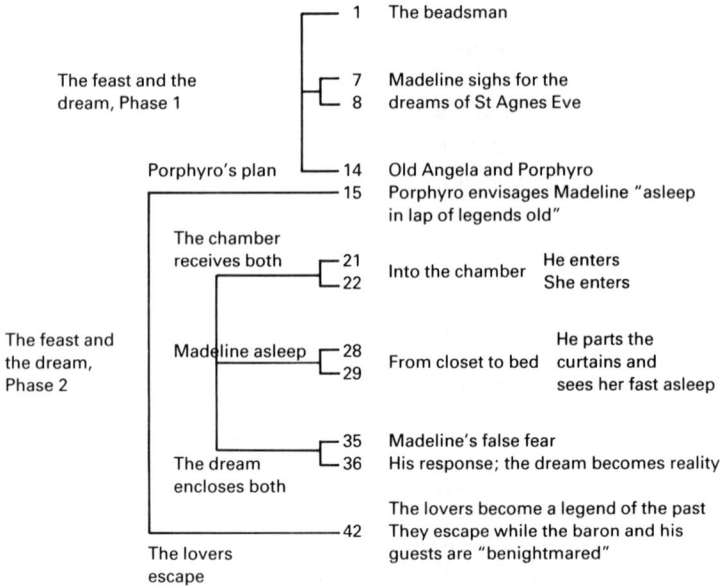

stage, and the action proper fills the remaining 28 stanzas (see Diagram A1). The first phase is framed by descriptions of coldness and death. In the opening stanza, the coldness is a physical fact, but in stanzas 2–4 it becomes the coldness of the old beadsman and "the sculptur'd dead" who "seem to freeze, / Emprison'd in black, purgatorial rails". Similarly in stanzas 11–13 (Keats 12–14), Porphyro is taken by old Angela into a cobwebbed room, "Pale, lattic'd, chill, and silent as a tomb". However, on this occasion the coldness encloses passionate warmth, just as the structure of this opening sequence encloses passionate love (see Diagram A2). The entry of the revellers in stanza 5 corresponds to Porphyro's entry in stanza 10(11): the spurious life of the former, though, contrasts with the true life of the latter. In between are five stanzas on Madeline and the legend of St Agnes Eve, and at the centre are three stanzas on the visions of delight promised to all virgins who obey the strict rules laid down. The suppressed stanza leaves no doubt about the nature of these delights:

'Twas said her future lord would there appear
Offering as sacrifice – all in the dream –
Delicious food even to her lips brought near:
Viands and wine and fruit and sugar'd cream,
To touch her palate with the fine extreme
Of relish: then soft music heard; and then
More pleasures followed in a dizzy stream
Palpable almost: then to wake again
Warm in the virgin morn, no weeping Magdalen.[3]

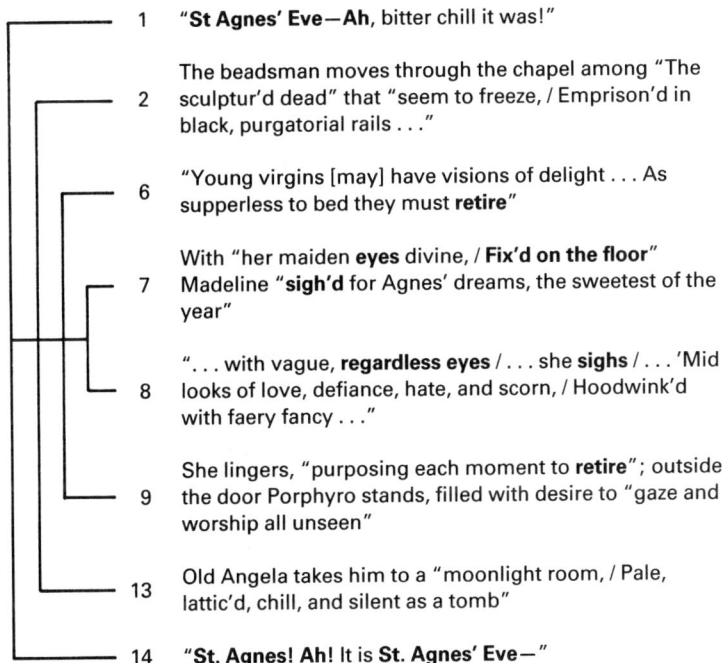

Diagram A.2 Keats, *The Eve of St. Agnes*. Stanzas 1–14

1 "St Agnes' Eve—**Ah**, bitter chill it was!"

2 The beadsman moves through the chapel among "The sculptur'd dead" that "seem to freeze, / Emprison'd in black, purgatorial rails . . ."

6 "Young virgins [may] have visions of delight . . . As supperless to bed they must **retire**"

7 With "her maiden **eyes** divine, / **Fix'd on the floor**" Madeline "**sigh'd**" for Agnes' dreams, the sweetest of the year"

8 ". . . with vague, **regardless eyes** / . . . she **sighs** / . . . 'Mid looks of love, defiance, hate, and scorn, / Hoodwink'd with faery fancy . . ."

9 She lingers, "purposing each moment to **retire**"; outside the door Porphyro stands, filled with desire to "gaze and worship all unseen"

13 Old Angela takes him to a "moonlight room, / Pale, lattic'd, chill, and silent as a tomb"

14 "St. Agnes! Ah! It is St. Agnes' Eve—"

The symmetry is created in part by events and in part by the repetition of the same or similar words. Madeline's *eyes* and her *sighs* are at the centre, while "visions of delight" are desired in stanzas 6 and 9. The substructure is framed by descriptions of the coldness of winter and of death; the "bitter chill" contrasts strongly with the warmth of the desire that fills the young lovers.

When the suppressed stanza is added between stanzas 6 and 7, the centre consists of three rather than two stanzas.

In the two stanzas that follow, "Thoughtful Madeline" sees nothing, but sighs for "Agnes' dreams, the sweetest of the year", and she is oblivious to all, except "the bliss before to-morrow morn". But for the suppressed stanza, the erotic character of this bliss would have been underestimated.

The suppressed stanza on the "Viands and wine and fruit", the "soft music", and further pleasures in "a dizzy stream" provides the subject of the second phase when the dream comes true. The second phase begins after Angela's thrice-repeated apostrophe to St Agnes Eve (14 or 15), when Porphyro conceives his "stratagem" on learning "His lady's purpose" in a stanza which again resounds with the rhyme words *told / cold / old* (15 or 16):

> But soon his eyes grew brilliant, when she told
> His lady's purpose; and he scarce could brook
> Tears, at the thought of those enchantments cold
> And Madeline asleep in lap of legends old.

Here, then, begins the second phase or cycle, where Madeline becomes "a peerless bride" (19 or 20) or a "lovely bride" (38 or 39). These symmetrically placed rhymes present the key concept of the second phase, whose three points of structural emphasis show (1) the entry into Madeline's chamber first of Porphyro and then of Madeline (21–22), (2) Porphyro's move from the closet to the bed (28–29), and (3) how the dream encloses both (35–36). To quote from the unexpurgated version of stanza 36: "See while she speaks his arms encroaching slow / Have zon'd her, heart to heart". Or, to quote from Woodhouse's comment, Porphyro "acts all the acts of a bona fide husband" so that the poem is rendered "unfit for ladies".[4]

As Diagrams A1 and A2 show, it is possible to see the 42 or 43 stanzas as combining overall symmetry with a division into 14+28 (or 14+1+28), where each substructure has its own symmetrical pattern. The structural precision is extraordinary: in the second cycle the centre shows Porphyro as he parts the curtains of the bed and gazes on Madeline, fast asleep, and this topos of being asleep reaches back to the beginning (in stanza 15 or 16) when he envisages her "asleep in lap of legends old" and forward to the end where the lovers escape while the baron and his guests are "benightmared". Also the beginning points forward to the end when the reader unexpectedly and abruptly discovers that it is he who has been as it were "asleep in lap of legends old". The chamber encloses the lovers in stanzas 21–22 (22–23), and in stanzas 35–36 (36–37) it is the

Diagram A.3 Keats, *The Eve of St. Agnes*. The Symmetrical Pattern of Events

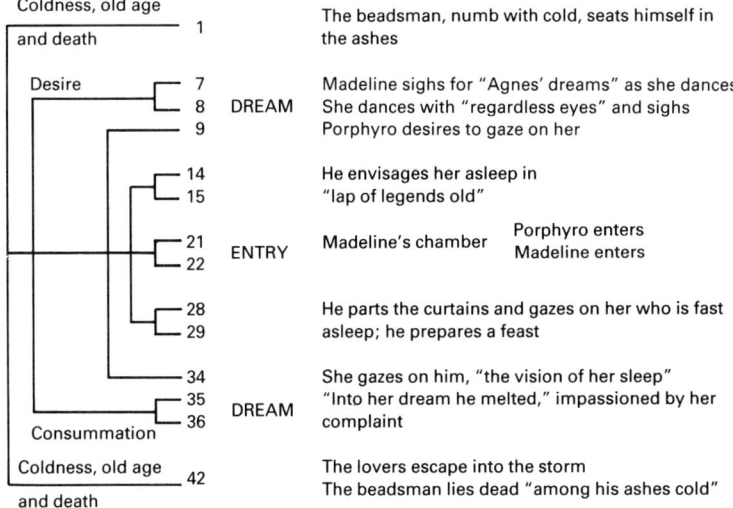

When the suppressed stanza is added between stanzas 6 and 7, the centre is stanza 21 (re-numbered 22) on Porphyro's entry into the bedchamber.

dream which encloses them as their love finds its consummation. Finally, the plan that is conceived in stanza 15 (16) finds not only its consummation but also its successful conclusion in the last stanza on the escape.

The overall symmetry is equally clear (see Diagram A3). The parallel between Madeline's absorption by the legend of St Agnes Eve in stanzas 7–8 (or 7–8–9), and the consummation in the stanzas equidistant from the end, has already been pointed out. It may be added that Porphyro enters the castle unobserved, desiring to gaze on his beloved Madeline (9 or 10), and that in the stanza equidistant from the end (34 or 35) it is Madeline who gazes on him, "the vision of her sleep". In stanzas 14–15 (15–16), he envisages her asleep, and he obtains his wish when, in stanzas 28–29 (29–30), he parts the curtains of her bed and gazes on her who is fast asleep. At the textual centre (21–22 or 22–23), Madeline's bedchamber is entered, first by Porphyro and then by Madeline.

The precision with which the story unfolds, with its pregnant parallels-with-a-difference and its pointed antitheses, helps to account for its appeal. The firmness of the structure invests the tale with a dramatic quality which makes it seem utterly realistic – so much so that it is with a sense of shock that we read in the last stanza, "And they are gone: ay, ages long ago / These lovers fled away into the storm". Spenser's compositional technique, therefore, served Keats well. The poem as a whole is framed by descriptions of death and decay, as it is by the rhyme words *cold / told / old*; this insistent repetition engenders a strong feeling of pathos, and the richness of life in the young lovers, their "purple riot" (16:3), is greatly enhanced by the contrast with the decayed deformity of old age.

The revisions show that Keats did not plan the structure in all its details before he began the composition; some effects were added in the process of revision. If we had had Spenser's foul papers it is possible that similar discoveries could have been made. The main outlines, though, must have been conceived as part of the original inspiration. It is unlikely that number symbolism is involved, tempting though it is to relate the 14+28 (or 14—1—28) structure to the idea of redemption (as in the 42 generations listed by Matthew in ch. 1). Porphyro, though, certainly is a Romantic redeemer unto life. It is equally doubtful that the ratio 1 : 2 between the first phase on the dream and the second on its realization should be taken to express the harmony between the two. This way of thinking surely belongs in the earlier period only.

Notes to Appendix

1. See Jack Stillinger, "The Text of 'The Eve of St Agnes' ," *Studies in Bibliography* 16 (1963), 207–12. Stillinger concludes that "the publishers forced the restoration of the original lines 314–22 [i.e. stanza 36], and it is almost as certain that they forced the rejection of the additional stanza inserted between VI and VII" (p. 210).
2. Quoted by Stillinger, p. 208, from *The Letters of John Keats*, ed. Hyder E. Rollins (1958), II, pp. 162–63.
3. All quotations are from John Keats, *The Poetical Works*, ed. H. W. Garrod (Oxford, 1939).
4. Quoted by Stillinger, p. 209.

Index of Names

Alberti, Leone Battista, 17
Albertus Magnus, 42
Allen, Don Cameron, xv
Ambrose, 134, 152, 372
Anderson, William S., xix n. 6
André, Yves-Marie, 61 f.
Apollonius of Rhodes, xii
Appleton Weber, Sarah, 401 n. 5
Aquinas, Thomas, 42, 43, 153
The Areopagus, 23
Aristophanes, 344
Aristotle, 60, 153, 159, 325, 326, 335, 337, 557, 564
Armstrong, A. H., xx n. 11
Augustine, Introduction, Chapter I *passim*, 154, 157, 164, 165, 166 n. 10, 183, 184, 187, 204, 227, 245, 324, 337, 372, 462, 495, 506, 528, 559; *Confessions*, xvii, xix, 12, 19, Chapter II, 173, 190, 193, 210, 247, 258, 262, 268, 270, 288, 304, 335, 366, 372–74, 381, 445, 451 f., 462–63, 465, 467, 476, 477, 479–81, 484–86, 509–10, 511, 513, 517, 518, 522, 563, 564; *De doctrina Christiana*, 6 f., 75, 129 n. 8, 133–38, 182, 302, 481; *Enchiridion*, 347; *De Genesi ad litteram*, 8; *De libero arbitrio*, 11, 100, 110, 335, 379, 428, 474–76; *De musica* VI, xi, 8 f., 169, *318*, 335; *De ordine*, 7 f., 9; *De Trinitate*, xiii, 75–79, 183–85, 411 f., 479, 483, 546 f.; *De vera religione*, xi, 9–11, 19, 65 f., 204, 355
Ausonius, 169

Baïf, Jean-Antoine de, 23
Baker-Smith, Dominic, 201 n. 5
Bartas, du, 25
Basil, Saint, 42
Battenhouse, Roy, 4, 69 n. 2
Battestin, Martin C., 62 f.
Baybak, Michael, 263
Becon, Thomas, 157, 482
Bede, 42, 138, 154
Bellarmine, Cardinal, 151, 172
Benlowes, Edward, 104
Beowulf, 164
Berlinghieri, Francesco, 17
Bernard, Saint, 156
Berosius, 369 n. 46
Bèze, Theodore de, 129 n. 10, 400
Blakemore, Stephen, 533 n. 13
Bober, Harry, 129
Bobrick, James, 566 n. 3
Boderie, see le Fevre
Bodin, Jean, 167 n. 25
Boethius, 13, 38, 41, 154
Bonaventure, xv f., 12–13, 25, 27, 41, 139, 152, 163 f., 187–88, 366, 564
Bongo, Pietro, 24, 39–45, 137, 143, 145, 159, 167 n. 23, 260 f., 324, 326 f., 354, 368 n. 10, 415, 438, 476, 477, 478, 479, 482, 486, 524, 547
Botticelli, 358
Bouelles, Charles de, 429
Bradford, Alan, 450, 459 n. 23
Brand, C. P., 206
Brooks-Davies, Douglas, 368 n. 11
Brown, C. C., 166 n. 15
Brouwer, Christoph, 201 n. 5
Bruno, Giordano, 23, 39, 65, 73 n. 58
Bullinger, Henry, 4 f., 69 n. 3, 132
Burchmore, David W., 369 n. 31
Burke, Kenneth, 129 n. 12
Butler, Christopher, xix n. 5, 24 f.

Cabala, 23
Calvin, 4, 12, 110, 335, 338, 345, 346, 369 n. 28
Canfield, J. Douglas, 547

INDEX OF NAMES

Capella, Martianus, 40, 184
Casaubon, 71 n. 39
Chassanæus, Bartholomæus, 167 n. 25
Cassiodorus, xii, 42, 78, 136, 138–51, 164, 167 n. 20, 167 n. 23, 175, 184, 274, 372, 439, 484, 565
Céard, Jean, 370 n. 46
Celtis, Conrad, 187
Chamberlain, David, 74 n. 87, 184, 201 n. 12, 202 n. 13, 202 n. 14
Chapman, George, 65, 313, 368 n. 15
Chastel, André, 17, 64
Chaucer, xv, 67, 535, 537
Cicero, 100, 101, 120, 339
Clement of Alexandria, 45
Clichtoveus, Jodocus, 39 f., 201 n. 11
Colet, John, xv, 22, 137, 167 n. 25
Collop, John, 21
Cooper, Antony, Earl of Shaftesbury, 60
Corrozet, Gilles, 264 n. 20, 399
Cowen, Painton, 161
Cowley, Abraham, xx n. 18, 22, 549 f.
Cummings, R. M., xx n. 7
Cusanus, Cardinal, 14, 22, 24, 25, 38, 41, 42, 44, 57

Dagens, Jean, 459 n. 26
Damianus, Petrus, 68 f.
Daniel, Samuel, xvii, 66 f., 369 n. 34, 565
Daniélou, Jean, 202 n. 18, 354
Dante, 64, 164, 351, 353
Davies, H. Neville, 367 n. 6, 402 n. 12, 458 n. 14, 534 n. 26, 536
Davis, Thomas M., 160
Davis, Walter, R., 167 n. 22
Dee, John, 23–24, 59
Defoe, Daniel, 79
de Foix, François, 23, 71 n. 39, 451–57 *passim*, 459 n. 26
Delany, Paul, 263
Dionysius the Areopagite, 21 f., 38, 42, 153
Donne, John, 18, 23, 71 n. 29, 200, 524

Dryden, John, xvii, xviii, 313, 368 n. 16, 462, 522 f., Chapter X, 563, 564, 566
Dürer, Albrecht, 187

E. K., xiv
Ellrodt, Robert, xiii, xv, 459 n. 25
Empedocles, 76
Erasmus, xiii f., xv, 71 n. 40
Eriksen, Roy, T., xix n. 1, 71 n. 25, 73 n. 58, 74 n. 89, 74 n. 90, 210, 263 n. 9, 458 n. 2, 505
Euclid, 59
Eugubinus, Augustinus Steuchus, 22, 167 n. 25
Euripides, 344
Eusebius, xiv f., 16, 25, 41, 51, 139
Evans, Maurice, 358 f., 370 n. 57
Everard, John, 4, 134, 166 n. 8, 451–55 *passim*

Fairfax, Edward, Chapter V
Fairfax, Thomas Lord, 71 n. 39, 456
Fernandius, Antonius, 155 f., 167 n. 25
Ferry, Anne, 129 n. 7, 367 n. 6
Fichter, Andrew, 89, 92 f., 109 f., 129 n. 5, 263 n. 9, 245, 246, 566 n. 1
Ficino, Marsilio, 14–18, 23, 25, 39, 70 n. 10, 64, 68, 459 n. 25, 482
Fielding, Henry, xvii, xviii, 60, 224 f., 267, 303, 342
Finny, Gretchen Ludke, 59
Fletcher, Giles, 33 f., 104, 167 n. 23, 197, 200, 202 n. 24, 246, 312 f., 368 n. 10, 388, 389, 393, 524, 528, 562
Fludd, Robert, 23, 24, 71 n. 39, 428
Forsyth, N., 533 n.
Fortunatus, Venantius, 169–72, 173
Fowler, A. D. S., xix n. 6, 74 n. 82, 165 n. 1, 345, 369 n. 38, 524
Foxe, 354
Fraunce, Abraham, 66
Frost, Kate Gartner, 202 n. 26, 524

Frye, Northrop, 484
Fulgentius, 344

Galinski, G. Karl, 264 n. 17, 342–45 *passim*
Garin, Eugenio, 74 n. 90
The *Gawain* poet, 164
Genesis A, 164
Gildon, Charles, 63
Gill, Alexander, 24, 152
Giorgio, 8, 18 f., 24–39, 40, 56, 60, 71 n. 40, 143, 153, 157, 457, 471, 486
Gordon, R. L., 74 n. 90
Goulart, Simon, 25
Gray, Thomas, xvii
Graziani, René, 355, 370 n. 54, 370 n. 56
Gregory the Great, 154 f., 157, 204, 372
Greville, Robert, 8, 72 n. 49

Hakluyt, 354
Hall, John, 398 f.
Hamilton, A. C., 264 n. 21, 318, 325, 326
Hardison, O. B., xiv
Harvey, Gabriel, 22, 66
Haubrichs, Walter, 129 n. 7
Haymo, bishop, 151
Heninger, S. K. Jr., xiv, xix n. 5, 71 n. 34, 76, 166 n. 17, 429, 458 n. 12, 458 n. 13
Herbert, George, 78, 129 n. 3, 131, 278, 313, 371 f., 391, 403–25, 426, 430, 436, 444, 445, 458, 565
Hercules, 111, 346, 385; see the Subject Index
Hermes Trismegistus, See the Subject Index under *Ancient Theology*, the *Hermetic Dialogues*, and *Syncretism*
Herrick, Robert, 44, 202 n. 20
Hieatt, A. Kent, 263
Hilarius, 152
Hill, Thomas, D., 202 n. 18
Hirst, Désirée, 24, 166 n. 8
Hobbes, 63
Höltgen, K. J., 372

Homer, 79, 92, 132
Homeyer, Helene, 201 n. 12
Horace, 34, 554
Hornik, Henry, 72 n. 57
Horton, Ronald Arthur, 325 f.
Hrotsvit, 183–87, 475
Hughes, Merritt Y., 472
Hugo of St Victor, 37 f., 42, 173, 183, 201 n. 11
Hugo, Herman, 388
Hurst, Andrée, xix n. 6
Hutcheson, Francis, 61
Hutchinson, F. E., 408 f., 421

Isidore, 154
Italicus, Silius, 343

Jackson Knight, W. F., xix n. 6
James, M. R., 159
Jerome, 34, 139, 156
Joachim of Fiore, 351, 353, 354
Johnson, Samuel, 558
Jonson, Ben, 173, 313, 346, 445
Jordan, Robert M., xv
Joukovsky, Françoise, 72 n. 57
Justin Martyr, 57

Keats, John, xv, 567–72
Knoespel, K. J., 59 f.
Kristeller, Paul Oskar, xiii f., xv
Kyd, Thomas, 73 n. 60

Landino, Christoforo, xi, 18, 63–65, 66, 203
Lapide, Cornelius à, 26, 40, 72 n. 49, 132, 154 f., 158, 165 n. 5, 166 n. 7
Lazzarelli, Ludovico, 456
le Fèvre, Guy, 16, 19, 29, 35–37, 38 f., 72 n. 57
le Fèvre, Nicolas, 19, 22, 37 f.
le Fèvre, Guy, Nicolas, and Antoine, 22
le Fèvre, Raoul, 344
Levine, J. Arnold, 551, 559 n. 8, 559 n. 9
Lewalski, Barbara K., 371 f.
Locke, John, xvi
Longinus, 270

INDEX OF NAMES

Lorinus, xx n. 22, 152
Luther, Martin, 4

Macrobius, 74 n. 87, 205, 263 n. 7, 437–38
McDonald, Sister Mary Frances, 129 n. 5
Maguire, Henry, 401 n. 6
Maillard, J.-F., 23, 72 n. 41
Mantuanus, 153
Marks, Carol L., 459 n. 35
Martz, Louis L., 165 n. 1
Marshall, Will, 415
Marvell, Andrew, 14, 173; *The Coronet*, 400 f.; *The Garden*, 196; *Upon Appleton House*, 29, 131, 165 n. 2
Maurus, Hrabanus, 165, 172–83, 184, 201 n. 11, 344, 353
Mersenne, Marin, xi, 24, *56–60*, 127, 133, 483–84
Miller, David L., 370 n. 60
Milton, John, Chapter IX; xiv, 4, 18, 24, 26, 35, 52, 54, 74 n. 90, 79, 102, 127, 128, 129 n. 10, 129 n. 12, 132, 133, 135, 140, 141, 154, 156, 158, 164, 185, 193, 197, 199, 200, 215, 245, 246, 247, 259, 261, 296, 305, 314, 328, 335, 339, 346, 347, 375, 449 f., 458, 562 f., 564, 566; *At a solemn Musick*, 433; *De doctrina Christiana*, 50, 134–35; *Epistle on the Marchioness of Winchester*, 540; *Nativity Ode*, 55, 151, 167 n. 23, 202 n. 24, 313, 524, 565; *Sonnet XVI* ("When I consider..."), 137
Miner, Earl, 165 n. 1
More, Sir Thomas, 166 n. 15
Moseley, C. W. R. D., 566 n. 5
Mulder, John R., 410, 458 n. 3

Nazianzen, 383
Nicomachus, 38
Nohrnberg, James, 267 f., 334, 354

O'Connell, Robert J., 80–82, 92, 129 n. 6

O'Meara, John, 129 n. 5
Origen, 41, 154
Orpheus, See Subject Index under *Ancient Theologians* and *Syncretism*

Panofsky, Erwin, 264
Paolini, Shirley S., 130 n. 18
Patrides, C. A., 71 n. 29
Patterson, Annabel M., xx n. 9, 204
Perella, Nicolas J., 402 n. 7
Pererius, Benedictus, 133, 158
Person, David, 71 n. 39
Petaut, 56
Philip of Mornay, 4, 24, 54–56
Phillips, James E., 28, 368 n. 18
Philo Judæus, 35, 55, 153
Pico della Mirandola, xv, xx n. 19, 4, 18–22, 51, 61, 132, 133, 155, 451
Pindar, 34
Plato, Introduction and Chapter I *passim*; see Subject Index under *Ancient Theologians*, *Lambda formula*, and *Syncretism*
Poole, Matthew, 132
Pope, Alexander, xvii, 545; *Epistle to Bathurst*, 555–58
Porphyrius, Optatianus, 169
Postel, Guillaume, 72 n. 57
Prescott, Anne Lake, xii, xix n. 5, 71 n. 36, 73 n. 67
Primaudaye, Pierre de la, 21, 24, 45–54, 324, 337–39, 369 n. 23
Proclus, 35
Prosper, Saint, 138
Pythagorus, Introduction and Chapter I *passim*; see Subject Index under *Ancient Theologians*, the *Tetractys formula*, and *Syncretism*

Quarles, Francis, *Emblemes*, xviii f., 82, 303, Chapter VII, 434, 462, 564; *Hierogliphikes*, 369 n. 26, 399, 547
Qvarnström, Gunnar, 200, 263 n. 8, 368 n. 10, 489, 524

INDEX OF NAMES 577

Ralegh, Sir Walter, 71 n. 39
Reeves, Marjorie, 351, 353
Reuchlin, John, 172
Reynolds, Henry, 22
Richard of St Victor, 157
Roche, Thomas P., 167 n. 21
Rogers, Daniel, 22 f.
Ronsard, Pierre, 23
Rose, Mark, 368 n. 8
Ross, Alexander, 158, 483
Rossi, Joan Warchol, 368 n. 19
Rudrum, Alan, 458 n. 15

Salutati, Coluccio, 342
Sanctius, Gasparius, 154, 156
Sardo, Antiocho, 156, 157
Scaliger, Julius Cæsar, 68
Secret, François, 72 n. 57
Seneca, 132, 344
Sidney, Sir Philip, 22, 24, 65
Sigwart, Christopher, 69 n. 2
Smith, D. E., 39 f.
Smith, John, xvi, 143
Spenser, Edmund, xi, xvii, xviii, 4, 28, 72 n. 51, 111, 124, 127, 133, 135, 149, 158, 159, 185, 203, 205, 206, 208, 210, 216, 220 f., 227, 245, 246, 258, 260, 261, Chapter VI, 377, 385, 387, 391, 393, 461, 464, 473, 492, 498, 499, 513, 518, 523, 529, 530, 548, 555, 561, 562, 563 f., 564, 566, 567, 572; *Epithalamion* 69, 173; *Mutability Cantos* 30, 362–63; *Prothalamion* 405, 458 n. 2; *The Shepheardes Calender* 22, 39, 47, 66, 67, 74 n. 88, 173, 312, 368 n. 19, 369 n. 25; *Sonnets* (dedicatory) 362–65

Tasso, Torquato, xi, xvii, xviii, 45, 63, 67 (on rhyme), 74 n. 87, 124, 127, 135, 158, 165, Chapter V, 267 f., 270, 274, 292, 293, 294, 303, 304 f., 310, 311, 312, 334, 342, 365, 366, 367 n. 1, 385, 387, 400, 462, 492, 510, 518, 523, 524, 529, 530, 555, 561, 562, 563, 564; *Del Giudizio sovra la Gerusalemme* 204 f.; *Discourses on the Heroic Poem* xiii, 18, 203 f.; *Il Mondo Creato* xii, xvii, 188–201, 439, 491, 521, 522, 523
Taylor, Edward, 172
Theocritus, 132
Thompson, Charlotte, 167 n. 21
Thomson, James, 314
Traherne, Thomas, 22, 436–58, 564
Troyes, Chrétien de, 164
Tyard, Pontus de, 23, 67

Vaughan, Henry, 78, 313, 424, *425–36*
Vaughan, Thomas, xvi, 428
Vieth, David, 559 n. 11
Vigerius, Marcus, 157, 158, 482
Villapandus, 56
Virgil, xii, xix n. 6, 79, 132, 344
Vitruvius, 32

Waddington, Raymond B., 19 f.
Walker, D. P., 71 n. 35, 71 n. 39
Webber Jones, Leslie, 138, 167 n. 20
Weinberg, Bernhard, 74 n. 80
Wickert, Max A., 201 n. 8
Williams, Arnold, 132 f., 133
Willichius, 40
Wills, Richard, 66
Wimphelingius, Iacobus, 172
Wind, Edgar, 226, 264 n. 18, 369 n. 43
Wion, Arnoldus, 172
Wither, George, 400
Wittreich, Joseph Anthony, 69 n. 6
Wolseley, Charles, 131

Xenophon, 224

Yates, Frances, xix n. 5, 23 f., 71 n. 40, 201 n. 10

Zeno, 43
Zinn, Grover A., 201 n. 7
Zwingli, 4, 69 n. 2

Subject Index

alphabetical composition, 152, 153, 154
aequalitas, *see* balance
allegorical mode, 21, 22, 37, 185, 204, 563 f.; mathematical, 60; based on correspondences, 37, 51; based on numbers and the laws of music, 38
ancient theologians, 22, 25, 26, 32 f., 34, 46, 48, 55 f., 69 n. 3, 71 n. 39, 165 n. 7
Aristotle's triple formula, 216, 255, 275, 278, 294 f., 303 f., 361, 365
Ark of Noah, 5, 37 f., 143, 145, 173, 183
art of memory, 37 f., 173, 187 f., 201 n. 10

balance reflects unity, 42; is a kind of unison, 58
balanced events, 42, 87, 88, 145, 157–58
Biblia Pauperum, 159–61
biblical references: *Canticles*, 154 f.; *Daniel 3*, 35; *Eph. 2:14*, 43; *Ex. 25–40*, 51; *Ez.*, 132 (*see* chariot, Ezekiel's vision); *Hebrews 8:5*, xii; *Job 25*, 156; *Job 38*, 31, 153; *Job 40*, 153; *Job 41:11–12*, 32; *Lament.*, 154; *Psalms*, 28, 68, 142–53, 173; *Ps. 119* (Vulg. *118*), 38 f., 142, 148 f., 152, 153, 154, 454 f., 457, 555; *Psalms of Ascent*, 149–53 (*see* the number 15); *Rev.*, 26, 27, 61; *Romans 1:20*, xii, xvi, xix, 10 f., 23 f., 37, 45, 54 f., 59, 64, 65, 78, 81, 99, 114, 130 n. 17, 152, 162; *Wisd. 8:1*, xi, xii, 3, 5, 10, 31 f., 65, 77, 100, 105, 405, 406; *Wisd. 11:21*, xi, 15, 16, 18, 41, 50, 59 f., 64, 81, 99, 120, 131, 139, 140, 143, 144, 145, 154, 184, 202 n. 15

Cabala, 25, 71 n. 40
Calvinism, 4
Cambridge Platonists, 6, 60, 62 f.
catalogue of trees, 271, 367 n. 6
centre, extended, 205–12, 216, 219, 221, 223, 258–59, 292–93, 295–97, 305, 311, 324, 366, 562; triple centre-piece, 162
chariot, Ezekiel's vision of, 5, 27, 38, 61, 132, 137, *155*, 156, 163, 192 f., 466, 471–72; of light, 192 f.; of paternal Deity, 158, 192, 471–73, 475, 483, 487–89, 530 f.
chastisement, 114, 230–31, 234, 250 f., 294, 296, 304, 373–74, 385, 387; *see* purification
Christ as creator, 33 (contains all numbers), 49, 55 (is the pattern of the world); *see* creation, Moses, music, and the circle; *in medio*, 19–20, 24, 27, 82, 150, 156–57, 159, 162, 163–64, 170, 172, 210; joins the beginning, middle, and end, 162 f., 182; *see* circle
circle of the alphabet, 38 f.; circle and centre, 157, 547–55; expresses the golden mean, 327, 365, 547 f.; circle of the octave, 431 f., 479; circle of perfection, 354; circle of return, 38 f.; circle of time, 162, 169; *see* octave, Christ *in medio*
circular form, 38 f., 142, 143, 144, 149, 150–51, 161, 162–63, 194, 197 f., 399 f., 400 f., 409, 415, 420–21, 423, 424, 435, 442, 449–50, 451, 467, 476, 540; in the Psalms, 143 f.; in the Bible, 17

concepts, primacy of, xviii, 185, 267, 303, 308, 328, 365, 367, 563, 564
concord, *see* order, harmony; *in malo*, 322, 327, 341–42
confessional mode, 128, 466
creation, divine and human, 11 f.; Mosaic account, 16, 189; its order a hymn of praise, 48; its study leads to salvation, 46–48; the world as a poem and the poem as a world, 11, 18, 60, 64; theatre of the world, 10, 32, 200 f.; *see* Moses, music

David compared to Horace and Pindar, 34
decalogue, *see* the number 10
departure from the established norm, 202 n. 24, 277, 312–14, 417 f., 426, 427, 435
design, *see* harmony, number, order
diapason, *see* octave proportion

emblems, Chapter VII; emblematic passages, 173, 240, 255, 260, 274 f., 283, 297–300, 303, 304, 361, 367
epic similes, submerged, 91, 94, 108, 331 f., 333, 511
Epicurean materialism, 63

form contradicts the contents, 170, 278, 391, 402 f.

gematria, 25

harmony, Chapter I (esp. 24–39, 76); based on due order, 35; based on symmetrical and graded arrangements, 10 f.; from dissonance, 158; of the elements, 15, 16, 36, 76 f.; equals obedience, 52, 141 f., 472; equals regeneration, 29; in hymns through their organization, 36 f.; *in malo*, 101, 187, 475, 491–92; Pythagorean and Platonic concept of, 75; the role of Satan in, 76 f.; *see* order
Hercules, 222, 342–45; the Choice of Hercules, xviii, 214, 224 f., 240, 248 f., 255 f., 303, 342–44, 346
Hermetic dialogues, 22, 23, 166 n. 8, 196, 450 f., 452–58, 459 n. 26

in bono/in malo distinction, 87, 89, 135 f., 143 and *passim*

ladder, Jacob's, 36, 37, 38, 60 f.; of creation, xvi, 37, 114 f., 483, 516; of the faculties of man, 122; of love, 118, 515 f., 519, 521; which is Christ, 37, 61; as double octave, 151 f.; *see* the number 15
lambda formula, 15 f., 17, 22, 33, 38, 52, 56 f., 77, 150, 154, 167 n. 23, 170, 205, 263 n. 7, 530, 566
latitudinarian divines, 63

magia naturalis, 237, 247
mean terms, 438
Moses, the perfect pattern of a poet, xiii, 5, 20 f., 132, 162 f.; source of all wisdom, 19, 29, 32 f., 35 f., 45 f., 48, 131, 166 n. 8
music, Chapter I *passim* (esp. 24–39), 141, 151, 204, 297, 389, 390, 391, 394, 418–19, 424, 428–29, 433, 434, 435, 536–37, 546, 564; Christ the original teacher of poetry and music, 33; Christ as an organ, 31; Christ taught the Apostles the "song" of the Gospels, 33; Christ taught David, 33; the Law and the Gospels as musical instruments, 33; music and Moses, 29; and Plato and Pythagoras, 59; a symbol of obedience, 484
musica humana, 53; *mundana*, 153, 405–06
musical consonances as images, 64

SUBJECT INDEX

musical laws govern rhyme schemes, 67, 205
musical rhythms, 141 f.
musical theology, 32, 36, 75, 183–85

number as sign, xiii, 7, 14, 60, 70 n. 18, Chapters III–IV *passim* (esp. 133–34, 136–38, 142, 155)
numbers, circular, 25 f., 157, 168 n. 37; *see* the number 8 and the octave
numbers, cubed and squared; 22, 26, 170, 183, 195, 479; *see lambda* formula
numbers, list of,
  1 see numbers and the Monad
  2 44, 186 f., 326, 388
  3 21 f., 29, 148, 150, 159, 169, *326–27*, 388, 438, 544, 545, 546; seen as circle and centre, 159; as the golden mean, 546
  4 20, 51 f., 137, 140, 148, 154, 155 f., 175, *182*, 188, 313, *410*, 426, *428* f., 435, 438, 471–73, 528, 529, 548, 555; as symbol of constancy, 156; imposes unity on multitude, 156; *see* tetractys formula, *quaternarius* and quaternions
  5 72 n. 57, 140, 148, 149, 424, 436, 449, 546
  6 24 f., 42, 75, 77, 140, 145, 149, 182, 289, 411, 546
  7 19 f., 29 f., 49, 70 n. 8, 132, 135, 137, 138, 140, 143, 147 f., 166 n. 15, 288 f., 313, 413, *415*, *436–39*
  8 17, 19, 22, 29 f., 143, 145 f., 148 f., 150 f., 161, 193, 195, 204 f., 312, 435, 436–37, 454–55, 546, 548 f.; as circular octave, 431 f., 433; as Christ, 17; *see* octave
  9 21 f., 136, 146, 149, 399
  10 25 f., 144, 146, 147, 151, 157, 175, 183, 190, 289, 406, 454, *482*, 533 n. 8, 545
  11 146, 150, 195, 362, 399, 426, 427, 428, 527, 555
  12 57, 143, *146* f., 150, 161, 164, 173, 182, 188, 289, 425, 454
  13 127, 137, 147, 150, 182, 412, 425, 492, 545
  14 288 f., 350 f., 424–25, 528
  15 78, 149, 150, 151, 167 n. 23, 388–89, 399, 427, 428, 442, 518–21, 528–29, 534 n. 26, *536–37*, 555; as double octave, 394, 427, 431
  17 143, 539, 545
  18 149
  19 260 f., 269, 278–79, 282, 292, 361
  22 38 f., 139, 147, 149, 152, 154, 555
  23 200, 278, 285–86, 292, 368 n. 10, 524, 534 n. 21, 540
  24 139, 183, 425, 435, 436
  25 147, 361
  27 22, 175
  28 174, 189, 195, *411*
  30 540
  33 138, 170, 189, 195, 249, 250, 251, 252, 255, 256, 260, 269, 276–77, 283, 284, 287, 288, 292, 329, *347*, 350 f., 362, 434, 527, 535–37, 549, 555
  35 170, 327
  36 77, 182
  39 188, 202 n. 20, 527
  40 7, *133–34*, 158, 162, 175
  42 187, 249, 250, 251, 260, 288 f., 350 f., 353, 492
  46 75
  49 187
  50 134, 139, 148, 425, 527, 539
  52 413
  60 429
  70 138, *524–27*, 549
  71 139
  72 139
  77 193–94
  80 138
  90 148
  100 149
  144 183

150 143
153 134, 137, 138
216 529 f.
327 529
360 529
numbers, transition from one number to another; from 7 to *8*; 143, 145 f., 149, 186, 195, 197, 202 n. 24, 373, *414* f., 417–18; from *11* to *12*, 148; from *50* to *51*, 148; from *70* to *80*, 148; *1–10* in sequence, 482–83
numerical concepts: the Monad 33, 142, 144; Multitude, 43 f., 144, 478, 488, 500, 501; multiplicity, 50, 476–77; Unity, xv f., Chapter I *passim* (esp. 35, 42–44, 50, 56), 476, 477, 478; Unity *in malo*, 102
numerical decorum, advocated, 140, 153; authorial comment on, 138, 140, 143, 151, 157, 169, 170, 172, 174, 204 f.; attributed to the Bible, Chapter III *passim*

octave proportion, xiii, 7 f., 8 f., 15, 29 f., 33, 58 f., 75–79, 101, 141, 145 f., 161, 169, 174, 185 f., 187–88, 189 f., 199, 205, 247, 250, 251, 252, 253, 256, 257, 260, 385, 389, 434; as a circle of return, 16 f., 150 f., transition from the octave to the unison, 484; *see* the numbers 8 and 15
opposites, reconcilable, 76 f; irreconcilable, 185–87, 202 n. 16, 261, 268, 314, 320–23, 325, 327–29, 332, 466
order, as image of God, 35; as numbers and ratios, 6–12; as meaning, 41 f.; as obedience, 46–48, 52; as peace, 31; defines beauty, 13; *see* harmony and Providential ordering
Orphic hymns, 38 f.

the particular and the universal, 86, 126 f., 173, 466 f.
Pindaric odes, 74 n. 90

poetry, art of, derived from divinity, Chapter I *passim* (esp. 21, 28–35, 68–69)
Providential ordering, xix, 5, 11, 80, 92–93, 169, Chapter VII *passim*, 405–10, 429, 480 f.; the artist imitates the hand of Providence, 12; *see* music, order, *Wisdom* 8:1 (biblical references)
purification 225–26, 227 f., 230–32, 234, 236, 252 f., *see* chastisement

quaternarius, quaternions, 36, 38, 52, 53, 72 n. 57, 76 f., 145, *154–56*, 182, 404, 426, 467, 472–73, 479 f., 482, 515 f., 545, 557, 558; *see tetractys* formula

rhetoric, xix n. 6, 59, 80, 94 f., 188, 270, 273–74, 396, 524–27
rhymes, repetition of, 204 f., 218, 220, 249, 254, 260, 269, 270, 271–74, 276–81, 308, 311; esp. Chapter VI *passim*

sin as discord, 60; as division and mutability, 42
spatial and linear reading, xviii, 82–85, 111 f., 126
Speculum Humanae Salvationis, 159–60
syncretism, xiii–xv, Chapter I *passim* (esp. 3 f., *6–12*, 32 f., 33, 41, 65, 69 n. 2 and n. 3), 78 f., Chapter III *passim* (esp. 132, 134, 137, 140, 145, 155, 161), 339, 411, 438–39, 450, 458, 482

the Tabernacle, 36, 38, 51, 60 f.
the Temple, 38, 75, 87
tetractys formula, 20, 51 f., 55, 137, 145, 150, 154, 156, 175, 183, 406; related to the Tetragrammaton, 36, 51
Tetragrammaton, 25 f., 36, 157, 479
Theatre of the World, *see* creation
topomorphical defined, xi

triadic patterns, 42, 78, 141, 161, 208–11
triplets, structural function of, Chapter X *passim*
types and typology, xv, 4 f., 16, 17, 19, 21, 32, 87, 132 f., 135, 137, 155, 159–61, 174, 175, 246, 259, 353, 354, 425, 499, 509 f.; Christocentric structure, 159–63; sequences in sacred art, 159–63; transition from the literal to the spiritual, 87, 98, 135–35, 214, 262, 303; typological structure, 294 f.

Unity, *see* numbers

Year of Jubilee, *see* the number 50